Education of the Interior

Essays in Honour of Professor Syed Ali Ashraf

Professor Syed Ali Ashraf

Education of the Interior

Essays in Honour of Professor Syed Ali Ashraf

Edited by
Shaikh Abdul Mabud

Foreword by
Professor Seyyed Hossein Nasr
George Washington University

Afterword by
Dr Anwar Ibrahim
Prime Minister of Malaysia

Bismi'Llāh al-Raḥmān al-Raḥīm

First published in the UK by Beacon Books and Media Ltd
Earl Business Centre, Oldham OL8 2PF, UK

Copyright © Shaikh Abdul Mabud 2025

The right of Shaikh Abdul Mabud to be identified as the author of this work has been asserted in accordance with the Copyright, Designs and Patents Act 1988. All rights reserved. This book may not be reproduced, scanned, transmitted or distributed in any printed or electronic form or by any means without the prior written permission from the copyright owner, except in the case of brief quotations embedded in critical reviews and other non-commercial uses permitted by copyright law.

First paperback edition published in 2025

www.beaconbooks.net

ISBN: 978-1-916955-39-4   Paperback
ISBN: 978-1-916955-40-0   Hardback
ISBN: 978-1-916955-41-7   eBook

Cover image by Ashraf-Ullah Azvog-unsplash
Photographs courtesy of author

Cataloging-in-Publication record for this book is available from the British Library

Contents

Transliteration System for Arabic, Persian, and Urdu — ix
Acknowledgements — xi
Foreword   *Seyyed Hossein Nasr* — xiii
Preface   *Shaikh Abdul Mabud* — xv

Introduction   *Shaikh Abdul Mabud* — 1

Part I: Reflections

Chapter 1 — 29
Civilizational Dialogue and the Islamic World
Seyyed Hossein Nasr

Chapter 2 — 39
The Aims of Education: The Forgotten Truths
Osman Bakar

Chapter 3 — 58
Islam and the West: Meaningful Dialogue and Peaceful Coexistence
Ahmad Salah Jamjoom

Chapter 4 — 62
Islam and the West in the Twenty-First Century
Akbar S. Ahmed

Chapter 5 — 77
Islamic Education and the Challenge of Secularism: Professor Syed Ali Ashraf's Critique of Secularism in Education in Muslim Countries: A Personal Appraisal
Ghulam Nabi Saqeb

Chapter 6 — 92
The Islamic Concept of Knowledge: Some Reflections on the Epistemological Assumptions in the Educational Thinking of Professor Syed Ali Ashraf
J. Mark Halstead

Chapter 7 — 116
Poems of Syed Ali Ashraf
Syed Ali Ahsan

Chapter 8 — 125
Islam and the West
Abdullah Omar Nasseef

Chapter 9 — 135
Exploring Professor Syed Ali Ashraf's Views on Religious and Secular Education
Shaikh Abdul Mabud

Chapter 10 169
    Faith-Based Education
        Peter Mitchell

Chapter 11 182
    Abraham, The Babylonian
        James Kinnier Wilson

Chapter 12 186
    The Definition of Religion
        Syed Farid Alatas

Chapter 13 205
    Professor Ashraf and His Contribution to Religious Education in England
        Sarah Smalley

Chapter 14 215
    Syed Ali Ashraf: Exploring Education through a Spiritual Lens
        Syed Ali Naqi

Chapter 15 228
    The Cosmic Triangle: God, Man and Nature in Syed Ali Ashraf's Philosophy of Education
        Iftekhar Iqbal and *Asiyah Kumpoh*

Chapter 16 245
    Skills of Discernment: An Essential but Neglected Aspect of Education in Religion
        Brenda Watson

Chapter 17 265
    Islamisation and Higher Education: Syed Ali Ashraf and the Secular Consequences of Religious Ideas
        Mujadad Zaman

Chapter 18 286
    Education of the Interior: Reflections on the Legacy of Syed Ali Ashraf
        Nadeem A. Memon

Chapter 19 304
    The Moral Theory of Five Cosmic Values: Islamic Moral Theory Based on Reason and Revelation
        Mashhad Al-Allaf

Chapter 20 325
    Spotlights on the Islamisation of Education from Syed Ali Ashraf's Perspective
        Muḥammad Al-Sayyid Al-Sayyid Al-Ṣaftī

Chapter 21 340
    Literary Activities of Professor Syed Ali Ashraf
        Mahmud Shah Qureshi

Chapter 22   348
  Between Utopia and Despair: The Impact of Environmental and
  Technological Millennialism on the Young
  Magnus Bradshaw

Chapter 23   374
  Natural Philosophy and Islamic Science: Is the Lack of Natural
  Philosophy the Reason for the Decline of Islamic Science?
  Hazim Shah

Chapter 24   391
  Syed Ali Ashraf: The Spiritual-Intellectual Guide on Islam and English
  Literature
  Nor Faridah Abdul Manaf

Chapter 25   404
  Islamic Scholarship: A Gateway to a Grand Destination
  Emajuddin Ahamed

Chapter 26   408
  Islamisation of Education: Contribution of Syed Ali Ashraf and
  a Global Muslim Perspective
  Ahmed Farid

Chapter 27   422
  Syed Ali Ashraf's Contribution to Teacher Education in Bangladesh
  Mohammad Nurul Haq

Chapter 28   427
  Islamic Education in the Light of Professor Ashraf's Philosophy
  M. M. Roisuddin Ahammad

Part II Reminiscences

Chapter 29   447
  Professor Syed Ali Ashraf: An Appreciation
  Peter Mitchell

Chapter 30   451
  A Few Memories of Syed Ali Ashraf at Cambridge: 1950–1952
  Norman J. L. Howlings

Chapter 31   455
  Professor Syed Abu Nasr Ali Ashraf: A Friend I Miss Forever
  A. M. M. Azhar Hussain

Chapter 32   459
  Reflections on the Life of Syed Ali Ashraf: Based on an Interview with
  His Sister-in-Law, Mrs Selina Ali
  Muhammad Abdul Jabbar Beg

Chapter 33   465
  Dignity Wrapped up in Humility: A Tribute to Professor Syed Ali Ashraf
  M. Harunur Rashid

Chapter 34   470
   In Memory of Syed Ali Ashraf: Reminiscences and Reflections
     Muhammad Ahsan

Chapter 35   489
   Professor Syed Ali Ashraf: A True Believer
     Rhoda Jal Vania

Chapter 36   496
   Dr Syed Ali Ashraf: Memoirs of a Student
     Farogh Naweed

Chapter 37   501
   Remembering Syed Ali Ashraf
     Muhammad Abdul Jabbar Beg

Chapter 38   511
   My Memories of Professor Dr Syed Ali Ashraf
     Imran N. Hosein

Chapter 39   524
   Professor Syed Ali Ashraf: Visits to Trinidad
     Waffie Mohammed

Chapter 40   534
   Reminiscing on Professor Syed Ali Ashraf
     Zainol A. Khan

Chapter 41   551
   Visionary Legacy: The Life and Dreams of Professor Ashraf
     A. K. M. Mohiuddin

Chapter 42   553
   In Remembrance of Syed Ali Ashraf
     Tosun Bayrak

   Conclusion *Shaikh Abdul Mabud*   556
   Afterword *Anwar Ibrahim*   560
   Appendix 1: Syed Ali Ashraf: Chronology of Events   562
   Appendix 2 Family Tree of Syed Ali Ashraf   565
   Contributors   567
   Index   579

Transliteration System for Arabic, Persian, and Urdu

Consonants

A = Arabic, P = Persian, U = Urdu

	A	P	U		A	P	U		A	P	U
ء	ʾ	ʾ	ʾ	ر	r	r	r	ق	q	q	q
ب	b	b	b	ڑ	-	-	ṛ	ك	k	k	k
پ	-	p	p	ز	z	z	z	گ	-	g	g
ت	t	t	t	ژ	-	zh	zh	ل	l	l	l
ٹ	-	-	ṭ	س	s	s	s	م	m	m	m
ث	th	s̱	s̱	ش	sh	sh	sh	ن	n	n	n
ج	j	j	j	ص	ṣ	ṣ	ṣ	ں	-	-	ñ
چ	-	ch	ch	ض	ḍ	ż	ż	ه	h	h	h
ح	ḥ	ḥ	ḥ	ط	ṭ	ṭ	ṭ	و	w	w	w
خ	kh	kh	kh	ظ	ẓ	ẓ	ẓ	ي	y	y	y
د	d	d	d	ع	ʿ	ʿ	ʿ	ے	-	-	e
ڈ	-	-	ḍ	غ	gh	gh	gh	ة	t, h	t, h	t, h
ذ	dh	ẕ	ẕ	ف	f	f	f	ال	al-, -l-	-	-

Vowels

Long	ا or ى	ā	Short	◌َ	a
	و	ū		◌ُ	u
	ي	ī		◌ِ	i

Doubled	ۑ	iyy (final form ī)	Diphthongs	وَ	au *or* aw
	وُ	uww (final form ū)		ىَ	ai *or* ay

Acknowledgements

I wish to express my deep gratitude to Sultan Omar 'Ali Saifuddien Centre for Islamic Studies, Universiti Brunei Darussalam and the Islamic Academy, Cambridge for making the writing and publication of this work possible. My sincere thanks to all the contributors who have cooperated with me at every stage of the production of this book. Without their cooperation, this work would not have seen the light of day. It saddens me that some contributors have passed away before the completion of this book, and I am deeply indebted to them for their invaluable contributions. I extend my heartfelt gratitude to Professor Seyyed Hossein Nasr for writing the Foreword, and to His Excellency Dr Anwar Ibrahim, Prime Minister of Malaysia, for contributing the Afterword. I am particularly grateful to Professor Osman Bakar and Dr Iftekhar Iqbal for their generous support during the manuscript preparation process. I am grateful to Professor Muhammad Ahsan for his journey to Pakistan and his efforts in meeting with Professor Ashraf's colleagues to gather invaluable information about him. I wish to express my sincere thanks to Dr Emin Poljarevic and Dr Nadeem Memon for their invaluable insights and constructive comments on specific sections of the text. I am deeply grateful to my daughters, Maliha and Fariha, for their invaluable comments on certain parts of the text and suggestions regarding its rearrangement. I also wish to thank my youngest daughter, Samiha, for obtaining information on Professor Ashraf from Cambridge University Library, which led to the improvement of certain parts of the text. I greatly appreciate Professor Khairudin Aljunied's assistance with the publication of the book. I wish to thank Mohamed Jabir Ali al-Hudawi for his meticulous attention to detail in formatting the references and bibliography. I wish to thank the publication team at Beacon Books, particularly Jamil Chishti, who gave me his unwavering support, and Siema Rafiq, who edited the manuscript and who offered invaluable help through the many stages of its production. Last but not least, I extend my heartfelt gratitude to my wife, Shajeda, for her enduring patience, understanding, and steadfast support and encouragement throughout the entire journey of writing this book. Above all, I am profoundly thankful to Allah, as without His divine help and guidance, none of this would have been achievable.

Foreword

The late professor Syed Ali Ashraf must be considered as one of the major figures in Islamic education during the past few decades. I first met him over fifty years ago and soon we became close friends and collaborators in many projects, leading to the organization of the First World Conference on Muslim Education held in Makkah in 1977, an unprecedented event in which Dr Abdullah Nasseef of Saudi Arabia also participated actively.

Coming from a family of educators, my father having been one of the founders of the modern educational system in Iran and being myself deeply immersed in educational matters in Iran where I had been both a dean and a university president, I found in Dr Ashraf a kindred soul. He was fully aware, like myself, through direct experience of the prevalent educational systems in most Islamic countries, that those systems were in reality a new form of Western intellectual and cultural colonialism, after formal political colonialism came to an end in most of the Islamic world after the Second World War. We both sought to revive the Islamic philosophy of education. Dr Ashraf travelled widely to spread the authentic Islamic philosophy of education, and the influence of his efforts can be seen from his home country of Bangladesh to England to even some Caribbean countries.

I congratulate the distinguished scholar Shaikh Abdul Mabud for the editing of this important volume and I pray that Dr Ashraf's teachings continue to resonate among Muslim educators everywhere. May God shower His Blessings upon his soul. *Wa'Llāh aʿlam.*

Seyyed Hossein Nasr
University Professor of Islamic Studies
George Washington University
Washington D.C.
October 2023

Preface
Shaikh Abdul Mabud

When I went to Cambridge in 1974 to do my PhD at the Cavendish Laboratory, a Bangladeshi student named Abdus Sattar, who was doing a PhD in Islamic Studies at Cambridge University, told me that he would like to introduce me to a professor from Bangladesh who lived in Cambridge. I happily agreed. This was Professor Syed Ali Ashraf. When we went to meet him at his house at 12 Gurney Way, we found that he was strolling along the street outside his house for an evening walk with Professor Syed Sajjad Husain. Both Professor Ashraf and Professor Sajjad Husain were at the time teaching English at King Abdulaziz University and were back from Saudi Arabia for the holidays. I had met Professor Sajjad Husain earlier in 1969 when he was the Vice-Chancellor of Rajshahi University where I did my undergraduate and master's. It was, however, my first encounter with Professor Ashraf. Both the gentlemen were smartly dressed and perhaps our arrival curtailed their pleasant walk. Soon we were invited into the house where we met Mrs Ashraf who welcomed us with kindness and generosity. I used to address her as *Khalamma*, a term often used to signify respect for and attachment to someone as a motherly figure. The lounge where we were seated was modest with signs of no luxury. I was amazed at the simplicity of their living. I still remember the affectionate way both the professors were talking to me. I was in my early twenties at that time and for me it was a humble experience of encountering two great professors, one of whom had been my Vice-Chancellor a few years ago. We left after an hour or so. Within a few days both the professors left for Saudi Arabia, but Mrs Ashraf stayed behind. I used to visit her frequently and would meet Professor Ashraf whenever he would return from Saudi Arabia. Professor Ashraf had a magnetic personality and my attachment to him grew fast. I came to know him closely and held him in great esteem for his scholarship and personal character. Little did I realise that this first meeting with Professor Ashraf was the beginning of a lifelong journey with him.

In 1976, I left Cambridge and went to Oxford, where I continued my PhD at the Clarendon Laboratory. Occasionally I went to Cambridge to meet with Mrs Ashraf and Professor Ashraf when he would come home from Saudi Arabia. Having completed my PhD, I returned to Bangladesh in 1978 and resumed my lectureship at Rajshahi University. I continued at Rajshahi until I left for the University of Utah in Salt Lake City, USA, in 1981, where I spent over two years doing research and teaching in the Department of Physics. While I was in Salt Lake City, I travelled to California once to meet with Professor Ashraf while he was visiting some of his relatives. Through my contact, I organised a lecture for him in California on an aspect of Muslim education. I spent a few days with him in California and then returned to Salt Lake City.

During my stay in Salt Lake City, I received a letter from Professor Ashraf inviting me to join the Islamic Academy, which he was establishing in Cambridge. It was a difficult decision, but as providentially ordained, I decided to leave the University of Utah and joined the Academy in October 1983 as its Deputy Director General. It was a turning point in my life: from research in physics to education.

The period from 1983 to 1998, when I worked at the Academy with Professor Ashraf as my colleague, was a period of intense activities of various kinds: research in education, lecturing, arranging seminars, editing an educational journal (*Muslim Education Quarterly*), organising interfaith dialogues, attending local meetings and international conferences, developing syllabuses, and writing articles and books, in addition to the administrative activities to run the Academy. My wife and the older children also used to help me with some of these activities. Professor Ashraf, a prolific writer, superb negotiator, and organiser, had a very busy life. He used to travel to various countries presenting keynote speeches in conferences, establishing contacts with scholars and organisations, and advising governments and organisations on the development and implementation of Islamic education. He shared most of his time between the UK, Saudi Arabia, and Bangladesh which he used as his base for the propagation of Islamic and faith-based education. During his absence he would entrust me with the responsibilities of running the Academy, which I carried out to the best of my ability, often in consultation with him over the phone if needed.

I accompanied Professor Ashraf to some of the countries he visited, including Saudi Arabia, Egypt, Malaysia, Holland, and Bangladesh. The purposes of my visits were for various reasons: to present papers at conferences, to train teachers to teach their subjects from the Islamic perspectives, and in Saudi Arabia it was to meet with the trustees of the Academy in relation to the official activities of the Academy. On one such visit in 1993, I was fortunate to perform Ḥajj with Professor Ashraf. In the early 1990s, he came to Jashore (a district in Bangladesh) at my request to visit my parents' graves. I seized this opportunity to organise a lecture for him in a hall at my house, which was attended by college teachers, Islamic scholars, and individuals interested in education.

Gradually Professor Ashraf became closer to my family. He would come to my house, which was only a few minutes' walk from his and meet my wife and children. My family would also visit him at his house on Metcalfe Road which was also the headquarters of the Islamic Academy until 1997. When our children, the older ones—Masum and Maliha, had any questions about their English novels, Professor Ashraf would explain them. He also used to come to my house every Thursday evening, when he was in Cambridge, to lead the spiritual session which consisted of the recitation of the Qurʾān, *Khatm-e Khwājegān*, *ṣalāt* and *salām* on the Prophet (pbuh) followed by supplication and a meal.

The Islamic Academy served as an intellectual hub for scholars to exchange ideas on spiritual and educational matters. In addition to publishing the *Muslim Education Quarterly* and other works, the Academy hosted meetings and seminars that provided a platform for this purpose, attracting many renowned scholars who visited the Academy either to present invited lectures or to discuss educational issues or simply to visit us. It was visited by Professor Ashraf's friends, colleagues and students and other scholars, some of whom came to the UK for other businesses. It was through the Islamic Academy that I had the opportunity to meet esteemed scholars such as Seyyed Hossein Nasr, Ismaʿil Raji al-Faruqi, Naquib al-Attas, Abdur Rahman Doi, William Chittick, Malik Badri, Tosun Bayrak, Martin Lings, Akbar S. Ahmed, Ahmed Paul Keeler, Imran N. Hosein, Hakeem Muhammad Saeed and many others. I had the privilege of associating and corresponding with some of these scholars for an extended period.

My work at the Academy has been enlightening and rewarding. In addition to my regular official duties, I had numerous opportunities to discuss regularly various philosophical and spiritual matters with Professor Ashraf, either during tea breaks, outside office hours, or even during weekends at his house. I have treasured these discussions in my mind, as they have significantly broadened my perspective not only on educational issues but also on human life and destiny. What I have presented in this work is based on my firsthand experience of working with him and understanding his philosophical and educational thoughts over a period of twenty-four years.

During the last few years of his life, Professor Ashraf was visiting Cambridge less frequently and spending more time in Dhaka. During his last visit to Cambridge, in the evening on Thursday 6 August 1998, he came to my house on Darwin Drive to lead the spiritual session as usual, as stated above. He left at 10:30 pm for his residence at the Islamic Academy building on Gilbert Road, where two gentlemen, Abdul Aziz Doughaiter (from Madinah) and Mustafizur Rahman (from London) were also residing. The next morning, Mustafizur Rahman called me and said that Professor Ashraf had not called them for the *Fajr* prayer. He was still lying in bed and not moving. I hurried to the Academy, checked, and found that he had passed away. I informed Mrs Selina Ali, his sister-in-law, Barrister Nazmul Hussain, a Trustee of the Academy, and the relevant government authorities. Barrister Nazmul Hussain and Mrs Selina Ali's family soon arrived from London. Professor Ashraf's body was then taken to

Addenbrooke's Hospital in Cambridge. After completing all the formalities, his body was transferred to the East London Mosque, where his *Janāzah* (funeral prayer) was performed the following day (the 8th) after the *Ẓuhr* prayer. His body was then taken to Heathrow Airport and flown from there on 9 August en route to Bangladesh. I accompanied him on the flight. We arrived at Dhaka on 10 August in the morning. He was buried on the same day next to Tahfizul Quranil Karim Fazil Madrasah at the Darul Ihsan University Campus in Savar, Dhaka.

One year after the passing of Professor Ashraf the trustees of the Academy promoted me to Director General, the post I still hold.

I am pleased to present this book to the reader on the 100th birth anniversary of Professor Ashraf. The contributors to this book have done an outstanding job recounting their experiences of encountering Professor Ashraf directly or through his writings. In a few cases, they have also contributed articles in areas that were important to Professor Ashraf.

Introduction
Shaikh Abdul Mabud

They know but the outer things in the life of this world, but of the End of things they are heedless. (Qurʾān 30:7)

The Prophet (pbuh) said, "Truly in the body there is a morsel of flesh, which, if it is sound, the whole body is sound, and if it is corrupted, the whole body is corrupted. Truly, it is the heart." (Bukhārī)

This collection of essays is a tribute to one of the eminent Islamic thinkers of the twentieth century, Professor Syed Abu Nasr Ali Ashraf. Most of the contributors to this book met Professor Ashraf personally. Some were his colleagues, some students, some friends, some classmates, and some relatives. A few of the contributors who never met Professor Ashraf are aware of his work. This is the first comprehensive and reliable account of Professor Ashraf's life, work, and philosophy to be produced in the English language. The book offers glimpses into important events in his life, delves into his philosophical concepts, provides critical analyses of his literary endeavours, recounts his interactions with distinguished scholars and spiritual leaders, and illuminates his personality and the underlying philosophy of his thoughts. On the one hand, this is a tribute to his legacy; on the other hand, it serves as a sourcebook on his life and work.

When I began compiling essays on him, I encountered the unfortunate reality that many of his colleagues, friends, and relatives had passed away. Locating and reaching out to those who still knew Professor Ashraf personally and could contribute to this volume posed a significant challenge. Moreover, many individuals who knew him were unable to provide written contributions. However, after persistent efforts, a substantial number of articles capturing various facets of his life were obtained and are presented in this book for our readers. While there are numerous aspects of his life and valuable work that deserve further elaboration, constraints on the book's length necessitated omitting such attempts. Nevertheless, plans are underway for a future volume dedicated to exploring Professor Ashraf's life and work in greater detail.

Professor Syed Ali Ashraf was a leading Islamic thinker of the twentieth century. He was an eminent educationalist, a great Sufi master, and an acclaimed poet in the Bengali language. He was versatile, creative, and prolific. He was a man who spoke out with conviction with the voice of a visionary. To his devoted followers he was a profound spiritual guide; to his friends and colleagues he stood out as reliable and respectful; to those in need he was compassionate, gentle, and generous; and to people of other religions ever ready to cooperate.

Peter Mitchell, Professor Ashraf's colleague at the University of Cambridge, aptly captures his extraordinary character when he says, "By any measure he was an outstanding person, showing clearly by his life and actions a combination of outstanding scholarship with deep personal piety."[1] Professor Akbar Ahmed spoke of him as, "Virtually unknown in the media, Ashraf was one of the half-dozen most important Muslim scholars of the last few decades."[2] Professor Mark Halstead described him as follows: "His intense personal faith, his prayerfulness and his spiritual insight and vision . . . will continue to provide an example and source of inspiration for Muslim and non-Muslim alike."[3] Professor David Thompson portrayed him as having a "gentle manner, a lovable character, and profound wisdom."[4] Professor Ghulam Nabi Saqeb compared him with such figures as ʿAbdul Qādir Jīlānī, Shaikh Muʿīnuddīn Chishty, Khwāja Niẓāmuddīn Awliyāʾ, and Mujaddid Alf Thānī in Sufi tradition.[5]

Renowned as an eminent educationalist, revered Sufi master, and celebrated poet in the Bengali language, his legacy embodies versatility, creativity, and prolificacy. With his intuitive insight, he fearlessly articulated his convictions, leaving an indelible mark on all who encountered his wisdom. Over the span of fifty years, his contributions have enriched scholars and researchers worldwide. As a trailblazer in Islamic education, his endeavours mark the dawn of a new era in the global Islamic education movement.

---

1 Peter Mitchell, "Syed Ali Ashraf: An Appreciation" see Chapter 29 of this book.
2 Akbar S. Ahmed, "Obituary: Syed Ali Ashraf," *The Independent*, Wednesday, August 13, 1998 (online version), https://www.independent.co.uk/arts-entertainment/obituary-professor-syed-ali-ashraf-1171311.html.
3 Mark Halstead, "Obituary: Syed Ali Ashraf 1925–1998," *British Journal of Religious Education* 21, no. 3 (1999): 133–134, DOI: 10.1080/0141620990210302.
4 David M. Thompson, "Professor Syed Ali Ashraf," *Fitzwilliam College Journal* X, no. 5 (March 1999): 37.
5 Ghulam Nabi Saqeb, "Islamic Education and the Challenge of Secularism: Professor Syed Ali Ashraf's Critique of Secularism in Education in Muslim Countries: A Personal Appraisal," see Chapter 5 of this volume.

Professor Ashraf's Early Life, Education and Professional Achievements

Professor Ashraf was born on 30 January 1924[6] into a family steeped in scholarly and spiritual heritage, tracing its roots to Shah Abu Ali Baghdadi, a fifteenth-century Sufi saint who journeyed from Baghdad to Delhi to spread the teachings of Islam. A short history of his arrival in Bengal and settling there has been described by Syed Ali Ahsan in his book, *Hôzrot Shah Ali Boghdadi*.[7] For generations, the descendants of this revered saint have been instrumental in disseminating the message of Islam in Bengal. The lineage of Professor Ashraf, extending back to this saintly figure, is illustrated in Appendix 2. From early childhood, he was immersed in a profoundly spiritual atmosphere, inheriting a rich legacy of spiritual teachings from both his paternal and maternal grandfathers. Their steadfast adherence to Sufi practices and teachings formed the bedrock of his upbringing. Even in his boyhood, he exuded a remarkable serenity and gentleness. His father, Syed Ali Hamed, served as a school inspector, while his mother, Syedah Qamrunnigar Khatun was a daughter of the renowned spiritual master, Syed Mukarram Ali, residing in Agla, Nawabganj, within the district of Dhaka, Bangladesh. Following in the footsteps of his ancestors, he devoted his life to the propagation of Islam from every position he held, whether as a university lecturer or vice-chancellor, as a Sufi Shaykh, or as a family man or friend. He envisioned a society that would be devoted to God, spiritually enlightened, morally upright drawing its nourishment from the fountain of Islamic spiritual and intellectual heritage, while ready to cooperate with people of other cultures and traditions. He believed, education—in its comprehensive sense, that is, education of the body, mind, and soul—is the most effective means through which human beings can be trained to attain these noble goals.

Professor Ashraf devoted his writings to several themes that are crucial to educational provisions in modern society. Numerous works authored by him, in both English and Bengali, extends over half a century, pre-dating the organisation of the World Conferences on Muslim Education. The corpus of

---

6 According to Syed Ali Naqi, Professor Ashraf's brother, his date of birth is 30 January 1924 (see Chapter 14 of this book). This date is engraved on his tomb at Savar, Dhaka. This is the date reported in *Bôrenyo: Syed Ali Ashraf Smarok Grôntho* (1999), p. 202, edited by Muhammad Ahsanullah Mia, Muhammad Ismail Husain, Mahmudul Hasan Yusuf, Muhammad Shamsuddoha, and Shah Waliullah Farhad, and published by Faculty of Religious Education, Darul Ihsan University, Dhaka, Bangladesh. However, according to the official record of Fitzwilliam College (Cambridge University) where he did his undergraduate and PhD, his date of birth is 1 January 1925 (see, note 4 above). This date was reported in an obituary published by me in *Muslim Education Quarterly*, no. 3, vol. 15, 1998 and Akbar S. Ahmed in the London newspaper, *The Independent* dated 13 August 1998 (online version 13 August).

7 Syed Ali Ahsan, *Hôzrot Shah Ali Boghdadi* (Dhaka: Syed ali Naqi, 1996).

his writings encompasses a wide array of topics, ranging from Muslim traditions, Islamic religion, Sharīʿah, and Sufism to literary criticism, philosophy of education, educational institutions, the teaching of English, teacher training, and social reform through religious regeneration. He derived the foundational principles of education from the Qurʾān and Sunnah which he strove to inculcate in every branch of knowledge. His thoughts consistently revolved around the innate nature of human beings and their relationship with God. What appeals to me particularly in him is the depth and sincerity of his thought and his genuine commitment to his principles. With deep commitment to faith and unswerving loyalty to tradition, he consistently maintained his fundamental philosophical position throughout his life. His passion for truth and his devotion to God and His Prophet were unparalleled.

He embarked on his academic journey by completing his Matriculation Examination at Armanitola Government School, Dhaka in 1940, followed by the IA (Intermediate of Arts) examination at Government Dacca Intermediate College in 1942. He attained his Bachelor's degree in English from the University of Dhaka in 1945, followed by a Master's degree in English from the same institution in 1946. His academic aspirations led him to the University of Cambridge, where he achieved significant milestones, including a BA (English Tripos, Fitzwilliam College) in 1952, a further MA in 1955, and a PhD in 1964.[8]

Syed Ali Ashraf showed sign of talents from an early age. Appointed Joint Secretary of the East Pakistan Literary Society (established in 1942) while still in his teenage years and already a burgeoning poet, he found himself immersed in the vibrant Bengali cultural milieu. This early involvement provided him with a profound understanding of the cultural landscape of Bengal, which later found full expression in his literary works, notably *Muslim Traditions in Bengali Literature* (1960) and *Literature, Society and Culture in East Pakistan 1947 to 1971* (1973), both published by Karachi University. Throughout his extensive academic career, Professor Ashraf held various positions at different educational institutions. He began teaching as a Lecturer of English at the University of Dacca in 1947. Subsequently, he served as the head of the English departments at Rajshahi University, Karachi University, and King Abdulaziz University during 1955–1977. Additionally, he worked as a Visiting Professor of English at Harvard University (1971) and New Brunswick University (1974) and held roles as a Fellow of Clare Hall (1973–1974), Fellow of Wolfson College (1982–1984) and Supervisor of English at the University of Cambridge. During 1980–1982, he served as the Director General of the Makkah-based World Centre for Islamic Education established by the Organisation of Islamic Conference. He also served as a Visiting Professor at the Department of Education, University of Cambridge (1982–1992). In 1983, he became the founding Direc-

---

8   Shamsuzzaman Khan, *Bangladesh Lekhok Porichiti* (Introduction to Bangladesh Writers) (Dhaka: Bangla Academy, 1984), 197.

tor General of the Islamic Academy, Cambridge, and later served as the Vice Chancellor of Darul Ihsan University, Dhaka, from 1990 until his passing.⁹

Naturally inclined towards Sufism, at the age of 22 he pledged his allegiance (*bayʿah*) to Hazrat Ghulam Muqtadir. Subsequently, he progressed on his spiritual path, successively becoming the disciple and later successor (*khalīfah*) of Hazrat Baba Zaheen Shah Taji, Hazrat Hafez Bazlur Rahman, Hazrat Syed Manzur Husain, Hazrat Dr Badiuzzaman, Al-Sayyid Muhammad ʿAlawi al-Maliki al-Husayni, and Shaikh Abdul Majid. Notably, Hazrat Dr Badiuzzaman entrusted him with the responsibility of leading his spiritual organisation, Jamāʿat-e Madīnah. Through these profound connections with Sufi masters, he ascended to a high position (*maqām*) within the spiritual realm. The wisdom acquired from this spiritual journey endowed him with a deep understanding of universal and timeless truths. Together with his dedication to Sufi practices, he remained steadfast in his adherence to the principles of Sharīʿah.

In addition to his ongoing educational pursuits, Professor Ashraf remained steadfastly committed to providing spiritual guidance to his disciples across various locations including the UK, the USA, Bangladesh, and Trinidad and Tobago. During his visits to these countries, he would meet with his disciples, engage in spiritual contemplation with them, and impart invaluable spiritual training. Moreover, he made a point of visiting Sufi Shaykhs (spiritual masters) in diverse regions to further his own spiritual advancement and to pay respect to them.

Professor Ashraf passed away in Cambridge on August 7, 1998. His body was transported to Bangladesh, where he was laid to rest at the Darul Ihsan University campus in Savar, Dhaka, on August 10, 1998.

The Context of His Work

In the 1950s, Professor Ashraf observed a rising tide of invasive secular ideology seeping into the Muslim world, impacting every facet of life in Muslim societies. This phenomenon stemmed from the legacy of British colonial rule. Over the preceding two centuries of colonial dominance, Muslims had endured multifaceted Western encroachments—cultural, religious, intellectual, military, and political—culminating in their physical subjugation and economic exploitation. The colonial powers implemented an education system designed to further their own interests, primarily aimed at exerting control, exploitation, and assimilation of the colonised population. This endeavour involved imposing the language, culture, and values of the colonising nation onto the indigenous populace, often with the intent of cultivating a class of local elites who would align with and serve the colonial administration and who would be "English in tastes, in opinions, in morals and in intellect."¹⁰ Con-

---

9   See Appendix 1, "Chronology of Events."
10 Lord Macaulay published an official minute on the method of education in the colonised

sequently, local languages, traditions, and knowledge systems were systematically marginalised or suppressed.[11] Moreover, colonial education sought to erode or replace traditional religious instruction with secular or Christian-oriented curricula. Initially influenced by Enlightenment philosophy and the increasing secularisation of the West, this education progressively shifted towards a more secular orientation, relegating religious roots in favour of a rationalistic approach that considered sense-experience and rationality, and not revelation, as valid sources of knowledge. Morality was regarded as a social product and not dependent on Absolute values. Based on an evolutionary vison of the world and human beings, Divine Truths were denied a place in secularised education systems.

After the end of colonial rule, Muslims began asserting themselves and working diligently across various fronts to establish their independence. However, the prolonged period of colonisation led to a shift in the mindset of the educated elite. Their efforts to develop their countries politically, economically, militarily, and intellectually were significantly influenced by a colonial mindset. This dynamic created tensions between two segments of Muslims: those educated in traditional madrasahs and those from modern colleges and universities. The modern educated elite, equipped with contemporary knowledge, were better positioned to assume leadership roles in governing the country. These individuals were also the ones who had benefited the most from the Empire, holding positions of influence and power while supporting imperial rule, and this trend continued into the Independent era. Consequently, graduates of madrasahs often found themselves marginalised, holding peripheral positions in society and lacking influence in national affairs, including the formulation of educational policies. This situation brought the two major groups at loggerheads with each other. From the nineteenth century onward, modernised Muslims started to emulate the West with the hope of regaining power but the more they followed the West, the more they drifted away from the spirit of Islam, and the more they were subjugated intellectually and politically. In many countries traditional Islamic education had been replaced by the Western style education system, the Divine Law (*Sharīʿah*) by civil law, and other traditional systems by policies that are often against the tenets of the faith of the Muslim masses. However, not all sections of Muslim society accepted this: the powerful sacred centres of Islam resisted such change. Hence a cultural duality appeared everywhere in the Muslim world. Professor Ashraf

---

countries on 2 February 1835 which was approved by William Bentinck on 7 March of the same year: "Minute by the Hon'ble T. B. Macaulay, dated the 2nd February 1835," Bureau of Education. Selections from Educational Records, Part I (1781–1839). Edited by H. Sharp. Calcutta: Superintendent, Government Printing, 1920. Reprint. Delhi: National Archives of India, 1965, 107-117.

11   Gauri Viswanathan, *Masks of Conquest: Literary Study and British Rule in India* (Columbia University Press, 1989).

observed that Western institutions of learning became the means for the spread of secular values and the criticism of the religious worldview. On the other hand, modernised Muslims failed to grasp that Islam is at once both progressive and orthodox, liberal and conservative, and innovative and imitative. He noticed that modernity maintains rigid opposition to revealed truths while a rigid understanding of tradition entails unreasonable resistance to scientific advancements. In all this Professor Ashraf observed a decline of religious sensibility alongside a rise in secular perspectives. He began writing with the goal of reinstating religious values within Muslim societies, aiming to counteract the impact of secularisation. Professor Ashraf's own reflections shed light on why, despite being a Western-educated Cambridge graduate himself, he was critical of modern education and chose to restructure the education of Muslims:

> I criticised the modern education system because it is based on a concept of human nature which does not recognise the human spirit and its relationship with God and thereby eliminates the possibility of revelations and God-given knowledge and guidance for mankind. It is also based on a worldview that propagates the concept of society producing values and thereby creating a tradition of values and a tradition of evolution of values. This worldview is fundamentally of this world and hence it does not rouse in the pupils' minds the slightest consciousness of life after death. It is difficult to keep religious consciousness alive in the hearts of children when all branches of knowledge are dominated by such a view of life and when teachers are expected not to teach from the religious point of view. For more than one hundred years teacher training institutes and colleges have been propagating this secularist approach. Even religious education is taught from a non-religious secularist point of view, not from the point of view of cultivating the religious sensibility. I therefore suggested and the scholars at the First World Conference agreed to recommend that research should be carried out to replace the secularist concepts at the roots of all branches of knowledge by concepts drawn from the Islamic frame of life and values as found in the Qurʾān and the Sunnah.[12]

The circumstances faced by Muslims in the mid-twentieth century provided the backdrop for his endeavours to invigorate the Muslim world with the essence of Islam. His mission was to instigate social reform by combatting secular influences in society and education, advocating for a form of education among Muslims rooted in their faith. He urged the Muslim intelligentsia to diverge from Westernisation and guide the masses back to the true path of Is-

---

12 Syed Ali Ashraf, preface to *Religion and Education: Islamic and Christian Approaches*, eds. Syed Ali Ashraf and Paul H. Hirst (Cambridge: The Islamic Academy, 1994), xi.

lam. Recognising education as the most potent tool for this transformation, he pursued a two-pronged approach: after the World Conferences on Muslim Education, when he started working at the Islamic Academy, he first emphasised the necessity of developing an Islamic theory of education across all branches of knowledge. Secondly, he sought to replace secular ideologies entrenched in various fields of study within contemporary curricula with principles derived from the Qurʾān and the Sunnah.

Upon relocating to Cambridge in 1974, he also noted the predominantly secular nature of the British education system. However, he found common ground with certain Christian individuals and organisations, sharing concerns about "increasing secularisation, rising materialism, and excessive individualism,"[13] as well as the marginalisation of religious voices in education.[14] The Islamic Academy, established by Professor Ashraf, provided a venue for forging a new era of collaboration between Muslims and other faith groups, in order to protect the presence of religious perspectives in educational discourse.

His Achievements and Impacts

Professor Ashraf's writings are critical, penetrating, analytical, and comprehensive. They have been written from both universal and Islamic perspectives, adapting to the specific topic under consideration. Transcending mere comprehension, he showed clarity of thought and depth of vision in grasping subtleties of philosophical propositions and complexities of situations. For instance, in 1957, during his tenure as the head of the Department of English at the University of Karachi, he participated in a conference in Michigan sponsored by the Near East Club under the State Department's Leader Exchange Program. At this event, he delivered a speech entitled "Democracy and Islam." In this address, he astutely observed that while democracy ostensibly pursued the ideal of freedom, he provocatively questioned, "Yet, a freedom leading to what?"—suggesting that the trajectory of human freedom must be guided in a manner that preserves, rather than undermines, our humanity. His profound concern for the erosion of morality in the modern age was evident, as he identified the dilution of moral principles as a significant factor contributing to the failure of democracy and the educational system. Donald Kurtz succinctly encapsulated his perspectives voiced during this conference in the following words:

> In contrasting the political philosophies of Islam and democracy, Prof. Ashraf saw nineteenth century Europe as the stage for dethroning the Christian ideals of morality and "replacement with the scientific con-

---

13 Ruth Deakin, *The New Christian Schools* (Bristol: Regius Press, 1989), 5.
14 Deakin, *The New Christian Schools*, 7.

cept of man under new multiple ideals." With the failure of an integrated moral law democracy itself crumbled, he said. Man sought to become a superman, and in the struggle lost his values. This, he said led to delinquency and the educational problem, "the great danger facing democracy."[15]

As early as the 1950s, Professor Ashraf expressed concern about the displacement of religious moral ideals from Western society, being replaced by a secular concept of humanity, resulting in the erosion of values and contributing to social ills and educational challenges.

Professor Ashraf was a prolific writer in both English and Bengali, with a remarkable oeuvre comprising over twenty-five authored or edited books, including six books of poetry. His mystical poetry explores themes related to spirituality, divine love, longing for the divine, inner journey, and the human soul's quest for transcendence. His educational writings have influenced many Muslims and some Christian scholars who have accepted his stance on the secularisation of education in modern times. His ideas are scattered in numerous writings in books, journals, newspapers, interviews, and lectures in both English and Bengali. Notably, he was the founding editor for several esteemed journals, such as *Venture* (Department of English, Karachi University), *Taj* (Islamic Education Society, Karachi), *Islamic Education Quarterly* (World Centre for Islamic Education, Makkah), *Muslim Education* (King Abdulaziz University), and *Muslim Education Quarterly* (Islamic Academy, Cambridge). Beyond print, Professor Ashraf's influence extended to radio and television platforms, where his lectures in the UK, Dhaka, and Trinidad and Tobago addressed various facets of Islamic religion, education, and social reform. Moreover, his lectures were delivered in many countries, including the USA, UK, Europe, Trinidad and Tobago, Saudi Arabia, Jordan, Egypt, Pakistan, India, Bangladesh and Malaysia focused on revitalising Muslim society across realms of knowledge and spirituality.

One of the most significant aspects of his work was the establishment of educational institutions wherever he went. Whether in Dhaka, Karachi, or Cambridge, he was dedicated to providing Islamic education by founding schools for children. His contributions were far-reaching, as seen in the establishment of research institutions like the Islamic Academy in Cambridge and the Institute of Higher Islamic Learning in Dhaka. He established language laboratories for teaching English language at Karachi University and introduced new methods of teaching the language. Among his notable achievements was the establishment of Darul Ihsan University in Dhaka[16] that demonstrates his com-

---

15 Donald Kurtz, "Pakistani Professor Sees Vagueness in Democracy," *The Michigan Daily*, May 16, 1957.
16 Unfortunately, eighteen years after Prof. Ashraf's passing, this university was shut down for illegally operating numerous branch campuses and selling higher degree

mitment to advancing integrated education at the tertiary level. He also established Tahfizul Qurʾānil Karim Fazil Madrasah at Savar, Dhaka that is based on an integrated system of Islamic education consisting of both religious as well as non-religious subjects such as physics, chemistry, etc. He developed a model curriculum for King Abdulaziz University's General Education program, which he submitted to Dr Abdullah Omar Nasseef, the then President of the university. Collaborating with partners, he developed curricula for institutions such as Dar al-Islam in New Mexico and schools under The Anjuman Sunnat-ul-Jamaat Association (ASJA) in Trinidad and Tobago. Teacher training was another priority for him, with numerous courses organised worldwide. He restructured the teacher education courses at Darul Ihsan University, Dhaka, while also coordinating teacher training programmes at Dar al-Islam and The Anjuman Sunnat-ul-Jamaat Association. Notably, Professor Ashraf and I were invited in July 1991 to conduct a teacher training workshop at the University of Technology Malaysia in Johor Bahru on the topic, "University Education and Modern Technology: The Islamic Approach." The main objectives were to (1) make teachers aware of the Islamic basis of education, (2) understand the Islamic structure of values and its maintenance in the technological education system; and (3) design a curriculum keeping in view the above two aspects of education.[17] In cooperation with the Cambridge University Department of Education he trained teachers of Religious Education (Islam) from British schools for several years. The organisation of the World Conferences on Muslim Education, the establishment of the Islamic Academy in Cambridge and Darul Ihsan University in Dhaka stand out as three of his major achievements, with far-reaching impact on Islamic education around the globe. In what follows, we delve into the first two, while the third one is described in Chapter 28.

World Conferences on Muslim Education and Their Impacts

Professor Ashraf moved to the UK in 1974, but divided his time between Dhaka, Cambridge, and Makkah where he had his own residences. While in Makkah, he made an international impact because of his organising the First World Conferences on Muslim Education in Makkah from March 31 to April 8, 1977. He describes the event that sparked the idea of holding the First World Conference in the following:

> When Shaikh Hassan Al-i-Shaikh, the Education Minister of Saudi Arabia, was returning from America, he was interviewed by some British journalists. The report that came out in the British papers was rather sarcastic. Al-i-Shaikh had talked to the journalists of expansion and modernisation of education in Saudi Arabia, and asserted that the

---

certificates.
17 Syed Ali Ashraf, "Editorial: University Education and Modern Technology: The Islamic Approach: A Malaysian Experiment," *Muslim Education Quarterly* 8, no. 4 (1991): 1–3.

country as a whole was so Islamic that this expansion of education would not erode the Islamic sensibility of the pupils. The journalists commented that this was a blinkered attitude produced by a mind not aware of modernisation and still trying to adhere to an outmoded way of life.

It was this comment that prompted me, and my friend Dr Motiur Rahman to write a letter to King Faisal, saying that unless steps were taken from now on, Saudi Arabia would fall into the same trap that Pakistan had fallen into. When Pakistan came into existence in 1947, the then Education Minister, Mr Fazlur Rahman invited all senior Muslim educationalists to give an Islamic character to the education system inherited from the British. The only solution suggested by them was the introduction of the teaching of *Islāmiyāt* (Islamic Studies) as an obligatory subject at all levels of education. They had failed to see the basic anti-religious, secularist approach that governed all other branches of knowledge....

I had worked in Karachi University as Head of the Department of English from 1956. I had seen the gradual erosion of the religious sensibility among the young, in spite of the obligatory teaching and learning of Islamic Studies at the undergraduate level.

We therefore wanted to point out the basic conceptual problem to the Saudi Government, and thought that at the very inception of Modern Education and its expansion, they were the right people to organise courses and thus give a lead to the Muslim World.

Our letter was sent in April 1974.[18]

Professor Ashraf and Dr Motiur Rahman's letter initiated the process, leading to a series of meetings and contacts, both private and official. Through these, basic principles and guidelines for the First World Conference were established. Over three years, a dedicated team of intellectuals, scholars, administrators, and supporters worked tirelessly to make the conference a reality. The organisation of the First World Conference on Muslim Education marked a significant milestone in the history of Muslim education. Professor Ashraf was one of the secretaries of this conference.[19] This conference produced a

---

18 Syed Ali Ashraf, *Islamic Education Movement: An Historical Analysis* (Cambridge: The Islamic Academy, 1990), 5-6.
19 The Organising Committee consisted of ten people with H. E. Shaikh Ahmad Salah Jamjoom as the chairman, Professor Syed Ali Ashraf and Dr Abdullah Muhammad Zaid as secretaries, and Dr Ghulam Nabi Saqeb as the assistant secretary. The Steering Committee consisted of forty people from various disciplines with H. E. Dr Muhammad Umar Zubair as the chairman; H. E. Shaikh Ahmad Salah Jamjoom, Dr Abdullah Omar Nasseef, Dr Jafar Abdul Rehman Sabbagh, and Dr Muhammad Ali Hibshi as the vice-chairmen; Professor Syed Ali Ashraf and Dr Abdullah Muhammad Zaid as secretaries;

comprehensive repertoire of concepts, theories, recommendations, and approaches to Islamic education. No conference on Muslim education of comparable magnitude has ever been organised before or since. As the secretary of the follow-up committee Professor Ashraf organised three other World Conferences on Muslim Education in Islamabad (1980), Dhaka (1981) and Jakarta (1982) dealing with curriculum designing, development of textbooks, and teaching methodologies and teacher education respectively. In the wider world, Professor Ashraf's name came to be associated with Islamic education following his organisation of these World Conferences. The aims of these conferences were the development of curricula, textbooks, and teacher training courses, with the intention of formulating a comprehensive educational plan for implementing an Islamic system of education in Muslim countries and for Muslim minorities residing in non-Muslim societies.[20] Later he helped organise two more World Conferences on Muslim Education in Cairo (1987) and Cape Town (1996).[21] He led these initiatives in collaboration with the Saudi Arabian government and a group of devoted scholars and educators. Throughout his educational endeavours, Professor Ashraf found unwavering support from two individuals: His Excellency Shaikh Ahmad Salah Jamjoom and His Excellency Dr Abdullah Omar Nasseef. They provided consistent practical, moral, and financial assistance, standing by him until his final days. They deserve sincere gratitude for their whole-hearted support in advancing Islamic education in the modern world. We also express our deep gratitude to all the scholars, too many to be mentioned here, who were involved in making these educational conferences a great success.

The World Conferences on Muslim Education initiated a transformative wave of Islamisation in education that reverberates to this day. In his book titled, "*Islamic Education Movement: An Historical Analysis*," Professor Ashraf vividly describes how he conceptualised these conferences, organised them, and delineates their profound impacts on the education of Muslims. Professor Saqeb described him as the individual who, "having masterminded the [First World] conference had further ideas as to how follow-up action should proceed."[22] Professor Osman Bakar called him "an irreplaceable figure" whose "post-conference role and contribution were perhaps even more challenging and significant for he had the unenviable task and responsibility of ensuring

---

and Dr Ghulam Nabi Saqeb as the assistant secretary.
20 Shaikh Abdul Mabud, "World Conferences on Muslim Education: Shaping the Agenda of Muslim Education in the Future," in *Philosophies of Islamic Education: Historical Perspectives and Emerging Discourses*, eds. Nadeem A. Memon and Mujadad Zaman (New York and London: Routledge, 2016), 129–143.
21 Mabud, "World Conferences," 135–36.
22 Ghulam Nabi Saqeb, "Some Reflections on Islamization of Education Since 1977 Makkah Conference: Accomplishments, Failures and Tasks Ahead," *Intellectual Discourse* 8, no. 1 (2000): 52.

that the resolutions of the conference were effectively carried out."[23] His keynote addresses at these conferences, compiled into a monograph titled *New Horizons in Muslim Education*, identified the problems of education in the Muslim world and offered suggestions to overcome them in a way that engages with the modern world.[24] The subsequent publications, comprising selected papers presented at these conferences, were consolidated into six books forming the "Islamic Education Series," all under the general editorship of Professor Ashraf.[25] These volumes effectively crystallised his visionary insights. Professor Ashraf says, "After the publication of these books the term 'Islamic education' acquired a new significance and a new dimension. Previously it used to mean education in Islamic studies. From then on it meant education whose conceptual and philosophical basis for each branch of knowledge was founded on principles drawn from the Qurʾān and the Sunnah."[26] As a pioneer of Islamic education in modern times, he spearheaded the modern Islamic education movement through these conferences and subsequent articles and editorial contributions to *Muslim Education Quarterly*. His efforts profoundly shaped contemporary understanding of Islam and its educational imperatives.

The World Conferences on Muslim Education, masterminded by Professor Ashraf, were a watershed in the history of Islamic education that laid the foundation of a worldwide movement for the Islamisation of education. As a result of these conferences, many organisations were created, educational institutions established, seminars organised, and journals launched to propagate and implement Islamic education.[27] They succeeded in establishing communication, mutual understanding, and cooperation among like-minded Mus-

---

23 Osman Bakar, "The Aims of Education: The Forgotten Truths." See Chapter 2 of this book.
24 The first chapter of this book was presented at the conference, on "Human Rights in Islam" held jointly by Kuwait University, International Association of Jurists and Arab Association of Lawyers in Kuwait in December 1980.
25 The following books in the "Islamic Education Series" were published by London: Hodder and Stoughton and Jeddah: King Abdulaziz University under the general editorship of Syed Ali Ashraf: Syed Sajjad Husain and Syed Ali Ashraf, eds., *Crisis in Muslim Education* (1979); Syed Muhammad Naquib al-Attas, ed., *Aims and Objectives of Islamic Education* (1979); Muhammad Hamid Al-Afendi and Nabi Ahmed Baloch, eds., *Curriculum and Teacher Education* (1980); Ismaʿil Raji Al-Faruqi and Abdullah Omar Nasseef, eds., *Social and Natural Sciences: The Islamic Perspective* (1981); Mohammad Wasiullah Khan, ed., *Education and Society in the Muslim World* (1981); Seyyed Hossein Nasr, ed., *Philosophy, Literature and Fine Arts* (1982).
26 Syed Ali Ashraf, *Islamic Education Movement: An Historical Analysis* (Cambridge: The Islamic Academy, 1990), 19.
27 They have been summed up by Professor Ashraf and Professor G. N. Saqeb who were the Organising Secretary and Assistant Secretary respectively of the First World Conference on Muslim Education. See Syed Ali Ashraf, "Editorial," *Muslim Education* 1, no. 3 (1983): 7 and Ghulam Nabi Saqeb, "Some Reflections on Islamization," 45–68. The Islamic education movement has progressed forward since these papers were written.

lim scholars all over the world. They created an atmosphere where Muslim scholars could ventilate their problems, shortcomings, and needs and share new ideas generated through discussion about education in both Muslim majority and Muslim minority countries. Departments of Education in various universities in Muslim countries and in the West started to introduce courses in Islamic education. Students from Muslim countries started doing PhD in Western universities on different aspects of Muslim education. Another major impact was that the heads of Muslim states, through their Makkah Declaration made at the Third Summit meeting held in 1981, stated that "all efforts should be made to remove from education all alien forces and make education Islamic in character."[28] In essence, these conferences were the beginning of a new era in the field of Muslim education. Professor Ashraf's leadership in organising these conferences was instrumental in catalysing the global movement for the Islamisation of education during the latter decades of the twentieth century.

The Islamic Academy

In response to the needs identified at the First World Conference on Muslim Education Professor Ashraf established the Islamic Academy in Cambridge on 18 June 1983 as a non-political educational charity dedicated to advancing the true goals of Islamic education. He served as the Director General of the Academy, and I as the Deputy Director General. The Board of Trustees consisted of His Excellency Shaikh Ahmad Salah Jamjoom (Chairman), His Excellency Abdullah Omar Nasseef and Barrister Nazmul Hussain.

The Islamic Academy strives to integrate faith into education across all fields, fosters open dialogue between Muslims and others, and revises educational curricula based on Islamic principles. It seeks to promote social harmony by identifying shared values and facilitating interfaith dialogue. Over the next three decades after its inception, the Islamic Academy evolved into a vibrant international hub for educational discourse, promoting collaboration among Muslim and non-Muslim educators in Britain. In partnership with the University of Cambridge, Professor Ashraf and I organised a series of seminars on Islamic and faith-based education during 1983 to 1998. The organising committee included one or more members from the Faculty of Education at the University of Cambridge, among them Professor Paul Hirst, Peter Mitchell, Dr Terence McLaughlin, and Jean Holm, whose valuable contributions deserve sincere acknowledgment. Following Professor Ashraf's passing, I sustained this collaboration for an additional fifteen years. These seminars, jointly sponsored by the Islamic Academy, and the Department of Education at the University of Cambridge, were attended by representatives from the six major religions recognised in the United Kingdom—Christianity, Islam, Juda-

---

28 Ashraf, "Editorial," *Muslim Education* 1, no. 3 (1983): 7.

ism, Hinduism, Buddhism, and Sikhism. The outcome of each of these seminars was published as *An Agreed Statement* or *Areas of Agreement*,[29] containing broad areas of agreement of the group present. These seminar reports were distributed to educational institutions, the Ministry of Education, education authorities, religious organisations, and political leaders in the UK. Additionally, they were shared with select university departments of education in various countries, resulting in significant impacts within their educational circles. In Cambridge, the Islamic Academy organised public lectures on educational issues and Islamic exhibitions. Additionally, it actively participated in the consultation processes regarding draft curricula for various subjects published by the British government, seeking the opinions of various stakeholders.

Immediately before the establishment of the Islamic Academy, on 7-8 May 1983, Professor Ashraf organised a seminar titled "Religion and Education in a Multi-cultural Society" at Wolfson College, Cambridge University. The seminar was jointly sponsored by the Cambridge University Department of Education and King Abdulaziz University. The outcome of this seminar was published as *Religion and Education in a Multi-cultural Society: An Agreed Statement*.[30] In 1983 Professor Ashraf also organised a public lecture series titled, "Religion as the Basis of Education" consisting of six lectures. The outcome of this series of lectures was published as a book, *Religion and Education: Islamic and Christian Approaches* (1994),[31] edited by Syed Ali Ashraf and Paul H. Hirst. These two events in 1983 served as a precursor to all subsequent seminars and lectures that the Islamic Academy organised in collaboration with Cambridge University.

The purpose of these seminars, lectures, and exhibitions, held in Cambridge, was to bring together Christian and Muslim educationalists on a common platform and to promote a deeper understanding of Islam among the people of the UK by exploring commonalities with people of different faiths. These lectures serve as a powerful testament to Professor Ashraf's unwavering dedication to authentically upholding the voice of religion in an era marked by the growing influence of secularism. Additionally, his contribution to the British education system, especially the teaching of Religious Education (RE) "continues to stand as an example for Muslim and non-Muslim cooperation in the field of education today."[32]

---

29 It should be noted that these documents did not attempt to represent the views of the School of Education of Cambridge University but were an expression of the opinions of the participants in their personal capacity.
30 University of Cambridge and King Abdulaziz University, *Religion and Education in a Multi-cultural Society: An Agreed Statement* (Cambridge: University of Cambridge Department of Education, 1983).
31 Syed Ali Ashraf and Paul H. Hirst, *Religion and Education*.
32 Sarah Smalley, "Professor Ashraf and his contribution to Religious Education in England," see Chapter 13 of this book.

Professor Ashraf's leadership at the Islamic Academy, Cambridge, saw the publication of over forty books, enriching educational discourse and practice globally. Published by the Islamic Academy and edited by Professor Ashraf and me, *Muslim Education Quarterly* quickly established itself as one of the foremost Islamic educational journals in the world. Through its local and international educational activities consisting of publications, conferences, seminars, lectures, meetings, and dialogues, the Islamic Academy established itself as a powerful voice for the Muslim community within a short time.

Philosophy of Professor Ashraf: The Framework for Educational Reform

Professor Ashraf's philosophical perspectives encompass several strands, the most important of which are articulated below. The concept of God is central in his philosophical thought, permeating his literary critiques, educational principles, and creative writings, including poetry and social commentary. Then Prophet Muhammad (pbuh) stands as the supreme exemplar for humanity, embodying the highest expressions (*uswatun ḥasanah*) of moral and spiritual qualities to be emulated. Faith and piety are intimately connected with moral and spiritual development to be pursued through education. He placed education in the total Islamic frame of reference which has three dimensions: (i) spiritual, (ii) intellectual and (iii) educational. The spiritual dimension is rooted in the concepts of *tawḥīd* (Unity of God, Unity of Creation and Unity of Religion), *risālah* (Prophethood) and *ākhirah* (Life after death or the Hereafter) that constitute the essential pillars of faith (*īmān*) and define the relation between human beings and God. He explained the intellectual and educational dimensions in the light of the spiritual dimension in a series of editorials in *Muslim Education Quarterly*.[33] He advocated for a fundamental shift in educational philosophy, aiming for a comprehensive restructuring of the entire education system:

> We needed a clear assessment of the shortcomings of the western concept of Man, of the sources and methods of acquiring knowledge in the West . . . We needed in short, a new philosophical perspective with a new starting point derived from the Islamic alterative, an alternative that gives a comprehensive worldview and a methodology in which the material, the ethical and the spiritual approaches are integrated.[34]

This Islamic alternative draws its foundations from the Qurʾān and Sunnah, while also embracing the intellectual and spiritual legacy of Islam. He

---

33 Syed Ali Ashraf, "Editorial," *Muslim Education Quarterly* 6, no. 3 and 4; 7, no. 1, 2 and 3; 8, no. 1, 2 and 3; 9, no. 1, 2, 3 and 4; 10, no. 1 and 3; 11, no. 3; 12, no. 1; 12, no. 2.

34 Syed Ali Ashraf, "Editorial: The Islamic Frame of Reference: (B) The Intellectual Dimension," *Muslim Education Quarterly* 7, no. 1 (1989): 1–2.

said that seven prerequisites are necessary before a country can draw up a proper plan to Islamise its education system: (a) a comprehensive worldview grounded in the Qurʾān and the Sunnah alongside a genuine dedication to it; (b) a recognition by authorities that the secular modern scientific method falls short in providing such a worldview and can undermine the Truth bestowed by Allah; (c) comprehension of the inseparable connection between the traditional intellectual (ʿaqlī) and transmitted (naqlī) branches of knowledge within the Muslim scholarly tradition, with a resolve to comprehend and adapt this tradition to address contemporary life challenges; (d) examination of the dynamics of human-human and human-nature relationships in the light of the God-human relationship outlined in the Qurʾān and Sunnah, aiming to identify the reasons for modern deviations from divine guidance and to redirect society towards Qurʾānic objectives; (e) restructuring of educational curricula to include obligatory courses on God-human relationships, alongside optional courses on human-human and human-nature relationships, providing specialisation opportunities; (f) Islamisation of lifestyles in a fundamental manner that fosters recognition of the universality and inherent purity of Islam by other religious groups; and finally, (g) the integration of traditional and modern educational systems into a cohesive framework rooted in faith in God and eternal values exemplified by the Absolute Qualities of God.[35] Ultimately, these prerequisites converge towards a singular objective: the necessity for a comprehensive Islamic framework to assess the present and plan for the future.

Professor Ashraf believes that the purpose of education is to honour and preserve the Trust (amānah) God bestowed upon humanity: "We did indeed offer the Trust to the Heavens and the Earth and the Mountains; but they refused to undertake it, being afraid thereof: but man undertook it" (Qurʾān 33:72, trans. A. Yusuf Ali). He connects this Trust with "All the Names" that God taught Adam (Qurʾān 2:31). He maintains that these "Names" represent not just individual objects, but the conceptual essence of those objects. When we mention "Man," "Horse," or "Table," we evoke the universal idea behind each term, rather than a specific instance. Each creation reflects one or more Qualities or Powers of God, making it a manifestation of His essence, as indicated by the term āyatullāh (Sign of God). God entrusted Adam (pbuh) with these Qualities, with the condition that he safeguard their integrity, honour them, and utilise them to fulfil his ultimate purpose—that is to uphold the Trust (amānah). The teaching of the "Names" involved the implantation of these Qualities within Adam's heart, granting him spiritual cognition of them. This knowledge, cognitive power, and trust in God's Qualities elevated Adam to the status of God's Viceregent (Khalīfatullāh). These Qualities form the foundation of all moral values, including Justice, Truth, Mercy, Love, Beauty, and

---

35 Syed Ali Ashraf, "Planning for the Islamisation of Education: Pre-requisites for a Model," *Muslim Education Quarterly* 6, no. 2 (1989): 1–3.

Charity. Human beings bear the responsibility of preserving and promoting these values, fostering their growth within individuals and society. Education, therefore, entails recognising this Trust within oneself and adhering to God's guidance to nurture these qualities within oneself and society.

Professor Ashraf observed that modern Western education tends to overly prioritise reason and rationality while undervaluing the significance of spirituality. It emphasises scientific inquiry at the cost of faith, fosters individualism, cultivates scepticism, and often dismisses non-demonstrable concepts. Furthermore, it maintains an anthropocentric rather than a theocentric perspective. Even when it does not directly oppose faith, it frequently marginalises it as inferior to reason. He contends that reason ought to defer to revelation, emphasising that revelation inherently embodies truth, even if rationality cannot fully comprehend it. As regards the status of reasoning, he is on the same page with the twelfth-century scholar, Al-Zarnūjī who said, "Reasoning does not reach everything in all respects just as vision does not reveal all things to the sight. Hence they [the people who seek truth from man alone] are excluded from and incapable [of the highest truth]. Consequently, they err and cause others to deviate from [the path of God]."[36]

However, Professor Ashraf acknowledges the crucial roles of rationality, autonomy, and critical reflection in fostering cognitive, affective, and spiritual development, yet his interpretation diverges from that of liberal educationalists. Rationality is indispensable in comprehending religion, as without it, understanding may be hindered. Autonomy is vital for individuals to embrace faith freely, but critical reflection gains depth when students have access to diverse modes of inquiry beyond mere rationality. The Qurʾān places reason and rationality within a broader context of creation and existence, going beyond mere logical analysis or conceptual abstraction. It emphasises that reality surpasses our limited epistemic constructs. There are various modes of understanding that pertain to different levels of reality. Rationality, often considered the highest form of knowledge, is insufficient to fully grasp the world of the spiritual as conveyed through revelation. If it were, philosophers throughout history would have universally accessed it. However, their failure to do so led to their denial of its existence. They do not realise, nor are they ready to accept or explore, the existence of a world that can only be understood through spiritual knowledge grounded in revelation.

He was therefore disturbed when he found that some educated Muslims have begun to question the very foundations of their culture[37] and in the name of *ijtihād* endeavour to modernise Muslim society with principles derived

---

36 Al-Zarnūjī, *Instruction of the Student: The Method of Learning*, trans. G. E. von Grunebaum and Theodora M. Abel, in *Classical Foundations of Islamic Educational Thought*, ed. Bradley J. Cook (Utah: Brigham Young University Press, 2010), 137.
37 Syed Ali Ashraf, "Editorial: The Islamic Frame of Reference: (B)," 1.

from a secular scientific worldview, unaware that such principles contradict the fundamentals of Islam. For Professor Ashraf *ijtihād* is indeed necessary for engaging with the emerging circumstances. He says, "What we have to do is to find out new ways and means of applying it [Sharīʿah] in new circumstances. That is the *ijtihād* that we must exercise."[38] However, he does not condone attacks on the foundational tenets of Islamic tradition under the guise of engaging in *ijtihād*, especially by individuals influenced by secularist ideologies from other cultures. Such endeavours risk not only undermining the philosophy and theology of the religion but also the religion itself.[39] This sentiment resonates with Allama Muhammad Iqbal's observation in early twentieth century expressed in his poem, "Ijtihad," wherein he remarked, "They don't change themselves but seek to change the Qurʾān instead."[40]

This perspective of Professor Ashraf is consistent with the viewpoint of Lebanese jurisconsult Muṣṭafā al-Rāfiʿī, who posits that "a mere statement of what seems best to reason or what reason judges to be beneficial without the support of evidence from the book of God and the Sunna cannot be considered the *ijtihād* of Islamic law.... Otherwise, it would be abrogating Islamic law and introducing a new law."[41] Professor Ashraf, therefore, criticised the formulation of a new epistemology of the Qurʾān using Western scientific terminology such as "paradigm," "holistic," and "progress," as some Muslim scholars have done. He asserted that Islamic education does not aim at development (*taṭawwur*), progress (*taqaddum*), or renaissance (*nahḍah*) as these terms are used in a secular context to denote improvement or advancement without specific reference to religious or spiritual elements.[42] He said that "The Spirit (*rūḥ*) of Man ... can control and guide the growth of Man only through *tajdīd* (renewal) and *tazkiyah* (purification)."[43] What is needed is reform (*iṣlāḥ*) and renewal (*tajdīd*) of the entire system as the Islamic objective is to attain the harmonious growth of the complete human personality, through the application of all their faculties—soul (*nafs*), spirit (*rūḥ*), intellect (*ʿaql*), and heart (*qalb*)—or as Naquib al-Attas has said, "the channels of the sound senses, true narrative, sound reason, and intuition."[44]

---

38 Syed Ali Ashraf, "Editorial—The Islamic Frame of Reference: The Intellectual Dimension II—The Methodology (*Uṣūl*)," *Muslim Education Quarterly* 7, no. 3 (1990): 9.
39 Seyyed Hossein Nasr, "Reply to Marietta Stepaniants," in *The Philosophy of Seyyed Hossein Nasr*, eds. Lewis Edwin Hahn, Randall E. Auxier, and Lucian W. Stone Jr., The Library of Living Philosophers, vol. 27 (Peru, IL: Open Court Press, 2000), 810–11.
40 Muhammad Iqbal, "Ijtihad," *Zarb-e Kalīm*.
41 Muṣṭafā al-Rāfiʿī, *Islamuna (Our Islam)* (Middlesex: The Muhammadi Research Trust, 1987), 72 and 73.
42 Syed Ali Ashraf, "Editorial: Recommendations of the Five World Conferences on Muslim Education: A Plan for Implementation," *Muslim Education Quarterly* 10, no. 1 (1992): 3.
43 Syed Ali Ashraf, "Editorial: Planning for the Islamisation of Education," 3.
44 Syed Muhammad Naquib al-Attas, *A Commentary on the Hujjat al-Siddiq of Nur al-Din al-Raniri*, (Kuala Lumpur: Ministry of Culture, Malaysia, 1986), 31.

Agreeing with Al-Attas on the need to instil all these four channels, Professor Ashraf observes that contemporary Western civilisation has predominantly relied on just two channels: the human senses and reason, divorced from intellection and intuition. He emphasised the importance of human intuition and concurred with Huston Smith when he said, "Human intelligence can never be replaced by machine intelligence because we are not ourselves thinking machines. Each of us has, and uses every day, a power of intuitive intelligence that enables us to understand, to speak, and to cope skilfully with our everyday environment."[45] The contemporary secular world's refusal to accept the other two channels—authentic narrative and intuition conveyed by the Messenger of God and people of knowledge—is the main reason for the moral and spiritual malaise afflicting society today. Professor Ashraf's frame of reference develops and expands organically from the rich tradition it stems from, rather than abruptly emerging from novel interpretations of the Qurʾān and the Sunnah. According to this, intellectual sciences (al-ʿulūm al-ʿaqliyyah) must be built upon the principles of transmitted sciences (al-ʿulūm al-naqliyyah). Only through such actions can we prevent ourselves from drifting amidst the myriad of evolving social values and navigate away from the quagmire of conflicting ideas. This will pave the way towards achieving our cherished goal of cultivating a society imbued with prophetic ideals.

Modern Muslim intellectuals, due to their modern schooling, have lost sight of the unifying principles of Islam—principles embodied in the concept of *tawḥīd* that connects all disciplines pertaining to intellectual sciences such as law, ethics, economics, physics, and biology to the Qurʾān and Sunnah. This lack of unifying vision leads to dispersion in the domain of knowledge, which in turn results in "an ever-increasing multiplicity of goals and desires, an ever-intensifying chaos." In this regard, Professor Ashraf's thought finds remarkable similarity with that of William Chittick when he says:

> What is striking about contemporary Islam's encounter with modernity is that Muslims lack the intellectual preparation to deal with the situation. Muslim intellectuals—with a few honorable exceptions—do not question the legitimacy of the modern gods. Rather, they debate about the best way to serve the new tyrants. In other words, they think that Islamic society must be modified and adapted to follow the standards set by modernity, standards that are built on the basis of *takthīr*. This is to say that innumerable modern-day Muslims are forever looking for the best way to adapt Islam to *shirk*.[46]

---

45 Huston Smith, *Beyond the Post-Modern Mind* (Illinois: Theosophical Publishing, 1989), 243.
46 William Chittick, "Can the Islamic Intellectual Heritage be Recovered?" *Iqbal Review* 39, no. 3 (1998): 21. *Takthīr*, meaning multiplicity, is the antonym of *tawḥīd*. *Shirk* is association of partners with God.

Nevertheless, social circumstances are perpetually evolving, and as science and technology progress we continually encounter new challenges. With the advancement of modernity, we find ourselves increasingly influenced by an educational philosophy that encourages scepticism, doubt, and critical thinking, rather than fostering unwavering faith, absolute certainty, and intuitive understanding. In the face of these changing circumstances, how do we adapt? How do we reconcile the new with the timeless tradition? Is such assimilation even possible? Professor Ashraf contemplates:

> This assimilation of the new is possible only when the interpretation of the new facts is based on the Islamic concept of human nature, the nature of society and external nature and the nature of God-Man-Nature relationship. This interpretation can be made by one who realises, believes and applies the Islamic world-view. . . . The only hypothesis that Islam demands is faith in God and the Prophet and the only process that it advises is action on the basis of the Absolute norm enshrined in the Attributes of God and exemplified through the character and conduct of the Prophet. The only experimental deduction and justification that it presents is the historically testified transformation of human beings leading to the establishment of a God-fearing (*taqwā*) society of people whose behaviour and conduct (*ʿamal*) manifested in practical terms the essentials (*ḥaqīqah*) and Universals of Truth (*Ḥaqq*), Justice (*ʿadl*), Righteousness, Honesty, Mercy, Charity, Knowledge and Beauty.⁴⁷

The renewal (*tajdīd*) of an individual's faith in God, the Prophet, and consequently, the Qurʾān and the Sunnah, becomes possible only through the purification (*tazkiyah*) of the mind from erroneous ideas, thoughts, desires, and devices. This process of renewal entails the cultivation of humanity's primordial nature, thereby reviving the original vitality of Islam. It necessitates not a progressive shift towards novelty but a retrospective movement towards the roots of Islam, achieved by assimilating contemporary elements into the foundational framework of Islamic tradition (Sharīʿah).⁴⁸ The true spirit of renewal (*tajdīd*) has been captured by Professor Ashraf in the following words:

> This renewal means the restoration of something of the primordial nature of Man and hence of the primordial vigour of Islam. It needs a movement not forward to something new, but backward to the origin of Islam through assimilation of the new into the matrix of the basic tradition of Islam (Sharīʿah), the rejection of the false be they theories

---

47 Ashraf, "Editorial: Recommendations of the Five World Conferences," 4.
48 Ashraf, "Editorial: Recommendations of the Five World Conferences," 4.

or hypotheses or ideas or methods about God, Man and nature and the reform of the existing conditions of society and the individual.[49]

Central to this renewal is the explicit rejection of falsehoods—whether they manifest as concepts, ideas, conjectures or methods—pertaining to God, humanity, and nature. This rejection paves the way for the restoration of authentic Islamic principles, promoting a return to the essence of Islam through the integration of modern elements into the religious tradition. Concurrently, it calls for a comprehensive reform of existing societal and individual conditions, aligning them with the core tenets of Islam.

Professor Ashraf's vision entails a genuine integration of Islamic and Western knowledge, wherein the two would converge and be united under the principles of Islam. When this happens, the boundary between religious and secular education disappears and so does the boundary between Islamic and Western knowledge. If this integration is not achieved, the duality between religion and other aspects of life will continue. However, he was against the practice of sporadically inserting Qurʾānic verses within a curriculum to give it an Islamic façade, while in truth, the underlying philosophy of the curriculum remained secular. He was deeply traditional but did not support blind traditionalism, advocating instead for engagement with the modern world and the development of innovative methodologies to tackle contemporary challenges with depth and insight. Following Al-Ghazālī, he challenged prevailing structures and premises within existing disciplines, emphasising the importance of infusing educational pursuits with both spiritual and intellectual vision.

Professor Ashraf's intellectual horizons transcended the confines of his academic disciplines, owing much to his formative years steeped in the ethos of Sufism. This upbringing left an indelible mark on his worldview, evident in his writings, religious observances, and interactions with others. During his undergraduate and PhD studies at Cambridge he came into direct contact with eminent scholars of English literature and Western culture such as R. N. Walters, T. R. Henn, F. R. Leavis, Sir Herbert Read, A. N. Jeffares, Raymond Williams, W. S. Ingram, Raymond O'Malley, Stephen Spender, John Wain, Anthony Hartley, and Robert Conquest. Interactions with this galaxy of scholars and exposure to their ideas deepened his understanding of English literature, society, and culture, broadening his perspective to appreciate the richness of British society. An established poet and writer in Bengali, he recognised the common threads among diverse cultures and appreciated the inherent goodness within all human beings. Rooted in profound religiosity, he cultivated a holistic perspective on life and existence, drawing from the timeless wisdom enshrined in the Qurʾān and Sunnah.

---

49 Ashraf, "Editorial: Recommendations of the Five World Conferences," 4.

Through his exploration, he discerned the universal applicability of Islamic principles, recognising their presence in societies influenced by diverse religious traditions. He, therefore, never hesitated to accept the truth irrespective of its source. This finds a remarkable parallel with Al-Ghazālī who said in his *Al-Munqidh min al-Ḍalāl*, "An initiate, a wise man, begins by recognising what is true and after that examines individual sayings. If one of these is truthful, he accepts it, whether the person who said it is in error or in truth."[50] This is the approach adopted by classical Muslim educationalists. For example, Ibn Miskawayh said, "The proper food of the rational soul is knowledge, . . . the acceptance of truth no matter where or with whom it may be, and the shunning of falsehood and lying whatever it may be or whence it may come."[51] This perspective is aligned with the wisdom conveyed by the Prophet (pbuh): "The wise statement is the lost property of the believer, so wherever he finds it, then he is more worthy of it."[52]

This Islamic approach to knowledge prompted Professor Ashraf to appreciate truths from sources beyond the Muslim tradition. He joined individuals and groups from various faiths to explore common ground and shared understanding in matters of faith and education. This perspective led him to accept teachings of universal value from esteemed Western authors such as St. Thomas Aquinas, Jacques Maritain, T. S. Eliot, W. B. Yeats, A. N. Whitehead, and Frithjof Schuon, just to mention a few. He went as far as to say that, "the Islamic approach could be comprehensive enough to incorporate within itself most of the essential elements of the secularist approach, especially when the secularist approach is governed by a concept of universal objective values."[53]

He endeavoured to discover common ground with people of other faiths and to work alongside them for the collective welfare of humanity. In his appraisal of a "Dialogue Conference" he attended in Wetherby, Yorks on 3–5 May 1974, he wrote in *Impact International*:

> From the Muslim point of view . . . as faith is the common ground on which we both [Christians and Muslims] stand, as secularisation of life is what we both oppose, as we want both to prevent the erosion of moral values and to revive the religious spirit in our communities, as

---

50 Al-Ghazali, "Section C: Danger of Philosophy, Part II," *Deliverance from Error and Mystical Union with the Almighty (al-Munqidh min al-Ḍalāl)*, trans. Muhammad Abulaylah, ed. George F. McLean (Council for Research in Values & Philosophy. March 2002), https://www.ghazali.org/books/md/index.html.
51 Miskawayh, "From the Second Discourse of the Refinement of Character," in *Classical Foundations of Islamic Educational Thought*, ed. Bradley J. Cook (Utah: Bringham Young University Press, 2010), 76.
52 Tirmidhī, Ḥadīth no. 2687.
53 Syed Ali Ashraf, "Editorial," *Muslim Education Quarterly* 1, no. 1 (1983): 1.

we want the Christians to be truly Christian and the Muslims to be truly Muslim we have a common platform on which to stand.[54]

This conviction remained steadfast throughout his lifetime. His aim was to cultivate a religious approach to life by bringing together the various significant religions recognised in the UK—Christianity, Islam, Judaism, Hinduism, Sikhism and Buddhism—advocating for the preservation of both unity and diversity among them. Unity is rooted in the notion of One Unique Supreme and Transcendental Reality, while diversity thrives within doctrinal and socio-cultural variations. Through his faith-based educational system, he envisioned a society where unity in diversity prevails, where both unity and diversity coexist harmoniously within the context of shared humanity, acknowledging the spiritual, intellectual, rational, and physical dimensions of human existence. His belief in the divine conception of humanity led him to embrace the inherent goodness present in all individuals, regardless of caste, creed, or faith, a principle he fervently advocated in his writings.

This book describes Professor Ashraf's endeavours to integrate faith and spirituality into the theory and practice of education, aiming for both individual and societal development. He advocates for a worldview based on the Qurʾān and the Sunnah, that recognises spirituality as intrinsic to human existence, permeating all aspects of reality. By nurturing spiritual growth alongside intellectual and moral development, this approach empowers individuals to cultivate God-consciousness (*taqwā*), inner peace (*iṭmiʾnān*), and a sense of purpose. This is achieved when life and events are interpreted with a God-centric meaning, motivating human beings to attain balanced growth in their total personality, both individually and collectively. Moreover, integrating faith and spirituality into education deepens our understanding of ethical values and social responsibility, helping us recognise the interconnectedness of all beings. This promotes harmony with nature and fosters environmental stewardship. In essence, Professor Ashraf's approach to education transcends mere academic achievement, aiming to foster holistic well-being and the flourishing of both individuals and communities. It promotes a vision of education that enriches not only the mind but also the heart and the soul, nurturing individuals who are knowledgeable, compassionate, ethical, and spiritually grounded.

Relevance of Professor Ashraf's Work Today

Professor Ashraf's work remains as relevant today as it was twenty-five years ago when he passed away, for several reasons. The valuable ideas of

---

54 Syed Ali Ashraf, "The Problem of the Secular: An Appraisal of the Christian-Muslim Dialogue conference, Wetherby, Yorks, 3–5 May," *Impact International Fortnightly*, 28 June-11 July 1974.

scholars such as Professor Ashraf, Professor Hossein Nasr, Professor Naquib al-Attas, and Professor Ismaʿil Raji al-Faruqi for making education Islamic in character are perhaps needed more today than when they were first proposed. Professor Ashraf's dream of developing Islamic principles of education for all branches of knowledge is yet to be fulfilled. Now, with many Islamic schools established in different parts of the world, there is a growing need for ideas to create Islamic curriculums, textbooks, and properly trained teachers. Although there are some excellent Islamic schools in operation in different places, many Islamic schools lack a unifying Islamic vision and struggle to integrate core Islamic principles with modern education. Some young scholars, having little or no awareness of the classical foundations of Islamic educational thoughts, tend to rely on modern theories that may appear to align with certain aspects of Islam superficially, but are completely irreconcilable with its essence. This book offers a wealth of ideas and guidance to fill such vacuums.

Some Muslim educationalists today selectively promote only those Islamic values that do not conflict with Western secular principles as a display of co-operation with the West. However, true Islamic education goes beyond merely promoting ethical values; it encompasses education of the body, mind, and soul, rooted in the core principle of *tawḥīd* (Unity of God), *risālah* (Prophethood) and *ākhirah* (Hereafter). Professor Ashraf's concepts of education will enlighten those who are sincerely trying to implement an Islamic system of education in our challenging times.

The Structure of the Book

The chapters within this book delve deeply into significant aspects of Professor Ashraf's life and his contributions. They are structured into two parts. Part I, titled "Reflections," is a compilation contributed by his friends, colleagues, relatives, and other educationalists. This part comprises twenty-eight chapters, predominantly focusing on his literary, philosophical, and educational endeavours. Included in this part are articles presented as Memorial Lectures, held in his honour at various locations, alongside discussions on broader topics that held significance for him. Additionally, these chapters provide insights into his organisational and spiritual activities, offering a comprehensive understanding of him as a scholar and a spiritual guide. Part II, titled "Reminiscences," contains fourteen chapters dedicated to personal encounters with Professor Ashraf. These chapters shed light on numerous incidents from his life, recounted by individuals who observed him closely, often on a daily basis for extended periods. Through these personal anecdotes, readers gain a deep understanding of Professor Ashraf as a person. The contributors to these chapters include his classmates, relatives, students, friends, and disciples, collectively offering a multifaceted portrayal of his character and legacy.

Bibliography

Ahmed, Akbar S. "Obituary: Syed Ali Ashraf." *The Independent*, Wednesday, August 13, 1998. https://www.independent.co.uk/arts-entertainment/obituary-professor-syed-ali-ashraf-1171311.html.

Ahsan, Syed Ali. *Hôzrot Shah Ali Boghdadi*. Dhaka: Syed ali Naqi, 1996.

Ashraf, Syed Ali. "The Problem of the Secular: An Appraisal of the Christian-Muslim Dialogue Conference, Wetherby, Yorks, 3–5 May." *Impact International Fortnightly*, 28 June–11 July, 1974.

Ashraf, Syed Ali. Preface to *Aims and Objectives of Islamic Education*, edited by Syed Muhammad al-Naquib al-Attas, ix–xiv. London: Hodder and Stoughton and Jeddah: King Abdulaziz University, 1979.

Ashraf, Syed Ali. "Editorial." *Muslim Education* 1, no. 3 (1983): 5–8.

Ashraf, Syed Ali. "Editorial." *Muslim Education Quarterly* 1, no. 1 (1983): 1–2.

Ashraf, Syed Ali, *New Horizons in Muslim Education*. London: Hodder and Stoughton and Cambridge: The Islamic Academy, 1985.

Ashraf, Syed Ali. "Editorial: Planning for the Islamisation of Education: Pre-requisites for a Model," *Muslim Education Quarterly* 6, no. 2 (1989): 1–4.

Ashraf, Syed Ali. "Editorial: The Islamic Frame of Reference: (B) The Intellectual Dimension." *Muslim Education Quarterly* 7, no. 1 (1989): 1–9.

Ashraf, Syed Ali. *Islamic Education Movement: An Historical Analysis*. Cambridge: The Islamic Academy, 1990.

Ashraf, Syed Ali. "Editorial: The Islamic Frame of Reference—The Intellectual Dimension II: The Methodology (*Uṣūl*)." *Muslim Education Quarterly* 7, no. 3 (1990): 1–10.

Ashraf, Syed Ali. "Editorial: Recommendations of the Five World Conferences on Muslim Education: A Plan for Implementation." *Muslim Education Quarterly* 10, no. 1 (1992): 1–6.

Ashraf, Syed Ali. Preface to *Religion and Education: Islamic and Christian Approaches*, edited by Syed Ali Ashraf and Paul H. Hirst, xi–xiv. Cambridge: The Islamic Academy, 1994.

Al-Attas, Syed Muhammad Naquib. *A Commentary on the Hujjat al-Siddiq of Nur al-Din al-Raniri*. Kuala Lumpur: Ministry of Culture, Malaysia, 1986.

Bakar, Osman. "The Aims of Education: The Forgotten Truths." See Chapter 2 of this book.

Chittick, William. "Can the Islamic Intellectual Heritage be Recovered?" *Iqbal Review* 39, no. 3 (1998): 9–25.

Deakin, Ruth. *The New Christian Schools*. Bristol: Regius Press, 1989.

Al-Ghazali. "Section C: Danger of Philosophy, Part II." *Deliverance from Error and Mystical Union with the Almighty (al-Munqidh min al-Ḍalāl)*. Trans by Muhammad Abulaylah. Edited by George F. McLean. Council for Research in Values & Philosophy, March 2002. https://www.ghazali.org/books/md/index.html.

Halstead, Mark. "Obituary: Syed Ali Ashraf 1925–1998." *British Journal of Religious Education* 21, no. 3 (1999): 133–134. DOI: 10.1080/0141620990210302.

Iqbal, Muhammad. "Ijtihad." *Zarb-e-Kalīm*.

Khan, Shamsuzzaman. *Bangladesh Lekhok Pōrichiti* (Introduction to Bangladesh Writers). Dhaka: Bangla Academy, 1984.

Kurtz, Donald. "Pakistani Professor Sees Vagueness in Democracy." *The Michigan Daily*, May 16, 1957.

Mabud, Shaikh Abdul. "World Conferences on Muslim Education: Shaping the Agenda of Muslim Education in the Future." In *Philosophies of Islamic Education, Historical Perspectives and Emerging Discourses*, edited by Nadeem A. Memon and Mujadad Zaman, 129–43. New York and London: Routledge, 2016.

Macaulay, Lord. "Minute by the Hon'ble T. B. Macaulay, dated the 2nd February 1835." Bureau of Education, 2 February 1835. Edited by H. Sharp. Calcutta: Superintendent, Government Printing, 1920. Reprint. Delhi: National Archives of India, 1965, 107–117.

Miskawayh. "From the Second Discourse of the Refinement of Character." In *Classical Foundations of Islamic Educational Thought*, edited by Bradley J. Cook, 75–87. Utah: Bringham Young University Press, 2010.

Mitchell, Peter. "Professor Syed Ali Ashraf: An Appreciation." See Chapter 29 of this book.

Nasr, Seyyed Hossein. "Reply to Marietta Stepaniants." In *The Philosophy of Seyyed Hossein Nasr*, edited by Lewis Edwin Hahn, Randall E. Auxier, and Lucian W. Stone Jr., 809–812. The Library of Living Philosophers, vol. 27. IL: Open Court Press, 2001.

Al-Rāfiʿī, Muṣṭafā. *Islāmunā (Our Islam)*. Middlesex: The Muhammadi Research Trust, 1987.

Saqeb, Ghulam Nabi. "Some Reflections on Islamisation of Education Since 1977 Makkah Conference: Accomplishments, Failures and Tasks Ahead." *Intellectual Discourse* 8, no 1 (2000): 45–68.

Saqeb, Ghulam Nabi. "Islamic Education and the Challenge of Secularism: Professor Syed Ali Ashraf's Critique of Secularism in Education in Muslim Countries: A Personal Appraisal." See Chapter 5 of this volume.

Smalley, Sarah. "Professor Ashraf and his Contribution to Religious Education in England." See Chapter 13 of this volume.

Smith, Huston. *Beyond the Post-Modern Mind*. Illinois: Theosophical Publishing, 1989.

Thompson, David M. "Professor Syed Ali Ashraf." *Fitzwilliam College Journal* 5 (March 1999): 37.

Tirmidhī, Ḥadīth no. 2687.

Viswanathan, Gauri. *Masks of Conquest: Literary Study and British Rule in India*. New York: Columbia University Press, 1989.

Al-Zarnūjī. *Instruction of the Student: The Method of Learning*. Translated by G. E. von Grunebaum and Theodora M. Abel. In *Classical Foundations of Islamic Educational Thought*, edited by Bradley J. Cook, 108–155. Utah: Brigham Young University Press, 2010.

Part I
Reflections

Chapter 1

Civilizational Dialogue and the Islamic World
Seyyed Hossein Nasr

Dedicated to the memory of Syed Ali Ashraf, pioneer in educational philosophy in the context of civilizational dialogue.

When discussing civilizational dialogue, it is necessary first of all to ask what we mean by civilization. For several centuries in the West, the power and glitter of the world dominated by modem civilization had made the very term civilization synonymous with modem Western civilization and all the other civilizations were considered as stages in the development of this particular civilization, which the Encyclopedists called *la civilization*. For a long time, intellectual discourse in the West had reduced the use of the term civilization to the singular and since the 19th century many a modernized Asian and African also surrendered to this Western view. But despite the overwhelming power of Western civilization, which itself came into being as a result of rebellion against the Christian civilization of the European Middle Ages, the other civilizations, although weakened in many ways, did not die out. And now, at the beginning of a new Christian century and millennium, there is again talk of civilizations in the plural, despite the aggressive spread to the farthest corners of the earth of global consumerism and with it some of the shallowest aspects of Western popular culture. No, the other civilizations have not died out, and some, especially the Islamic, are in fact seeking to revive themselves. It is therefore necessary to turn to that which enjoyed a remarkable universality among various traditional human collectivities which have occupied the world over the millennia, before dealing with the contemporary situation.

I

The term civilization is related to the word *civitas* or city in European languages, *civitas* itself being derived from the Greek root *kei* which means to lie outstretched. "A city is thus a 'lair', in which the citizen 'makes his bed' on which he must lie."[1] The question then arises as to who occupies this city. The

---

1   Anand K. Coomaraswamy, *What is Civilization? And Other Essays* (Ipswich: Golgonooza

Sanskrit Word for city, *pur*, reveals the answer, for it is also the root of the word *purusa* or Universal Man (*al-insān al-kāmil*) of Islamic metaphysics. The dweller of the ideal city is *purusa* who is, according to the Upanishads "the citizen in every city,"[2] or as Philo has said, going even further, "As for lordship (*kyrios*), God is the only citizen."[3] This city which is at once cosmic, social, and microcosmic, is the origin of the traditional understanding of civilization. This city at once transcends the human order and penetrates into the traditional civilizations but in different forms and according to the religious norms which are the foundations of all civilizations. All the realities that comprise the life of a tradition are contained in the particular "City of God" whose manifestation on earth has created the particular civilization in question. Moreover, each human being contains this "City" within himself and is able to realize it if he or she is able to perfect himself or herself spiritually. Traditionally speaking, the truly civilized man is one who has realized this *civitas Dei* within himself and gained the inner vision with which he is able to realize that the only master of this city is the Immortal Spirit within and not his rebellious ego. Without this realization, man lives in barbarism even if he invents the fanciest of gadgets.

From another point of view, it might be said that every traditional civilization is dominated by a "Presiding Idea,"[4] or a heavenly given dispensation whose spirit guides that civilization and whose form determines its particular formal structure in conjunction with the ethnic genius of the people destined to create and be members of that civilization. That "Presiding Idea" may also be identified with religion in its most universal sense (*al-dīn* in Arabic). A traditional civilization remains always aware of this at once transcendent and immanent reality. The people of such a civilization have always lived in a space which is like the space of a circle with an immutable Supreme Center and have experienced time always in relation to the Origin, which is also their End, that is, the *alpha* and *omega* of their existence.[5] Traditional civilizations never lost sight of either the Center or the Origin.[6]

Press, 1989). In Islamic languages, the terms for civilization are also related to the city as traditionally understood. In Arabic the word civilization, *al-ḥaḍārah*, is derived from the root *ḥḍr* meaning a place of settlement or town or city. In Persian and many other Islamic languages such as Urdu and Turkish, the term *tamaddun* or *madaniyyah* usually used for civilization are also related to the word *madan*, which likewise means town or city.

2   Coomaraswamy, *What is Civilization?* 2.
3   Coomaraswamy, 2.
4   See Marco Pallis, "Chapter 22: The Present State of Tibetan Art," in *Peaks and Lamas* (London: Cassell and Company Limited, 1942), 343–66.
5   As we have had occasion to mention elsewhere, there are numerous treatises on traditional metaphysics and philosophy in the Islamic world with precisely the title *al-Mabda' wa'l-ma'ād* in Arabic or *Āghāz wa anjam* in Persian, both terms meaning origin or beginning and end.
6   "The whole existence of the peoples of antiquity, and of traditional peoples, in general,

This common vision does not of course mean that the "Presiding Idea" is the same in every traditional civilization, despite the inner unity that binds them together. As Marco Pallis writes,

> The fact is that every civilization that can be called authentic is endowed with a principle of unity peculiar to itself, which is reflected in varying degrees, in all the institutions of the civilization in question. By a principle of unity is meant a predominant idea, corresponding to a given aspect of the truth, which has been recipient of particular emphasis and for the expression of which, if one may so put it, that civilization shows a peculiar 'genius.'[7]

The inner or transcendent unity to which we have referred does not in any way annul the reality of the principle of unity peculiar to each traditional civilization. Consequently, as traditionally understood, there are multiple civilizations each with its own particular formal order and "mandate from Heaven" yet with remarkably similar perspectives on the nature of reality resulting from the universal truths which through different forms have created, presided over and sustained traditional civilizations over the ages.[8]

In contrast to all that has been said, modem civilization, which was created in the West on the basis and also in opposition to many of the basic tenets of Latin Christian civilization, but which has now spread to all the four corners of the globe, is based on the absolutization of terrestrial man, on a Promethean individualism, rationalism and humanism. For the most part it has substituted the kingdom of man for the kingdom of God.[9] It no longer possesses a transcendent "Presiding Idea" as did all traditional civilizations and the ethical and spiritual values that are present in it are the heritage of the Christian civilization which it has sought to supplant. In fact, strictly speaking, one cannot speak of modem Western civilization as a new civilization. Rather, it is both a continuation of and reaction against Western Christian civilization.

From the traditional point of view in the present day situation all civilizations have decayed and fallen from their ideal except that the Oriental civilizations began to decay in a passive way during the past few centuries and Western civilization in an active way since the Renaissance.[10] More recently,

---

is dominated by two presiding ideas, the idea of Center and the idea of Origin." Frithjof Schuon, *Light on the Ancient World*, trans. Lord Northbourne (Bloomington, Indiana: World Wisdom Books, 1984), 7.

7 Marco Pallis, *The Way and the Mountain* (London: Peter Owen Ltd, 1991), 178.

8 See René Guénon, "Principles of Unity of the Oriental Civilizations," in his *Introduction to the Study of Hindu Doctrines*, trans. M. Pallis (London: Luzac & Co., 1945), pp. 19 ff.

9 See Tage Lindbom, *The Tares and the Good Grain: Or the Kingdom of Man at the Hour of Reckoning*, trans. Alvin Moore, Jr. (Macon, Ga: Mercer University Press, 1983).

10 "All civilizations are in decline, but in different ways; the decline of the East is passive and that of the West is active. The fault of the East in decline is that it no longer thinks;

a certain type of decadence associated with Asia and Africa in modern times is now beginning to appear in the West and that active decay in the form of deviation from traditional norms is in non-Western civilizations. This reality must be considered in any serious civilizational dialogue.

Today, we see on the globe several major and a few smaller civilizations including the Western, the Eastern European and Russian, the Islamic, the Indian, the Chinese and Japanese, the black African and the various remnants of indigenous civilizations and cultures. Some like Samuel Huntington would count South America as a civilization separate from the Western and the Japanese as a civilization distinct from the Chinese.[11] There are also many sub-sets within each of these civilizations distinguished by ethnicity, nationalism, various religious interpretations, languages, and other factors. Nevertheless, the reality of these civilizations can hardly be doubted.

There are today no intact traditional civilizations. Nevertheless, there is a major difference between modern Western civilization and the others in that it is this civilization which represents most of all modernism and is still powerful enough to project its world view and values upon other civilizations whereas the reverse is not true. If there had been a movement to carry out civilizational dialogue six centuries ago, the situation would have been very different. Each civilization would have then been based on that "Presiding Idea" which offered remarkable similarities with the "Presiding Idea" of another civilization despite obvious differences. If they were to discuss the nature and goal of human life, there would be remarkable resemblances. When one reads the list of basic virtues in Confucianism and Neo-Confucianism, it is as if one were reading an Islamic text on ethics. And most important of all they would all agree that all external reality of the cosmos and of man is derived from and based upon an Ultimate Reality, which is both beyond and within all things. They would have little difficulty understanding each other on the metaphysical level, whether they were speaking of *Brahman, Atman,* the One, *Ahura mazda, Deus, Allāh* or for that matter *nirvana*.[12] Such of course is not the case of modern Western civilization in which there are still Christian and Jewish elements but in which a secularist and scientistic discourse dominates much of public life as well as philosophy, science and the arts. Today, civilizational dialogue means,

---

that of the West is that it thinks too much and thinks wrongly. The East is sleeping over truths; the West is living in error." This quote is in: Frithjof Schuon, *Spiritual Perspectives and Human Facts*, trans. Mark Perry, Jean-Pierre Lafouge and James S. Cutsinger, ed. James S. Cutsinger (Indiana: World Wisdom, Inc., 2007), 17–8.

11 Samuel P. Huntington, *The Clash of Civilizations and the Remaking of World Order* (New York: Simon and Schuster, 1996), 40–48.

12 On how the Buddhist perspective can be integrated into the understanding of this wisdom or *philosophia perennis*, see Seyyed Hossein Nasr, "Reply to Sallie B. King," in Library of Living Philosophers, vol. 28, *The Philosophy of Seyyed Hossein Nasr*, eds. Lewis Edwin Hahn, Randall E. Auxier, and Lucian W. Stone, Jr. (Chicago and La Salle, Illinois: Open Court, 2001), 221-31.

on one hand, dialogue between traditional civilizations weakened and modernized to various degrees, and on the other hand, between each of those civilizations and the modern and post-modern Western in which there still exist important religious and spiritual elements but which is also the driving force behind all the ideas and ideals which seek to destroy the very foundations of the still existing albeit weakened traditional civilizations

To carry out serious dialogue under these difficult conditions, one must first of all remember that all the civilizations of which we have knowledge, those still living and those which have perished, have been created by a religion or the "Presiding Idea" already mentioned. Chinese civilization is based on Confucianism and Taoism, Western civilization on Christianity, Islamic civilization on Islam as Roman civilization was based on the Roman religion and Egyptian civilization on the Egyptian religion. This does not mean that a civilization does not borrow from what came before it, but a new dispensation from Heaven integrates various elements of what went before into a new unity reflecting its own spiritual genius. The Christian civilization of Europe certainly owes much to Greece and Rome but is not simply their continuation. There is nothing more different from a Roman temple than a Romanesque Church or from a Greek temple a Byzantine Church. It is the new spirit blown by a new religion upon the "material" and "earthly" elements to which it is sent that creates a civilization with its own distinct social structure, ethical norms, sciences, and the arts.

Because of this centrality of religion in the creation of each civilization, understanding between religions, which are the sources of values and ideals of these civilizations, and accord between religions lie at the heart of civilizational dialogue if this dialogue is also to lead to mutual respect and understanding. It is here that the traditional perspective of perennial philosophy, which sees an inner truth that unites the religions on the supra-formal and universal level without in any way violating the sanctity of their particular formal structures, becomes so important in the current discussion about civilizational dialogue. If this dialogue is to result in understanding, one must first of all accept what Frithjof Schuon has called "the transcendent unity of religions"[13] and realize that despite differences of a formal order all authentic spiritual paths "lead to the same summit."[14] Nothing is more important for civilizational dialogue than a common understanding of first principles even between non-Western

---

13 See Frithjof Schuon, *The Transcendent Unity of Religions* (Wheaton, Chennai: Quest Books, The Theosophical Publishing House, 1993). See also Seyyed Hossein Nasr, "Chapter 9: Principial Knowledge and the Multiplicity of Sacred Forms," in *Knowledge and the Sacred* (Edinburgh: Edinburgh University, 1981), 280–308; and Seyyed Hossein Nasr, "Chapter 3: Religion and Religions," in *Religion and the Order of Nature* (Oxford: Oxford University Press, 1996), 3–38.

14 See Ananda K. Coomaraswamy, "Chapter 3: Paths that Lead to the Same Summit," in *The Bugbear of Literacy* (Bedfont, Middlesex: Perennial Books, 1979), 42–63.

civilizations and the West where many of these principles have been discarded by the dominating paradigm but nevertheless survive not only among Jews and Christians, but even to a large extent among those who have turned their back consciously or unconsciously upon the religion of their ancestors.

II

It is not accidental that at the dawn of this new millennium the call for civilizational dialogue rather than clash should come from the Islamic world, more specifically from Sayyid Muhammad Khatami, the president of The Islamic Republic of Iran, a land which has been one of the major *foci* of Islamic civilization during the past thirteen centuries and before that period the heart of a major empire and civilization. The Islamic world has always been aware of itself as a unified civilization bound together by Islam as both religion, in the ordinary sense of the term, and a complete way of life. The Islamic world stretched form the very first century of its existence form the heart of France to the borders of China. It created a civilizationally unified world with two distinct zones, the Arabic and the Iranic or Persianate, to which later zones were added. It contained within itself such diverse ethnic groups as Arabic, Iranian, Turkic, Indian, Malay, Black African, European, and even Chinese. It was witness to not only much greater geographical and climatic differences than Western European civilization, but also a greater diversity of ethnicities and languages. The main language of Western Christendom was Latin, and all the European languages save for very small linguistic groups belong to a single family whereas the three main languages of the Islamic world, namely, Arabic, Persian and Turkish belong to three totally different families of languages. Yet, very early in its history, Islam had a powerful awareness of itself as a distinct civilization while it integrated many elements of previous civilizations especially in the domain of the arts and sciences into its universe.

Classical Islamic historians even wrote about the religious and philosophical as well as historical significance of other civilizations, as we see in the works of al-Ṭabarī, al-Masʿūdī and the like. One of them, Ibn Khaldūn, was the father of what one might call civilizational studies and wrote with exceptional depth about the rise, continuity, and decline of civilizations.[15] Another major Islamic historian, Rashīd al-Dīn Faḍl-Allāh, was the author of the first universal history ever written, a work which dealt with the Franks and the Chinese and nearly everyone in between.[16] In fact Islamic civilization was the only one before modern times to have had experience of nearly every other major

---

15 See Ibn Khaldun, *Muqaddimah*, trans. Franz Rosenthal, 3 vols., (Princeton: Princeton University Press, 1967); Muhsin Mahdi, *Ibn Khaldun's Philosophy of History* (London, George Allen & Unwin, 1957).

16 See Rashīd al-Dīn Hamadānī, *Kitāb jāmiʿ al-tawārīkh*, 2 vols., ed. E. Blochet (Leiden: Brill, 1911).

civilization of the world. It inherited much of the learning, the sciences and philosophy and the technology of ancient Egypt, the Mesopotamian civilizations, ancient Greece, ancient Persia, and to some extent Rome, India and even China, and on the basis of what it had inherited created the vast traditions of Islamic science and philosophy which also influenced the West deeply.[17] It also learned many ancient artistic and architectural techniques into which it breathed the spirit of the Islamic revelation, thereby creating a very distinct art whose influence is to be seen to this day in South and Central America in the form of *mudejar* art. And once it came into existence, Islamic civilization had direct contact with and experience of the Chinese and Indian civilizations in the East, the Byzantine and Western Christian worlds in the West and the Black African world to the South, not to speak of Mesopotamia, Egypt and Persia which became part of the Islamic world. In contrast to the West where experience of other civilizations, except for the Islamic, was combined with the advent of modernism, Islam had full awareness of many other civilizations and also religions before modem times. For a thousand years it saw itself as both the central and the most powerful of all civilizations, hence the extreme shock of the realization of its weakness before the modern West brought home to the heartland of the Islamic world with the Napoleonic conquest of Egypt in 1798, combined with the sudden weakness and strings of defeat of the Ottomans in Europe as well as the destruction of Muslim power in India by the British.

From the 18th century Islamic civilization began to weaken to various degrees in different areas. Much of the Islamic world became colonized by various European powers, chief among them the British, the French, the Dutch, and the Russians. From the 19th century onward modernized Muslims, seeking to emulate the West with the hope of gaining power and therefore making themselves independent, began to weaken Islamic civilization in the name of trying to save it and this process continued to accelerate up to the end of the first half of the 20th century. At first there was much resistance but governmental authorities, controlled by either colonial powers or modernized Muslims who did their bidding, usually won the day. Islamic dress began to change in favour of Western dress, as did art, architecture, and city planning. Western style educational systems were established everywhere to introduce Western science and learning at the expense of Islamic ones. Even laws, which had been that of the Sharīʿah or Divine Law based on the Qurʾān and the traditions (Ḥadīth) of the Prophet of Islam, were changed in many lands in favour of Western legal codes. Many thought that soon nothing would be left of Islamic civilization.

---

17 On the transmission of the ancient sciences and the rise of Islamic science and learning see Seyyed Hossein Nasr, *Islamic Science: An Illustrated Study* (London: World of Islam Festival Publishing Company Limited, 1976), 3–12.

Yet, despite the unbelievable havoc brought about in nearly every domain, Islamic civilization did not die out completely because the religion of Islam which had created it was still very strong. From the 1950s onward, along with the revival of Islamic thought and rejection by many newly educated Muslims of the complete and blind imitation of the West, which itself was beginning to experience a major crisis in the domain of values, gradually some aspects of Islamic civilization began to be renewed. This process is still very much going on and because it seeks to reassert the Islamic identity of the Islamic world rather than simply to emulate a West no longer completely certain of where it is going itself, it is often construed as being anti-Western. For obvious political reasons, opposition to Western "interests" in the Islamic world is often interpreted as being opposition to the West itself, whereas the current revival of things Islamic makes no claim whatsoever about the West's right to do what it wants in its own world. But because the West has "interests" in various Islamic countries which it wants to protect and it is still more powerful and dominant than all non-Western civilizations, some of these attempts at self-assertion by Muslims take extreme forms, often using Western ideologies to combat the West. In many places they find no other channel for the achievement of their goals, which should normally be through peaceful means. But these extremist actions, no matter how much aggrandized in the Western media, are secondary factors compared to the larger reality of the desire of Islamic civilization to re-assert its own identity and preserve its own religious and cultural ethos even under the unprecedented pressures that it faces. The vast majority of Muslims have no desire to have clashes with other civilizations nor wish to have "interests" in the Gulf of Mexico or the English Channel, which would then need to be protected through clashes. In fact, where there are clashes in the Islamic world today, such as in Palestine Kashmir or Chechnya, it is always the question of Muslims seeking to protect their rights, freedoms or land that has either been taken away or is being threatened, and not to conquer others and then try by force to rule over them.

III

There are numerous factors today which oppose dialogue and understanding between civilizations and even within civilizations. There are economic interests, ethnic and nationalistic assertions, and even the missionary zeal of imposing one's views on others by either political or economic means. But there are also forces which seek to heal rifts both within each civilization and among civilizations, realizing that without accord with other men and with God's creation there is no future for human life on earth. Man's future seems to hinge between clash or dialogue of civilizations. Men and women of good will, whether Jewish, Christian, or Muslim, Hindu or Buddhist or even some outwardly agnostic now realize that there is no way for the human species to survive save through dialogue and accord even with those with whom we disagree on principles. In the present context there must first of all be a civilizational dialogue between members of what remains of the traditional civilizations on the basis of the unity of that transcendent Truth which binds them together. Then there must be an accord on the basis of mutual respect and the acceptance of the thesis of agreeing to disagree even with those who do not accept the traditional principles. If an accord could be created between the religions including those in the West where secularism has become victorious in so many domains, civilizational dialogue leading to understanding would become much more facilitated. And then on the basis of that mutual understanding a greater accord could be created at least on the level of action between those who accept a transcendent Principle and an ultimate goal of human life beyond the purely mundane and earthly and those who do not.

Every civilization today, each in its own way, is faced with an unprecedented crisis. There are wars, the breakdown of social order, the weakening of ethical norms and most ominously the destruction of the natural environment for which all the civilizations are to blame. Each civilization should be given the freedom based on mutual respect to turn its attention to its own spiritual, intellectual, and social problems. And on the basis of mutual respect various civilizations must be able to join hands in facing global problems such as the environmental crisis or the spread of new biotechnologies without consideration of their ethical consequences. These problems recognize no national or civilizational boundaries and only dialogue and accord and not clash or brutal military or economic force can hope to confront and solve them.

In this complicated process upon whose success depends the future of humanity, Islam and Islamic civilization are destined to play a central role. Islam is the last major religion of this cycle of human history and the Qurʾān speaks explicitly of the veracity of religions sent to mankind before Islam. As for Islamic civilization occupying the middle belt of the world, by geography as well as by its historical experience, it is suited in every way to carry out civilizational dialogue with various civilizations and be itself a bridge between East and West, reflecting the light of that blessed olive tree to which the Qurʾān refers as being neither of the East nor of the West as it is also the message of surrender to the Lord Who is the Lord of all the Easts and all the Wests.

Bibliography

Coomaraswamy, Anand K. "Chapter 3: Paths that Lead to the Same Summit." In *The Bugbear of Literacy*, 42–63. Bedfont, Middlesex: Perennial Books, 1979.

Coomaraswamy, Anand K. *What is Civilization? and other essays.* Ipswich: Golgonooza Press, 1989.

Guénon, René. "Principles of Unity of the Oriental Civilizations." In *Introduction to the Study of Hindu Doctrines.* Translated by Marco Pallis. London: Luzac & Co., 1945.

Hamadānī, Rashīd al-Dīn. *Kitāb jāmiʿ al-tawārīkh.* 2 vols. Edited by E. Blochet. Leiden: Brill, 1911.

Huntington, Samuel P. *The Clash of Civilizations and the Remaking of World Order.* New York: Simon and Schuster, 1996.

Ibn Khaldun, *Muqaddimah: An Introduction to History.* Translated by Franz Rosenthal. 3 vols. Princeton: Princeton University Press, 1967.

Lindbom, Tage. *The Tares and the Good Grain: Or the Kingdom of Man at the Hour of Reckoning.* Translated by Alvin Moore, Jr. Macon, Ga: Mercer University Press, 1983.

Mahdi, Muhsin. *Ibn Khaldun's Philosophy of History.* London: George Allen & Unwin, 1957.

Nasr, Seyyed Hossein. *Islamic Science: An Illustrated Study.* London: World of Islam Festival Publishing Company Limited, 1976.

Nasr, Seyyed Hossein. "Chapter 9: Principial Knowledge and the Multiplicity of Sacred Forms." In *Knowledge and Sacred*, 280–308. Edinburgh: Edinburgh University, 1981.

Nasr, Seyyed Hossein. "Chapter 1: Religion and Religions." In *Religion and the Order of Nature*, 3–38. Oxford: Oxford University Press, 1996.

Nasr, Seyyed Hossein. "Reply to Sallie B. King." In Library of Living Philosophers. Vol. 28. *The Philosophy of Seyyed Hossein Nasr,* 221-31. Edited by Lewis Edwin Hahn, Randall E. Auxier, and Lucian W. Stone, Jr. Chicago and La Salle, Illinois: Open Court, 2001.

Pallis, Marco. "Chapter 22: The Present State of Tibetan Art." In *Peaks and Lamas*, 343–66. London: Cassell and Company Limited, 1942.

Pallis, Marco. *The Way and the Mountain.* London: Peter Owen, 1991.

Schuon, Frithjof. *Light on the Ancient World.* Translated by Lord Northbourne. Bloomington, Indianan: World Wisdom Books, 1984.

Schuon, Frithjof. *The Transcendent Unity of Religions.* Wheaton, Illinois and Chennai, India: Quest Books, Theosophical Publishing House, 1993.

Schuon, Frithjof. *Spiritual Perspectives and Human Facts.* Translated by Mark Perry, Jean-Pierre Lafouge and James S. Cutsinger. Edited by James S. Cutsinger. Indiana: World Wisdom, Inc., 2007.

Chapter 2

The Aims of Education: The Forgotten Truths

Osman Bakar

Introduction

The main thesis presented in this chapter is that our modern systems of education have failed to address the fundamental human needs viewed in their totality, mainly because many thinkers and practitioners of education only have a vague understanding of what these fundamental human needs themselves mean. I refer to these needs as the forgotten truths in education, meaning that contemporary education would continue to be crisis-ridden unless we return to these forgotten truths. This chapter discusses the most important of these truths and their epistemological roles and functions in any proposed educational reform that is worthy of the name within the historical perspective of the revival of traditional Islamic thought in the post-colonial era. In particular, it addresses the issue of how to harmonize education of time-honoured human values that are at the core of humanness with education to generate new knowledge for society's changing needs, both of which are necessary to the sustainment of society.

The main objective of this chapter is twofold. First, to identify and restate several of what may now be viewed as the main forgotten truths pertaining to the fundamental aims of education that, in the Islamic perspective, constitute its true purpose. Second, to reformulate the identified forgotten truths in the light of the present key challenges confronting Muslim education.

The forgotten truths that we have in mind are not truths that have disappeared a long time ago from the collective memory of the Muslim ummah. Rather, the forgotten truths in question were last resurrected in modern times only about half a century ago when the so-called religious revival swept the Muslim world and indeed the whole ummah, including Muslim minority communities in both the East and the West, but only to disappear again from the radar of Muslim consciousness a generation later. In historical terms, half a century ago is only a recent past. So, it seems that in modern civilization, changes are occurring more rapidly and more fleeting than ever not only in the technological domain but also in the realm of ideas. From the traditional Islamic point of view, this kind of phenomenon of change and the attitudinal change that accompanies it, often for the worse, is a real cause for worry, especially when viewed in the light of the dominant philosophical belief in contemporary human thought that deifies change for the sake of change to the point of denying the very idea of permanence itself.

The traditional belief based on the teachings of the Qurʾān and the Prophetic Ḥadīths affirms the position that the human mind needs to be continuously nourished by permanent truths that are to be complemented with truths of a transient nature. In other words, human needs are partly permanent and partly transient and changing with time. The rationale of the traditional Islamic position insisting on the idea of permanent truths as basic nourishments for the soul, particularly for its part that we call intellect-reason (al-ʿaql), and hence the idea of permanent human needs, is provided by the very nature of Reality itself. Both the Divine Reality and the human reality that, according to the Qurʾān, bears within itself the signs of God (āyātuʾllāh)[1] dictate the fundamentality of the idea of permanent truths in human consciousness. It is education in its broad sense that provides the process of nourishment of the soul with absolute and relative truths furnished by both divine revelation (waḥy) and rational inquiry. If the process of intellectual nourishment in question has proved to be ineffective resulting in the permanent truths that serve as its staple food to be marginalized and subsequently forgotten, as what has actually happened to the truths about the true purpose of education, then there is an urgent need to conceive of a new educational curriculum and pedagogy that would be efficacious in delivering a good understanding of the forgotten truths.

The Islamic Revival and the Historic 1977 Makkah Conference on Education

The forgotten truths in question that had resurfaced in the 1960s in the writings of a number of Muslim scholars soon came to enjoy wide currency especially among students and academics following the initial wave of the revival during the early 1970s. Apparently, the single most important event of the decade that helped thrust these forgotten truths to take center stage in the emerging consciousness of post-colonial Muslim intellectuals, particularly education policy makers and activists, was the historic First World Conference on Muslim Education held at Makkah on 31st March to 8th April 1977.[2] Judging

---

1 Qurʾān 41:53.
2 Shaikh Abdul Mabud, "World Conferences on Muslim Education: Shaping the Agenda of Muslim Education in the Future," in *Philosophies of Islamic Education, Historical*

from the enormous response it received from the global ummah and, more importantly, the big impact it had on Muslim education generally, this conference must be regarded as perhaps the most significant scholarly event in the intellectual history of the ummah in modern times.

However, the Makkah Conference partly owed its impressive success to the religious revival fervour that had already gripped the Muslim ummah years before it was convened. A brief discussion of the new Muslim frame of mind that was taking shape prior to the Makkah Conference would help us to better contextualize the historic event. In this respect, two big international events ought to be mentioned. The earlier and more important one was the First Islamic Summit Conference held in Rabat, Morocco on 22–25 September 1969 that made the historic decision to establish the Organization of Islamic Conference (OIC) with twenty-five participating states as its founding members.[3] The Rabat Conference was convened by King Faisal of Saudi Arabia (reign: 1964–75) in the wake of the arson attack on the Al-Aqsa Mosque in Israeli-occupied Jerusalem, Islam's third holiest city, just over a month earlier.[4] The other was the First International Conference on Science and Technology in the Muslim World held in Riyadh, Saudi Arabia in 1975.[5] The Riyadh Conference was also linked to the name of King Faisal. It was scheduled to be officiated by King Faisal on 26th March 1975 but had to be postponed to a later date in the same year due to his assassination only the day before. The Rabat Conference was particularly significant as a contributing factor to the genesis of the Islamic awakening at the very beginning of the 1970s. It fostered a new sense of Muslim unity that had not been seen since the end of Western colonialism. It was greeted with enthusiasm, especially by the Muslim intelligentsia and youths who openly expressed their fervent hope that the OIC would be a catalyst for change and the revival of Islam in the post-colonial Muslim world.[6] Without doubt, the formative years of the OIC during the first half of the decade were themselves an important integral component of the early wave of Islamic revival.

Perspectives and Emerging Discourses, eds. Nadeem A. Memon and Mujadad Zaman (London: Routledge, 2016), 129–43. Hereafter, the First World Conference on Muslim Education will be referred to as Makkah Conference.

3   Officially established on 25th September 1969, the OIC changed its name to Organisation of Islamic Cooperation on 28th June 2011 during the 38th Council of Foreign Ministers Meeting in Astana, Kazakhstan. With the current membership of fifty-seven countries the OIC is the second largest inter-governmental body in the world after the United Nations.

4   The arson attack took place on 21st August 1969. The attacker was an Australian Christian extremist named Denis Michael Rohan.

5   Hereafter, this Conference will be referred to as Riyadh Conference.

6   On a personal note, I am happy to recall my own involvement in the leading youth movement in Malaysia in the 1970s, ABIM (Muslim Youth Movement of Malaysia), which gained popular support in its thought perspectives and activities in the early part of the decade thanks to the inspiring developments that the OIC had generated.

The Riyadh Conference was also significant, but it was to be appreciated from another point of view, namely the scientific and the technological. The conference was primarily about the conditions of science and technology in the contemporary Muslim world. The rationale of having the conference was not unrelated to the issue of Islamic revival that was then widely discussed by Muslim academic circles and university students, including in the West. On the contrary, there was a close connection between the issue of Islamic revival and the convening of the Riyadh Conference.[7] The close connection was underscored by the fact that the organizers of the conference—the newly established Faculty of Engineering at King Abdul Aziz University in Riyadh—included intellectual-activists who played an important role in spearheading the Islamic revival movement in the early 1970s. One of the ideas that were very much in the minds of the revivalists was the importance of science to Islam. There was a deep awareness that contemporary Islam was weak in science and technology, but during its golden age (particularly from the tenth to the twelfth centuries CE) Islamic civilization led the world in this field. Consequently, the pursuit of Muslim scientific and technological progress was viewed as an indispensable component of the religious revival agenda. In the light of this view, therefore, it was a matter of great urgency that the Muslim world should strive to restore its eminence in the field. The Riyadh Conference was primarily to help globalize the revivalist scientific and technological agenda.

For some of the revivalists—thinkers and activists—though small in number but intellectually quite influential in society, the interest in science and Islam assumed the form of a quest for a civilizational revival of Islamic philosophical perspectives on science. The pioneering figure in this quest was Seyyed Hossein Nasr, an Iranian-American scholar of Islam who wrote in the 1960s several influential works on science in Islamic history and civilization.[8] Nasr refers to as Islamic science the form of science that was cultivated in Islamic civilization throughout its history and which he would like to be revived in the contemporary world. As he has argued, the usage of the term Islamic science presupposes its fundamental differences with modern science with respect to philosophical foundation and value orientation. Although Nasr has helped revive the interest in science in classical Islamic civilization, especially the idea of its religious character that distinguishes it from modern science,

---

7   I was invited to present a paper at the conference not as an academic but as a representative of the revivalist-oriented ABIM.
8   His most influential works on this broad subject published in the 1960s are: Seyyed Hossein Nasr, *An Introduction to Islamic Cosmological Doctrines* (Cambridge, Massachusetts: Harvard University Press, 1964) and *Science and Civilisation in Islam* (Cambridge, Massachusetts: Harvard University Press, 1968). These writings had a considerable impact on the minds of young Muslim academics and students in the 1970s, including this author.

the Riyadh Conference did not discuss the ideological or philosophical dimension of Islamic science along the lines he has articulated. Although there were papers dealing with the religious dimension of the Muslim pursuit of science, the Riyadh Conference was mainly concerned with issues of scientific and technological development in Muslim countries. However, through his writings on Islamic science that were replete with persuasive arguments for its new cultivation in the Muslim world, albeit with a philosophical bent, Nasr helped create an intellectual environment that was conducive to the convening of the Riyadh Conference.

Looking back now into more recent history, we could see quite clearly that the restatement and reformulation of many forgotten truths in the treasury of Islamic thought in the writings of a number of prominent modern Muslim scholars that appeared in the 1960s together with the Rabat and Riyadh Conferences had helped to significantly pave the way for the 1977 Makkah Conference. The Makkah Conference was indeed a logical follow-up to the intellectual, religious and political developments in the 1960s and 1970s pertaining to the legacy and revival of Islam. Nasr's two works previously cited and Syed Muhammad Naquib al-Attas' first great work, *The Mysticism of Hamzah Fansuri*[9] are good examples of writings of the period that influenced the Islamic intellectual development leading to the Makkah Conference. An event of global and civilizational significance that is also worthy of mention in this brief discussion on the pre-Makkah Conference Islamic intellectual climate is the World of Islam Festival held in London in the spring of 1976.[10] Described as a unique and cultural event that in concept and in scale was no less than an attempt to present one civilization—in all its depth and variety—to another with the underlying message of Unity, the Festival provided a good civilizational experience of Islam not just for the West to whom it was targeted but also for Muslims, particularly the modern educated, who had practically little knowledge of their own civilization. The key exhibitions during the three-month Festival were "The arts of Islam" and "Science and technology in Islam." Given its depth and variety and scale, the World of Islam Festival as best represented by the two exhibitions could not but have generated some genuine interest in Islamic civilization among the visitors to the exhibitions.

Held hardly a year after the London Festival, the Makkah Conference could still feel the intellectual heat and Islamic euphoria generated by the Festival that it could take advantage of to serve its own purposes, both immediate and long-term. It is worth noting that there were individuals who attended both the events. They experienced a kind of emotional, if not also intellectual, link

---

9 This work was highly influential among Malay academics and students in the 1970s, especially among the revivalist intellectual-activists.
10 The Festival that lasted for three months from April to June 1976 was opened by Queen Elizabeth II.

between the two global events. In fact, some individuals, including this author, could even relate the intellectual and emotional links that connected the Rabat and Riyadh Conferences to the London Festival, and then to the Makkah Conference. For this author, the intellectual link in question was provided by the resurrected forgotten truths, and the emotional link by the sense of Islamic revival that was associated with each event. The Makkah Conference is especially significant from the perspective of our present discussion, since it provided the best intellectual platform to have been convened till then for expounding the most pertinent forgotten truths for the renewal of Islamic educational ideals.

One of the core concerns of Muslim intellectual-activists during the decade prior to the Makkah Conference was the issue of modern Western secularism and the pervasive philosophical challenges that it posed to Muslim education in both theory and practice. This ideological issue was to dominate the discussions at the Makkah Conference. Not surprisingly at all that this was what transpired at the conference, given the already widely held view among Muslim scholars and university students well before the convening of the conference that secularism in contemporary education is the greatest stumbling block of ideas to the realization of Islam's educational ideals. In the light of this pre-conference awareness of the challenges of secularism to Muslim education[11] among many modern educated Muslims, the main aims and objectives of the conference—"to define the principles, aims and methodology of the Islamic concept of education" and "to suggest ways and means of realizing the aforementioned principles in practice"[12]—struck a chord with the speakers and participants of the conference. The conference strengthened the belief that to fully understand the Islamic concept of education in its depths and breadths and to practically realize it in the contemporary world would demand a dismantling of many key philosophical, pedagogical and curricular facets of the secular system of education that is sought to be replaced.

In this chapter we will be discussing some of the forgotten truths pertaining to the fundamental aims of education that were sought to be revived, reaffirmed and resuscitated at the Makkah Conference by three of its most prominent speakers, namely Syed Muhammad Naquib al-Attas, Seyyed Hossein Nasr, and Syed Ali Ashraf. Prior to the conference, al-Attas, a leading Malay thinker of the twentieth century, had been disseminating his captivating views on Islamic philosophy of education and his Islamic critique of secularism. There was a great interest among students and youths of the early 1970s in Malaysia to know the Islamic concept and philosophy of education and in what im-

---

11 For an insight into modern developments in Muslim education that led to the organisation of the conference, see Syed Ali Ashraf, *Islamic Education Movement: An Historical Analysis 1977–1990* (Cambridge, UK: The Islamic Academy, 1990).
12 See Mabud, "World Conferences on Muslim Education," 131.

portant respects it differs from the modern secular education that then prevailed side by side with what had survived of the traditional system of Islamic education in the worldwide Muslim communities.[13] Al-Attas had shared his "preliminary thoughts" on the aims of education and the modern knowledge problem with Malaysian university academics, students and youths, through public talks and lectures that were organized for him.[14] These important intellectual events were mostly held in 1975–6 prior to his appointment at Temple University as Visiting Scholar and Professor of Islamics[15] during the Fall 1976 and Spring 1977 Semesters. The main organizer of these events was the Muslim Youth Movement of Malaysia (ABIM) and its allied student organizations.

Mainly through the work of its leader Anwar Ibrahim, who was later to become Malaysia's Deputy Prime Minister (1993–8), ABIM had forged then a close ideological relationship with al-Attas whom it considered as the main source of intellectual inspiration for its educational thought and activities. The context of the time is important to be noted. The 1970s were the first decade of the so-called Islamic revival, a worldwide phenomenon that demonstrated an impressive display of united efforts and programmatic collaboration of Muslim youths, intellectuals and ulama in empowering Islam as a total way of life in the modern world and restoring its lost dignity as a religion and as a civilization. It was the first time in the post-colonial era that the world

---

13 The traditional system of Islamic education that survived the onslaught of modernism as still found in the *madrasahs* and other religious schools was just a fragment of what was known as the transmitted sciences (*al-ʿulūm al-naqliyyah*). The intellectual sciences (*al-ʿulūm al-ʿaqliyyah*) were taught in modern schools from a different philosophical and methodological perspective that was often at odds with the traditional Islamic perspective. For an overview of post-Ibn Khaldun period progressively widening gulf between the two categories of sciences in higher Muslim education until the post-colonial era, see Osman Bakar, "The Role of Islam in Higher Education Policies of Muslim countries," in *Contemporary Higher Education Needs in Muslim Countries: Defining the Role of Islam in 21st Century Higher Education*, eds. Osman Bakar, Eric Winkel, and Airulamri Amran (Kuala Lumpur: IAIS Malaysia, 2011), 24–31.

14 If I may mention here, I had the opportunity of organising some of these intellectual events. During the period 1974–81 when I was closely associated with al-Attas as his informal student, quite often he would grant me the privilege of sharing his thoughts on many intellectual issues confronting the contemporary Muslim ummah, particularly in the Malay world. See Osman Bakar, *Advancing Comparative Epistemology and Civilisational and Futures Studies: The Global Role of the New ISTAC-IIUM* (Kuala Lumpur: ISTAC-IIUM Publications, 2019), 37–8.

15 Al-Attas' appointment was initiated and arranged by the late Ismaʿil R. al-Faruqi, who was then a Professor at the University. Al-Faruqi was another notable scholar to be associated with the 1977 Makkah Conference. He was co-editor with Abdullah Omar Nasseef of another book in the earlier mentioned Islamic Education Series. See Ismaʿil R. al-Faruqi and Abdullah O. Nasseef, eds., *Social and Natural Sciences: The Islamic Perspective* (London: Hodder and Stoughton and Jeddah: King Abdulaziz University, 1981). Al-Attas' stint at Temple University turned out to be consequential for Islamic thought in the second half of the twentieth century.

had seen such a religious phenomenon sweeping the global Muslim ummah in both scale and intensity. The revival was to impact all sectors of life of the ummah, not only the socio-political but also the intellectual and spiritual. Anwar Ibrahim, a student of al-Attas at the prestigious University of Malaya in the late 1960s and ABIM's best known leader, established himself as an influential and respected international Muslim youth leader by riding "the wave of Islamic revival," the equivalent Malay term for which he himself had coined and popularized in the 1970s.[16]

It was during this revivalist-charged intellectual environment that al-Attas articulated his Islamic philosophy of education as a response to the modern secular Western education that gripped the educational life and thought of practically the whole Muslim world. His response was essentially intellectual and philosophical in nature. It was befitting the challenge of the day—modern secular education—whose nature was clearly also intellectual and philosophical. More precisely, al-Attas' response was epistemological, meaning that it pertains to visions or theories[17] of knowledge.

One of the core issues in al-Attas' epistemological response was about the real purpose of education as viewed from the Islamic perspective. In his view, this issue must be addressed with clarity in the light of Islamic intellectual and spiritual tradition. At the Makkah Conference, in his keynote paper[18] entitled "Preliminary Thoughts on the Nature of Knowledge and the Definition and Aims of Education,"[19] he reaffirmed the traditional view that "the [primary] aim of education in Islam is to produce a good man,"[20] and only secondarily as a "good citizen" whose value is "measured in terms of the pragmatic or utilitarian sense of his usefulness to state and society and the world."[21] It was on the basis of this central idea of the "good man" that he articulated in the paper his philosophy of education. The historical context of his statement is worth revisiting, especially for the attention of everyone who is deeply con-

---

16 The Malay term in question was "gelombang kebangkitan Islam."
17 In Greek the original meaning of *theoria* from which the English word 'theory' is derived actually means 'vision.'
18 Al-Attas wrote and completed the paper while he was at the Department of Religion, Temple University, Philadelphia, USA shortly before presenting it to the Makkah Conference.
19 The paper was published together with other selected papers of the conference in a book that he himself edited with an introduction. See Syed M. N. al-Attas, ed., *Aims and Objectives of Islamic Education* (London: Hodder and Stoughton and Jeddah: King Abdulaziz University, 1979). The book is one of the six books in the Islamic Education Series, published under the general editorship of Syed Ali Ashraf, that materialised from the conference. The paper was also included as a chapter in al-Attas' *Islam and Secularism* but with the title "The Dewesternization of Knowledge." See Chapter V, 127–60. Another book in the series was co-edited by Syed Ali Ashraf to whom the present volume is dedicated. See Husain and Ashraf, *Crisis in Muslim Education*.
20 Syed M. N. Al-Attas, *Islam and Secularism* (Kuala Lumpur: ABIM, (1978), 144.
21 Al-Attas, *Islam and Secularism*, 141.

cerned with the issue of the need for qualitative improvement of education in our present times.

His paper at the Makkah Conference was an articulation of this epistemological response. His masterly dissection of modern Western epistemology in the light of the traditional Islamic epistemology has exposed it as being endowed with a problematic anatomy, created as it were out of conflicting elements that is characteristic of the worldview and values of modern Western civilization itself.[22] The mainstream modern Western epistemology posits a marginal role for religion in the pursuit of knowledge, but instead confers the central role to science that itself has deviated from its true purpose. From the perspective of traditional Islamic epistemology, quite clearly the modern West has done a great injustice to the role of religion in knowledge acquisition and in the creation of a sustainable knowledge culture. As argued by al-Attas, misguided as it were by an epistemology that is characterized by inherent contradictions, the modern West was lured into an epistemological adventurism that led to the crowning of science as its new "religion" replacing Christianity, at least in the domain of knowledge if not in many other domains as well. The West, says al-Attas, "has defined knowledge in terms of the effort of science as control of nature and society," whereas the true purpose of knowledge to which "it no longer attaches any significance and reality," is "the improvement and identification and elevation of his personality and the desire to learn about the Divine order of the world and salvation."[23]

In conformity with his traditional perspective, al-Attas explains in greater details his conception of the good man. "The concept of a 'good man' in Islam," he says, "connotes not only that he must be 'good' in the general social sense understood, but that he must also first be good to his self, and not be unjust to it."[24] The good man as conceived by him is fundamentally constituted of praiseworthy qualities in four dimensions of humanness: man's worship (*ʿibādah*) and obedience (*ṭāʿah*) to God;[25] man's role as vicegerent of God (*khalīfatuʾllāh*) shouldering "the weighty burden of trust (*amānah*)";[26] justice (*ʿadl*) to oneself and, by extension, to others;[27] and man's spiritual, moral and ethical conduct (*adab*).[28] These four qualitative achievements of humanness that enter into the definition of the good man are intellectual and spiritual in nature and closely related to each other. Thus, al-Attas relates worship

---

22 Al-Attas, *Islam and Secularism*, 128.
23 Al-Attas, *Islam and Secularism*, 148–9.
24 Al-Attas, *Islam and Secularism*, 141.
25 Al-Attas, *Islam and Secularism*, 133.
26 Al-Attas, *Islam and Secularism*, 134.
27 Al-Attas, *Islam and Secularism*, 135.
28 Al-Attas, *Islam and Secularism*, 142–4. For al-Attas' detailed discussion of *adab* in Islam and its loss within the ummah as the main cause of its present dilemma and predicaments, see this book's Chapter IV.

(*ʿibādah*) to *adab* and justice. He also relates *khilāfah* (vicegerency) to *amānah* (trust) and *ʿadl* (justice). He expresses the close relationship between *ʿibādah* and *adab* by emphasizing that "*ʿibādah* in its entirety is but another expression of *adab* towards God."[29] This means that *adab* is not just about one having the right and proper relations with fellow humans but also with God. As al-Attas puts it, *adab* in its comprehensive sense reflects "the condition of justice."[30] With this explanation of the essential relationship between *adab* and justice, we are able to better understand and appreciate the meaning and significance of his statement, "loss of *adab* implies loss of justice, which in turn betrays confusion in knowledge."[31]

It is clear from his paper at the Makkah Conference that while expounding his conception of "the good man" al-Attas had resurrected several fundamental traditional Islamic doctrines that lie at the heart of Muslim education. In speaking of the forgotten truths pertaining to the fundamental purpose of education, it is to be emphasized that it is not the idea of "the good man" itself that has been forgotten. Prior to the Islamic revival of which we are speaking, the great majority of Muslims still cherished the traditional idea of the good man. Nor had the ideas of vicegerency (*khilāfah*) and worship and servitude (*ʿibādah*) been entirely forgotten. Rather, what had been forgotten was the real knowledge underlying each of the four dimensions of humanness that has to be actualized in the good man and the knowledge that connects these dimensions to each other and integrates them into a single portrait of the good man. In al-Attas' view, the main substance of this lost knowledge was the true conception of man and knowledge of the Divine order in the cosmos. It was his main goal to revive this lost knowledge through his paper presentation at the Makkah Conference.

Seyyed Hossein Nasr, another important scholarly figure at the Makkah Conference,[32] concurs in many of his writings with al-Attas' view on this forgotten truth about the true purpose of knowledge and about the real purpose of science understood as a particular branch of knowledge. Simply put, Nasr affirms the traditional Islamic view that the true purpose of seeking knowledge is to know God. But Nasr is known to have expressed this purpose in different ways in his different writings some of which had appeared much earlier than the works of al-Attas. For example, in his *Science and civilization in Islam* (1968) Nasr affirms that "the aim of all the Islamic sciences—and, more generally speaking, of all the medieval and ancient cosmological sciences—is to show the unity and interrelatedness of all that exists, so that in contemplating

---

29 Al-Attas, *Islam and Secularism*, 100.
30 Al-Attas, *Islam and Secularism*, 99.
31 Al-Attas, *Islam and Secularism*, 99.
32 Nasr was the editor of another book in the Islamic Education Series output of the Makkah Conference. See Seyyed H. Nasr, ed., *Philosophy, Literature and Fine Arts* (London: Hodder and Stoughton and Jeddah: King Abdulaziz University, 1982).

the unity of the cosmos, man may be led to the unity of the Divine Principle, of which the unity of Nature is the image."[33] By "all the Islamic sciences" Nasr means all the branches of knowledge or all academic disciplines. In fact, in this book he provides a treatment of the epistemic position and significance of each of the natural, social, and human sciences known to have been cultivated in Islamic civilization, thus significantly underlining the broader semantic field of science to which he subscribes. In this expression of the true purpose of knowledge, Nasr identifies human knowledge about God with human knowledge of the unity of the Divine Principle, meaning the Divine Attributes and Qualities as signified by God's Most Beautiful Names (*al-asmā' al-ḥusnā*). The idea of the possible attainment[34] of knowledge of the unity of the Divine Principle through knowledge of the unity of Nature and, more generally, through knowledge of the unity of the cosmos, as emphasized by Nasr, is of fundamental importance to both Islamic epistemology and Islamic philosophy of education. This idea that has its basis in the Qur'ān itself[35] attests to the harmony and unity of religion and science and their complementary but interactive roles in knowledge creation and acquisition that ought to be repeatedly reminded in teaching and learning. The educational perspective that issues from this idea is one in which there is a well-defined pedagogical role for science in the teaching and learning of theology and likewise a well-defined pedagogical role for theology in the teaching of science, especially its philosophy.[36]

In a post-Makkah Conference work *Knowledge and the Sacred* (1981), however, Nasr defines the highest form of knowledge to be sought by man as knowledge of "the Ultimate Reality as the Transcendent, the Beyond and the objective world as a distinct reality on its own level, and the Ultimate Reality as the Immanent, as the Supreme Self underlying all the veils of subjectivity and the many "selves" or layers of consciousness within him."[37] In this profound expression of the true purpose of knowledge, however, which employs philosophical language, Nasr identifies man's knowledge about God with his knowledge of the Ultimate Reality as the Transcendent and the Ultimate Reality as

---

33 Seyyed H. Nasr, *Science and Civilization in Islam* (Cambridge: Harvard University Press, 1968), 22.
34 Indeed, in Islamic civilization, this possibility became a reality in the lives of a multitude of scientists, artists, and ordinary believers over the centuries.
35 "If there were, in the heavens and the earth, other gods besides God, there would have been confusion in both!" (Qur'ān 21:22). See Abdullah Y. Ali, *The Meaning of The Holy Qur'ān: Text, Translation and Commentary* (Kuala Lumpur: Islamic Book Trust, 2005), 660.
36 For a comprehensive discussion of the various facets of the relationship between religion and science that could provide the necessary materials for their respective pedagogical roles, particularly in their mutual enhancement, see Osman Bakar, *Tawhid and Science: Islamic Perspectives on Religion and Science*, 2nd ed. (Shah Alam: Arah Publications, 2008).
37 Seyyed H. Nasr, *Knowledge and the Sacred: The Gifford Lectures* (Edinburgh: Edinburgh University Press, 1981), 3.

the Immanent and of their respective manifestations or disclosures (*tajallī*) in both the macrocosmic universe and in the microcosmic universe which is the multi-layered human reality itself. But Nasr emphasizes the important principle that knowledge about God must go hand in hand with knowledge of the cosmic order, viewed not as an independent order of reality but rather as God's creation or manifestation. In other words, in the Islamic perspective, the emphasis on theology is not made at the expense of the cosmological and natural sciences. Nor is it made at the expense of the psychological sciences, including the cognitive, since sciences of the subjective world comprising the many different layers of the self or human consciousness are included in Nasr's description of the highest form of *knowledge* to be pursued by man. Certainly, from the point of view of Islamic epistemology, these sciences are neither neglected nor limited in Muslim education. But Islam does insist on a God-centric approach to the study of the cosmic and human orders. This insistence on studying and knowing these orders in the light of God's relations with them is what essentially distinguishes the Islamic from the modern secular study of it. In practically every page of the Qurʾān calls are made on man to reflect on the cosmic and human phenomena in their relations to the Divine Attributes and Qualities that manifest them. The most frequent Divine Attributes mentioned in the Qurʾān are Knowledge (*ʿilm*), Power (*qudrah*), and Wisdom (*ḥikmah*).

Although in *Knowledge and the Sacred* Nasr has expressed the main substance of the most important knowledge in Muslim education quite differently from his expression of it in *Science and Civilization in Islam*, the two expressions actually lead to the same conclusion. The conclusion inferred is that the true purpose of education is to know the Divine Attributes and Qualities as signified by God's Beautiful Names and to know the universe and man in the light of this theological-metaphysical Reality. The meaning of this conclusion is perfectly clear. An integral education from the Islamic perspective would have to be founded on the beautiful Divine Names. However, between the two of Nasr's expressions of the theological-metaphysical Reality to be known the second provides additional knowledge about the Divine Names that would be useful to the Muslim philosophers in their task of transforming the Names into educational principles. I have in mind Nasr's reference to the "Ultimate Reality as the Transcendent" and the "Ultimate Reality as the Immanent." The additional knowledge alluded to in Nasr's second formulation pertains to the distinction between two kinds of Divine Names, namely Names of incomparability (*tanzīh*) in reference to the Transcendent Reality and Names of similarity (*tashbīh*) in reference to the Immanent Reality. In my view, the best explanation in Islamic thought of the difference between these two kinds of Divine Names is given by the Sufi thinker, Muḥyī al-Dīn Ibn al-ʿArabī (1165–1240).

Ibn al-ʿArabī maintains that true knowledge of God and creation can only come through combining the perspective of incomparability and the perspective of similarity.³⁸ Without this combination, a student of theology and cosmology would fall into a lopsided view of Divine Reality and creation. To demonstrate that God combines attributes of incomparability and similarity, Ibn al-ʿArabī cited among others this Qurʾānic verse: "Nothing is like Him, and He is the Seeing, the Hearing."³⁹ "Nothing is like Him" emphasizes the attribute of incomparability; "He is the Seeing, the Hearing" emphasizes attributes of similarity, since these two attributes are shared by human beings and other creatures, though in imperfect forms. Despite this very clear scriptural support for the theological position that affirms combination of incomparability and similarity in Divine Attributes many Muslim thinkers and religious scholars overemphasized incomparability at the expense of similarity. Ibn al-ʿArabī has an explanation for their lopsided view of Divine Reality: they rely on reason to know the nature of things, including Divine Nature, but "the rational faculty can grasp God's Unity and transcendence, while imagination is needed to perceive the multiplicity of His self-disclosures (*tajallī*) and His immanence."⁴⁰ This view of Ibn al-ʿArabī is of particular significance to Muslim education, since it addresses the issue of how best to teach theology, especially the doctrine of Divine Unity (*al-tawḥīd*).

Nasr's insistence on knowledge of the Divine Reality together with knowledge of the cosmos viewed as the theatre of God's self-disclosures will find precious support from Ibn al-ʿArabī in the form of his combined incomparability-similarity and the corresponding reason-imagination approach to that knowledge and also his extremely useful God's Self-Disclosure Principle to the study of natural and social sciences.

At the Makkah Conference Nasr presented a paper entitled "The Teaching of Philosophy."⁴¹ The paper provided him with a golden opportunity to restate traditional Islamic philosophy in its whole depth and breadth and to emphasize the need for it to be resuscitated in contemporary times. He reminded the conference that the term Islamic philosophy refers to not only the *falsafah* of the Peripatetic school (*al-mashshāʾī*) but also philosophical ideas found in the other Islamic intellectual schools, including the perspectives of *uṣūl al-fiqh* (principles of jurisprudence) and *kalām* (dialectical theology). Nasr mentions four major areas of intellectual concern to Islamic philosophy. First, the formulation and application of the ideas of wisdom (*ḥikmah*), universality,

---

38 William Chittick, *The Sufi Path of Knowledge: Ibn al-ʿArabī's Metaphysics of Imagination* (Albany: SUNY Press, 1989), 69. For Chittick's detailed discussion of Ibn al-ʿArabī's views on the two perspectives, see 68–76.
39 Qurʾān 42:11. See Ali, *Meaning of the Holy Qurʾān*, 1041.
40 Chittick, *Sufi Path of Knowledge*, 70.
41 Seyyed H. Nasr, "The Teaching of Philosophy," in *Philosophy, Literature and Fine Arts*, ed. Seyyed H. Nasr (London: Hodder and Stoughton and Jeddah: King Abdulaziz University, 1982), 3–21.

certitude, and the supra-individual character of the Truth (*al-ḥaqq*).⁴² Second, knowledge about the nature of things leading to and based on the idea of Divine Unity (*al-tawḥīd*).⁴³ Third, the formulation of Islamic worldview.⁴⁴ And fourth, the issue of method of disciplining the mind in general and method of thinking that is applicable to the various sciences in particular.⁴⁵ Nasr's discussion of Islamic philosophy at the Makkah Conference brings into sharp focus important truths related to the idea of Divine Unity. It is quite clear that Islamic philosophy as Nasr has explained it would play an important role in the resuscitation of these truths through education.

Syed Ali Ashraf, the mastermind of the Makkah Conference in his capacity as its organizing secretary, also presented a paper entitled "Islamic Principles and Methods in the Teaching of Literature."⁴⁶ His most important message in the paper is that it is possible for literature to serve as an instrument or vehicle for progressive advancement in man's self-awareness or consciousness "of his relationship with God, with nature and with the world at large."⁴⁷ He maintains that the highest form of self-awareness is the awareness of "all the attributes of Allah expressed through His Names."⁴⁸ This awareness was granted to Adam by God when He taught him His Names. The main aim of the teaching of literature in the Islamic perspective is to rekindle the fire of imagination (*khayāl*) within man that would help unite the Spirit and the self in an expanding relationship to the point of him attaining the highest form of self-awareness as earlier mentioned. In other words, literature is to primarily help man discover his true self, who is God's own reflection.

The foregoing discussion of the papers of al-Attas, Nasr and Ashraf, shows remarkable convergence in their views on the fundamental truths that need to be resuscitated in contemporary Muslim education. These truths pertain to knowledge of Divine Unity and knowledge of the spiritual conception of man.

The Post-Makkah Conference: A Brief Renaissance

The Makkah Conference succeeded in generating a new intellectual momentum in the Muslim world in the post-colonial era. It produced a new intellectual climate with Islamic characteristics and generated new intellectual currents and movements of Islamic inspiration, the most prominent of which was, undoubtedly, the Islamization of knowledge movement. Several intellec-

---

42 Nasr, "The Teaching of Philosophy," 5.
43 Nasr, "The Teaching of Philosophy," 5.
44 Nasr, "The Teaching of Philosophy," 4.
45 Nasr, "The Teaching of Philosophy," 4, 13–6.
46 The paper is published in the same volume together with Nasr's "The Teaching of Philosophy," 22–40.
47 Syed Ali Ashraf (1979), "Islamic Principles and Methods in the Teaching of Literature," in Nasr, *Philosophy, Literature and Fine Arts*, 23.
48 Ashraf, "Islamic principles and methods," 23.

tual schools of thought or positions emerged on the meaning and significance of Islamization of knowledge and its implementation agenda.[49] These schools centered around several scholars who either had presented key papers or participated in the conference. The most prominent of these schools were those led by Muhammad Naquib al-Attas, Ismaʿil Raji al-Faruqi, Seyyed Hossein Nasr, Syed Ali Ashraf and Ziauddin Sardar. Al-Attas, who claims to have originated the idea of Islamization of knowledge,[50] founded in September 1987 a postgraduate center in Kuala Lumpur known as the International Institute of Islamic Thought and Civilisation (ISTAC), an autonomous institute of International Islamic University Malaysia,[51] with generous government support. Several years earlier (1981), al-Faruqi co-founded an international organization, the International Institute of Islamic Thought (IIIT) based in Virginia, the United States with the established objective of advancing the cause of Islamization of knowledge. The Institute grew rapidly, spreading its wings of influence to the whole Muslim world and even to Muslim minority communities in the West.

Unlike al-Attas and al-Faruqi, Nasr did not have an organization to help him realize his vision of Islamization of knowledge. However, the organization deprivation and having to live in exile in the United States a year after the Makkah Conference amidst the Iranian Islamic Revolution (1978) did not prevent him from producing many great works relevant to the Islamization of knowledge agenda. His lack of physical organization was compensated by his stature similar to the Muslim universal figure of old with scholarly interests in many fields of study and the intellectual capacity to produce great literary works. His intellectually productive traditionalist school was also a compensating factor. Nasr himself may be viewed as an institution. As noted earlier, even before the Makkah Conference Nasr has produced works relevant to Islamization of knowledge, particularly the natural sciences.[52]

Ashraf, as organizing secretary, had significantly contributed to the success of the Makkah Conference. His post-conference role and contribution were perhaps even more challenging and significant for he had the unenviable task and responsibility of ensuring that the resolutions of the conference were effectively carried out. He helped organize five follow-up World Conferences in five different capitals of the Muslim world, partly to help sustain the

---

49 On these positions, see Bakar, *Tawhid and Science*. Also, see Leif Stenberg, *The Islamization of Science: Four Muslim Positions Developing an Islamic Modernity* (Stockholm: Almqvist & Wiksell, 1996).
50 See Wan Mohd N. Wan Daud, *The Educational Philosophy and Practice of Syed Muhammad Naquib al-Attas: An Exposition of the Original Concept of Islamization* (Kuala Lumpur: ISTAC, 1998).
51 Established in May 1983, IIUM was the first of four Islamic Universities to be sponsored by the OIC.
52 On Nasr's major contribution to the Islamisation of the natural sciences, see Bakar, *Tawhid*, 236–40.

intellectual momentum generated by the Makkah Conference. When the OIC established the World Centre for Islamic Education in Makkah in 1980 Ashraf was appointed as its first Director-General. From the point of view of his contribution to the Islamization of knowledge agenda it was The Islamic Academy that he set up in 1983 in Cambridge, the United Kingdom with the support of his able Deputy, Shaikh Abdul Mabud that had helped provide him with the best intellectual platform for the realization of his educational goals. In this respect, the journal he founded in the same year and edited, *The Muslim Education Quarterly*, was instrumental to the success of the Academy. The journal gained increasing popularity among Muslim academics interested in issues of Islamic education.

In the immediate years of the post-Makkah Conference era, another notable intellectual group contributing to the discourse on Islamization of knowledge but by way of critique of the concept was the *Ijmalis*, a group of Muslim intellectuals, created in 1983 by Ziauddin Sardar and his friends.[53] The group with Sardar as its coordinator was small but intellectually active. Apart from Gulzar Haider, an architect, all members of the group were accomplished critics. But without a common fundamental intellectual perspective that could bind them together like the ones that bound the traditional Islamic intellectual schools the group could hardly survive long. Conferring on their group the common trait of *ijmalis*, that is "those who value Beauty," did not appear to be sufficient to sustain the group's existence. Individually, however, members of the group continue to be productive in their respective areas of concentration. Sardar was particularly prolific both before and after the Makkah Conference. His numerous works covering many academic disciplines, including environmental sciences, science and technology studies, and futures studies are mostly relevant to the debate on Islamization of knowledge. Undoubtedly, taken together, the works of members of this group were a major source of influence on Muslim intellectual discourse in the last quarter of the twentieth century.

The first two decades of the post-Makkah Conference period (1977–97) may be described as the new Islamic intellectual and educational renaissance in the post-colonial era. Revival of Islamic thought was visible both in depth and breadth. Also visible was the new institutionalization of Muslim education at all levels. Particularly heartening was the growth of educational institutions at the tertiary level. But the Islamization of knowledge movement suffered its first setback when al-Faruqi was assassinated in 1986. It lost another irreplaceable figure when Ashraf died in August 1998. In 1999 Anwar Ibrahim, a prime mover of Islamization lost his deputy premiership when he was sacked by Mahathir Mohamad. In 2002 al-Attas lost ISTAC, a key institu-

---

53 For a critical discussion of the intellectual position of this group, see Stenberg, *Islamization of Science*.

tion in Islamization of knowledge, that he had helmed for fifteen years during which he trained many young intellectuals from various parts of the Muslim world. This was when his appointment as Founding-Director of the Institute was terminated with Anwar no longer around on whom he could rely for support. Given all these important developments that could only be described as negative, it was not at all surprising that as a generation was coming to pass after the Makkah Conference, the Islamization of knowledge movement generally underwent a decline. The decline needs to be arrested by reaffirming and resuscitating the fundamental aims of education that were agreed upon at the Makkah Conference.

Reformulating the 'Newly' Forgotten Truths

In the light of the foregoing discussion, our present focus on reformulation is given to the following truths that were revived by the Makkah Conference but that are now again in eclipse due to numerous reasons. One of these reasons was the various developments just mentioned. Earlier identified as the truths and knowledge related to the fundamental aims of education that need a new emphasis in contemporary Muslim education and that need to be taught anew are truths about the Divine Reality and Unity and the corresponding science, that is, ʿilm al-tawḥīd, and truths about the human reality and their corresponding science, namely ʿilm al-insān (spiritual anthropology). It is only within the framework of these truths and knowledge that the fundamental aim of education to produce the good man could be realized.

Knowledge of Divine Unity in Muslim education should be formulated in terms of God's Most Beautiful Names (al-asmāʾ al-ḥusnā). Both Names of Incomparability and Names of Similarity are to be learnt and known by students through their respective self-manifestations (ẓuhūr) or self-disclosures (tajallī) in the natural and human worlds. Students are required to memorize these Divine Names and learn about their self-disclosures that are either directly observable in the natural or human worlds or hidden from view. Names of similarity are known by reflecting on similarities between divine and creaturely qualities, while Names of incomparability are known by reflecting on their differences. A student's knowledge of God's self-disclosures requires help from the various branches of knowledge. The level of knowledge required would correspond to the level of education of the student in question. It is extremely important to emphasize the important role to be played by the various academic disciplines, especially science, in the teaching of theology or ʿilm al-tawḥīd.

Knowledge of spiritual conception of man or human reality in its spiritual dimensions that is to be emphasized in contemporary Muslim education would focus on four dimensions of humanness or the good man. These are man the servant of God (ʿabduʾllāh), man the vicegerent of God (khalīfatuʾllāh), the just man (ʿādil), and man of excellent character (adīb). These dimensions of humanness need to be formulated in terms of virtues that define "man of the *wasaṣṭiyyah* ideal" or the golden mean character. The emphasis here is on character building of students that is not divorced from the understanding of the real issues that are now shaping the human condition. Whenever and wherever possible and appropriate, the virtues to be cultivated in the individual student should be conceptually connected to the Divine Attributes and Qualities as expressed through God's Most Beautiful Names. In this way, the link between human virtues and Divine Attributes is preserved in the consciousness of students thereby helping to shape their life and thought in accordance with the fundamental aims of education.

Bibliography

Ali, Abdullah Y. *The Meaning of The Holy Qurʾan: Text, Translation and Commentary*. Kuala Lumpur: Islamic Book Trust, 2005.

Al-Attas, Syed M. N. *Islam and Secularism*. Kuala Lumpur: ABIM, 1978.

Al-Attas, Syed M. N. *Aims and Objectives of Islamic Education*. London: Hodder and Stoughton, 1979.

Al-Attas, Syed M. N. *The Mysticism of Hamzah Fansuri*. Kuala Lumpur: University of Malaya Press, 1970.

Ashraf, Syed Ali. *Islamic Education Movement: An Historical Analysis*. Cambridge, UK: The Islamic Academy, 1990.

Ashraf, Syed Ali. "Islamic Principles and Methods in the Teaching of Literature." In *Philosophy, Literature and Fine Arts*, edited by Seyyed H. Nasr, 22–40. London: Hodder and Stoughton, 1982.

Bakar, Osman. *Advancing Comparative Epistemology and Civilisational and Future Studies: The Global Role of the New ISTAC–IIUM*. Kuala Lumpur: ISTAC Publications, 2019.

Bakar, Osman. *Tawhid and Science: Islamic Perspectives on Religion and Science*, 2nd ed. Shah Alam: Arah Publications, 2008.

Bakar, Osman. "The role of Islam in higher education policies of Muslim countries." In *Contemporary Higher Education Needs in Muslim Countries: Defining the Role of Islam in 21st Century Higher Education*, edited by Osman Bakar, Eric Winkel, and Airulamri Amran, 24–31. Kuala Lumpur: IAIS Malaysia, 2011.

Chittick, William C. *The Sufi Path of Knowledge: Ibn al-ʿArabī's Metaphysics of Imagination*. Albany: State University of New York Press, 1989.

Daud, Wan Mohd N. Wan. *The Educational Philosophy and Practice of Syed Muhammad Naquib al-Attas: An Exposition of the Original Concept of Islamization*. Kuala Lumpur: ISTAC, 1998.

Al-Faruqi, Ismaʿil R. and Abdullah O. Nasseef, eds. *Social and Natural Sciences: The Islamic Perspective*. London: Hodder and Stoughton, 1981.

Husain, Syed Sajjad and Syed Ali Ashraf, eds. *Crisis in Muslim Education*. London: Hodder and Stoughton, 1979.

Mabud, Shaikh Abdul. "World Conferences on Muslim Education: Shaping the agenda of Muslim education in the future." In *Philosophies of Islamic Education, Historical Perspec-*

tives and Emerging Discourses, edited by Nadeem A. Memon and Mujadad Zaman, 129–143. New York: Routledge, 2016.

Nasr, Seyyed Hossein. *An Introduction to Islamic Cosmological Doctrines.* Cambridge: Harvard University Press, 1964.

Nasr, Seyyed Hossein. *Knowledge and the Sacred: The Gifford Lectures, 1981.* Edinburgh: Edinburgh University Press, 1981.

Nasr, Seyyed Hossein. *Science and Civilization in Islam.* Cambridge: Harvard University Press, 1968.

Nasr, Seyyed Hossein, ed. *Philosophy, Literature and Fine Arts.* London: Hodder and Stoughton, 1982.

Stenberg, Leif. *The Islamization of Science: Four Muslim Positions Developing an Islamic Modernity.* Lund Studies in the History of Religion 6. Stockholm: Almqvist & Wiksell 1996.

Chapter 3

Islam and the West: Meaningful Dialogue and Peaceful Coexistence[1]

Ahmad Salah Jamjoom

In 1977 we succeeded in organizing the First World Conference on Muslim Education under the auspices of King Abdulaziz University, with the help of Dr. Abdullah Omar Nasseef, Professor Syed Ali Ashraf and some other colleagues of ours. At this conference we examined the prevailing philosophy of education for all branches of knowledge and made recommendations for a system which integrates both the secular and the divine. Five world conferences have been held after this in Pakistan, Bangladesh, Indonesia, Egypt and South Africa in 1980, 1981, 1982, 1987 and 1996 respectively. These conferences dealt with curriculum design, textbook development, teacher education, and evaluation and implementation. As a result of these conferences several Islamic universities and colleges and many schools and educational institutions have been set up throughout the world. Professor Ashraf was a key person in all these activities and conducted his research and educational movement form Cambridge-based Islamic Academy.

Speaking about Global Islam and the West, which is the theme of this lecture, I would like to say the following:

This is a vast subject. I will briefly talk about three points. First, there are welcome signs that the West is searching for an understanding of Islam rather than put labels on it, e.g., fundamentalist, militant, terrorist and the like. Second, the search for understanding should lead to real dialogue between leaders, not merely discussion amongst academics. Third, the lesson of history is that meaningful dialogue, not clash of beliefs or civilizations, is in the interest of the West itself as well as other civilizations.

---

1 Presented at the First Syed Ali Ashraf Memorial Lecture titled, "Global Islam and the West: challenges and opportunities in the 21st century" held at Mill Lane Lecture Rooms, University of Cambridge on 27 October 1999.

Changing Perceptions of Islam in the West

Particularly since the Second World War, and increasingly so in the last thirty years, the interest of the West in Islam has been generated due to two reasons. Firstly, the resources in the Muslim world and secondly, investigation into parties and groups in the Muslim world to assess their impact on domestic politics and eventually regional and international relations. The interest in the Islamic parties is to judge how genuine they are in their commitment, what is their timeframe and whether they wish to come to power within the rules of the existing political system or are willing to take the risk of operating outside the establishment rules for achieving their manifesto.

Today's seminar talks of "Global" Islam. It shows greater understanding and the impact of globalization. HRH Prince Charles, Prince of Wales, demonstrated this understanding a few years ago by declaring that he would prefer the title "Defender of Faith" instead of the historical title, "Defender of the Faith."[2] If Britain is a multi-cultural society, surely globalization has made this planet a multicultural global village.

It is said that the West's perceptions of the Muslim World have been divided by politics. For instance, the Khomeini revolution was equated by the West with the French Revolution such that powerful allies of the poor Shah would not allow him even to be buried in their country; but when it was feared that Khomeini's revolution would not be stopped at exploration within Iraq, suddenly the revolutionaries became "fundamentalists." Jews and Muslims lived in the Middle East in harmony for centuries until the Balfour Declaration sowed the seeds of religious hatred. In Afghanistan, the Mujahideens were eulogized by the West as great freedom fighters against the "evil empire of communism." Yet the same Mujahideens having served their purpose, have become the accursed lepers living in the Middle Ages. Saddam, for nine years a bulwark against militant mullahs of Iraq, is being despised with greater vengeance than the "evil empire." Whether in former Yugoslavia, Indonesia or Kashmir, there is less sensitivity to Muslims rivers of blood than the environmental concerns for Potomac River or River Thames, for example.

---

2 In 1994, Prince Charles triggered a controversy when he said that he would be defender of faiths rather than Defender of the Faith, a title conferred on King Henry VIII of England by Pope Leo X in 1521. In 1544, it was recognized by Parliament as an official title of the English monarch and has been borne by all subsequent sovereigns. However, Prince Charles clarified his position in 2015 in an interview with BBC Radio 2, saying, "As I tried to describe, I mind about the inclusion of other people's faiths and their freedom to worship in this country. And it's always seemed to me that, while at the same time being Defender of the Faith, you can also be protector of faiths." See Harriet Sherwood, "King Charles to be Defender of the Faith but also a defender of faiths," *The Guardian* online, Friday 9, Sept 2022.

From Clash to Dialogue

After the end of the Cold War, Huntington's prediction of a clash of civilization has been often referred to as a conflict between Western democracy and Islamic ideology as the two gladiators, which must clash. This means that we have not moved forward since the zealot jingoism of the Crusades. Surely, we should do better. The outstanding contributions of the West to human civilization are the industrial revolution, technology, organization, and communications. But the Muslim World is not necessarily a jungle of barbarians. Their influence and indeed empires were from Spain to Indonesia, from Central Asia to Africa. In medicine, science, mathematics, and philosophy particularly, the bridge from Greek philosophers to the modern world is a result of some of their contributions. So, the dialogue, even if among the unequal, must be with an understanding that both sides have to give; they have to receive from the other the heritage, the wisdom and the lesson of their own history. Maimonides, the well-known Jewish scholar, happily served Muslim rulers. Thousands of Jews and Christians fleeing from persecution in Christian states found asylum and comfort in the Ottoman Empire.[3]

I should warn against the tendency of some intellectuals, both in the West and in the East, Muslims and non-Muslims, who are fanning indiscriminate fires of "Protestant Reformation" in Islam. It is true that Islam is for all times and all places, but the Qurʾānic injunctions are not to be "doctored" in the garb of modern solutions to today's problems. Mustapha Kamal must be given great praise for transforming the sick man of Europe into modern Turkey. Yet, how many sociologists and historians would approve of his suppression of Islam? There has to be a golden mean between Kamalism and shutting the gate of Ijtihād.[4] The former will lead to complete secularism and the latter will keep the Muslim world frozen while the rest marches on by leaps and bounds.

Lessons from History

I said that a meaningful dialogue between the West, the Muslim world and indeed other cultures like China and the Far East is in the interest of the West itself. How did the great empires say, the Roman Empire or the Islamic Empire end? It was not by foreign aggression but from the weakness within the system, which the rulers refused to recognize. Every so often it was the lust for power of the rulers, which made them blind, deaf, and dumb to what was happening at their doorsteps. They were possessed with the belief that they could not do wrong, and fault was always with the foreign nations who must be despised and cursed. Only, for example, the frenzied destruction of life and

---

3 Gemmina Alberico, in "Golden Age of the Ottoman empire," https://ottomanempiregroupnine.weebly.com/religion-and-law.html.
4 Deduction of the laws of Sharīʿah for emergent issues and new phenomena employing the principles of the Qurʾān and Sunnah.

property in Oklahoma, the ravages of the day-traders are symptoms of growing pressure points within.[5]

Let me quote from the Holy Qurʾān, which encourages the diversity of cultures and nations. It strongly enjoins that there is no compulsion in religion.[6] Again, the purpose of making mankind into different brotherhoods and tribes is that they may "know each other,"[7] not that they may despise and crush each other. The emphasis on enlightenment and knowledge in Islam is so fundamental that the very first verse[8] revealed to the Holy Prophet (peace be upon him) begins with the word *iqraʾ*, which may be translated as: "read" or "acquire knowledge" or "seek enlightenment."

Meaningful dialogues will make even clearer that the core values of most religions, indeed the religions of the Abrahamic tradition, have a common thread in righteousness, mercy, forgiveness, equity, love, and charity. Perhaps if the common threads are woven at the present time into a mosaic fabric, humanity will emerge more elevated. The spirit of the values of Islam and the spirit of the values of democracy are not inimical but they overlap.

Let us hope that the year 2001, which has been declared by the United Nations as the year of Dialogue among Civilizations,[9] will make an inspiring beginning to the next millennium.

Bibliography

Alberico, Gemmina. In "Golden Age of the Ottoman empire." https://ottomanempiregroupnine.weebly.com/religion-and-law.html.

Sherwood, Harriet. "King Charles to be Defender of the Faith but also a defender of faiths." *The Guardian online*, Friday 9, Sept 2022. https://www.theguardian.com/uk-news/2022/sep/09/king-charles-to-be-defender-of-the-faith-but-also-a-defender-of-faiths.

United Nations. "United Nations year of dialogue among civilizations, 2001 launched with headquarters round table discussion." Press release, GA/9747, 5 September 2000. https://press.un.org/en/2000/20000905.ga9747.doc.html.

---

5   The Oklahoma City bombing was a domestic terrorist truck bombing of the Alfred P. Murrah Federal Building in Oklahoma City, Oklahoma, United States, on April 19, 1995.
6   Qurʾān 2:256.
7   Qurʾān 49:13.
8   Qurʾān 96:1.
9   United Nations, "United Nations year of dialogue among civilizations, 2001 launched with headquarters round table discussion." Press release, GA/9747, 5 September 2000, https://press.un.org/en/2000/20000905.ga9747.doc.html.

Chapter 4

Islam and the West in the Twenty-First Century[1]

Akbar S. Ahmed

Introduction

It is an honour and a pleasure to be asked to deliver the first Syed Ali Ashraf Memorial Lecture. Both the man we are here to honour and the subject of the lecture are worthy of our most serious attention.

In my talk I will point out why some of the most influential current global theories about Islam's relations with the West are inadequate. I will then explore an alternative method of understanding what is happening in the Muslim world through the Muslim quest for Islamic social and political models. We will discuss Muslim political structures and leadership in order to explain Islam's present predicament and its sometimes-thorny relations with the West. In concluding we will suggest ways to improve mutual understanding. In the process a host of important questions will be raised, not all of which will find answers in this paper. But the questions will point to the need for urgent thinking on the subject of Islam and its relations with the West.

Islam cannot be ignored as a global force. The evidence to support this contention is plentiful: An understanding of Islam is important in our world because there are about fifty Muslim states and Islam has over one billion followers with abundant vitality and passion whose span is now truly global. Muslims control much of the oil and gas reserves of the world; Muslims live in the West in large numbers; the challenge to Israel by Islamic organizations like Hamas, the resurgence of Islam in countries that matter strategically to the West like Turkey and the nuclear ambitions of several Muslim countries make Islam important. More Muslims have made an impact in the global media—

---

[1] Presented at the First Syed Ali Ashraf Memorial Lecture titled, "Global Islam and the West: challenges and opportunities in the 21st century" held at Mill Lane Lecture Rooms, University of Cambridge on 27 October 1999.

positively or negatively—Benazir Bhutto, Saddam Hussain, Muammar Gaddafi, Yasser Arafat, for examples, than those of any other civilization. (Can even informed people in the West name any Russian leader apart from Gorbachev and Yeltsin? And how many can name any Indian or Chinese leader?). We saw how during the Gulf War a regional Muslim crisis drew in the West, economically, politically, and militarily; a Muslim crisis had rapidly escalated into a world crisis.

Into the millennium, I will suggest, the real clash will not be between Islam (or Hinduism or Confucianism) and the West—nor between religious and secular positions—but between two distinct emerging world views of the coming time: one that foresees and in an important sense engenders the not too distant future as a nightmarish urban hell, pessimistic, anarchic, bleak, violent and out of control with man a poor second to machine (powerfully depicted by Hollywood from the 1980s onwards like *Blade Runner* and *Terminator* I and II); and one that foresees a future that respects tradition and values the past, that holds the hope of dignity, piety and, above all hope for the human race. Battle lines will be blurred and unexpected allies stand shoulder to shoulder. As many people in the West want a bright future as in the rest of the (Muslim) world we need to be aware of the common objectives and be able to evolve a common strategy.

Seeing Saladin

Leading up to and during the Gulf War the West perceived Saddam Hussein as 'Hitler.' Civilization as they knew it had to be defended against the barbaric Hitler, a conceptual if not genealogical descendant, it was suggested, of the equally barbaric Attila the Hun; indeed, the Germans were—and are sometimes in private still—contemptuously called Huns. The loyal ally Saudi Arabia—then depicted as cute and cuddly, a perception now changing—had to be protected from the monster.

The Iraqis in turn responded as Muslims normatively do in a crisis. Saddam was seen by many as a Muslim champion, a Salahuddin—or Saladin in Western folklore—and the confrontation was increasingly cast in Islamic terms. On Iraqi TV Saddam was shown saying his prayers and the Muslim declaration of faith, *Allāhu Akbar*, God is great, was hastily stitched onto the Iraqi flag—judging from the unusually inelegant calligraphy. From a straightforward clash concerning strategic access to oil, which is why Iraq invaded Kuwait in the first place and why the West was so alarmed, a deeper clash of cultural values rooted in history had emerged.

For the purposes of our argument, it is the selection of Saladin, who symbolizes a Muslim leader of integrity representing the finest in his culture and the tolerant humane side of Islam, that is of interest. Saladin was a God-fearing ruler preferring to spend his spare time with scholars and books. He achieved one of the greatest military and political triumphs of his time: the re-capture of Jerusalem. When Saladin died there was no equivalent of the secret Swiss Bank account, no chalets in the south of France; he died like a simple soldier with the proverbial sword and saddle to his name and little else. Saddam clearly is no Saladin. But when in crisis ordinary Muslims look for a Saladin figure. It is a sociological reflex. Today Muslims are desperate for good leadership.

The failure of the political leadership has far-reaching anthropological ramifications for the small-scale traditional societies facing rapid change and confronting the irresistible advance of alien values and images. The effects of the impact on the family, the household, the core of society, are as enormous as uncertain.

Because the leadership is seen as weak and ineffective against the forces of (largely Western) globalization ordinary traditional parents feel vulnerable and threatened. Images of sex and violence disturb them, and they worry about the impact on their family. In particular, TV is considered the Trojan horse. Never before in history have alien values and images been able to penetrate the most inaccessible Muslim home in the most remote mountain or desert in so full a manner.

Conflict or Understanding?

How are we to capture a truly global phenomenon in the spirit of true understanding—when Islam is said to be behind the bombs exploding at the Borobudur temple in Indonesia, or the explosion in Oklahoma, when again Islam is suspect, when world figures commenting on it show the diversity of western responses to it: for Prince Charles it has much to give to our world and he would happily be defender of faiths and not just the Christian faith; for the NATO Chief it is the new enemy after Communism—in one viable coherent, theoretical and methodological frame? Can the traditional approach in the social sciences still assist us in our search considering that we are dealing with global geopolitics at the same time, as we are able to discern links to village social life? Are the traditional methods of the political scientists and anthropologists no longer of much use in studying contemporary Islam?

For both Islam and the West—considering that there is a remarkable similarity in their vision of globalization or universalism, although perhaps approached from different angles—this stand-off is intellectually dubious, empirically weak and morally suspect. Nonetheless, it is the extravagant expressions of the conflict that have captured the imagination of ordinary people of both sides: for non-Muslims in the West, the suicide bombers in Israel and Lebanon or the explosions in New York or the blowing up of the passenger plane over Lockerbie; for Muslims, the burning of Turk families in Germany or the torture camps in Bosnia or the long-standing indifference to the plight of the Palestinians and Kashmiris. Why have these images become a metaphor for the confrontation?

These questions intrigue us while providing us a clue as to how Muslims respond to crisis and leadership. The answers will help us to understand not only Muslim society but Muslim relations with the West.

Global Theories

In the last few years Muslims have simplified global issues and interpreted a series of developments, on the surface clearly unconnected, as a well-laid plan by the West to humiliate and even subjugate them: *The Satanic Verses* controversy, the collapse of the BOCI Bank, the Gulf War, the rape and death camps of Bosnia.

In this milieu of suspicion even scholarly exercises—Professor Samuel Huntington's essay, "The Clash of Civilizations?"[2] Francis Fukuyama's *The End of History and the Last Man*[3] and Felipe Fernandez-Armesto's *Millennium*[4]— are seen as part of the global conspiracy against Islam, part of a bludgeon-Islam-out-of-existence school of thought. Even Baudrillard, seeing the world through postmodern spectacles, a starburst of kaleidoscopic, jostling images, holds out little hope. The rich West confronts "the distress and catastrophe" of Africa, Asia (which is the Muslim world) and Latin America in a mutually self-destructive, symbiotic relationship.[5] Few, too few, alas, who study Islam as a global contemporary phenomenon see Islam in a less than sensationalist manner (one of the few, in spite of its alarmist title, is the level-headed and objective *A Sense of Siege: The Geopolitics of Islam and the West* by Graham Fuller and Ian Lesser[6]).

Writers like Huntington, Fukuyama and Armesto have confirmed the popular negative stereotype of Muslims in the West and given it the fig-leaf of academic respectability. Stimulating as the theses were, they were flawed as we will see below and further muddied the already murky waters. They are influenced, in part I suspect, by the nervous twitching of a civilization predisposed to entering a new millennium—and we need to be reminded that the concept is a Christian one however global its impact—with heightened anxiety. Such theses feed into the end of millennium mood which suggests dramatic, apocalyptic happenings: perhaps a major, all but inevitable, final show-down between Islam and the West? It is a critical moment in relations between Islam and the West.

---

2 Samuel P. Huntington, "The Clash of Civilizations?" *Foreign Affairs* 72, no. 3 (Summer 1993): 22–49, https://doi.org/10.2307/20045621.
3 Francis Fukuyama, *The End of History and the Last Man* (New York: Free Press, 1992).
4 Felipe Fernandez-Armesto, *Millennium; A History of the Last Thousand Years* (New York: Free Press, 1995).
5 Jean Baudrillard, *The Illusion of the End*, trans. Chris Turner (Cambridge: Polity Press; Stanford: Stanford University Press, 1994), 69. Original in French: Jean Baudrillard, *L'illusion de la fin, ou, la grève des événements* (Paris: Galilée, 1992).
6 Graham E. Fuller and Ian O. Lesser, *A Sense of Siege: The Geopolitics of Islam and the West* (Colorado: Westview Press, 1995), RAND Study.

In an important if negative sense Muslims have become part of the cultural and political landscape of the Western media. They are reduced to stereotypes and caricature. Are the serious Western thinkers making an attempt to rectify this?

Huntington's Clash of Civilizations?

In his influential essay "The Clash of Civilizations?" Professor Huntington argued that future conflicts will be cultural, not ideological or economic in content.[7] Islam was singled out as a potential enemy of civilization in an argument that was as deterministic as simplistic (Huntington's thesis derived from established Orientalist thinking: "we are facing a mood and a movement far transcending the level of issues and policies and the governments that pursue them. This is no less than a clash of civilizations," wrote Bernard Lewis in "The Roots of Muslim Rage"[8]). "Islam has bloody borders," concluded Huntington.[9] But so do Christianity, Judaism and Hinduism (ask, respectively, the Bosnians and Chechens, the Palestinians and the Kashmiris); and where does this dangerously deterministic argument take us except to a clash of civilizations? Is this merely a self-fulfilling prophecy?

Islam as the enemy of civilization of the West locked in a life-and-death confrontation which echoes a thousand years of history is all very well as a journalistic cliche—indeed it is a seductive idea as we develop our own arguments—but from a Harvard Professor, as serious scholarship, it is disappointing. There are several chinks in Huntington's armour. Let us begin with the most obvious.

Isn't the real clash, the cause of the turmoil, to be located *within* Islam (in Algeria, in Egypt, in Afghanistan, in Pakistan) and the target the Muslim leadership? For Muslims, their leadership has failed (it is caricatured by stories of the hidden, illegal wealth looted from the people to be kept abroad and the corruption and cruelty at home); hence the depth of their despair, the extent of their anger and desperation of their response. Bombs in bus stops and bazaars which kill innocent citizens are deplorable acts and not Islamic. But they will continue to take place as Muslim anger grows. We, therefore, need to understand not only Muslim leaders but their relationship with their people, their appreciation of Islam, their perception of the past and the regional context within which they live.

But beware of simplification, of creating monoliths even in one country. Each country is driven by ethnic, sectarian and political rivalries. Take Paki-

---

7   Huntington, "The Clash," 22.
8   Bernard Lewis, "The Roots of Muslim Rage," *The Atlantic Monthly* 266, no. 3 (September 1990): 60.
9   Huntington, "The Clash," 35.

stan: ethnic Sindhis battle immigrant *muhājirs*[10] in the Sindh province; Shia-Sunni rivalry costs lives annually and political intolerance between the main parties is reduced to personal vendettas. Those in the cities lead different lives and have different values to those in the rural areas. In the tribal areas of Baluchistan and the Frontier Provinces tribal codes still determine behaviour. Different legal and administrative systems that overlap and fuse—a bewildering mixture of Islamic, British colonial and tribal tradition—further complicate life. Can we then talk of an "Islamic" monolithic Pakistan facing up to an equally monolithic West as does Huntington?

Besides, the global strategic and security interests of the West are directly related to Muslim lands and many Muslim nations are seen as important allies. Of the nine "pivotal states" identified in a recent article by Western experts around which America forms its foreign policy, five were Muslim—Algeria, Turkey, Egypt, Pakistan, and Indonesia.[11] Strategic imperatives scramble Huntington's neat theory.

What about the 20 million Muslims permanently settled in the West Huntington conveniently ignores? Where do they line up? Surely, they are a bridge between the two civilizations? Huntington needs to recognize that an entire generation of young Muslims is coming of age in the West. There is a strong middle-class component among them in America and they are integrated into the social and political structure. Into the next millennium we can expect influential figures in public life from this generation. Perhaps what is most significant is that they see themselves as *both* Muslim and American (or British or French). In the next few years we can expect Muslim Congressmen/Senators in the USA and MPs in the UK.

What about the serious efforts, at global level, perhaps for the first time on this scale and frequency, of influential individuals at increasing mutual understanding? Although the influence of individuals is limited in an age of intense even perverse iconoclasm several have spoken on the need to view Islam on its own terms, in terms of the global community and not as the Other or more simplistically as the new enemy after Communism.

The Prince of Wales' initiative to bring better understanding between his civilization and Islam, which began with his celebrated lecture at Oxford in 1993 on Islam and the West, is one example.[12] The speech was widely reported in the Muslim world and gained the Prince wide-spread respect. The King of Saudi Arabia, known to be one of the most powerful and inaccessible monarchs on earth, broke all protocol to drive to the Prince's hotel late at night to congratulate him when the Prince visited his country shortly after the lecture.

---

10 Lit. immigrants. Here, those Muslim migrants from India who settled in urban Sindh.
11 Robert S. Chase, Emily B. Hill and Paul Kennedy, "Pivotal States and U.S. Strategy," *Foreign Affairs* 75, no. 1 (January–February 1996): 37, https://doi.org/10.2307/20047466.
12 H.R.H. The Prince of Wales, "Islam and the West" (lecture, Oxford Centre for Islamic Studies, Sheldonian Theatre, Oxford University, October 27, 1993).

The movement for global dialogue is a two-way process. From the Muslim world we can identify key players who mirror the spirit of dialogue we see in the Pope and the Prince of Wales. Going west to east, King Hassan of Morocco, King Hussein and his brother Crown Prince Hassan of Jordan, Benazir Bhutto of Pakistan, Muhammad Mahathir of Malaysia; the Aga Khan, who has a worldwide following, are also note-worthy names in this list. They are a big draw on major university campuses (like Ivy League and Oxbridge) and the think-tanks (Chatham House or Davos).

We need to ask Huntington about leaders like Benazir Bhutto of Pakistan and Tansu Çiller of Turkey? They are seen in Western capitals as modern, liberated women who the West can do business with. Their message is a simple but effective one. If you do not support us and we are thrown out, you will have to deal with less pretty and more hairy faces who don't like you and will oppose what you stand for. The processes of globalization and the media were therefore used effectively by both Muslim and non-Muslim in such cases.

Some of Huntington's premises are wildly inaccurate. "A Confucian-Islamic connection has emerged to challenge Western interests, values and power," he asserts. The blood-curdling image is calculated to conjure up in the Western mind—traditional stereotypes of hordes of yellow devils and mad mullahs in a fanatical alliance to destroy the West.

The shaky edifice of Huntington's argument is built on the friendly relations between China and Pakistan. Yet the foundations were laid in the 1960s by Mao's Communists, the avowed enemies of Confucianism, and Ayub Khan, a straightforward military dictator who was opposed by the Islamic parties.

The relationship developed partly as a geo-political reflex to contain India, then a staunch ally of the Soviets; neither Confucian nor Islamic ideology nor anti-Western sentiment had much to do with it. On the contrary, Pakistan was a key member of the global Western security structure designed to check the Soviets. Pakistan also played a singular role in opening the door to China for the USA.

The End of History?

History, for Fukuyama, has come to an end. The technology, market compulsions and consumerism of the Western liberal democracies have triumphed over rival global ideologies. But there is a fly in the ointment: Islam. Islam is a threat to liberal practice and democracy, a force of disruption in the tranquility at the end of history.[13] For Islam it is the end of the road, the end of its history.

For Fukuyama, Islam is a cliche. He outrageously, equates Islam to "European fascism"[14] as if we were back to the deployment of Hitler to damn the opposition. The main entry in the reference to Islam in his index is under "Is-

---

13 Fukuyama, *The End*, 45–46.
14 Fukuyama, 236.

lamic fundamentalism" and then, if anyone has missed the point, cross-referenced to "Fundamentalist Islam." There is no other entry under Fundamentalist—no Christians, Jews, Hindus in spite the clear global evidence of exuberant fundamentalism in these religions—except that of Islam. "Fundamentalism" is equated to fanaticism, extremism and violence.

Fukuyama does not help his case or himself: there is neither a single Muslim author in his bibliography nor, more surprisingly for an expert working in Washington, the acknowledged American experts like Professors John Esposito, Clifford Geertz, Roy Mottahedeh, James Piscatori and Edward Said. To compound matters, Huntington's influence is clear from five entries that refer to his work in the bibliography.

Another influential author also echoes Fukuyama. Contemplating the end of the cycle Felipe Fernandez-Armesto in *Millennium* noted the fate of Islam: "As the end of the millennium approaches, the Islamic revolution seems to be over and Islamic revival seems stymied."[15] But his masterly historical survey is selective. His two chapters on Islam pick on the violent and confrontational—the titles are indicative of the attitude: "The tower of darkness" and "The maze of God;" Khomeini and the violence in Iran dominate the discussion. While writing, incorrectly as it happens, of Muslim rulers like Alauddin Khilji (1291–1316), the ruler of Delhi, who "aped the Prophet of Islam and devised a new religion,"[16] we learn next to nothing of Islamic art, architecture, poetry and science.

Surveying the world in the millennium, Fernandez-Armesto predicts a shift in economic and political influence from the "white West" to the "yellow East" (to use his phraseology) and notes Islam, in the middle, will be left out. Yet Muslims form an important part of the "yellow East." There are more Muslims in Malaysia, Indonesia and Brunei, Muslim countries at the take-off stage, than in the Arab world.

Muslims can reject Fukuyama's and Fernandez-Armesto's theses out of hand. The rhythm of history for them is now picking up after it was suspended for almost two centuries under European colonization and half a century under post-colonial rulers overly impressed by non-Islamic models. History was not ending; it was just beginning for Muslims; they were dreaming global dreams.

Looking for a General Theory

We will plunge traditional left and right social scientists—now floundering around for new moorings—into paroxysms of fury by suggesting that we explore a model that will explain Muslim behaviour in the Qur'ān, their holy book.

---

15 Fernandez-Armesto, *Millennium*, 574.
16 Fernandez-Armesto, 105.

This is not entirely an original route to take. Weber had persuasively shown us the way when Marx had proclaimed God dead and economic and material factors as all-important in explaining social and political behaviour. Weber illustrated one part of the Western work ethic with reference to a certain kind of religious behaviour and thought. His analysis of political ideal-types was also useful in explaining political authority. But inherent in the Weberian models of authority is the assumption that societies move along a secular path, that leadership would be provided by a rational bureaucracy set in a working democracy. Weber looked to the future and in his theories runs the assumption that the bureaucratic structure is the best, most rational model. Charismatic leadership, another Weberian model, was inherently dangerous. In the West there has always been suspicion of men of charisma, of the hero on horseback.

Weber got it right for most of Europe. Today faceless bureaucrats run many of its governments on the basis of rules and regulations. Charisma or imagination or compassion are well controlled. This is a dull but safe civilization. John Major, the archetypical bureaucratic politician of the 1990s, is even coloured in grey by the cartoonists to depict this personality and mind.

But even Weber could not foresee the collapse of the civilized veneer and easy reversion to primordial tribalism and savagery in Europe. Germany half a century ago, just decades after Weber was writing, and the Balkans in the 1990s illustrate for us how fragile the notion of a staid and safe European civilization based on respect for human life and liberty really is.

No self-respecting political or social scientist, reared in the secular or liberal tradition of the West, would dream of looking at the Qurʾān for explanations of behaviour. Muslim social scientists themselves remain in awe of Western social theories and look around for easy answers in Ivy League or Oxbridge or London university departments (that is why so much of their work appears to be a second-hand version of second-rate material). They need to look closer home for an alternative explanation, to the Qurʾān. By analyzing Muslim society through this method we approach an authentic native model while becoming aware of the emptiness of words like fundamentalist, revivalist or resurgent. We are not only rejecting phrases and concepts that have been borrowed from one culture and applied to another but also exposing their weakness. We are also able to provide a stronger, more coherent, explanation of social and political behaviour. We are therefore looking for a general theory that would make sense of contemporary Muslim society and its interaction with the world.

We suggest that the explanation for the turbulence, unrest, and anger in the Muslim world, which often expresses itself in anti-Western rhetoric, lies in the Muslim political structures and leadership. Because the modern state is so intrusively powerful political leadership becomes a defining factor in ordinary lives affecting social, economic, and religious issues.

Because of the conflation of several systems—European imperialism, Islamic, tribal, dynastic—there is in fact a hotchpotch of systems jostling, overlapping, and colliding in the Muslim world. Hence the confused environment fraught with tension. Muslims may be exemplary as individuals but the systems within which they work are falling apart. The scope for a strong man or woman to impose his will is unlimited.

Muslim Political Leadership

Our thesis is that if the political leadership in its behaviour, ideas and politics is close to the Islamic ideal as laid out in the Qur'ān and the life of the Prophet (peace be upon him), friction in society is minimum; the further from the Islamic ideal, the greater the tension in society.[17] Political leadership is locked in a dynamic and inescapable relationship with Islam which commentators are quick to point out but not able to explain.

The Qur'ān provides a clear idea of an ideal Muslim ruler which Muslims attempt to live up to, sometimes successfully, sometimes not. What is more important is that they are judged by ordinary Muslims by how much their behaviour corresponds to the ideal laid out in the Qur'ān. We shall look to the Qur'ān for answers but read the Qur'ān not only as the divine word but as a sociological text.

The concept of leadership in Islam is a simple one. The Muslim leader represents both moral and political authority. He thus leads his men in prayer and in battle. At the core of the Muslim world view are the concepts of ʿadl (justice) and iḥsān (compassion)—and this includes all sections of society, especially women and the young. The clearest and most unambiguous model of leadership is provided by the example of the holy Prophet whose behaviour is derived from the Holy Qur'ān. The model rests in the Prophet being acknowledged as the insān kāmil or the perfect human being. It is the conscious or unconscious desire of every Muslim to live up to this model. It therefore puts pressure on the leadership to emulate this example. Ordinary Muslims are constantly reminded of it through the sermons in the mosque and the writings of the Muslim scholars. Failure to live up to it in leadership involves widespread criticism. There can be no disjunction between this model and 'pragmatic' political behaviour which may involve immorality, tyranny or injustice. People will not accept the latter as an Islamic model. That is why many leaders who become dictators or tyrants while tolerated for a time are eventually rejected or have such a poor reputation in history.

---

17 This idea was explored in a general sense in Akbar S. Ahmed, *Discovering Islam: Making Sense of Muslim History and Society* (London: Routledge and Kegan Paul, 1988).

The Gentle Face of Islam

We need to ask Muslims where is the tradition of compassion and tolerance? Why have many Muslims abandoned one of the most powerful and endearing features of Islam? Why is the resistance invariably expressed in violence—as in Iran, Afghanistan, Algeria, Pakistan, and Egypt? Why are the gentle teachers and mystics of Islam not heard?

The Muslims most prominent in the British media are known because of the noise they make and heat they generate. They fit into pre-conceived ideas of Muslim fanatics and extremists. It is natural, therefore, that Professor Syed Ali Ashraf, whom we are here to honour, one of the most distinguished Muslim scholars living in Britain, is virtually unknown in the media. This is a pity as Professor Ashraf was one of the half-dozen most important Muslim scholars of the last few decades. He made an international impact as the organizing secretary of the First World Conference on Muslim Education held in Makkah in 1977. He then helped organize five follow-up World Conferences in different capitals of the Muslim world. In 1980 he was appointed the first Director General of the World Centre for Islamic Education, set up by the Organization of Islamic Conferences in Makkah.

In the 1980s Professor Ashraf moved to Cambridge, which he loved from the time he completed his Ph.D. here. The Islamic Academy was set up and Professor Ashraf became its Director General. Aided by his trusty Deputy, the indefatigable Dr Abdul Mabud, also from Bangladesh, he produced a stream of books and organized seminars. The journal he edited, *Muslim Education Quarterly*, was begun in 1983, and is still continuing.

In the last decade of his life Professor Ashraf made a significant contribution to education in Britain. Collaborating with the University of Cambridge, a series of seminars and books resulted. His book, *Islam*, is part of the GCSE course on World Religions. During his last years he struggled successfully to set up a university in Dhaka, called Darul Ihsan University. As Vice Chancellor he divided his time between Dhaka and Cambridge.

His soft way of speaking, affectionate manner and hospitable nature made him a much loved figure. Because of his erudition most people who came in contact with him thought of him as a teacher; many saw him as a spiritual mentor. With his ordinary clothes and humble appearance it was easy to mistake him for a country bumpkin. But this Professor rubbed shoulders with Presidents and Prime Ministers. It was always startling to hear him enunciate clear English, a language he taught most of his life and loved passionately. I first met Professor Ashraf in 1962 when he was head of the English department, Karachi University. Over the last two decades we became friends, and I respected him for his learning and genuine commitment to understanding between different faiths. He always had time for me, however busy his schedule, always supportive of my endeavours. I will miss his wisdom and affection.

What Needs to be Done

For the future, Muslim leaders need to pay serious heed to the social, demographic and educational trends in their countries. Muslim population growth percentages are among the highest in the world, the literacy rates among the lowest, the figures for health facilities poor and the life expectancy below average. The uneven spread of income per capita between countries like the Arab Gulf States and Bangladesh reflects the uneven picture within most Muslim countries with affluent corrupt elites living the extravagant and wasteful high life in the capital cities amidst the miserable squalor of the shanty towns. The gap between rich and poor is growing ominously wide. All this when a large percentage of the population is young, jobless and restless for radical change. For many, Islam is the only natural way out.

In the short term the prospects for a harmonious relationship between Islam and the West look uncertain, even pessimistic. In the longer term a great deal will depend on whether those who encourage dialogue and understanding will succeed or not.

What can be done to improve matters? The first steps are to stop demonizing each other; for Muslims to stop seeing a global conspiracy all around them—they need to re-build an idea of Islam which includes justice, integrity, tolerance and the quest for knowledge—the classic Islamic civilization—not just the insistence on the rituals. Reducing a sophisticated civilization to simple rituals encourages simple answers: reaching for guns and explosives, for instance. Today, piety and virtue are judged by political action—often equated to violence—not sustained spirituality.

We all know that ʿilm or knowledge and the use of the mind are highly emphasised in Islam. The Islamic emphasis on ʿilm should help to create an image of Muslims not as book burners but as book writers. Yet, we know that many Muslims are falling behind in the acquisition of ʿilm. How can the leadership challenge the modern or postmodern world around us without understanding its key concept? How many understand postmodernity, existentialism, or structuralism?

Indeed, most would dismiss such knowledge as irrelevant. ʿIlm is something the Muslim leadership needs to emphasize again and again through action, through speeches, through deeds. And by this I do not only mean grades or marks in school or college. I am also talking about an attitude, a frame of mind. For instance, we need, living in Britain, to open our minds to the best that Britain can offer us where it is compatible with our own religious traditions. Take the examples of libraries, schools and parks. If you look around, you will see learning and good sense and respect for human values.

We need to wake up to the world in which we are living. If we whine and complain on the one hand, then we must take action to remedy the problem on the other. We cannot do one without the other. In this case, I heard the whining about the Western media, but I saw little action on behalf of the community as a whole. One example is the film *Jinnah*.

As for the importance of a film like *Jinnah* let me make a broader comment on films. *True Lies, Executive Decision, The Siege, Air Force One*—these are major Hollywood blockbusters with the biggest stars of the 1990s in them. The two contrasting images of the all-American male hero and the universal Muslim villain are both depicted in straightforward caricature.

While the Americans are depicted as clean-cut—all-American heroes—the Muslims appear as unshaven, irrational, fanatic psychopaths, bent on blowing up as much of America as possible to further the glory of 'Allah.' The language of the divine Qurʾān—language that reduces men to tears and ecstasy according to its European translator Marmaduke Pickthall—of some of the greatest works in literature in human thought, in poetry and in ideas is reduced and equated to that of the villain wanting to blow up New York or Washington. To a non-Muslim audience, Arabic is now the chosen language of the terrorist and therefore equated to terror through these films.

We are not told what the Muslim is avenging and why. We are not told of the killings, the brutality and the torture of Muslim groups in the Middle East, in the Balkans or in South Asia. There is no link between cause and effect. This is not only the shaky foundation of a legitimate argument in a story, but a feeble political image of the realities of the late twentieth century.

The West must confront the fact that it has made Muslim leaders such as Khomeini, Gaddafi and Saddam the most hated villains in popular Western media culture. This is both dangerous reductionism on the part of the West and cultural humiliation for Muslims (as these leaders are by no means universally accepted by Muslims). Yet how many in the West know of other alternative Muslim models of leadership like Jinnah, the Quaid-i-Azam? (The fault is partly that of Muslims; for years his negative portrayal in Sir Richard Attenborough's *Gandhi* was accepted as the truth until the film *Jinnah*.)

How many know (and this question is also posed to Muslims) that the notion of the greater *jihād*, commonly misunderstood as an aggressive act of religious war in the West, which derives from the word to strive, was explained by the Prophet as the attempt to control our own base instincts and work towards a better, more harmonious world? The lesser *jihād* is to battle physically for Islam; that too only against tyranny and injustice.

Because the world media equates the word fundamentalist to extremist, fanatic Muslims we need to ask how many media people pause to ask the question: can we legitimately use a term devised to describe something in one culture (a certain brand of Christian behaviour and thought) to another distinct culture? As Muslims by definition believe in the Qur'ān—however actively they may follow its instructions—they are technically all fundamentalists. So is, then, every Muslim on earth today an extremist and a fanatic?

Because of the global power of the West the initiatives in understanding must come from the West. The West must back off; it must treat Islam in its reporting and in its handling with the dignity due to a world religion. The problems of the unhappy people of Bosnia, Palestine, Chechnya and Kashmir have not been solved. There can be permanent peace only if that happens. Violence is possible at any time as young men give way to desperation and anger whatever the consequence.

The West must put pressure on Muslim governments—and it is interlocked with almost all of them either through acts of commission or omission—to get their act together, to ensure justice and provide clean administration. It must send serious signals to the ordinary Muslim people—through seminars, conferences, meetings—that it does not consider Islam as the enemy however much it may disagree with certain aspects of Muslim behaviour.

The West needs to understand the Islamic expressions of revolt as movements against corruption and lack of justice, not as anti-Western. Expressions of commitment will continue and they will cause global turmoil but the West needs to know that these expressions do not mean Muslims want a theocratic order run by mullahs (and Iran remains a one-off example); that when given a choice (as in Pakistan) the electorate have rejected religious parties at the polls.

The common problems in this shrinking world need to be identified: drug and alcohol abuse, divorce, teenage violence and crime, ethnic and racist prejudice, the problems of the aged and the poor; the challenge of the growing sense of anarchy and rampant materialism; the sexual debasement of women and children; the depletion of our natural resources and ecological concerns. On all these issues Islam takes a strong, enlightened position. This is the real Islamic *jihād* and, if it is properly harnessed and understood, it can provide fresh, sorely needed strength to these most crucial of global issues.

In conclusion: We have seen how some of the most eminent Western global thinkers have got it so wrong regarding Islam. While pointing out their inadequacies we have suggested an alternative method to examine Islam and thereby understand its relations with the West. We have underlined the contemporary Muslim political urgent re-thinking is required in the corridors of power.

In the end, may I say that the coming time is a time of great challenges and opportunities? As Muslims, it is our destiny to reach out to them. For the first time in history the atmosphere has changed substantially and the wall of silence and prejudice that usually met Muslim endeavours has been shaken. Although there is much work to be done, there are also positive signs.

There are today many more opportunities for Muslim youth than existed a generation ago. Muslim leaders now need to awaken Muslims and move them into positive channels. It is no secret that Muslims as a whole are falling behind as a community when compared to other communities in terms of education and financial strength. Once again, the leaders of the community need to look beyond their own family, or their own clan or ethnic group and reach out into the community as a whole, helping them, directing them and providing whatever assistance is possible to move them in the right directions.

I believe we are at the crossroads in the relationship between Muslims and non-Muslims. I believe the next years will determine which road we take: conflict and confrontation or consensus and harmony. Those of us who believe in the latter pray that the Islamic vision based in compassion and justice prevails in the millennium.

Bibliography

Ahmed, Akbar S. *Discovering Islam: Making Sense of Muslim History and Society*. London: Routledge and Kegan Paul, 1988.

Baudrillard, Jean. *The Illusion of the End*. Translated by Chris Turner. Cambridge: Polity Press; Stanford: Stanford University Press, 1994.

Chase, Robert S., Emily B. Hill and Paul Kennedy. "Pivotal States and U.S. Strategy." *Foreign Affairs* 75, no. 1 (January–February 1996): 33–51. https://doi.org/10.2307/20047466.

Fernandez-Armesto, Felipe. *Millennium: A History of the Last Thousand Years*. New York: Free Press, 1995.

Fukuyama, Francis. *The End of History and the Last Man*. New York: Free Press, 1992.

Fuller, Graham E., and Ian O. Lesser. *A Sense of Siege: The Geopolitics of Islam and the West*. Colorado: Westview Press, 1995. RAND Study.

Huntington, Samuel P. "The Clash of Civilizations?" *Foreign Affairs* 72, no. 3 (Summer 1993): 22–49. https://doi.org/10.2307/20045621.

Lewis, Bernard. "The Roots of Muslim Rage." *The Atlantic Monthly* 266, no. 3 (September 1990): 47–60.

The Prince of Wales, H.R.H. "Islam and the West." (Lecture, Oxford Centre for Islamic Studies, Sheldonian Theatre, Oxford University, October 27, 1993).

Chapter 5

Islamic Education and the Challenge of Secularism: Professor Syed Ali Ashraf's Critique of Secularism in Education in Muslim Countries: A Personal Appraisal[1]

Ghulam Nabi Saqeb

It is an honour indeed for me to be invited to take part in this memorable event marking the Second Memorial Lecture for my respected colleague and intimate friend and brother in Islam with whom I had the unforgettable opportunity of interacting and working for the best fifteen years of my life in the cause of Islamic education at Makkah. Before I proceed to articulate his views on secularism in education, I would like, if I may, to say something about the character of Professor Ashraf as I knew him as a person and in his practical life. This prelude is timely, as it will lend authenticity to my statements about his views. It will be equally inspiring for the audience who would fully appreciate the intensity of the impact which Professor Ashraf's personality used to make upon the people and the issues that he dealt with.

I first came to know Professor Ashraf in 1974 when we were both appointed to the King Abdulaziz University, Makkah Campus, Faculty of Education, he as Head of the Department of English, and I as an Assistant Professor in the Department of Education and English. Instantly there developed between us a bond of cordiality and empathy. However, our relationship blossomed into a lifelong mutual appreciation and respect when in 1975 we both began to work, he as the Secretary and I as the Assistant Secretary, to organise the First World Conference on Muslim Education that was later held in Makkah in April 1977. For two years together we worked day and night, preparing blueprints of the

---

[1] The Second Professor Syed Ali Ashraf Memorial Lecture held at Sundarban Hotel, Dhaka on 8 August 2000, sponsored jointly by the Islamic Academy, Cambridge and Darul Ihsan University, Dhaka, Bangladesh.

conference rationale, designing programs of the plenary and committee sessions, meeting scholars and administrators to hold discussions and obtain approvals, managing budgets and making various arrangements for invitations, visa arrangements, accommodation, reception, transportation, and a host of other facilities pertaining to the comfort of the participants to the conference. These participants were not only to be our guests but also pilgrims to the two Holy places, *Bayt-Allāh*[2] at Makkah and *Masjid al-Nabawī*[3] at Medina; and, obviously, keen to spend longer times at these two Holy mosques. It was our utmost desire not only to make the Conference most successful but also to do our best to please our guests and to satisfy all their wishes.

The magnanimous government of His Majesty King Khalid bin Abdulaziz and Crown Prince Fahd bin Abdulaziz and the King Abdulaziz University had entrusted us with confidence and responsibility. Organising this historic and extremely significant event was a great challenge. Professor Ashraf masterminded the whole event and worked with extreme enthusiasm. I helped a great deal. Together we intellectualised the various themes of the Conference and ran about in making all the various arrangements. But his role was so well pronounced that I have always felt happier to give most credit to Professor Ashraf for the success of the Conference which, thanks to Allah, became one of the most successful and consequential international conferences held anywhere in the world. Over 300 scholars representing various academic disciplines and hailing from Muslim as well as non-Muslim countries were officially invited from overseas, but more came on their own and a considerable number came from within the country. Working together in this program was an extremely rewarding experience, especially for me. It was then that I became aware of some splendid qualities of Professor Ashraf. He had many qualities of head and heart, but I will mention only the most prominent ones that impressed me most.

First, and above all others, must remain his devout religiosity, profound spirituality, and an unremitting piety. He was a godly man to the core of his existence. This quality permeated through all his ideas and actions. He had completely drowned himself in the love of Allah and the love of the Prophet, peace be upon him. I watched him pray with complete absorption in Makkah. I accompanied him to Medina where we used to spend the last ten days of Ramaḍān. He used to dip deep into the fountain of love of the Prophet and would still come out thirstier for it. I accompanied him to visit the shrines of *Awliyāʾ Allāh*[4] in many countries that we travelled to together. At every shrine he used solemnly to get absorbed in seeking blessings and trying to be in com-

---

2   Meaning, "House of Allah," the Kaʿbah, which is a cubical structure at the centre of Masjid al-Ḥaram in Makkah, considered to be the most sacred site in Islam.
3   The Prophet's Mosque.
4   Lit. friends of Allah; saints.

munion with the souls of the inmates. No matter how busy he was, prayers and *dhikr* (remembering God) always remained his top priorities, never to be ignored, never to be postponed. His devotion generated in him a capacity to achieve comprehensive excellence. Such indeed are the people whom Allah has described in the Holy Qurʾān in the following words:

> Men whom neither traffic nor merchandise can divert from the Remembrance of Allah, nor from regular Prayer . . . that Allah may reward them according to the best of their deeds, and add even more for them out of His Grace (Qurʾān 24:37–38, trans. Abdullah Yusuf Ali).

His second quality was his intellectual clarity and consistency. He was always well focused. I never saw him taking notes and preparing for intricate discussions and debates that we held almost every day. If we finished our deliberation session at ten o' clock at night, early the next morning he would be ready with new points for discussion. I could not understand how and when he developed new ideas, but they were always there, ready when required. He never noted things in his diary, but he always remembered them and had an unfailing memory. I remember he used to tell me that ideas came to him in flashes.

His third unusual quality was that he was gifted with a pleasant, charming and winsome personality through which he could influence people and win their hearts. He was able to win over people of diverse, even opposite views to his own. Imagine him, being of a Sufi bent of mind, working in Saudi Arabia among staunch Wahhabi Ulema and university administrators who were also his pay masters. He never engaged in futile debates or doctrinal controversies with them. Some grinned and complained in secret, but none ever produced anything to supersede his views. All became converted to his views on Islamic education. Often with a sweet smile, he would bring about a viable compromise in tricky situations without sacrificing his basic thesis. It was entirely due to Professor Ashraf's charm that we had the constant support of two wonderful Saudi personages, the dynamic Shaikh Ahmad Salah Jamjoom, Chairman of the Organising Committee of the First World Conference, and the visionary Dr Abdullah Omar Nasseef, the then Rector of King Abdulaziz University, Jeddah. Both always helped us in every way.

This brings me to mention another of his qualities which was useful for us in our public dealings. He was a broad-minded man. This quality held him in high esteem even in England where he set up the Islamic Academy and began working for Islam amongst the most committed British secularists and anti-religious academics. I remember that Professor Paul Hirst, the well-known professor of educational philosophy was at first opposed to Professor Ashraf's views on secularism. But with his persuasive analyses of the religious views and his convincing style, Professor Ashraf soon prevailed upon Professor Hirst who then became a close ally. Similarly, Peter Mitchel, Professor Hirst's colleague, began to appreciate Professor Ashraf's views on secularism and remains until today a committed supporter of the Islamic Academy.

Professor Ashraf was the only Muslim scholar in Britain who could gather together British intellectuals from various religious and non-religious beliefs and engage them in meaningful discussions and debates which led to the production of Agreed Statements on very delicate and controversial educational issues, for example, faith-based curriculum, moral and spiritual values in education, sex education in schools and the role of the family. It was this quality of broad-mindedness which inspired participants at the recently held seminar in last March[5] to unanimously pay tribute to late Professor Ashraf. They all commended the ability of the Islamic Academy for making it possible for intellectuals of so divergent viewpoints to respond to its invitations and to attend its seminars.

With all his religiosity, however, he was also a very shrewd man, a skillful planner, and a tactful negotiator. He knew the art of getting things done. He was a believer and a rationalist, a traditionalist and a modernist, at the same time. In matters of faith, he was a blind believer, but when it came to public dealings, he would become a pragmatist. Sometimes, he would employ a very mysterious, I should say, mystical tact to obtain concessions from difficult people in authority. I think that in this quality he was like many distinguished Sufi masters such as Shaikh ʿAbdul Qādir Jīlānī, Shaikh Muʿīnuddīn Chishty, Khwāja Niẓāmuddīn Awliyāʾ, Mujaddid Alf Thānī and others (may Allah reward them). These intellectual and spiritual giants had to deal with despotic sultans, crafty viziers, and powerful generals but with their charm and wisdom, they captivated them and won concessions from them for the good of the common Muslims. Like them, Allah Almighty had added His *barakah* (blessings) in everything that Professor Ashraf set out to do.

Last but not least, I come to yet another superb quality that he possessed. Of this aspect of him, I trust you here would be more intimately aware than myself as an outsider. I always found Professor Ashraf extremely kind to his family. He was generous to his brothers and other relatives but his affection for his wife was exemplary. I have never seen anybody more loving and caring for his wife than Professor Ashraf. I knew Mrs. Ashraf well—may Allah bless her soul. During her youthful days he treated her like a queen and during her final illness he showed her extreme care and patience. I used to see him holding her hand like a slave boy and taking her for a walk. I used to tell my friends

---

5 The reference is to the seminar held on 20–21 March 1999 at Homerton College, Cambridge which resulted in the document, *Old Age, Education and Religion: Areas of Agreement*, sponsored by The Islamic Academy, Cambridge and School of Education, University of Cambridge.

that if one single quality would take Professor Ashraf to paradise, it was his kindness to his beloved wife. Indeed, they were a loving couple.

Professor Ashraf's Critique of Secularism and Secularisation

Now I come to explain Professor Ashraf's attitudes and ideas about Islam and secularism. With his profound and inalienable conviction in the Islamic faith and the Islamic worldview, Professor Ashraf would never accept secularism as a viable philosophy for education. He critically analysed secularism, exposed its inner inconsistencies and its anti-Islamic assumptions. He strongly argued against the persisting influence of secularism and Westernisation on the minds and sensibilities of certain Muslim educationists who had been educated under Western systems of thought. He was sure that they had not critically examined its inner logic. Almost all of them started their writings, their discourses with the philosophical theories of Greek philosophers such as Plato and Aristotle or post-Renaissance, post-Enlightenment humanists like Erasmus, Rousseau, Bacon, Kant or their later counterparts like John Dewey, Freud, and others, as they were considered in the West to be the prophets of liberalism, rationalism, democracy, progressivism, and modernisation. These labels mesmerised modernist Muslims who wrongly hoped that by following their philosophies, Muslims would come out of their inherited backwardness in education.

Secularism was now no longer understood in its original connotation as the separation of the spheres of the church and the state in public affairs. Its champions had successively, over a period of centuries, turned it into a movement for the denial of the Divine authority and Revelation as a source of knowledge. The end product of secularism in the West was the near complete loss of faith in God by the Western man. Western thinkers had openly pronounced that God was dead! Given below are excerpts of Professor Ashraf's writings explaining his views on Western secularism vis-à-vis the Islamic concepts on the natures of Man, Knowledge, and Education.

Muslim Intellectuals and the Lure of Western Materialism

Muslim scholars, according to Professor Ashraf, were caught in the web of the visible materialistic progress of the West oblivious of the inner and invisible conflicts generated by the modern Western worldview. In his writings, Professor Ashraf exposed the superficiality of ideas and understanding among those Muslim intellectuals who could not resist the lure of secularism and its by-products. He divided them into the following categories.

(a) Those Muslims who have just adopted empirical and pragmatic concepts of the West without analysing their shortcomings or their conflicts with Islamic beliefs.

(b) Those Muslims who do not probably understand the relationship between Western philosophical thinking and the evolution of the Western society and who have been advising Muslims to learn from empiricism and rationalism in order to advance in this world.

(c) Those who have tried to draw from their limited knowledge of Western philosophy and tried to impose their philosophical thinking on Muslims hoping that in this way they will be able to bring about a holistic change in the Muslim world. They think that the classical concepts of Islamic jurisprudence are dead and gone and a new *fiqh* (jurisprudence) can be produced on the basis of their study of Islamic epistemology.[6]

Professor Ashraf regarded the upholders of Western rationalism and empiricism as completely misguided as they ignored the fundamental difference between the Islamic and the Western worldviews. He argued that our thought processes have not undergone scientific evolution based on Aristotelian dualism. Nor has it been influenced by modernism or postmodernism. Suddenly we are faced with a confusing arena where postmodernist materialism is at odds with Kant's notion of human reason. He warned that "It is an absurdity if we adopt ideas and thoughts which are at loggerheads with traditional Muslim ideals."[7]

Secular Beliefs

According to Professor Ashraf, "The secularists disbelieve in God and creation because they do not want to utilise their own inner spirit to realise this truth. They reject the validity of revealed knowledge, because they do not take the help of their *qalb* (a spiritual organ, 'heart') on which it was revealed[8] and through which only one can proceed beyond logic and facts into the Reality of the Spirit."[9] They only believe either in sense perception or in reason that is divorced from spiritual intuition or intellection—in other words from the *qalb*. By asserting the evolution of intelligence from non-intelligence they lose the sense of humility which awareness of the transcendent source generates and become proud of their individualities. Professor Ashraf asserts that "this pride prevents intelligence, where it has become rationalism, from rising to its source."[10] The secularists deny the Spirit and replace it with matter and believe that it is from matter that consciousness springs forth, as it is some

---

6   Syed Ali Ashraf, "Editorial," *Muslim Education Quarterly* 3, no. 1 (1985): 1.
7   Syed Ali Ashraf, "Editorial," *Muslim Education Quarterly* 14, no. 4 (1997): 3.
8   The Qurʾān came down upon the heart of the Prophet: "Verily this is a Revelation from the Lord of the Worlds: With it came down the spirit of Faith and Truth to thy heart" (Qurʾān 26:192–194).
9   Syed Ali Ashraf, "Education and Values: Islamic vis-à-vis the Secularist Approaches," *Muslim Education Quarterly* 4, no. 2 (1987): 4.
10 Ashraf, "Education and Values," 4.

kind of power associated with complex mechanisms such as the human brain. Instead of accepting the evidence of the Spirit, Professor Ashraf argues, the secularists deny its existence and nature using a methodology that lacks intellectual perspicacity, imagination and a sense of proportion which is precisely a consequence of their pride.[11]

Antagonism between Secular and Islamic beliefs

Professor Ashraf regards the secular and Islamic concepts of the relationships between education and values as being completely antagonistic:

> Though both may use the same terminology and say that education is a 'life-long process of learning from experience, developing and modifying one's knowledge in the light of ever-new experiences,' whereas the empiricist educationists speak of the 'educational process' as 'its own end' and conceives of 'growth' as relative to nothing 'save growth' and that 'there is nothing to which education is subordinate save more education,' the Islamic educationist speaks of the 'educational process' as goal-orientated and conceives of 'growth' as relative to the Absolute that makes man conscious of the final . . . growth into *Khalīfatullāh* (viceregent of God) whose complete example . . . is Prophet Muhammad, peace be on him.[12]

This growth in knowledge and virtue through education is likewise endless for humanity, since God is infinite and Absolute, and the Prophet is the supreme example of human perfection.

The difference between the secular and Islamic concepts of education and values, insists Professor Ashraf, is irreconcilable because "the secularist empirical theory abruptly rejects spiritual reality without any justification and posits physical existence as the only reality." Religion accepts advances in scientific knowledge, and thus knowledge about the universe and its organisms, as legitimate, but emphasises the need to understand, apply, and practise this knowledge within a framework of values. One the other hand, both empiricists and rationalists demand that educational framework be continually changed in response to changing social circumstances. They discuss the moral and cultural pluralism of industrial societies, asserting their superiority over religious communities by highlighting their tolerance and the acknowledgment of various moral, aesthetic, and cultural viewpoints as equally valid. Professor Ashraf challenges this relativistic perspective. Instead, he reminds us that

> Islam is both theoretically and historically found to be tolerant of other religions and cultures and of different moral and aesthetic views,

---

11 Ashraf, 4–5.
12 Ashraf, 10.

but it never considers all views to be equally valid. That is why in all traditional Muslim countries, non-Muslim children were never forced to take the same education that Muslim children were getting. It is only the secularist modern countries which do not allow Muslims to have their own system, and which compel Muslim children to read what the secularist system demands.[13]

The Nature of Knowledge in Islam

Professor Ashraf firmly links knowledge as understood in Islam with Allah Almighty, the Creator of the Universe and everything in it. One of His attributes is *al-ʿalīm*, the Knowledgeable, the Omniscient One, the Knower, One whose knowledge extends to all that is near and far, seen and unseen, apparent and hidden, present and future. He is nearer to us than our neck vein. He is Unique in His own Perfection. He has brought us into existence by His Own Will. He is present wherever we are. Islam, he explains, follows the natural process of asserting man's ultimate connection with God. Professor Ashraf asserted,

> Islam, therefore, does not separate intelligence from its 'supra individual' transcendent source. Intellection therefore connects man to God. . . . when true *īmān* (faith) enters a man's soul, he loves God and the Prophet more than himself, his family, clan, tribe or nation or entire humanity. As this intellection is active through Spirit and as the greatest manifestation of the Spirit is in the *qalb* of a *muʾmin* (believer), knowledge and love are integrally related, intellectual realisation and emotive response are immediate and sacred.[14]

The urge in Man to transcend the narrow boundaries of their self is natural but the human pride that ties down its *modus operandi* to the material domain preventing it from connecting to the Supreme Spirit from which it is derived. When Man strivers to seek nearness to God, he elevates his inner being and begins to realise his own nature. This urge for transcendence stems from the love for Allah and is so innate and unquestionable, that "its naturalness is its rationality and justification."[15] When Man starts to experience the transcendence, doubt begins to melt away and he begins to be drowned in the Light of God and *know* the purpose of creation. When love of God prevails, the love of the created world becomes only for His sake. This can be compared with what John Haldane says: "The primary purpose for which we were created is certainly *not* that of loving ourselves, as the ethical egoist might have it, but

---

13 Ashraf, 11.
14 Ashraf, 5.
15 Ashraf, 5.

nor is it that of loving one another. Rather it is that of loving *God*." This is not incompatible with an ethic of brotherly concern as we are "fellow creatures brought into existence by the one and only Divine creator."[16]

It is because of its subjective nature that secularists object to spiritual experience of and Man-God relationship. But is subjectivity inherently unreliable? Isn't subjectivity an aspect of Man's inner nature? Man has been granted freedom to choose and it is this limited freedom that man employs to make his individual choice. By exercising this individual choice, they either deny the demands and needs of their inner nature or accept them and thus transcend the demands and needs of the material self and decide to follow the guidance that brings that control and pleasure that "surpasseth all understanding."[17] The inner nature of man, asserts Professor Ashraf, is fully conscious of the Absolute. This is because such attributes of God as Justice, Righteousness, Patience, Kindness, Mercy, Charity as enshrined in the Names of God lie implanted in the depth of human beings. He maintains that the Names of God mean His Qualities and Powers which are His Attributes, the powers that He uses to bring anything into existence. Certain Attributes of God have been implanted within the heart of Adam[18] which man has inherited and it is through these attributes that "man can understand the essence of Nature and his own relationship with it, just as his forefather Adam, peace be upon him, understood it and taught the angels what they did not know.",[19] It is through the Divine spark that reside in man that they can realise that everything in existence is a sign and reflection of Reality.

As Man lives in this contingent, time-ridden world, he is subject to laws of nature that is endowed with both outward and inward aspects, and as he is also a spiritual being whose essence is not of this world, he must travel from the outward towards the inward. Professor Ashraf Asserts that it is not possible to gain knowledge in the real sense of the term unless man is able to have Spiritual control over his own self:

> He must also combine the two and bring the physical and the spiritual into harmony, but as God had breathed into him from His own Spirit,[20] his senses, his reason and his imagination must be under the complete, harmonious, control of his spirit. The descent of the Qurʾān on the *qalb* of the Prophet and the complete passivity demanded of the Prophet by

---

16 John Haldane, "Catholic Education and Catholic Identity," in *The Contemporary Catholic School: Context, Identity and Diversity*, ed. Terence McLaughlin, Joseph O'Keefe SJ and Bernadette O'Keeffe (London: Falmer Press, 1996), 134–135.
17 Ashraf, "Education and Values," 5.
18 Qurʾān 2:33.
19 Ashraf, "Education and Values," 5–6.
20 Qurʾān 15:29.

God indicate and repeatedly affirm the necessity of Spiritual control over man's being if man wants to acquire that Knowledge of God, and thus fulfil the goal and the purpose of his existence.[21]

In order that man can achieve this end, they have been made conscious of both the means and ends through the Prophet and the Revelation. This has been briefly summed up in the Ḥadīth Qudsī in which it is related that Gabriel was sent by God to teach Muslims through the Prophet the essence of ends and means. From this Ḥadīth we know that to achieve the goal three things are essential: *īmān* (Faith), *Islām* (Law) and *iḥsān* (the Way). God alone is worthy of worship, a concept contained in the "two attestations of faith"—to believe in the Unity of God (*tawḥīd*) and the Prophethood (*risālah*) of Muhammad, peace be upon him. This implies an all-encompassing and uncompromising monotheism proclaiming the primacy, supremacy, sovereignty, and Unity of God.

In order to attain God's nearness Man must follow God's guidance—sent to Man through His messengers. As Prophet Muhammad is the supreme human example (*uswatun ḥasanah*), the necessity of obedience to the Prophet is an essential Islamic concept enshrined in the "two attestations of faith" stated above. Following the Way (Sunnah) of the Prophet helps one overcome one's ego and make the self ready for the whole-hearted worship of God. *Tawḥīd* and *ittibāʿ* (obedience) of the Prophet further imply that the means of attaining the goal for which man has been created, is complete servitude. It corroborates what God says in the Qurʾān, "I created jinn and man only to worship me (Qurʾān 5:54)." For Professor Ashraf knowledge is connected to action as they together lead to the nearness to God. He says, "Both the acquisition of the Knowledge of Revelation and of the Sunnah and the cultivation of the psychological attitude that makes whole-hearted surrender to God and His Prophet possible are necessary."[22]

The Qurʾān says, "If you love God, then follow me [the Prophet], God will love you (Qurʾān 3:31)." Love, Knowledge and surrender to God of one's own fee will are integrally related. Knowledge is the starting point for attaining the status of *Khalīfatullāh* (vicegerent of God), but love has been given a significant status because the Prophet has said that a person cannot be considered to have true faith if he does not love God and the Prophet more than himself, his family, tribe or nation and entire humanity. It means different people have different degrees of faith, as they have different degrees of knowledge:[23] "Are those who know equal to those who do not know (Qurʾān 39:9)?"

---

21 Ashraf, "Education and Values," 8.
22 Ashraf, "Education and Values," 8.
23 Ashraf, "Education and Values," 8.

The Role of Education in Islam

The aim of education is to produce a good man. For Muhammad Naquib al-Attas, the fundamental concept of education in Islam is "the inculcation of *adab* (*tádīb*), for it is *adab* in the all-inclusive sense I mean, as encompassing the spiritual and material life of man, that instils the quality of goodness that is sought after."[24] "The fostering of a sound religious belief ... is the main task of education," says A. K. Brohi.[25] "Education, according to Islam, is a means of training body, mind and soul through the imparting of knowledge of all kinds, i.e. fundamental as compulsory and specialised as optional."[26] Professor Ashraf distinguishes education from instruction: "Education helps in the complete growth of an individual's personality whereas instruction merely trains an individual or a group to do some task efficiently. ... The outlook of an educated man is not static but is modified and mellowed as he applies principles to practice and his outlook is enriched by experience."[27]

The mainstream system of education in the modern world is based on Godless secular philosophy, but a religious system of education is formulated on the principles of religion. Whereas religions provide a norm and a sense of accountability to God, and belief in the next world and hence a check on selfishness, racial or cultural pride, secularism can lead to power struggle between the races without any check that is divinely ordained. By separating religious and governmental institutions secularism claims to allow for diversity and equal treatment of all individuals regardless of their beliefs or backgrounds, but it is not supported by the reality on the ground. Secular morality has many aspects shared with religion, but it is not based on a permanent source of values, although it can be based on principles such as empathy, compassion, fairness, and respect for human rights. These values, developed by social experience, are based on concepts that ignore or deny any notion of the Absolute. These values are cultivated through education and contribute to the development of a society where religion is considered a private matter. Paradoxically, it talks about spirituality while denying the human spirit as a gift of breath and life from God upheld by all major religions of the world including Islam, Christianity, and Judaism.

---

24 Syed Muhammad al-Naquib al-Attas, introduction to *Aims and Objectives of Islamic Education*, edited by Syed Muhammad al-Naquib al-Attas (Kent, UK: Hodder and Stoughton, and Jeddah: King Abdulaziz University, 1979), 1.
25 Syed Sajjad Husain and Syed Ali Ashraf, eds., *Crisis in Muslim Education* (Kent, UK: Hodder and Stoughton, and Jeddah: King Abdulaziz University, 1979), 30.
26 King Abdulaziz University, *Conference Book: First World Conference on Muslim Education* (Mecca, and Jeddah: King Abdulaziz University, 1977), 15.
27 Syed Ali Ashraf, preface to *Aims and Objectives of Islamic Education*, edited by Syed Muhammad al-Naquib al-Attas (Kent, UK: Hodder and Stoughton, and Jeddah: King Abdulaziz University, 1979), ix.

Islam unites in itself both the spiritual and temporal aspects of life as it regulates not only the individual's relationship to God but also human relationships in a social setting. The Qurʾān and Ḥadīth are concerned with social legislation and the politico-moral principles for constituting and ordering the community. This is why Professor Ashraf believed that education should be grounded in religious principles or teachings. It is the overarching framework of knowledge and values within which all aspects of education must operate. It is this framework that reflects the Unified Truth of religion. Professor Ashraf believes:

> If education, including teaching in all branches of knowledge, is guided by the religious approach to life, the true nature of man is nourished and developed, the interrelationship among all branches of knowledge understood and appreciated and all faculties of a human being grow in such a way that the autonomy of each branch of knowledge is seen in the context of Unified Truth and not in segregation, the hierarchy of knowledge is realized and established and all branches of knowledge are seen in their proper perspective within the orbit of the supreme knowledge that man can attain, that of Man's relation with God.[28]

Man will be able to fulfil the duties and obligations demanded by religion only when his education makes him conscious of God to the level of attaining *iḥsān*, that is, worshipping God as though he 'sees' Him. He must see God before him, and if he is unable to do, he must be conscious of the fact that God is seeing him—that is, the spiritual attainment described in Ḥadīth Jibrīl. When God-consciousness impinges on his personality, affects his cognition, controls and guides his motivation and engenders a positive orientation towards self, others, Nature and God, he becomes a truly purified person.[29] It must be remembered that for this reason, Professor Ashraf has named the University that he founded at Dhaka as the Darul Ihsan University.

The divine dimension of education has to be realised to understand what is required to formulate an Islamic system of education and what it aims to achieve. Man's commitment through intrinsic faith leads him to a process of continuous self-evaluation and continuous growth and progress towards perfection. With the continuous inflow of God's grace man is able to attain righteousness, through ʿilm (knowledge), good conduct (ʿamal ṣāliḥ) and sincerity (ikhlāṣ) of intention (niyyah), which helps him grow continuously till his death. When he responds to Sharīʿah with all sincerity he is elevated to a state where

---

28 Syed Ali Ashraf, "A View of Education—an Islamic Perspective," in *Schools for Tomorrow: Building Walls or Building Bridges*, ed. Bernadette O'Keeffe (London: The Falmer Press, 1988), 73.

29 Ashraf, "Education and Values," 9.

the heart (*qalb*) and the intellect (*ʿaql*), that is, his rationality and spirituality work in unison. But trials and tribulations will always accompany Man as a test destined by God, and "the tension between personal commitment and institutional constraints continuously requires individualised solution."[30] Education in Islam not only purifies the self, but also envisions through its education system a society of righteous people through whom God's law will prevail. Islamic civilisational regeneration will be possible only when righteous people are committed to establish Islamic values in their own lives and an Islamic order in society. This dual role of education has been succinctly captured by Professor Ashraf in the following words:

> Education thus becomes a twofold process—one of acquiring external knowledge breeding extrinsic faith and the other, through internal realisation, of the intrinsic meaning and worth of that knowledge in training man to play his individual, societal, cultural, and civilisational role in a world perspective. The individual thus becomes the meting point of the two forces—one of which is the unique individuality of the person in whom some specific quality of God has been implanted.... The secularists also stress this individuality. But they reject the other universal, eternal force that unifies mankind and Nature and brings man into direct contact with God.[31]

Although Professor Ashraf was deeply committed to Islam, for a multi-faith multicultural society, he argued for a pluralistic approach that respects diverse beliefs and cultures.[32] For this reason, the Islamic Academy, Cambridge organised a number of seminars jointly with the University of Cambridge on different areas of education and invited all major faith groups of the United Kingdom to participate in these seminars. A consensus existed among the participants that education should encompass a broad range of knowledge, including religious studies, but should be based on beliefs in a Transcendental Reality, the existence of the spiritual dimension in each human being, eternal and fundamental values, and the need for divine guidance. This approach did not favour one particular religion over others.[33]

---

30 Ashraf, 9.
31 Ashraf, 9–10.
32 Shaikh Abdul Mabud, "Professor Syed Ali Ashraf: A Pioneer of Faith-Based Education," in *Great Muslim Leaders: Lessons for Education*, eds. Melanie C. Brooks and Miriam D. Ezzani (North Carolina: Information Age Publishing, 2023), 57–67.
33 The Islamic Academy and University of Cambridge, *Faith as the Basis of Education in a Multi-faith Multi-cultural Country: Discussion Document II*. Seminar sponsored by the Islamic Academy, Cambridge and the Department of Education, University of Cambridge (Cambridge: The Islamic Academy, 1991), 8.

Conclusions

Thus, through his powerful writings, Professor Ashraf has adopted an approach like the great Imam Al-Ghazālī and Muhammad Iqbal, who each in his own way and in his own time, exerted concerted efforts (*jihād*) to avert the rising tide of anti-Islamic flood of secularism entering the inner domains of Islamic education. The holding of the First World Conference on Muslim Education in 1977 was a breakthrough and a watershed for the reconstruction of Islamic thought and education on Islamic lines. The five subsequent World Conferences on Muslim Education have further paved the way for the implementation of the programmes recommended by the first Conference.

Today, there is an emergent and progressive growth of research, publications, and efforts at the individual and institutional levels to expand the horizon of understanding on Islamisation of knowledge and education proposed in the World Conferences on Muslim Education. Hundreds of schools have emerged to implement the rationale of Islamisation of knowledge and education at the grassroots level. Thousands of teachers all around the Islamic world and in non-Muslim countries are becoming seriously involved in the silent revolution that we—Professor Ashraf, our associates and I—set in motion at Makkah in 1977. Various Muslim organisations like the International Institute of Islamic Thought (IIIT), the Islamic Academy Cambridge, the Islamic Foundation (Leicester), the Union of Muslim Organisations (UMO) and its National Muslim Educational Council and many regional and national organisations have seriously undertaken the task of Islamisation of education in earnest. The establishment of the International Islamic universities at Islamabad, Kuala Lumpur, Chittagong, and other places has been a great step forward. The International Islamic University at Kuala Lumpur alone is avowedly engaged in the task of Islamisation of Knowledge and integration of the Revealed and Acquired knowledge in its various faculties. It would be now safe to say that no Muslim scholar and educator has any reason knowingly to embrace secular Western concepts of education and try to put them in practice in the Muslim world. Secularisation in the Islamic world is now perhaps being perpetuated subtly through the Muslim political leaderships and the upper ruling classes who, by and large, do not represent true Islamic norms and values. To conclude, I have no doubt that the late Professor Ashraf's movement against the penetration of Godless secular concepts into the Islamic world is making headway. More and more Muslim scholars are becoming aware of the challenges of *kufr* (unbelief) that confront the present-day Muslim education. With this awareness will hopefully come the determination to combat and eradicate the roots of secularism from the Islamic psyche.

Bibliography

Ashraf, Syed Ali. Preface to *Aims and Objectives of Islamic Education*, edited by Syed Muhammad al-Naquib al-Attas, ix–xiv. Kent, UK: Hodder and Stoughton, and Jeddah: King Abdulaziz University, 1979.

Ashraf, Syed Ali. "Editorial." *Muslim Education Quarterly* 3, no. 1 (1985): 1–4.

Ashraf, Syed Ali. "Education and Values: Islamic vis-à-vis the Secularist Approaches." *Muslim Education Quarterly* 4, no. 2 (1987): 4–16.

Ashraf, Syed Ali. "A View of Education—an Islamic Perspective." In *Schools for Tomorrow: Building Walls or Building Bridges*, edited by Bernadette O'Keeffe, 69–79. London: The Falmer Press, 1988.

Ashraf, Syed Ali. "Editorial," *Muslim Education Quarterly* 14, no. 4 (1997): 1–4.

Al-Attas, Syed Muhammad al-Naquib. Introduction to *Aims and Objectives of Islamic Education*, edited by Syed Muhammad al-Naquib al-Attas, 1–15. Kent, UK: Hodder and Stoughton, and Jeddah: King Abdulaziz University, 1979.

Haldane, John. "Catholic Education and Catholic Identity." In *The Contemporary Catholic School: Context, Identity and Diversity*, edited by Terence McLaughlin, Joseph O'Keefe SJ and Bernadette O'Keeffe, 126–135. London: Falmer Press, 1996.

Husain, Syed Sajjad and Syed Ali Ashraf, eds. *Crisis in Muslim Education*. Kent, UK: Hodder and Stoughton, and Jeddah: King Abdulaziz University, 1979.

The Islamic Academy and University of Cambridge. *Faith as the Basis of Education in a Multi-faith Multi-cultural Country: Discussion Document II*. Seminar sponsored by the Islamic Academy, Cambridge and the Department of Education, University of Cambridge. Cambridge: The Islamic Academy, 1991.

King Abdulaziz University. *Conference Book: First World Conference on Muslim Education*. Mecca, and Jeddah: King Abdulaziz University, 1977.

Mabud, Shaikh Abdul. "Professor Syed Ali Ashraf: A Pioneer of Faith-Based Education." In *Great Muslim Leaders: Lessons for Education*, edited by Melanie C. Brooks and Miriam D. Ezzani, 57–67. North Carolina: Information Age Publishing, 2023.

Chapter 6

The Islamic Concept of Knowledge: Some Reflections on the Epistemological Assumptions in the Educational Thinking of Professor Syed Ali Ashraf

J. Mark Halstead

Allah will exalt to high degree . . . those who have knowledge. (Qurʾān 58:11, trans.)

Say: Are those equal, those who know and those who do not know? (Qurʾān 39:9, trans.)

The high status accorded to the pursuit of knowledge in Islam is well known. The Arabic word for knowledge (*ʿilm*) and its derivatives occur with great frequency in the Holy Qurʾān. The Prophet Muhammad himself was urged to pray for an increase in knowledge.[1] A ḥadīth of the Prophet reminds believers that "seeking for knowledge is obligatory for every Muslim man and woman,"[2] and another says that "he who goes forth in search of knowledge is in the way of Allah till he returns."[3]

However, it would be a mistake to assume that this emphasis on knowledge licenses *any* pursuit of *any* knowledge. Knowledge in Islam is subject to two major constraints. The first relates to its religious origin. The Holy Qurʾān makes it clear that knowledge is a characteristic of God Himself, and that all knowledge comes from Him.[4] This means that knowledge must be approached reverently and in humility, and that there cannot be any true knowledge which is in conflict with religion and divine revelation, only ignorance. The

---

1 Qurʾān 20:114.
2 *Ṣaḥīḥ al-Bukhārī*.
3 *Jāmiʿ al-Tirmidhī* and *Sunan al-Dārimī*.
4 Qurʾān 49:16; 2:216.

second relates to its purpose. There is no notion in Islam of the pursuit of knowledge for its own sake. Seyyed Hossein Nasr points out that in Arabic "to know" ultimately means "to be transformed by the very process of knowing."[5] Ibn Khaldūn pours scorn on the man "who knows about tailoring but does not know tailoring,"[6] and al-Ghazālī says,

> Be sure that knowledge alone is no support ... If a man reads a hundred thousand scientific subjects and learns them but does not act upon them, his knowledge is of no use to him, for its benefit lies only in being used.[7]

Like money, knowledge is not to be accumulated for its own sake but must be put to use. And the appropriate use for knowledge on a Muslim perspective is to help people to acknowledge God, to live in accordance with Islamic law and to fulfil the purposes of God's creation. Knowledge which does not serve these purposes may be considered useless.

All this implies a concept of knowledge which is very different from dominant western concepts. Professor Ashraf has over many years been a powerful exponent of this Islamic concept of knowledge and its educational implications. At the heart of his exposition is the belief that God has granted knowledge to human beings to help them to follow the right path and to fulfil their role as God's vicegerents on earth (khalīfatullāh).[8] This implies

- that knowledge is not merely "an intellectual awareness divorced from spiritual realization,"[9] for people's emotions, morals and faith are all governed by what they know;[10]
- that knowledge which is acquired through "human intelligence and imagination" is unreliable and of secondary importance compared to knowledge originating from divine revelation;[11]
- that though there is no "bar to the acquisition of knowledge," the purpose of knowledge must be borne in mind and care taken not simply to pursue knowledge for its own sake;[12]

---

5   Quoted in Hasan Gai Eaton, "'Knowledge and the Sacred': Reflections on Seyyed Hossein Nasr's Gifford Lectures," *The Islamic Quarterly* 26, no. 3 (1982): 141.
6   Ibn Khaldun, *Muqaddimah*, trans. Franz Rosenthal, Vol. 3 (Princeton, NJ: Princeton University Press, 1967), 354–55.
7   Quoted in Abul-Wafa al-Ghuneimi al-Taftazani, "Islamic Education: its principles and aims," *Muslim Education Quarterly* 4, no. 1 (1986): 70.
8   Syed Ali Ashraf, *New Horizons in Muslim Education* (London: Hodder & Stoughton, 1985), 3.
9   Ashraf, *New Horizons*, 4.
10 Ashraf, *New Horizons*, 40.
11 Ashraf, *New Horizons*, 9.
12 Ashraf, *New Horizons*, 5, 39.

- that by separating knowledge and values from their religious source, the process of secularization that has occurred in the West has destroyed the ideal of *khalīfatullāh*;[13]
- that the aim of education in Islam is to contribute to the balanced (spiritual, moral and intellectual) development of human beings and to produce good Muslims who acknowledge God's supremacy and who know how to use their knowledge for the benefit of themselves, their community and humanity at large.[14]

The importance from a Muslim perspective of this restatement of Islamic principles in relation to the concept of knowledge and education cannot be over-emphasised. Wan Daud[15] suggests that while there has been "admirable commitment and enthusiasm" among Muslims both in Muslim countries and in the West to establish Islamic schools and colleges, these are often not based on a strong theoretical foundation. Particularly in the West, such schools have frequently been established in response to perceived inadequacies in the state system of schooling, and they have been happy to contribute to the preservation of Muslim identity and help children to take pride in their religion, without generally thinking through the principles on which the distinctive education they provide is based, nor the way they should deal with the philosophical and epistemological problems posed for Muslims by modern secular scientific knowledge. Much contemporary discussion on Islamic education, Wan Daud maintains, betrays "weak theoretical foundations, simplistic interpretation, and intemperate application, which do not do justice to its true ideals and heritage."[16] Professor Ashraf belongs to a small company of Muslim scholars of the last fifty years (among whom I would also list A. L. Tibawi, F. Rahman, S. H. Nasr, S. M. N. al-Attas and I. R. al-Faruqi) who have understood this situation and have given high priority to the need to think seriously about education and the concept of knowledge which underpins it.

The aim of the present chapter is to bring together Professor Ashraf's key ideas on the concept of knowledge from a variety of sources and to provide a critical discussion of these ideas. The chapter is therefore divided into two main sections. The first examines Professor Ashraf's views on the definition of knowledge, the sources of knowledge, the nature of knowledge, the classification of knowledge, Islamic and western conceptions of knowledge, the need for Islamization of knowledge and the relationship between knowledge and education. The second section provides a critical discussion of these views

---

13 Ashraf, *New Horizons*, 9.
14 Ashraf, *New Horizons*, 4–5, 39.
15 Wan Mohd Nor Wan Daud, *The Educational Philosophy and Practice of Syed Muhammad Naquib Al-Attas: an exposition of the original concept of Islamization* (Kuala Lumpur: International Institute of Islamic Thought and Civilization, 1998), 26.
16 Wan Daud, *Educational Philosophy and Practice*, 24.

from a positivist and rationalist perspective, and draws attention to the gulf that exists between Islamic and western ways of thinking about the nature of knowledge. The conclusion highlights the difficulties encountered by Muslims, especially those living in the West who are faced with these conflicting and incompatible perspectives, and explores ways of encouraging dialogue and mutual understanding in the future.

An Islamic Concept of Knowledge

Professor Ashraf did not write extensively on knowledge as a separate topic, though he did produce one paper entitled "The Islamic Concept of Knowledge" for presentation to a meeting of the Philosophy of Education Society at Cambridge.[17] However, his epistemological assumptions permeate his more extensive writings on education and the curriculum, and he was at the forefront of the early work on the Islamization of knowledge. The central account of knowledge contained in the Cambridge paper, which draws heavily on al-Ghazālī and medieval Islamic scholarship, is thus expanded and modified in other publications, especially his book *New Horizons in Muslim Education*[18] and in a series of editorials and articles for the *Muslim Education Quarterly* on "The Islamic Approach to Education,"[19] the "Islamisation of Education"[20] and "The Islamic Framework of Reference."[21] These are the main sources used for the current chapter.

Definition of knowledge

Professor Ashraf offers the following Islamic definition of knowledge: the "acquisition of certainty (*yaqīn*) regarding God, His attributes and action [and] regarding Self and the Universe."[22] This definition needs some contextualisation and explanation. Following Ibn Hazm, Al-Ghazālī in *The Incoherence of the Philosophers*[23] has distinguished two meanings of the term 'definition.' The first

---

17 Syed Ali Ashraf, "The Islamic Concept of Knowledge," (Unpublished paper presented to a meeting of the Philosophy of Education Society at Homerton College, Cambridge, 1986).
18 Ashraf, *New Horizons*.
19 Syed Ali Ashraf, "Editorial: The Islamic Approach to Education and the National Curriculum," *Muslim Education Quarterly* 6, no. 4 (1988).
20 Syed Ali Ashraf, "Editorial: Islamisation of Education: Need for the Islamic Frame of Reference," *Muslim Education Quarterly* 6, no. 3 (1989); Syed Ali Ashraf, "Editorial: Islamisation of Education: The Islamic Frame of Reference II," *Muslim Education Quarterly* 6, no. 4 (1989).
21 Syed Ali Ashraf, "Editorial: The Islamic frame of Reference: (B) the Intellectual Dimension," *Muslim Education Quarterly* 7, no. 1 (1989); Syed Ali Ashraf, "Editorial: The Islamic Frame of Reference: The Intellectual Dimension II," *Muslim Education Quarterly* 7, no. 2 (1990); Syed Ali Ashraf, "Editorial: The Islamic Frame of Reference: The Intellectual Dimension II—the Methodology," *Muslim Education Quarterly* 7, no. 3 (1990).
22 Ashraf, "Islamic Concept of Knowledge," 1.
23 A. H. M. I. M. Al-Ghazālī, *Incoherence of the Philosophers (Tahāfut al-Falāsifah)*, trans. Sabih

(ḥadd) provides a precise specification of the distinctive characteristic(s) of the object defined. The second (rasm) describes the salient characteristics or nature of the object through division (qismah) and example (mithāl).[24] There is wide agreement that knowledge need not and cannot be defined by ḥadd. This is because knowledge is limitless and thus defies the limitations set by a precise definition,[25] because humans have a natural understanding of the term since knowledge is a human attribute,[26] and because every definition of knowledge presupposes knowledge and this makes the definition tautological.[27] However, there is an abundance of rasmī definitions of knowledge (some of which are discussed in Rosenthal,[28] and in Wan Daud.[29] It is not immediately clear which category Professor Ashraf's definition falls into, but it is not dissimilar to the fuller definition offered by al-Attas,[30] which describes knowledge as the arrival of the meaning of a thing (or object of knowledge) in the soul of the subject, and the soul's arrival at the meaning of that thing. The first half of this definition is an acknowledgement that all knowledge emanates from God, while the second is an acknowledgement that the seeker for knowledge is an active agent; and 'soul' is used here as the seat of human reason, emotion and spiritual discernment.

The emphasis on certainty in Professor Ashraf's definition of knowledge is significant from an Islamic perspective. It implies an acceptance of the prevailing understanding of knowledge as true belief, but does not limit the concept of true belief to propositions for which there is objective evidence. True belief may be intuitional as well as rational, and may involve our spiritual capacities as well as our powers of reasoning. Following al-Ghazālī, Professor Ashraf identifies three sources of certainty:[31] lack of doubt through knowledge based on authority (ʿilm al-yaqīn), lack of doubt through evidence either from sensory experience or from logical thinking (ʿayn al-yaqīn); and faith through direct experience of the soul (ḥaqq al-yaqīn). These sources of knowledge will be

---

    Ahmad Kamali (Lahore: Pakistan Philosophical Congress, 1963).
24 Franz Rosenthal, "Muslim Definitions of Knowledge," in *The Conflict of Traditionalism and Modernism in the Muslim Middle East*, ed. Carl Leiden (Austin: University of Texas Press, 1966).
25 Syed M. N. Al-Attas, *Islam and the Philosophy of Science* (Kuala Lumpur: International Institute of Islamic Thought and Civilisation, 1989), 16.
26 Syed M. N. Al-Attas, "Preliminary Thoughts on the Nature of Knowledge and the Definition and Aims of Education," in *Aims and Objectives of Islamic Education*, ed. S. M. N. al-Attas (London: Hodder & Stoughton and Jeddah: King Abdulaziz University, 1979), 30.
27 Wan Daud, *Educational Philosophy and Practice*, 101.
28 Franz Rosenthal, *Knowledge Triumphant: The Concept of Knowledge in Medieval Islam* (Leiden: E.J. Brill, 1970).
29 Wan Daud, *Educational Philosophy and Practice*, ch. 2.
30 Syed M. N. Al-Attas, *The Concept of Education in Islam: A Framework for an Islamic Philosophy of Education* (Kuala Lumpur: Muslim Youth Movement of Malaysia, 1980), 17.
31 Ashraf, "The Islamic Concept of Knowledge," 1.

discussed in the next section, but it is important to note at this stage that, particularly in Sufi thought, certainty is not limited to what can be proved empirically or through rational debate, but may be achieved through a different form of reason or spiritual experience in which particular aspects of reality are understood. As Bakar points out, ḥaqq al-yaqīn is "free from error and doubt" because it is "not based on conjecture or mental concepts, but it resides in the heart and thus involves the whole of man's being."[32] The heart is central to the kind of knowledge that comes from mystical experiences, such as the sweetness of love.[33] Doubt, scepticism, conjecture and contention are to be avoided because the ultimate goal of human existence is happiness and spiritual fulfilment, and happiness involves "certainty on the ultimate matters concerning the nature of reality."[34]

Sources of knowledge

The three sources of knowledge outlined in the last paragraph are re-examined in different ways throughout Professor Ashraf's subsequent writings,[35] and are eventually restructured into four categories which, following al-Attas, he calls the sound senses (or experience), true narrative (or authority), sound reason, and intuition.[36] Of these four ways of acquiring knowledge, Professor Ashraf regards perception and observation through the bodily senses as the least reliable.[37] They do help individuals to acquire some knowledge of empirical realities, including the experiences of enjoyment and suffering, but they are incomplete because they are tentative, always open to challenge, and incapable of recognising the transcendent. The second channel for the acquisition of knowledge is what al-Attas calls "true narrative," which is of two kinds. There is the narrative of scholars, scientists, religious leaders and their writings, and there is the narrative of the Messenger of God himself. The authority of the former depends on their authenticity, which is open to critical discussion and challenge; though when the authority of individuals is linked to a chain of authorities culminating in the Prophet Muhammad, this authority will be confirmed in the light of faith and widely accepted in the Muslim world. The authority of the Messenger of God, however, is absolute.

---

32 Ashraf, "The Islamic Concept of Knowledge," 42.
33 Mulyadhi Kartanegara, *Essentials of Islamic Epistemology: A Philosophical Inquiry into the Foundation of Knowledge* (Brunei Darussalam: UBD press, 2014), 36–7.
34 Wan Daud, *Educational Philosophy and Practice*, 77.
35 Ashraf, "Editorial: The Islamic Approach to Education," Ashraf, "Editorial: The Islamic frame of Reference: (B) the Intellectual Dimension;" Ashraf, "Editorial: The Islamic Frame of Reference: The Intellectual Dimension II—the Methodology."
36 Ashraf, "Editorial: The Islamic frame of Reference: (B) the Intellectual Dimension;" cf. Syed M. N. Al-Attas, *A Commentary on the Hujjat al-Siddiq of Nur al-Din al-Raniri* (Kuala Lumpur: Ministry of Culture, 1986), 31–33.
37 Ashraf, "The Islamic Concept of Knowledge," 1–2; 1988, p. 14.

The third way of acquiring knowledge is through the use of reason. However, in Islam the rational dimension cannot be isolated from other dimensions of the intellect (ʿaql), including the spiritual. When humans try to divorce their rational powers from the power of the heart or the spirit, logic, argument and rational debate can lead them away from God.[38] It is not the power of reason alone, but the combination of reason, wisdom and spiritual insight and understanding, that distinguishes human beings from animals and brings them to an understanding of God. Reason is thus closely linked to the fourth source of knowledge, intuition. Intuition refers not only to the direct and immediate apprehension by the knowing subject of self, of other selves, of an external world, of values and of rational truths (such as the truth that two are greater than one, or that a person cannot be in two different places at once, which even an infant understands).[39] It refers also to our understanding of things that cannot be fully understood by reason alone, such as the moral implications of knowledge. And for Sufis at least, it refers also to that inner illumination or mystical experience which produces a direct and immediate apprehension of religious truths, of the reality and existence of God.[40] The highest example of this is prophetic consciousness, but it is also experienced by those who live close to God and are thus able to transcend the limited knowledge of this world.[41]

Nature of knowledge

In common with many Muslim scholars, Professor Ashraf distinguishes between two types of knowledge (sometimes called *naqlī* (transmitted) and *ʿaqlī* (intellectual): see note 20, MEQ 6 (3), p. 1), and also argues that there is an essential unity between them. The distinction is linked to the origin of the knowledge but ultimately concerns the nature of the knowledge and the degree of certainty attached to it. The first type, which Professor Ashraf variously calls "revealed knowledge,"[42] "perennial knowledge"[43] or "true knowledge,"[44] is a direct gift from God. It is derived from the Qurʾān and the Sunnah and includes all Sharīʿah-oriented knowledge. He even goes so far as to claim that it is this type of knowledge that is meant by the word *ʿilm*.[45] Because of its origin, this "longstanding Qurʾānic epistemology" has an absolute character and provides an Islamic framework of reference which he argues should be

---

38 Ashraf, "The Islamic Concept of Knowledge," 2
39 Ashraf, "The Islamic Concept of Knowledge," 3; Ashraf, "Editorial: The Islamic frame of Reference: (B) the Intellectual Dimension," 3.
40 Kartanegara, *Essentials of Islamic Epistemology*, 94–102.
41 Ashraf, *New Horizons*, 32; Ashraf, "The Islamic Concept of Knowledge," 3–4; Ashraf, "Editorial: The Islamic Approach to Education," 14–15.
42 Ashraf, "Editorial: Islamisation of Education: The Islamic Frame of Reference II," 4.
43 Ashraf, *New Horizons*, 26.
44 Ashraf, "Editorial: The Islamic Frame of Reference: The Intellectual Dimension II," 1.
45 Ashraf, "Editorial: Islamisation of Education: The Islamic Frame of Reference II," 4.

the basis of any Islamic educational system.[46] The second type, which is called "acquired knowledge," is a product of human intelligence, imagination, experience, observation, research and rational enquiry.[47] As such, it has a more relative character and is capable of development and variation, though in the West it is the only category which is actually called "knowledge."

Professor Ashraf explores the idea that this distinction can be applied to the content as well as to the origin and nature of knowledge. Thus at one stage he wishes to suggest that "true knowledge" is knowledge that concerns the relationship between humans and God, whereas "acquired knowledge" concerns either the relationship between humans and humans or the relationship between humans and the natural world.[48] However, it is clear that these two types do not neatly divide up the content of knowledge into two categories. For example, Muslims' understanding of their duties towards each other and towards the natural world is derived largely from revealed knowledge, as is their understanding of human nature and the fusion of body and spirit which makes up human beings.[49]

Professor Ashraf is at pains to emphasise the unity of knowledge,[50] but what this means in effect is that revealed knowledge should take priority over acquired knowledge. Acquired knowledge on this view is only valid insofar as it remains consistent with the Sharīʿah as the source of values.[51] All other knowledge is to be reviewed in the light of revealed knowledge; and where the basic ideas of any subject or discipline are found to be "at variance with Islam," then Muslims must "question the validity and adequacy of that branch of knowledge."[52] Therefore, there is no room for the autonomy of the disciplines. Al-Attas makes essentially the same point, though rather less bluntly:

> The first knowledge unveils the mystery of Being and Existence and reveals the true relationship between man's self and his Lord, and since for man such knowledge pertains to the ultimate purpose of knowing, it follows that knowledge of its prerequisites becomes the basis and essential foundation for knowledge of the second kind, for knowledge of the latter alone, without the guiding spirit of the former, cannot truly lead man in his life, but only confuses and confounds him and enmeshes him in the labyrinth of endless and purposeless seeking.[53]

---

46 Ashraf, "Editorial: Islamisation of Education: Need for the Islamic frame of Reference," 1–2.
47 Ashraf, *New Horizons*, 9.
48 Ashraf, "Editorial: The Islamic Frame of Reference: The Intellectual Dimension II," 1.
49 Ashraf, "Editorial: Islamisation of Education: The Islamic Frame of Reference II," 4–5; Ashraf, "Editorial: The Islamic frame of Reference: (B) the Intellectual Dimension," 2.
50 Ashraf, *New Horizons*, 44.
51 Ashraf, *New Horizons*, 26.
52 Ashraf, *New Horizons*, 42.
53 Al-Attas, "Preliminary Thoughts on the Nature of Knowledge," 31.

In this both Ashraf and al-Attas are following al-Ghazālī and rejecting earlier philosophers like al-Fārābī, Ibn Sīnā (Avicenna), Ibn Rushd (Averroes) and the Muʿtazilites, who were closer to the Aristotelian tradition of the pursuit of truth with the help of human reason. Al-Kindī, for example, had already asserted the supremacy of reason over revelation in matters of morality, and al-Fārābī went further in asserting the insufficiency of revelation and the priority of philosophy over religion in many areas of knowledge.[54] With the advent of al-Ghazālī, however, this rationalistic school of thought lost ground. Al-Ghazālī reasserted the dominance of religion over reason and gave superior status to revelation as a source of knowledge.[55] In *The Incoherence of the Philosophers*[56] he argued that it was impossible for the rational faculties to attain to certainty without the help of revealed knowledge and spiritual understanding. Al-Ghazālī's influence on all subsequent Muslim thinking about the nature of knowledge has been immense. By the time of Ibn Khaldūn, the twofold nature of knowledge was widely accepted, and Ibn Khaldūn himself discussed education under the headings of *naqliyyah* (transmitted sciences, such as theology and jurisprudence) and *ʿaqliyyah* (intellectual sciences, such as medicine and mathematics). In more recent times, under the influence of the West (as we shall see below), *naqliyyah* sciences lost status, becoming just one of many subjects, and the essential integration of the two types of knowledge was lost; as a result, Islamic education became separated from modern education and two different systems started functioning in Muslim countries.[57] For more than twenty years, Professor Ashraf devoted himself to the task of reasserting the twofold nature of knowledge and grounding an Islamic approach to education on the integration of these two types of knowledge.

Classification of knowledge

In his *Book of Knowledge*,[58] al-Ghazālī suggests a number of ways of classifying knowledge. The first uses the criterion of obligatoriness to distinguish knowledge which is requisite for every individual (*farḍ ʿayn*), such as the five pillars of Islam, and the concepts of permitted and prohibited, from knowledge which is needed within the community but is not required for everyone (such as engineering or medicine). The second kind of knowledge (*farḍ kifāyah*) can be classified into knowledge which is based on the *Sharīʿah* (e.g., jurisprudence, ethics and the Arabic language) and knowledge which is not (e.g., philosophy). The second kind of knowledge can also be classified into

---

54 Cf. Osman Bakar, *Classification of Knowledge in Islam* (Cambridge: Islamic Texts Society, 1998).
55 Ashraf, *New Horizons*, 27–32.
56 Al-Ghazālī, *Incoherence of the Philosophers*.
57 Ashraf, *New Horizons*, 34–5.
58 A. H. M. I. M. Al-Ghazālī, *The Book of Knowledge* (*Kitāb al-ʿIlm*), trans. Nabih Amin Faris (Lahore: Sh. Muhammad Ashraf, 1962).

what is praiseworthy (e.g., medicine and arithmetic) and what is blameworthy (e.g., astrology and magic).[59]

On this view it is clear that not all branches of knowledge are of equal status, an idea which Professor Ashraf develops more explicitly. He argues that knowledge should not be acquired for its own sake but to transform the personality and develop people's morals, emotions and faith as well as their intellect, and that this implies a hierarchy of knowledge.[60] Spiritual knowledge has the highest priority, because this relates to a person's relationship with God and ultimate destiny. Knowledge of moral values is next in importance, as morals govern both individual and collective behaviour as well as the relationship between humans and the natural world. Next comes knowledge that disciplines the intellect, then knowledge that controls the human imagination, and finally knowledge that helps people gain control over their bodily senses. Professor Ashraf argues that education must work its way through the hierarchy in reverse order, but never lose sight of spiritual realisation as the final goal.

Islamic and Western Conceptions of Knowledge

Professor Ashraf argues that there is common ground between the ancient Greek and the Islamic concepts of knowledge. He says that in the Aristotelian tradition knowledge was seen as the understanding of reality and the causes of observable phenomena and hence as the means of getting closer to God,[61] and claims that "by Islamizing the Greek concept of good, and by reinterpreting their hierarchical scheme of knowledge," Muslim scholars were able to "give a certain pattern and order to education."[62] Even though (as we have seen) al-Ghazālī denounced the Muslim philosophers, he did not discard Greek knowledge or even the Greek concept of knowledge, but simply sought to make them Islamic by incorporating them into the Islamic framework.[63] The common ground which Professor Ashraf finds between Greek philosophy and Islam is still, he argues, to be found between Islam and the other great world religions today.[64]

However, he is emphatic that Muslims cannot compromise with secular beliefs and values.[65] This leads him to attack both positivism and secular humanism because these sideline the highest sources of authority in Islam, undermine the status of fundamental values, and deny the essentially spiritual nature of humanity by "their assumption that only those data are reliable

---

59 Ashraf, *New Horizons*, 32–3; cf. Wan Daud, *Educational Philosophy and Practice*, 241.
60 Ashraf, *New Horizons*, 39–40.
61 Ashraf, *New Horizons*, 7, 34.
62 Ashraf, *New Horizons*, 35–6.
63 Ashraf, *New Horizons*, 44, 60–61.
64 Ashraf, "Editorial: The Islamic Approach to Education," 2–3.
65 Ashraf, *New Horizons*, 11.

which are demonstratable."⁶⁶ The real problem with contemporary education, Professor Ashraf maintains, is that most disciplines (including not only the natural sciences, but history, sociology, economics and politics) are now being studied "without any reference to the ultimate principles of things or first or efficient causes, or universal and immutable values."⁶⁷ This puts Muslims in a difficult position: they cannot believe in the basic assumptions of Islamic culture and civilisation and at the same time accept the assumptions of modern western civilisation.⁶⁸ Professor Ashraf believes that the only answer is for Muslims to create Islamic schools of thought in all modern branches of knowledge.

The Islamization of knowledge

In an important paper delivered to the First World Conference on Muslim Education held at Mecca in 1977, al-Attas maintains that it is "confusion and error in knowledge" that is the ultimate cause of the contemporary problems facing Muslim society, including social injustice and inadequate leadership.⁶⁹ He argues that since knowledge exists *in minds* (things that exist *out there* being merely *objects of knowledge*) the nature of the knowledge depends on the spiritual, moral and intellectual qualities of the mind or soul which has received or created it.⁷⁰ Modern western knowledge is thus infused with western secular values, and is inappropriate for Muslims because of its secular associations. However, he maintains that "in the minds of good Muslims ... every bit of information [or] idea from any source whatsoever, can be Islamized or put in its right and proper place within the Islamic vision of truth and reality."⁷¹ Islamization is therefore a key process in countering the influence of western secularism and purging Muslim institutions of insidious western influences.

These then are the roots of the "Islamization of knowledge" thesis—a term said to have been coined by al-Attas,⁷² though it was shortly to be taken up by al-Faruqi and developed into a major scheme for the reconstruction of Muslim thought.⁷³ Professor Ashraf's view of the Islamization of knowledge thesis is ambivalent. On the one hand, he maintains that "if Muslim scholars can formulate religious substitutes for secular concepts for all branches of knowledge and can implement a proper system of education, that itself will be an eye-

---

66 Ashraf, *New Horizons*, 62–3.
67 Ashraf, *New Horizons*, 34–5.
68 Ashraf, *New Horizons*, 11.
69 Al-Attas, "Preliminary Thoughts on the Nature of Knowledge," 2–9.
70 Wan Daud, *Educational Philosophy and Practice*, 306.
71 Wan Daud, *Educational Philosophy and Practice*, 309.
72 Ashraf, "Editorial: The Islamic frame of Reference: (B) the Intellectual Dimension," 2; Yasien Mohamed, "Islamization of Knowledge: A Comparative Analysis of Faruqi and Rahman," *Muslim Education Quarterly* 11, no. 1 (1993): 27.
73 I. R. Al-Faruqi, *Islamization of Knowledge: General Principles and Workplan* (Washington: International Institute of Islamic Thought, 1982).

opener for modern society in the West."⁷⁴ On the other hand, he criticises the plan because it accepts western classifications of knowledge as unproblematic even though these are based on the western scientific worldview.⁷⁵ He also makes it clear that on his view what is involved is much more than Islamizing existing branches of knowledge or substituting secularist concepts with Islamic ones; these are only the first steps in countering the pervasive process of secularisation. More fundamental is learning how to "acquire knowledge in the real sense, of Matter, Mind, Spirit, Soul, God and the whole creation and their interrelationship."⁷⁶ This involves exploring the sources of knowledge established in Islam and the methodology followed by eminent Muslim thinkers. Al-Attas⁷⁷ argues that mastering the disciplines of the religious sciences (farḍ ʿayn) will naturally Islamize the disciplines of philosophy and the human sciences (farḍ kifāyah). Other critical discussions of the "Islamization of knowledge" thesis are found in Ali,⁷⁸ Bugaje,⁷⁹ Choudhury,⁸⁰ Dzilo,⁸¹ Maiwada,⁸² Mohammed,⁸³ Rahman⁸⁴ and Shafiq.⁸⁵

Knowledge and Education

Professor Ashraf defines Islamic education as

> an education which trains the sensibility of pupils in such a manner that in their ... approach to all kinds of knowledge they are governed by the deeply felt ethical values of Islam. They are trained and men-

---

74 Ashraf, *New Horizons*, 20.
75 Ashraf, "Editorial: The Islamic frame of Reference: (B) the Intellectual Dimension," 2.
76 Ashraf, "Editorial: The Islamic frame of Reference: (B) the Intellectual Dimension," 2; cf. Ashraf, *New Horizons*, 12.
77 S. M. N. Al-Attas, "Introduction," in *Aims and Objectives of Islamic Education*, ed. S. M. N. al-Attas (London: Hodder & Stoughton and Jeddah: King Abdulaziz University, 1979), 8–10.
78 Mohammad Mumtaz Ali, "Reconstruction of Islamic Thought and Civilisation: the case of Islamization of knowledge," *American Journal of Islamic Social Sciences* 16, no. 1 (1999).
79 U. Bugaje, "Contemporary Muslim Response to the Challenge of Knowledge: separating the grain from the chaff," *Encounters: Journal of Inter-Cultural Perspectives* 2, no. 1 (1996).
80 Masudul Alam Choudhury, "A Critical Examination of the Concept of Islamization of Knowledge in Contemporary Times," *Muslim Education Quarterly* 10, no. 4 (1993).
81 Hasan Dzilo, "The Concept of 'Islamization of Knowledge' and its Philosophical Implications," *Islam and Christian-Muslim Relations* 23, no. 2 (2012). DOI:10.1080/09596410.2012.676779
82 Danjuma A. Maiwada, "Islamization of Knowledge: Background and Scope," *American Journal of Islamic Social Sciences* 14, no. 2 (1997).
83 Yasien Mohamed, "Islamization: A Revivalist Response to Modernity," *Muslim Education Quarterly* 10, no. 2 (1993); Mohamed, "Islamization of Knowledge."
84 Fazlur Rahman, "Islamization of Knowledge: A Response," *American Journal of Islamic Social Sciences* 5, no. 1 (1988).
85 S. Shafiq, "Islamization of Knowledge: Philosophy and Methodology and Analysis of the Views and Ideas of Ismaʿil R. al-Faruqi, S. Hossein Nasr and Fazlur Rahman," *Hamdard Islamicus* 18, 3 (1995): 63-75.

tally so disciplined that they want to acquire knowledge not merely to satisfy an intellectual curiosity or just for material worldly benefit but to grow up as rational, righteous beings and to bring about the spiritual, moral and physical welfare of their families, their people and mankind. Their attitude derives from a deep faith in God and a wholehearted acceptance of a God-given moral code."[86]

The goals of education are laid down by revealed religion and therefore have an objective quality; they do not vary according to individual opinion or experience. It follows therefore that the curriculum should be designed in accordance with the Islamic understanding of the nature of knowledge and the nature of man, especially his spiritual nature. It is for this reason, as we have already seen, that Professor Ashraf argued strongly at the First and Second World Conferences on Muslim Education for the reclassification of knowledge into (a) "perennial" or divinely revealed knowledge and (b) "acquired" knowledge (i.e., knowledge derived from reason, which is only recognised if it is consistent with perennial knowledge), and for the integration of these into a unified Islamic curriculum.[87]

Professor Ashraf stresses that religious teaching must be brought to life for children of all ages. This involves encouraging students to "think for themselves about religion,"[88] so that they know how to resist irreligious ideas and know how to put their religious knowledge to use in contemporary life. However, he rejects the need for encouraging children to engage in critical questioning of everything, including the Qurʾān. Similarly, he rejects the need for the scientific verification of everything on the basis of empirical evidence, which he says makes individuals their own authority as they seek to critically evaluate all knowledge.[89] The logic of his position requires taking the Qurʾān and Sunnah as foundational truths, and aiming to use education to develop the intellect on the basis of these spiritual truths and moral values. He further maintains that this kind of education "is good for both the Muslims and the non-Muslims."[90]

These values also have an important impact on the role of the teacher. Teachers have a double responsibility towards their students. First, they are a source of authority in relation to knowledge and have a responsibility to use this authority to train their students' personality, strengthen their faith in God and guide their spiritual and moral development, as well as to develop their intellectual powers. Second, they have to set an example to their stu-

---

86 Syed Sajjad Husain and Syed Ali Ashraf, eds., *Crisis in Muslim Education* (London: Hodder & Stoughton, 1979), 1.
87 Ashraf, *New Horizons*, 26, 56, 104, 110.
88 Ashraf, *New Horizons*, 42.
89 Ashraf, *New Horizons*, 76.
90 Ashraf, "Editorial: The Islamic Approach to Education," 9.

dents through their character, conduct and faith in God. It is much more important for teachers to exemplify spiritual and moral values than for them to exemplify intellectual prowess and a spirit of critical enquiry.[91]

Critical Discussion

The purpose of this section is first to examine the coherence of the view of knowledge expounded above from the perspective of western foundationalist epistemologies (including empiricism, positivism and rationalism), and second to consider whether the approach to education to which it gives rise is in any way compatible with western approaches to education. This discussion clearly has practical implications for the recognition of Islamic education as a viable alternative to the dominant forms of liberal education that are found in western societies, but these implications are not explored here. The chapter will conclude with an examination of the possibility of continuing dialogue between Islam and contemporary western traditions within the philosophy of knowledge.[92]

Definition of Knowledge

To define knowledge as "the acquisition of certainty" is immediately problematic from a foundationalist perspective, the more so when this certainty is a matter of religious belief. Sometimes 'certainty' refers to the strength of one's personal conviction, but as Wittgenstein points out, "One does not infer how things are from one's own certainty."[93] Outside the realm of pure mathematics (where the proofs of theorems may be conclusive) it is often argued that there are no objective, demonstrable certainties.[94] Of the three sources of certainty which Professor Ashraf describes, the first, authority, is of doubtful value, because even the most authoritative person may be wrong. White argues that "there are no moral experts on the good life,"[95] and most liberal educationalists would agree that growth to adulthood should be marked out by an increasingly critical and reflective attitude to tradition and authority. The second source of certainty, sensory experience and logical thinking, is also problematic. If certainty implies that there is no possibility of being wrong, then it is clear that it cannot be achieved either by sense impressions or by reasoning. As far as sense impressions are concerned, we might make mistakes, we might imagine things that are not true, we might be under a continuous illusion; the most we can hope to achieve are plausible conjectures or highly probable hy-

---

91 Ashraf, *New Horizons*, 74–78.
92 Cf. Norazmi Anas et al., "The Integration of Knowledge in Islam: Concept and Challenges," *Global Journal of Human Social Science* 13, no. 10 (2013): 51–55.
93 Ludwig Wittgenstein, *On Certainty* (Oxford: Blackwell, 1975), 6.
94 Cf. A. J. Ayer, *The Problem of Knowledge* (Harmondsworth: Penguin, 1956).
95 Patricia White, *Beyond Domination: an essay in the Political Philosophy of Education* (London: Routledge & Kegan Paul, 1983), 10.

potheses. As far as reasoning is concerned, pure reason produces only abstract truths, not truths about states of affairs in the world; in combination with sense impressions it also provides a way of critically examining beliefs and identifying mistakes. But once the principle of critically examining beliefs is accepted, it is difficult to maintain, as does Professor Ashraf, that some beliefs (notably religious ones) should remain immune to such criticism; yet of course if they are subjected to rational critical investigation, their certainty may be eroded.

As for the third source of certainty, direct experience of the soul, it is not clear what this means or how it is to be distinguished from illusion. Phillips and Burbules[96] tell the story of a woman who appeared on a television documentary about the recovery of memories of childhood events. The woman was in a trance-like condition as she recalled that, as a fertilised ovum, she had been trapped in her mother's fallopian tube for a short period. The recollection was cathartic for her and the validity of the memory was enthusiastically endorsed by the therapist and other members of the therapy group. It seems clear that the event was a valid experience for her (perhaps a "direct experience of the soul") which relieved her longstanding trauma, but the facts on which it was based (both the trapped ovum and her recollection of it) seem literally unknowable, and hence it seems unavoidable that any objective assessment would dismiss the whole event as an illusion.

Sources of Knowledge

It is clear, as we have seen, that from the perspective of both empiricism and western rationalism, the sources of knowledge which Professor Ashraf discusses do not guarantee the kind of certainty which he claims. However, Popper brings a different perspective to the question of the sources of knowledge. He argues that philosophers who attempt to demonstrate the reliability of a knowledge claim by pointing to the secure foundation on which the claim is based are on the wrong track. "The proper epistemological question is not one about sources," he maintains; "rather, we ask whether the assertion made is true—that is to say, whether it agrees with the facts."[97] On this view, knowledge is conjectural; even though it is based on the best available evidence, it must be held provisionally and must be open to revision when new evidence comes to light which challenges its reliability.

As we have seen, Professor Ashraf's approach to what he calls "acquired knowledge" has something in common with this view. He sees acquired knowledge as susceptible to development and variation in the light of new evidence. But whereas Popper would not distinguish between revealed and acquired

---

[96] D. C. Phillips and Nicholas C. Burbules, *Postpositivism and Educational Research* (Lanham, MD: Rowman & Littlefield, 2000), 38–40.

[97] Karl Popper, *Conjectures and Refutations: The Growth of Scientific Knowledge* (New York: Basic, 1965), 27.

knowledge, but would expect both equally to be subject to the challenges of critical investigation and revision when new information comes to light, Professor Ashraf wishes first to make an exception of "revealed knowledge" and second to bring "acquired knowledge" into line with "revealed knowledge" through the process of Islamization. This means in effect that "acquired knowledge" is not open to free critical debate or to radical challenge or change as a result of testing the assertion or examining its consequences or revising it in the light of new evidence, except within the bounds predefined by religion. The effect of this is to play down the importance of certain skills within education, such as questioning, verifying, criticising, evaluating and making judgments, in favour of the uncritical acceptance of authority.

The Nature and Classification of Knowledge

In terms of all western foundationalist epistemologies, the division of knowledge into "revealed knowledge" and "acquired knowledge" is extremely problematical. The first problem is whether "revealed knowledge" comes under the category of knowledge at all. The second problem is whether "revealed knowledge" deserves the special status which it is accorded within the Islamic concept of knowledge. Let us look at each of these more closely.

If knowledge is defined as true belief for which there is adequate evidence (as A. J. Ayer, for example, proposes), then it is hard to see how "revealed knowledge" comes under the category of 'knowledge' at all. Indeed, from a foundationalist perspective it would be considered inappropriate to claim to 'know' that God exists since there is no agreement as to what kind of evidence would verify or refute such a claim. Ultimately, Muslims claim to find such evidence in 'intuition', which is considered to be an aspect of the spiritual capacity of the human intellect or soul.[98] But this terminology is imprecise and impossible to conceptualise with any clarity, and it is difficult to find any objective criteria that can be used to settle the matter when the truth claims or 'intuitions' of Islam come into conflict with the truth claims or 'intuitions' of other religions or world views. It emerges that Muslims are classifying as 'knowledge' something which western philosophers would classify as 'belief.' (Similarly, Muslims classify as 'ignorance' something which western philosophers would simply call a different belief.)[99] The use of the term 'knowledge' in this case draws attention to the strength and importance and centrality of the belief in the Islamic worldview, but conceptually (from a rationalist perspective) it remains a 'belief' because of the absence of objective evidence. Al-Attas[100] concedes that in Islam the concept of knowledge includes faith and belief, and justifies this, as we have seen, by claiming that true beliefs are not

---

98 Wan Daud, *Educational Philosophy and Practice*, 105–6.
99 Cf. Wan Mohd Nor Wan Daud, *The Concept of Knowledge in Islam and its Implications for Education in a Developing Country* (New York: Mansell, 1989), 78–9.
100 Al-Attas, "Preliminary Thoughts on the Nature of Knowledge," 33.

just propositional but may also be intuitional, but he does not explore the logical difficulties implicit in this view—that in a situation of conflicting 'beliefs' there are no objective grounds for prioritising one set of intuitions over the others.

The Muslim view of "revealed knowledge" as the best form of knowledge adds further conceptual problems, since from a rationalist perspective this is tantamount to elevating 'belief' to a higher status than 'knowledge.' The process of "Islamization" involves bringing 'knowledge' (i.e., belief for which there is adequate evidence to justify universal acceptance) into line with 'belief' (i.e., belief for which there is inadequate evidence to justify universal acceptance), and from a rationalist perspective this is topsy-turvy. The dominance of "revealed knowledge" also has a crucial impact on critical openness and free critical debate, which in western liberalism are seen as the best ways of advancing the pursuit of truth. In Islam, critical openness is only meaningful among those who share a commitment to the fundamental truths revealed by God, and academic freedom is restricted by the need to pursue agreed goals in line with Islamic principles. There is no space for the autonomy of the subject or discipline as understood in the West, because nothing exists outside religion. Muslims can never be free to pursue their research wherever it leads, irrespective of religious considerations, because they must always be guided by religion, and if they go astray others have the responsibility to bring them back to the right path.

Knowledge and Education

The kind of education which is based on the Islamic concept of knowledge as expounded by Professor Ashraf is inevitably open to accusations of indoctrination from a foundationalist perspective. Indoctrination is a complex concept, but it is commonly applied to any school which has "the intention of committing children to a set of beliefs."[101] particularly if the aim is to make the beliefs unshakeable ones[102] and if they are beliefs of a restricted number of people where the restriction follows from their inability "to provide publicly acceptable evidence for their truth."[103] It is sometimes argued that indoctrination may occur unintentionally, if teachers take for granted certain beliefs in their teaching[104] or speak of their beliefs with a particular "emotional warmth."[105] What makes indoctrination immoral on a western perspective is

---

101 Robin Barrow, *The Philosophy of Schooling* (Brighton: Harvester, 1981), 150.
102 J. P. White, "Indoctrination," in *The Concept of Education*, ed. R. S. Peters (London: Routledge & Kegan Paul, 1967), 189; Antony Flew, "Indoctrination and Religion," in *Concepts of Indoctrination*, ed. I. A. Snook (London: Routledge and Kegan Paul, 1972), 75.
103 James Gribble. *Introduction to Philosophy of Education* (Boston: Allyn & Bacon, 1969), 34.
104 White, "Indoctrination," 189.
105 Edwin Cox, *Problems and Possibilities for Religious Education* (London: Hodder & Stoughton, 1983), 65.

that it implies a lack of respect for persons by denying them "independence and control over their own lives."[106]

On all these counts, the Islamic education proposed by Professor Ashraf is a model case of indoctrination, since the purpose of such education is first and foremost to inculcate belief in Islamic doctrines. Even if we try to soften this conclusion by arguing (as I have done elsewhere: cf. Halstead[107]) that the purpose of Islamic education is to encourage belief not enforce it (it is in any case a central Islamic belief that there is no compulsion in religion[108]) and to offer guidance to children until they are old enough to make up their own minds, it remains the case that teaching belief as if it were the most important kind of knowledge is likely to predispose children to accept it without question.

Conclusion

Professor Ashraf has performed a great service in setting out a clear and unambiguous if uncompromising statement of Islamic principles in relation to the concepts of knowledge and education. His statement maintains the purity of the Islamic perspective and draws on central Islamic traditions which can be traced back to the earliest days of Islam. As we have seen, he argues that Muslims can never compromise with secular beliefs and values or try to combine belief in the basic assumptions of Islamic culture and civilisation with belief in the assumptions of modern western civilisation.[109] He also condemns as "absolutely wrong" those who argue that *new* values and principles should be derived from the *Sunnah* to replace the current rather 'dated' ones and help Muslims to respond to the needs and challenges which they face in the contemporary world.[110] However, as we have seen, the epistemological framework which Professor Ashraf espouses, with the priority it gives to a form of knowledge that transcends human rationality and the senses, is deeply opposed (and perhaps even found incoherent) by western philosophers working in the equally uncompromising positivist and rationalist traditions.

It is hard to avoid the conclusion that the huge gulf that exists between Islamic and western foundationalist conceptions of knowledge is "ultimately unbridgeable."[111] A number of Muslim scholars besides Professor Ashraf have recognised the impossibility of compromise. Al-Attas writes that "there exist such profound and absolute differences between Islam and western cul-

---

106 John Kleinig, *Philosophical Issues in Education* (London: Croom Helm, 1982), 65.
107 Cf. J. Mark Halstead, *The Case for Muslim Voluntary-Aided Schools: Some Philosophical Reflections* (Cambridge: Islamic Academy, 1986), 27–9.
108 Qurʾān 2:256.
109 Ashraf, *New Horizons*, 11; Ashraf, "Editorial: The Islamic Frame of Reference: The Intellectual Dimension II—the Methodology," 7.
110 Ashraf, "Editorial: The Islamic Frame of Reference: The Intellectual Dimension II—the Methodology," 2–3.
111 Seyyed Hussein Nasr, quoted in Eaton, "'Knowledge and the Sacred,'" 144.

ture that they cannot be reconciled."¹¹² Safi writes rather more wistfully of the need to "understand why the revealed secures the respect of the intelligentsia in one religious tradition while it becomes a source of embarrassment in another."¹¹³

All this makes life difficult for Muslims living in the West (and for Muslims in Muslim countries whose education is based on western epistemologies—though I do not have space to deal with their case here), and equally difficult for western authorities searching for a form of education which is appropriate for their Muslim minorities. If Muslims live as citizens in the West, they are living in a society where the split between the secular and the religious is regarded as fundamental; yet to treat the former as a public and the latter as a private matter offends against the cherished Muslim belief in the unity of knowledge (*tawḥīd*) and the centrality of religion. Muslims are dependent on the explosion of western knowledge because of the comparative intellectual stagnation in the Muslim world,¹¹⁴ but if they allow their children to receive an education based on western epistemology, they must wave goodbye to any hope of restoring to divine revelation the "authority to furnish the ontological and ethical foundations" of all other areas of knowledge.¹¹⁵ However, if Muslims in the West seek to insulate themselves from the broader society, this means that they are unable to enjoy full citizenship and unable to influence the way that western society develops; yet they may feel that they have much to contribute here, particularly in the spiritual and moral domain and in restoring a sense of the sacred in everyday life.¹¹⁶

But let us not end on too pessimistic a note. I have argued elsewhere that the education of Muslim minorities in the West should be made up of three components.¹¹⁷ The first is education for cultural identity, the second education for democratic citizenship and the third education for cross-cultural understanding. Education for cultural identity would allow for Muslims to be taught the beliefs and values of their community (both the local minor-

---

112 Quoted in Wan Daud, *Educational Philosophy and Practice*, 72.
113 L. M. Safi, "Towards an Islamic Theory of Knowledge," *Islamic Studies* 36, no. 1 (1997): 50.
114 U. Bugaje, "Contemporary Muslim Response to the Challenge of Knowledge: separating the grain from the chaff," *Encounters: Journal of Inter-Cultural Perspectives* 2, no. 1 (1996), 58.
115 Safi, "Towards an Islamic Theory of Knowledge," 39.
116 Seyyed Hossein Nasr, *The Need for a Sacred Science* (New York: State University of New York Press, 1993).
117 J. Mark Halstead, "Voluntary Apartheid? Problems of Schooling for Religious and Other Minorities in Democratic Societies," *Journal of Philosophy of Education* 29, no. 2 (1995); J. Mark Halstead, "Schooling and Cultural Maintenance for Religious Minorities in the Liberal State," in *Citizenship and Education in Liberal-Democratic Societies: Teaching for Cosmopolitan Values and Collective Identities*, ed. Kevin McDonough & Walter Feinberg (Oxford: Oxford University Press, 2003). DOI 10.1093/0199253668.003.0011

ity community and the worldwide community of believers) and to be initiated into their religious and moral practices. Education for democratic citizenship would enable them to understand the political beliefs and values of the state in which they live and enter fully into the rights and responsibilities of citizenship. Education for cross-cultural understanding would encourage understanding of, tolerance and respect for, and dialogue with, other groups in culturally diverse societies. Each of these components has epistemological implications.

Education for Islamic cultural identity will only make sense if it is based on a consistent Islamic epistemology. Islamic identity cannot be preserved unless children receive an education based on a strong theoretical foundation including knowledge of the spiritual dimensions of life and of their religious and moral duties as Muslims. The work of Professor Ashraf and others in clarifying the Islamic concept of knowledge is of vital importance here.

Education for citizenship, on the other hand, requires Muslims to have some familiarity with dominant forms of western epistemology. If their Islamic identity represents, as it were, the mother tongue of Muslims living in the West, then citizenship is the second language in which they must become fluent if they are to enjoy the privileges of citizenship and lead successful lives in the broader society in which they live (just as, according to the Qurʾān, the Prophet Yusuf rose to prominence in a society which did not share his beliefs and values).

Education for cross-cultural understanding involves, among other things, a willingness to learn about and engage in dialogue with other groups, in order to achieve some degree of understanding of their position. Professor Ashraf was active for many years in promoting dialogue between religions through the many seminars he organised at Cambridge, and he even went out of his way to encourage dialogue with faith groups which currently do not enjoy a high standing in the West (such as the Scientologists and the Unification Church). It is possible that dialogue with other epistemological approaches may be similarly worthwhile and productive. Professor Ashraf sometimes gives the impression that he views western epistemology as a single undifferentiated mass of secular ideas opposed to Islam, but of course this would be an oversimplification. I want to argue in conclusion that Muslims may find significant grounds for dialogue with traditions of epistemology other than empiricism, positivism and rationalism—particularly continental and other non-foundationalist philosophies.

Al-Zeera has led the way with her ground-breaking discussion of interpretive and constructivist approaches to knowledge and her support for naturalistic methods of enquiry such as phenomenology, hermeneutics, heuristics and narrative enquiry, which she argues are appropriate within an Islamic framework for "the production of Islamic knowledge."[118] She appears to use the latter term to mean roughly what Professor Ashraf calls "acquired knowledge," though like him she argues that all knowledge must be constructed in line with Islamic principles in order to give it the necessary wholeness. There is plenty of other fertile ground for dialogue between Muslims and European philosophers, including Fichte's emphasis on the unity of knowledge and his belief that striving towards unification with God is the ultimate explanation for all knowledge and action;[119] Hegel's view that the philosopher is not so much an active judge of truth as a passive follower who allows the truth to unfold itself to him;[120] Schopenhauer's discussion of intuitive knowledge;[121] and Buber's distinction between the realms of I-Thou (a direct form of knowing through a relationship with God) and I-It (an indirect and symbolic form of knowing).[122] Even among philosophers whose work lacks a religious content, it is possible for Muslims to find stimulating ideas like Derrida's most famous aphorism "There is nothing outside the text," which has a remarkably Islamic ring to it.[123] It is not impossible that, through creative interaction with philosophers such as these, Muslims may find new ways, more accessible to western thought, of expressing the fundamental, unchanging principles and essential values of Islam which Professor Ashraf has expounded so clearly from a Muslim perspective.

---

118 Zahra Al-Zeera, *Wholeness and Holiness in education: an Islamic Perspective* (Herndon, VA International Institute of Islamic Thought, 2001), 104.
119 Johann Gottlieb Fichte, *Samtliche Werke*, Vol. 1 (Berlin: Walter de Gruyter, 1971).
120 Georg W. F. Hegel, *Phenomenology of Spirit*, trans. A. V. Miller (Oxford: Oxford University Press, 1977).
121 Arthur Schopenhauer, *The World as Will and Representation*, Vol. 1 (New York: Dover, 1969).
122 Martin Buber, *I and Thou* (New York: Charles Scribner's Sons, 1958); Martin Buber, *The Knowledge of Man: A Philosophy of the Interhuman* (Atlantic Highlands, NJ: Humanities Press International, 1988).
123 Jacques Derrida, *Writing and Difference* (Chicago: University of Chicago Press, 1967).

Bibliography

Ali, Mohammad Mumtaz. "Reconstruction of Islamic Thought and Civilisation: the case of Islamization of knowledge." *American Journal of Islamic Social Sciences* 16, no. 1 (1999): 99–109.

Anas, Norazmi, Ahmad Z. E. Alwi, Mohd. H. H. Razali, Roose N. Subki and Nor A. A. Bakar. "The Integration of Knowledge in Islam: Concept and Challenges," *Global Journal of Human Social Science* 13, no. 10 (2013): 51–55.

Ashraf, Syed Ali. *New Horizons in Muslim Education*. London: Hodder & Stoughton, and Cambridge: The Islamic Academy, 1985.

Ashraf, Syed Ali. "The Islamic Concept of Knowledge." Unpublished paper presented to a meeting of the Philosophy of Education Society at Homerton College, Cambridge, 1986.

Ashraf, Syed Ali. "Editorial: The Islamic Approach to Education and the National Curriculum," *Muslim Education Quarterly* 6, no. 4 (1988): 1–6.

Ashraf, Syed Ali. "Editorial: Islamisation of Education: Need for the Islamic frame of Reference," *Muslim Education Quarterly* 6, no. 3 (1989): 1–6.

Ashraf, Syed Ali. "Editorial: Islamisation of Education: The Islamic Frame of Reference II," *Muslim Education Quarterly* 6, no. 4 (1989): 1–6.

Ashraf, Syed Ali. "Editorial: The Islamic frame of Reference: (B) the Intellectual Dimension," *Muslim Education Quarterly* 7, no. 1 (1989): 1–8.

Ashraf, Syed Ali. "Editorial: The Islamic Frame of Reference: The Intellectual Dimension II," *Muslim Education Quarterly* 7, no. 2 (1990): 1–3.

Ashraf, Syed Ali. "Editorial: The Islamic Frame of Reference: The Intellectual Dimension II—the Methodology," *Muslim Education Quarterly* 7, no. 3 (1990): 1–7.

Al-Attas, Syed M. N. "Introduction." In *Aims and Objectives of Islamic Education*, edited by Syed M. N. al-Attas, 1–15. London: Hodder & Stoughton and Jeddah: King Abdulaziz University, 1979.

Al-Attas, Syed M. N. "Preliminary Thoughts on the Nature of Knowledge and the Definition and Aims of Education." In *Aims and Objectives of Islamic Education*, edited by Syed M. N. al-Attas, 19–47. London: Hodder & Stoughton and Jeddah: King Abdulaziz University, 1979.

Al-Attas, Syed M. N. *The Concept of Education in Islam: A Framework for an Islamic Philosophy of Education*. Kuala Lumpur: Muslim Youth Movement of Malaysia, 1980.

Al-Attas, Syed M. N. *A Commentary on the Hujjat al-Siddiq of Nur al-Din al-Raniri*. Kuala Lumpur: Ministry of Culture, 1986.

Al-Attas, Syed M. N. *Islam and the Philosophy of Science*. Kuala Lumpur: International Institute of Islamic Thought and Civilisation, 1989.

Ayer, A. J. *The Problem of Knowledge*. Harmondsworth: Penguin, 1956.

Bakar, Osman. "The Meaning and Significance of Doubt in al-Ghazzali's Philosophy," *The Islamic Quarterly* 30, no. 1 (1986): 31–44.

Bakar, Osman. *Classification of Knowledge in Islam*. Cambridge: Islamic Texts Society, 1998.

Barrow, Robin. *The Philosophy of Schooling*. Brighton: Harvester, 1981.

Buber, Martin. *I and Thou*. New York: Charles Scribner's Sons, 1958.

Buber, Martin. *The Knowledge of Man: A Philosophy of the Interhuman*. Atlantic Highlands, NJ: Humanities Press International, 1988.

Bugaje, U. "Contemporary Muslim Response to the Challenge of Knowledge: separating the grain from the chaff," *Encounters: Journal of Inter-Cultural Perspectives* 2, no. 1 (1996): 43–69.

Choudhury, Masudul Alam. "A Critical Examination of the Concept of Islamization of Knowledge in Contemporary Times," *Muslim Education Quarterly* 10, no. 4 (1993): 3–34.

Cox, Edwin. *Problems and Possibilities for Religious Education*. London: Hodder & Stoughton, 1983.

Derrida, Jacques. *Writing and Difference*. Chicago: University of Chicago Press, 1967.

Dzilo, Hasan. "The Concept of 'Islamization of Knowledge' and its Philosophical Implications," *Islam and Christian-Muslim Relations* 23, no. 2 (2012): 247–256. DOI:10.1080/09596410.2012.676779.

Eaton, Hasan Gai. "'Knowledge and the Sacred': reflections on Seyyed Hossein Nasr's Gifford Lectures," *The Islamic Quarterly* 26, no. 3 (1982): 138–148.

Al-Faruqi, I. R. *Islamization of Knowledge: General Principles and Workplan*. Washington: International Institute of Islamic Thought, 1982.

Fichte, Johann Gottlieb. *Samtliche Werke*, Vol 1. Berlin: Walter de Gruyter, 1971.

Flew, Antony. "Indoctrination and Religion." In *Concepts of Indoctrination*, edited by I. A. Snook, 82–90. London: Routledge and Kegan Paul, 1972.

Al-Ghazālī, A. H. M. I. M. *The Book of Knowledge* (*Kitāb al-ʿIlm*). Translated by Nabih Amin Faris. Lahore: Sh. Muhammad Ashraf, 1962.

Al-Ghazālī, A. H. M. I. M. *Incoherence of the Philosophers* (*Tahāfut al-Falāsifah*). Translated by Sabih Ahmad Kamali. Lahore: Pakistan Philosophical Congress, 1963.

Gribble, James. *Introduction to Philosophy of Education*. Boston: Allyn & Bacon, 1969.

Halstead, J. Mark. *The Case for Muslim Voluntary-Aided Schools: Some Philosophical Reflections*. Cambridge: Islamic Academy, 1986.

Halstead, J. Mark. "Voluntary Apartheid? Problems of Schooling for Religious and Other Minorities in Democratic Societies," *Journal of Philosophy of Education* 29, no. 2 (1995): 257–272.

Halstead, J. Mark. "Schooling and Cultural Maintenance for Religious Minorities in the Liberal State." In *Citizenship and Education in Liberal-Democratic Societies: Teaching for Cosmopolitan Values and Collective Identities*, edited by Kevin McDonough & Walter Feinberg, 273–296. Oxford: Oxford University Press, 2003.

Hegel, G. W. F. *Phenomenology of Spirit*. Translated by A. V. Miller. Oxford: Oxford University Press, 1977.

Husain, Syed Sajjad, and Syed Ali Ashraf, eds. *Crisis in Muslim Education*. London: Hodder & Stoughton, 1979.

Ibn Khaldun. *Muqaddimah*. Translated by Franz Rosenthal, Vol. 3. Princeton, NJ: Princeton University Press, 1967.

Kartanegara, Mulyadhi. *Essentials of Islamic Epistemology: A Philosophical Inquiry into the Foundation of Knowledge*. Brunei Darussalam: UBD press, 2014.

Kleinig, John. *Philosophical Issues in Education*. London: Croom Helm, 1982.

Maiwada, Danjuma A. "Islamization of Knowledge: Background and Scope." *American Journal of Islamic Social Sciences* 14, no. 2 (1997): 275–282.

Mohamed, Yasien. "Islamization: A Revivalist Response to Modernity." *Muslim Education Quarterly* 10, no. 2 (1993): 12–27.

Mohamed, Yasien. "Islamization of Knowledge: A Comparative Analysis of Faruqi and Rahman." *Muslim Education Quarterly* 11, no. 1 (1993): 27–40.

Nasr, Seyyed Hossein. *The Need for a Sacred Science*. New York: State University of New York Press, 1993.

Phillips, D. C., and Nicholas C. Burbules. *Postpositivism and Educational Research*. Lanham, MD: Rowman & Littlefield, 2000.

Popper, Karl. *Conjectures and Refutations: The Growth of Scientific Knowledge*. New York: Basic, 1962.

Rahman, Fazlur. "Islamization of Knowledge: A Response." *American Journal of Islamic Social Sciences* 5, no. 1 (1988): 3–11.

Rosenthal, Franz. "Muslim Definitions of Knowledge." In *The Conflict of Traditionalism and Modernism in the Muslim Middle East*, edited by Carl Leiden, 117–133. Austin: University of Texas Press, 1966.

Rosenthal, Franz. (1970) *Knowledge Triumphant: The Concept of Knowledge in Medieval Islam* (Leiden: E. J. Brill).

Safi, L. M. "Towards an Islamic Theory of Knowledge," *Islamic Studies* 36, no. 1 (1997): 39–56.

Schopenhauer, Arthur. *The World as Will and Representation*, Vol. 1. New York: Dover, 1969.

Shafiq, S. "Islamization of Knowledge: Philosophy and Methodology and Analysis of the Views and Ideas of Isma'il R. al-Faruqi, S. Hossein Nasr and Fazlur Rahman." *Hamdard Islamicus* 18, 3 (1995): 63–75.

Taftazani, Abul-Wafa al-Ghuneimi. "Islamic Education: its principles and aims," *Muslim Education Quarterly* 4, no. 1 (1986): 66–74.

Wan Daud, Wan Mohd Nor. *The Concept of Knowledge in Islam and its Implications for Education in a Developing Country*. New York: Mansell, 1989.

White, J. P. "Indoctrination." In *The Concept of Education*, edited by R. S. Peters, 177–191. London: Routledge & Kegan Paul, 1967.

White, Patricia. *Beyond Domination: An Essay in the Political Philosophy of Education*. London: Routledge & Kegan Paul, 1983.

Wittgenstein, Ludwig. *On Certainty*. Oxford: Blackwell, 1975.

Zeera, Zahra. *Wholeness and Holiness in Education: An Islamic Perspective*. Herndon, VA: International Institute of Islamic Thought, 2001.

Chapter 7

Poems of Syed Ali Ashraf[1]

Syed Ali Ahsan

Like all forms of art, poetry serves as a powerful medium for human reactions and responses. Every aspect of life—be it a situation, a behaviour, or a scenic view—evokes a unique response within our minds. The reception of visual and auditory stimuli, as well as contemplation of written words, fuels our emotional reactions and thoughts. We endeavour to shape these reactions in diverse ways, channelling them through the medium of song, painting, sculpture, architecture, and poetry. An architect, too, is an artist in their own right; they craft artistry in the form of buildings. An architect's canvas is an empty space, and they employ construction techniques to bring their artistic vision to life. Through a delicate balance of interior and exterior spaces, and by employing unique methodologies, they transform emptiness into a tangible architectural design. The architect's mind is deeply influenced by the surrounding environment and its historical context, all of which find expression in the architectural blueprint. Similarly, painting is a means of beautifying life. Through the skilled use of sketches and colours, painters translate their visions and beliefs onto the canvas. The vibrant ambiance created by the sun's rays caressing the Earth's objects finds its reflection in the artist's paintings. In the same vein, music and sculpture can also be described as arts of reflection. Musicians convert the full spectrum of human emotions into a myriad of audible vibrations, creating profound reactions in their audience. Sculptors mould and carve three-dimensional materials into lifelike forms, infusing them with a sense of consciousness and vitality. These artistic expressions are the results of human reactions to the world around us, transformed into beautiful and meaningful works of art.

Observation stands as the foundational pillar in the creation of poetry. The poet relishes savouring the sweetness that comes from observing his desires,

---

1 Translated by the Editor from the original Bengali version: Syed Ali Ahsan, "Syed Ali Ashrafer Kôbita," in *Syed Ali Ashrafer Kôbita* by Syed Ali Ashraf (Dhaka: Shilpotoru Prokashôni, 1991), 9–18.

emotions, pain, and moments of leisure. Nonetheless, it is an undeniable truth that no single observer can encapsulate the entirety of our vast world within their purview. Furthermore, amidst the whimsical meanderings of a poet's creative endeavours, how much of any subject can they truly apprehend? Thus, there exists an inherent limitation to the scope of what can be observed and subsequently transmuted into verse. The compendium of observations gathered by a Bengali poet will invariably differ from those of a poet dwelling in the arid expanse of the Sahara Desert. Similarly, it will diverge from the perceptual realm of an English poet.

Yet, when a poet wields the power of keen observation, what facets of an object do they perceive, or what essences do they uncover? Do they scrutinize the kaleidoscope of colours, or do they delve into the resonating vibrations that emanate from the inner depths of the objects themselves? In the multifarious observations of distinct poets, a solitary object takes on myriad forms—sometimes in its contours, at other times in its vivid chromatic tapestry, occasionally as a vessel for emotions, and sometimes simply as an object of aesthetic pleasure.

In all similitudes of the Holy Qurʾān, I witness the unquestionable and profoundly remarkable portrayal of the multifaceted tapestry of human experience. Those who have chosen to embrace delusion, rather than being steered towards the path of honesty, are likened to individuals such as:

> Their example is that of one who kindled a fire, but when it illuminated what was around him, Allah took away their light and left them in darkness [so] they could not see. (Qurʾān 2:17, trans. *Saheeh International*)

Continuous darkness gradually becomes tolerable to the eyes, but when a sudden intense burst of light illuminates everything only to be extinguished abruptly, the subsequent darkness feels exceedingly deep and profound to the eyes. In this comparison, we witness the depiction of the image of that profound and absolute darkness.

Here is another similitude:

> Or [it is] like a rainstorm from the sky within which is darkness, thunder and lightning. They put their fingers in their ears against the thunderclaps in dread of death. But Allah is encompassing of the disbelievers. The lightning almost snatches away their sight. Every time it lights [the way] for them, they walk therein; but when darkness comes over them, they stand [still]. And if Allah had willed, He could have taken away their hearing and their sight. Indeed, Allah is over all things competent. (Qurʾān 2:19–20, trans. *Saheeh International*)

In the above comparison, the significance of experience has been elevated by rendering it readily discernible.

Throughout history, poets have endeavoured to illuminate the realm of human experiences and allow the warmth of those experiences to flow through their readers. Some have achieved remarkable success in this endeavour. We are endeavoring to uncover the history of that poetic prowess and determine its underlying causes. When dissecting the reasons behind the triumph of Homer's poetry, Aristotle noted that the events depicted in epic poems possess dramatic qualities akin to those found in tragedies.[2] These events are centred around a central mode of action, meticulously structured and executed, complete with a well-defined beginning, middle, and end. By harnessing this narrative framework of introduction, development, and culmination, epic poetry offers a pleasure akin to the well-crafted journey of life itself. Unlike historical accounts, where events unfold in a sequential fashion, epic poems focus on individual pivotal events. In historical records, every event in the lives of one or more individuals during a given period is typically documented, even if the events are unrelated. However, epic poems diverge from this approach. For example, although the *Iliad* is based on the Trojan War, it does not encompass the entirety of the war's events. While the war had a clear start and end, the epic poem selectively highlights only a portion of the overall narrative. Homer selectively picked certain events from the war. All these events orbit around a single, central theme.

The purpose of the above discussion on the significance of poetry is to gain insight into a poet's perspective. This understanding helps us discern the situations, events, or beliefs that trigger a poet's creative expression. From ancient times to the present day, Bengali poetry has predominantly served as a vehicle for the representation of faith and belief, even though these beliefs have taken various forms throughout different historical periods.

The earliest Bengali Buddhist lyrics, known as "Chôrjapôd," revolved around the themes of worldly attachments and the quest for relief from painful experiences, which Buddhists refer to as *nirvana*. Notably, these Buddhist compositions did not involve surrender to a Supreme Power, as Buddhist thought does not embrace the concept of a Supreme Being. Nevertheless, they expressed a form of faith, rooted in the pursuit of liberation from suffering and the cycle of birth and rebirth.

Similarly, the "Baishnab" (Vishnu) poems also centre around themes of faith and surrender. During the Middle Ages, Sufi devotees in both Bengali and Hindi literature wrote allegorical stories of surrender to the Supreme Being through the metaphor of love. Alaol's poetry exemplifies Bengali poems containing such allegorical narratives with subtle, suggestive meanings, and he was not alone in this trend.

---

2   James C. Hogan, "Aristotle's Criticism of Homer in the Poetics," *Classical Philology* 68, no. 2 (April 1973): 95–108.

As the Modern Age dawned, Bengali poetry started to reflect the practicalities of life, critical life situations, and the emotions of hope and despair. Michael Madhusudan Datta epitomized this shift in focus. However, despite Madhusudan's profound influence, Rabindranath Tagore's emergence brought forth a new dimension of belief. Rabindranath, shaped by an environment of religious consciousness influenced by his father's sincere adoption of Sufi beliefs, incorporated these beliefs into his works such as *Gitanjoli*, *Noibedya*, and *Kheya*. In these poetic volumes, Rabindranath made an endeavour to explore the characteristics of the Supreme Lord and assert the right to surrender in a distinctive manner.

Following the devastations of the First and Second World Wars, Europe experienced severe turmoil that permeated every facet of life, profoundly impacting matters of faith. Following the collapse of all forms of stability, endeavours to foster a pervasive sense of hopelessness were seen everywhere. We won't delve into the specifics of this history, but it is noteworthy that Bengali poetry was not immune to the influence of these global events. This era gave rise to poets like Bishnu Dey, Jibonanando Das, and Sudhindranath Datta. Sudhindranath Datta made a daring proclamation, stating, "Perhaps there is no God; living creatures are helpless from birth."[3] Atheism became the prevailing ethos in poetry during this period, compounded by Marxist materialism. The Bengali poetry of the 1930s bore the imprint of these pessimistic themes, marking a significant turning point. However, this transformation faced resistance from two formidable poets: Kazi Nazrul Islam and Jasimuddin. Both poets harboured steadfast religious faith and their popularity enabled them to challenge and defeat atheism.

In the 1940s, a group of Muslim poets introduced a fresh wave in Bengali poetry. Among them, Farrukh Ahmed sought to infuse Islam with a romantic spirit. Farrukh aspired to reinvigorate Islam, breathing new life into it. His book of poems, *Saat Sagorer Majhi* ("Boatman of Seven Seas"), was characterized by a captivating blend of romanticism, dreamlike imagery, and enchantment, which served as its primary allure. He endeavored to depict the ideals, beliefs, and awareness of Islam within the framework of an enchanting dream. As a result, his poems not only brought delight to believers but also resonated with non-believers, a resonance that endures even today. Farrukh's poems centered around the concept of challenging the dangers of the sea to reach distant attractions and to keep the journey within reach as a central theme.

More recently, Syed Ali Ashraf endeavoured to give poetic expression to the fundamental principles and impassioned appeals of Islam. He had been absent from the realm of Bengali poetry for an extended period due to his prolonged stay abroad, which has obscured his influence on our poetic land-

---

3 Sudhindranath Datta, "Biprolap," in *Sôngbôrto* (in Bengali) (Calcutta: Cygnet Press, 1953), 39.

scape. A poet's presence in the evolution of a language's poetry is most keenly felt when they are consistently visible in the fabric of that language's daily life. Unfortunately, Syed Ali Ashraf's extended absence makes it nearly impossible to fully grasp his impact on the history of our poetic trends. Nevertheless, had he been more consistently engaged in our national life, his profound sentiments and thoughtfulness could have played a pivotal role in shaping the structural changes within our poetry.

Syed Ali Ashraf's entry into the realm of Bengali poetry occurred with the publication of his book *Choitra Jôkhon* in 1958. In this collection, one can discern the profound influence of English poetry on Syed Ali Ashraf's literary sensibilities. Notably, the first two poems in *Choitra Jôkhon* were composed in the style of Robert Browning's monologues, a stylistic choice hitherto unexplored in the Bengali language. This style had not undergone scrutiny to determine its compatibility with established Bengali poetic conventions, making Syed Ali Ashraf the pioneering figure in this examination. Regrettably, this innovative style was only tested in two poems, but Syed Ali Ashraf deserves commendation for his pioneering effort in this regard.

Yet, despite the exploration of English poetic styles in this collection, the core focus remains on the poet's personal beliefs. According to Syed Ali Ashraf, the mere expression of a belief, opinion, or idea does not qualify as poetry unless it is shaped by life's challenging experiences. As long as a belief remains an abstract concept acquired through knowledge, it remains beyond the realm of poetry. Syed Ali Ashraf underscores the importance of alignment between a poet's personal life and their beliefs. While he is a proponent of Western literary styles, he rejects the notion, prevalent in the West, that poetry serves as a luxury for imaginative indulgence. Instead, he articulates that the purpose of his poetry is to "express the realization of unexpressed truth," thereby introducing a novel dimension to Bengali poetry.

In his poem "Boni Adôm" ("Children of Adam"), Syed Ali Ashraf delves into the capacities and rights of humanity while elucidating their vulnerabilities. Islamic philosophy posits that humans are representatives of God on Earth and encourages them to embrace the virtues of Allah. Simultaneously, it acknowledges the extent of human weakness and helplessness, as individuals may succumb to temptation and moral decay under Satan's influence. Man possesses the divine power bestowed by God, while also being susceptible to the influence of Satan. In "Boni Adôm," an attempt is made to unveil this enigmatic aspect of human nature. Syed Ali Ashraf's introductory propositions in the poem illuminate the complexity of the human character:

O Boni Adôm,
We are the drifting Moon in the Earth's embrace,
In gradual growth and decay,
In our twilight-life's profound emptiness.

I've witnessed, time and time again,
The spectrum of daytime palace, once radiant and grand,
Crumble to dust with night's marauding enchantment,
Each day I've seen,
The radiant Syrian forgets the flavour of life each time,
As untimely maladies take their toll,
Turning Hasina Banu's doe eyes into leaden balls.

Sufi theologians emphasize the ascetics' duty to unearth, through rigorous ascetic practices, the names that Allah imparted to Adam, the first human. In the Qurʾān, it is stated that these names were concealed from the angels. But what is the deeper meaning behind this concept of the "names"?[4]

Sufi ascetics have persistently delved into the significance of these mystical names. In this world, humanity is immersed in a realm of stark contrasts—between compassion and deception, virtue and vice, and victory and defeat. Ascetics undertake the arduous journey of unravelling truths within these contrasting shades. Syed Ali Ashraf, a student of Dhaka and Cambridge Universities and a distinguished professor of English literature, was not only an academic but also a devoted Sufi ascetic in his personal life. He traversed the intricate steps of Sufi practices, forging his identity with unwavering self-confidence. Many of his poems bear the imprint of this profound quest.

Syed Ali Ashraf's second poetry book, titled *Bisôngoti* (1974), delves into the significance of the term *sôngoti*, which denotes unity, appropriateness, or fairness. By adding the prefix *bi* to it, the word transforms into "the unity or coordination that evolves in a unique manner." Through this word, Syed Ali Ashraf endeavours to elucidate the concept of *fanāʾ fillāh* (annihilation in Allah), a central theme in his work.

At the initial stage of meditation, an ascetic embarks on a journey of self-understanding. Gradually, they merge with a spiritual mentor or a *pīr*, ultimately seeking to realise the divine presence of Allah. *Bisôngoti* mirrors the aspiration for annihilation in the Will of Allah. The depth of poetic expression in *Bisôngoti* reaches its zenith within the pages of his subsequent work, *Hijrôt* (1984), where Syed Ali Ashraf's thought patterns attain their full depth. The poem serving as a preface to *Hijrôt* is titled "Asfala Saafeliin." In its concluding verses, the poet explicitly articulates his profound aspiration—to attain annihilation in Allah:

Let my faith's embrace, O Rahim,[5] prevail,
O Rahmanur-Rahim,[6] strengthen the frail.
In the heart's eastern mountain's pristine glow,

---

4 Qurʾān 2:31.
5 The Compassionate
6 The Merciful, the Compassionate.

May sadness vanish, its radiant flow.
Let scars of disgrace from the mind be erased,
With faith's affectionate downpour, they shall be effaced.
In the contented soul, may riches unfurl,
Like golden fields laden with paddy, a tranquil swirl.
Today, let me adorn the roses so fair,
With dew's brief glaze, a moment to share.
Eternally, as the simoom's amber hue,
I'll blend with Sahara's sands, winds that blew.
On the path from negation to affirmation's grace,
Uplift me, uplift me, O Rab,[7] embrace.
O Qahharu,[8] O Musabbiru,[9] in Your glorious name,
I find strength and purpose, ever the same.

In this poetry collection, "Hijrôt"[10] and "Labbaek" stand as a new addition to Bengali literary treasure. These verses mark an unprecedented milestone in the history of Bengali poetry, introducing a form previously uncharted. *Hijrôt* maps the poet's profound spiritual voyage. Forsaking worldly attachments like love, greed, gains, and losses, the poet embarks on a migration towards the divine, seeking the closest communion with Allah and His Prophet. This poem finds kinship with T. S. Eliot's "Ash Wednesday," both employing symbolic representations that stir the depths of the soul's spiritual essence.

Divided into four distinct parts, the first captures the pain of relinquishing family ties and simultaneous attraction towards it while steadfastly embracing renunciation. The second paints a vivid canvas of self-dissolution amid the rigours of spiritual practice. The third part masterfully articulates the joy of drawing near to Allah and the Prophet, conveyed through exquisite allegorical imagery:

In which tumultuous waves did this sand dune wall succumb,
In the arid heart's depths, igniting a frenzied deluge's drum?
From which celestial realm did Shraban's[11] shower descend,
Filling the heart's inner chambers with a rhythm enlightened,
The recurring, dazzling brilliance of lightning within the cloud's embrace,
Upon the tips of white waves, pure swift brilliance they chase.
I hear, deep within, the boundless sky's call,
In the endless deluge, the sandy land, submerged, enthralled.
In the vanishing wings of this sky, sea, and storm,
My well-tended abode has drifted to distant shore, transformed.

---

7 The Lord
8 The Subduer.
9 The Fashioner.
10 "Hijrôt" is the title of a poem in Syed Ali Ashraf's book of poems, *Hijrôt*.
11 Shraban is the fourth month of the Benali calendar.

In the poem's fourth part, we discern the resonance of William Butler Yeats' "Sailing to Byzantium." Just as Yeats yearned for eternal life, our poet, too, craves eternity in a transient world, having attained proximity to Allah and the Prophet. Ashraf perceives Madinah Munawwarah[12] as the embodiment of this enduring essence, discovering a "peaceful immortality" (*nirbedôn ômôrôtto*) within the Prophet (pbuh). With profound insight, Ashraf reinterprets a familiar Bengali allegory, infusing it with fresh, symbolic significance. In doing so, he charts a new path, providing us with a wholly innovative direction to explore:

> Today, the barriers of time lie shattered,
> As the rose of memory intertwines with the lotus of dream.
> In the depths of his cerulean gaze,
> The Day of Judgment shines brilliantly, unveiled.
> Harmoniously, the peace-giving creative light radiates,
> Merging with the celestial realm shattered with dormant darkness.

The poem "Labbaek" portrays the spiritual journey, a *hijrah* (migration) of the soul, ignited by the deep resolve to embark on the Hajj pilgrimage. The purpose behind this divine *hijrah*, undertaken by Prophet Muhammad (pbuh), was to establish the Kingdom of Allah on Earth. Along this path of establishment, there existed both conflict and combat, but also an unwavering sacred determination. Every devout Muslim experiences a taste of this *hijrah* when they perform Hajj with resolute commitment. The rituals of Hajj serve as a profound connection to one's religious heritage. Ali Ashraf masterfully weaves these rituals into his poetry, leveraging his profound faith to illuminate the comprehensive journey of Hajj for his readers. He unveils the intricate tapestry of this pilgrimage through twelve ritualistic acts. However, his portrayal is not a mere description; it is a humble narrative that resonates with the genuine emotions that well up within the heart of a devout Muslim during their Hajj journey. With exquisite allegory, the poet captures the intense sentiments that surged within him as he stood at the threshold of the sacred Kaʿbah, encapsulating a moment of profound spiritual significance.

> May the heart's desires dissipate,
> Lest the wandering mind lose its way
> On the anticipated path of circling;
> May the heart be cleansed of all vanity,
> Or else its reflection in the mirror of truth
> Shall be tainted by darkness.
> In my humblest hopes, I seek only Your arrival,

---

12 The city of Madinah, Arabic *Al-Madīnah*, also called *Al-Madīnah al-Munawwarah* ("The Luminous City") or *Madīnat an-Nabī* ("City of the Prophet").

In the cycle of light, the first and the last,
May my heart find fulfilment.

Sufi mysticism, a realm of profound complexity, dwells within the realm of perception, requiring realization that transcends the ordinary. It can be dissected through theological discourse, yet its essence remains elusive when translated into the realm of poetry. For poetry is the art of words, and the subject must harmonize with the nuanced shades of meaning woven by those words.

In the tapestry of Bengali poetry, we encounter the poetic odyssey of Ali Ashraf, a pursuit of divine communion—the quest for closeness to God. Ashraf's verses offer fresh pathways to spiritual enlightenment, and as such, they beckon to all seekers of wisdom. In the realms of Sufi thought, Ashraf's poems stand as luminous guides, inviting every soul to partake in their transformative journey.

Bibliography

Ahsan, Syed Ali. "Syed Ali Ashrafer Kôbita." In *Syed Ali Ashrafer Kôbita* (in Bengali) by Syed Ali Ashraf. Dhaka: Shilpotoru Prokashoni, 1991.

Datta, Sudhindranath. "Biprolap." In *Sôngbôrto* (in Bengali). Calcutta: Cygnet Press, 1953.

Hogan, James C. "Aristotle's Criticism of Homer in the Poetics." *Classical Philology* 68, no. 2 (April 1973): 95-108.

Chapter 8

Islam and the West[1]

Abdullah Omar Nasseef

Islam is the religion of all prophets.[2] Every prophet was sent by the Almighty Allah, and they called people to adhere to the Orders and Commands of Allah, to follow His Message and to submit to Him completely. That is why Islam is not a new religion. Islam, in its complete and final form, was revealed to Prophet Muhammad (peace be upon him).[3]

Islam is a religion and a comprehensive conduct of life for all Muslims, in fact, for all humanity. Although Muslims are following this great religion, today we see that they are not following it properly. Consequently, they cannot present themselves as saviours of the world. Often the question which is raised by non-Muslims is: if your religion is so great and has all the ingredients of success for life in this world and salvation in the hereafter, then why the Muslims are not following it. Allah has made it clear in His Book that if we do not abide by His Guidance, we will suffer.[4] So, Muslims are required to follow and abide by the Orders of Allah. Allah has given us the best religion, Islam, and we do not follow its injunctions. Muslims do not adhere to the principles of their religion, fearing it will circumscribe their lives and curtail their freedom. Therefore, they adapt themselves to un-Islamic ways derived from the West.

Muslims should return to the universality and globality of the message of their great religion which does not prevent them from presenting it to people. I believe, Islam has the panacea for the problems faced by the Muslims as well as by the non-Muslims. Today, the world has been reduced to a global village with breathtaking technological innovations and devices like computer, internet, satellite communication, etc. These devices have invaded people's privacy

---

1 Presented at the First Syed Ali Ashraf Memorial Lecture titled, "Global Islam and the West: challenges and opportunities in the 21st century" held at Mill Lane Lecture Rooms, University of Cambridge on 27 October 1999.
2 Qurʾān 2:136. All Qurʾānic translations in this chapter are from *Sahih International*.
3 Qurʾān 5:3.
4 Qurʾān 9:63.

leaving no aspect of life hidden from public sight. In this age of globalization, every idea and every concept get universalized. That is why we should present Islam in its true form and with its sound principles which are universal—so that we can tackle some of the problems, which are growing every day and are affecting everybody—educating large segments of people about the message of Islam.

Though our society and community have become internationalized and globalized, our education system is problem ridden. It is bereft of ethical or moral values. But the picture was completely different in the past, when people, no matter which religious denomination they belonged to, whether Muslims or Christians or Jews, used to educate their children on sound principles of ethics and values which prevented them from going astray, from easily falling prey to evil forces. But nothing like that exists today in our education programme.

Besides educational programmes, our curriculum has not fulfilled the requirements of our young people. It has not fulfilled their ambitions and failed to solve their social problems. As a result, we see all kinds of problems happening in the school, both primary and secondary. Teachers are facing those difficulties every day, as our children are not being trained morally and spiritually to develop the strength of character and to face un-Islamic fads and trends. They are not told how to solve their social and psychological problems, how to overcome the difficulties they are facing in society, as all societies, whether rich or poor, urban, or rural, face various problems. That is why, we must speak clearly and firmly about the educational system, which should be integrated with values, ethics and parental guidance so that every individual human being is properly educated in every aspect of life, be it material or spiritual, which, at present, very few religions have attempted to do.

Islam accords great importance to spirituality and emphasizes the purification of the soul. Even human emotions, sentiments and intentions do not escape its attention. Therefore, an all-around revolution in the field of education covering all aspects of human life, theoretical as well as practical, is required. Before I present the universal and eternal principles of Islam as a World Order, able to face the problems besetting the new generation of the coming millennium, I would like to discuss some of the problems which people are confronted with and probe the causes of those problems.

Problems

Let us begin with the serious problems which people are facing, particularly in the Muslim communities today. The first among them, that comes to my mind, is the co-education system prevalent in Muslim and non-Muslim societies. The rulers and educationists think that this system will create a better society. But in reality, it is creating problems at school and in society at large. Challenges arising from co-education in schools are widespread. There are inherent natural differences between boys and girls that hinder their easy interaction. When we conducted a survey of co-ed schools, we observed girls standing separately in one place with boys standing at some distance.

One of the drawbacks of the co-education system is the emergence of premarital relations between boys and girls before maturity. One of the English newspapers, either *The Times* or *The Daily Telegraph*—I cannot remember exactly—published a story of a 12-year-old boy, who met a 10-year-old girl and made her pregnant. If the boy thought that at that age, he could be a good father, he was not right. In other words, it means that even if such a girl continues her pregnancy and gives birth to a baby, it will be a 'fatherless' baby. Looking at the current trends it can be said that the problems created by these premarital relations will aggravate in the future. Today, we can see in many societies the phenomenon of single parenthood. In these societies, children are facing great psychological and physiological problems. They do not have the benefit of a natural harmonious family, because in the natural well-knit family, the father and the mother jointly educate their children when they need it most. It is one of the great teachings of Islam that parents have the responsibility, especially the mother, to raise their children, rear them up in infancy and educate them at the age when they should start receiving education. This places a single parent family at a great disadvantage. This is only part of the problem.

The other problem is the lack of kindness in many modern families. Kindness is essential for the sound and congenial growth of children. In a family, when both parents are busy earning their livelihood and place the child in the care of a nanny or a baby-sitter, there is no scope for the development of such fine feelings as kindness. When parents return home after work, they are too tired to give any time to their children. They do not have time to provide much needed emotional bond which is necessary for sound mental development. Similarly, there are many other problems which people are not taking seriously but as time goes on, we find that the youth encounter various psychological problems.

Similarly, another problem which our society is facing is disrespect for parents. We see children revolting against their parents, because during that phase of life the youth hanker after freedom and do not like any restrictions on the fulfilment of their raw instincts and passions. They think their parents are dictators, they are preventing them, creating hindrance to their freedom. In an Islamic environment, this parent-child relationship has been tackled very carefully. During this impressionable age, children should be kept under surveillance and provided with proper guidance until they become mature and are able to regulate their lives and choose the right direction. The parents will provide avenues for recreation too, but that kind of recreation will be wholesome and keep the children away from unhealthy pursuits. Because of the lack of this parental authority the family is broken these days. The children find life at home dull and without any attraction, where parental love, affection and understanding are missing. On the other hand, the parents think that the children are out to assert their authority. This is a problem which is affecting almost every family now. It has become an international problem, a global problem.

This troubled relationship between parents and children may lead to several other complications later when the parents grow old and there is nobody to take care of them. The children are now young males and females, being independent and leave the parental control at the age of around 18. In the West, many such young people set up their own separate homes and have little emotional attachment to their parents. The society and government try to solve these problems by setting up Old People's Homes for the aged and elderly people. In this kind of society fine human sentiments of kindness, affection and sympathy do not exist. In Islam, one cannot ignore the importance of a harmonious society, which is a collection of healthy families.

So, if an individual is brought up in an uncongenial atmosphere without proper education, counselling and guidance, where the relationships between the parents and children are not on a sound footing, the young men and women fall prey to such vices as homosexuality, drug abuse, smoking, intoxication and other social evils. They are far away from any religious guidance, moral values, and ethics, which help to keep society intact. The immediate effect is that family life breaks down and society develops on fault lines, comprising individuals who are against any religion, against any code of conduct, order or principles in life and therefore behave in an abnormal way.

These problems started to be widely visible 30 or 40 years ago and are growing from bad to worse. We must think of some solutions to these problems. It must be remembered that Islam is not against freedom of expression, freedom of faith, and private ownership, but there are certain guidelines which ensure the protection of the individual, the family, the society and the harmonious flow of life because life is a blend of all kinds of relations and interactions. If these relations and dealings with people are not regulated properly, everything goes wrong.

I believe, today if we revise and revolutionize our education system based on moral and spiritual principles, things will be on a sound footing. The revision of our educational system requires that we tackle some of the problems prevailing in our society, such as free sex, drug addiction and the kinds of films which encourage permissiveness, breed crime and promote terrorism. The media is harming society more than anything else. As we see, the children who do not have proper schooling, watch television programmes, read obscene books and magazines and while away their time on the internet eventually turn away from the Straight Path.[5] They become engaged in trivial matters. They do not

---

5   The Straight Path refers to *al-ṣirāt al-mustaqīm*, mentioned in *Sūrat al-fātiḥah*, the first chapter of the Qurʾān. This is the path of the righteous people.

think about how to build their nation, how to develop their economy, how to set up their army and so on.

So, we must address this situation. To begin with, the media must be reformed. We can keep the recreation part of the media and improve upon it. We may also introduce new things needed to build the new generation on a sound basis enabling it to develop the nation and solve some of the economic and social crises and maladies the community is suffering from. These are, in short, some of the problems which Islam seeks to tackle. It is always wise to solve a problem as soon as it raises its head and before it gets public attention and causes untold damage to society at large.

Today, man's misdeeds and over-exploitation of the earth's resources have damaged the environment and its ill effects are all too evident. Enormous resources are being squandered on arms race; the prospects of a nuclear war are hovering over our heads as well as the fears of terrorists. All these problems are caused by the lack of a proper educational system, as improperly educated people cannot differentiate between what is right and what is wrong. Then they go after their personal gains, without caring for others, polluting the water and the air, and damaging the atmosphere. These are only some examples.

If we think deeply about the roots of the problem, we will find that this is happening because the individuals are not properly educated and consequently, they do not pay heed to other individuals, and become self-centred and avaricious. They tend to disregard the interests of society. Exposed to an exploitative economic system these people grow to become selfish and greedy, geared to making money without bothering about the means and caring for others. Such improperly educated young people become spendthrift, they do not save and recklessly spend whatever they earn. When they grow up, they wish to have homes of their own, but they cannot afford them. They have no option but to take loans from banks on which they must pay interest throughout their life. Thus, young people begin their career with a large amount of debt. All their expenses are met by borrowing on interest, so much so that at the time of death, they still have loans to pay back. So, an improper education lands such young people in an exploitative economic system which, in turn, engenders a host of social problems and spoils social relations.

The whole world has now shrunk into a global village after globalization and internationalization of the world community and world trade. These problems, therefore, touch every human. So, we must devise solutions which will benefit the whole mankind. Islam has an answer to all the problems human beings face today. Not a theoretical framework, it provides practical solutions for every situation. Muslims can prosper, build up a civilization comparable to any other in the past or the present. They built up a civilization from which everybody benefited, and which contributed to other civilizations. Western civilization owes a great deal to that civilization. For more than a thousand years the Islamic civilization remained preponderant, correcting the behaviour of the society, and bringing harmony, peace and justice in the world. That is why even today, people from the East and the West, from the Muslim world and non-Muslim societies, appreciate that period of the Muslim glory. Therefore, people of wisdom should get together and develop a world order which will benefit every human being and every society. This requires a lot of courage, proper education and hard work. We cannot repair society without careful preparation.

The United Nations has drafted various charters, like those of human rights, the children's and women's rights, etc. But unfortunately, these are based on false grounds and have ingredients of destruction in them. People think that they are doing good, but they are not. These covenants have failed to solve any problems, rather they create more crises, problems and miseries for societies. One must raise one's voice to stop now before it is too late. The UN called 20 years ago for a new world order, because the communists sat on one side and the capitalists on the other side, and neither was able to provide humanity with real happiness. Committee after committee has held deliberations, but nothing solid has been done.

Principles of Islam

I want to present here Islamic principles in their international, global form, to solve the problems of the Muslims, the non-Muslims and the international community. These principles are very helpful and positive. They lay down the foundation for a prosperous world with sound principles. Of course, they are not for an imaginative society, but based on pragmatic considerations. In its heyday Islam eliminated individual and social problems as much as possible. Even now, acting on the Islamic principles we can eliminate poverty from Africa, for example, and also other countries, eradicate Aids and other diseases, improve the quality of air and water, eliminate drug abuse and overcome narrow-mindedness and terrorists in all societies.

The religion of Islam is an embodiment of moral principles and has all the ingredients of a world order that can bring happiness to mankind at large. Some Islamic principles that can address issues of grave concern are mentioned here:

Islam is the universal religion for all people and for all times. God says: "Say, [O Muhammad], 'O mankind, indeed I am the Messenger of Allah to you all, [from Him] to whom belongs the dominion of the heavens and the earth'" (Qurʾān 7:158). In the same sequence, the Prophet of Islam says: "O people! Your Lord is one, and your father is one. There shall be no preference for an Arab over a non-Arab nor a non-Arab over an Arab, and neither a White over a Black nor a Black over a White except by piety,"[6] and "You all are children

---

6   *Musnad Aḥmad*, 23489.

of Adam, and Adam was created from Dust."[7] He also said: "All creatures are the dependents of God. The most beloved of them to God is he who is most beneficial to his family."[8] What evidence can be there than this regarding the universality of Islam?

Islam recognizes the existence of a human brotherhood based on mutual acquaintance and affection among mankind. God says: "O mankind, indeed We have created you from male and female and made you peoples and tribes that you may know one another. Indeed, the most noble of you in the sight of Allah is the most righteous of you" (Qurʾān 49:13). Although Islam lays stress on universal brotherhood of human beings, it however recognizes peculiarities and diversities within the framework of fair play and justice to all. God says: "'O People of the Scripture, come to a word that is equitable between us and you—that we will not worship except Allah and not associate anything with Him and not take one another as lords instead of Allah'" (Qurʾān 3:64).

Islam regards other faiths with respect, in conformity with God's injunction. God says: "There shall be no compulsion in [acceptance of] the religion" (Qurʾān 2:256) and also: "For you is your religion, and for me is my religion" (Qurʾān 109:6).

The principles of equity among individuals and communities rank high in the Islamic doctrine. God says: "Indeed, Allah orders justice and good conduct and giving to relatives and forbids immortality and bad conduct and oppression" (Qurʾān 16:90). He also says: "And do not let the hatred of a people prevent you from being just. Be just; that is nearer to righteousness" (Qurʾān 5:8).

Islam lays great emphasis on the strict observance of charity and good deed towards the followers of other religions who do not transgress. God says: "Allah does not forbid you from those who do not fight you because of religion and do not expel you from your homes—from being righteous toward them and acting justly toward them. Indeed, Allah loves those who act justly" (Qurʾān 60:8).

Islam attaches great importance to the fulfilment of obligations regardless of the parties involved. God says: "And fulfill the covenant of Allah when you have taken it, [O believers], and do not break oaths after their confirmation while you have made Allah, over you, a witness. Indeed, Allah knows what you do" (Qurʾān 16:91). To further interpret this commandment, it is reported in certain traditions of the Noble Prophet that "He whoever kills a man who has entered into an accord with the Muslims would never smell the scent of paradise."[9] This means that, contrary to common erratic belief, Islam recognizes and respects the existence of a zone of treaty, besides the Islamic zone and the war zone.

---

7   Sunan al-Tirmidhī, 3955.
8   Ṣaḥīḥ al-Bukhārī, quoted in Mishkat al-Maṣābīḥ, 3:1392.
9   Ṣaḥīḥ al-Bukhārī, 6914.

Islam lauds any treaty or alliance that is bound to help the wronged and deter the wrong doer. It is reported in the traditions of the Noble Prophet that he once said: "I was a witness to an alliance which was concluded in the house of ʿAbdullāh ibn Judʿān which I cherish more dearly than an entire herd of red-coloured camels. Were I to be invited to a similar treaty after the emergence of Islam, I would have accepted the invitation."[10] The alliance in question is of course none other than the alliance called *Ḥilf al-fuḍūl* (League of the Virtuous) which was concluded to repel injustice and lend support to the wronged. Islam views the question of preservation of the environment seriously. As a result, destruction of the environment is absolutely prohibited; to the extent that, Muslim soldiers are prohibited from cutting down fruitful trees or killing animals. God says: "And when he goes away, he strives throughout the land to cause corruption therein and destroy crops and animals. Allah does not like corruption" (Qurʾān 2:205).

Islam prevents its followers from debating with the followers of other religions except in the best manner. God says: "And do not argue with the People of the Scripture except in a way that is best, except for those who commit injustice among them" (Qurʾān 29:46). He also says: "Invite to the way of your Lord with wisdom and good instruction and argue with them in a way that is best. Indeed, your Lord is most knowing of who has strayed from His way, and He is most knowing of who is [rightly] guided" (Qurʾān 16:125). It goes without saying that debate with the followers of other religions from the Islamic point of view is one that is both meaningful and conducive to agreement rather than mere show.

Islam is a religion of love and cooperation. It is reported in the traditions of the Noble Prophet that: "None of you will be considered a true believer until he likes for his brother that which he likes for himself."[11]

Islam is a religion that attaches great importance to the intellect and encourages intellectual activity, for the revelation is the Word of God, while the intellect is but a gift from Him. The Sender of the revelation is the One Who created the intellect. There should be no contradiction between that which is sent down and that which is created, for they are all from God.

Islam is a religion of knowledge as God says: "Say: 'Are those who know equal to those who do not know?'" (Qurʾān 39:9). In addition to the Qurʾānic verses on the importance of knowledge, there are numerous sayings of the Noble Prophet in this regard. In fact, it was such exhortations that helped Muslims to enjoy a scientific renaissance that enriched the human civilization and was influential in Europe's own renaissance, especially in the fields of mathematics, geometry and ophthalmology. The Muslims also excelled in the fields

---

10 *Al-Sunan al-Kubrā*, 13080.
11 *Ṣaḥīḥ al-Bukhārī*, 12; *Ṣaḥīḥ Muslim*, 45.

of geography and surveying.[12] In one of the letters that he wrote describing his voyages, Columbus quoted an essay titled, *Ymago Mundi e Mappa Mundi* (The Imagined World and its World Map) by a French scholar named Pierre d'Ailly which Columbus studied and annotated. In this essay, d'Ailly quoted many ancient scholars including Averroes whose writings inspired Columbus to make his epochal voyages.[13] There is no doubt that the Arabs alone were the representatives of civilization in the Middle Ages and as such were able to repel Europe's barbarism caused by the raids of the northern communities.

Islam stands for mutual responsibility. That is, not only does it impose on its followers, the obligation of not harming others, but it also obliges the Muslim to prevent one individual from causing harm to another with all his might, to safeguard his life, wealth, and honour. Failure to do so amounts to sin, and the injured person is entitled to hold such negligent person responsible before the court and demand compensation for the injuries he had suffered, for instance, failure to save a person from an outbreak of fire, or a blind man from falling into a pit. Thus, it is easy to show that all the basic human rights are enshrined in the teachings of Islam. Man indeed, is honoured by God, and his natural disposition is inclined towards peace. God says: "We have certainly created man in the best of stature" (Qurʾān 95:4). He also says: "And formed you and perfected your forms" (Qurʾān 64:3).

Consequently, man is entitled to certain rights throughout the span of his life and at death. God says: "And do not spy or backbite each other" (Qurʾān 49:12). He also says: "Do not enter houses other than your own houses, until you ascertain welcome and greet their inhabitants. That is best for you" (Qurʾān 24:27). Of course, all these obligations must be observed regarding both Muslims and non-Muslims. For the Prophet, according to al-Bayhaqi, has prohibited entrance into houses belonging to the people of the Book or making use of their crops and fruits without their permission. Also, a man must not be addressed in a manner he dislikes. God says: "O you who have believed, let not a people ridicule [another] people; perhaps they may be better than them; nor let women ridicule [other] women; perhaps they may be better than them. And do not insult one another and do not call each other by [offensive] nicknames" (Qurʾān 49:11). Moreover, man's life is inviolable. He must not be punished for offences committed by others. God says: "And no bearer of burdens will bear the burden of another" (Qurʾān 35:18).

Likewise, a person is considered innocent until he is proven otherwise, and he must not be liable to punishment without warning. God says: "O you who

---

12 For a detailed discussion of Muslim contribution to science and technology see: Seyyed Hossein Nasr, *Islamic Science: An Illustrated Study* (London: World of Islam Festival Publishing Company, 1976); Salim T. S. al-Hassani, *1001 Inventions: The Enduring Legacy of Muslim Civilization*, 3rd ed. (Washington, DC: National Geographic, 2012).
13 Mary Ames Mitchell, "Crossing the Ocean Sea," 2015, accessed 7 February 2023, https://crossingtheoceansea.com/OceanSeaPages/OS-62-ColumbusNewProposal.html.

have believed, avoid much [negative] assumption. Indeed, some assumption is sin" (Qurʾān 49:12). He also says: "O you who have believed, if there comes to you a disobedient one with information, investigate, lest you harm a people out of ignorance and become, over what you have done, regretful!" (Qurʾān 49:6). And He says: "And never would We punish until We sent a messenger" (Qurʾān 17:15). All the fundamental freedoms such as freedom of opinion and conviction which have only recently been discovered by man, are guaranteed by Islam.

Islam also guarantees the right of ownership and use of common property such as the earth, oceans, rivers, wild animals, and fish. In Islamic jurisprudence, men are equal partners in as far as water, fire and grazing lands are concerned. There should be no transgression against the property of others, and the estate of the deceased goes to his legal heirs. People are close associates with regard to the equitable and good utilization of natural resources. Moreover, all means of earning a livelihood such as exchange of trades, leasing and loans are all permissible in Islam, except of course, such earnings that come from robbery, extortion, usury, deceit, and gambling.

Finally, society owes obligation towards the poor and the vulnerable. They should not be left to languish and perish. Even the wayfarer has the right to be guided, fed and provided for by other people. In short, man, either male or female enjoys rights throughout the various stages of their life within the limits of justice and goodness. God says: "And women shall have rights similar to the rights against them, according to what is equitable" (Qurʾān 2:228).

Bibliography

Al-Hassani, Salim T. S. *1001 Inventions: The Enduring Legacy of Muslim Civilization*, 3rd ed. Washington, DC: National Geographic, 2012.

Mitchell, Mary Ames. "Crossing the Ocean Sea." 2015. Accessed 7 February 2023. https://crossingtheoceansea.com/OceanSeaPages/OS-62-ColumbusNewProposal.html.

Nasr, Seyyed Hossein. *Islamic Science: An Illustrated Study*. London: World of Islam Festival Publishing Company, 1976.

Chapter 9

Exploring Professor Syed Ali Ashraf's Views on Religious and Secular Education

Shaikh Abdul Mabud

Introduction

According to the Holy Qurʾān, humanity's purpose is to seek knowledge, with the first word of Revelation, *Iqrà* (Read), intricately tied to this pursuit. The acquisition and dissemination of religious knowledge (*ʿilm*) hold a central place in the Islamic tradition. They are regarded as acts of worship themselves, thus underscoring the paramount importance of knowledge in Islam. The verses of the Qurʾān and the sayings of the Prophet (pbuh) are replete with the importance of knowledge and exhortations to seek it. Throughout Islamic history, education, including seemingly secular subjects like mathematics and medicine, has been imbued with sacred significance. However, the influence of a secularised Western civilisation over the past century has fractured the unity of the Islamic educational system. This fragmentation has spawned competing educational paradigms, resulting in division within Islamic societies and among individual Muslims. In modern secular contexts, education has often been reduced to a commodity, with individuals seen as consumers, and the acquisition of knowledge primarily perceived as a means for social advancement and wealth accumulation. On the other hand, from the Islamic perspective, the aim of education is to nurture individuals who embody goodness and righteousness, sincerely worship Allah, adhere to Sharīʿah, and align their lives with the divine will. Worship in Islam transcends mere ritualistic acts. It encompasses all facets of life—faith, thought, emotion, and deeds—in accordance with the teachings of the Holy Qurʾān and the Sunnah of the Prophet. Education serves the noble purpose of guiding humanity towards attaining this comprehensive understanding and living a righteous life.

Professor Ashraf was deeply troubled by the prevalence of secular education in the Muslim world, seeing it as running counter to the core tenets of Islam. This concern prompted him to critically analyse the modern educational system, of which he was a product, revealing its detrimental impacts on the holistic human development. Through extensive writings, he delved into the essence of education from an Islamic perspective, proposing remedies to mitigate the adverse consequences of secular education on both individuals and society. This chapter examines Professor Ashraf's perspectives on education based on the Qurʾān and Ḥadīth, alongside an analysis of contemporary secular education as practised in mainstream systems across the globe today. He lived for considerable periods of time in Bangladesh, Pakistan, Saudi Arabia and the United Kingdom and had firsthand experience of the education systems of these countries. He noted that the education systems of these countries are basically guided by the philosophy of secular education. Although Islamic subjects are taught in the mainstream systems of Muslim countries, the tendency to break loose from the bondage of religion is evident in the syllabus and curriculum at all levels of education, but the extent of such departure from religion varies across the Muslim world. This phenomenon can be attributed to the decline of institutional religion and emphasis on materialistic goals and aspirations. Professor Ashraf noted that the attempt to dissociate education system from the influence of religion started with the era of colonisation, which itself was a result of the progressive internal decay of the Muslim society. The integral unity of the education system, which was a reflection of the unitary principle of Islam (*tawḥīd*) and was still to be observed two hundred years ago, started to crumble under foreign rulers and their stooges. Christian educationalists have also noted the dominance of secular philosophies in educational institutions. For example, Baroness Cox says: "We are in danger of selling our spiritual birthright for a mess of secular pottage. Many of our children are in schools where they are denied the experience of religious worship at all, and where teaching about Christianity has either been diluted to a multi-faith relativism or has become little more than a secularised discussion of social and political issues."[1] This situation has progressively worsened.

Professor Ashraf's philosophy of education resonates profoundly with the essence of Islamic revelation. He derives his educational principles from the Qurʾān, Sunnah and the intellectual and spiritual heritage of Islam. Drawing from his experience of working in the education sectors of Bangladesh, Pakistan, and Saudi Arabia, he gained firsthand insight into the adverse effects of secular education within these Muslim-majority countries. Residing in the UK for over two decades, he keenly observed the detrimental impact of secular education on Muslim pupils attending British schools. Utilising his wealth

---

[1] Caroline Cox, foreword to *The Crisis in Religious Education*, ed. John Burn and Colin Hart (London: Educational Research Trust, 1988).

of experience, he engaged in a discussion about the ramifications of secular education for both Muslim-majority and minority nations. This chapter delves into the fundamental tenets of his educational philosophy, addressing key issues such as educational aims and objectives, provisions for a plural society, and religious and moral education. It explores his perspectives on education within Islam and provides a critique of secular education, examining its impact both within the Muslim world and British educational systems. The chapter is structured into four sections:

1. Principles of Education: Examining secular and Islamic perspectives, with subsections dedicated to secular education and education in Islam.
2. Moral Education.
3. British Education Systems: This section is further divided into three subsections focusing on education for the British plural society, Faith School versus State School, and Religious Education.
4. Conclusion.

Principles of Education: Examining Secular and Islamic Perspectives

Secular Education

Secular education pertains to an educational system or institution that is not affiliated with any specific religion or belief system. Its primary aim is to impart knowledge and instruction without bias toward any faith or doctrine, emphasising the clear delineation between religious influence and academic pursuits. A related term, liberal education, embodies a learning approach that prioritises a wide array of subjects, fosters critical thinking and intellectual curiosity, and encourages exploration of diverse perspectives while promoting analytical skills development. Secularism forms an integral part of liberalism, where the reduction of religious influence in education correlates with increased liberalism. Conversely, heightened religious involvement in education diminishes its liberal nature. Professor Ashraf's critique of secular education is based on a traditional Islamic framework, that is derived from the Qurʾān, Ḥadīth and the spiritual traditions of Islam. His scathing criticism of secularism—of the kind that makes social interactions the source of values and considers all values to be relative to historical period and social situations—is a recurrent theme in his writings. In his article, "Education and Values: Islamic vis-à-vis the Secularist Approaches," published in *Muslim Education Quarterly*[2] he made an in-depth analysis of secularism and secularisation and their incompatibility with Islam. From a traditional perspective education

---

2 Syed Ali Ashraf, "Education and Values: Islamic vis-à-vis the Secularist Approaches," *Muslim Education Quarterly* 4, no. 2 (1987).

is a conserver of absolute human values and the guardian of tradition. This differs from the secularist-modern perspective on education, which views it as a means to enhance human well-being within the confines of the material world, devoid of adherence to fundamental, unchanging moral or spiritual values. The rationalistic stance adopted by secularists frequently leads to tensions between schools and families, especially when children from those families dissent from the imposed perspectives. While it is widely acknowledged that rationality may struggle to address non-material matters like the mind, meaning, morality, and ultimate origins, problems arise when secularists enforce their viewpoints on all students via a uniform education policy. In doing so, they often overlook other important educational values, including pluralism, diversity, and tolerance. Islamic education is goal oriented, but this is in sharp contrast to the secularist position asserted by R. S. Peters, a proponent of liberal education:

> Education, then, can have no ends beyond itself. Its value derives from principles and standards implicit in it. To be educated is not to have arrived at a destination; it is to travel with a different view.[3]

Liberal education proposed here is a non-authoritarian education for the development of a mind free from all impediments and constraints. Thiessen explains liberal education as a form of education that "avoids dogmatism, authoritarianism, and indoctrination. It aims for autonomy where individuals are free to reason and to critically evaluate the beliefs of others as well as their own beliefs."[4] It does not support subordination of one's mind to others. In the modern world, the concept of subordination of humans to certain absolute values has been overthrown in favour of "a belief in the perfection of man, in personality and 'all the bunkum that follows from it.'"[5] When the "central abstract ideas" are compromised by notions grounded in the primacy of humanity, individuals liberate themselves from the constricting dictates of religious laws. They then assume the authority to formulate and reformulate laws in alignment with evolving social circumstances, thereby embracing a newfound freedom to shape their legal and ethical frameworks. Implicit in the decision to reject divine law is the concept that humans are perfectly capable of legislating laws for themselves. However, the idea that perfection resides within humanity is a fundamental error that often escapes secular educationalists.

Professor Ashraf observed that secular philosophy that is at the roots of modern education does not support the application of Islamic religious princi-

---

3   Richard S. Peters, "Education as initiation," in *Philosophy of Education an Anthology*, ed. Randall Curren (Oxford: Blackwell, 2007 [1965]), 67.
4   Elmer J. Thiessen, "R. S. Peters on Liberal Education—A Reconstruction," *Interchange* 20, no. 4 (Winter, 1989): 5.
5   W. E. Collin, "Beyond Humanism: Some Notes on T. E. Hulme," *The Sewanee Review* 38, no. 3 (Jul-Sep. 1930): 335.

ples in education and thus undermines the development of the total personality of a human being.[6] He highlighted several drawbacks of secular humanism. He argued that religion asserts absolute truths based on revelations, challenging the relativistic approach of secular humanism. It claims moral authority derived from divine teachings, thereby challenging secular humanists who derive their morality from human reason and societal consensus, often based on principles such as human rights or utilitarianism. Additionally, religion offers metaphysical explanations for existence, purpose, and the afterlife, which conflict with secular humanist views grounded in naturalism and empirical evidence. Moreover, religion challenges the epistemological foundations of secular humanism by advocating for faith-based knowledge over empirical inquiry leading to conflicts over the validity of different ways of knowing. Professor Ashraf contested these secular notions and asserted that the true purpose of education is "to become a wholehearted servant of God." He critiqued certain philosophical perspectives of such people as John Vaizey, Bertrand Russell, R. S. Peters, Laszlo Versenyi, William Hitt, and other humanist-secularist writers contending that their secular outlook does not differentiate between the universal and the absolute, as well as the local and relative. Furthermore, their approach fails to discern between revealed knowledge and acquired knowledge, disregards the existence of fundamental, unique, and immutable moral and spiritual values, and outright denies the concept of faith in the hereafter.[7]

Professor Ashraf, valuing dialogue and seeking common ground for enhanced cooperation, offers a balanced critique of those who hold differing perspectives. He respects the traditional viewpoints of Jewish, Christian, and Hindu scholars, acknowledging their foundations in beliefs surrounding God, human spirituality, and the accountability inherent in the concept of the Day of Judgment. He supports such views expounded by non-Muslim scholars and theologians such as A. N. Whitehead, M. V. C. Jeffreys, T. E. Hulme, Jacques Maritain and St. Thomas Aquinas who support the essential roles of religion in guiding educational activities. The greatness of Professor Ashraf's mind becomes apparent as he selectively cites specific statements or ideas from these scholars that align with his philosophical or religious stance, despite his disagreement with the overall philosophical position of these scholars. Professor Ashraf observes that secular humanists grapple with a profound epistemological dilemma stemming from their ontological uncertainties. They perceive humans as products of evolution, positing consciousness as arising from inert matter through intricate biological processes. Their worldview is characterised by a reliance on natural laws, devoid of divine influence, and they posit

---

[6] Bernadette O'Keefe, introduction to *Schools for Tomorrow: Building Walls or Building Bridges*, ed. Bernadette O'Keefe (London: The Falmer Press, 1988), 5.

[7] Syed Ali Ashraf, preface to *Aims and Objectives of Islamic Education*, ed. Syed Muhammad al-Naquib al-Attas (London: Hodder and Stoughton and Jeddah: King Abdulaziz University, 1979).

empirical evidence and rational inquiry as paramount for understanding reality. Rooted in empiricism, reason, and scepticism, their epistemology favours observation, experimentation, and critical thinking over revelation or faith. Professor Ashraf contends that such perspectives, devoid of acknowledgment of divine guidance, lead to what is viewed in Islamic terminology as *kufr* or disbelief. While secular humanists prioritise rationality, evidence, and scepticism in their pursuit of knowledge, Professor Ashraf highlights a fundamental divergence in worldview, emphasising the Islamic perspective of reality as imbued with divine purpose and guidance.

Professor Ashraf agrees with Naquib al-Attas when he says that secularisation has brought about "the disenchantment of nature," "the desacralization of politics" and "the deconsecration of values."[8] He asserts that "by separating values from their religious source (God and His attributes), the process of secularization has destroyed the concept of man's nobility and grandeur, his ideal of *Khalīfatullāh* and the objective and universal norm by which Man could be judged."[9] The effect of secularisation has been to reduce the Islamic concept of *ʿilm* to a worldly form of knowledge that changes the value system held sacred in the Islamic society. Nasr notes that "modernism and modern education became the most important means for furthering the value system of the modern world, for the spread of secularization and the criticism of the religious worldview."[10] However, some very profound criticisms of modern secular thoughts have also come from university circles in the West.

Professor Ashraf asserts, "It is impossible to compromise between Islam and secularism. . . . There cannot be a compromise between *kufr* [disbelief] and *īmān* [belief], faithlessness and faith, secularism and Islam."[11] Nasr agrees with Professor Ashraf when he says, "secularism destroys this vision of unity and the integration of all human activity within a Divine norm and pattern."[12] Christian scholars have also expressed deep-rooted criticism of the pervasive influence of secularism. Archbishop Rowan Williams goes as far as to say that secularism is a most powerful cause of certain forms of modern religiousness: "secularism—a functional, instrumentalist perspective, suspicious and uncomfortable about inaccessible dimensions—is the hidden mainspring of certain kinds of modern religiousness."[13] The kind of secularism that Professor Ashraf is so vehemently opposed to includes "programmatic secularism"

---

8 Syed Ali Ashraf, *New Horizons in Muslim Education* (London: Hodder and Stoughton and Cambridge: The Islamic Academy, 1985), 9.
9 Ashraf, *New Horizons*, 9.
10 Seyyed Hossein Nasr, "Modern Education: Its History, Theories, and Philosophies," in *Education in the Light of Tradition*, ed. Jane Casewit (Bloomington, Indiana: World Wisdom, 2011), 105.
11 Ashraf, *New Horizons*, 11.
12 Seyyed Hossein Nasr, *Islam in the Modern World* (New York: HarperOne, 2010), 236.
13 Rowan Williams, *Faith in the Public Square* (London: Bloomsbury, 2012), 15.

that Archbishop Rowan Williams describes as the situation where "any and every public manifestation of any particular religious allegiance is to be ironed out so that everyone may share a clear public loyalty to the state unclouded by private convictions, and any signs of such private convictions are rigorously banned from public space."[14] This kind of secularism in its pure form is "a doomed enterprise, bound to fail . . . it has changed the face of education at every level."[15] Going one step further, there are those who speak of the religious dimension to life "as an additional dimension of the *rational form* of consciousness"[16] and that "Religion . . . originates in experiences of awe, an emotion to which human beings are subject when they are confronted with events, objects, or people which are of overwhelming significance to them."[17] Such statements sever religion from its divine source, relegating it to mere human constructs. According to R. S. Peters, religious judgments are not grounded in either revelation or religious facts; rather, they stem from emotional experiences of awe.[18] Such a narrow rationalistic approach to education has been criticised as "it focuses one-dimensionally on the development of the child's cognitive faculties."[19]

In secular or liberal education, all beliefs and practices are considered questionable and revisable as they are not based on verified or verifiable knowledge. The remarkable achievements of science and technology, that have given human beings ever expanding control over nature, serve to cast corrosive doubt on the validity and objectivity of all other claims to understanding and knowledge particularly those rooted in religious perspectives. As a result of this, educational policy is formulated in non-religious terms emphasising the cultivation of rational autonomy. The validity of this rationalistic view of education is, however, now itself coming under more scrutiny. There is an ongoing debate about whether religious scepticism or agnosticism should be regarded as the only legitimate rational conclusion on religious matters.[20] After all, "the truths of science ultimately rest on man-made conventions."[21] Pro-

---

14 Williams, 3.
15 Williams, 15.
16 Stefaan E. Cuypers. "The Life of Reason—R. S. Peters' Stoic Philosophy of Education," *Kultura Pedagogiczna* 1 (2015): 30.
17 Stefaan E. Cuypers. "The Life of Reason," 30.
18 Peters, R. S. (1973) *Reason and Compassion* (London: Routledge & Kegan Paul), 106.
19 Stefaan E. Cuypers. "The Life of Reason," 28.
20 David L Johnson, "Beyond Modernism: from Theory to Activism," in *Earth, Empire and Sacred Text: Muslims and Christians as Trustees of Creation* (London: Equinox Publishing Limited, 2010), 111–152. Huston Smith, *Beyond the Post-Modern Mind* (New York: The Crossroad Publishing Company, 1982). Paul Hirst, introduction to *Religion and Education: Islamic and Christian Approaches*, ed. Syed Ali Ashraf and Paul H. Hirst (Cambridge: The Islamic Academy, 1994), 3.
21 Arthur Fine, "Scientific Realism and Antirealism," in *Routledge Encyclopedia of Philosophy, Volume 8*, ed. Edward Craig (New York: Taylor & Francis, 1998), 581.

fessor Ashraf contended that religious truths can be verified through their effects on social transformation and by experiential realisation. These realisations can vary depending on the spiritual attainment of the individual and the aspects of reality that are realised.

However, as stated above, Professor Ashraf is not against accepting knowledge from non-Muslim sources, but such knowledge must conform to the spirit of Islam. He has identified numerous perplexities afflicting certain Muslim educationalists, stemming from their oversight in critically analysing secular perspectives in education through the intellectual lens grounded in the Qurʾān and Sunnah. He noted that certain Muslim scholars are actively participating in dialogues with secular educationalists, yet they may not be fully aligned with the rich intellectual and spiritual heritage of Islam themselves. If Muslim intellectuals wish to engage in meaningful discourse with the modern West, they should assess the secular paradigm through the lens of the traditional Islamic worldview and subject it to constructive criticism. Only through this approach can genuine dialogues take place. Without taking this initial step, modernist Muslims often find themselves conceding ground to the prevailing secular humanistic worldview. Professor Ashraf asserts,

> Muslims cannot believe in the basic assumptions of Islamic culture and civilization together with these assumptions of modern Western civilization. They cannot believe in a God-created universe in which natural phenomena are portents (or āyāt) of God and at the same time regard them as nothing more than materials which can be plundered for temporary gain. Can one accept Adam as the first man created by God and at the same time believe in evolution? How can the viewer believe in man's destiny as Khalīfatullāh when all modern scientific and psychological theories teach many confused notions of 'self'? If it is accepted that values are dependent on changing circumstances ... and all norms are regarded as time and space-bound and not derived from absolutes, how can Divine Law as given in the Qurʾān and the Sunnah be immutable against which man can measure his own actions objectively?[22]

In his criticism of modern secularists, Professor Ashraf often refers to the writings of such classical scholars as Al-Kindī, Al-Fārābī, Ibn Sīnā, Ibn Khaldūn and Al-Ghazālī. He finds Al-Ghazālī's methodology of integrating rationality, divine spirituality, and religiosity as particularly fitting for the contemporary time marked by a deficiency in spiritual and religious awareness. He noted, "even though Ghazzali denounced the Muslim philosophy he did not discard Greek knowledge."[23] He only rejected the science of metaphysics that discuss-

---

22 Ashraf, *New Horizons*, 11.
23 Ashraf, *New Horizons*, 44.

es God (ulūhiyyāt).²⁴ In his *Al-Munqidh min al-Ḍalāl*, Ghazālī cautions about the danger of philosophy and also of rejecting philosophy.²⁵ As there was a close similarity between Greek and Islamic approaches and ideas, Ghazālī modified the Greek approach and Islamised the concepts. However, Professor Ashraf believes that the concept of modern education and that of Islamic education are so fundamentally different that full integration is not possible, except marginally and only in certain closely related subjects.²⁶ William Chittick has noted that modern education, based on the presuppositions of the Enlightenment that rejected all traditional notions of truth, authority, hierarchy and human nature, is "profoundly incompatible with Islamic education, which serves the needs of the human soul in its quest to return to God in the best possible manner."²⁷

Professor Ashraf argued that when the spiritual dimension of human nature is overlooked or dismissed, and the rational aspect is detached from the Spirit of Man, reliance on logical thinking becomes the sole avenue for acquiring knowledge. In a worldview where everything is perceived as evolving and inherently changing, no knowledge can be deemed absolute, permanent, or certain. All knowledge becomes grounded in hypotheses, rendering it inherently tentative: science does not believe in absolute truths, nor does it claim to have attained the final truth. Still, it progresses through the exercise of rationality. Arguing for rationality to be the arbiter of all kinds of knowledge, Moshman boldly asserts, "Genuine rationality is unpredictable, open-ended, and potentially subversive. To educate for rationality is to facilitate processes of reflection and reconstruction from which nothing—not even rationality itself—is secure."²⁸ Secular educational paradigm, devoid of religious content, fosters doubt, scepticism, and critical inquiry rather than faith, certainty, and intuitive understanding. It steers individuals toward a more utilitarian and pragmatic mindset, or at best, a narrowly logical and rationalistic one. Thus, the fundamentals of religion stand to be sacrificed at the altar of rationality as the core tenets of religion may be compromised or set aside when subjected to rational scrutiny or logical analysis. The ultimate goal of the secularist is not the pursuit of "Truth" but enhancing human skills and shaping the environment for material benefit. Truth, for them, is contingent on hypothesis

---

24 Mohd Fakhrudin Abdul Mukti, "Al-Ghazzali and His Refutation of Philosophy," *Journal Usuluddin* 21 (2005): 1–22.
25 Al-Ghazālī, "Section C: Danger of Philosophy, Part II," *Deliverance from Error and Mystical Union with the Almighty (al-Munqidh min al-Ḍalāl)*, trans. Muhammad Abulaylah, ed. George F. McLean (Council for Research in Values & Philosophy. March 2002), https://www.ghazali.org/books/md/index.html.
26 Ashraf, *New Horizons*, 44.
27 William C. Chittick, "The Goal of Islamic Education," in *Education in the Light of Tradition*, ed. Jane Casewit (Bloomington, Indiana: World Wisdom, 2011), 85.
28 David Mosham, "Rationality as a Goal of Education," *Educational Psychology Review* 2, no. 4 (1990): 359–60.

or tentative knowledge. However, scientific theories concerning Life, Matter, Nature, and Human Beings, formed on unverified hypotheses like the theory of evolution, are inherently biased and constrained.[29] The West has excelled in developing techniques for material progress but has faltered in devising a methodology that harmonises the Spirit and the Body, the Absolute and the changing.[30] This separation, inherent in Western schools of thought, obscures the interrelationship that unifies the Secular and the Divine leading to destructive consequences for human life and thought. Mitchell observes that "perhaps the most serious adverse consequences were the loss of a holistic vision of the world coupled to a fragmentation of knowledge and an increasing growth of relativism in the area of beliefs and values."[31]

Education in Islam

Professor Ashraf's Islamic educational philosophy starts with the Qurʾānic concept that God created human beings for His worship: "And I did not create the jinn and mankind except to worship Me" and "Say, 'Indeed, my prayer, my rites of sacrifice, my living and my dying are for Allāh, Lord of the worlds.'" (Qurʾān 51:56 and 6:162). The teaching and learning processes must begin and end with obedience to God. This idea is based on the Islamic principle that all phenomena including educational activities must be understood within a religious framework. Professor Ashraf, therefore, defined Islamic education as

> an education which trains the sensibility of pupils in such a manner that in their attitude to life, their actions, decisions and approach to all kinds of knowledge, they are governed by the spiritual and deeply felt ethical values of Islam. They are trained, and mentally so disciplined, that they want to acquire knowledge not merely to satisfy an intellectual curiosity or just for material worldly benefit, but to develop as rational, righteous beings and bring about the spiritual, moral and physical welfare of their families, their people and mankind. This attitude derives from a deep faith in God and a whole-hearted acceptance of a God-given moral code.[32]

Here Professor Ashraf is not discussing "Islamic education" in the traditional sense, referring to a subject focused on the teaching and learning of the

---

29 In science, it is essential to recognise that theories are continually subject to scrutiny and refinement as new evidence emerges. Some scientific theories remain unverified or are still debated within the scientific community.
30 Syed Ali Ashraf, "Editorial: Recommendations of the Five World Conferences on Muslim Education: A Plan for Implementation," *Muslim Education Quarterly* 10, no. 1 (1992): 3.
31 Peter J. Mitchell, "Education, Religion and Transcendental Values," *Muslim Education Quarterly* 14, no. 2 (1997): 10.
32 Syed Sajjad Husain and Syed Ali Ashraf, ed., *Crisis in Muslim Education* (London: Hodder and Stoughton and Jeddah: King Abdulaziz University, 1979), 1.

Qurʾān, Ḥadīth, Fiqh, etc. Instead, he is advocating for an educational system where Islam plays a central role in all subjects taught and learned. In these broad educational aims he is no different from classical scholars such as al-Ghazālī, Miskawayh and al-Zarnūjī. The writings of all the classical Muslim educationalists are centred on seeking true knowledge and obeying God and His messenger and purifying mind and behaviour. For example, in his *Tahdhīb al-Akhlāq*, the Persian philosopher Ibn Miskawayh (932–1030) writes,

> He who has the chance in youth to be trained to follow the morality of the Law [Sharīʿah] and to be required to observe its duties and requirements until they become as habits to him . . . is indeed the happy and the perfect one, and it is his duty to praise God (mighty and exalted is He!) abundantly for this gift and immense favor.[33]

Professor Ashraf emphasises that fostering religious belief (*īmān*), translating it into practice (*ʿamal*), and cultivating a moral life are the core objectives of education. He asserts that genuine education inherently intertwines with religious principles that are enshrined in the concepts of *tawḥīd* (unity), *risālah* (prophethood) and *ākhirah* (afterlife).[34] He saw education as a process that promotes the balanced growth of the total personality of a human being—that is, their physical, intellectual, moral, spiritual, and imaginative aspects—to be attained through the inculcation of religious beliefs and values instead of an approach dominated by concepts that stress rationality at the expense of faith. Islamic education, with its focus on the training of the body, mind and soul is aimed at producing human beings who aspire to fulfil the purpose of creation which is the worship of God in a comprehensive sense, that is the total submission to God in all situations. In this perspective, education serves as the holistic cultivation of the total human being, aimed at equipping individuals with the knowledge and principles essential for living an Islamic way of life. Professor Ashraf discerns a fundamental distinction between education and instruction, contending that education contributes to the holistic development of an individual's personality, fostering moral and spiritual growth whereas instruction merely imparts training to individuals or groups for the proficient execution of specific tasks.[35] The First World Conference on Muslim Education—of which Professor Ashraf was an organising secretary—formulated the principal aim of education as follows: "The aim of Muslim education is the creation of the 'good and righteous man' who worships Allah in the true sense of the term, builds up the structure of this earthly life according

---

33 Miskawayh, "From the Second Discourse of the Refinement of Character," in *Classical Foundations of Islamic Educational Thought*, ed. Bradley J. Cook (Utah: Bringham Young University Press, 2010), 76.
34 Syed Ali Ashraf, "Editorial: Islamisation of Education: Need for the Islamic Frame of Reference," *Muslim Education Quarterly* 6, no. 3 (1989): 2–6.
35 Ashraf, preface to *Aims and Objectives*, ix.

to the Sharīʿah (Islamic law) and employs it to subserve his faith."[36] Professor Ashraf brought this concept to bear on all his educational considerations. He asserted,

> Religion thus provides an all-comprehensive norm of man . . . This norm has a stability because the values are regarded as absolutes derived from the absolute attributes of God which are being continually realized in a relative context in time and space. Contextual change only leads to change in emphasis and focus, modification and alteration of stress and relative importance of certain values in different periods and areas. It does not mean any change in values. Religion thus provides a meaningful goal for education. According to religion this goal is revealed to man and thus it has an objective status. It is not concocted by man or just derived from experience. All experience is tied down to time and space, hence relative.[37]

The "all-inclusive" and "meaningful" aim of education is to equip students with the necessary tools to lead a life in harmony with God's commandments, enabling them to achieve happiness in this world and the hereafter. This can be accomplished through an educational system that integrates teachings from both realms and contributes to the total growth of the students. His integrative perspective on education and religion widens into a metaphysical worldview grounded in a Qurʾānic understanding of life, the world, and eternity. A human being, as *Khalīfatullāh* (vicegerent of Allah) who cultivates within themselves the attributes of Allah, can attain limitless spiritual and intellectual progress. As this progress depends on knowledge, there is no bar to the acquisition of knowledge. Achieving the holistic development of a human being involves nurturing spiritual, moral, intellectual, imaginative, emotional, and physical dimensions. Professor Ashraf views this comprehensive growth within the framework of "Man's relationship with God, Man, and Nature."[38]

The holistic education of Professor Ashraf stresses that the true meaning of human activities is unveiled when they are aligned with a sense of devotion and servitude to God. This servitude must be accepted freely out of love for God who can be known by His Attributes such as Knowledge, Truth, Love, Mercy, Kindness, Charity, Justice, Freedom, Goodness, and Beauty. God's Attributes provide norms for human beings to live by. As Prophet Muhammad (pbuh) is the perfect human example of these norms in spirit and application, love for the Prophet generates love for God. Professor Ashraf firmly held that "Education must therefore make man aware of those attributes and the life

---

[36] King Abdulaziz University, *Conference Book: First World Conference on Muslim Education* (Jeddah and Mecca: King Abdulaziz University, 1977), 76.
[37] Ashraf, preface to *Aims and Objectives*, xii.
[38] Ashraf, *New Horizons*, 5.

and character of the Prophet so that love is generated by that knowledge."[39] Knowledge generates love and love leads to action. The truest expression of faith is in action. Therefore, no matter how well-designed an education system may be, its value remains dormant unless put into practice following the Prophetic norm. The Prophet was of "an exalted character" (khuluqin ʿaẓīm),[40] and the "example per excellence" (uswatun ḥasanah)[41] for humanity. The Prophet himself said, "I have been sent to complete the excellence of virtues."[42] The purpose of education is therefore to attain these virtues and fulfil "God's will through the exercise of his [human being's] will and through action (ʿamal) in this world."[43] Professor Ashraf continues:

> The system of education must be so designed that it reflects not just any man but the Universal Perfect Man (al-insān al-kāmil). As the Prophet, peace be upon him, is the person in whom that Perfect Man is realized, and as the concept of education in Islam pertains to man alone, the system of education conceived in Islam has always been a system that describes the model of man as perfected in the sacred person of the Holy Prophet.[44]

The basis of relating education to the obedience of the Prophet is based on the Qurʾānic teaching that "Whoever obeys the Messenger has truly obeyed Allah" (Qurʾān 4:80). The function of this education system is to help attain the status of God's representative (Khalīfatullāh) by emulating the Prophet as following practical examples of the Prophet is true submission to God.

For Professor Ashraf, knowledge of God gained through education should not be merely an intellectual acquisition but an assimilation of certain truths by the learner. Unless human beings have certainty (yaqīn) in those truths, their assimilation is not possible. This certainty is only possible through faith: "Faith is a spiritual gift and knowledge is an intellectual acquisition through the use of man's intellect (ʿaql). . . . Islam demands an acceptance by qalb (heart) and obedience first and then seek assistance from ʿaql (intellect)"[45] The function of education is to create an enquiring mind but doubting the existence of God and the teaching of the Prophet is destructive of human spirituality as it cuts them off from the source of their own spirit. He says, "That which

---

39 Syed Ali Ashraf, "A View of Education—An Islamic Perspective," in *Schools for Tomorrow: Building Walls or Building Bridges*, ed. Bernadette O'Keeffe (London: The Falmer Press, 1988), 74.
40 Qurʾān 68:4.
41 Qurʾān 33:21.
42 Al-Bukhārī, *Adab al-Mufrad*, Book 14, Ḥadīth 273.
43 Ashraf, "A View of Education," 75.
44 Ashraf, "A View of Education," 75.
45 Ashraf, "A View of Education," 74 and 76.

destroys faith is not really knowledge but a form of ignorance (*jahl*)."[46] The roles and limits of doubt in Islam should be properly understood. When Imam Ghazālī started to doubt his own faith (*īmān*), he did not turn to disbelief (*kufr*), but he left his home and prestigious position at Nizamiyyah Madrasah and went out in search of God, the One he doubted. He neither had certainty about God nor His non-existence, but his conscious decision to search for God with the full force of his spiritual faculties shows that he believed in His existence although he had not realised Him. His doubt was thus a desire to know the Unknown. Doubt as a perpetual state of mind and doubt as a gateway into truth are not the same; the former being a veil on the human spirit and the latter a gateway to the realisation of the Truth.

In addition to the primary sources—the Qurʾān and Ḥadīth—the Islamic education system should also draw from the Islamic classics on education and the vast intellectual heritage of Islam. Islamic education should, therefore, be based on

> a total framework of concepts and value regarding every aspect of life derived from the Qurʾān and the Sunnah and the long-standing tradition of knowledge established by *mufassirūn* (interpreters of the Qurʾān), *muḥaddithūn* (interpreters of ḥadīth); metaphysicians, philosophers, *ʿārifūn* (gnostics), Sufi *ʿulamāʾ* and *fuqahāʾ* (jurists). The Qurʾān and the Sunnah are the basic, primary source but intellectual and experiential interpretations have thrown considerable light on different aspects of their vast store of knowledge.[47]

Professor Ashraf's comprehensive framework necessitates an exploration of Islam's rich religious, spiritual, and intellectual heritage across multiple disciplines: Qurʾānic exegesis, Ḥadīth, Sufism, philosophy, and more. While classical Islamic scholars generally integrated education into broader philosophical or sociological discussions, virtually all Qurʾānic exegetes have touched upon the concept of education within their great works of *tafsīr*. For instance, luminaries like Ibn Kathīr, Al-Ṭabarī, Al-Rāzī, Ibn al-Qayyim al-Jawziyyah, and Ibn ʿĀshūr offer profound insights into the Qurʾānic perspective on education, stressing its significance and offering guidance on acquiring knowledge and wisdom in the Islamic tradition. Ibn ʿĀshūr's *Alaysa al-ṣubḥu bi-qarīb* provides a meticulous account of Islamic education, its methodologies, curricula, and avenues for educational reform. Bediuzzaman Said Nursi, through his profound work, *Risale-i Nur*, pioneered significant advancements in education by integrating traditional madrasah teachings with modern scientific education. His seminal initiative aimed at establishing Madrasatʾuz Zahra, in Eastern Turkey, symbolised his commitment to this educational synthesis. Ḥadīth

---

46 Ashraf, "A View of Education," 74.
47 Syed Ali Ashraf, "Editorial: Islamisation of Education," 1–2.

scholars such as Imām al-Bukhārī, Imām Muslim, Imām al-Tirmidhī, and Imām al-Nawawī, through their compilations of authentic Ḥadīth literature, have enriched the understanding of Islamic education, etiquette, and moral values, elucidating their vital role in a Muslim's life. Notably, Muslim Sufis like Al-Ghazālī, Jalāl al-Dīn Rūmī, Ibn ʿArabī, and Ibn ʿAṭāʾ Allāh, renowned for their profound spiritual insights and practices, emphasise the importance of education, especially spiritual and moral education, within Islam. Their teachings shed light on the spiritual dimension of education, emphasising the significance of both inner and outer knowledge in the journey toward spiritual enlightenment and proximity to the Divine. Islamic philosophers such as Ibn Sīnā delve into the role of education in nurturing human intellect and moral character, while Ibn Khaldūn, in his seminal work *Muqaddimah*, explores education's pivotal role in the ascent and decline of civilisations, underscoring its impact on societal institutions and cultural development. Al-Fārābī, in his *Kitāb ārāʾ ahl al-Madīnah al-Fāḍilah*, discusses the ideal city-state and the role of education in fostering virtuous citizens. Ibn Rushd, in *Tahāfut al-Tahāfut*, examines the interplay between reason, revelation, and education in Islamic thought, advocating for the compatibility of reason and revelation and the utility of philosophy in elucidating religious truths. Conversely, Al-Ghazālī critiques philosophical thought, advocating for the primacy of revelation over reason in his work, *Iḥyāʾ ʿulūm al-dīn* which emphasises spiritual education and self-purification within the Islamic tradition.

Moreover, scholars like Ibn Saḥnūn, Al-Qābisī, Al-Zarnūjī, Ibn Jamāʿah, and Miskawayh have expounded upon various facets of education in their respective treatises, encompassing educational theories, curriculum development, teaching methodologies, and character formation. Their contributions enrich the philosophical understanding of education within the Islamic paradigm, addressing its theoretical foundations, practical applications, and broader societal implications, thus informing contemporary discussions on Islamic education. The collective works of all these scholars serve as nothing less than elucidations of the teachings found within the Qurʾān and Ḥadīth, collectively shaping the aims and objectives of Islamic education providing clear guidance on curriculum development, teacher education and educational management. Their contributions provide us with the essential theoretical foundations upon which to build our education systems, enabling us to address the challenges of the present era. This not only ensures stability and continuity within our educational traditions but also equips us to effectively respond to the demands of the modern age.

The educational framework described above is crucial for both individual and societal reform and safeguarding against the infiltration of divisive ideologies. To imbue education with Islamic principles, authorities must not merely espouse these values verbally but demonstrate how this comprehensive perspective offers a balanced understanding of humanity. Islamic scholars ought to supplant secular and anti-religious interpretations of Nature, Society, and Humanity with concepts rooted in the Qurʾān and Sunnah. Moreover, they should elucidate how this approach can shield society from the dehumanising effects of technology, empower individuals to harness these forces responsibly, and guide them toward personal fulfilment through integrated development. Without a clear understanding of the purpose of human existence, without envisioning harmony between humanity and nature, and without acknowledging the spiritual quest for ultimate Truth as the paramount objective, the pursuits of knowledge may lead to spiritual detachment, selfishness, and intellectual isolation.

Professor Ashraf's concept of Islamic education encompasses the inculcation of *tawḥīd*, the oneness of God, and the Prophetic examples, emphasising their profound implications for all aspects of life. It champions lifelong learning and transmission of knowledge across diverse fields, with the aim of nurturing individuals holistically. This holistic approach not only prioritises intellectual growth but also places significant emphasis on spiritual, moral, and emotional development. Professor Ashraf emphasises the vital importance of harmonising all human faculties—*qalb* (heart), *ʿaql* (intellect), *rūḥ* (spirit) and *nafs* (soul). He advocates for the incorporation of authentic narratives (Revelation), spiritual practices, and moral refinement as indispensable components in the educational pursuit. Education in Islam requires the cultivation (*tarbiyah*) of a balanced and virtuous personality, drawing upon the teachings of Islam. Individuals are encouraged to pursue excellence (*iḥsān*) in all their endeavours, guided by values such as honesty, integrity, compassion, and justice. Moreover, they are called to embody humility, respect, kindness, and empathy in their interactions with others, actively engaging in community service and contributing positively to society. This educational framework promotes cooperation, solidarity, and compassion, particularly towards those in need. Furthermore, his vision seeks to harmonise faith and reason, underlining the compatibility between religious beliefs and rational inquiry, while recognising the primacy of revealed knowledge conveyed by the Prophet. Critical thinking, reflection, and intellectual engagement are fostered within the context of Islamic teachings, enriching the educational experience and preparing individuals to navigate the complexities of the modern world with wisdom and discernment.

Moral Education

In Islam, morality is part of religion, and the moral norm is set by the Qurʾān and Sunnah of Prophet Muhammad (pbuh). Engaging in immoral actions involves violating established norms and committing sinful acts. Individuals possess the inherent freedom either to embrace this norm for their own benefit or disregard it, leading to their own detriment.[48] Universality and permanence are the basic characteristics of human nature; therefore, Professor Ashraf believes that fundamental moral values (sing. *khulq*; pl. *akhlāq*) are also universal and permanent. The moral sense is intrinsic. That is why there is a remarkable consensus on core moral values among major world religions, and indeed, many of these values are shared by secular humanists as well.

Values and value-consciousness are innate in the human Spirit: "This Spirit is endowed with moral perception."[49] Values such as Justice, Truth, Mercy, Love, Creativity, and Destruction are enshrined in the Names of God. God has endowed human beings with these values. As every human being is endowed with Spirit, they have "basically the same spiritual consciousness with intellect, imagination, intelligence and feelings and the same innate consciousness of supreme values."[50] Professor Ashraf has stressed that morality is innate and supported his argument by giving the example of small children who can possess a sense of justice and an appreciation of love, beauty, and truth.[51] That morality is innate has some support among linguistics, political philosophers, and psychologists. In *Moral Minds: How Nature Designed Our Universal Sense of Right and Wrong* Marc Hauser says, "morality is best understood in much the same way as Noam Chomsky described language: as the product of an innate and universal mental faculty. . . . it is human nature to unconsciously and automatically evaluate the moral status of human actions: to judge them as right or wrong, allowed or forbidden, optional or obligatory."[52] Professor Ashraf believes that moral wisdom is not exclusive to those who adhere to established faiths, asserting that human beings, through their innate nature and reasoning, can attain some comprehension of right and wrong. He considers innate sense of moral values as "the product of the impingement of a Supreme Being on the material self of the human being."[53] However, he contends that without the guidance of God's revelation, individuals may fall short of achieving a complete and accurate understanding of both the nature of reality and moral principles. This guidance includes understanding God's promise of reward for adhering to the moral principles and the potential consequences for deviating from them.

---

48 Syed Ali Ashraf, "Editorial: Islamic Education and Moral Development I—The Metaphysical Dimension," *Muslim Education Quarterly* 8, no. 1 (1990): 1.
49 Ashraf, "Editorial: Islamic Education and Moral Development I," 1.
50 Syed Ali Ashraf, "Islamic Education and Moral Development," in *Religion and Education: Islamic and Christian Approaches*, eds. Syed Ali Ashraf and Paul H. Hirst (Cambridge: The Islamic Academy. 1994), 144.
51 Ashraf, "Editorial: Islamic Education and Moral Development I," 1–2.
52 Paul Bloom & Izzat Jarudi, "The Chomsky of Morality? A View of Morality as the Product of an Innate Mental Faculty—rather like language," *Nature* 443 (26 October 2006). See also Marc D. Hauser, *Moral Minds: How Nature Designed Our Universal Sense of Right and Wrong* (New York: HarperCollins, 2006).
53 Ashraf, "Islamic Education and Moral Development," 144.

Two commendable goals of secular education are to produce good individuals and good citizens, but Professor Ashraf argues that in the absence of a defined set of moral values none of these aims is attainable.[54] Kretzschmar asks, "Thus, lacking an objective transcendent moral Being, on what basis can human beings be obliged to resist self-gratification and promote the well-being of others?"[55] On the other hand, for secular educationalists such as Peters, "moral education is indistinguishable from the ideal of a liberal education."[56] Liberals believe that the religious dimension of a rational morality has nothing to do with religious education such as a Christian or an Islamic one.[57] Secular scholars advocate for the autonomy of morality, asserting that moral principles exist independently and are not inherently tied to any religious framework. Professor Ashraf argues that morality is much deeper than that. It is rooted in the pre-natal covenant (mīthāq, ʿahd) between God and human souls that they will accept God as their Lord:

> Education through the study of the texts with faith should enable the rational soul to assert its supremacy and confirm and affirm the covenant within the total self of the human being so that the total self is able to accept the guidance (hudā) granted by God and fulfil the Trust through action (ʿamal) and thereby perform the job of worshipping God.[58]

The acceptance of the guidance and fulfilling the Trust will lead to a moral life. Values and ethical principles find their true meaning when viewed in this context. Morality is not "dry-as-dust logic alone that would make a true human being. Heart is fully involved in this process."[59] That is why the outlook of a moral person evolves and becomes more nuanced as they apply principles to practice, enriched by their experiences. Human beings should act out of love for God and His Prophet as "mechanical action can become cruel."[60] Referencing the Qurʾān, Professor Ashraf highlights that all prophets, including Abraham, Moses, and Jesus, provided their followers with the ideal norm of values and Prophet Muhammad, the last Prophet, provides the humanity with the best human norm (uswatun ḥasanah). The Prophet said, "I was sent to per-

---

54 Husain and Ashraf, eds., *Crisis in Muslim Education*, 38.
55 Louise Kretzschmar, "Convergence and Divergence: A Christian Response to Prozesky's "Global Ethic" and Secular Spirituality," *Journal for the Study of Religion* 31, no. 1, Festschrift for Martin Prozesky (2018), 123.
56 Richard S. Peters, *Moral Development and Moral Education* (London: George Allen & Unwin Ltd., [1970] 1981), 81.
57 Stefaan E. Cuypers. "The Life of Reason," 30.
58 Syed Ali Ashraf, "Editorial: Islamic Education and Moral Development II—The Metaphysical Dimension," *Muslim Education Quarterly* 8, no. 2 (1991): 2.
59 Ashraf, "Islamic Education and Moral Development," 152.
60 Ashraf, "Editorial: Islamic Education and Moral Development II," 3.

fect good character."[61] Following the Prophet is to aspire for excellence being inspired by faith and led by virtues. A moral and ethical life is a spiritual life and a life of virtue. It is a life of having faith and trust in God, remembrance of God, and a life or worship, love and hope.

Professor Ashraf envisioned an educational system aimed at instilling moral and spiritual virtues in students, guiding them towards piety and selfless devotion. He emphasised that moral education's primary focus should be on purifying the heart (*qalb*) through faith. He asserted that to be moral is to be a complete human being, whose head and heart work in coordination, and love for the good is evident through good deeds.[62] He stressed that "Knowledge of the moral principles is important but the manifestation of morality in action is more important both individually and in the community."[63] This is because in Islam faith (*īmān*) and action (*'amal*) go hand in hand. Education should enable students to discern right from wrong, even if it contradicts their personal preferences. Upon leaving school, students should possess a sense of social justice and awareness of both personal morality and broader societal issues. He viewed any action contributing to the comprehensive growth of an individual's personality as moral.

Without a foundation in moral principles, education has the potential to produce individuals who lack human values, effectively creating human monsters. Professor Ashraf says,

> A man may be a great general, an efficient carpenter or a first-class pilot, a lawyer, a mechanic or a pathologist, a renowned doctor, a chemical engineer or a chartered accountant, but may still remain a semi-educated, ill-mannered, immoral, unrighteous or unjust man. Similarly, a man may be a very fine painter, a good poet, or his love of beauty may be highly delicate and sensitive, but he may, at the same time, be cruel or brutal, or an untruthful, unsocial individual. He could be highly selfish and deliberately ignore his duty towards his neighbours or even towards his wife and children. We can say that people who have specialized in certain educational fields are well-instructed persons, but we cannot necessarily regard them as truly educated.[64]

Education should be more than just the acquisition of knowledge; it should also be a means to cultivate moral values and virtues. The evolution of mass education over the past two centuries has increasingly disregarded the crucial aspect of moral development in students, neglecting their moral upbringing. Without moral education, Kretzschmar writes, "society would be exposed

---

61 Imam Malik, *Al-Muwaṭṭa'* 1614.
62 Ashraf, "Islamic Education and Moral Development," 154.
63 Syed Ali Ashraf, "Editorial: Islamic Education and Moral Development II," 4.
64 Ashraf, preface to *Aims and Objectives*, ix.

to doctors, mine-owners and presidents who could abuse their positions and power."[65] Jeffreys asserts that "It stands to reason that if education is supremely concerned with the quality of people, it needs the inspiration of some vision of what human beings ought to be."[66] Shockingly, throughout history, some of the architects of terrible atrocities were highly educated individuals lacking in moral fortification. This raises the question: shouldn't education, which encompasses influences from family, school, and society, also prioritise the cultivation of virtues that elevate human nature? Education devoid of moral guidance only serves to enhance efficiency in evildoing, creating individuals who are educated but morally bankrupt. Enes Karić states:

> Moral tuition implies, above all, a recognition of the higher purpose and superior reasons for learning, knowledge, and instruction. Moral tuition is grounded in culture, culture in faith, and faith in the Ultimate Purpose, God. To know the laws of hydraulics, to know how to make water conduits is a matter of education; to clean oneself with water, however, is a matter of upbringing, of culture. To know the formula for soap and to make soap is a matter of science; to use soap when it is necessary is a matter of upbringing. To capture enemy troops in wartime is a matter of military skill and knowledge; to spare their lives and preserve their dignity is a matter of upbringing.[67]

Just as education shapes the intellect, moral tuition nurtures the inner conscience and enlightens the heart itself. Therefore, education and moral tuition are two inseparable components of humanity's developmental journey. Education lacking moral guidance risks transforming into a destructive force, harming both nature and human society. If our education fails to establish a groundwork of moral principles and neglects to instil a profound understanding of what it means to be human, such education is inherently flawed. It is not surprising that Pring concludes his lecture on "Education as a Moral Practice" by asserting that "teaching should be regarded as a moral practice."[68]

The trajectory of human development cannot avoid the inculcation of moral and spiritual values that provide it with vigour and stability which is essential in these days of confused and disintegrating values.[69] For Professor Ashraf moral wisdom can be gained from both natural laws (reason and innate nature ingrained in human beings) and God's revelation and Prophetic practice. The total framework of values is also dependent on the concept of faith in

---

[65] Louise Kretzschmar, "Convergence and Divergence," 113.
[66] M. V. C. Jeffreys, *The Aims of Education (Glaucon)* (London: Pitman, 1972), xiv.
[67] Enes Karić, "Moral Tuition and Education," in *Education in the Light of Tradition*, ed. Jane Casewit (Bloomington, Indiana: World Wisdom), 37–38.
[68] Richard Pring, *Philosophy of Education: Aim, Theory, Common Sense, and Research* (London: Continuum, 2004), 25.
[69] M. V. C. Jeffreys, xiv.

the hereafter (*ākhirah*). As love for God and the Prophet are the major means of strengthening this faith, this includes both intellectual awareness and innate response. Morality has a foundation in the human experience of God's love and human love for God, others, and the entire creation. Human beings are more than mere reason. Professor Ashraf emphasised the importance of placing human intellect in a deeper and wider perspective, enabling it to comprehend that the human self is capable of delving into a far richer and deeper level of understanding, where the spiritual and moral dimensions of human existence play an inevitable role.

British Education System

Education for the British Plural Society

Professor Ashraf made a remarkable contribution to the British education system, particularly in the realm of religious education. He observed that the predominantly secular British education system, catering to a substantial number of Muslim pupils, exhibited similar detrimental effects of secularism as discussed earlier in this chapter. An additional challenge arises as Muslim students, being in a minority context, face the risk of eroding their religious and cultural identities. His critique of the British education system was informed by the philosophical perspective delineated earlier in the text and in the introduction. He passionately engaged in a long struggle to make education rooted in the concept of human beings' relationship with God and argued for faith-based education through a common faith framework for a multifaith, multicultural country such as the UK. His core principles were promotion of faith through education and living together in harmony with people of other faiths, and he carefully constructed an educational rationale to justify his approach. Clearly, when Professor Ashraf discusses faith-based education within a pluralistic society, he is not specifically addressing any singular religion, be it Islam or Christianity, to avoid accusations of bias. Instead, he highlights the universal attributes shared by all world religions, emphasising the common threads of belief in a Transcendental deity and the imperative for divine guidance as foundational principles shaping educational endeavours. His edited book, *Religion and Education: Islamic and Christian Approaches*[70] shows his deep commitment to faith and desire to search for common educational grounds for people of all faiths in a multifaith, multicultural and multiethnic country.

Professor Ashraf realised that developing an education system that satisfies all groups in a multi-denominational country is a difficult task. To maintain a balance between the achievement of social integration and preservation of cultural identity of different groups, or "the legitimate demands of

---

70 Syed Ali Ashraf and Paul H. Hirst, eds., *Religion and Education: Islamic and Christian Approaches* (Cambridge: The Islamic Academy, 1994).

pluralism and difference", or to resolve the "tensions between universalism and particularism"[71] is a serious challenge posed by modern society in a globalised world. The United Kingdom, which is a multifaith, multicultural, multiethnic country with cultural roots in Christianity, follows a primarily secularist policy in education. Various approaches such as theories of assimilation, integration, pluralism, and multiculturalism have been adopted to integrate diverse communities into the dominant cultural fold of the country, but assimilationist and integrationist theories have utterly failed, and pluralist and multicultural approaches attained a limited success. In order to satisfy the educational needs of the British society, the Swann Committee proposed a concept of "education for all" that adopts "mainly a secular outlook which views religion as a cultural phenomenon and principally a private matter."[72] The Swann Report sought to "develop appropriate ways of integrating all pupils into an all embracing pluralist culture" by adopting a mainly secular outlook which views religion as a cultural phenomenon and principally a private matter.[73] Professor Ashraf argued that being integrated into a comprehensive cultural entity based on a humanistic democratic and pluralistic philosophy may lead to apparent "unity in diversity" and may cultivate "multicultural outlook" and "tolerant attitude" to all faiths but will eventually alienate the minority groups from their cultural roots and religions, as "culture is integrally related to values and values are derived from religion."[74] He strongly defended the need to preserve the identity of the immigrant groups living in the UK as the secular curriculum was eventually going to destroy their cultures that are indissolubly linked to their religions. For him, the greatest danger of the secularist policy was that it "does not provide children with certainty and a reliable, sustaining and accepted and acceptable norm to fall back upon."[75]

Professor Ashraf was acutely aware of the happenings in the British education system and interacted cooperatively with fellow educationists in the British academia. He argued that if the curriculum and methods of teaching and school ethos are not based on "the absolutes in human nature" but on "the philosophy of changing values that are dependent on external and social

---

71 Terence H. McLaughlin, "Liberalism, Education and the Common School," *Journal of Philosophy of Education* 29, no. 2 (1995): 239.
72 *Education for All: Report of the Committee of Enquiry into the Education of Children from Ethnic Minority Groups* (London: Her Majesty's Stationery Office, 1985), 5, https://education-uk.org/documents/swann/swann1985.html. This is generally known as "The Swann Report (1985)."
73 Jürgen Habermas, "A 'post-secular' society – what does that mean?" *Reset Dialogues on Civilizations* (June 2–6, 2008), para 3. This is a paper presented by the author at the Istanbul Seminars organised by Reset Dialogues on Civilizations in Istanbul from June 2nd to the 6th, 2008, https://www.resetdoc.org/story/a-post-secular-society-what-does-that-mean/
74 Ashraf, "A View of Education," 70.
75 Ashraf, "A View of Education," 71.

change," the result will be "not unification of society or 'unity in diversity' but more stress on diversity without any roots in unity."[76]

His clarity of vision, honesty and integrity and willingness to cooperate with British scholars and educationalists and policymakers—at times fearlessly presenting his own views that often ran counter to the secular philosophy of the mainstream education system—gained him respect from both Muslim and non-Muslim scholars at British institutions.[77] He urged the authorities to consider seriously the reality of the existence of different faiths in our society. He noted that the following of a singular curriculum at school, which does not promote diverse approaches to education, consistently fail to meet the needs of the children from the Muslim and other minority communities, and as a result they suffer from low esteem, low aspirations, and low confidence.

For education in a democratic pluralist society the Swann Committee stressed the need for "the acceptance by all groups of a set of shared values distinctive of the society as a whole" that would maintain and support "the essential elements of the cultures and lifestyles of all the ethnic groups within it."[78] Professor Ashraf supported the idea of shared values, but he tried to find these in the religious beliefs and spiritual values of the major religious communities living in the UK: Christians, Muslims, Jews, Hindus, Sikhs and Buddhists. What he wanted for Muslims, he wanted for others too: to foster religious belief and strengthen spiritual values. The existence of "religious pluralism" is a reality, and Professor Ashraf wanted to maintain this religious differentiation in a plural society, and he rejected the Swann Committee's "integrational pluralism" as it was rooted in "a secular approach to religion and all religious communities." He said,

> If the curriculum, the methods of teaching and the school ethos are based on the philosophy of changing values that are dependent on external social change and not on the philosophy of the absolutes in human nature which provide the unchanging universal norms of truth, justice, righteousness, freedom, pity, mercy, honesty, compassion and charity, Muslim children will suffer from the conflict that people suffered in England in the nineteenth century and the sense of loss, uncertainty and insecurity that is prevalent in the twentieth century.[79]

As opposed to the common frame of belief upheld in the name of humanism, democracy, universality and rationalism, he proposed a Common Frame of Reference that is based on "the common spiritual attitude to life that is

---

76 Ashraf, "A View of Education," 71.
77 Peter Mitchell, "Professor Syed Ali Ashraf: An Appreciation." See Chapter 29 of this book.
78 *Education for All*, 6.
79 Ashraf, "A View of Education," 71.

bred by the Judaeo-Christian-Islamic beliefs in God, man's accountability to God and afterlife."⁸⁰ The source of this Framework is the Absolute values that were enunciated by messengers of God: "In matters of faith, He [God] has laid down for you [people] the same commandment that He gave Noah, which We [God] have revealed to you [Muhammad] and which We enjoined on Abraham and Moses and Jesus: Uphold the faith and do not divide into factions within it" (Qurʾān 42:13). Professor Ashraf was aware that the manifestation of the fundamental values that Muslims, Christians, and Jews share are different, but "the roots of most of those which are regarded as fundamental values are the same."⁸¹ He wanted to stress what unites them rather than what divides. He passionately believed that:

> There is no reason therefore why this Common Frame of Reference should not be the basis of educational planning for the faith-communities living in this country and should not be the source of unity in diversity. We shall then accept the difference not only in customs, conventions and rituals but also in the nature and method of the manifestation and expression of those Absolutes in different societies.⁸²

An exploration into the foundations of major religions reveals the presence of shared enduring values, which followers can utilise to live together harmoniously. This helps the believing communities come together as they share beliefs in the existence of a Transcendental Reality, the human spirit, the need for divine guidance, and moral and spiritual values. To have faith at the basis of education does not take away the autonomy of disciplines, nor does it restrict the use of rational faculty, but it helps to see all branches of knowledge in the context of a "Unified Truth" in their "proper perspective within the orbit of the supreme knowledge that man can attain, that of Man's relation with God."⁸³

Through the organisation of two seminars, organised jointly by the Islamic Academy and the Cambridge University Department of Education, entitled, "Faith as the Basis of Education in a Multi-faith Multi-cultural Country,"⁸⁴ the organisers wanted to explore "if there were any values which we all shared,

---

80 Ashraf, "A View of Education," 71.
81 Ashraf, "A View of Education," 73.
82 Ashraf, "A View of Education," 72–73.
83 Ashraf, "A View of Education," 73.
84 The first of these seminars (held on 15–17 September 1989) was attended by representatives of Islam and Christianity. The second one (held on 16–17 September 1990) was attended by representatives of Islam, Christianity, Judaism, Hinduism, Sikhism and Buddhism. The outcomes of these seminars were later published as booklets: *Faith as the Basis of Education in a Multi-faith Multi-cultural Country: A Discussion Document* (Cambridge: The Islamic Academy, 1990) and *Faith as the Basis of Education in a Multi-faith Multi-cultural Country: Discussion Document II* (Cambridge: The Islamic Academy, 1991).

which would more adequately encapsulate afresh in a pluralist society the religious perspective on education and which could help to transform the schooling we provide for our young.[85] These seminars, which were organised at the initiative of Professor Ashraf, suggested principles and guidelines of a common core curriculum for state schools in the UK so that all subjects could be treated and taught as "having religious presuppositions without at the same time destroying the appropriate autonomy of each subject."[86] Emile Lester argues that "autonomous choice is not identical to rational choice, and educating for autonomy does not require discouraging students from relying heavily upon the authority of religious communities or Scripture."[87]

The British education system predominantly adopts a secular approach, thereby marginalising the religious voice and the cultures and identities of minority groups. Professor Ashraf's proposal to base education on faith aims to tackle these issues effectively. He concluded his book *Religion and Education* with the following words: "If this book, *Religion and Education*, rouses in the minds of readers the desire to go beyond the present worldviews, including the modern scientific worldview, to see the world through a mind freed from the narrow concept of logical reasoning, then I think it has fulfilled its primary job."[88] This succinctly encapsulates his aspirations for a faith-based education within a plural society. His was advocating for an educational system in a pluralistic society that derives its principles from the primacy of the revealed word of God, shared by major religious groups, with reason being subservient to it—a central tenet of his educational philosophy.

Faith School versus State School

For a multicultural, multireligious society like the UK, Professor Ashraf strongly advocated for the establishment of Muslim voluntary-aided schools to cater to the educational needs of Muslim children, allowing them to pursue their educational aspirations. He found support from prominent educationalists such as Paul Hirst, Terence McLaughlin, Peter Mitchell, and Mark Halstead. They were convinced that such schools provide the best way for Muslims to achieve the dual objectives of preserving, maintaining, and transmitting their religious faith while offering a high standard of general education for their children. The problem of maintained schools where majority of Muslim children go is that they are dominated by concepts that stress "rationality

---

85 The Islamic Academy, *Faith as the Basis of Education in a Multi-faith Multi-cultural Country: Discussion Document II* (Cambridge: The Islamic Academy, 1991), 6.
86 The Islamic Academy, *Faith as the Basis of Education*, 18.
87 Emile Lester, "A More Neutral Liberal Education: Why Not Only Liberals, but Religious Conservatives Should Endorse Comparative Religious Education in Public Schools," *Polity* 39, no. 2 (Apr. 2007): 179–207 and 183.
88 Syed Ali Ashraf, "Conclusion," in *Religion and Education: Islamic and Christian Approaches*, eds. Syed Ali Ashraf and Paul H. Hirst (Cambridge: The Islamic Academy. 1994), 217.

and ignore faith, doubts and not spiritual certainty, changing values and not essential unchanging norms, worldly life and this worldly culture and not life in the other world and culture governed by spiritual certainties."[89] This secular approach affects other faith communities also. The issues faced by Catholic schools have been discussed in detail in *The Contemporary Catholic School: Context, Identity and Diversity*. One of the contributors to the book, McClelland quoted Professor Ashraf approvingly by saying that the Christian view of education as spiritual fulfilment "is not far distant from the view of Islam, carefully presented by Syed Ali Ashraf":[90]

> True humanism lies not in playing with some intellectual counters but in purifying the self of all forms of narrowness and greed and this is possible when the love of God is generated within the soul. The sense of eternal values which are already there in that soul has to be nurtured and refined and given free play in the context of the society and humanity as a whole.[91]

He was aware that despite goodwill on all sides, due to financial and other reasons only a few voluntary schools could be established, and a vast majority of Muslim children would have to go to maintained schools.[92] He believed that "as Muslims do not consider any human law superior to the divine law, they will resist anti-Muslim laws and create cores of resistance in the hearts of their children to such laws. At the same time Muslims will readily accept all the basic human values which they commonly share with other religions or ethical or humanist groups."[93] He made the British Muslims aware that they have to undertake certain responsibilities themselves for the proper education of their children: "On the one hand they have to fight at the intellectual and academic level with those who are preaching secularism dogmatically and trying to justify it as if it is the only rational philosophy of life in a multi-cultural society. On the other, they have to get their own children trained and disciplined to think in terms of Islam."[94]

---

89 Ashraf, "A View of Education," 76–77.
90 V. Alan McClelland, "Wholeness, Faith and the Distinctiveness of the Catholic School," in *The Contemporary Catholic School: Context, Identity and Diversity*, eds. Terence H. McLaughlin, Joseph O'Keefe SJ, and Bernadette O'Keeffe (London: The Falmer Press, 1996), 157.
91 Syed Ali Ashraf, "Responding to the Challenge of Secularism," in *Aspects of Education* 51 (1994). Quoted in V. Alan McClelland, "Wholeness, Faith and the Distinctiveness of the Catholic School," in *The Contemporary Catholic School: Context, Identity and Diversity*, eds. Terence H. McLaughlin, Joseph O'Keefe SJ, and Bernadette O'Keeffe (London: The Falmer Press, 1996), 157.
92 Ashraf, "A View of Education," 77.
93 Syed Ali Ashraf, foreword to *The Case for Muslim Voluntary-Aided Schools: Some Philosophical Reflections*, by J. Mark Halstead (Cambridge: The Islamic Academy, 1986), vi.
94 Ashraf, foreword to *The Case for Muslim Voluntary-Aided Schools*, vii.

He realised that in a modern society where all spheres of life are dominated by secular concepts, and erosion of fundamental religious values cannot be avoided, the home and the mosque have a responsibility to help children develop within their hearts forces of resistance to counter evils in society. Muslim children living in the UK should be taught the importance of cooperating with people of other faiths and living in harmony with them and encouraged to contribute to the welfare of the society to the best of their ability. Likewise, "it is necessary to remove from the hearts of white British children the shadow of the Crusades generated by . . . propaganda, false presentation of Islam and the Prophet and stereotypes and myths in history and religious education texts."[95] British children should also be made aware of the contribution of Islamic civilisation to the West through diverse cultural, scholarly, and scientific modes, which will broaden their vision, bring flexibility in their minds, and help them accept Islam and Muslims as an integral part of British society.[96]

Religious Education

All state-funded schools in England must teach religious education (RE). Religious education is a component of the basic curriculum (but not the National Curriculum)[97] and is compulsory for all pupils in local authority maintained schools aged 5 to 18 years. The teaching of RE occupies a central place in Professor Ashraf's educational curriculum, but he found a serious flaw in the way it is taught in state schools. As a member of Cambridgeshire SACRE (Standing Advisory Council for Religious Education), he took an active part in reviewing the locally agreed syllabus for religious education (RE). He observed that one of the drawbacks of modern education is that it speaks of moral, rational, aesthetic, and social sensibilities but neglects "religious sensibility" which is considered to be something private and personal. In the state schools it is assumed that education may inform about religions, but it should not cultivate religious sensibility. By religious sensibility he meant "that element in human nature that makes human beings aware of the transcendent *selfless* norms of Justice, Truth and all such values that pull the heart away from selfishness towards selflessness, strengthen it and compel the heart to transcend subjective interests and establish that which is just and true."[98] In his charac-

---

95 Ashraf, "A View of Education," 78.
96 Ashraf, "A View of Education," 78.
97 The "basic" school curriculum includes the "national curriculum," as well as relationships, sex and health education, and religious education. The national curriculum is a set of subjects and standards used by primary and secondary schools so children learn the same things. It covers what subjects are taught and the standards children should reach in each subject. (See: The National Curriculum at https://www.gov.uk/national-curriculum).
98 Syed Ali Ashraf, "The Religious Approach to Religious Education: The Methodology of Awakening and Disciplining the Religious Sensibility," in *Priorities in Religious Education: A Model for the 1990s and Beyond*, ed. Brenda Watson (London: The Falmer Press, 1992), 83.

teristic way, he wanted to see faith commitment and loyalty to tradition at the centre of RE. To cultivate religious sensibility is to help pupils appreciate the teachings of religion in a deeper way by relating their own life experiences with the "norm of conduct for the society that derives its principles from the immutable, transcendent absolutes of justice, truth and other virtues."[99] Modern education has no qualm about teaching in a balanced way taking account of the whole life, but it normally ignores the question of religious awareness, as teachers are afraid of stimulating religious sensibility for fear of indoctrination. For Professor Ashraf, religious sensibility, so essential for balanced development of pupils, should be cultivated through exploring the great "Religious Tradition" of human beings and developing moral integrity and respect for other religions without succumbing to relativism.[100] This is possible only when one is ready and willing to cooperate in the common interest as part of one's own faith. In order to teach RE in a way that inculcates religious sensibility in pupils, the religious teachers themselves should be religious or have a sympathetic attitude to religion. Some of his colleagues were opposed to this idea but Michael Donley agrees with Professor Ashraf when he poses such questions as, "Could a tone-deaf person teach music? How then can someone not attuned to the spiritual dimension, or who denies its very existence, hope to teach meaningfully in this area of the curriculum?"[101]

One of the guiding principles of Professor Ashraf's philosophical perspective is rooted in the Islamic belief that prophets from various religions conveyed the same essential truths across civilisations. This notion led him to propose the existence of a shared tradition transcending religious boundaries. He points to the unity of human beings beneath the variety of expressions of religious beliefs and apparently conflicting worldviews and asks faith groups in a multireligious country to look at what he terms as the "Religious Tradition" of human beings. In this tradition, behind the external manifestation of rituals of different faiths there are common beliefs in a Transcendental Reality, the spiritual nature of human beings, common unchanging moral values, the need for divine guidance and life after death. RE should be taught in the context of the "Religious Tradition" of the world and not in the context of the scientific worldview or sociological study of religion.[102] In doing this Professor Ashraf does not situate spirituality outside of theology, nor promote religious relativism or syncretism. By focusing on the "essential principles common to all religions" Professor Ashraf not only attempts to comply with the legal requirements but also promote genuine understanding among people of

---

99 Ashraf, "The Religious Approach," 82.
100 Ashraf, "The Religious Approach," 89–90.
101 Michael Donley, "Teaching Discernment: An Overview of the Book as a Whole from the Perspective of the Secondary School Classroom," in *Priorities in Religious Education: A Model for the 1990s and Beyond*, ed. Brenda Watson (London: The Falmer Press, 1992), 188.
102 Ashraf, "The Religious Approach," 90.

all faiths. As religious and cultural diversity can enrich just as it can disrupt unity of society, making the fundamental religious principles as the common grounds for conversation among different faiths is expected to lay the foundation of a harmonious society. Professor Ashraf believes that undue influence of secularism has made obligatory RE not merely partial, but defective. In her "Editorial Introduction" in the book, *Priorities in Religious Education*, Watson says,

> He [Professor Ashraf] has a high view of the true function of religion which is to "uplift the heart beyond the narrow confines of the material worldly self, an expansion of the heart beyond all calculations, a transcendence which for Muslims, Christians, Hindus, Sikhs and Jews cannot occur without the presence of a supreme being, God."... Writing as a Muslim, he presents a powerful case for a truly world-religions approach which shows real respect for what is at the heart of particular diverse traditions. There is much in common to be drawn on "from the great moral and religious literature of the world irrespective of particular religious doctrines"; he terms this "the Religious Tradition." Religious education must help pupils to overcome narrow sectarianism and prejudice and realise "for example, those who follow Jesus Christ or Muhammad should not condemn each other. If religious education cannot succeed in doing this, that education and its methodology must be seriously defective."[103]

In a society fractured by prejudice, intolerance, and sectarian interests, Professor Ashraf's quest for a shared identity might seem like a distant hope. However, dismissing it would only exacerbate the challenges faced by an educational framework already criticised for its perceived selectivity in embracing pluralism.

Conclusion

This article delves into the educational insights of Professor Ashraf, offering an understanding of his foundational philosophy across various educational domains. It explores his perspectives on education, curriculum development, teacher training, and moral cultivation. His vision of Islamic education is comprehensive, drawing from the foundational principles of the Qurʾān and Sunnah, as well as the rich intellectual and spiritual heritage of Islam. His approach aims to nurture the holistic development of individuals, integrating spiritual, moral, and intellectual dimensions. Moreover, the article delves into Professor Ashraf's critique of secular education, which has predominantly shaped educational systems in many Muslim countries. Through this explora-

---

103 Brenda Watson, "Editorial introduction," in *Priorities in Religious Education: A Model for the 1990s and Beyond*, ed. Brenda Watson (London: The Falmer Press, 1992), 61.

tion, readers gain valuable insights into both Islamic and secular educational frameworks, as Professor Ashraf reflects on their convergence and divergence. His critique is grounded in Islamic principles, emphasising the centrality of revelation while also recognising the importance of rationality as a tool for understanding religion and guiding education. To achieve the overarching educational goal of fostering the complete growth of human personality, Professor Ashraf underscores the necessity for all human faculties—*qalb* (heart), *rūḥ* (spirit), *ʿaql* (intellect), and *nafs* (soul)—to harmonise. He advocates for the guidance of authentic narratives, spiritual practices, and moral refinement as indispensable elements in this endeavour.

British education systems also served as a platform for him to apply his philosophical perspectives to the secular approach to education. Recognising the universal themes among religions, which resonate with fundamental Islamic teachings, he advocated for an inclusive educational framework accommodating all faiths for the mainstream education in the UK. Engaging in dialogues with representatives of diverse faiths, he promoted understanding and common ground, paving the way for social harmony and peaceful coexistence among Britain's religiously diverse populace. He emphasised the importance of safeguarding the cultural identities of minority groups within the diverse British society, which risked erosion under a uniform secular curriculum. Proposing curriculum reforms that respects and celebrates minority cultures and religions, he warned of the adverse effects on self-esteem, confidence, and academic attainment among pupils from these communities, if neglected. For plural societies, he advocated for an education system grounded in a Common Frame of Reference that is based on the Judaeo-Christian-Islamic beliefs in God, man's accountability to God and in afterlife. He proposed revitalising religious education (RE) to nurture religious sensibility among pupils, advocating for the teaching of RE in the universal "Religious Tradition" shared among major faiths. His advocacy for faith-based schools, a religiously informed approach to RE, and his efforts in training RE teachers at Cambridge University and elsewhere represent significant contributions not only to the British educational landscape but also to countries worldwide grappling with the erosion of minority cultures within mainstream educational systems.

Through unwavering commitment to integrating faith into education, he continuously strove to elevate the discourse and practice in this vital field in both Muslim majority and minority countries. However, while acknowledging the merits of logical analysis and philosophical discourse, Professor Ashraf underscores the importance of morality in education. He argues that even a well-developed and balanced education proves futile if individuals educated in such a manner behave immorally, posing a threat to humanity. Despite potential areas of agreement with secularists on aspects like morality, autonomy, and addressing social issues like substance abuse and bullying, Professor Ashraf's critique of secular philosophies of education and science, particularly their neglect of revelation as a valid source of knowledge, faces staunch opposition, highlighting a classic and enduring challenge in the discourse.

Challenging the primacy of rationality in secular critiques, Professor Ashraf contends that rationality alone cannot fully grasp the truths revealed through revelation, citing its inherent limitations in grasping the depth of spiritual truths. In contemporary discourse, Professor Ashraf's critique aligns with the intellectual framework of Imam Ghazālī. Drawing from Ghazālī's approach, he systematically questions secular philosophy, employing both rational and religious perspectives. This critical examination leads to the gradual dismissal of secular arguments, culminating in the assertion that spiritual realisation, transcending superficial manifestations, is the exclusive path to truth. He posits that the profound truth of Islam is realised within the innermost core of individuals, achievable only through inner spiritual education, which is reflected in Islam's historical transformative impact on human life and society. Central to Professor Ashraf's educational vision are values rooted in divinity, intrinsic to the structure of reality, advocating for their integration into educational systems. In the words of Peter Mitchel, "such values . . . are not mere human constructs. Their origin is with God and they point towards His own perfections."[104]

Professor Ashraf realised that even if Muslim scholars diligently engage in research and successfully formulate authentic Islamic concepts to confront the encroachment of secularised ideas, relying solely on formal education will not be adequate. There should be a proper *application* of education so that individuals and communities can harness the benefit of education. Confronting the broader issue requires concerted efforts to instil resistance to the creation of modernised and mechanised environment, modern scientific attitudes, and the pervasive influence of entertainment industries promoted by television and the internet. In essence, a holistic approach, encompassing both educational reform and a reorientation of societal attitudes, is imperative to fortify Muslim society against the pervasive influences of secular education and secularisation.[105]

---

[104] Peter J. Mitchell, "Education, Religion and Transcendental Values," *Muslim Education Quarterly* 14, no. 2 (1997): 9.
[105] Ashraf, *New Horizons*, 12.

Bibliography

Ashraf, Syed Ali. Preface to *Aims and Objectives of Islamic Education*. Edited by Syed Muhammad al-Naquib al-Attas, ix–xiv. London: Hodder and Stoughton and Jeddah: King Abdulaziz University, 1979.

Ashraf, Syed Ali. *New Horizons in Muslim Education*. London: Hodder and Stoughton, and Cambridge: The Islamic Academy, 1985.

Ashraf, Syed Ali. Foreword to *The Case for Muslim Voluntary-Aided Schools: Some Philosophical Reflections*, by J. Mark Halstead, 5–9. Cambridge: The Islamic Academy, 1986.

Ashraf, Syed Ali. "Education and Values: Islamic vis-à-vis the Secularist Approaches," *Muslim Education Quarterly* 4, no. 2 (1987):1–4.

Ashraf, Syed Ali. "A View of Education—An Islamic Perspective." In *Schools for Tomorrow: Building Walls or Building Bridges*. Edited by Bernadette O'Keeffe, 69–79. London: The Falmer Press, 1988.

Ashraf, Syed Ali. "Editorial: Islamisation of Education: Need for the Islamic Frame of Reference, *Muslim Education Quarterly* 6, no. 3 (1989): 1–6.

Ashraf, Syed Ali. "Editorial: Islamic Education and Moral Development I—The Metaphysical Dimension." *Muslim Education Quarterly* 8, no. 1 (1990): 1–5.

Ashraf, Syed Ali. "Editorial: Islamic Education and Moral Development II—The Metaphysical Dimension," *Muslim Education Quarterly* 8, no. 2 (1991): 1–6.

Ashraf, Syed Ali. "The Religious Approach to Religious Education: The Methodology of Awakening and Disciplining the Religious Sensibility." In *Priorities in Religious Education: A Model for the 1990s and Beyond*. Edited by Brenda Watson, 81–91. London: The Falmer Press, 1992.

Ashraf, Syed Ali. "Editorial: Recommendations of the Five World Conferences on Muslim Education: A Plan for Implementation," *Muslim Education Quarterly* 10, no. 1 (1992): 1–6.

Ashraf, Syed Ali. "Islamic Education and Moral Development." In *Religion and Education: Islamic and Christian Approaches*, edited by Syed Ali Ashraf and Paul H. Hirst, 142–158. Cambridge: The Islamic Academy, 1994.

Ashraf, Syed Ali, and Paul H. Hirst, eds. *Religion and Education: Islamic and Christian Approaches*. Cambridge: The Islamic Academy, 1994.

Ashraf, Syed Ali. "Responding to the Challenge of Secularism." In *Aspects of Education* 51 (1994).

Bloom, Paul and Izzat Jarudi, "The Chomsky of morality? A View of Morality as the Product of an Innate Mental Faculty—rather like language," *Nature* 443 (26 October 2006): 909–910. See also Marc D. Hauser, *Moral Minds: How Nature Designed Our Universal Sense of Right and Wrong* (New York: HarperCollins, 2006).

Al-Bukhārī. *Adab al-Mufrad*, Book 14, Ḥadīth 273.

Chittick, William C. "The Goal of Islamic Education." In *Education in the Light of Tradition*, edited by Jane Casewit, 85–92. Bloomington, Indiana: World Wisdom, 2011.

Collin, W. E. "Beyond Humanism: Some Notes on T. E. Hulme." *The Sewanee Review* 38, no. 3 (Jul–Sep. 1930): 332–339.

Cox, Caroline. Foreword to *The Crisis in Religious Education*. Edited by John Burn and Colin Hart. London: Educational Research Trust, 1988.

Cuypers, Stefaan E. "The Life of Reason—R. S. Peters' Stoic Philosophy of Education." *Kultura Pedagogiczna* 1 (2015): 21–38.

Donley, Michael. "Teaching Discernment: An Overview of the Book as a Whole from the the Perspective of the Secondary School Classroom." In *Priorities in Religious Education: A Model for the 1990s and Beyond*. Edited by Brenda Watson, 183–194. London: The Falmer Press, 1992.

Education for All: Report of the Committee of Enquiry into the Education of Children from Ethnic Minority Groups. London: Her Majesty's Stationery Office, 1985. https://education-uk.org/documents/swann/swann1985.html.

Fine, Arthur. "Scientific Realism and Antirealism." In *Routledge Encyclopedia of Philosophy*, edited by Edward Craig. Taylor and Francis, 1998. Accessed March 15, 2024. doi:10.4324/9780415249126-Q094-1.

Al-Ghazālī. "Section C: Danger of Philosophy, Part II." *Deliverance from Error and Mystical Union with the Almighty (al-Munqidh min al-Dalal)*. Translated by Muhammad Abulaylah. Edited by George F. McLean. Council for Research in Values & Philosophy, March 2002. https://www.Ghazālī.org/books/md/index.html.

Habermas, Jürgen. "A 'post-secular' society – what does that mean?" Reset Dialogues on Civilizations. June 2–6, 2008. https://www.resetdoc.org/story/a-post-secular-society-what-does-that-mean/.

Hulmes, Edward. "Unity and Diversity: The Search for Common Identity." In *Priorities in Religious Education: A Model for the 1990s and Beyond*. Edited by Brenda Watson, 124–139. London: The Falmer Press, 1992.

Husain, Syed Sajjad and Syed Ali Ashraf, eds. *Crisis in Muslim Education*. London: Hodder and Stoughton and Jeddah: King Abdulaziz University, 1979.

Islamic Academy, The. *Faith as the Basis of Education in a Multi-faith Multi-cultural Country: Discussion Document II*. Cambridge: The Islamic Academy, 1991.

Jeffreys, M. V. C. *The Aims of Education (Glaucon)*. London: Pitman, 1972.

Johnson, David L. *Earth, Empire and Sacred Text: Muslims and Christians as Trustees of Creation*. London: Equinox Publishing Limited, 2010. Huston Smith. *Beyond the Post-Modern Mind*. New York: The Crossroad Publishing Company, 1982. Paul Hirst. Introduction to *Religion and Education: Islamic and Christian Approaches*, edited by Syed Ali Ashraf and Paul H. Hirst, 1–3. Cambridge: The Islamic Academy, 1994.

Karić, Enes. "Moral Tuition and Education." In *Education in the Light of Tradition*, edited by Jane Casewit, 37–38. Bloomington, Indiana: World Wisdom, 2011.

King Abdulaziz University. *Conference Book: First World Conference on Muslim Education*. Jeddah and Mecca: King Abdulaziz University, 1977.

Kretzschmar, Louise. "Convergence and Divergence: A Christian Response to Prozesky's "Global Ethic" and Secular Spirituality." *Journal for the Study of Religion* 31, no. 1, Festschrift for Martin Prozesky (2018): 112–134.

Lester, Emile. "A More Neutral Liberal Education: Why Not Only Liberals, but Religious Conservatives Should Endorse Comparative Religious Education in Public Schools." *Polity* 39, no. 2 (Apr. 2007): 179–207.

Mabud, Shaikh Abdul. "World Conferences on Muslim Education: Shaping the Agenda of Muslim Education in the Future." In *Philosophies of Islamic Education: Historical Perspectives and Emerging Discourses*, edited by Nadeem A. Memon and Mujadad Zaman, 129–143. New York and London: Routledge, 2016.

Malik, Imam. *Al-Muwaṭṭa'* 1614.

McClelland, V. Alan. "Wholeness, Faith and the Distinctiveness of the Catholic School." In *The Contemporary Catholic School: Context, Identity and Diversity*, edited by Terence H. McLaughlin, Joseph O'Keefe SJ, and Bernadette O'Keeffe, 155-161. London: The Falmer Press, 1996.

McLaughlin, Terence H. "Liberalism, Education and the Common School." *Journal of Philosophy of Education* 29, no. 2 (1995): 239-55.

Miskawayh. "From the Second Discourse of the Refinement of Character." In *Classical Foundations of Islamic Educational Thought*, edited by Bradley J. Cook, 75-87. Utah: Bringham Young University Press, 2010.

Mitchell, Peter J. "Education, Religion and Transcendental Values." *Muslim Education Quarterly* 14, no. 2 (1997): 5-15.

Mitchell, Peter. "Professor Syed Ali Ashraf: An Appreciation." See Chapter 29 of this book.

Mosham, David. "Rationality as a Goal of Education." *Educational Psychology Review* 2, no. 4 (1990): 335-364.

Mukti, Mohd Fakhrudin Abdul. "Al-Ghazzali and His Refutation of Philosophy." *Jurnal Usuluddin* 21 (2005): 1-22.

Nasr, Seyyed Hossein. "Reply to Marietta Stepaniants." In *The Library of Living Philosophers*, vol. 27, *The Philosophy of Seyyed Hossein Nasr*, edited by Lewis Edwin Hahn, Randall E. Auxier, and Lucian W. Stone Jr., 809-812. IL: Open Court Press, 2001.

Nasr, Seyyed Hossein. "Modern Education: Its History, Theories, and Philosophies." In *Education in the Light of Tradition*, edited by Jane Casewit, 105-109. Bloomington, Indiana: World Wisdom, 2011.

O'Keefe, Bernadette. Introduction to *Schools for Tomorrow: Building Walls Or Building Bridges*, edited by Bernadette O'Keefe, 1-10. London: The Falmer Press, 1988.

Peters, Richard S. "Education as initiation." In *Philosophy of Education: an Anthology*, edited by Randall Curren, 55-67. Oxford: Blackwell, 2007 [1965].

Peters, Richard S. *Moral Development and Moral Education*. London: George Allen & Unwin Ltd., 1981 [1970].

Peters, Richard S. *Reason and Compassion*. London: Routledge & Kegan Paul, 1973.

Pring, Richard. *Philosophy of Education: Aim, Theory, Common Sense, and Research*. London: Continuum, 2004.

Thiessen, Elmer J. "R. S. Peters on Liberal Education—A Reconstruction." *Interchange* 20, no. 4 (Winter, 1989): 1-8.

Watson, Brenda. "Editorial introduction." In *Priorities in Religious Education: A Model for the 1990s and Beyond*. Edited by Brenda Watson, 60-64. London: The Falmer Press, 1992.

Williams, Rowan. *Faith in the Public Square*. London: Bloomsbury, 2012.

Chapter 10

Faith-Based Education[1]

Peter Mitchell

In our modern world education grows in importance. The extraordinary expansion in knowledge, the sophistication of the skills required in modern living, the growth of technology, the challenge of almost instantaneous communications as well as our deeper appreciation of the rich and complex cultural heritage of humankind have all helped to stimulate a public demand for a better and more extensive education. Increasingly societies are having to expend more and more resources on its provision. Indeed, the well-being of any contemporary society, both in its economic prospects and in its quality of life, seem inexorably linked to the excellence or otherwise of the education it can offer its young. Of course, society's prosperity and well-being depend on the complex coming together of many other services and activities, yet without the provision of a sound educational foundation it is extremely unlikely that in the long term either individuals or the community will be able to flourish. However, the provision of a good modern educational system is very costly and calls for a considerable effort from both individuals and the community. If, therefore, such expenditure and effort are to be justified, it is important to be certain that the right kind of education is offered to the young and that it is of the appropriate type and quality. It is the purpose of this chapter to examine and support one such approach to education—faith-based education. It has to be emphasised at the very beginning that advocacy however compelling cannot remove the need for adequate resources, astute planning and imaginative leadership. In education it is essential that the practical and the theoretical go hand in hand.

We must, therefore, first set out the main characteristics of such an education. Faith-based education can be varyingly described. Professor Ali Ashraf defined it thus: "The education here conceived presupposes faith and operates within its sphere, rather than faith being treated as something extraneous to

---

[1] Presented at the Third Professor Syed Ali Ashraf Memorial Lectures, held on 12 August 2001 in Trinidad, West Indies.

education and external to its major objectives. It sets forward an approach to education which reflects the presuppositions of faith." It thus starts from the conviction that any approach to education must be value laden. Education is never neutral. It always reflects a particular perspective on life. The shape given to the curriculum, the weight allocated to different subjects, the measures it contains for success and failure, the overall objectives of the teaching and learning all reflect value decisions, some deliberate and many others taken for granted by educational planners. Sometimes the values embodied in such decisions are internally inconsistent with each other creating incoherence in the system and confusion to teachers and students alike. So, for example, a system can by implication seem to advocate personal success at all costs while also teaching the importance of service to others. Or an educational system can reflect unthinkingly the spirit of the age or even passing fashions and so its coherence and long-term success can be undermined by random and sometimes contradictory changes. Obviously change is often necessary. An educational system has to cater for the needs of today, not the circumstances of yesterday. And it is often extremely difficult to balance the demands of different values. But faith-based education claims to offer a coherent set of values drawn from the wisdom of the great religions that can help educationalists manage change and achieve consistency in their objectives.

Second, recognising the supreme importance of values in education, faith-based education seeks to give these values a sure foundation. Values, it argues, are not free standing, open to random choice. They have to be firmly located in a way of life. Faith-based education goes further. Recognising that customs and traditions may vary between people and over time, it argues that values are more fundamental and must be tied to and arise from the way things are, in this case reflecting the nature of God our Creator and the reality of the spiritual aspect of human nature. Such values, it affirms, as truth, justice, righteousness, mercy, love, compassion, and care towards all creation are therefore not human creations, open to change and optional, but are part of the structure of reality and their practice is essential if human life is to flourish. It stands in sharp opposition to attitudes to life such as that exemplified by thinkers such as Nietzsche who urges us to extinguish pity and praises the powerful and the predator. And it does this because such a self-regarding and adversarial way of life ignores our dependence on God and our mutual interdependence on each other, a mutual dependence that can only be fruitful and not destructive if it is based upon and arises from those divinely given values without which human life cannot flourish.

Third, it follows that a faith-based education in its fullest sense operates best in the context of a believing community. It requires the acceptance by parents and teachers alike of the supreme importance of those transcendental values given to humankind and of the spiritual aspect of human nature bestowed upon us by our Creator. Obviously, there are those who freely accept the importance of such values, who stress the spirituality of human beings and who see education as directing young people towards truth, beauty and goodness, but who do not attribute the foundation of all this to a Divine source. Faith-based education is distinctive in that it strongly affirms that without such a Divine foundation such an education would be built upon sand and that the power and binding nature of such values would not be properly appreciated. It similarly follows that such an approach to education is not confined to one particular religion. In spite of their obvious differences, the major world religions show a surprising agreement on those fundamental values that should guide human life and on their Divine source. Faith-based education, therefore, need not be divisive or sectarian. It could lead to strong cooperation and joint enterprises where the importance and centrality of such universal values to education is widely accepted.

Fourth, the values fundamental to faith-based education means that it has to be open in character rather than closed. By recognising the universal range and Divine origin of the values it espouses, it is committed to helping pupils to appreciate and value communities other than their own. So, whilst individuals need to learn how to become active and responsible citizens of their own society, they also have to avoid being caught up in ethnocentric feelings that prevent them seeing the whole world and all of humankind as part of the Divine creation and their need to respect the rights and freedoms of others. Faith-based education has to seek to replace a narrow with a wider perspective on life that is prepared to celebrate diversity and repudiates any form of xenophobia. The arena in which the values to which it adheres are to be exercised cannot to be limited to any one group or nation. The acceptance of universal values requires an inclusive, all-embracing perspective on life.

Fifth, faith-based education has to be open in a further way. Education has to fulfil many functions in the process of forming the minds and characters of young people and enhancing their skills and individual potentialities and gifts. But at the heart of the educational enterprise is the need for individuals to acquire and test new knowledge. There are many disputes as to how and when this should be done, what topics this should include and to what uses such knowledge should be put. It is also undeniable that no one person could possibly learn everything that is now known. Selection is both imperative and inevitable. But it is also true that human knowledge is often unstable, needing to be corrected and replaced as further research and experience uncover new information and fresh ways of understanding. The curricula of educational establishments are therefore always in need of revision and correction. Faith-based education approaches these phenomena with confidence and humility: confidence because of its belief that God has given human beings the capacity to explore and understand the world in which we live and so any new knowledge is to be welcomed; and humility because it recognises that human beings are finite and that their knowledge will always be incomplete and limited. It therefore accepts the need for Divine guidance and for those universal values which lie at the heart of things, and which should be binding on our use of such knowledge as well as on our treatment of others. Finding the correct balance between treasuring the wisdom of the past and being open to new knowledge and technologies is never easy. Nevertheless, according to its own principles faith-based education has to be open to the future for that is where its recipients will have to live.

Sixth, faith-based education recognises the need to transcend the cognitive. Education has to consist of more than the acquiring of knowledge or learning how to reason. Human beings are thinking creatures, but they also feel and act. It is one thing to learn of the needs of others, it is another to feel concern for them and to be motivated to act on that concern. It is a common place in educational discussions to speak of educating the emotions. Learning to appreciate another's feelings and to be able to empathise with them is much harder for some than for others, often depending to a large extent on the quality of an individual's home and community life outside school or college. It is here that cooperation between home and school becomes even more important. However, faith-based education wishes to go further than this. It recognises that there is a conflict between selfishness and altruism in each individual, a battle that is often mirrored in the wider society. All the major religions explore this conflict and offer advice and direction on its resolution. Faith-based education wishes to help pupils draw on this advice and learn to appreciate the nature of the altruistic lifestyle. Furthermore, it recognises that the ultimate values upon which this depends cannot become part of the student's life by reason alone. Only when they are willingly followed can such values be grounded and nourished in both personal and social life. Such a willing cannot be coerced, but only won. For this reason, faith-based education has to exemplify the values upon which it is based both by the role models it commends and the methods it employs.

Seventh, and more controversially, faith-based education accepts the transcendental nature of ultimate reality. It sees this life from the perspective of eternity. Death, it affirms, is not the end. Human beings are mortal, but they are not extinguished by death. The world religions from their own points of view affirm this reality and urge humankind to live with this perspective in view. How is faith-based education to reflect this without becoming embroiled in controversies posed by the particularities of the different religions? First, by offering an alternative to the materialist's view that this world is all there is, and that death is the end. Second, by showing to students the difference it makes to see one's actions and responses to the challenges and tests of life from this perspective, which can be both reassuring and beneficent as well as demanding. Third, by exploring its implications for the way we treat human life and as well as other living creatures.

Given that these are some of the main features of faith-based education, what benefits, if any, could it bring? To do this I want now to explore three major ways of envisaging the contribution education can make to the community's and individual's well-being and the difference faith-based education could make in each of these three areas.

Economic Progress

No society can succeed in the long term that spends more than it in some way earns. Indeed, to be able to add to its economic base seems essential if a society is to prosper. What has been of major controversy over the past one hundred years is how this is to be done and what relationship should there be between individual and community ownership, effort and need. What is not controversial is the general belief that a sound and effective education system can help add to the long-term economic prospects of a society. Why this should be so is not all together clear. Indeed, some have argued that a developed educational system is more an evidence of a prosperous society rather than a net contributor to its economic wealth. What seems increasingly obvious is that a modern society requires a highly skilled workforce and education is seen as an important way of achieving this. It can also be argued that a democratic society in which freedoms and enterprise can flourish requires a sophisticated and literate electorate and that it is democratic societies that have proved to be the most prosperous. But to achieve a well-informed electorate willing and able to settle its disputes by means of the ballot box requires a well-developed educational system.

What, it might be argued, can a faith-based education has to do with all this? Surely what is required to secure the economic wealth of both individuals and the community are skills and technical know-how very distant from the concerns of faith-based education as we have described it. But this would be to take a very superficial view of what economic prosperity consists of. In spite of arguments to the contrary, economics is not so easily separated from the demands of morality. Moral judgements are required at every stage of the economic process. From initial questions about the acceptability or dangers of modes of production to questions concerned with human health and the environment and with the justice and fairness of methods of wealth distribution value questions arise. Similarly, moral questions are raised about the responsibilities of the individual, where possible and appropriate, to engage in economic activity and the responsibilities of society and the individual for those in economic need.

One central aim of faith-based education with its emphasis on eternal values is to help students develop the ability to apply such values to the questions of everyday life. Someone nurtured in an educational environment where it is natural and normal to raise such value questions is much more likely to be able to respond to the challenges posed by later economic activities and to take an informed part in the consequent debates. Faith-based education is therefore not separate from questions of economic activity and unconcerned with so called worldly affairs. Far from it. But it does insist that syllabuses concerned with the development of economic and technical skills should have integrated within them an examination of the value questions their exercise raises. Questions of greed and generosity, of personal choice and responsibility, of exploitation and human dignity and of justice and fairness cannot be separated from the problems of economics nor ignored in the educational treatment of such topics.

Economics and education are tied together in another way. Research, with a few exceptions, increasingly suggests that an individual's educational outcomes and their future economic status are positively linked. That is, the higher their educational achievements the more the individual is likely to earn. Obviously, there are always exceptions, but the trend seems well established. This phenomenon has given rise to a whole series of vigorous educational debates which this is not the place to explore except for two areas where faith-based education ought to have something important to say. First, it has recently been noticed that the more prosperous people become the more they expand their aspirations to have more; bigger houses, a more affluent lifestyle and the like. The values embedded in faith-based education offer an alternative vision of life built amongst other things upon care for others rather than a careless hedonism. Pupils at least have the right to appreciate what this alternative vision means. Second, it is too easy for pupils and schools alike to measure pupils in terms of their success and failure. Faith-based education is committed to recognising the intrinsic worth of every human being as a creature of God and in showing this in the way pupils are treated in school. Economic success has too often been linked to the exercise of power both individually and in the community of nations. Faith-based education can offer to pupils an alternative view, that it is better to give than to receive, and that service rather than domination is the way to a fulfilled life.

Cultural Transmission and Intellectual Growth

Education however is not primarily concerned with economics but with handing on to the next generation their intellectual and cultural inheritance and providing them with the skills, attitudes and motivations that will enable them to live successfully and fully in the future. It is also intended to help them add to that inheritance themselves, as they are able. In the main schools and colleges have responded to these tasks by offering their students a broad-based curriculum that grows increasingly specialised as students get older. Again from such a programme there have been spun innumerable educational controversies concerning, for example, the selection and content of the subjects and topics to be studied, the nature and standard of the skills to be mastered, the balance between breadth and depth necessary for the successful mastering of subjects, the time and necessity for specialisation, the best methods of assessment, the relationship between pupil choice and freedom and their long-term interests, etc. Without attempting to adjudicate in such disputes, many of which require close attention to the local circumstances of particular institutions and places, some general principles regarding faith-based education can be enunciated.

One reason given for studying a range of different subjects on the curriculum is that they embody logically distinct ways of thinking with their own concepts and appropriate tests for truth, their own language or modes of expression and their own selected models of achievement. So history is distinct from geography and both are not to be confused with mathematics or science. Great poetry cannot be evaluated mathematically, nor painting be seen as a scientific statement. Subjects in this sense are autonomous, and though their relationships to each other are complex, for they are all studying the same universe, they each present a distinctive way of viewing some aspect of reality that to be meaningful must not be confused with another. But this seems to empty faith-based education of significance at the heart of the educational enterprise. Academic study has its own impetus. Subjects have to stand on their own feet and be tested by their own criteria.

In one sense all this must be true. Progress in the world of academic study and imaginative and artistic expression has depended on accepting in general terms this picture and using the techniques and skills so developed to understand more of the world and our complex experiences of it. But this is only part of the picture and on its own can be misleading. To see the whole as the gift of God and our own part in it as persons responsible to the Deity can transform our understanding of the aspects of the whole captured by the individual subjects. It is part of the task of faith-based education to help students to grasp something of this wider picture and the consequences for us as part of it.

We can go further. Plato required his chosen students in his ideal academy to study mathematics for fifteen years before they were allowed to study his transcendental teachings. Why do this? Partly because Plato thought that the strenuous nature of mathematical thinking would help his students think logically, partly because Plato thought thinking about the truths of mathematics would get his students more capable to thinking about a non-sensible reality not open to what he saw as the vagaries and haphazard nature of the natural world, but above all because he thought the study of mathematics would prepare his students to appreciate more the transcendent source of truth, beauty and goodness that lay at the heart of everything. We may not agree with Plato with his ideas on the place to be given to mathematical education or on his pessimism about the study of nature, but we can see what he was getting at. He believed that the study of topics chosen at his academy would not only serve practical and pragmatic purposes but would, if properly approached, help his students to appreciate more the transcendent source of all things. In other words, there was a reciprocal relationship between his foundational beliefs and the subjects studied at his institution, each illuminating the other.

How to achieve this symbiotic relationship between the beliefs and values upon which faith-based education rests and the subjects studied at school is a challenging and demanding task requiring detailed and informed work. It becomes even more imperative when we look at subject syllabuses in many educational institutions. Often the religious perspective is entirely missing, and the contributions religious insights could make to many of the most pressing problems of the day are ignored.

Being true to the faith perspective raises other challenges for the faith-based educator. It is obvious that there are other perspectives that challenge those based on faith. These are most glaringly obvious in the areas of science and of ethics, but they can occur almost anywhere. Even if the teacher fails to raise these issues, the students will, whether silently or vocally. Honesty and openness can be the only policy here, especially since these are amongst the values upon which faith-based education rests. The faith perspective has to and can commend itself by its own quality not by censorship or repression. What has to be remembered is that there is no neutral standpoint from which judgements of this kind can be made. Often the most important thing is to uncover the hidden presuppositions that give the disputes their force. The most intractable problems often arise in the area of science where often the stark alternative is sometimes posed as science or religion. It is this alternative that has to be resisted. Science and religion seek to answer different questions in distinctive ways. Properly understood, it is logically impossible for there to be a contradiction. This only arises when one subject tries to answer questions posed in the language of the other. Of course there is scientism that sees itself as the enemy of religion, but this is itself a particular ideology and not itself a scientific theory, and is a view that poses its own problems and contradictions.

It can therefore be argued that an open faith-based education, far from hindering the intellectual and emotional development of students, can, by providing them with a coherent and stable base from which to work, increase their confidence and motivation as they learn to explore and make their own the complex and rich intellectual and cultural world that is their inheritance. And by throwing fresh and often challenging light on the various academic disciplines, faith-based education can help enhance and make more intelligible their study.

Education can also be seen in a much more pragmatic and utilitarian light where the emphasis is on providing students with those technological and practical skills that will enable them to survive and prosper in an increasingly complex material world. Indeed many of the contemporary changes in education can be directly traced to the commercial and industrial demands of society. Achieving a balance between this necessary recognition of the importance of the vocational element in education and its broader tasks of forming the minds and characters of students is not easy. Vocational direction can, for example, often be a strong motivating drive for many young people.

Faith-based education offers two comments on this. First, a skills-based or vocational education can on its own never be enough. Human beings cannot live only for the world of work. The human spirit needs nourishment. A reductionism that treats humans only as subjects for employment seriously underestimates what it is to be human. Second, the world of work is not to be despised. Human beings need to able to contribute as they are able to the well-being of the whole. But such an ambition has to be shaped by those moral and spiritual values which lie at the heart of faith-based education. Vocational education is value laden and students have to be made acutely aware of this.

Social Cohesion

Society's well-being depends not only on its material and cultural wealth however this to be measured, but also on the ability of its citizens to work and live together with a high level of reciprocal trust. "Societies work best, and have always worked best," claims Robert Rotberg, "where citizens trust their fellow citizens, work cooperatively with them for common goals, and thus share a civic culture."[2] Collective action upon which social life depends requires its participants both to exhibit trust in each other and to be trustworthy. Such networks of reciprocal or mutual trust do not spring up overnight. They have to be built up over the years. One important source of this is those voluntary societies and associations, which exist in many countries, especially in those nations where the right of free association is well established. Religious groups are one example amongst many of such volunteerism. Where such trust and confidence in others is missing and is replaced by fear, hostility and dislike, societies will lack cohesion and be liable to disintegration or even violence. The existing strength or otherwise of such networks of social bonding based on mutual trust can be called a society's social capital. And for political stability and government effectiveness, says Robert Putnam, "social capital may be even more important than physical or human capital."[3]

Home and schools are where children first learn to trust and be trustworthy both in their interactions with adults and with each other. By living, working and playing together in social groups they can experience the benefits of and need for trust and trustworthiness. Schools have an important role in establishing and reinforcing such attitudes. They can do this in a variety of ways. First, by being places of safety worthy of the trust of the child and by being

---

2 Robert I. Rotberg, "Introduction: Social Capital and Political Culture in Africa, America, Australasia, and Europe," in *Patterns of Social Capital: Stability and Change in Historical Perspective*, ed. Robert I Rotberg (Cambridge: Cambridge University Press, 2001), 1.
3 Robert D. Putnam, Robert Leonardi and Raffaella Y. Nonetti, *Making Democracy Work: Civic Traditions in Modern Italy* (Princeton: Princeton University Press, 1993), 15.

consistent and fair in the way students are treated rather than inconsistent and arbitrary.

Second, schools also have to exhibit trust in the child and expect high standards of trustworthiness. Schools will achieve these things in different ways according to their circumstances, but evidence suggests that where the structures of the school encourage pupils to undertake self-regulated tasks and be responsible for their own actions and the well-being of others, trust and trustworthiness is more likely to be nourished than in those institutions based upon hierarchies of coercive power and control.

Third, almost inevitably because of human frailty, schools and pupils will fail to live up to such high standards. Schools need some clearly defined process in which a fresh start can be made and forgiveness experienced.

Fourth, whilst it is true that trust and trustworthiness are learnt primarily through experience and behaviour, schools have an important cognitive task in this area. There is a marked distinction between trust and trustworthiness learnt in the home and with close friends where the ties are based on natural bonds of affection and the more impersonal relationships of the wider world. Pupils have to learn to extend their circle of trust and trustworthiness beyond that of their family and immediate peers. This can be very difficult to achieve. With young children trust in strangers is the last thing caring parents would want to encourage, rather the opposite. In the wider world adults achieve wisdom and discernment in this area by engaging in joint enterprises through their membership of voluntary groups and associations. Part of the problem arises through failing to distinguish between relations of trust based upon affection and relations of trust in an institution based on beliefs in the justice and fairness of that institution and in the worthwhileness of the joint action that membership of the institution requires. Moving from the personal and intimate to the impersonal and institutional requires thought and reflection as well as experience. Its achievement is part of the educational task of the school.

Unfortunately, not all homes offer security and affection in which trust and trustworthiness can be naturally nourished. Here schools have a difficult pastoral task in which they often need the help of other agencies. What seems to be true, however, that it is extremely difficult to develop trust in the structures and fairness of social institutions in those who learnt suspicion and fear of others in their early years.

However, though all this may be true, what, it may be asked, has it particularly to do with faith-based education? Surely all that is claimed about social capital and education must apply to every school and not just those connected with faith-based education. Indeed, citizenship education is increasingly recognised as a proper task for all schools and what is said above is an important part of it. It is important not to deny this. All schools have such a duty. We have, therefore to ask, "What, if anything, is the distinctive contribution that faith-based education can make to this task?"

There are several ways of answering this. First, a faith-based education arising from a believing community and the free choice of parents, provides an important bridge between the relations of trust and trustworthiness based on bonds of affection and intimate relationships and those appropriate in the wider world. By recognising the importance of pupils' rootedness in their own immediate faith community and providing a place of safety where their cultural and religious identities are reaffirmed and valued, a broader sense of community-located trust and trustworthiness can begin to be established. And in as much as the faith-based education is open in the ways previously characterised, far from creating social division as its critics suppose, such an education can be an important factor in adding to the social capital upon which both individuals and society depends.

Second, the values upon which the cooperative style of life envisaged by the concept of social capital rests; that is, trust and trustworthiness with their close associates of honesty, justice, love, compassion, forgiveness, care for others; are all drawn from those fundamental values upon which the whole idea of faith-based education rests. It can therefore be claimed that faith-based education offers a firm foundation upon which the whole can rest. It is not merely one way of life amongst others but helps to draw us closer to reality.

Third, someone who believes that in spite of the vagaries of life, the universe is essentially beneficent because it depends for its existence on God in whom all perfections rest, will have a very different attitude to life than the person who sees the world as the product of haphazard chance and empty of value except in so far as we place value on it. This confidence that we are in the final analysis able to be secure in the love of God and in the final triumph of good is itself a strong motivating factor in working cooperatively towards such a goal. It is this positive vision of life that is the driving force of faith-based education and which it wishes to advocate.

Fourth, we have so far talked of cooperative action based on trust and trustworthiness as good in itself and as needing no justification. But this cannot in isolation be the whole truth. The direction or goal of the activity must also be subjected to moral as well as pragmatic scrutiny. It is the claim of faith-based education that because it rests on absolute values it contains within itself the dependable moral criteria by which the goals as well as the mode of cooperative activity can be judged. Helping pupils to engage in this self-reflective scrutiny is an important task of faith-based education.

Fifth, it is easy for cooperative action based on trust and trustworthiness to be corrupted in another and more subtle way. For such actions to become effective and long lasting in society they have to be embedded in networks of trust. It is all too easy for the person seeking their own selfish ends at the expense of others to use such networks to further their own or their family's advantage and to use their social connections and social relationships in achieving selfish and unjust goals. A democratic society is especially alert to this, giving rise to the checks and balances intended to prevent nepotism and the like. Faith-based education wishes to go further than this. Because of its emphasis on the interiority of human action it seeks to establish in pupils virtues of character which would counter this and to provide them with the necessary skills of discernment that they are able distinguish good from evil.

Sixth, trust and trustworthiness cannot be coerced. They are very different from compliance or obedience which the state or other institutions might be able to obtain through fear or punishment. Their very nature demands that they be the exercise of free people. For this reason some have argued that they can be seen at their best in a participating free democratic and plural society. But this requires that different groups in such a society should be able to exhibit mutual reciprocal trust and cooperation. Faith-based education points the way as to how this might be achieved by its emphasis on the fact that we are all creatures of God whatever our race, nation, gender or religion and that commitment to one's own faith ought to make the individual more able to appreciate other faiths and respect them.

However, trust and trustworthiness are not enough to achieve a truly cohesive society. What is missing goes to the heart of what it means to be human. Human beings cannot in an ultimate sense live alone. Even those who choose to do so depend on skills and language learnt from others. We are in a radical sense dependent in a myriad of ways on each other. In our earliest years and when we experience the frailty of illness or advancing years this dependence become more obvious, but as MacIntyre points out, it is a fundamental and unpredictable part of our human condition.[4] Even the concept of education carries with it the idea of dependence on the teaching of others for the skills and knowledge we need. To treat those with disabilities or handicaps as different from ourselves is to misunderstand our own situation. And because this human dependence is mutual it carries with it ideas of care. Giving and receiving is an essential part of the human condition. This is not neatly balanced and reciprocal, a type of market exchange, but it arises from particular situations and circumstances. Coming to appreciate the nature of our dependence on each other and learning to expand and express our duty of care to others becomes an important task of education.

This leads us to the heart of faith-based education with its fundamental belief that we depend absolutely on God and that in expressing our care for others and for the natural world we are expressing and reflecting something of the Divine Reality in the way we live. Many others would share this duty of care, but it is the claim of faith-based education that it gives to this duty an absolute foundation by locating it in the basic structure of Reality itself.

---

4   Alasdair MacIntyre, *Dependent Rational Animals* (London: Duckworth, 1999).

Bibliography

MacIntyre, Alasdair. *Dependent Rational Animals*. London: Duckworth, 1999.

Putnam, Robert D., Robert Leonardi, and Raffaella Y. Nanetti. *Making Democracy Work: Civic Traditions in Modern Italy*. Princeton: Princeton University Press, 1993.

Rotberg, Robert I. "Introduction: Social Capital and Political Culture in Africa, America, Australasia, and Europe." In *Patterns of Social Capital: Stability and Change in Historical Perspective,* edited by Robert I Rotberg, 1-18. Cambridge: Cambridge University Press, 2001.

Chapter 11

Abraham, The Babylonian

James Kinnier Wilson

Introduction

The concern of this study is with one of the honoured Messengers of Islamic history and religion,—Abraham, *al-khalīl*, "the friend of God." The writer is privileged to present these notes in a volume dedicated to the memory of Syed Ali Ashraf.

One might think that, by now, everything that can be known about Abraham and his times has already been said, and in many places. The *Encyclopaedia of Islam* and its bibliography, supplemented to the present time by entries in the *Index Islamicus*, provides a wealth of information, under "Ibrāhīm," on the revered name, of his search for God beyond the statues, and of the great story of the Kaʿbah. But one item, perhaps, is missing: it would remain to explain convincingly the name itself. As understood in the Old Testament, the name means "the father of a multitude." Thus, in Genesis 17:5, one reads: "Behold . . ., no longer shall your name be Abram; your name shall be Abraham, for I have made you to be 'the father of a multitude' of nations." But what, then, of the earlier name "Abram"? As suggested in many commentaries and as accepted also by the New English Bible,[1] Abram has been thought to mean "High Father," the second element being taken to be from the Hebrew *rûm*, "to be high."

A New Proposal

This note believes that the name is Babylonian and means "Beloved Father," from *abu*, "father," and *rāmu*, the past participle of *râmu*, "to love."[2] As it happens, vol. 14 of the *Assyrian Dictionary* devoted to the letter "R," is now

---

1 *The New English Bible with the Apocrypha* (Oxford: Oxford University Press and Cambridge: University Press, 1970), 16, note f.
2 For transliteration of Akkadian words used in this chapter see: Arthur Ungnad, *Akkadian Grammar*, 5th ed., trans. Harry A. Hoffner, Jr. (Atlanta, Georgia: Scholars Press, 1969), 13–29.

to hand,³ and therein through numerous references the meaning of the verb in question may be amply confirmed. The word *abu*, "father," if it is necessary to say so, is documented in the *Assyrian Dictionary*, vol. 1, pp. 67ff.,⁴ but importantly it includes examples of *abu* used as an "honorific title" in formal address.

However, *abu râmu* is not "Ab-ram," so it remains to explain that, as I have myself had occasion to mention in a discussion of certain Nimrud texts, "unqualified singular nouns forming part of Akkadian names seem not to have been inflected."⁵ This means that while in Babylonian (or, in "Akkadian," as thus to include the Assyrian language) the endings *-u(m)*, *-a(m)*, and *-i(m)*, express the nominative, accusative and genitive cases—the bracketed (*m*) is known as "mimation" and corresponds exactly to the "nunation" of classical Arabic—these endings were dropped in the writing, as no doubt also in the pronunciation, of proper names.

Many examples attest the correctness of this rule. Thus the Akk. *šamšu*, Arab. *šams*, means "the sun," but the name of the sun god was Shamash (Akkadian: šamaš). The word for "sea" was *tâmtu*, originally *tiāmtu(m)*, but Marduk's well-known adversary in the Babylonian *Epic of Creation* was "Tiamat." Assurbanipal, king of Assyria, will not here need any introduction, but the name is indeed *Assur-bān-apal*, "Assur created the son," with *apal* being the uninflected form of *aplu*, "son," or "heir." Similarly, *Nabû-kudur-uṣur*, the transcribed writing of "Nebuchadrezzar" means, "O Nabû, protect the 'boundary stone'"—the latter term was evidently an honoured name for the founder of a family—with *kudur*, usually written *ku-dur*, being the uninflected form of *kudurru*. One could mention additionally, and as an example of a partial non-inflection of an element in royal names, the interesting and fully phonetic writings of Sargon I of Akkad as *šar-ru-um-ki-in* (not *ki-nu-um*), as so given in the study of Joan Westenholz on this king.⁶ The name means "the legitimate king," and was a "throne name," not that given at birth.

From these examples, and others that could be cited, it will be seen that there is good support for transforming *abu râmu* as a proper name into Abram. The name would be a title, clearly suitable for a respected patriarch, and the name, if thus Babylonian, would link attractively with the tradition that Abraham's native city was "Ur of the Chaldees," as thus chronicled in Genesis 11:31 and 15:7, and in Nehemiah 9:7. Since in its origins Ur was a Sumer-

---

3   Erica Reiner and Martha T. Roth, eds., *The Assyrian Dictionary of the Oriental Institute of the University of Chicago*, Vol. 14, R (Chicago, Illinois: The Oriental Institute, 1999).
4   Erica Reiner, ed., *The Assyrian Dictionary of the Oriental Institute of the University of Chicago*, Vol. 1, A (Chicago, Illinois: The Oriental Institute, 1964), 67ff.
5   J. V. Kinnier Wilson, *Cuneiform Texts from Nimrud*, vol. 1, *The Nimrud Wine Lists* (British School of Archaeology in Iraq, 1972), 127. https://www.bisi.ac.uk/wp-content/uploads/publications/CTN1_wine_lists.pdf.
6   Joan Goodnick Westenholz, *Legends of the Kings of Akkade: The Texts*, Mesopotamian Civilizations (Winona Lake, Indiana: Eisenbrauns, 1997), 52.

ian city—its excavation by C. Leonard Woolley in the 1920s was a milestone in Mesopotamian archaeology—the allusion to "the Chaldees" may suitably refer to a Semitic or Babylonian settlement in the city, most probably in "post-Sumerian" times.

Concerning Sarah, or "Saray"

Further support for the above proposal is perhaps to be seen in the name of Abraham's wife, Sarah. In Genesis 17:15, one learns that her original name was Saray, and such a form would accord well with the -*ay* or -*aya* endings of Akkadian female names which are thought to be "hypocoristic," that is endearing or familiar, in their significance. In fact, a female proper name written as *Sa-ra-a-a* has long been known from a letter originating in one of the Nineveh archives,[7] and, at least in earlier years, this name, supposedly "Saraya," was thought to be associable with the biblical "Saray."[8] However, a more certain argument for a Babylonian connection derives from etymology. The common adj. *sarru*, or *sāru*, has the general meaning of "dishonest" or "deceitful," but it is used also to describe a palm tree which is "unfruitful" or "barren."[9] This latter meaning, if it should apply equally to women, would exactly meet the requirement of Sarah's name and condition.

Conclusion

Since the interest of this study is with names, it may be said in conclusion that the name of "Ismā-El," that is, of Abraham's son by his Egyptian handmaid, Hagar, was doubtless a West Semitic form, perhaps specifically Canaanite. It was in any case *not* Babylonian; the equivalent name in that language would have been "Išmē-il." Indeed, one could think that, after he left Babylonia, Abraham put behind him the unhappy memories of his early life. A close reading of Genesis 24:4 with verse 10 relates that what he called "my country" was no longer Babylonia: it was "Aram-naharaim," that is, northern or Upper Mesopotamia, the land to which he first travelled after his departure from Ur. Yet one memory of that city will have lived with him for ever; for it was there beyond the statues, beyond even the rising and setting of the sun and moon,[10] that Abraham, *Khalīl Allāh*, found the truth and the reality of the Lord of the Worlds Whose light he was to follow all his days.

---

7 Robert Francis Harper, *Assyrian and Babylonian Letters* (Chicago: University of Chicago Press, 1892–1914), No. 220, line 2.
8 Leroy Waterman, *Royal Correspondence of the Assyrian Empire*, III (Ann Arbor, Michigan: University of Michigan Press, 1931), 89 and references; Knut Leonard Tallqvist, *Assyrian Personal Names*, reprinted ed. (Hildesheim: Georg Olms Verlag, 1966), 193.
9 Wolfram von Soden, *Akkadisches Handwörterbuch* (Wiesbaden: Harrassowitz Verlag, 1959ff.), 1030; Jeremy Black, Andrew George and Nicholas Postgate, eds., *A Concise Dictionary of Akkadian*, 2nd printing (Wiesbaden: Harrassowitz Verlag, 2000), 318.
10 Qur'ān 6:75–78.

Bibliography

Black, Jeremy, Andrew George, and Nicholas Postgate, eds. *A Concise Dictionary of Akkadian*. 2nd printing. Wiesbaden: Harrassowitz Verlag, 2000.

Harper, Robert Francis. *Assyrian and Babylonian Letters*. Chicago: University of Chicago Press, 1892–1914.

The New English Bible with the Apocrypha. Oxford: Oxford University Press and Cambridge: University Press, 1970.

Reiner, Erica and Martha T. Roth, eds. *The Assyrian Dictionary of the Oriental Institute of the University of Chicago*. Vol. 14, R. Chicago, Illinois: The Oriental Institute, 1999.

Reiner, Erica, ed. *The Assyrian Dictionary of the Oriental Institute of the University of Chicago*. Vol. 1, A. Chicago, Illinois: The Oriental Institute, 1964.

Tallqvist, Knut Leonard. *Assyrian Personal Names*. Reprinted ed. Hildesheim: Georg Olms Verlag, 1966.

Ungnad, Arthur. *Akkadian Grammar*, 5th ed. Translated by Harry A. Hoffner, Jr. Atlanta, Georgia: Scholars Press, 1969.

von Soden, Wolfram. *Akkadisches Handwörterbuch*. Wiesbaden: Harrassowitz Verlag, 1959ff.

Waterman, Leroy. *Royal Correspondence of the Assyrian Empire*, III. Ann Arbor, Michigan: University of Michigan Press, 1931.

Westenholz, Joan Goodnick. *Legends of the Kings of Akkade: The Texts*, Mesopotamian Civilizations. Winona Lake, Indiana: Eisenbrauns, 1997.

Wilson, J.V. Kinnier *Cuneiform Texts from Nimrud*, vol. 1, *The Nimrud Wine Lists*. London: British School of Archaeology in Iraq, 1972. https://www.bisi.ac.uk/wp-content/uploads/publications/CTN1_wine_lists.pdf.

Chapter 12

The Definition of Religion

Syed Farid Alatas

The Problem

A crucial part of the process of knowledge acquisition is the grasping and formulation of definitions of things. It is through definition that we are able to distinguish one concept from another, and one phenomenon from another. Incorrect definitions can create misunderstandings of objective realities. For example, defining socialism as a political economic system founded on collective ownership of the factors of production is very different from defining it as a system based on the state ownership and control of the means of production. The former would tend to convey a more positive view of socialism. The same is true of other concepts. This chapter deals with problems relating to the definition of religion.[1]

Definition is the beginning of understanding of a concept, which in turn is an abstraction in the mind from objects that the mind attempts to understand. A definition is the concise version the statement of a concept and signifies the essence of the object that is referred to by the concept.[2] An example of such an object is religion. The definition of religion can be said to be the formulation of the concept, that is, the formal and concise statement of the concept.

Any definition of religion must necessarily distinguish between the universal and particular aspects of religion. In other words, those traits which are found in all religions and which are, therefore, essential must be distinguished from those traits that are peculiar to certain religions.

---

1   This chapter draws on material from Syed Farid Alatas, "Religion and Concept Formation: Transcending Eurocentrism," in *Eurocentrism at the Margins: Encounters, Critics, and Going Beyond*, ed. Lutfi Sunar (London: Routledge, 2016), 87-101.
2   For an exposition of definition, see Zainal Abidin Baqir, *The Problem of Definition in Islamic Logic: A Study of Abū al-Najā al-Farīḍ's Kasr al-Manṭiq in Comparison with Ibn Taymiyyah's Kitāb al-Radd ʿalā al-Manṭiqiyyīn* (Kuala Lumpur: International Institute of Islamic Thought and Civilization ISTAC, 1998).

Failure to make this distinction is a result of confusing the universal with the particular. Certain traits of a particular religion may be seen to be universal traits of all religions. The result would be the false construction and understanding of religions through the traits and characteristics of one particular religion. This is indeed what had happened with the study of religion in the modern social sciences. There had been a strong tendency to read into the concept of religion traits associated with one religion, Christianity. This problem is due to the continuing prevalence of Eurocentrism in the human sciences.

This chapter is an attempt to explain the problem of the definition of religion that characterizes the modern human sciences as well as provide a more satisfactory definition that overcomes the problem of confusion between the universal and the particular. I discuss some key conceptual works in this regard, including those of Joachim Matthes and Syed Hussein Alatas and Edward Said.

The Definition of Religion

The term "religion" as it is used in the modern human sciences is derived from the Latin *religio*. The trajectory of *religio* was such that it began as an inclusive term when it referred to the cults in and around Rome but remained exclusive when applied solely to Christianity for centuries, and then returns as a more inclusive definition during the nineteenth century. Still, the problem of definition continues to be debated. One of the points of debate concerns the question of inclusive versus exclusive definitions of religion. The debate surrounds the issue of the relative merits and demerits of inclusive and exclusive definitions of religion.

The Inclusive Definition of Religion

Syed Hussein Alatas discusses various problems of the definition of religion, including that of conceptual inflation. This refers to the tendency to generalize or dilute the meaning of a term such that precision and clarity are sacrificed.[3] Conceptual inflation involves increasing the range of empirical reality to which a particular concept refers but which are not included in people's religious experience.

Alatas notes that the term religion had been erroneously extended to include other phenomena such as "Hitler's Nazism and American Baseball." He also discusses Erich Fromm's conception of religion which includes (i) a set of doctrines, whether theistic or non-theistic; (ii) an attitude (humanitarian, authoritarian); (iii) an outcome of psychological tendencies such as love, masochism, sadism insecurity; and (iv) a private obsession that takes the form of

---

[3] Syed Farid Alatas, "Problems of Defining Religion," *International Social Science Journal* 29, no. 2 (1977): 226.

neurosis such as ancestor worship, a cult of cleanliness, etc.[4] This then raises the question of how to distinguish religious from non-religious phenomena.[5] If the above traits listed by Fromm are taken as part of the definition of religion it becomes impossible to distinguish religions from naturalistic ways of life.[6]

Such a loose concept of religion is the result of what Alatas calls conceptual inflation, which he borrowed from Huizinga's Dutch phrase *inflatie der termen*. Huizinga gave the example of the term "Renaissance" which became so general that it lost its value.[7]

What is required for this conceptual inflation is pluralistic reductionism. Alatas notes that there are two kinds of reductionism. One explains a phenomenon in terms of a single cause, and the other in terms of a number of causes. The latter is termed pluralistic reductionism.[8] As far as the concept of religion is concerned, it is being pluralistically reduced, as it were, to the characteristics of non-religion. An example would be replacing the idea of the "instinctive search for God" with that of the search for meaning to the environment and the creation of a reified symbol. This is at odds with the phenomenological sense of religion in which God is not a symbol but a reality.[9] The result of such a reductionism is that the concept of religion is reduced to certain traits to the exclusion of others. The exclusion of other traits renders the concept so general that the distinction between what is usually understood as religion and non-religion is removed.

The reason for the conceptual inflation of the concept of religion is that secular humanism rebelled against religion and dispensed with the supernatural, prayer, the holy, and life after death. There is, therefore, resistance to establishing religious phenomena as qualitatively independent and distinct.[10]

The Exclusive Definition of Religion

The opposite of conceptual inflation is conceptual deflation, which takes place when the concept is "diminished in scope, so as to exclude relevant potential content as much as possible. Conceptual deflation is often the result of reductionism.[11]

Herbrechtsmeier might accuse Alatas himself of conceptual deflation because the latter includes as a key trait in the definition of religion belief in a supernatural being or beings. Herbrechtsmeier, on the other hand, notes that

---

4   Erich Fromm, *Psychoanalysis and Religion* (New Haven: Yale University Press, 1950), 29, quoted in Alatas, "Problems of Defining Religion," 222.
5   Alatas, 219.
6   Alatas, 222.
7   Johan Huizinga, *De Wetenschap der Geschiedenis* (Haarlem: Tjenk Willink, 1937), 70–71, quoted in Alatas, 226.
8   Alatas, 229.
9   Alatas, 230.
10 Alatas, 231–2.
11 Alatas, 227, 229.

Buddhism is largely devoid of such a belief in supernatural beings but it has all the other features of religion such as temples, ritual practices, a sacred canon, pilgrimage sites, reverence for saints, and priest-monks.[12] The claim that the Theravada *dharma* (central teachings) is derived from a superhuman Buddha is a distortion of Buddhism because it is not Buddha's being superhuman but his being transcendental, referring to the residing of his transcendental spirit in the teachings or *dharma*, that makes the *dharma* valid.[13]

Herbrechtsmeier suggests that Western scholars often brought in ideas of religion into non-Western contexts that do not fit the experience and understanding of the peoples that they study, resulting in the etic concept of religion not allowing for an empathic and non-distorted understanding of the variety of emic religious phenomena outside of the West. An example is the Western association of religion with worship of supernatural beings.[14]

To the charge that the emic concept of religion is being falsely attributed to Buddhist understandings Alatas would say that while it may be true that Buddha himself did not preach about a supernatural being, millions of Buddhists in Asia do believe in supernatural beings. In fact, he uses the example of Buddhism to make the point that the basis of enumerative induction, by which the concept of religion is derived, is empirical reality. In the case of Buddhism, what matters is not what some agnostic Buddhists and Western scholars say about the absence or presence of supernatural beings in Buddhism but rather whether millions of Buddhists in Asia actually understand and practise Buddhism in a way that is consistent with the definition of religion as suggested by Alatas.[15]

What emerges from the above discussion on inclusive and exclusive definitions of religion is the idea that both conceptual inflation and deflation are partly outcomes of the superimposition of Western ideas and experiences of religion onto religious phenomena outside of the West. What is interesting and relevant for our purposes here is the nature of the constructions of other "religions" that result from such superimposition. We have already seen how both the concept of religion (as in the conceptual inflation of "religion") as well as the definition of a specific religion (as in the characterization of Buddhism as theistic, as claimed by Herbrechtsmeier) may be outcomes of Western understandings. This raises the crucial question of the nature of such Westernized constructions (of "religion" in general, as well as specific religions) which is what I turn to next.

---

12 William Herbrechtsmeier, "Buddhism and the Definition of Religion: One More Time," *Journal for the Scientific Study of Religion* 32, no. 1 (March 1993), 7. https://doi.org/10.2307/1386910.
13 Herbrechtsmeier, "Buddhism and the Definition of Religion," 11.
14 Herbrechtsmeier, 1.
15 Alatas, "Problems of Defining Religion," 222.

Deflation and Eurocentrism: The Intellectual Christianization of "Religion"

The emergence and development of the concept of religion can be seen in a number of historical stages, that is, those of pre-Christian Rome, early Christianity (the Catholic Church), the modern period (Renaissance, Reformation, Enlightenment) and the nineteenth century.

The etymological approach is the least fruitful for our purposes but is, nevertheless, necessary in order to begin to think of the connotations of "religion." As stated above, "religion" originates from the Latin *religio*. The three verbs *relegere* (to conscientiously observe), *religari* (binding oneself to one's origin and goal) and *reeligere* (goal) are possible derivations of *religion* and refer to different but converging religious attitudes.[16]

In pre-Christian Rome, *religio* was a collective term referring to the cultic patterns and ceremonies at the shrine of a god.[17] When Rome became Christian, Christianity became the dominant belief system, and all other cults were either absorbed or eliminated. *Religio* in early Christianity was frequently used during the first four centuries but appeared less often from the fifth century on. Prior to that, when Christianity as a religion existed alongside many rivals, the term was applied. However, by the fifth century these rivals were largely eliminated and the term came to be less frequently used.[18] In fact, there was no need to continue to apply *religio* to Christianity as Christianity was the only legitimate belief, so it was just known as the Church.[19] To the extent that it was used during this period, it had as varied meanings as ritual practices, worship (of God), piety, the bond between God and man, and the structural organization of the Church and its various ecclesiastical levels.[20]

In the early modern period, the phrase "Christian religion" came to be used more frequently to refer to Christianity with the appearance of the Christian Platonist, Marsilio Ficino's *De Christiana Religione* in 1474.[21] Greek words in the New Testament were translated into English as "religion" and referred to (i) correct religious observances or worship; (ii) a recognized structure of ethical behaviour; and (iii) obedience to the Christian faith,[22] as opposed to unchristian worship and behaviour.

---

16 Karl Rahner, *Encyclopedia of Theology: The Concise Sacramentum Mundi* (New York: Crossroads, 1989).
17 Wilfred Cantwell Smith, *The Meaning and End of Religion: A Revolutionary Approach to the Great Religious Traditions of Mankind* (London: SPCK, 1962), 21.
18 Smith, *The Meaning and End of Religion*, 24–5.
19 Joachim Matthes, "Religion in the Social Sciences: A Socio-Epistemological Critique," *Akademika* 56, no. 1 (2000): 56.
20 Smith, *The Meaning and End of Religion*, 25, 26, 29.
21 Smith, 33, 36.
22 George Arthur Buttrick, *The Interpreter's Dictionary of the Bible: An Illustrated Encyclopedia Identifying and Explaining All Proper Names and Significant Terms and Subjects in the Holy*

But with Luther and the Protestant Reformation *religio* took on an oppositional meaning. *Christiana religio* came to refer to Christian beliefs and a way of life separate from the institution of the Catholic Church. It was oppositional to the clergy, that is, it was the laymans' religion. It was also during this period that *religio* begins to take on a broader meaning closer to the way it is understood today, that is, a system of ideas, beliefs, or doctrine[23] and not just piety, the bond between God and man, or worship. A work that marks this change is Hugo de Groot's *De Veritate Religionis Christianae*.[24] In addition to this radical shift, there were two other important transformations that *religio* went through. One is its generalization to include non-Christian beliefs and practices and the other is its entry into the social sciences.

In the early days of the history of *religio* the term was applied mainly to Christianity. However, early English translations of the Bible do use *religio* to refer to Judaism as well, although this is held to refer to the outer expressions rather than the inner spirit. This is the sense in which the term is used for Judaism in English translations of the Bible from the fourteenth to seventeenth centuries.[25] But *religio* was still far from the more universal notion of religion of which Christianity was just one example.

Matthes notes that an early proof of the generalization of the concept of religion to belief systems other than Christianity is to be found in Jean Bodin's 1593 work, the *Colloquium Heptaplomeres* (*Colloquium of the Seven about the Secrets of the Sublime*).[26] This colloquium contains a fictitious discussion between six representatives of various belief systems and is an early instance of inter-religious dialogue in Europe. Three of the representatives, a Catholic, a Lutheran and a Calvinist, by then were traditionally regarded as having *religio*. Bodin also includes a Muslim, a proponent of a "religion of reason" and a "religious universalist."[27] As Matthes notes, it is very significant that Bodin brought in a Muslim into this debate, even though Islam was widely regarded as wrong belief at best. Matthes makes the very interesting point that the way that this fictitious colloquium was structured clearly demonstrates that Bodin regarded all six belief systems as "religion."[28]

Scriptures, including the Apocrypha: with Attention to Archaeological Discoveries and Researches into the Life and Faith of Ancient Times, vol. 4 (New York: Abingdon Press, 1962), 32

23 Smith, *The Meaning and End of Religion*, 40.
24 Smith, 39, n. 107.
25 James Hastings, ed., *A Dictionary of the Bible Dealing with Its Language, Literature, and Contents Including the Biblical Theology*, 4 vols., (Edinburgh: T & T Clarke, 1902), 225.
26 Matthes, "Religion in the Social Sciences," 56; Jean Bodin, *Colloquium of the Seven about Secrets of the Sublime* (*Colloquium Heptaplomeres de Rerum Sublimium Arcanis Abditis*), trans. Marion Leathers Daniels Kuntz (Princeton: Princeton University Press, 1593, 1857, 1975).
27 Matthes, "Religion in the Social Sciences," 56.
28 Matthes, 56.

By the nineteenth century, "religion" in the sense of a community of adherents with institutionalized beliefs and practices and referring to belief systems other than Christianity was becoming widespread. It is here that we see the hidden construction of "religion" after the image of Christianity, as related very ably by Matthes.[29] While "religion" meant all beliefs, when European scholars wrote about religions other than Christianity, there was the implicit or explicit comparison with Christianity which resulted in problematic constructions, that is, supposedly emic conceptions that were falsely attributed to believers. To understand this, it is necessary to consider what is involved in the logic of comparison.

The logic of comparison is such that the two things to be compared are subsumed under a third unit which is at a higher level of abstraction.[30] For example, apples and pears are subsumed under fruits. This third term is the *tertium comparationis*. The problem arises if the characteristics of the third term are not sufficiently general but are derived largely from one of the units that are being compared.

In the comparison between Christianity and Islam both are subsumed under the third term, religion. The problem with this is that the characteristics of religion are derived from Christianity to begin with. Therefore, the supposedly general scientific concept "religion" is culturally defined by Christianity and Islam is looked at in terms of Christianity rather than compared to Christianity in terms of a general concept "religion."

The danger of the intellectual or what Matthes calls the 'hidden' cultural Christianization of other religions[31] is the reading into other religions the attributes of Christianity because the comparative dimension of religion was derived exclusively from Christianity. The result is a distortion or loss of meaning.

This is what Alatas refers to as conceptual deflation, that is, the concept is diminished in scope, reducing the range of empirical reality that it can refer to. When applied to certain realities there is, therefore, a loss of reality.[32] The only difference in the case of intellectual Christianization is that the deflation is not made explicit. The deflated concept is not defined as such. In fact, the assumption is that "religion" is defined in such a manner that it is sufficiently universal to include what in the past were considered non-religions or heathenisms. But because the Christian elements remain dominant albeit unarticulated features of the concept or, if having been consciously expunged were

---

29 See also Asad's discussion on how religion emerged as an historical category in the West and had come to be seen and applied as a universal concept. Talal Asad, *Geneologies of Religion: Discipline and Reasons of Power in Christianity and Islam* (Baltimore and London: Johns Hopkins University Press, 1993).
30 Matthes, "Religion in the Social Sciences," 96.
31 Matthes, 98.
32 Alatas, "Problems of Defining Religion," 229.

unwittingly smuggled back in, the definition of religion is exclusive. The idea of the intellectual Christianization of "religion" presupposes a more general notion of constructions of which the former is a type. This general notion is based on the critique of Orientalism by Edward Said.

Said describes Orientalism as not just a learned field or discipline, but a "theoretical stage affixed to Europe." The Orientalist, like a dramatist who puts together the drama, constructs images of the Orient in a way that betrays the influence of the history and cultural climate of his society.[33] Orientalism represents more Western knowledge of the Orient rather than true discourse about the Orient.[34] Said makes a distinction between early or pre-modern Orientalism and modern Orientalism. Pre-modern Orientalism, formally beginning in 1312 as a result of the establishment of chairs in Arabic, Greek, Hebrew and Syriac at universities in Avignon, Bologna, Oxford, Paris and Salamanca,[35] was articulated and elaborated by prominent European authors such as Ariosto, Milton, Marlowe, Tasso, Shakespeare, Cervantes and others, all of whom helped sharpen the image of the Orient.[36]

Early Orientalism was not simply ignorant of the Orient, it was characterized by a complex ignorance of the Orient.[37] The image of the Orient was not only far from reality but also complex. The Orient was seen to be hostile to Europe but also weak and defeated, although always a threat, in contrast to a powerful Europe that speaks on her behalf, as when Aeschylus has the Persian queen speak rather than the Persians speaking on their own volition.[38] Said makes a very interesting point about early Orientalism. In the encounter between East and West the Orient neither remains as something completely novel to the Occident nor as something completely well-known. Instead a "new median category emerges, a category that allows one to see new things, things seen for the first times as versions of a previously known thing."[39] An example of a new thing was Islam, at least to medieval Europeans, which was gradually dealt with by being considered as a fake version of something known, that is, Christianity.[40] Here Said is speaking of the European Christian view of Islam, which developed and spread in poetry, scholarly controversies and popular superstition.[41]

---

33 Edward W. Said, *Orientalism* (New York: Vintage Books, 1979), 63.
34 Said, *Orientalism*, 6, 63.
35 Said, 49–50.
36 Said, 63.
37 R. W. Southern, *Western Views of Islam in the Middle Ages* (Cambridge, M.A.: Harvard University Press, 1962), 14, quoted in Said, 55.
38 Aeschylus, *The Persians*, trans. Anthony J. Podlecki (Englewood Cliffs, N. J.: Prentice-Hall, 1970), quoted in Said, 57.
39 Said, 58–9.
40 Said, 59.
41 Said, 61. See also William Wistar Comfort, "The Literary Role of the Saracens in the French Epic," *PMLA* 55, no. 3 (September 1940), quoted in Said, 61, n. 40.

My concern is not so much with the Christian or Western views of non-Western religions as such but with the intellectual Christianization of these "religions," that is, the attribution of Christian-like traits to other belief systems as a result of the application of Christian concepts and categories to these belief systems. This can be seen as a special case of the Western view of other religions. Said comes close to discussing this problem when he refers to the analogical constraint that acts on European Christian thinkers. They assumed that "Mohammed was to Islam as Christ was to Christianity."[42] In early Orientalism, the Europeans referred to Islam not as Islam but as Mohammedanism, a consequence of this analogical constraint. With Jesus and Muhammad juxtaposed in that way, the "truth" must be that the latter is a fake, an imposter.[43] An early observer of Islam in this manner was St. John of Damascus.[44] The Europeans attributed to Islam the intention to deceive by posing as the true religion. Islam could then be rejected on the grounds that it was Christian heresy. This is an instance of the intellectual Christianization of Islam because Islam is not looked at on its own terms, in terms of how it sees itself. Rather, Islam is viewed much like any other Christian heretic claim that had to be rejected by the Church. Islam is first Christianized and then rejected on the grounds that it is fake Christianity.

The late eighteenth and early nineteenth centuries was the period of the emergence of modern Orientalism. There began to be far greater emphasis on the scientific study of the Orient. This was partly due to the translations of newly discovered Arabic, Sanskrit and Zend texts as a well as the awareness of a new kind of relationship between the Orient and the West, symbolized by the Napoleonic invasion of Egypt in 1798.[45] Modern Orientalism retained its original features as a thought style founded upon an ontological and epistemological distinction between the Occident and the Orient, which formed an important part of the collective consciousness of European scholars and lay people alike, and which was functional in the domination, restructuring and authorizing of the Orient.[46] This was not unrelated to the fact that Europeans were not just reading, writing and talking about the Orient but were also governing it. Practically all the sciences were complicit in the development of modern Orientalism. The Orient could not represent itself but had to be spoken on behalf of by the West,[47] as Orientals were irrational, backward

---

42 Said, 60.
43 Norman Daniel, *Islam and the West: The Making of an Image* (Edinburgh: Edinburgh University Press, 1960), 33, quoted in Said, *Orientalism*, 60.
44 See Daniel J. Sahas, *John of Damascus on Islam: The "Heresy of the Ishmaelites,"* Leiden: E.J. Brill, 1972.
45 Said, *Orientalism*, 42–3.
46 Said, 2–3.
47 Said, 6.

and uncivilized. Hence, the "free-floating mythology of the Orient" that went hand-in-hand with more scholarly and scientific research.[48]

The intellectual Christianization of Islam is found in modern Orientalism as well. Engels had referred to Islam as a fake religion.[49] While Marx and Engels regarded all religions as founded on illusion, they nevertheless understood Christianity to be a universal religion while Islam was an Oriental religion.[50] The Orientalist, Duncan Black MacDonald was of the opinion that Islam was second-order Arian heresy.[51]

What reality is lost, what is the distortion done to belief systems other than Christianity as a result of this intellectual Christianization? Let us consider the case of Hinduism. According to Smith, "'Hinduism' is . . . a particularly false conceptualization, one that is conspicuously incompatible with any adequate understanding of the religious outlook of the Hindus. Even the term 'Hindu' [an Indian or non-Muslim inhabitant of India] was unknown to the classical Hindus. 'Hinduism' as a concept certainly they did not have."[52] The term 'Hindu' has its origins in antiquity as the Indo-Aryan name of the river Indus, which is its Greek transliteration.[53] It is from this usage that the terms 'Hindu' and 'Hinduism' gradually acquired their descriptive and geographical denotations. Muslim scholars such as al-Bīrūnī (973-1048 CE), writing in Arabic, used the term *al-Hind* to refer to the Indian subcontinent, but when they referred to the people of that subcontinent or aspects thereof they were referring to what they considered the indigenous and non-Muslim inhabitants of India.[54] In Persian and Urdu the corresponding geographical term to *al-Hind* was *Hindustān*. Things *Hindustānī* referred to whatever was indigenous to India and non-Muslim.[55] The English "Hindu" probably derived from the Persian. The term "Hindu" appears in the *Gaudiya Vaishnava* texts of the sixteenth cen-

---

48 Said, 53.
49 Karl Marx, and Friedrich Engels, *Selected Correspondence* (Moscow: Foreign Languages Publishing House, 1953), 96, quoted in Alatas, "Problems of Defining Religion," 234.
50 Karl Marx, and Friedrich Engels, *On Religion* (Moscow: Progress Publishers, 1975), 178.
51 Duncan Black Macdonald, "Whither Islam?" *The Muslim World* 23, no. 1 (January 1933): 2.
52 Smith, *The Meaning and End of Religion*, 61, quoted in Robert Eric Frykenberg, "The Emergence of Modern 'Hinduism' as a Concept and as an Institution: A Reappraisal with Special Reference to South India," in *Hinduism Reconsidered*, eds. Günther-Dietz Sontheimer, and Hermann Kulke (New Delhi: Manohar Publishers, 1989), 102, n. 3.
53 Smith, *The Meaning and End of Religion*, 249, n. 46, quoted in Frykenberg, "The Emergence of Modern 'Hinduism'," 83.
54 Abū al-Rayḥān Muḥammad bin Aḥmad al-Bīrūnī, *Taḥqīq mā lil-hind min maqūlah maqbūlah fī al-ʿaql aw mardhūlah*, Hyderabad: Majlis Dāʾirat al-Maʿārif al-Uthmāniyyah, 1377/1958 [c1030]. For the English translation see Muhammad ibn Ahmad al-Biruni, *Alberinu's India: An account of the religion, philosophy, literature, geography, chronology, astronomy, customs, laws and astrology of India about AD 1030*, trans. Edward C. Sachau. 2 vols., (Delhi: Low Price Publications; London: Kegan Paul, Trench, Trubner & Co. Ltd, 1910).
55 Frykenberg, "The Emergence of Modern 'Hinduism'," 84.

tury (probably as a result of Muslim influence).⁵⁶ The usage here is consistent with that in the Muslim texts of the premodern Arabs and Persians. Even in the modern period, this negative definition of Hinduism is found as evident in the Hindu Marriage Act. The Act defines a Hindu, among other things, as one "who is not a Muslim, Christian, Parsi or Jew by religion . . ."⁵⁷

The terms "Hindu" and "Hinduism" in reference to religion, and a unitary one at that, was for the most part, a modern development. In the eighteenth century it began to be used to denote an Aryan, Brahmanical or Vedic-based high culture and religion by European Orientalists such as Halhed, Jones and Müller.⁵⁸ It is this usage that was adopted by the early Indian nationalists themselves like Ram Mohan Roy, Gandhi and Nehru.⁵⁹ This 'new' religion was founded on the ontology and epistemology contained in the *Varnāsramadharma* and encompassed the entire cosmos, detailing as part of its vision a corresponding stratified social structure.⁶⁰

What is important in these developments as far as the intellectual Christianization of Indian beliefs systems is concerned is that (i) the belief systems of the inhabitants of the Indian subcontinent (excluding Muslims, Jews, Christians and Parsis) came to be regarded as religion; (ii) the belief systems were seen to constitute a single religion; and (iii) were founded on a system of Brahmanical doctrines based on the *Chatur-Veda* (Four Vedas).⁶¹ It is in these senses that characteristics of Christianity were read into Indian beliefs. Gradually, the "newly-christened" Hinduism also came to encompass the 'low' tradition or what is nowadays referred to as "popular," "temple," "bhakti," "village," or "tribal" Hinduism.⁶²

This is a construction at odds with indigenous thinking and experience as there was never such a thing as a single all-encompassing religion (or *dharma*, for that matter) called Hinduism or any other name that can be traced to the Vedas and that characterize the beliefs of the non-Muslim, non-Jewish, non-Christian, non-Parsi population of India. Instead, what happened was a process of reification, that is, an ideal type of the "Hindu" religion was constructed and assumed to be a description of the real Indian society. As Deshpande

---

56 O'Connell, Joseph T., "The Word 'Hindu' in Gauḍīya Vaiṣṇava Texts," *Journal of the American Oriental Society* 93, no. 3 (July September 1973), 340-343, quoted in Frykenberg, "The Emergence of Modern 'Hinduism'," 84.
57 J. Duncan M. Derret, *Introduction to Modern Hindu Law* (Bombay: Oxford University Press (Indian Brach), 1963), 18-9.
58 Frykenberg, "The Emergence of Modern 'Hinduism'," 85-6.
59 Frykenberg, 86.
60 Frykenberg, 86.
61 Frykenberg, 86.
62 Frykenberg, 87.

suggests, this is a "case of simulated identity which over the years has been accepted as true identity."[63]

Looking at South Indian examples, Frykenberg tells us how this happened in practical terms beginning in the nineteenth century. Modern Hinduism is a form of corporate, organized and "syndicated" religion which arose in South India and by which highly placed and influential groups of Brahmans, supported by Brahmanized non-Brahmans, did most of the defining, the manipulating, and the organizing of the essential elements of what gradually became, for practical purposes, a dynamic new religion. Moreover, this process of reification, this defining and organizing of elements which they did, occurred with the collaboration, whether witting or unwitting, with those who governed the land.[64]

This was facilitated by the process centralization, rationalization, and bureaucratization of information which had two bases. One was the interaction between local officials and the rulers, examples of which are the patronage of cultural events and the policy with respect to temples and their administration. The latter entailed the collection and preservation of information (historical, archaeological, artistic) that served to concretize a concept that was gradually developing in the minds of colonial scholars and administrators, and local elites.[65] The other refers to movements outside of the state structure that acted as lobbies and pressure groups that sought to bring about changes to the structure in line with their aspirations or which acted to counter Christian proselytization.[66]

I have suggested that the intellectual Christianization of "religion" is a special case of the application of an exclusive definition of religion. The exclusivity of the definition is smuggled into the concept unwittingly. The result is a specific type of construction of religion determined in the first place by the elements smuggled into the concept of religion to begin with. I have argued that the elements smuggled into the understanding of Islam and "Hinduism" are derived from Christianity. The result is a distortion and loss of meaning, and a failure to consider the meaning of religion from the perspective of the understanding and experience of its adherents.

Another illustration of the same problem is from the well-known sociologist, Anthony Giddens. His textbook, *Sociology*, is widely used in introductory courses to the discipline at the undergraduate level. In the chapter on religion, not only are the main concepts used for the study of religion derived from Christianity, as in the section of types of religious organization,[67] the impres-

---

63 G. P. Deshpande, "The Plural Tradition," *Seminar* 313, 23–5, (1985), quoted in Frykenberg, 101.
64 Frykenberg, 89.
65 Frykenberg, 89, 91–2, 94.
66 Frykenberg, 95-6.
67 Anthony Giddens, *Sociology*, 3rd ed. (Cambridge: Polity Press, 1997), 446–449.

sion is given that these apply to the study of non-Christian religions. For example, in his discussion on religion in the United Kingdom, Giddens refers to church membership in the country to note the increase and decrease of church attendance among different religions. He notes that forty percent of adults attended church on Sundays in 1851 and that this number had dropped to about ten percent in the late 1990s.[68] What is problematic is that in a table that Giddens presents that provides data on church membership in the United Kingdom between 1970 and 1994, the data is given not only for various Christian churches, but also for Muslims, Sikhs, Hindus, Jews and others.[69] In other words, the impression is given that the idea of the church as a religious body is a universal category that applies equally to all religions and not just Christianity.

The problem of the loss of meaning was noted decades ago by Syed Muhammad Al-Naquib Al-Attas. In a lecture delivered at the International Islamic Conference held under the auspices of the Islamic Council of Europe in 1976, he says that the concept conveyed by the term *dīn*, "which is generally understood to mean *religion*, is not the same as the concept of religion as interpreted and understood throughout Western religious history."[70] He goes on to say that when we refer to Islam in the English language as a religion, we actually understand by that the *dīn* and all the meanings implied by the concept of *dīn*.[71] The failure to understand by religion as *dīn*, when the term religion is applied to Islam, would result in the loss of meaning and distortion of the Islam as understood, experienced and practised by Muslims.

James Spickard's important book on alternative sociologies of religion questions the mainstream perspective that confines its understanding of religion to belief in the context of religious institutions. He then considers approaches from outside of the mainstream, Eurocentric sphere to examine if there are alternative ways of understanding religion, such as those suggested by the Confucian, Islamic and Navajo traditions.[72] For example, what would it be like to look at religion, as Ibn Khaldun did, as a form of social solidarity rather than as belief and doctrine.[73]

---

68 Giddens, *Sociology*, 460.
69 Giddens, 461.
70 Syed Muhammad Naquib al-Attas, *Islam: The Concept of Religion and the Foundation of Ethics and Morality* (Kuala Lumpur: Muslim Youth Movement of Malaysia (ABIM), 1976), 1.
71 Al-Attas, *Islam: The Concept of Religion*, 1.
72 James V. Spickard, *Alternative Sociologies of Religion: Through Non-Western Eyes* (New York: New York University Press, 2017).
73 Syed Farid Alatas, *Applying Ibn Khaldun: The Recovery of a Lost Tradition in Sociology* (London: Routledge, 2014).

Towards a Universal Definition of Religion

The application of a universal concept of religion would not result in such distorting constructions of individual religions because the elements that make up the universal concept of religion are derived from all religions, apply to all of them with varying degrees of significance and are, therefore, neutral, in the sense that one is not led by the very concept of religion to read into a particular religion the traits of another. The neutrality of the universal concept of religion would extend to all related concepts in the study of religion. A universal concept of religion implies neutrality for all other concepts applied in the description and analytical study of religion. The reverse is also true. A non-universal concept of religion, such as an exclusive one, would render all other concepts in the study of religion non-universal.

Therefore, the use of the conceptual vocabulary of one religion to talk about another religion is not in itself a problem if the concept of religion in operation is the universal one. For example, in the sociology of religion concepts such as sect and denomination are defined in terms of another concept, that of the church. Since the idea of the church as a religious organization does not exist in other religions, the use of concepts like denomination and sect for other religions runs the risk of resulting in an intellectual Christianization of these religions. In Islam, for example, the terms denomination and sect cannot be used to refer to the Sunni and Shiʿite branches of Islam as they both imply a certain relationship vis-à-vis a church, which is non-existent in Islam. The problem lies in the non-universality of terms like sect and denomination.

Alatas' argument is as follows. He develops a definition of religion on the basis of enumerative induction. Enumerative induction refers to the exhaustive enumeration of the traits of religion derived from the various dimensions of religious life, that is, the psychological, the social and the philosophical.[74] He lists the following traits of religion as identified by scholars of religion by way of enumerative induction:[75]

1. belief in a supernatural being or beings
2. a corresponding invisible order or dimension
3. a personal relationship between humans and the supernatural being or beings
4. specific rites and beliefs sanctioned or required by the supernatural being or beings, such as belief in an afterlife, prayer, etc.
5. the distinction between the sacred and the profane in life with corresponding division of activities and objects such as rituals or places of worship

---

[74] Alatas, "Problems of Defining Religion," 215.
[75] Alatas, 215–6.

6. belief that the supernatural communicates with humans through human messengers
7. ordering life in harmony with the conception of truth as established by the supernatural being or beings
8. belief that revealed truth supersedes that resulting from human efforts
9. the establishment of a community of believers such that religion informs both individual as well as collective life.

These are what Alatas calls the permanent characteristics of religion which must be distinguished from the variable traits, that is, those traits that are not essential and universal characteristics of religious life and experience.[76] Examples of variable traits that he cites are the presence of magic or religions representing a particular nation or group. Apart from enumerating the traits of religion, religion can also be defined in terms of its function such as the integration of group and individual life or the differentiation of action according to notions of right and wrong, good and bad.[77] Alatas then points out that the traits and function of religion could be condensed into a single concept, that of meaning.

Were one to condense the traits and function of religion into a single sentence containing a minimum number of concepts one would find the concept of meaning predominant. It is not fear, hope for security in this world or the hereafter, the desire for reward or mere conditioned habit that motivates a genuinely religions person in his devotion: it is the sense that life has a particular meaning, and only one single meaning, which is that provided by his faith. Whatever psychological states flow out in the form of overt religious behaviour, underlying it is always this profound sense of meaning.[78]

Religions as they are found in the empirical world and throughout history conform to the above definition of religion as the definition itself is a result of enumerative induction from the phenomena of religion. The methodology of concept formation is such that the general concept of religion is derived from its inductive base, the total phenomena of particular cases of religion, from which common characteristics, including ideas, overt behaviour, psychological processes, and the hierarchy of significance attached to them within each religion, are selected. This selection determines the constant of our general concept, but before we start selecting, we must have a notion of what a general concept should be, which in turn is subject to continual modification by particular cases, so that it cannot avoid being a dynamic concept. It must always be fed from below. If the particular cases remain constant in their fundamentals over a considerable time, a relatively constant general concept, applica-

---

76 Alatas, 216.
77 Alatas, 217.
78 Alatas, 218.

ble to existing cases, can be derived. Such a concept of religion exists and is applicable to all known cases. It is used here to define types of phenomena designated by historical consensus, as religious and differing from the type designated as non-religious.[79]

The logic of concept formation in enumerative induction is not circular. It is not that a decision is first made as to what the empirical religions are and then the traits of the general concept are derived from them. These traits may be derived from any particular religion and then found to exist in other belief systems that we designate as religion.

The classical Islamic tradition method, conveyed by the term *manṭiq*, referred to the conventions that made it possible to distinguish right from wrong.[80]

In general, the procedures involved include the formulation of definitions (*ḥudūd*) that refer to the essence (*māhiyāt*) of phenomena, and arguments that lead to judgment or apperception.[81] Knowledge, therefore, is either conception (*taṣawwur*), that is, the perception of the essence of things, or it is apperception (*taṣdīq*) or the judgement establishing the correspondence between the concept and the phenomenon in question. *Taṣawwur* entails the knowledge of the five universals (*al-kullīyāt al-khams*), that is, genus (*jins*), differentia (*faṣl*), species (*nawʿ*), property (*khāṣṣah*) and general accident (*al-ʿaraḍ al-ʿām*).[82] Ibn Khaldun noted that every phenomenon possesses its own essence as well as accidental conditions or properties that attach themselves to the phenomenon. If one knows the essence or the nature of events as well as the accidental conditions that attach themselves to those events, it would help one to distinguish truth from falsehood because it leads to a critical approach to historical information.[83]

Obtaining knowledge of the five universals involves a process of abstraction from phenomena which takes place until the highest genus is reached. The early Muslims studied and further developed Greek logic in order to aid the process of analogical reasoning to ensure that the process of abstraction proceeds in the correct manner.

Applied to the case of religion, the definition of religion is the statement of its essence and refers to what Alatas calls the permanent characteristics of

---

79 Alatas, 221–2.
80 Muhsin Mahdi, *Ibn Khaldûn's Philosophy of History: A study in the Philosophic Foundation of the Science of Culture* (London: George Allen & Unwin, 1957),160.
81 Ibn Khaldūn, *Muqaddimah*, III, 91 [III, 137]. The first set of page numbers refers to the Arabic edition by Abdesselam Cheddadi. See Ibn Khaldūn, *Al-Muqaddimah*. Page numbers in square brackets refer to Rosenthal's English translation of the *Muqaddimah* from which quotations are taken. See Ibn Khaldûn, *The Muqadimmah—An Introduction to History*.
82 Ibn Khaldūn, *Al-Muqaddimah*, III, 94 [III, 142].
83 Ibn Khaldūn, *Al-Muqaddimah*, I, 53 [I, 72–73].

religion, which must be distinguished from its variable traits, that is, those traits that are not essential. The genus is that part of the essence of religion which is predicable of another phenomenon that otherwise differs from religion. For example, it can be said that religion is a belief system. When we specify the genus of a thing, we are placing it under the category of a higher universal, that is, the genus. The differentia refers to that part of the essence that allows us to differentiate one species from another. An example would be monotheistic and polytheistic religions. The essential property refers to traits or characteristics which are essential for the thing to be what it is. For example, religions require belief in the supernatural. This is an essential property of what it means to be religion. A particular religion may believe in a particular deity as a supernatural being, but this would be a property that is particular to that specific religion and is not an essential property of religion. Rather, it should be understood as an accidental property of religion.[84]

Conclusion

The example of religion illustrates the backwardness of concept formation in the modern human sciences. It is a wonder that supposedly scientific fields of study, with all the rigour, precision and cogency that are claimed for their practitioners, remain parochial when it comes to the appropriateness and relevance of key concepts. The example of religion also illustrates the persistent and perennial problems of Eurocentrism and Orientalism in contemporary knowledge production in the human sciences. There is a need to go beyond recognition and critique of the problem towards active concept formation and theory building. One way to do this is to deal with the problem of definition as they relate to concept formation. In the case of the concept of religion, what can be learnt is that concept formation is a process that requires our being mindful of the cultural origins of key terms and the possible distortion that results from not taking into account the distinction between the universal and the particular. Such mindfulness requires serious attention to the problem of definition.

---

84 That is, there is a universal definition of religion which specifies belief in a supernatural being(s) as the essence. But specific religions have different conceptions of that supernatural being. In Islam it is *Tawḥīd*, Trinity in Christianity. Neither *Tawḥīd* nor Trinity can be said to be essential to the definition of religion. *Tawḥīd* is essential to the definition of Islam, but not religion in general.

Bibliography

Aeschylus. *The Persians*, Translated by Anthony J. Podlecki. Englewood Cliffs, N. J.: Prentice-Hall, 1970. Quoted in Edward W. Said. *Orientalism*, New York: Vintage Books, 1979.

Alatas, Syed Farid. "Problems of Defining Religion." *International Social Science Journal* 29, no. 2 (1977): 213–234.

Alatas, Syed Farid. *Applying Ibn Khaldun: The Recovery of a Lost Tradition in Sociology*. London: Routledge, 2014.

Alatas, Syed Farid. "Religion and Concept Formation: Transcending Eurocentrism." In *Eurocentrism at the Margins: Encounters, Critics, and Going Beyond*, edited by Lutfi Sunar, 87-101. London: Routledge, 2016.

Asad, Talal. *Genealogies of Religion: Discipline and Reasons of Power in Christianity and Islam*. Baltimore and London: Johns Hopkins University Press, 1993.

Al-Attas, Syed Muhammad Naquib. *Islam: The Concept of Religion and the Foundation of Ethics and Morality*. Kuala Lumpur: Muslim Youth Movement of Malaysia (ABIM), 1976.

Al-Bīrūnī, Abū al-Rayḥān Muḥammad bin Aḥmad. *Tahqīq mā lil-hind min maqūlah maqbūlah fī al-ʿaql aw mardhūlah*. Hyderabad: Majlis Dāʾirat al-Maʿārif al-Uthmāniyyah, 1377/1958.

Al-Biruni, Muhammad ibn Ahmad. *Alberinu's India: An account of the religion, philosophy, literature, geography, chronology, astronomy, customs, laws and astrology of India about AD 1030*. 2 vols. Translated by Edward C. Sachau. Delhi: Low Price Publications and London: Kegan Paul, Trench, Trubner & Co. Ltd, 1910.

Baqir, Zainal Abidin. *The Problem of Definition in Islamic Logic: A Study of Abū al-Najā al-Farīḍ's Kasr al-Manṭiq in Comparison with Ibn Taymiyyah's Kitāb al-Radd ʿalā al-Manṭiqiyyīn*. Kuala Lumpur: International Institute of Islamic Thought and Civilization ISTAC, 1998.

Bodin, Jean. *Colloquium of the Seven about Secrets of the Sublime* (*Colloquium Heptaplomeres de Rerum Sublimium Arcanis Abditis*). Translated by Marion Leathers Daniels Kuntz. Princeton: Princeton University Press, 1593/1857/1975.

Buttrick, George Arthur. *The Interpreter's Dictionary of the Bible: An Illustrated Encyclopedia Identifying and Explaining All Proper Names and Significant Terms and Subjects in the Holy Scriptures, including the Apocrypha: with Attention to Archaeological Discoveries and Researches into the Life and Faith of Ancient Times*. 4 vols. New York: Abingdon Press, 1962.

Comfort, William Wistar. "The Literary Role of the Saracens in the French Epic." *PMLA* 55, no. 3 (September 1940): 628–59.

Daniel, Norman. *Islam and the West: The Making of an Image*. Edinburgh: Edinburgh University Press, 1960.

Derret, J. Duncan M. *Introduction to Modern Hindu Law*. Bombay: Oxford University Press (Indian Brach), 1963.

Deshpande, G. P. "The Plural Tradition." In *Seminar* 313 (1985): 23-25.

Fromm, Erich. *Psychoanalysis and Religion*. New Haven: Yale University Press, 1950.

Frykenberg, Robert Eric. "The Emergence of Modern 'Hinduism' as a Concept and as an Institution: A Reappraisal with Special Reference to South India." In *Hinduism Reconsidered*, edited by Günther-Dietz Sontheimer, and Hermann Kulke, 82-107. New Delhi: Manohar Publishers, 1989.

Giddens, Anthony. *Sociology*. 3rd ed. Cambridge: Polity Press, 1997.

Hastings, James, ed. *A Dictionary of the Bible Dealing with Its Language, Literature, and Contents Including the Biblical Theology*. 4 vols. Edinburgh: T & T Clarke, 1902.

Herbrechtsmeier, William. "Buddhism and the Definition of Religion: One More Time." *Journal for the Scientific Study of Religion* 32, no. 1 (March 1993): 1-18. https://doi.org/10.2307/1386910.

Huizinga, Johan. *De Wetenschap der Geschiedenis*. Haarlem: Tjenk Willink, 1937. Quoted in Syed Farid Alatas. "Problems of Defining Religion." *International Social Science Journal* 29, no. 2 (1977): 213-34.

Ibn Khaldūn, ʿAbd al-Raḥmān. *Al-Muqaddimah*. 5 vols. Edited by ʿAbd al-Salām al-Shaddādī [Abdesselam Cheddadi]. Casablanca: Bayt al-Funūn wa al-ʿUlūm wa al-Ādāb, 2005.

Ibn Khaldūn. *The Muqadimmah—An Introduction to History*. 3 vols. Translated from the Arabic by Franz Rosenthal. London: Routledge & Kegan Paul, 1967.

Macdonald, Duncan Black. "Whither Islam?" *The Muslim World* 23, no. 1 (January 1933): 1-5. https://doi.org/10.1111/j.1478-1913.1933.tb00229.x.

Mahdi, Muhsin. *Ibn Khaldûn's Philosophy of History: A study in the Philosophic Foundation of the Science of Culture*. London: George Allen & Unwin, 1957.

Marx, Karl, and Friedrich Engels. *On Religion*. Moscow: Progress Publishers, 1975.

Marx, Karl, and Friedrich Engels. *Selected Correspondence*. Moscow: Foreign Languages Publishing House, 1953. Quoted in Syed Farid Alatas. "Problems of Defining Religion." *International Social Science Journal* 29, no. 2 (1977): 213-34.

Matthes, Joachim. "Religion in the Social Sciences: A Socio-Epistemological Critique." *Akademika* 56, no. 1 (2000), 85-105.

O'Connell, Joseph T., "The Word 'Hindu' in Gauḍīya Vaiṣṇava Texts." *Journal of the American Oriental Society* 93, no. 3 (July-September 1973): 340-43. https://doi.org/10.2307/599467.

Rahner, Karl. *Encyclopedia of Theology: The Concise Sacramentum Mundi*. New York: Crossroads, 1989.

Sahas, Daniel J. *John of Damascus on Islam: "The Heresy of the Ishmaelites."* Leiden: E.J. Brill, 1972.

Said, Edward W. *Orientalism*. New York: Vintage Books, 1979.

Smith, Wilfred Cantwell. *The Meaning and End of Religion: A Revolutionary Approach to the Great Religious Traditions of Mankind*. London: SPCK, 1962.

Southern, R. W. *Western Views of Islam in the Middle Ages*. Cambridge, M.A.: Harvard University Press, 1962.

Spickard, James V. *Alternative Sociologies of Religion: Through Non-Western Eyes*. New York: New York University Press, 2017.

Chapter 13

Professor Ashraf and His Contribution to Religious Education in England

Sarah Smalley

Introduction

Professor Syed Ali Ashraf was a man whose interests ranged across many areas of scholarship and learning, expertise, and practical action. The focus of this chapter is on just one of them: the work he did in relation to religious education as a curriculum subject in the school education system.[1] It is a measure of Professor Ashraf's vision and far-sightedness that many of the ideas he put forward in the 1980s about religious education are widely accepted now but were highly unusual then. He saw the importance of bringing together Muslim and non-Muslim scholars and organisations to work together on a shared agenda—that of encouraging teaching and learning about Islam in a way that was true to its traditions but also acknowledged the context of a society where many different religions and beliefs sat alongside one another.

The Context for Religious Education in the 1980s

The education system in the late 1970s and early 1980s was in the process of change in many respects, as was the society it reflected and served. RE in its traditional form was being challenged, at least implicitly, by the secularisation of society in general. This included a belief in many quarters that religion had had its day and would gradually be replaced by a rational, secular, and scientifically based worldview. Another factor was the growing awareness, particularly in education circles, of the significant numbers of children from religious backgrounds such as Islam, Hinduism, and Sikhism in schools in some parts of the country.

---

1   This article refers to the system in maintained schools in England. During the period of Professor Ashraf's engagement in RE, the same system applied in Wales, but this is no longer the case since devolution of education to the Welsh Assembly in 1998.

If RE was to help prepare pupils for life in this religiously, culturally, and philosophically plural society, it needed to do two things. Firstly, it had to help all children and young people to explore ultimate questions and human experience, whilst taking account of the fact that some were not from religious backgrounds and had parents who did not wish them to be brought up in a faith. Secondly, the subject needed to take account of the experience of many other young people from a variety of faith backgrounds for whose parents religion was a central part of their lives.[2] RE was no longer religious *instruction*—nurture in the Christian faith—but religious *education*, a more broadly based and inclusive enterprise.

The result in RE terms was not, as Robson puts it, "simply a branch of piety. Its aim was the study of major religions as contemporary living faiths, using the material they provided to challenge pupils to think seriously about the meaning and purpose of life, but without imposing in advance any predetermined answers."[3] Pioneering work by the Schools Council during the 1970s had a major influence on some of the new Agreed Syllabuses for religious education, for example in Birmingham (1975) and Hampshire (1978). For the first time, these were "multifaith" syllabuses rather than documents which took Christianity, and more specifically Christian instruction and nurture, as their starting point. However most serving teachers had little in their background or training which would equip them to teach a form of religious education which required knowledge and understanding of five major faiths in addition to Christianity, nor to deal with young people's questions and challenges in an open and non-confessional way.[4]

This was the context into which Professor Ashraf stepped. He saw the urgent need for teachers and schools to be supported in taking on the challenge of teaching children in mainstream primary and secondary schools about Islam, lack of knowledge and resources notwithstanding.

Partnership between Muslims and non-Muslims

During the 1980s and early 90s, Ashraf produced a series of publications through the Islamic Academy of which he was Director General. An important, and indeed an unusual, characteristic of all these publications was that

---

2   Tariq Modood, "Culture and Identity," in *Ethnic Minorities in Britain: Diversity and Disadvantage*, eds. Tariq Modood, and Richard Berthoud (London: Policy Studies Institute, 1997), 301.
3   Geoff Robson, "Religious Education, Government Policy and Professional Practice, 1985–1995," *British Journal of Religious Education* 19, no. 1 (1996), 14, https://doi.org/10.1080/0141620960190103.
4   In 1988 this was codified in the Education Reform Act as a requirement that pupils should be taught about "Christianity and the other principal religions represented in this country." This was interpreted in subsequent documentation to mean teaching about Buddhism, Hinduism, Judaism, Islam, and Sikhism.

they were the outcome of a partnership between Muslim scholars involved in Islamic education and non-Muslim educationalists involved in the organisation of religious education or the training of teachers. Representatives of both groups were bought together on a number of occasions to organise residential seminars which allowed Muslims and non-Muslims to engage in dialogue on the issues under discussion and to produce a tangible outcome which could be shared more widely.

As well as emphasising the right of Muslim communities in the UK to have their religion and way of life respected through accurate teaching, Ashraf drew attention to the fact that some of the core values of Islam were also shared by the wider community. This provided openings and opportunities for Muslims to make contributions to British society. Islam "upholds many of the basic values that are similarly adhered to by the wider British community. This strength of Islam which enables it to contribute to the general good ought not to be underestimated, for harmony in a pluralist or multi-faith society such as our own depends on minority groups sharing a common core of values with the rest of society as well as at the same time being able to retain their own identity."[5]

In 2009 when there are Muslim members of both houses of parliament, when Muslims are widely (if still not widely enough) represented in the professions, business, the media, charities and voluntary organisations and other aspects of public life, it is not easy to remember back to the period a quarter of a century earlier when public awareness about Islam and Muslims barely existed. The debate about Islam and public life in the early years of the 21st century has often been inextricably tied to issues of war and terrorism, but Ashraf's point about Islam's capacity for contributing to the general good of society through the identification of shared values alongside the recognition of distinctiveness is gradually being expressed and recognised in the public arena.[6]

Professor Ashraf took seriously the responsibility of practising what he preached in this regard. He was the respected Muslim representative for many

---

5   The Islamic Academy, *The Teaching of Islam in British Schools: An Agreed Statement* (Cambridge: The Islamic Academy, 1985), 3.
6   An example is the foundation in 2005 of the Three Faiths Forum, representing Muslims, Christians and Jews who work together for peace and reconciliation (www.threefaithsforum.org.uk). The establishment of Islam Awareness Week during the autumn every year has provided an opportunity to highlight work done in the community by Muslims in the health and welfare services, in neighbourhood businesses, in support for religious education in schools and so on (www.iaw.org.uk). Another interesting example is the development, within the Shi'ah Muslim community, of the practice of donating blood to the health service as a symbolic alternative to the traditional drawing of blood through self-flagellation in Ashura processions of witness. See, www.world-federation.org.

years on Cambridgeshire Standing Advisory Council on Religious Education (SACRE), at a time when such representatives were the exception rather than the norm they are today. As such, he was able to perform a dual role, providing knowledgeable and authoritative advice to the local authority on matters to do with Islam, and responding to concerns of Muslim parents about the religious education their children received in their schools. He felt that Muslim parents should have the confidence to allow their children to take part in school RE classes, and to refrain from exercising their legal right to withdraw their children from the subject. Rather, parents should seek reassurance from teachers about the purpose and nature of such lessons.

The logical corollary of this was that teachers needed to be sure they were teaching RE in a way that respected the rights of children and parents to hold to their religious beliefs, and that "openness" in the RE context should mean respectful enquiry rather than critical agnosticism. Ashraf's emphasis was on both the rights and the responsibilities of all parties: the rights of Muslim parents and children to have their faith and traditions respected, the rights of all parents to be assured that religious education lessons would contextualise but not undermine their home faith or belief, and the right of educators to be supported by parents in school lessons aimed at spreading mutual understanding and awareness whilst respecting religious difference. In each case parents and educators alike had a responsibility to make sure these rights and expectations were upheld.

As well as recognising the many areas where Muslims and non-Muslims held shared values, Ashraf saw the wisdom of articulating such commonalities in publishded statements which could then form a basis for policy or action. As a young teacher in the early 1980s I was initially rather surprised by the number of "discussion documents" and "agreed statements" which seemed a central part of the Islamic Academy's output.[7] It soon became clear to me that such statements, far from being a substitute for action, were an essential starting point. In a potentially controversial area, agreement needed to be visible and recorded as a joint basis for shared future work. The practice of identifying areas of agreement before tackling areas of dispute is now a commonplace, for example in international peace negotiations, but Professor Ashraf was rather ahead of his time in applying it to religious education.

---

7   See, for example, the following documents published by the Islamic Academy, Cambridge: Ashraf, ed., *The Teaching of Islam in British Schools* (1985); *Resources for the Teaching of Islam in British Schools: An Agreed Statement* (1986). Ashraf had applied a similar approach to the question of the education of Muslim young people through the perspectives of their own faith in *New Horizons in Muslim Education* (Kent, UK: Hodder and Stoughton, and Cambridge: The Islamic Academy, 1985).

Representation of Islam in an Educational Context

Ashraf was strongly committed to the proper, accurate and authentic portrayal of Islamic beliefs and practices. The Islamic Academy booklet on resources for the teaching of Islam in British schools identified a major problem in the dearth of resources that were "accurate, authentic and informative, and not biased, prejudiced or based on stereotypes."[8] Many, according to Ashraf, contained errors and demonstrated attitudes which would be unacceptable to most devout Muslims. In 1986 he organised a seminar (along the lines described above) to analyse existing resources; the outcome was that the participants found a serious shortage of reliable and engagin materials: "There is a lack of books for pupil use which adequately draw on personal testimony in such a way that the non-Muslim reader can hear the voice of faith. There is, therefore, a need for books at the pupils' level which will enable them to encounter genuine Muslim experience."[9]

This is a problem which teachers, writers and publishers continue to grapple with. How can a religious perspective be illustrated effectively unless the children or young people who present such personal testimony come across as full and rounded young humans? (This problem exists in the representation of all religious traditions and is perhaps even worse as far as Christianity is concerned.) Great strides have been made, and websites such as "Children talking" show both how much young people have to say about religion and religious issues. Even if their voices cannot always be relied upon absolutely for orthodox presentations of their faith tradition, they are certainly authentic and give a powerful impression of the impact of Islam on believers' lives.[10] The pioneering work of Ashraf and others gave impetus to the development of much greater awareness of this issue, which resulted in guidelines such as those produced by the Religious Education Council of England and Wales to encourage publishers of RE resources to take seriously the need for accuracy and authenticity.[11]

The need for reliable resources was related to another issue in religious education. In the early 1980s only relatively small numbers of serving teachers of RE had had any training in teaching about faiths other than Christianity. Agreed syllabuses (the documents which set out the curriculum for religious education in each local authority) might include limited opportunities for

---

8   Islamic Academy, *Resources for the Teaching*, 4.
9   Islamic Academy, *Resources for the Teaching*, 7.
10 "Children and young people talking in RE," National Association for Teachers of Religious Education, www.natre.org.uk.
11 "Why RE Matters," Religious Education Council of England and Wales, accessed June 25, 2023, https://religiouseducationcouncil.org.uk/. In 2008 the Department for Children, Families and Schools felt sufficiently concerned about the issue of resources for RE that a major research project to review resources currently available was set up, led by Professor Robert Jackson, University of Warwick.

children to learn about different faiths and beliefs, but in general 'comparative religion' as it was then known, was still a bit of a novelty for many schools and teachers, and the shortfall in suitable resources was compounded by a woeful lack of teacher knowledge. And the teachers themselves needed to be well prepared: Ashraf's list, in *The Teaching of Islam in British schools*,[12] sounds quite daunting even now: teachers needed accurate knowledge, to be able to present material on Islam in such a way as to be recognisable to a believing Muslim, to make it intelligible, relevant and interesting to pupils, and to be properly trained, with access to Islamic Studies courses. When primary teachers today graduate with sometimes as little as a few hours training to cover pedagogy and subject knowledge in all the 'major faiths' covered by a locally agreed syllabus, this particular battle is still clearly far from being won.

Professor Ashraf tried to address this problem in a practical way, seeing that if his ideal was for authentic, accurate and empathetic understanding of Islam, an ideal provider of training was the Islamic Academy itself. Weekend courses gave teachers of religious education a chance to meet and talk with communicative and well-informed Muslims who could discuss questions of Islamic beliefs and how they shaped Muslim lives. It is hard to remember, now, the fact that people in many parts of the UK, including teachers, had never met or talked to a Muslim apart from an occasional pupil. In our own time, twenty-five years later, a rich diversity of Muslim cultures is represented in Britain—there are self-confident and successful members of Turkish, Pakistani, Bengali, Nigerian, Egyptian, Iraqi, Somali, Moroccan, Malaysian, Palestinian and Iranian Muslims who live and work in Britain and are part of our educational environments, workplaces, and neighbourhoods in many parts of the country. Alongside these Muslims of Asian, African, and Middle Eastern origins there are also increasing numbers of British born Muslims, both converts and British born Muslims from a range of cultural heritages. Teachers, particularly RE teachers, encounter pupils from all these backgrounds and would probably now be amongst the sections of the population with the greatest knowledge about Islam.

Muslim Children in British Schools

Another area of great concern to Professor Ashraf was that of the experience of Muslim children and young people in the education system of England and Wales. In the 'Agreed statement' on the teaching of Islam in British schools, he identified many of the issues over which Muslim parents were troubled in relation to school life, going much further than the teaching of religious education. These included recognition of religious requirements in relation to dress for girls, participation in mixed sex swimming and other physical education lessons and activities, provision of halal food and the option to

---

12 The Islamic Academy, *The Teaching of Islam in British Schools*.

withdraw from sex education lessons, the provision of facilities for Muslim prayer and attendance at Friday congregational prayers. In addition to these aspirations for children in schools, there was the hope that where possible single sex secondary schools would be provided, Muslims should be represented on school governing bodies and Voluntary Aided Muslim schools should be established.[13] Many of these were aspirations with simple practical solutions which many schools and local authorities had accepted, some twenty years on—though there are still cases where schools or sometimes individual teachers fail to meet the needs of their Muslim pupils in a way that respects their rights to fulfil religious requirements.

However, Ashraf's greater concern was the danger that he believed a secular education system posed to children. He outlined as the purpose of education in Islam, "to enable man to fulfil the purpose of his creation, of his coming into the world . . . to become a wholehearted servant of God."[14] He put forward the view that an education system which aimed to produce scepticism and proceeded through doubt was destructive of the balanced growth of the individual and called for religious and moral teaching to be the governing and guiding principle underpinning the curriculum. Understanding early on that even if there were to be a wholesale expansion in the number of Muslim Voluntary Aided schools in urban areas with comparatively large concentrations of Muslim population, there would still be large numbers of Muslim children unable to attend them outside such areas.[15]

His call was therefore for all schools to develop a "faith based" curriculum.[16] Always a man of keen practical understanding, he saw that the only realistic way this might come to pass in England and Wales was if people of goodwill in all religious traditions made common cause in calling for the education system to be based on values they held in common, acknowledging their religious source. Such a system would prevent religion being marginalised and recognise a need for their education to help children and young people see some relationship between the material and spiritual realms of experience. In some respects, this was reflected in the requirements of the Education Reform Act (1988), in which the aims of education were to include the spiritual and moral development of the child. This was a move closer to Ashraf's vision of an education philosophy based on "the totality of the human being in whom spirit, heart, intellect, reason and senses work in cooperation and in unison."[17]

---

13 The Islamic Academy, *The Teaching of Islam in British Schools*, 9.
14 Syed Ali Ashraf, "A View of Education—an Islamic Perspective," in *Schools for Tomorrow*, ed. Bernadette O'Keefe (London, New York and Philadelphia: Falmer Press, 1988), 74.
15 The implications of this point were more recently developed in detail in Saied R. Ameli, and Arzu Merali, *British Muslims' Expectations of the Government* (London: Islamic Human Rights Commission, 2004).
16 The Islamic Academy, *Faith as the Basis of Education in a Multi-faith, Multi-cultural Country: Discussion Document II* (Cambridge: The Islamic Academy, 1991).
17 The Islamic Academy, *Faith as the Basis of Education*, 11.

When the Ofsted inspection system was introduced into schools in 1993, with a requirement to make judgements on the extent to which schools promoted the spiritual, moral, social and cultural development of all pupils, the impetus for schools to take seriously these dimensions as the underpinning of the whole curriculum and other aspects of school activity was strengthened still further. However it was clear that in this context, "spiritual" was to be interpreted in a non-religious way; it included learning about and reflecting on religious beliefs, practices and values, but its aim was not to promote a religiously spiritual form of development. A further move in the direction of articulating a common vision was to be found in the revised version of the National Curriculum, which included a set of shared values to underpin the work of schools.[18] These were not grounded in religion, but were endorsed by some hundreds of organisations (including religious ones) across the country; they set out shared beliefs on the self, relationships, society and the environment.

The main enemy of faith-based education, in Ashraf's view, was a secularist approach to life which emphasised materialistic goals and aspirations, an approach whose values were man-made, without any religious foundation, promoting doubt rather than faith, and ignoring the "education of the interior." However, he was willing to acknowledge that even amongst people who did not identify with any religious tradition, there were many who shared some of the values he looked to inculcate.

Ashraf's Legacy to Education in England and Wales

In some respects, the education system has moved closer to the ideals put forward by Syed Ali Ashraf in the 1980s and 90s. There is now much more sympathetic understanding of Islam in the education system; whilst problems still arise, the majority of schools try hard to meet the religious needs of all their pupils, including Muslim ones, in terms of making it possible for them to meet religious requirements in terms of food, dress, appropriate curriculum approaches and materials. Teachers of religious education are by and large a great deal better informed about Islam than was the case twenty years ago. There is still considerable room for improvement but many of the resources available for teachers to use in the RE classroom when exploring Islam and Muslims are more accurate, authentic, interesting, and attractive—not perfect, but better than they were. A number of state-funded Muslim schools have been established, offering the full National Curriculum but with a school ethos grounded in the values of Islam. On the other hand, and this would surely have been the key point for Ashraf, most Muslim children continue to be educated in schools with a basically secular outlook and to live in a society where many people, not just Muslims and not just those from other religious backgrounds, feel a sense of alienation from the dominant materialism of society.

---

18 Qualifications and Curriculum Authority, *Curriculum 2000* (London: 2000).

This means that for Muslim parents and educators alongside those of other religions and beliefs, there is also an increased sense of needing to find ways of co-existing in a pluralistic society which acknowledge the values of all, not just the religious and not just the secular. Recent steps towards this have included, for example, the Toledo Guiding Principles on religion and belief in public schools in Europe.[19] These set out principles based on the values of reciprocity, respect, and inclusion—for example that teaching about religions and beliefs must be provided in ways that are fair, accurate and based on sound scholarship. But a key phrase is "religion and belief," not just "religion." From Ashraf's perspective, this might have been a step too far in the direction of inclusion. However, it seems likely, on the basis of his accommodation to living in a religiously plural society, that he would have agreed with the principle of reciprocity, whilst feeling that a child could never receive an education in the fullest sense of the word unless it was based on faith.

But perhaps his most important legacy was the one which finds expression in the ways people of different faiths and beliefs are working together, up and down the country in branches of the Inter Faith Network, of SACREs, of Faith Forums, of discussion groups and football matches, of joint neighbourhood action groups and many, many other activities. From the very first, he saw and believed in the value of person-to-person dialogue and discussion as a way through the potential hostilities and misunderstandings which can so easily come about between people of different backgrounds and perspectives. His commitment to dialogue is even more necessary today in our world of problems related to terrorist activity carried out in the name of Islam, the social fracturing generated by British involvement in Iraq and Afghanistan, the anguish and anger related to failures to find justice and peace in Israel/Palestine, and the countless smaller but no less deeply felt causes of resentment, mistrust and antagonism between people of different beliefs. His answer—for people to sit down together and work until they have found some principles they can agree on—is an answer for education in Britain and indeed the world, as valuable now as it was when Ashraf made it a central commitment. His work continues to stand as an example for Muslim and non-Muslim cooperation in the field of education today.

---

19 Organisation for Security and Co-operation in Europe, *Toledo Guiding Principles about Religions and Beliefs in Public Schools* (Warsaw: ODIHR, 2007).

Bibliography

Ameli, Saied R., and Arzu Merali. *British Muslims' Expectations of the Government*. London: Islamic Human Rights Commission, 2004.

Ashraf, Syed Ali. *New Horizons in Muslim Education*. Kent, UK: Hodder and Stoughton, and Cambridge: The Islamic Academy, 1985.

Ashraf, Syed Ali. "A View of Education—an Islamic Perspective." In *Schools for Tomorrow*, edited by Bernadette O'Keefe, 69-79. London, New York, and Philadelphia: Falmer Press, 1988.

The Islamic Academy. *Faith as the Basis of Education in a Multi-faith, Multi-cultural Country: Discussion Document II*. Cambridge: The Islamic Academy, 1991.

The Islamic Academy. *Resources for the Teaching of Islam in British Schools*. Cambridge: The Islamic Academy, 1986.

The Islamic Academy. *The Teaching of Islam in British Schools: An Agreed Statement*. Cambridge: The Islamic Academy, 1985.

Modood, Tariq. "Culture and Identity." In *Ethnic Minorities in Britain: Diversity and Disadvantage*, edited by Tariq Modood, and Richard Berthoud. London: Policy Studies Institute, 1997.

Organisation for Security and Co-operation in Europe. *Toledo Guiding Principles about Religions and Beliefs in Public Schools*. Warsaw: ODIHR, 2007.

Qualifications and Curriculum Authority. *Curriculum 2000*. London: 2000.

Religious Education Council of England and Wales. "Why RE Matters." Accessed June 25, 2023. https://religiouseducationcouncil.org.uk/.

Robson, Geoff. "Religious Education, Government Policy and Professional Practice, 1985-1995." *British Journal of Religious Education* 19, no. 1 (1996): 13-23. https://doi.org/10.1080/0141620960190103.

Chapter 14

Syed Ali Ashraf:
Exploring Education through a Spiritual Lens[1]

Syed Ali Naqi

Shāh Walī Allāh, in his book *Ḥujjat Allāh al-Bālighah*, asserts that the Prophet, may the peace and blessings of God be upon him, told that God decrees a great event after every hundred years."[2] This aligns with the Ḥadīth stating that "God will send to this community at the beginning of every century someone to renew its religion for it."[3] In essence, every century, Allah bestows upon the world an individual through whom religious reawakening occurs, societal refinement is achieved, and a revolutionary transformation permeates all aspects of human life grounded in religious faith.

Shāh Walī Allāh attributes this phenomenon to the recurring turmoil in matters of religion that plagues each century, resulting in rampant indiscipline, ignorance, and a dearth of knowledge within human societies. This deterioration leads to societal corruption, obstructing the practice of genuine wisdom and shrouding the world in darkness. These exceptional individuals, through their appearance, usher in a religious, educational, intellectual, and scientific revolution, dispelling various forms of religious fanaticism and narrow-mindedness. They bring order and cohesion to society and nations, all guided by the rekindled religious principles. These remarkable personalities are commonly referred to as *mujaddid* (reformers) or *muḥyīddīn* (revivers of the faith). For instance, approximately a thousand years after the passing of Prophet Muhammad (pbuh), Aḥmad Fārūqī Sirhindī (1564–1624) emerged, known as Mujaddid-e Alf-e Thānī or the reviver of the second millennium. Such luminaries appear in every century, earning the title of the century's *mujaddid* or reformer. They possess profound knowledge in matters of Sharīʿah

---

1 Translated by the Editor from the Bengali version. This chapter was written in 2002.
2 Shāh Walī Allāh, *The Conclusive Argument from God: Shāh Walī Allāh of Delhi's Ḥujjat Allāh al-Bālighah*, trans. Marcia K. Hermansen (Leiden: Brill, 1995), 268.
3 *Abū Dāwūd* IV:109, no. 4290, Malāhim I.

(Islamic law), *ṭarīqah* (spiritual path), *ma'rifah* (spiritual knowledge), and *ḥaqīqah* (ultimate truth), providing education and guidance to humanity. They excel in both spiritual and worldly knowledge.

Islamic history, moreover, abounds with individuals blessed with profound esoteric and exoteric knowledge, dedicated to establishing Allah's religion on earth. Although we cannot assert that Syed Ali Ashraf was a *mujaddid* prophesied in the Ḥadīth sated above, he was undoubtedly a spiritual personality who was endowed with a diverse range of qualities and his profound impact on the Muslim society's transformation is evident through his global educational, intellectual, and spiritual endeavours. He was born on 30 January 1924 at his maternal uncle's residence in Agla Purbo Paṛa village on the outskirts of Dhaka district, Bangladesh. Quite some time before his birth, one of his brothers tragically passed away at just seven months old. As a result, his mother was profoundly devastated, and one night in a dream, she witnessed a beautiful lady clad in a white saree who approached her, cradling a baby boy in her arms, and asked, "Would you like to have him?" His mother shouted, "This is my baby, give him to me." Before his birth, his mother saw in another dream that there was a dazzlingly bright half-moon in the sky of Agla and in her lap was a bright star. The radiance was so intense that it illuminated every speck of dust on the leaves of every tree in Agla, rendering them distinctly visible. As a result of these dreams, his mother felt that she was on the verge of welcoming a blessed son into her life.

When Syed Ali Ashraf was three months old, he was afflicted with pneumonia, which was hard to cure then. In this difficult situation, his mother frequently wept and feared that she might lose him, just as she had lost her previous son. At that time, Ashraf's maternal grandfather, Syed Mukarram Ali, a spiritually enlightened person, instructed his daughter, i.e., Ashraf's mother, to go to sleep with the baby son, and he himself sat down in *murāqabah* (spiritual meditation). After a long time, Ashraf's mother woke up and saw that her father had left and her son was completely cured. While asleep, she had a dream that she would often recount to us. She had seen that she was walking over an expansive field while carrying the baby son. While walking, she saw a large tree under which Prophet Ibrahim (*'alayhis salām*) was seated. She approached Prophet Ibrahim with her son, and he offered a prayer on his behalf. It seems that this supplication contributed to his subsequent success in life.

His childhood was spent at Agla. When he was a few months old, his maternal grandfather Syed Mukarram Ali died. He spent his education life in Dhaka. He was admitted in class three at Armanitola Government School from where he passed his Matriculation Examination securing 5th position. He passed the Intermediate of Arts Examination from the Government Dacca Intermediate College by achieving the 6th position. He attained the first position in first class in the BA English Honours at Dhaka University in 1945, earning a gold medal for his outstanding achievement. After he passed his MA with distinction in

1946, he had three job offers—lecturer at Dhaka College, Civil Supply officer, and lecturer at Dhaka University, but he chose to join the English Department of Dhaka University as a lecturer.

Syed Ali Ashraf was the 11th descendant of Dhaka's renowned saint Hazrat Shāh ʿAlī Baghdādī as shown in Appendix 2 of this book. His father was Syed Ali Hamed who had five sons and five daughters. Among them Syed Ali Ashraf was the fourth child. The eldest among the five sons, Syed Ali Ahsan, is a renowned educationist, writer, poet, litterateur, and a national professor. Another brother, Dr Syed Ali Reza, was a well-known homeopath of Bangladesh. Fourth among his brothers, Syed Ali Naqi, is a professor of History and one of the founders of Darul Ihsan Trust and Darul Ihsan University. Throughout his active life, he remained closely intertwined with Syed Ali Ashraf, actively engaging in various aspects of thought, planning, and all other affairs related to Syed Ali Ashraf. Presently, in his role as Syed Ali Ashraf's successor, he diligently upholds and carries forward the legacy of his spiritual endeavours. The youngest brother Syed Ali Taqi was involved with teaching in his initial life. Currently, he is passing through a period of frail health.[4]

Spiritual Attainment

Syed Ali Ashraf's family had a rich spiritual lineage, stretching from Hazrat Shāh ʿAlī Baghdādī to his own generation, with all the male members being spiritually enlightened individuals affiliated with various Sufi orders (*tarīqah*). His father and mother used to discuss and practise Sufism at home. From there Ali Ashraf became attracted to Sufism. The profound influence of his family deeply shaped his character and beliefs. He was naturally drawn to Sufism, and at the age of 22, shortly after completing his MA written examination, one morning, he gave *bayʿah* (pledge of allegiance) to Hazrat Ghulam Muqtadir at Kamrangirchar, located across the Buriganga River in Dhaka. Later that same day, in the late afternoon, Hazrat Ghulam Muqtadir visited his home and expressed his delight to Ali Ashraf's mother, saying that in his lifetime, he had accepted many *murīds* (disciples), but he had never encountered anyone as exceptional as Ali Ashraf. Hazrat Ghulam Muqtadir was very old at that time.

Under his mentor's guidance, Syed Ali Ashraf made significant strides in his spiritual journey, but he still had a long path ahead when his guide passed away in 1957. At that time, he was Reader and Head of English Department at Karachi University. He was very much struck with grief at the demise of his spiritual guide. During this period, Ali Ashraf met Professor M. M. Ahmad, the Dean of the Faculty of Arts at Karachi University, who embraced him as a younger brother. Professor Ahmad, a *khalīfah* (successor) of Karachi's illustrious saint, Hazrat Baba Zaheen Shah Taji, introduced Syed Ali Ashraf to his

---

4   Syed Ali Ahsan passed away in 2002, Syed Ali Reza in 2001, and Syed Ali Naqi in 2008.

own spiritual guide. From then onwards, Ali Ashraf used to visit Baba Zaheen Shah regularly. Towards the beginning of 1958, Baba Zaheen Shah instructed him to undergo *chillah* which is a vigorous spiritual practice of asceticism or austerity and solitude in Sufism. During a span of forty days, all non-essential communication is strictly prohibited, and one must completely abstain from worldly pleasures and pursuits. This time is devoted primarily to various spiritual practices, including *dhikr* (remembrance of God), *murāqabah* (meditation), *tilāwah* (recitation of sacred texts), and *shogal* (spiritual exercises). Even while serving as the departmental head at Karachi University and actively participating in various endeavours, he remarkably fulfilled his *chillah* duties. In June of the same year, Baba Zaheen Shah conferred upon him *khilāfah* (successorship) from himself and on behalf of Hazrat Ghulam Muqtadir.

After the demise of his father in July 1958, Syed Ali Ashraf came to Dhaka and made me and one of our nieces his disciples. I had then only just completed the Intermediate of Arts examination. At that time the method of his spiritual training was such that every disciple had to remain at a fixed spiritual station (*maqām*) for an extended period of time. Each year, he would journey from Karachi to Dhaka during the summer vacation, where he resided for two months. During this period in Dhaka, his focus was solely on imparting teachings related to a specific *laṭīfah*, a subtle spiritual organ. In this way, he used to help every disciple to advance on the spiritual path with firmness.

During the Bangladesh War of Liberation, he resided in Karachi. Throughout this period, he generously extended financial assistance to numerous Bengalis and freely shared his wisdom with them. Baba Zaheen Shah wished to install Syed Ali Ashraf as his *Gaddī Nashīn*[5] successor after him. However, following the tumultuous events of the 1971 war, Baba Zaheen Shah advised him to depart from Pakistan, assuring that this move would enable him to undertake even greater endeavours.

In either 1961 or 1962, he embarked on a journey to what is now Bangladesh, then known as East Pakistan, from Karachi. His destination was a remote village named Boro Khata in Hatibandha, Rangpur, where he had the privilege of meeting a revered blind saint of extraordinary stature, belonging to level of *ghawth* in the spiritual hierarchy, known to the locals as "Andho Hafez." Among the populace, there existed a deep-rooted belief that the saint possessed the miraculous power to heal illnesses and fulfil wishes through his prayers. This remarkable figure was none other than Hazrat Hafez Bazlur Rahman.

Their initial encounter left a lasting impression, as Hazrat Hafez Bazlur Rahman was able to recognise the spiritual potential in Ali Ashraf. In a rare

---

5   The prevailing spiritual head of a *Khānqāh* is called *Gaddī Nashīn*. In Urdu, *Gaddī* means a seat and a person who sits on that is called *Nashīn*. However, this term is specifically used for the current spiritual leader of a *Khānqāh* or tomb.

gesture, he conferred upon him *khilāfah*, despite his customary reluctance to accept disciples. In private conversations, Hazrat Hafez Bazlur Rahman would confide that finding a worthy disciple was an exceedingly rare occurrence. Thus, Syed Ali Ashraf received *fayḍ* (spiritual grace) from Hazrat Hafez Bazlur Rahman. Once he remarked that every time Ali Ashraf lifted his hands in prayer, his supplications were unfailingly answered.

Following the birth of Bangladesh, Ali Ashraf decided to leave Karachi for the United Kingdom. During his time there, he received an invitation from King Abdulaziz University in Saudi Arabia to lead its English Department. It was in Saudi Arabia that he would cross paths with a person of great spiritual eminence, named Hazrat Syed Manzur Husain, belonging to the Naqshbandī Order of Sufism. At the time, Hazrat Manzur Husain held a significant spiritual position called *qayyūm-e zamān* in Sufism. His principle was that he would never accept anyone as a disciple without the explicit guidance of his spiritual mentor.

In a profound and transformative connection, Syed Ali Ashraf became a disciple of Hazrat Manzur Husain, receiving the *khilāfah* from him to the extent that Ali Ashraf held his spiritual guide's words as sacrosanct. He firmly believed that the spiritual guide's decisions and directives were beyond question, viewing them as repositories of mercy and sources of profound wisdom. Through this philosophical stance, he saw the potential for both spiritual growth and the enrichment of one's intellect.

While residing in Makkah in 1978, Syed Ali Ashraf met Hazrat Dr Badiuzzaman, a revered Sufi shaykh possessing an elevated status of a *ghawth*. Dr Badiuzzaman hailed from Mirwarishpur in the Noakhali district of Bangladesh and had established a spiritual organisation known as Jamā'at-e Madīnah (*Madinar Jamaat*, in Bengali) with thousands of devout followers. This organisation drew its name from the profound spiritual knowledge he had acquired directly from Madinah through the divine guidance of Prophet Muhammad (pbuh). Following the directives of Prophet Muhammad (pbuh), Hazrat Badiuzzaman provided accessible spiritual instruction and guidance to individuals, seamlessly combining the teachings of the Qādiriyyah and Chishtiyyah Orders. Through this unique process, individuals could swiftly complete the *sulūk* (spiritual path) and achieve a profound spiritual connection with Prophet Muhammad (pbuh) known as *ziyārah*.

Hazrat Dr Badiuzzaman, in his advanced age, contemplated the critical matter of succession for Jamā'at-e Madīnah. It was during his encounter with Syed Ali Ashraf that he recognised the chosen successor he had long sought. In accordance with the instructions of the Prophet (pbuh), he conferred upon Ali Ashraf the esteemed *khilāfah* and entrusted him with the entire responsibility of Jamā'at-e Madīnah.

Through his association with such Sufi masters, Syed Ali Ashraf ascended to a lofty position (*maqām*) within the spiritual realm. The knowledge he gleaned from this spiritual journey led him to a profound understanding of the universal and timeless truth. This truth, bestowed upon humanity by Allah immediately upon creation, carried a tremendous responsibility. It encompassed qualities such as kindness, the ability to discern good from bad, truth from falsehood, unwavering faith in goodness, and above all, belief in Allah. Syed Ali Ashraf firmly believed that every individual was endowed with these qualities from birth, which education refined and developed over time. This foundational belief underpinned his spiritual philosophy, leading him to advocate, "Many different types of questions can arise in the mind. However, try to evaluate those by accepting this belief as a hypothesis."

Based on this belief, he discerned truth in such a way that it became the cornerstone of his life philosophy and educational principles. He lived his life guided by this truth, shaping his family and social life, as well as all his individual and collective endeavours, around this belief. He understood that truth could be identified through belief and sought to enrich every individual with this knowledge base. He endeavoured to impart education and guidance rooted in this philosophy to his disciples, not only in Bangladesh but also across the globe, including America, England, and Canada. In his view, a truly human person tries to stay away from evil, gains mastery over their desires, and acts in alignment with their conscience.

This perspective led to a life characterised by exemplary actions, as he believed that by living in this manner, one would continuously receive Allah's blessings. This led to his clarity of vision allowing him to discern good from bad, truth from falsehood, and he maintained that the success or failure of every action rested with Allah. He used to say, "I have come to this world with a purpose, and I will continue to work, drawing strength from the blessings of relentless *jihād*. Syed Ali Ashraf firmly held his ground throughout his seventy-four years of life, guided by the belief that courageous individuals proceed with their actions while placing their faith in Allah, even in the face of danger. It is about such people that Allah says, "Behold! verily on the friends of Allah there is no fear, nor shall they grieve" (Qurʾān 10:62, trans. Yusuf Ali).

Syed Ali Ashraf held that spiritual devotion was the sole path to realising truth, and the knowledge required for the realisation of the truth was spiritual knowledge. This spiritual knowledge could only be attained by only a certain belief. Syed Ali Ashraf clearly knew what that belief was and what that knowledge was. That is, unwavering belief in *tawḥīd* (monotheism) and a commitment to following all the instructions given by Allah through the Holy Qurʾān. The knowledge based on this belief is true experiential knowledge. The foundation of the spiritual philosophy that leads to the understanding of God's gnosis is rooted in this belief.

Philosophy of Education

He constructed his educational philosophy upon a foundation of spiritual principles, firmly maintaining that the primary objective of education was to nurture the profound connection between individuals and their Creator. Within his educational framework, he categorised all knowl'edge into three distinct domains: religious sciences, human sciences, and natural sciences. Building upon this framework, he meticulously designed a comprehensive curriculum and took proactive measures to produce textbooks and train educators to impart this philosophy effectively.

Syed Ali Ashraf staunchly held the belief that all knowledge originates from a divine source, and he advocated for the integration of religion as the cornerstone of education. In his classification of knowledge, he delineated three distinct categories. Firstly, he identified religious sciences as disciplines concerned with the profound relationship between human beings and Allah. This encompassed the study of sacred texts like the Qur'ān, Ḥadīth, *tafsīr*, *fiqh*, *uṣūl al-fiqh*, as well as the Arabic language. Secondly, Ashraf categorised human sciences, which pertained to the interactions and relationships among human beings. These encompassed subjects such as Bangla, English, geography, history, social sciences, and economics, shedding light on the intricate web of human society. Lastly, he placed natural sciences in the third category, focusing on the interaction of humanity with the natural world. These included fields like physics, chemistry, biology, medicine, and astronomy, revealing the connection between humans and the physical universe. In essence, Syed Ali Ashraf's vision sought to harmonise education by grounding it in religious principles while encompassing the full spectrum of human experience, from spirituality to societal dynamics and the natural world.

Professor Syed Ali Ashraf embodied a unique fusion of Islamic upbringing and a profound connection with modern Western knowledge. His mission was to combat the moral decay stemming from extreme modern lifestyles. Recognising that the convergence of religious and modern education held the key to global progress, he aimed to bridge the gap between these two distinct educational systems. In his astute observation, there existed two parallel education systems for Muslims—modern education, devoid of religion, and religious education, isolated from modernity. Those immersed in modern education often lacked knowledge of religion, while those grounded in religious education remained largely ignorant of modern scientific advancements. This stark division troubled him deeply.

During the British colonial era in India, some Muslim intellectuals perceived that English education was permeating Indian culture with the values of the British, often at odds with their own beliefs. To safeguard Indian Muslims from this cultural intrusion, two religious education institutions were established in Deoband and Saharanpur. These institutions produced a cadre of scholars well-versed in religious teachings but ill-prepared to bridge the gap between religion and modernity. Their contributions were commendable, significantly mitigating the spread of atheism brought by the British, yet they failed to realise the untapped wealth of modern knowledge attainable through the teaching of English. While they were diligently disseminating Islamic knowledge through religious institutions, modern education was advancing unchecked and unchallenged in secular educational institutions.

In the 20th century, Syed Ali Ashraf emerged as a visionary who understood that the solution lay not in excluding modern education but in harmonising it with religious teachings. He aimed to eliminate religious ignorance within modern education and address the deficiency of religious values within secular education. From 1956 to 1973 he was the Head of the English Department of Karachi University. A seasoned educationist, Sufi ascetic, and a teacher at various Oriental and Western educational institutions, he recognised the need to transform the Western secular education paradigm into a comprehensive religious education system. However, this vision did not entail a mere replication of traditional religious teachings, as practised in our country, focused solely on the study of the Qurʾān, Ḥadīth, *tafsīr*, *fiqh*, *uṣūl al-fiqh*, and *manṭiq*.

Syed Ali Ashraf envisioned an educational revolution, blending the best of both worlds. His strategy aimed at creating a seamless educational system wherein students could simultaneously acquire religious knowledge and modern wisdom. This revolutionary approach resonated not only within our nation but sent ripples throughout the global education landscape, establishing Syed Ali Ashraf as a trailblazer in the field of education worldwide.

Education Movement

During the 1970s, while serving as the Professor and Head of the English Department at Karachi University, Syed Ali Ashraf became acutely aware of how Western education and its curriculum had permeated global consciousness, leading people to perceive worldly life as the only life worth pursuing. He articulated his reservations about the limitations of modern education through various writings. He convincingly argued that acquiring proficiency in modern knowledge alone should not define an educated person. He often questioned the common practice of labelling teachers, poets, writers, engineers, doctors, pilots, civil servants, and others as "educated," especially when some of them engaged in immoral and dishonest behaviour within society. According to him, these individuals were skilled in their respective fields but not necessarily educated in the broader sense.

This contemplation prompted him to delve into the fundamental definition of education and the essential structure of a curriculum. He encapsulated his thoughts in a proposal, which he sent to King Faisal of Saudi Arabia. Subsequently, in 1974, he received an invitation from King Abdulaziz University, where he assumed the role of Professor and Head of the English Department and came into contact with notable figures such as Abdullah Omar Nasseef and Shaikh Ahmad Salah Jamjoom, Minister of Commerce under the Saudi government. Through discussions with them, Syed Ali Ashraf's proposal for organising an international Islamic educational conference gained traction.

Upon my first visit to Makkah in 1975, I found that scholars from various countries gathered at Ashraf's residence to discuss the idea of this educational conference. Discussions were also held almost daily at the flat of Professor Muhammad Qutb. Prominent participants included Ustadh Muhammad al-Mubarak, Dr Abdullah Zayd, Dr Abdullah Omar Nasseef, Shaikh Ahmad Salah Jamjoom, Dr Ghulam Nabi Saqeb, and Dr Hussain Hamed Hassan and others. Together, they formed an organising committee to bring the First World Conference on Muslim Education to fruition in 1977.

It is important to highlight that, under the guidance of Dr Abdullah Omar Nasseef, who served as the Secretary General of Abdul Aziz University at the time, the plan for an international conference was adopted. Subsequently, Abdur Rahman, the Controller of Examinations, and Shaikh Usman, the Legal Adviser of King Abdul Aziz University, joined the group. These dedicated individuals engaged in continuous discussions, both day and night, while Ali Ashraf diligently prepared a memorandum and formulated the policies for the forthcoming world conference. This proposal was submitted to Dr Abdullah Omar Nasseef through the Dean of the Education Faculty, Dr Abdul Aziz Khoja. Dr Nasseef then presented it to the University's President, Dr Abduh Yemeni. In 1975, during the University's convocation, Dr Yemeni formally announced the upcoming First World Conference on Muslim Education. To organise the conference, an organising committee was established, with Shaikh Ahmad Salah Jamjoom as its Chairman and Syed Ali Ashraf and Abdullah Zayd serving as Secretaries. This organising committee delineated the conference's aims and objectives, which were as follows:

1. To define the principles, aims and methodology of the Islamic concept of education.
2. To suggest ways and means of realising the above principles in practice.
3. To formulate methods of securing mutual understanding and co-operation among Muslim scholars all over the world.[6]

During this pivotal conference, the primary goal was to establish a philosophy of education aimed at eliminating the secular underpinnings of education. At its core, this philosophy was rooted in faith, specifically, belief in

---

6 King Abdulaziz University, *Conference Book: First World Conference on Muslim Education* (King Abdulaziz University, 1977), 3.

the monotheism of Allah, that is, faith in *tawḥīd*. Distinguished educators and individuals connected to the field of education from around the world gathered at this conference. Through unanimous agreement among these scholars, a redefined definition of education emerged:

> Education should aim at the balanced growth of the total personality of Man through the training of Man's spirit, intellect, the rational self, feelings and bodily senses. Education should therefore cater for the growth of man in all its aspects: spiritual, intellectual, imaginative, physical, scientific, linguistics, both individually and collectively and motivate all these aspects towards goodness and the attainment of perfection. The ultimate aim of Muslim education lies in the realisation of complete submission to Allah on the level of the individual, the community and humanity at large.[7]

The success of this conference was greatly indebted to the support of the Saudi government, with special recognition for the invaluable contributions of Shaikh Ahmad Salah Jamjoom and Dr Abdullah Omar Nasseef. This committee extended invitations to Heads of State worldwide, proposing the Islamisation of education. The first positive response came from the government of Pakistan, leading to the convening of the Second World Conference on Muslim, Education in Islamabad in 1980. During this conference, the outlines of a curriculum were devised from an Islamic perspective, introducing the idea that students could excel in their national language, English, and mathematics alongside memorising the Qurʾān. This marked a significant departure from prior practices.

The Third World Conference on Muslim Education took place in Dhaka in 1981. At that time, Bangladesh was led by President Ziaur Rahman and Prime Minister Shah Azizur Rahman. Prior to the organisation of this conference, at the Prime Minister's invitation, Syed Ali Ashraf and Dr Abdullah Omar Nasseef had visited Dhaka, where they informed President Ziaur Rahman about the Islamisation of education. President Ziaur Rahman endorsed the idea and promptly initiated the establishment of an institute. During the 1980 winter session of the parliament, a law was passed, creating the Institute of Islamic Education and Research. Dr Mumtazuddin Chowdhury was appointed as its Director, with my role as Deputy Director. The Third World Conference on Muslim Education brought together 34 educators from various foreign countries. The conference's central theme was "textbook development." It delved into how textbooks could be authored from an Islamic standpoint, aligning with the curriculum formulated during the Second World Conference. Committees were established within the Institute to evaluate subjects such as literature,

---

7   King Abdulaziz University, *Conference Book*, 78.

mathematics, science, geography, history, and Islamiyat from an Islamic perspective. These committees conducted thorough reviews over a year and presented their findings to the government in 1982. The Bangladesh Textbook Board agreed to create textbooks based on these perspectives. Unfortunately, subsequent progress on this initiative by the Bangladesh government was limited.

The Institute of Islamic Education and Research continued to conduct research on various aspects of Islamisation of education. However, in 1982, following the tragic assassination of President Ziaur Rahman, the Institute was incorporated into the Islamic University located in Kushtia, Bangladesh and eventually, the organisation was dissolved altogether, halting all ongoing research efforts.

In 1982, Jakarta, Indonesia hosted the Fourth World Conference on Muslim Education, focusing on teacher education and teaching methodology from an Islamic perspective. Educators participating in the conference engaged in in-depth discussions and formulated a comprehensive list of recommendations, emphasising the need to train teachers in accordance with Islamic principles.

Following this conference, a five-year hiatus ensued. This pause was necessary to monitor the progress of those at the forefront of the Islamisation of education during this period. In March 1987, the Fifth World Conference on Muslim Education took place in Cairo, Egypt. Its primary purpose was to assess the effectiveness of the recommendations generated from the previous four World Conference on Muslim Education, held in various Muslim countries. This conference attracted participants from various Muslim nations in Africa and Asia, including Malaysia, Indonesia, Pakistan, Bangladesh, Sudan, and Nigeria. The conference's aims and objectives were discussed thoroughly.

It was evident that education, particularly in developing countries, is predominantly governed by governments. Consequently, initiating changes in the education system depends largely on government initiatives. For meaningful change to occur in any education system, key stakeholders, such as teachers, education policy makers, curriculum designers, and educational administrators, must fully embrace Islamic principles and thinking. It is essential to recognise that all the ongoing efforts in the field of Islamic education in various Muslim countries are driven primarily by non-governmental organisations. Syed Ali Ashraf, deeply involved in these endeavours, served as a source of inspiration for numerous educational institutions worldwide. Notably, he influenced institutions like Omdurman University in Sudan, Islamic University in Malaysia, and Darul Ihsan University in Bangladesh, guiding them in aligning their educational philosophies with his vision of faith-based education.

For a considerable duration, he had harboured the aspiration of founding an Islamic university. The vision of Darul Ihsan University persisted, gradually evolving into a tangible reality as an institute was established towards realising this vision. In March 1988, an international curriculum committee was formed, with Professor Dr Syed Ali Ashraf serving as its chairman. The committee included the following members: Syed Abul Hasan Ali Hasani Nadwi, Dr Hashim Mahdi, Shaikh Badruddin, National Professor Syed Ali Ahsan, Dr Ayub Ali (now deceased), Dr M. Shamsher Ali, Dr Mustafizur Rahman, and Professor Syed Ali Naqi. Professor Syed Ali Naqi served as the Member Secretary of this committee, which convened for an intensive 15-day period to develop a comprehensive syllabus spanning from 1st to 12th grades. The core objective of this syllabus was to ensure that every Muslim boy and girl not only excelled in modern education but also established a strong foundation in Islamic knowledge.

During the committee's deliberations, Shaikh Badruddin proposed the idea of implementing this syllabus through the establishment of an Islamic institute. This proposal received unanimous approval, leading to the formation of the Institute of Higher Islamic Studies.[8] In July 1989, the process of student admissions commenced, and by the last week of October, the institute was in full operational mode. On 28 December of the same year, the then President, Hussain Muhammad Ershad, laid the foundation stone of this institute, situated on land acquired through the personal finances of Syed Ali Ashraf, in Bolibhôdro, Savar, near Dhaka. The institute, which was the beginning of Darul Ihsan University, was inaugurated with a joyful ceremony. In July 1990 Darul Ihsan University was established as the first private university in Bangladesh. In 1993, the government of Bangladesh accredited it as a private university. After Darul Ihsan University was established, the Institute of Higher Islamic Learning was absorbed into it. Following the passing of Syed Ali Ashraf in August 1998, the institution was renamed the Syed Ali Ashraf Institute of Higher Islamic Learning. Today, it operates under the Religious Science faculty of Darul Ihsan University. On the same site in Savar, he also established Tahfizul Quranil Karim Fazil Madrasah (residential) in 1992.

Syed Ali Ashraf held the lifelong position of *Gaddī Nashīn* (enthroned leader) within the spiritual organisation called Jamāʿat-e Madīnah, mentioned earlier. His spiritual stature was of a very high order. Prior to his passing, he bestowed the honour of *khilāfah* upon his younger brother, Syed Ali Naqi, who currently assumes the responsibilities of the Jamāʿat-e Madīnah organisation while imparting the teachings of Syed Ali Ashraf in the realm of spirituality.

---

8   Later called the Institute of Higher Islamic Learning.

Bibliography

Abū Dāwūd IV:109. No. 4290, Malāhim I.

King Abdulaziz University. *Conference Book: First World Conference on Muslim Education.* Mecca: King Abdulaziz University, 1977.

Walī Allāh, Shāh. *The Conclusive Argument from God: Shāh Walī Allāh of Delhi's Ḥujjat Allāh al-Bālighah.* Translated by Marcia K. Hermansen. Leiden: Brill, 1995.

Chapter 15

The Cosmic Triangle: God, Man and Nature in Syed Ali Ashraf's Philosophy of Education

Iftekhar Iqbal and *Asiyah Kumpoh*

Syed Ali Ashraf was a leading Islamic thinker of the twentieth century who devoted himself to the development of educational ideas and institutions which were rooted in Islamic faith. At the same time, he articulated a universalist discourse on collective human existence and wellbeing that appealed to a broad set of non-Islamic worldviews. In this pursuit he was in intimate conversations with the wider world of religions and epistemic bases. This malleable duality of his thoughts took him not only to bridge Islamic scholarship and global discourses of moral and ecological questions, but also to excavate the relationship between the self and the universal. This chapter suggests that Syed Ali Ashraf's ability to locate Islam and globality in the same wavelength and to connect the self and the universal originated in a transcendental approach to God, Man and Nature—a cosmic triangle that was poignantly articulated in his pedagogic thoughts.

With decolonization of most of the Muslim world following the Second World War, Muslim thinkers were invested in different areas of reconstruction of public life. Some advocated Islamization of political process and a minority among them encouraged revolutionary path to Islamization of the state; some intellectuals suggested a complete disassociation of the Muslim world from what they perceived as continuing cultural domination of the West. On the other spectrum of the postcolonial debates, there was a renewed call to implant Western secular values in preference to Islamic worldview. Syed Ali Ashraf took a different path and was among the group of scholars who believed that knowledge and education were key to post-colonial reconstruction of Muslim societies. In that pursuit, Syed Ali Ashraf put Islam at the core of his intellectual endeavours and devoted his life to the development of educational ideas and institutions across the Muslim world and beyond.

What distinguishes Syed Ali Ashraf from many contemporary Muslim thinkers is that beyond his commitment to the cultural and spiritual advancement of the Muslim community, he attempted to articulate a universal paradigm that would appeal to both Muslim and non-Muslim worldviews. In this pursuit he was in intimate conversations with the wider world of religions and epistemic bases. This flexibility of his thoughts made him both a profound Islamic scholar and a globally-oriented thinker. This chapter is an exploration into the inclusive, universal aspects of his thoughts relating to the purpose and practice of education, with a particular focus on how this strand of his thoughts accommodated ecological concerns. This is important because this aspect of his thought has not yet been probed deeply and that the current environmental crisis of global scale demands a greater scrutiny of this issue.

Syed Ali Ashraf's quest for universalist thought is fortified by his employment of transcendental approach and the idea of immanence in the study of the triangular relationship between God, Man and Nature. The question of transcendence leaves him in critical engagement with the modern secular worldview which thrives on the idea that changing temporality, rather than permanence or transcendence, is what is real. It is therefore useful to start with his critique of the modern secular worldview. This discussion will be followed by an exploration of his thoughts on the cosmic triangle of God-Nature-Man and their applications in education.

I
A Critique of the Modern-Secular Worldview

Syed Ali Ashraf picks up his critique of secularism at the base of Enlightenment liberalism by suggesting that secular education leads to the creation of an anthropocentric mind.[1] This is premised on the understanding that securing the centrality of human was the main undercurrent of the European Enlightenment. Yet the form of anthropocentrism as particularly engrained in the secular educational process leads not only to the displacement of the idea of a supreme being, but it also perpetuates human's conflictual relations to nature. In this secular premise the "deconsecration of [divine] values" is connected with the "disenchantment of nature."[2] This strand of critique of the secular leads him to take stock of the environmental degradation created through human predominance in the post-Enlightenment era.

A second set of Syed Ali Ashraf's critique of the secular involves the question of morality. He suggests that in a secular education system "moral development is seen in terms first of patterns of moral thinking which, it is ex-

---

1 Syed Sajjad Husain and Syed Ali Ashraf, eds., *Crisis in Muslim Education* (Kent; UK: Hodder and Stoughton, and Jeddah: King Abdulaziz University, 1979), 2.
2 Syed Ali Ashraf, *New Horizons in Muslim Education* (Kent; UK: Hodder and Stoughton, and Cambridge: The Islamic Academy, 1985), 9.

pected, leads to moral actions"[3]—a process linked to cognitive development. According to secularist and relativist philosophy social interactions form the source of values, implying that all values are contingent on historical processes and evolving social conditions. He suggests that the latter instance leads to contested philosophies of life and cultures and so to the denial of anything called universal Truth. This is the backdrop in which material development and industrial progress create a pool of different relative contexts that pull different sections of the society further apart, resulting in more exclusivity than inclusivity.[4] In this context, Syed Ali Ashraf shared the emerging sentiment prevalent in the Western critique of scientific objectivity and modernist metanarratives.[5]

A third set of Syed Ali Ashraf's critique refers to the secular crisis of group conflicts based on different ideologies. Reference to these ideological differences could be understood from the vantage point of the Cold-War time bipolar contestations between capitalist and communist statecraft and the worldviews which dominated the period when he made much of his contributions. Within these contested ideological bases, he found one issue shared between them, which he identified as the "narrow concept of logical reasoning."[6] He refers to Huston Smith's *Beyond the Post-Modern Mind* to underline the importance of not just looking further in "horizontal" direction, but also in "vertical" direction. His critique of the secular is, therefore, not confined to its perceived focus on the dominance of the rational individual, but he also contests the notion that secularist approaches were governed by the concept of "universal objective values."[7] His critique of the secular frequently refers to the opposite: on the secular paradigm's lack of the universal and in this he shares the critique of transcendentalist scholar, Frithjof Schuon, who argued that rational mode of knowledge "in no way extends beyond the realm of generalities and cannot by itself reach any transcendent truth."[8]

Syed Ali Ashraf's other critique of the secular-modernist worldview comes from the fear of the breaking-up of "traditional integrated human personality" into many disjointed personalities, owing to, as Gilbert Durand has suggested, "an excessive concern with the world of things—(the world of *res* is

---

3   Syed Ali Ashraf and Paul H. Hirst, eds., "Islamic Education and Moral Development," *Religion and Education: Islamic and Christian Approaches* (Cambridge: The Islamic Academy, 1994), 156.
4   Ashraf and Hirst, appendix to *Religion and Education*, 225.
5   For example, Bruno Latour and Steve Woolgar, *Laboratory Life: The Construction of Scientific Facts*, 2nd ed. (Princeton, New Jersey: Princeton University Press, 1986); Jean-François Lyotard, *The Postmodern Condition: A Report on Knowledge* (The University of Minnesota Press, 1984).
6   Ashraf and Hirst, *Religion and Education*, 217.
7   Syed Ali Ashraf, "Editorial," *Muslim Education Quarterly* 1, no. 1 (1983): 1.
8   Ashraf and Hirst, *Religion and Education*, 63. Here Syed Ali Ashraf refers to Frithjof Schuon, *The Transcendent Unity of Religions* (London: Faber & Faber, 1953), 11-2.

here opposed to the world of *voces*)—thus confining man's image to the world of phenomena."⁹

Thus, at the core of Syed Ali Ashraf's critique of the secular-modernist worldview lie the "free" individual who is disproportionately idolized; relativity that destabilizes the inclusiveness of society and its moral system; an objective and rational value regime that is devoid of the quality of transcendence; and the materiality of consumerism. As he observes, these forms of individualism, relativism, rational choices, and positivist practices took centre stage in the post-Enlightenment era and gradually penetrated the educational institutions displacing religion from the core of pedagogic process as epitomized in the 1957 Harvard conference on education that removed religion from the humanities, social sciences, and natural sciences.[10] Where does this set of critiques lead him in his exploration of the faith in the field of education?

This leaves Syed Ali Ashraf with a choice in terms of the epistemic bases of human relations to the world they live in, with an eye to the limits of anthropocentrism—a choice that accommodates God and Nature alongside the Human. This approach not only gets him to see harmonizing elements running between religion and science, but it also allows him to appreciate the significance of the triangular and balanced relationship between God, Nature, and Human. He insists on the deeper significance of "Man's relationship with God, Man and Nature."[11] This issue will now be discussed in a little more detail.

II
A Metaphysical Approach to Nature

The modern secular everyday practices nurture an existential duality in which nature is diminished into exploitable resources and then made an object of environmentalist conservation. The ontological vacuum that defines this contradiction in modern civilization, according to Syed Ali Ashraf, emerges from the process of desacralization of nature. His critique of the modern-secular worldview of man's relation to man and nature eventually draws from wider epistemic sources and summons arguments from both Western and non-Western discourses. He endorses Bertrand Russell's criticism of utilitarianism as a basis of relationship among humans and counters John Dewey's classificatory technical efficiency.[12] He also invokes Lewis Mumford's critique of the "metropolitan interest" and Freud's discovery of the "death wish" among urban dwellers in discussing the rapid urbanization as a result of disas-

---

9   Syed Ali Ashraf, "Editorial," *Muslim Education Quarterly* 3, no. 1 (1985): 1. In this Syed Ali Ashraf refers to Gilbert Durand, *On the Disfiguration of the Image of Man in the West* (Boston: Golgonooza Press, 1977), 3–4.
10 Husain and Ashraf, *Crisis in Muslim Education*, 2.
11 Ashraf, *New Horizons*, 5; for a note on need to appreciate the links between human life and external nature see also Hussain and Ashraf, *Crisis in Muslim Education*, 3.
12 Ashraf, *New Horizons*, 15.

sociation from nature.¹³ In addition to utilitarian philosophy and urbanization, the factor that distances humans from nature is the increasing technological advancement including the use of "auto-brains." From the perspective of the danger of "divorce from nature and mechanical way of living," Syed Ali Ashraf noted: "As immediate utility is the sole goal, technical experts exploit society and nature to their detriment. Forests are destroyed, rivers polluted and hills denuded, and thus an imbalance is created in the environment."¹⁴

This disconnect between the actor and affective action sits oddly with the Islamic understanding of nature, as Syed Ali Ashraf notes: "They [Muslims] cannot believe in a God-created universe in which natural phenomena are portents (or *āyāt*) of God and at the same time regard them as nothing more than materials which can be plundered for temporary gain."¹⁵ In this context, he echoes Seyyed Hossein Nasr. As early as the 1960s, in the context of the environmental debates around Rachel Carson's newly published book *Silent Spring*, Nasr explored man's place in Nature which stands as an example of the cosmic harmony that emanates from one Supreme Being.¹⁶ A more focused discussion on the metaphysics of Nature in the context of environmental degradation appeared in Nasr's other book in 1968 which drew references from Taoism, Hinduism, Buddhism, Christianity, and Islam to explore the relationship between man and nature.¹⁷ Against the Baconian quest to win over and dominate Nature, Nasr had referred to the Qurʾānic idea that Nature was the signs of God (*āyāt*) and that humans were the custodians of Nature as God's vicegerent (*khalīfatullāh*).¹⁸

While Nasr made significant references to the idea of God, Man and Nature in explaining the precarious contemporary environmental situation, Syed Ali Ashraf brought these ideas into an organic triangular relationship. From a Qurʾānic or generally monotheistic religious perspective, man is superior to nature, which is also clearly the case with science's relation to nature. The difference between the Qurʾānic and scientific representation of the human-nature relationship is that while science is optimistic about the linear progress of human power over nature, Qurʾān indicates that human predominance over nature could be taken away by God at any time because human is merely a custodian of nature, not its owner.¹⁹ This destabilizes the teleology of science, which is understood in the context of the Qurʾān's warning against aggression

---

13 Ashraf, 13.
14 Ashraf, 17–8.
15 Ashraf, 11.
16 Seyyed Hossein Nasr, *An Introduction to Islamic Cosmological Doctrines* (London: Thames and Hudson, 1964).
17 Seyyed Hossein Nasr, *Man and Nature: The Spiritual Crisis in Modern Man* (London: Mandala, 1968).
18 Nasr, *Man and Nature*, 95–6, 131.
19 Ashraf, *New Horizons*, 15.

against nature and the command that mankind must fulfil their obligations and duties to God and His creatures (*ḥuqūq Allāh* and *ḥuqūq al-ʿibād*).[20]

But how capable are human beings to perform their duties to the rest of the God's creation? This question hinges on the very Spirit and attributes of God that were instilled in human being at the time of the creation of Adam. The human being was first empowered with God's Spirit and attributes and was then sent to the habitable earth and its non-human occupants as God's vicegerent. This is where the cosmic triangle between God, Man and Nature is forged. The violation of nature, therefore, is a violation of God's own Will. Syed Ali Ashraf in this context points out emphatically that: "Nature is not neutral. It reveals the divine purpose and therefore man is expected not to upset nature and forcibly redirect its energies in directions which are not normal."[21]

Moving beyond the anthropomorphic conception of man's relationship to nature, the Cosmic Triangle reveals that the relationship between Man, Nature and God primarily hinges on morality and religious ethics. As mentioned earlier, the Qurʾān emphasizes man's accountability towards nature, fulfilling his role of viceregency. This not only means that man should sincerely appreciate the life, diversity and beauties of nature, but also nurture curiosities invoked by nature, which should develop man's reverence towards God's infinite creativity and power. For instance, verses 3–4 of *Sūrah Al-Raʿd* of the Qurʾān allude to the significance of water to the diverse natural things such as vineyards, mountains, fruits, and crops. Verses 6-10 of *Sūrah Al-Qāf* indicate man should reflect on the environment and the universe to attain higher knowledge of the infinite Being.

God's laws and grace that govern nature should also remind man of the purpose and order of such laws and the infinite Being that governs the laws. Kurniawan notes that God's law of nature is not humanly comprehensible, but it helps humans discover and understand God as an infinite Being.[22] In addition, modern science also demonstrates the regularity and sustenance of nature's orders and laws within their own functioning and dependence on one another.

Hence, these laws of nature should foster an ecological ethic in man to respect the intrinsic value that nature possesses. However, Sher Zada suggests that the metaphysical and moral aspects of nature are only manifest to those "with sound spiritual vision and sensitive, appreciative and feeling-full heart."[23] In other words, only man with moral consciousness will be able to

---

20 Ashraf, "Editorial," *Muslim Education Quarterly* 3, no. 1, 2.
21 Husain and Ashraf, *Crisis in Muslim Education*, 84; see also Syed Ali Ashraf, "Editorial," *Muslim Education Quarterly* 4, no. 1 (1986): 7.
22 Deni Wahyudi Kurniawan, "Human Responsibility towards Environment in the Qurʾān," *Indonesian Journal of Islam and Muslim Societies* 2, no. 2 (December 2012): 315. https://doi.org/10.18326/ijims.v2i2.293-322.
23 Sher Zada, "Nature: Its Moral and Metaphysical Dimensions," *The Dialogue* 10, no. 3

derive and decipher the inspirations drawn from nature. A more significant implication is that, to make the cosmic triangle relationships work, nature should evoke moral consciousness in man; otherwise, nature loses its meaning and function in the cosmic triangle relationships. Relating this point to the earlier discussion on man's disassociation from nature and the changing emphasis on nature from being exploitable resources to becoming critical issue for conservation, the one solution to address the desacralization of nature and environmental imbalance is through Islamic philosophy of education that essentially focuses on moral training and character building.

Bilgrami and Ashraf pointed out that there are two main streams of knowledge in Islam: the external stream that deals with morality and rituals and the internal stream which aims at building self-discipline and purity of heart.[24] These streams are undoubtedly interconnected concepts. The main emphases of Muslim education have always been on personal spiritual and ethical development (*tarbiyah*), understanding of society through social and moral education (*tādīb*) and knowledge transmission (*taʿlīm*), and these dimensions of education mould all aspects of Muslim life.

Syed Ali Ashraf further demonstrated that education should not be seen as intellectual resources only, particularly when it comes to moral knowledge. One's possession of moral knowledge should be translated into moral action for one's personal and common benefit, which eventually enlightens and transforms one's personality.[25] Nasseef conducted a critical analysis of education from an Islamic perspective arguing that a person endowed with modern scientific wisdom "must understand how he can use this [scientific] knowledge for the betterment of man, society, the environment and the universe."[26] Hence, with a deep-rooted ecological conscience, modern science with a strong moral foundation can be utilized for both human benefit and environmental conservation.

Modern science tends to posit its idea, promoting modernization and technological advancement for human benefit with little consideration for its environmental implications. Syed Ali Ashraf insisted that the conflict between selfishness and selflessness can be resolved by the purification of the human soul whereby man would "sacrifice all material interests for the sake of vindicating, preserving and furthering truth, justice and love."[27] In this context, *tādīb*, which emphasizes moral education and sensibility, critically addresses

---

(2015): 256.
24 H. H. Bilgrami and Syed Ali Ashraf, *The Concept of an Islamic University* (Kent, UK: Hodder and Stoughton, and Cambridge: The Islamic Academy, 1985), 6.
25 Syed Ali Ashraf, "Islamic Education and Moral Development," in Ashraf and Hirst, *Religion and Education*, 155.
26 Abdullah Omar Nasseef, "Science Education and Religious Values: An Islamic Approach," in *Religion and Education*, ed. Ashraf and Hirst, 34.
27 Ashraf, "Islamic Education," 148.

man's disconnection with nature and man's negligence of God's supreme authority over nature.

From the point of view of Syed Ali Ashraf's focus on Islamic educational philosophy and practices, it is not difficult to infer his approach to an alternative vision to the secular worldview on education. He suggests that Islamic education stands for "spiritual and deeply felt ethical values of Islam."[28] But how does this ethical certainty couched in Islam leave a place for other, non-Islamic worldviews? Is there a universal that operates beyond the secular-modernist master narrative and accommodates both Islamic and other religious approaches to education? If so, how does it work in theory and practice? He offers a metaphysical approach to this question.

An important issue for this chapter is the approaches by which Syed Ali Ashraf's explicitly Islamic understanding of God-human-nature relations is accommodative of other faiths. This is a question that borders on the recent scholarly call to move beyond "Ecotheology" and delve deeper into the realm of "Ecometaphysics." Ecotheology as a branch of the study of nature from the vantage point of religious scriptures still needs to be foundational but "with the crucial qualification that Theology is rightly contextualized from a transtheistic metaphysical perspective."[29]

III
Inter-faith Platform for Education

As suggested earlier, Islam is central to Syed Ali Ashraf's worldview of God-Man-Nature triangle, yet his position about Islam and knowledge is conducive to an interfaith dialogue. Although he may have used the term "Islamization of Knowledge" as popularized by Isma'il Razi al-Faruqi, Naquib al-Attas and others, he seems to have an ambiguous appreciation of this term as he would often use instead "Islamization of Approach to Knowledge."[30] This is because this term, at least semantically, suggests that "Islam" and "Knowledge" are two separate epistemic categories in which "knowledge" stands open to be "Islamized." His preference for "approaches to knowledge" leaves room for other religion's contributions towards such "approaches" without being couched in the doctrinal certainty of a particular religion.

Syed Ali Ashraf's call to a faith-based universal approach to education is linked with the question of the "life-purpose" and remit of education. "An in-

---

28 Syed Sajjad Husain and Syed Ali Ashraf, introduction to *Crisis in Muslim Education* by Husain and Ashraf, 1. Syed Ali Ashraf has contributed extensively in the concept, scope and practices of Islamic education as reflected in his published work and in the essays in this volume. These issues do not fall within the scope of this essay.
29 Manzoor A. Shah and M. Maroof Shah, "Krishnamurti's environmental critique of traditional religion: A critical appraisal from perenialist perspective," *European Journal of Science and Theology* 4, no. 2 (June 2008): 61–78.
30 Ashraf, "Editorial," *Muslim Education Quarterly* 1, no. 2.

formed man or a trained expert is not necessarily an educated man," he contends, and suggests that proper education entails an inter-faculty assemblage of spiritual, moral, intellectual, emotional, and physical aspects of human personality. The fruit of this multiple dimensions of education is tested by the nature of "Man's relationship with God, Man and Nature."[31] Collective wellness in society, according to him, lies in the seamless relationship within this trio. This concept of religious education provides an outline of intellectual training aiming not merely to master knowledge about God and His exegetical realm, but also about appreciation of the linkages between divinity, nature and the individual that speaks to social wellness and ecological preservation. This "unity of approach" is where a transcendent norm takes shape and provides a clue to an alternative to the secular universal. Syed Ali Ashraf suggests:

> This norm must transcend time and space, and all human formulations of what "time" and "space" stand for, otherwise we shall be grounded into nationalism or regionalism, or at best the concept of a worldly "heaven". It must transcend the "individual" "I", otherwise we shall welter in the inferno of our personal "rights" or military dictatorships or "racist" riots and forget forever that "I" have only responsibilities to bear. *God, Man* and *Nature (including all creatures) have rights* over me.[32]

Since he locates knowledge in the traffic that emanates *from* God (divinity) rather than *towards* God (theology), he finds no difficulty in co-existing with other forms of divine approaches. Unity lies, he asserts, in the concept of "One Unique Supreme and Transcendental Reality" which is at the centre of the concept of God or Deity in Judaism, Christianity, Islam, Hinduism or Sikhism and the Transcendental Reality in Buddhism. He suggests that "diversity is maintained at the doctrinal level and at the socio-cultural level necessitating knowledge and understanding of each other and assimilation as far as possible of each other's diverse attitudes and approaches."[33]

One way of appreciating Syed Ali Ashraf's connective threads between God, Man and Nature is to understand how the idea of God permeates through all religions providing a common ground of human relations in time and space. If the secular-modernist consumerism is at the centre of ecological exploitation, then the inter-faith consolidation of the idea of a supreme divinity could contribute towards ecological preservations. Syed Ali Ashraf in this context shares Nasr's pioneering insight, but the point of departure for him lies in his efforts to advance this cause of the triangle through a pedagogical lens.

---

31 Ashraf, *New Horizons in Muslim Education*, 5.
32 Ashraf, "Editorial," *Muslim Education Quarterly* 3, no. 1, 2.
33 Ashraf and Hirst, *Religion and Education*, xiii.

He places his arguments about interfaith education in Britain, a religiously diverse society, which is also a place where the ontology of secularism has a very strong root. But the faith groups in the UK all believe in a

> Transcendental Reality, i.e. a Reality that transcends all limitation that particular qualities impose upon an object. With the exception of the Buddhists they believe this Reality to be the Essence of the Being whom they worship and whose name in English is 'God'. Buddhists do not deny the presence of God, yet neither do they affirm Him. But they too believe in the transcendental character of truth.[34]

He further notes that common to all these faiths are the notion of spirituality and the idea and practice of "Truth, Justice, Righteousness, Mercy, Love, Compassion and care towards all creation."[35] These thoughts were the kernel of discussions in a conference titled "Faith as the Basis of Education in a Multi-Faith, Multi-Cultural Country" held jointly by the Department of Education of Cambridge University and the Islamic Academy, Cambridge. The first segment of the conference, held in 1989, featured exchanges of Islamic and Christian perspectives on the multi-faith framework of education, while the second, held in 1990, facilitated conversations on the subject among the Buddhist, Christian, Hindu, Jewish, Muslim, and Sikh educationists. Syed Ali Ashraf was instrumental in organizing these events and compiling the recommendations for a multi-faith education that the 1990 segment of the conference produced. The set of recommendations was a well-crafted document that avoided any suggestions for diluting doctrinal diversity and promoting a syncretistic religious approach, but attempted to capture the common beliefs of nearly all religions regarding "human nature, God, and a framework of eternal values."[36]

Once Man's relationship with Man, via an abstract understanding of the power and place of the Divine, is deepened, ecological challenges and overcoming them become easier, because God as a common coordinator is as immanent in man as in nature. The proposed "common-faith" framework for the curriculum suggested that within the family of beliefs and values there should be "Awareness of the Absolute Values in God's Qualities reflected in the Creation, i.e. Humankind and Nature (or awareness of the reflection of transcendent values in creation)."[37] It recommends an inner understanding of knowledge's relations with faith, virtue, action, power, wealth and sociopolitical environment, and national development. These will eventually lead to the intellectual ability to justify a learner's "practice in the light of human beings' relationship with God, other human beings and the natural world."[38]

---

34 Ashraf and Hirst, 223.
35 Ashraf and Hirst, 223
36 Ashraf and Hirst, appendix to *Religion and Education*, 219.
37 Ashraf and Hirst, 230–31.
38 Ashraf and Hirst, 233

The conference also suggested that natural sciences and mathematics should not only include issues of logical reasoning, conceptualisation and generalisation, but also to make the students grasp the "principles of existence that religion has taught and the role of intuition and imagination in scientific research." On the top of this, they need to be able to "understand the relationship between the religious concept of Man and Nature as the reflection of God's Qualities and the scientific concepts."[39]

The use of education for the promotion of ecological preservation was most strongly recommended for the social and cultural studies of ecological concerns:

> The study of society and culture should be presented in such a manner that an insight into relational and environmental processes as envisaged in religion is developed in the minds of the students, their sense of selfless service is strengthened, and they acquire the habit and love of living in harmony with external nature. They will need to learn how to resist ruthless selfishness that corrupts social sensibility and know how to direct science and technology for the betterment of human relationships and the maintenance of the world's ecosystem as envisaged in religion.[40]

Syed Ali Ashraf elaborates this further in his recommendations for promoting aspects of integration instead of confrontation in the broader discipline of Natural Sciences. He suggests that the Islamic concept is to know the basic laws of the universe to be able to control and use it beneficially, but "without disturbing or corrupting external nature." He provides the example of ecological implications of flattening hills to build a city.[41]

This small example of anthropogenic intervention into nature is an invitation to Syed Ali Ashraf's larger educational philosophy that seeks to restore the visibility of God's signs and presence in nature. At the root of this restoration lies, according to him, the dismantling of the dogma of evolution. The trans-religious question of educational programmes that are sensitive to nature ultimately rolls back to the contested ideas of divine creation and evolution, particularly since the latter informs the clinical separation of God from modern disciplines of natural, human, and social sciences. Syed Ali Ashraf suggests that although Aristotle pointed to the interrelationship between God and Matter, his equal focus on their eternal and infinite Realities led to a long line of materialist worldviews with Laplace, Alfred Lyell and others culminating in Darwin and flourished through Huxley and others. Relying on the serious critique of evolutionism that surfaced only after the post-WWII period,

---

39 Ashraf and Hirst, 234.
40 Ashraf and Hirst, 234.
41 Husain and Ashraf, *Crisis in Muslim Education*, 84–5.

such as those from Frithjof Schuon and Seyyed Hossein Nasr, Syed Ali Ashraf poses a simple question: "Is it logical or scientific to say that blind inert matter can produce a conscious rational being with an intelligence to understand, and with eyes to see and ears that hear?"[42]

In addressing this question, Syed Ali Ashraf does not deny the process of evolution in nature, but he asserts that this could happen only with the actualization of possibilities latent in a particular being or thing and these possibilities are sourced in God because "no transformation of species is possible unless God wants it."[43] This attachment of God's will to the evolutionary potential of a being or a thing makes nature and the whole universe divine and sacred. It is from this perspective, not from the perspective of Darwinian natural selection with a lethal potential for racial, social and political exclusionism, that he suggests: "External nature, the universe, man's environment including all living things, are also Divine works, to be treated as a sacred trust entrusted to Man for the sake of his own ability, also for him to know God and His immutable principles and qualities manifested through them."[44] In other words, human beings are no different than a plant or a lump of mud, with the crucial exception that they are shaped in perfect physical form and endowed with certain divine attributes.[45] It is in this larger context of the immanence of God in both living and non-living, human and non-human that it is possible to argue that not only major revealed religions but elements of animism can also be meaningfully engaged in conversation about the triangular links between God, Nature and Human.

There is a fairly strong argument that revealed religions with a focus on human agency and next-worldly orientations are potentially less sensitive to nature than the animist religions which are essentially pro-nature. This understanding is bolstered by the Gaia hypothesis, as propounded by James Lovelock, which considers the planet Earth as the epitome of the autonomous power of nature, capable of self-regeneration and growth. This, again, connects back to Aristotle's holonic appreciation of Matter's infinite possibilities, but debates continue on the exact status of the Gaia hypothesis other than being either pseudo-scientific or pseudo-divine. It does not acknowledge external divine power while it is also unable to stand the test of scientific experiments. Operationally, this hypothesis is susceptible to the same criticism that revealed religions are subjected to from animistic school of scholars, in that it is not a good enough antidote to planetary decline. In other words, if a focus on human agency in revealed religions is a barrier to environmental sustainability, the idea of autopoietic power of the earth system could be considered a

---

42 Syed Ali Ashraf, "Editorial," *Muslim Education Quarterly* 4, no. 1 (1986): 2.
43 Ashraf, "Editorial," *Muslim Education Quarterly* 4, no. 1, 3.
44 Ashraf, "Editorial," *Muslim Education Quarterly* 4, no. 1, 7.
45 Qurʾān 15: 29; 32: 9

barrier to the development of an urgent sense of responsibility toward repairing its anthropogenic wounds by humans. In this context animism, although immensely eclectic in accommodating multiple values and ideas regarding nature, exposes itself to the need for conversations about a divine protocol of creation existing outside of nature, prompting "invisible, but felt presence of divinity."[46] Syed Ali Ashraf's following notes reflect on the possibility of meaningful conversations between revealed and animistic religions.

> Matter and material objects will not then be treated as 'non-living' dead objects, but will be approached with a sense of the sacredness inherent in them because God's particular powers and qualities are manifested in them. The distinction between 'living' and 'non-living' in the physical world will then be replaced by a distinction between the geological, vegetable, animal and human spheres.[47]

The Cartesian critique of empiricism was advanced by the discourse of the power of reasoning that was not of this world, something that was implanted in the human soul. But the rationalist doorway to metaphysics did not foreclose empiricism's capability of leading to metaphysics. Edward Wilson, one of the foremost evolutionary biologists, introduced himself as a "successor of Darwin" and asserted that it would be "foolish to deny dogmatically the possibility of some form of superior intelligence." So although rationalists and empiricists have recourse to different methods to knowledge, some of them seem to reach the same metaphysical nodal points about a supreme intelligence. In this scheme of metaphysics, however, religion is seen as, in the word of Wilson, "tribal."[48]

Yet in the nodal point of empirical and rationalist metaphysics lies clues to the possibility of conversations between science, philosophy and a divine creator. Wilson's own pioneering contribution is centred on the life and behaviour of ants, with the suggestion that ants are a highly intelligent community with work patterns and behaviour that can be used to understand the human community and also the love of nature itself. This cutting-edge anthropo-entomology took a major precedent in instruction from Buddha when he told a group of monks to avoid a road full of insects. The Bible instructs human to watch the ants and be wiser.[49] A full chapter of the Qurʾān is titled "The Ant," in which it is noted how Prophet Solomon heard an ant asking her peers to take

---

46 Dan Smyer Yü, "The Critical Zone as a Planetary Animist Sphere: Etho-graphing an Affective Consciousness of the Earth," *Journal for the Study of Religion, Nature and Culture* 14, no. 2 (2020): 273. http://dx.doi.org/10.1558/jsrnc.39680.
47 Ashraf, "Editorial," *Muslim Education Quarterly* 4, no. 1, 8.
48 Carl Zimmer, "E.O. Wilson, a Pioneer of Evolutionary Biology, Dies at 92," *The New York Times*, December 27, 2021, https://www.nytimes.com/2021/12/27/science/eo-wilson-dead.html.
49 *Holy Bible*, New International Version, Proverbs 6:6.

shelter from his advancing army.[50] These common religious understanding of smaller members of the biotic community and their corroboration by the latest biological sciences, calls for a revisit of the secular pedagogic approach of separating nature from the divine.[51] A reconciliation is possible, Syed Ali Ashraf would suggest, if humans see all living and non-living entities as signs of God.[52] It is this appreciation of the signs of God in nature that helps one to "hate the wantonness that distorts, corrupts and twists and tortures nature." It is this understanding of the divine signs that helps one to realize that:

> It is inhuman and impious and unjust to treat animals or trees with cruelty, even to walk on the earth with pride or to breed animals in the most unnatural way just to fatten them in order to kill them. He must know the natural process in order to preserve, maintain and sustain it as God's representative on the earth, and not in order to change it, and then suffer the consequences of creating a Frankenstein.[53]

Conclusion

How does faith in an eternal supernatural being influence the educational development of a human being? This is a central line of query in Syed Ali Ashraf's thoughts, and he sought to explore this in solidarity with institutions and scholars from other faiths. Such an exposition of a faith-based approach to education is not without its critique. Some of the faith-based thoughts on education that he and his non-Muslim colleagues espouse have been termed as "medieval" that, as historian Francis Robinson in the reviews of some of the works on faith-based education suggests, "stands as an important manifestation of the Muslim mind at the dawn of the fifteenth century."[54] Robinson is right to find medieval flavour in these discourses, yet these also reflect on continuous debates about metaphysical quest for 'truth' and reality from Socrates to Donald Davidson. The problem of recognition and refutation of certain ideas lies at different epistemic plains. History of doubt is as old as the history of faith and, as Alec Ryrie, has recently shown powerfully that doubt is not merely a philosophical issue, but also historical, e.g. the ordinary people's doubt, anger and anxiety about the particular historical phase of a religion, such that emanated from popular suffering at the hands of the Church

---

50 Qurʾān 27: 9–19.
51 Bert Hölldobler and Edward O. Wilson, *The Ants* (Cambridge, MA: Harvard University Press, 1990).
52 For an assessment of the universe, humans, animals, and plants as signs of God's creation rather than evolution, see Shaikh Abdul Mabud, *Theory of Evolution: An Assessment from The Islamic Point of View* (Cambridge: The Islamic Academy, 1991).
53 Ashraf, "Editorial," *Muslim Education Quarterly* 4, no. 1, 8.
54 Francis Robinson, "Review," *Modern Asian Studies* 15, no. 4 (October 1981): 891. https://doi.org/10.1017/S0026749X00008829.

during the Reformation and post-Reformation era as they dealt with religious authorities in their everyday life.[55] This is as medieval a problem as ancient or postmodern, as anxieties and anger about abuses in many faith-based institutions flares up. The problem, therefore, lies not in the epistemic premise of a religion, but in its operational deviances.

As Syed Ali Ashraf has shown, it was the loss of enchantment of God and Nature to the Mammon, in its various reincarnations, that has remained as steady as medieval as neoliberal. It is the battle between two different kinds of enchantments, spiritual and material, that has remained constant. That is why rather than displacing religion, capitalism reigns as another form of sacralization and enchantment, which both the socialist and the capitalist share.[56]

Coming back to the question of the triangle, the bulk of writings of Syed Ali Ashraf centres on the question of the essential relationship between God, Man and Nature. In this, Man takes an intermediary role, but the central issue is that all these entities have nature—God nature, human nature and nature's nature. Without cultivating God's attributes, the human cannot develop a positive approach to his/her inner nature and to the external nature. Only through cultivating God's attributes within themselves and locating their place within this triangular relationship humans can regain the power to behave responsibly towards nature. In this broader context, Syed Ali Ashraf is not contented with his critique of the modern rational and empirical mind plugged into scientism, he is equally sceptical of the monologic relationship between Man and God that excludes external nature which is the manifestation of God's attributes. This opens a broader engagement in ways in which human reality is flourished not in being a rational individual who "thinks" as a Cartesian being, but one who also lives to relate. This relationality, this triangular relationality, is key to Syed Ali Ashraf's thought about an educated human being. It is then possible to argue that it is through a truly God-conscious human that the age of Anthropocene can also be the age of Nature. This is summed up succinctly in his own words:

> The development of personality is seen in the context of Man's relationship with God, Man and Nature. Therefore, the organization of disciplines and arrangement of subjects are planned with reference to Man as an individual, Man as a social being and Man as a being who must live in harmony with Nature. His individuality, his collective existence and his existence as a natural entity are all conditioned by his relationship with God.[57]

---

55 Alec Ryrie, *Unbelievers: An Emotional History of Doubts* (Cambridge, MA: Harvard University Press, 2019).
56 Eugene McCarraher, *The Enchantments of Mammons* (Cambridge, MA: Harvard University Press, 2019).
57 Ashraf, *New Horizons*, 5.

Bibliography

Ashraf, Syed Ali and Paul H. Hirst, eds. *Religion and Education: Islamic and Christian Approaches.* Cambridge: The Islamic Academy, 1994.

Ashraf, Syed Ali. "Editorial." *Muslim Education Quarterly* 1, no. 1 (1983): 1-2.

Ashraf, Syed Ali. "Editorial." *Muslim Education Quarterly* 3, no. 1 (1985): 1-4.

Ashraf, Syed Ali. *New Horizons in Muslim Education.* Kent, UK: Hodder and Stoughton, and Cambridge: The Islamic Academy, 1985.

Ashraf, Syed Ali. "Editorial." *Muslim Education Quarterly* 4, no. 1 (1986): 1-9.

Ashraf, Syed Ali. "Islamic Education and Moral Development." In *Religion and Education: Islamic and Christian Approaches*, edited by Syed Ali Ashraf and Paul H. Hirst, 142-176. Cambridge: The Islamic Academy, 1994.

Bilgrami, Hamid Hasan, and Syed Ali Ashraf. *The Concept of an Islamic University.* Kent, UK: Hodder and Stoughton, and Cambridge: The Islamic Academy, 1985.

Hölldobler, Bert, and Edward O. Wilson. *The Ants.* Cambridge, MA: Harvard University Press, 1990.

Holy Bible. New International Version. Biblica, Inc, 2011.

Husain, Syed Sajjad, and Syed Ali Ashraf, eds. *Crisis in Muslim Education.* Kent, UK: Hodder and Stoughton, and Jeddah: King Abdul Aziz University, 1979.

Kurniawan, Deni Wahyudi. "Human Responsibility towards Environment in the Qurʾān." *Indonesian Journal of Islam and Muslim Societies* 2, no. 2 (2002): 293–322. https://doi.org/10.18326/ijims.v2i2.293-322.

Latour, Bruno and Steve Woolgar. *Laboratory Life: The Construction of Scientific Facts.* 2nd ed. Princeton, New Jersey: Princeton University Press, 1986.

Lyotard, Jean-François. *The Postmodern Condition: A Report on Knowledge.* The University of Minnesota Press, 1984.

Mabud, Shaikh Abdul. *Theory of Evolution: An Assessment from The Islamic Point of View.* Cambridge: The Islamic Academy, 1991.

McCarraher, Eugene. *The Enchantments of Mammons.* Cambridge, MA: Harvard University Press, 2019.

Nasr, Seyyed Hossein. *An Introduction to Islamic Cosmological Doctrines.* London: Thames and Hudson, 1964.

Nasr, Seyyed Hossein. *Man and Nature: The Spiritual Crisis in Modern Man.* London: Mandala, 1968.

Nasseef, Abdullah Omar. "Science Education and Religious Values: An Islamic Approach." In *Religion and Education: Islamic and Christian Approaches*, edited by Syed Ali Ashraf, and Paul H. Hirst, 30–59. Cambridge: The Islamic Academy, 1994.

Robinson, Francis. "Review." *Modern Asian Studies* 15, no. 4 (October 1981): 886–891. https://doi.org/10.1017/S0026749X00008829.

Ryrie, Alec. *Unbelievers: An Emotional History of Doubts.* Cambridge, MA: Harvard University Press, 2019.

Schuon, Frithjof. *The Transcendent Unity of Religions.* London: Faber & Faber, 1953.

Shah, Manzoor A., and M. Maroof Shah, "Krishnamurti's environmental critique of traditional religion: A critical appraisal from perenialist perspective." *European Journal of Science and Theology* 4, no. 2 (June 2008): 61–78.

Yü, Dan Smyer. "The Critical Zone as a Planetary Animist Sphere: Etho-graphing an Affective Consciousness of the Earth." *Journal for the Study of Religion, Nature and Culture* 14, no. 2 (2020): 271–90. http://dx.doi.org/10.1558/jsrnc.39680.

Zada, Sher. "Nature: Its Moral and Metaphysical Dimensions." *The Dialogue* 10, no. 3 (2015): 254–66.

Zimmer, Carl. "E.O. Wilson, a Pioneer of Evolutionary Biology, Dies at 92." *The New York Times*. December 27, 2021. https://www.nytimes.com/2021/12/27/science/eo-wilson-dead.html.

Chapter 16

Skills of Discernment: An Essential but Neglected Aspect of Education in Religion

Brenda Watson

The chapter argues that teaching skills of discernment should form a crucial part of education in religion. Four ways of knowing are outlined to which children and young people deserve to be given access. The all-important need to guard against dogmatism is met by acknowledging our own unavoidable limitations. Certainty which is provisional and partial is all that we can properly claim, but it is enough. Problems faced both by the secularist West and by religious communities in meeting the need for discernment are discussed, and a detailed example of the application of criteria is given.

It is in a spirit of deepest respect for Professor Ashraf that I write this chapter. His work has been enormously influential in promoting creative dialogue between Islam and the West. He brought a critical and perceptive eye to the educational scene in Britain whilst engaging positively with its achievements.

The events of September 11th and after have shown the crucial importance of widespread understanding of religion, and especially the need to judge what is genuine religion from the many counterfeits on offer. The nature of religion has been pushed centre-stage for many who care about the peace of the world.

Education in religion should play a major role in helping the young to learn powers of discernment. The need is to develop the latent capacity of all children to think and reflect, in order to protect them and the world from their falling prey to propaganda of all kinds, some highly sophisticated. There is less chance of people being dazzled by the rhetoric of extremists if they are helped to think deeply for themselves about the nature of real religion.

Such education should be available for all children and young people everywhere, whether or not they have formal Religious Education as such. By Religious Education indeed I do not mean just a discrete subject on the timetable in schools as happens in Britain and other countries. Religious Education concerns how we educate the young into understanding of religion. Reflection upon it can be encouraged in the home, in the local community, in church, synagogue, mosque or temple, as well as in school. Religious nurture within communities offers a crucially important arena for learning such skills.

What is Religion?

Education needs to focus on this question. Public reaction to the current crisis has highlighted the difficulties of answering it. Jonathan Sacks, Chief Rabbi for Britain, commented in *The Times* on October 8, 2001: "As a religious believer, I must face the fact that religion is not always a good thing. Usually it speaks to the best in us, but it can sometimes speak to the worst. Religion is like fire. It warms, but it also burns; and we are the guardians of the flame."[1]

Here religion is understood both as a sociological phenomenon and as an individual commitment. The analogy is apt for both senses. Extreme vigilance is needed in guarding the flame. Religion as practised can be destructive as well as creative.

One common reaction to the dark side of religion is to deny that this is religion. This may well be the case from the point of view of ideal religion. Yet to argue, as Yasmin Alibhai-Brown did in a recent interview: "Any religion that oppresses, as far as I am concerned, is not a religion but a political system which uses religion"[2] is not adequate. This can appear to be walking away from the problem. As another letter in *The Times* put it: "There can be not a scintilla of doubt that these terrorists were faithful Islamic believers."[3]

Nor is the problem mitigated by those who simply state with William Rees-Mogg: "Anyone who reads the Quran or studies the life of the Prophet will know that this madness has no place in the religion of Islam."[4] Is he here implying that the terrorists had not read the Qurʾān or known the life of Muhammad? The document containing final detailed instructions to the hijackers was revealing. Much of it looked like a highly devotional manual which anyone who was trying to love God could applaud. The hijacking was not the work of people indifferent to religion, but of people immersed within it.

---

1 Jonathan Sacks, "As the bombs fall, this is our greatest challenge," *The Times*, October 8, 2001.
2 Yasmin Alibhai-Brown, "All Due Respect," *Third Way*, November 2001, 18–22. This is an interview with Richard Wilkins, https://books.google.co.uk/books?id=qFVE-VUDiB4C&pg=PA18&dq=%22richard+wilkins+talks+to+yasmin+alibhai-brown+mbe%22&hl=en&sa=X&ved=0ahUKEwiJvc6isOPLAhWJbBoKHb7lAqEQ6AEIHTAA-#v=onepage&q=%22richard%20wilkins%20talks%20to%20yasmin%20alibhai-brown%20mbe%22&f=false.
3 Leon Marks, letter to the editor, *The Times*, October 3, 2001.
4 William Rees-Mogg, "The fears that gave rise to this evil man," *The Times*, October 8, 2001.

The difficulty in reality concerns interpretation. And this raises the question: is there a correct interpretation such that others can be measured beside it? If the terrorists' interpretation is flawed, it is the task of scholars to point out why it is flawed and how it is flawed. The task then is to communicate to people the interpretation of the religion in such a way that both Muslims and non-Muslims everywhere can understand. Similarly Christian scholars should be doing the same thing regarding the interpretation of the Bible, so that reprehensible and dangerous misinterpretation of verses in scripture such as has led, for example, to anti-Semitism, can be guarded against.

Another approach to the crisis, which re-defines religion, is that advocated by Robert van de Weyer in his book *Islam and the West: A New Political and Religious Order post September 11*. Heavily influenced by the secularist West, he sees the way forward as one of *open religion* in which tolerance and love are the supreme virtues—a religion which transcends all questions of truth-claims.

This approach ignores the centrality in religious commitment of love for God. Instead, it echoes Western philosophers' dismissal of religion as authority-based and fear-based. He states baldly without comment: "The fear of some kind of divine retribution, and the hope of divine reward, is the ultimate reason why people adhere to religious doctrines for which there is no compelling evidence."[5]

He fails to add "in his view"! He equates the dogmatic remarks of a leading American Christian evangelist with doctrinal Christianity and implies that only fundamentalists, whether Muslim or Christian, are concerned about truth. "The doctrines of organised Christianity and Islam have quite simply been rendered absurd; indeed, acceptance of religious dogma of any kind involves intellectual dishonesty."[6]

This prompts the response: upon what is his dogmatism based other than that he utters it?! By what criteria does he judge *intellectual honesty*?

But he admits that we cannot just get rid of religion because "human beings seem innately religious. . . . Stamping out religion is no more realistic than stamping out sex; and, just as we make a moral distinction between good sexual relationships and bad, so we must distinguish between good and bad religion."[7] In other words, having dismissed the truth-claims of religion, he still sees discernment required on pragmatic grounds.

The Need for Discernment

In this he is justified. We are familiar, in everyday life and in other areas of knowledge and experience, with the fact that some people are closer than

---

5 Robert Van De Weyer, *Islam and the West: A New Political and Religious Order Post September 11* (Hampshire: O Books Alresford, 2001), 95.
6 Van De Weyer, *Islam and the West*, 90.
7 Van De Weyer, *Islam and the West*, 91–92.

others to the skills and understanding concerned with a particular area of knowledge. For example, we speak of a good historian or a good scientist, and the academic subjects associated with these areas of knowledge or skill are concerned with learning what makes them 'good.' Anyone can set themselves up as an historian or scientist, but not everyone is worth being considered as such. Education must be concerned with helping people to understand and handle the criteria by which judgment can be made. If the historian becomes a propagandist, it is for the educated person to see through the propaganda and deny it the name of history. If the scientist does not bother to experiment, to study carefully the evidence and to consult with the scientific community as a whole, then however much he or she may claim to be a scientist we should not accord the status of scientific pronouncements to what he or she says.

It is equally essential to distinguish between "good" and "bad" when people claim to be religious. This distinguishing in religion is rendered peculiarly difficult but also peculiarly important, because of the many ways in which people can delude themselves and others with regard to high ideals and beliefs. Thus, believers can equate their own will with the will of God. Cromwell had to wrestle with precisely this point. "I beseech you, in the bowels of Christ, think it possible you may be mistaken," he wrote in desperation to Covenanters inflexible in regarding their own view of God as completely right and everyone else's as wrong.[8]

In a perceptive article entitled "Bin Laden hijacks history for his holy war" Ben Macintyre articulated the evil nature of the Crusades. "Few would dispute that the Crusades involved war crimes on a massive scale, a whipping-up of religious hatred for the purposes of pillage and political consolidation in fractured Europe, a largely unprovoked war waged against a deeply cultured people."[9]

Almost everyone today would agree. Why is it that intelligent and sensitive people everywhere can evaluate such behaviour like this? Upon what considerations does such condemnation rest? Gut-reaction maybe, but one then has to ask why *this* gut-reaction and not one of approval for the Crusades? Because of cultural brain-washing? Yet it is hard to see why. If so, such revulsion transcends all boundaries of culture. Most Christians today are as disgusted as any other people by such events.

Furthermore, the motivation was explicitly religious. "Enter upon the road to the Holy Sepulcher, wrest that land from the wicked race . . . *Deus lo volt!* God wills it." Ben Macintyre adds: "The words are those of Pope Urban II in 1095, but their modem incarnation is Osama bin Laden."

---

8   Godfrey Davies, *Oxford History of England: Early Stuarts 1603 – 1660* (Oxford: Oxford University Press, 1937), 167.
9   Benedict Macintyre, "Bin Laden hijacks history for his holy war," *The Times*, October 27, 2001.

Once again, it would be hard for any moderates to disagree. Yet many in the modem world appeal to dissent. Thus the majority of people have shown immediate rejection of terrorism, but not all. And those who do espouse it commonly do so explicitly on religious grounds.

In addition to dealing with the question of why extremism is attractive to some, there is urgent need for clearer thinking on a range of associated issues such as:

(i) What constitutes religion in its essential nature?
(ii) How does religion relate to culture?
(iii) What are the priorities which ought to govern human life?
(iv) Are values such as tolerance enough for a pluralist world?
(v) How can we engage people everywhere in a search for peace?

The Practice of Discernment

Discernment, however, appears to be a slippery matter dependent on individual assessment and not amenable to public debate. Is this really so however? Let us return to the Crusades. It is worth asking what exactly *was* wrong about them such that intelligent and sensitive people everywhere today are appalled by such behaviour. The Crusades involved at least four types of strongly negative thinking:

1. moral crime—cruelty and wanton destruction of largely innocent people which violates a basic sense of moral justice;
2. psychological deviation—hypocrisy: claiming to be God-fearing Christians whilst actually driven by a variety of personal, political and economic motives which as outsiders with hindsight we can easily perceive (cf. Runciman.[10]);
3. logical/linguistic deviation—stereotyped tribalism creating a false *them-and-us* situation which cannot be supported by logical argument;
4. religious crime—violence and hatred in the name of a God of love.

Disgust at what happened therefore rests on at least four different ways of knowing:

1. *An inbuilt sense of moral fairness.* This is the immediate direct apprehension of certain deeds and attitudes as inherently morally wrong. Professor Ashraf noted that every child has the capacity to sense moral right and wrong as distinct from humanly-devised rules and regulations.[11] Even

---

[10] Steven Runciman, *A History of the Crusades* (Cambridge: CUP, 1966) is still the standard text.
[11] Syed Ali Ashraf, "Islamic Education and Moral-Development," in *Religion and Education: Islamic and Christian Approaches*, eds. Syed Ali Ashraf and Paul Hirst (Cambridge: Islamic Academy, 1994), 143.

from the midst of Western philosophy Kant spoke of his sense of awe for "the starry heavens above and the moral law within."[12]

2. *Common sense knowledge of persons, including especially oneself.* This involves appreciating the strength of the temptations open to human beings due to fear and self-interest. Thus in analysing behaviour the strength of hidden motives must be gauged. Integrity is a major and much valued characteristic of people whose influence on others is beneficial. Its presence can be detected, but not using sense perception on its own; it uses empirical observation and enquiry but transcends it. Whether *common* or not it is potentially available for all. A striking example chosen at random is the maid in *The Secret Garden* who stands out as a shining character able to befriend the desperately lonely child because of her knowledge in personal relationships and the bringing-up of the young. She had been on no management skills course! Her knowledge however transformed Mary's life, just as Mary's knowledge went on to transform the life of her supposedly crippled cousin.[13]

3. *Careful reasoning.* Thus, for example, because a cause must precede what it causes, it is inept stupidity to blame for a crime innocent members of a group often centuries after a crime was committed. This is a basically logical point with very far-reaching implications if appreciated.

4. *Religious intuition.* Thus the humble, submissive, prayerful awareness of the love of a gracious God can detect outrage committed in God's name. Such awareness may be far wider spread than secularists may be inclined to believe. Recent research by the psychologist Olivera Petrovich, for example, parallels what has just been said about the moral sensibility of very young children.

Studies in Britain and Japan have indicated that children by the age of four have a fundamental concept of God which is not naively anthropomorphic. She comments: "What is striking about those findings is that the Japanese culture excludes any concepts of transcendent causality from its religious system." The concept is not, therefore, culturally-derived.[14]

To summarise the argument so far: those who enthusiastically supported the Crusades in the Middle Ages, and those who today embrace the cause of violent religious extremism anywhere in the world are failing in these ways of knowing.

---

12 Immanuel Kant, *Critique of Practical Reason*, vol. 5, 161–2.
13 Frances Hodgson Burnett, *The Secret Garden* (New York: F. A. Stokes, 1911).
14 Olivera Petrovich, "Postmodemity: Science points to God," *UPI*, May 4, 2001, para 11. 23rd instalment of the UPI series, "Christ and postmodernity," https://www.upi.com/Archives/2001/05/04/Postmodernity-Science-points-to-God/5336988948800/.

1. Their sense of moral fairness does not embrace mutuality but is one-sided, aggrieved only by injustice against themselves; injustice which they may perpetrate against others does not trouble them.
2. They are immature as human-beings, self-centered and able to perceive other people's hypocrisy but not the own. They can see the splinter in someone else's eye but not the beam in their own! They are little aware of the enormity of temptation facing everyone, including themselves, to selfishness and disreputable motives.
3. Their reasoning is faulty. Thus they fail to examine the sheer illogicality of tribalism which, because of its incapacity to distinguish individuals from the total entity, translates *an-eye-for-an-eye* into *many-innocent-eyes-for-one-eye*.
4. Their concept of God is confused and mistaken. Their view of God is of a vengeful, aggressive, selfish Power. A famous book entitled *Your God Is Too Small* by J. B. Philips[15] points to a profound truth which Voltaire's quip summarised: "If God made us in His image, we have certainly returned the compliment!"[16]

The Impossibility of Incorrigible Certainty

It is important however to note that the ways of knowing have to be worked at. None can supply infallible knowledge.

1. Direct immediate moral sense can be so influenced by custom and conditioning that it can turn right round, supplying terrorists with a sense of the justice of their cause because they have no interest in justice for anyone else. It is also the case that the application of fundamental principles of right and wrong has many grey areas where highly reasonable and responsible people can disagree. It is over-stress on this insight that has led so many in the West down the slippery slope of relativism. But the truth embodied within relativism must not be ignored, even as its dismissal of any moral absolutes must be resisted.
2. Knowledge of person can be notoriously fickle and unreliable, as life and literature alike can show. Misreading people's character, hate masquerading as love or self-interest, charming manners as devious ambition, and so forth.
3. Reason on its own is also inadequate. It is not the umpire *par excellence* of what constitutes knowledge which liberal Western philosophical tradition has tried to make of it. Thus people with short-term selfish objectives can see that violence pays, as it did for the Norman adventurers who set up kingdoms in the Levant as a result of the Crusades. Furthermore, the hi-

---

15 J. B. Philips: *Your God Is Too Small* (London: Epworth Press, 1932).
16 Voltaire, *Le Sottisier de Voltaire* (Paris: Garnier Frères, 1880), xxxii.

jackers of September 11 were highly rational people using reason to secure their ends.
4. It is terrifyingly easy for people to claim and genuinely think that they are worshipping God, being submissive to God, loving God by following their own bent. Being sure is no guarantee of truth. Hasan Askari has wisely noted: "I shall try to put forward the religious viewpoint remaining aware all the time that like any other point of view it is tentative, all too human, for to remember this is the very demand of my religious conscience, for to be modest with regard to even the strongly held religious convictions is the only way to remember the Immensity of the Transcendental and Inscrutable Reality."[17]

Equating what we think with what God wills is a most dangerous temptation to the religious person. There is a famous quotation from C. S. Lewis at the end of *The Great Divorce* where he is discussing the question of heaven and hell: he writes that in the end there are only two types of people, those who say to God, "Thy will be done," and those to whom God says, "*Thy* will be done."[18]

The possibility of error does not however render all our attempts at reaching truth useless. For if we cannot claim absolute incorrigible certainty, neither can we claim complete ignorance. Timothy Williamson, whose recent book is described as "a new way of doing epistemology for the twenty-first century," began the Preface: "If I had to summarise this book in two words, they would be *knowledge first*. It takes the simple distinction between knowledge and ignorance as a starting point from which to explain other things, not as something itself to be explained."[19] In all walks of life the ways of knowing can and do provide the partial and provisional certainty necessary to live and to move forward.

Relief from the anxiety of acknowledging the impossibility of incorrigible certainty can be obtained from reflecting on possible metaphors for knowledge. The metaphors which tend to govern thinking today in the West go largely unrecognised and unacknowledged. A particularly powerful one is what may be called the accountancy metaphor; according to this, what is credit and what is debit can be neatly put in columns and added up producing justified, definite certainty and therefore deserved to be called *knowledge*. Another prominent metaphor is that of walking *on terra firm* in a straight line as on an old Roman road. *Knowledge* is moving in clear-cut logical steps from one position to another without deviation.

---

17 Hasan Askari, "Can Education Have a Religious Foundation Today? An Islamic Approach," in *Religion and Education*, eds. Ashraf and Hirst, 6.
18 C. S. Lewis, *The Great Divorce: A Dream* (London: Collins Fount, 1945), 75.
19 Timothy Williamson, preface to *Knowledge and Its Limits* (Oxford: Oxford University Press, 2000), v.

Yet other metaphors are not only possible but far more true to the experience of gathering knowledge which we all have to do in order to exist at all and sustain any quality of life. Kierkegaard once remarked that we have to learn to live over 70,000 fathoms of water.[20] So the metaphor of sailing or swimming—not in a straight line but responsive to the ever-fluctuating currents around one—is more apposite. Similarly, a metaphor such as gardening is apt, where tremendous knowledge of such factors as plants, weather, soils, and artistry is needed to produce a garden—all skills which cannot be neatly translated into ticks and crosses on a balance-sheet.

We have to accept that our certainties have to remain provisional (cf. 5. Pierce[21]). As Richard Bailey notes: "Doubts and a recognition of our own limitations can encourage us to continue inquiring and learning about the world, and, perhaps more importantly, remain open to the possibility of our own errors."[22] But the difference between blindness and perception remains as a firm anchor.

Yet the practice of such discernment and willingness to teach it appears not to be well understood by many today, whether secularists or religious people.

Unwillingness to Facing the Need to Teach Skills of Discernment

1. *The secularist objection*: In the liberal West, teaching skills of discernment ought to present no theoretical problem for Religious Education as the rhetoric of openness, autonomy and pupil choice in beliefs and values clearly requires it: otherwise, how are pupils to choose? Yet such education in Britain appears mostly conspicuous by its absence! Religious Education in the latter decades of the last century was mostly concerned with the apparently safe area of description on religious practice and beliefs without encouraging or helping towards enquiry into their truth. For such enquiry might have compromised the over-arching value of tolerance. Search for a faith by which to live has normally been left at a personal level. Grounds for choosing are left obscure, unlike in the teaching of other areas of the curriculum such as Science and History.

---

20 Soren Kierkegaard, "Concluding Unscientific Postscript," in *The Essential Kierkegaard*, eds. Howard V. Hong and Edna H. Hong (Princeton, New Jersey: Princeton University Press, 1978), 207.
21 Charles Sanders Pierce, *Collected Papers of Charles Sanders Peirce*, vol. 1, *Principles of Philosophy and Elements of Logic*, ed. Charles Hartshorne and Paul Weiss (Cambridge, MA: Harvard University Press, 1931). The classic statement of fallibilism is in Section 1.120.
22 Richard Bailey, "Overcoming Veriphobia—Learning to love truth again," *British Journal of Educational Studies* 49, no. 2 (June 2001): 163, https://doi.org/10.1111/1467-8527.t01-1-00169.

The underlying reason for this is the *fact/belief divide*[23] which has been widely conditioned into people, whereby thinking and knowledge are the province only of facts empirically or scientifically demonsratable (at least in principle) or of pragmatic objectives. Beliefs and values, not being amenable to such clear-cut objective verification, are presumed to be beyond the pale concerning what can be called *knowledge*. Of course, believers think they *know*, but in fact they only *think* they know. There is no point therefore in trying to distinguish what is sound and wholesome and nearer to truth in beliefs from what is less so. The most complete philosophical expression of this view is to be found in Positivism.[24]

On such grounds religion can be adequately understood as purely sociological/psychological phenomena. For secularists who have already dismissed the notion of any real truth or insight in religion, their only interest is in how and why people believe, not what they believe and its validity. Therefore, the question of whether labels such as *Christian, Muslim* or *Buddhist* are meaningfully applied in a particular instance is of no consequence.

The ease with which Religious Education has pursued the phenomenological path illustrates how deeply secularism has become ingrained in the West. Instead of challenging secularism Religious Education has been impregnated by it. A more nuanced approach to the subject is indeed now being advocated, but it still stops short of serious attention to how children are supposed to evaluate truth-claims. Whole generations have been brought up *not* to think about beliefs and values except just in a personal way.

The way forward here is to challenge the validity of the fact/belief divide. The time is ripe because of the powerful postmodernist mood in the West today which denies the validity of the positivist heroic model of knowledge. Yet as Appleby *et al.* note: "Despite this generation's well-broadcast scorn for positivism, positivism has left as its principal legacy an enduring dichotomy between absolute objectivity and totally arbitrary interpretations of the world of objects."[25] Furthermore, even an excellent defence against postmodernism such as Richard Bailey provides in a recent stimulating article does not really dismantle the fact/belief divide; for the secularist viewpoint is still taken for granted, thus leaving religion languishing as outside the realm of knowledge.[26] It is high time that, on its own grounds, the weaknesses of the fact/belief divide be shown up.

---

23 I have discussed this term elsewhere: Brenda Watson, "Evaluative RE? A response to two articles by Andrew Wright on Hermeneutics and Religious Understanding," *The Journal of Beliefs and Values* 21, no. 1, (2000): 63–72. https://doi.org/10.1080/13617670050002336.

24 cf. Ludwig Wittgenstein, *Tractatus Logico-Philosophicus* (New York: Harcourt, Brace & Company, and London: Kegan Paul, 1922): 4.11. 6.52. 6.53.

25 Joyce Appleby, Lynn Hunt, and Margaret Jacob, *Telling the Truth about History* (New York: Norton, 1994), 246.

26 Bailey, "Overcoming, "159–172.

2. *A difficulty for religious people*: The problems of religious communities are different but tend to lead to the same result. The strength of emphasis on ritual, recitation of scripture, habits of living nurtured in the young in the home and the local community as the right way to live, can easily lead to conditioning whereby a child growing up in that atmosphere rarely questions these matters.

External practice is conveyed very successfully, but the inner purpose fails often to be adequately communicated. Individually devout people do penetrate the distinction between outer and inner orientation, but often they do not articulate it—they live it and by it, but others do not necessarily pick up clearly what it is. The handing-on of the faith in such situations can easily lead inadvertently to a closure of the mind and heart to real thinking about the faith and about the faiths which other people hold.

The way forward therefore is through a deepening of religious understanding. One of the reasons why I believe Professor Ashraf was unafraid of engagement with other religions and with the secularist West was because he had penetrated to the spiritual centre of his religion. He was acting not from a cultural base but from a devout love for God—the Oneness at the heart of reality and all genuine religion. Indeed, we need to examine afresh why we have religions in separate compartments—a sociological convenience? a cultural *fait accompli*, an unavoidable aspect of our limitations as human-beings? Such compartmentalising contradicts the luminous centre of religions and their *raison d'être*, if it is the case that God is One, creator of all, who loves all and reveals Himself to individuals, groups, and communities in ways appropriate to them.

This carries the corollary that the outward manifestations and forms in which such love for God clothes itself are perceived as not the essence of religion but rather a means towards it. They may be essential, in that we are finite creatures linked to a specific time and place, but ultimately disposable when they have done their work, like the scaffolding to build a house, or like the raft to cross the waters in the Buddhist analogy.

The result is probably what van de Weyer meant by *open religion*. But where he based his on a denial of truth-claims, the transcendence for which I am arguing is based on ever-deepening understanding of and commitment to the truth-claims. In the process, the religious believer may indeed encounter dross which must be discarded. Religious imagery frequently returns to the metaphor of fire mentioned by Jonathan Sacks. The mystics of the world religions experience fire as purification whereby the true gold of love for God is revealed.

Teaching Criteria for Discernment

The strong middle ground between secularists and religious people insists on helping people forward in skills of discernment for themselves, whilst being fair both to religion and to the case against religion in material presented to them. What skills are these? As a modest contribution to what needs to be a long and on-going debate, may I suggest the learning of some specific criteria for discernment?[27]

Before outlining these, it is important to note that these criteria should not be understood as rigid rule-like principles to be applied in so-called objective fashion to any problem for a neat solution to emerge. Rather they are considerations to be mulled over, reflected upon, and considered constantly in the laboratory of life in its total messiness and complexity. They are not rules for a cerebral game pursued in an ivory tower, in an isolated clinically tidy room remote from the actual decision-making we all of us have to do all the time.

Therefore, it will never be possible to demonstrate these criteria in such a way that all normally intelligent human beings can agree. They remain obstinately subjective and personal in application and interpretation. But they also have a public face. They can and should be discussed openly in the search for what is objectively true and realistic. One can express the point quite forcibly. The criteria are considerations which it would be reprehensible to overlook in coming to judgments. Failure to take account of them produces over-hasty conviction. By reflecting upon them they become ways of assessing of nature of reality in a manner which will affect how we live.

A further point about the criteria is that they are inter-dependent, operating on each other. It is the cumulative effect of them that can produce conviction. The criteria include the following four, related to the ways of knowing, already discussed:

1. *Moral consequences.* "By their fruits ye shall know them"—how far is the likely outcome of this belief beneficial and creative *for all* rather than destructive? The principle of reciprocity is a universal principle applicable to all people encountered, not just to some. Any religious practice which actually contradicts moral awareness causes one to suspect that something has gone wrong: either the belief producing such an outcome is false, or the belief is true but ignored in practice.

2. *Personal Wholeness.* This has two aspects at least: (i) Is the belief as comprehensive of experience as possible, or is it exclusive, and dismissive of many other aspects? Is it potentially welcoming to all insights? The focus here is on signs of prejudice and one-sidedness. (ii) Is the belief held with integrity, or is there serious mismatch between stated belief and behaviour?

---

[27] There are many other possible criteria some of which I outline in Brenda Watson, *The Effective Teaching of Religious Education* (Harlow, Essex: Longman, 1993; 1999), chap. 7.

3. *Logical/linguistic coherence.* Is the belief logically satisfying or is there anything contradictory or inconsistent about it? Is a logical fallacy present such as using a generalization with the implication of *all* when *some* is appropriate? Much depends here on how language is understood. For example, does the belief depend on a literal reading of what is metaphorical?

4. *Spiritual Intuition.* Is the belief close to the spirit of the religion as a whole? Is it authentic or inauthentic in its development from what began the religion? How a religion started is obviously crucial to what can claim to be distinctive and essential to it. There may indeed be many features of the earliest form of the religion which are transient and culturally conditioned, and which later authentic development may therefore discard. But such discarding depends upon acknowledging what was distinctive and precious in the first place.

This is so crucial a question that perhaps it needs developing further. Usually, our judgments on this are based on the cultural and religious groupings to which we belong or with which we come into significant contact. An example from Christianity might concern the role of the Virgin Mary. Is a custom such as genuflecting before an image of Mary authentic or inauthentic development? A Roman Catholic may see such genuflection as loyalty to the Christian tradition and yet a convinced Protestant may see this as not. From the Roman Catholic point of view, if devotion to the human Jesus is what matters, then veneration of his mother makes sense, provided that she is not worshipped alongside Jesus. If on the other hand, as with the Protestant, the eradication of idolatry is what matters most, then the possibility that such veneration could be or become idolatry, pandering to a seemingly ubiquitous human desire for go-betweens in the worship of God, would pronounce that veneration as inauthentic development.

In understanding the reasons in each case, a significant step forward can be taken, enabling middle ground to be expressed as perhaps: honouring Mary in this way may be authentic development but not essential, and needing to be guarded against abuse.

Criteria Applied to the Interpretation of Scripture

Scripture is appealed to as a major means of ensuring that faith is sound and authentic; it is the source of religious inspiration and seen as offering guidance for behaviour now. Yet scripture produces many different interpretations. Publically-available criteria by which to assess interpretations are urgently needed.

It may be helpful if, as a Christian, I share with readers the kind of criteria which I believe may help to guard against abuse of a text, and ensure readers gain real spiritual insight.

(i) What is the context in which a text comes? Did it just apply to the time when it was written or is it of universal significance? If these questions are not asked, inappropriate theological or revelatory information may be extrapolated from what were culturally-conditioned phenomena.

(ii) Is this text of major importance considering the sense of scripture as a whole, or is it out-of-step? All texts are not equally illuminating: they need to be placed in levels of importance and inspiration and closeness to divine revelation, or even to admit that particular passages could be false by comparison with those texts which are central. If this is not done, it may be easy to ignore inconsistency between an interpretation of an individual text and the main thrust of scripture as a whole.

(iii) Are there signs of mistakes or misunderstandings in the text? Behind this lies the need to appreciate that the Bible has been mediated through human beings who lived at a particular time and place, spoke a particular language, and had particular needs and concerns and concepts. Therefore, mistakes or misunderstandings due to limited vision may have influenced the text.

Example of the Criteria Used

The following may act as an example of how such criteria can enable valid judgment-making concerning inauthentic development within a religion. The example is how Christians need to deal with the anti-Semitism with which Christianity has been implicated. Such development is inauthentic to Christianity on at least the following grounds:

1. The *moral consequences* of such violent behaviour against Jews which indirectly was contributory to the Holocaust have been horrendously immoral. A trail of hatred and destruction and nearly two millennia of suspicion and stereotyping is hardly an edifying instance of the fundamental moral principle, "Do unto others as you would they do unto you."

2. The *Personal Wholeness* test shows serious mismatch here between using the symbol of the self-sacrifice of the Cross as a means of pursuing hatred. Jesus sought to heal by means of forgiveness and acceptance, not to inflame anger. The words put on his lips as he was nailed to the cross, "Father, forgive them, for they know not what they do,"[28] indicates the kind of approach which is required of those who claim to be his followers. Christians who think that it is their Christian duty to hate Jews are deceiving themselves.

3. Anti-Semitism embodies *logical/linguistic incoherence*: it rests on confusing individuals and communal entities. This results in the creation of nonexistent abstract concepts and treating them as though existent. In fact, there is no such thing as *Judaism*; the word stands for real people who are Jews; the

---

28 Luke 23:34.

same is true regarding *Christianity,* it does not exist per se but only as a generalization for real people who are Christians. Presumably all Jews have something in common and all Christians similarly, otherwise the terms *Judaism* and *Christianity* could not be used at all. But this does not mean that they have everything in common or even much. If the members of a group are deeply conflicting over important matters, prioritising what they have in common, such as claiming to follow Christ, will cause crucial differences to be hidden from sight and hence presumed negligible. If some Christians think that following Christ involves hating Jews and others think the opposite, this conflict is so serious in its effects that it dissolves the simplistic notion of such comments as *Christianity is not anti-Semitic.*

4. Does *spiritual intuition* suggest that the belief is in the spirit of Christianity as a whole? Is it authentic? Apart from reasons already given under the first three points, authentic development of Christianity could not lead to anti-Semitism. It is contrary to Christian experience as manifest in the lives of its saints and scholars, for example in George Herbert's poem "Love."[29] The notions of enmity and human judgement are anathema to those who have made even the beginnings of understanding the love of God as revealed in Jesus.

This conclusion is supported by the criteria for evaluating biblical texts. An example of the damage done by *faulty* exegesis is Matthew 27:24-26. This has been used to justify Christian persecution of the Jews through the centuries:

> When Pilate saw that he was getting nowhere, and that there was danger of a riot, he took water and washed his hands in full view of the crowd. "My hands are clean of this man's blood," he declared. "See to that yourselves." With one voice the people cried, "His blood be on us and on our children." (REV)

To read anti-Semitism out of this text is to fail to apply all three criteria discussed above.

(i) *Ignoring the impact of context in the assessment of significance of a passage*
Even according to the traditional acceptance of Matthew the disciple of Jesus being the author of this gospel, anyone thinking about the text should have realised that it was a Jew who was writing this. Modern scholarship has stressed that this gospel has Jewish Christians particularly in mind, so that once again, the notion of anti-Semitism in a racial sense is simply ruled out as impossible. Jesus was a Jew. All the first disciples were Jews. The gospel of

---

29 George Herbert, "Love," *The Temple: Sacred Poems and Private Ejaculations* (Cambridge: Thomas Buck and Roger Daniel, 1633). See also in *Herbert Grierson and Geoffrey Bullough, Oxford Book of Seventeenth Century Verse* (Oxford: Clarendon Press, 1934), 388.

Matthew goes to enormous trouble to underline the Jewish foundations of the Christian movement.

Furthermore, the context of the passage is the trial of Jesus in Jerusalem. This shows that the text refers to particular people, not the nation as a whole. Jews living since were not there. They could not possibly be responsible for Jesus's death. As Carson puts it:

> Matthew certainly knows that *all* the first disciples were Jews. Thus the Gospel's denunciations of the Jews are not more severe than those of many Old Testament prophets, and in both instances it is understood that a faithful remnant remains. So what Matthew actually says cannot be judged as anti-Semitic. It is only when Matthew's account is read as a description, not of Jesus' trial, but of later church-synagogue relations, that it begins to bear anti-Semitic nuances.[30]

(ii) *Regarding every passage as divinely inspired*

The most conspicuous failure is ignoring the intention of the gospel as a whole. The phrase *His blood be upon us and upon our children* is a Hebrew expression for inherited responsibility incurred in the death of a person (e.g. 1 Kings 2:33). It echoes traditional patterns of tribal solidarity which relate to the ancient concept of the blood-feud based on blood-guilt. How can such an ancient cultural practice still be adhered to in the light of the teaching also recorded by Matthew in the Sermon on the Mount of "Love thine enemy"?[31] This is the complete opposite of such an interpretation. It cannot possibly fit in with an anti-Semitic reading of this text.

(iii) *The absence of a critical eye for errors and linguistic/textual incongruities in a passage*

There is an inconsistency between interpreting Matthew's *people* (verse 25) as meaning the whole of Judaism, for in 26:5 Matthew tells of a fear that the people might cause a riot if something was done to Jesus, and 27:24 alludes to Pilate's fear of a riot. So obviously there were many supporters of Jesus among the Jew's. Therefore, all Jews could not possibly be meant by the 'people' of verse 25.

Facing the Abuse of Religion

What is serious however is the difficulty with which the inauthenticity of anti-Semitism for Christianity seems to be greeted. Recent correspondence with a Rabbi who has played a most valuable part in Jewish/Christian dialogue pinpointed this for me.[32] In a letter I likened anti-Semitism within Christian-

---

30 Donald A. Carson, "Matthew," in *Expositor's Bible Commentary: Matthew-Luke*, vol. 8, ed. Frank E. Gaebelein (Grand Rapids, MI: Zondervan, 1984), 571.
31 Matthew 5: 44.
32 Rabbi Tony Bayfield, Correspondence with author, January 31, February 6, 2001. He

ity to a cancerous development, not an authentic one. He responded that that does not help anyone for it is simply defining Christianity as everything that Christians have believed and taught which is good.

But he had, I think, missed the point on two grounds. Firstly, to argue that anti-Semitism is a cancerous inauthentic development within Christianity is not to generalise about Christianity, seeing it as though through rose-coloured spectacles; it is to relate to one precise development Christianity has, I believe, been associated with other inauthentic developments. Most religious believers tend to regard their own tradition as consisting only of the good most of the time. Indeed, that is why they are religious believers because they automatically perceive that mistakes, wrong-doing, hypocrisy and so forth, are mismatches. Indeed, this is why Christians, who today discover the role that some Christians have played in anti-Semitism, are normally absolutely horror-struck, as, for example, James Carroll in his book *Constantine's Sword*.[33] This reaction shows that it does not form part of authentic Christianity at all.

The second point I would make in answer to the Rabbi is that for all parties, Jews as well as Christians, to acknowledge inauthentic development helps to take the nastiness out of traditional hostility between religions. Indeed, if it is not acknowledged, one easily ends up in a situation in which, for example, Christians feel aggrieved for being expected to apologise for what they have never approved of or have been responsible for anyway. Similarly, it helps the earlier aggrieved party, the victims of aggression, to go on hating their presumed oppressors without distinguishing between the true and the false amongst them. Indeed, a creative way forward really does depend upon acknowledging this all-important distinction.

This relates to a further point. The crisis over what constitutes knowledge and what religion happens to be is why I believe that so few Christians have really taken the full force of serious crimes such as the Crusades committed in the name of Christ. It is not that Christians today do not acknowledge that they were crimes. Nor is it that they should acknowledge blame for them, for that is to pander to a primitive and now inappropriate form of tribalism. Clearly Christians today are not responsible for the Crusades. But I believe that there are two things which they should do.

Firstly, they need to show how and why such crimes were and are crimes against the very spirit of Christianity—the true heresies to be expelled. Speaking as a Christian, I think that Christian leaders have not repeatedly made clear that, for example, violence in Northern Ireland in the name of Christ is blasphemy and non-Christian; those who perpetrate it put themselves outside the

---

wrote a most impressive final chapter in *Christian-Jewish Dialogue: The next steps*, ed. Marcus Braybrooke (London: SCM Press, 2000).

33 James Carroll, *Constantine's Sword: The Church and the Jews* (Boston: Houghton Mifflen Company 2001).

bounds of following Christ. This needs to be constantly stated, otherwise we allow the perpetrators of violence to use the power of religion in their cause.

Secondly, Christians need to examine whether there are not features of what they do today which may have contributed to such colossal failure to be Christian. *Today* something should be done about renouncing such features, so that every effort be made to help Christians in the future to avoid the errors of the past. One example for Christians is a simplistic way of describing the Bible as the *Word of God*, for this can be applied by literalist-minded people to any verse unless the three criteria referred to above are taken into consideration.

Education in Discernment

Education in religion should embrace all four ways of knowing and their associated criteria in the teaching of skills of discernment. Translated into simple enough language and with concrete examples close to children's experience, such skills can and should be communicated to quite young children.[34]

Regarding the fundamental difference in unprovable starting point between religious people and secularists, the way forward is the way of dialogue. This offers the secularist, as much as the religious person, a way of avoiding dogmatism whilst holding on to the integrity of one's own commitment. In this respect it is important to note that the same quality of openness towards religion needs to be practised by secularists as that summarised by Yasmin Alibhai-Brown when she told how her mother brought her up to believe: "There is one God, but there are different roads to that one God. We have got one; other people have got others. Never look down on other people's faith."[35]

A pluralist world has to find creative ways of including controversy that is of accepting that we all do think differently, without this collapsing into relativism. Proper attention paid to criteria for discernment in a spirit of dialogue may facilitate this. The problems of dialogue are enormous, but as Peter Mitchell writing in 1994 noted prophetically: "In an age of balancing nuclear terror, the difficulties of dialogue seem better than the carnage of conflict."[36] Ability to take part in such dialogue should be the outcome of education in religion.

---

34 See, e.g., Elizabeth Ashton, *Religious Education in the Early Years* (London: Routledge, 2000).
35 Alibhai-Brown. "All Due Respect," 18.
36 Mitchell. P., "Can Education Have a Religious Foundation Today?" in *Religion and Education*, eds. Ashraf and Hirst, 28.

Bibliography

Alibhai-Brown, Yasmin. "All Due Respect." *Third Way*, November 2001, 18-22. https://books.google.co.uk/books?id=qFVE-VUDiB4C&pg=PA18&dq=%22richard+wilkins+talks+to+yasmin+alibhai-brown+mbe%22&hl=en&sa=X&ved=0ahUKEwiJvc6isOPLAhWJbBoKHb7lAqEQ6AEIHTAA#v=onepage&q=%22richard%20wilkins%20talks%20to%20yasmin%20alibhai-brown%20mbe%22&f=false.

Appleby, Joyce, Margaret Jacob, and Lynn Hunt. *Telling the Truth about History*. New York: Norton, 1994.

Ashraf, Syed Ali. "Islamic Education and Moral-Development." In *Religion and Education: Islamic and Christian Approaches*, edited by Syed Ali Ashraf and Paul H. Hirst, (142-158). Cambridge: Islamic Academy, 1994.

Ashton, Elizabeth. *Religious Education in the Early Years*. London: Routledge, 2000.

Askari, Hasan. "Can Education Have a Religious Foundation Today? An Islamic Approach." In *Religion and Education: Islamic and Christian Approaches*, edited by Syed Ali Ashraf and Paul H. Hirst. Cambridge: Islamic Academy, 1994.

Bailey, Richard. "Overcoming Veriphobia—Learning to love truth again." *British Journal of Educational Studies* 49, no. 2 (June 2001): 159-72. https://doi.org/10.1111/1467-8527.t01-1-00169.

Burnett, Frances Hodgson. *The Secret Garden*. New York: F. A. Stokes, 1911.

Carroll, James. *Constantine's Sword: The Church and the Jews*. Boston: Houghton Mifflen Company, 2001.

Carson, Donald. A "Matthew." In *Expositor's Bible Commentary: Matthew-Luke*. Vol. 8, edited by Frank E. Gaebelein. Grand Rapids, MI: Zondervan, 1984.

Davies, Godfrey. *Oxford History of England: Early Stuarts 1603-1660*. Oxford: Oxford University Press, 1937.

Grierson, Herbert, and Geoffrey Bullough. *Oxford Book of Seventeenth Century Verse*. Oxford: Clarendon Press, 1934.

Herbert, George. "Love." *The Temple: Sacred Poems and Private Ejaculations*. Cambridge: Thomas Buck and Roger Daniel, 1633.

Kant, Immanuel. *Critique of Practical Reason*. Vol. 1.

Kierkegaard, Soren. "Concluding Unscientific Postscript." In *The Essential Kierkegaard*, edited by Howard V. Hong and Edna H. Hong, 187-246. Princeton, New Jersey: Princeton University Press, 1978.

Lewis, C. S. *The Great Divorce: A Dream*. London: Collins Fount, 1945.

Macintyre, Ben. "Bin Laden hijacks history for his holy war." *The Times*. October 27, 2001.

Marks, Leon. Letter to the editor. *The Times*. October 3, 2001.

Mitchell, P. "Can Education Have a Religious Foundation Today." In *Religion and Education: Islamic and Christian Approaches*, edited by Syed Ali Ashraf and Paul H. Hirst. Cambridge: Islamic Academy, 1994.

Petrovich, Olivera. "Postmodemity: Science points to God." *UPI*, May 4, 2001. 23rd instalment of the UPI series. https://www.upi.com/Archives/2001/05/04/Postmodernity-Science-points-to-God/5336988948800/.

Philips, J. B. *Your God Is Too Small*. London: Epworth Press, 1932.

Pierce, Charles Sanders. "Charles Sanders Pierce, *Collected Papers of Charles Sanders Peirce*. Vol. 1, *Principles of Philosophy and Elements of Logic*, edited by Charles Hartshorne and Paul Weiss. Cambridge, MA: Harvard University Press, 1931.

Rees-Mogg, William. "The fears that gave rise to this evil man." *The Times*. October 8, 2001.
Runciman, Steven. *A History of the Crusades*. Cambridge: CUP, 1966.
Sacks, Jonathan. "As the bombs fall, this is our greatest challenge." *The Times*, October 8, 2001.
Van De Weyer, Robert. *Islam and the West: A New Political and Religious Order Post September 11*. Hampshire: O Books Alresford, 2001.
Voltaire. *Le Sottisier de Voltaire*. Paris: Garnier Frères, 1880.
Watson, Brenda. "Evaluative RE? A response to two articles by Andrew Wright on Hermeneutics and Religious Understanding." *Journal of Beliefs and Values* 21, no. 1 (2000): 63-72. https://doi.org/10.1080/13617670050002336.
Watson, Brenda. *The Effective Teaching of Religious Education*. Harlow, Essex: Longman, 1993; 1999.
Williamson, Timothy. Preface to *Knowledge and Its Limits*. Oxford: Oxford University Press, 2000.
Wittgenstein, Ludwig. *Tractatus Logico-Philosophicus*. New York: Harcourt, Brace & Company and London: Kegan Paul, 1922.

Chapter 17

Islamisation and Higher Education: Syed Ali Ashraf and the Secular Consequences of Religious Ideas

Mujadad Zaman

The status held by knowledge in Islamic belief places it beyond the confines of epistemic inquiry, a tool for objective verity or invention merely. To limit knowledge in this way would be to make exiguous the free and munificent gift, a benefaction of the Divine, offered to humankind as a repose through which Divine communion is achieved.

It is thus unsurprising then that Islam, as a world religion, gives knowledge a place of honour, perhaps unparalleled by other faiths.[1] And yet its status equally belies a potential for destruction, if left untethered to the moral bounds bequeathed by God. Without due reverence then, it is a gift equally ruinous. In the Islamic scripture, the story of the Fall draws upon this theme wherein the two protagonists, Adam and Iblīs (Satan), both epitomize, damnation as well as the redemptive qualities of penitence, in their respective operations with knowledge. Iblīs sees his demise at the hands of an impertinence brought to bear by the haughty and ill use of knowledge. "I am better than he," says Iblīs in the great heavenly revolt and acts upon it by willfully dismissing the command of God to prostrate before Adam.[2] His words of rebellion are met with a non-act of compliance and for his betrayal, he stands as the maligned saint, the first Faust, who polished the mirror of his soul only to see himself.[3] His role is now bound to an existence to tempt and compromise humanity, he is the eternal tragedian, bound to what he hates. And for this treachery, he is

---

1 Franz Rosenthal, *Knowledge Triumphant: The Concept of Knowledge in Medieval Islam* (Leiden: Bril, 2007), 2.
2 Qurʾān 38:76; 18:50.
3 Maḥmūd Shabistarī, *Garden of Mystery: Gulshan-e Rāz of Mahmud Shabestari*, trans. Robert Abdul Hayy Darr (Cambridge: Archetype, 2007), 142.

given Divine reprieve yet without the promise of return.[4] Adam's fate, and the fate of his children, on the other hand, dawns the potential to be received once more into heavenly grace, on condition that moral and sacramental probities are kept, as did Adam in offering repentance to God. Iblīs is left in the wilderness of estrangement, damned by that which once gave him his honour. He is, as Milton describes, left cogitating on the tools of his destruction; upon the very nature of thought and knowledge itself:

> The mind is its own place, and in itself
> Can make a Heav'n of Hell, a Hell of Heav'n.
> What matter where, if I be still the same,
> And what I should be, all but less than he
> Whom thunder hath made greater?[5]

That the sentence of Iblīs was delivered on account of his use of knowledge is significant, since he laid claim to the dark impulses of the mind which made "heaven a hell for him," to rephrase Milton. The burden of knowledge is however, not Iblīs' alone. Questions regarding the nature of knowledge, its definitions, use, value and moral demands are the perennial ventures of human intellectual endeavour. Evidence of this remains that such queries about knowledge and its nature are, in one way or another, amongst the most onerous questions facing humanity in the 21st century.[6] In the context of Islamic discourses over knowledge, in recent history, they have been addressed not least through the "Islamisation of Knowledge" thesis and its corollary musings on the nature of education.[7] The thesis, a concatenation of ideas on knowledge and education, appeared in the light of the preponderance of modern secularity, with an aim to offer ways for Muslims to think upon and practise education authentically according to Islam's normative beliefs and values. Appearing as a consequence of the First World Conference on Muslim Education in 1977,[8] the Islamisation of knowledge and its influence over the past half century remain amongst the most noted contributions of its kind. And whilst the landscape has shifted since the days of the first conference, it stands in many ways, as a Kuhnian moment for many Muslim intellectuals, a theorisation of Islamic education which could work outside the traditional centers of learning

---

4 Qurʾān 15:36.
5 John Milton, *Paradise Lost* (London: Penguin, 2014), Book I, lines 254–258.
6 Nico Stehr and Bernd Weiler, eds., *Who Owns Knowledge? Knowledge and the Law* (New Brunswick: Transaction Publishers, 2008), 17–24.
7 Amy Kind and Peter Kung, eds., *Knowledge Through Imagination* (Oxford: Oxford University Press, 2016), 1–40.
8 Shaikh Abdul Mabud, "World Conferences on Muslim Education: Shaping the Agenda of Muslim Education in the Future," in *Philosophies of Islamic Education: Historical Perspectives and Emerging Discourses*, eds. Nadeem A. Memon, and Mujadad Zaman (New York: Routledge, 2016), 130.

within the Muslim world. Whilst its metabolism has held together less well, being repudiated much in common chorus with a critique of its philosophical foundations, a final adjudication on the theory is only as valuable once measured by being amongst the first attempts at producing a "big theory" on the subject. In this light, the present chapter ruminates, using such a proviso, to consider the theory and work of, arguably one of its most articulate adherents, Syed Ali Ashraf, to reckon his oeuvre as against the contemporary philosophical discourses and critique within the wider spectrum of academic discontent surrounding education. Far from judging the verity of the Islamisation thesis through his works, we shall take Ashraf's oeuvre as part of a continuing and persistent trend of critique within higher education today. This chapter therefore considers not only the specific details and individual merits of the Islamisation of education, as rendered through the works of Ashraf, but also uses it as a means through which to explore contemporary debates in the philosophy of education. There are three issues which are prevalent in the literature and open problems in the fundamental issues facing education, specifically, the university today. These are firstly, a conception of humankind, student-teacher relations and finally debates over the ends of education. In all these cases, we will discuss what and how Ashraf's ideas may offer, specifically how religious ideas may converse with and find a home in secular institutions of learning.

Arbitrating Islamic Education

The work of Ashraf represents, in due measure to the intellectual locale of its time, a desire amongst some 20th century Muslim intellectuals, for a revision of secular social norms whose ontological pervasiveness had, up until that point, obviated the articulation of a sacred, and thus authentic in their estimation, conception of the faith.[9] Vindication through scripture and use of historical precedent to enunciate the values of Islam, would thus enable a fullness of human identity and eudemonic ends envisaged by religion.[10] It is in this sense, that history stands as a figure which is to be 'dealt' with specifically, since modernity offers a radical transference wherein humankind is alienated from its own sense of self.[11] The great hope being that the ability to harness

---

9   Abdullah Saeed, "Fazlur Rahman: A Framework for Interpreting the Ethico-legal Content of the Qurʾan," in *Modern Muslim Intellectuals and the Qurʾan*, ed. Suha Taji-Farouki (Oxford: Oxford University Press, 2006), 37–66.
10 Such ideas fall within the great many scopes of academic study. Where Ashraf intersects specifically within this context is via his fellow collaborators from the First World Conference on Muslim Education in 1977 (Mecca); amongst prominent of these figures being Seyyed Hossein Nasr. For an account of these ideas see Seyyed Hossein Nasr, *Traditional Islam in the Modern World* (London: Kegan Paul International Ltd., 1987); Seyyed Hossein Nasr, *The Need for a Sacred Science* (New York: SUNY Press, 1993).
11 Thinking on the nature of history, as a subject of the modern, is not however uncommon

the convictions born from the authority of scripture, the prophetic manner (*sunnah*) and the consequent intellectual heritage of Islam will help to reorientate one in the tumult of modernity's sway.[12] The First World Conference on Muslim Education in 1977 was a site of such intention namely, to explicate an Islamic vision of Islamic knowledge and education as well as to, and importantly, expostulate the evitable problems of modern world. Thus, Ashraf contemplating on his contribution to the conference explains:

> I criticised the modern education system because it is based on a concept of human nature which does not recognise the human spirit and its relationship with God and thereby eliminates the possibility of revelations and God-given knowledge and guidance for mankind. It is also based on a worldview that propagates the concept of society producing values and thereby creating a tradition of values and a tradition of the evolution of values. This worldview is fundamentally of this world and hence it does not rouse in the pupils' mind the slightest consciousness of life after death. It is difficult to keep religious consciousness alive in the hearts of children when all branches of knowledge are dominated by such a view of life and when teachers are expected not to teach from the religious point of view. . . . I therefore suggested and the scholars at the First World Conference agreed to recommend that research should be carried out to replace the secularist concepts at the roots of all branches of knowledge by concepts drawn from the Islamic frame of life and values as found in the Qurʾān and the Sunnah [Prophetic example].[13]

This ontological bearing, outlined above, is communed with an epistemic conjunction for Ashraf, wherein discursive knowledge creation is harnessed by the reception of, and deportment towards, Divine knowledge. In bearing up on these rudiments of intellectual thought and activity, the Islamisation of knowledge promulgates a kind of cautious renewal of these ideas in conjunction with the demands of the modern world. Its features in this regard can be surmised as (a) a trenchant critique of modernity,[14] (b) reacquainting

---

and restrained to modernity's perturbations. A parallel tradition is found in the development of early modern philosophy in Indo-Islamic scholarship. Jonardon Ganeri, *The Lost Age of Reason: Philosophy in Early Modern India 1450-1700* (Oxford: Oxford University Press, 2014), 117–162.

12 For an earlier 20th century account of such intellectual confrontations with modernity, Leor Halevi, *Modern Things on Trial: Islam's Global and Material Reformation in the Age of Rida, 1865-1935* (New York: Columbia University Press, 2021), 7–30, 251–266.

13 Mabud, "World Conferences on Muslim Education," 131-32.

14 Such debates are to be found elsewhere and evident in the discourses of the time of Ashraf. R. S. Peters argues in the *Education and the Education of Teachers* (1977) that "With the coming of industrialism, however, and the increasing demand for knowledge and skill consequent on it, 'education' became increasingly associated with 'schooling' and

the metaphysical and historical values of Islam, (c) forging disciplinary unity with a conception of knowledge, and (d) conceiving knowledge, learning, and praxis as the moral embodiment of education, necessary for an ethical vista of life.[15] In Ashraf's rendition of the hypothesis we may state as bearing a 'strong' version of the theory since he argues that "This challenge [creating Islamic conceptions of education] is now one for modern intellectuals. It is this new intellectual class which guides and governs the minds of younger generations. Therefore educational reform is necessary. This is not just the reform of basic concepts of sociology, economics, political science, ... but a rewriting of textbooks on the basis of Islamic concepts. It is a gigantic task."[16]

Of the works authored by Husain and Ashraf, *Crisis in Muslim Education*, arguably stands as a compendious illustration of Islamisation written in large part for educators, intellectuals, policy makers, and the general reading audience, to articulate the breadth of the problem. Published in 1979, its popularity amongst Muslim audiences cannot be underestimated and along with the works of other notable theorists of Islamic education at this time, it set in motion an influential critique of western learning. In the work, Ashraf's tone is nonconciliatory and yet sympathetic. It argues for lapses faced by the global Muslim community; the lapses of colonialism, and the dredging of traditional institutions and life, left anemic from the preponderance of modernity's schizophrenic mien towards deliverance from the past and yet unknowing the present.[17] In the light of such disarray, Ashraf approaches the dilemma with the same reliance on traditional Islamic belief and values that are evident throughout his oeuvre. And thus, his condensing of the matter into a polarity of educational options for the Muslim community to cogitate upon and confront helps crystalize his position:

> There are at present two systems of education. The first, traditional, which has confined itself to classical knowledge, has not shown any keen interest in new branches of knowledge that have emerged in the

---

with the sort of training and instruction that went on in special institutions. This large-scale change, culminating in the development of compulsory schooling for all, may well have brought about such a radical conceptual tightening up that we now tend to use the word only in connection with the development of knowledge and understanding. We distinguish now between 'training' and 'education,' whereas previously people did not." R. S. Peters, "Education and the Educated Man," *Journal of Philosophy of Education* 4, no. 1 (January 1970): 8.

15 Syed Muhammad Naquib al-Attas, *Islam and Secularism* (Kuala Lumpur: ISTAC, 1993); Hasan Dzilo, "The Concept of 'Islamization of Knowledge' and its Philosophical Implications," *Islam and Christian-Muslim Relations* 23, no. 3 (2012): 247-256.
16 Syed Sajjad Husain and Syed Ali Ashraf, introduction to *Crisis in Muslim Education* (Kent, UK: Hodder and Stoughton, and Jeddah: King Abdulaziz University, 1979), 4.
17 A similar critique is made by a number of social critics in this period as well as of modernity more generally. Cf. Zygmunt Bauman, *Intimations of Postmodernity* (New York: Routledge, 1992), 26-67.

West nor in new methods of acquiring knowledge important in the Western system of education. ... The second system of education imported into Muslim countries, fully subscribed to and supported by all governmental authorities, is one borrowed from the West. At the head of this system is the modern University which is totally secular and hence non-religious in its approach to knowledge.[18]

The "solution"[19] here is that the "creation of a third system, embracing an integrated system of education, is necessary but integration is not an easy process."[20] Ashraf's work is then a commentary on the necessary uneasiness of this endeavour. Since there is an understanding that the manner and contours of modernity's secular manifestation, with the pageantry of secular worldviews, willfully hinder our ability for self-actualization, a reclamation of traditional Islamic ideals is itself an exceedingly difficult task.

Despite the intellectual effort, judging the *influence* or *impact* of Ashraf is equally difficult since it has spawned as a lasting rumination on Islam and education in the modern world. And in this sense, his influence has been a powerful and prevailing presence in the intellectual market of ideas available and used, critiqued in equal measure by Muslim intellectuals since. Therefore, the work of Ashraf and others must be nominated as amongst the first apparent coordinated attempt at the incredulous task of intellectually confronting educational dilemmas in the 20th century and beyond. Niyozov and Memon summarize these contributions:

> Without examining Islamization it is not possible to understand modern Islamic education as a discipline. Islamization is not a minor filtering or gate keeping conduit: it is a broad-based, diverse and evolving epistemological, ontological, and pedagogical strategy that aims to counteract not just Western and secular, but also any other non-Western, and in some cases, not-so-proper-Muslim encroaches into Muslim psyche and society. Islamization is an alternative paradigmatic endeavor: it is based on the premise that all knowledge can and need to be understood from within an Islamic worldview.[21]

---

18 Husain and Ashraf, *Crisis in Muslim Education*, 16–17.
19 Ashraf's statement here should not be seen as merely an eradication of the problem, such that modernity can merely be done away with and its globalized interconnectedness. Rather drawing on its operative use, it pertains to sensibilities towards an Islamic mien which may become a source of relief for the situation, which is itself, as Ashraf admits, "not an easy process."
20 Husain and Ashraf, *Crisis in Muslim Education*, 17.
21 Sarfaroz Niyozov and Nadeem Memon, "Islamic Education and Islamization: Evolution of Themes, Continuities and New Directions," *Journal of Muslim Minority Affairs* 31, no. 1 (2011): 14.

Ashraf and the Tenor of Modern Educational Critique

The contemporary University stands as amongst the most significant and arguably successful institutions whose medieval heritage has made a comfortable home within the contemporary landscapes of modern life. Amongst the successes of the institution has been its significance in economic sustainability, national prestige, individual well-being, etc. The ubiquitous presence of the modern University attracts, however, both laudation and discontent. It seems evident that as the institution has gained prominence, it has come under greater scrutiny and social critique.[22] This is in part due to its operations within a "fragile" society in that modern life is determined by instability and a "fluid" mien which the institution itself cannot escape.[23] These critiques range from the utilization of the academic profession, the rise of neo-liberal values in the administrative culture of the institution, to the increasing demands placed upon academics to serve, what seems, an never ending list of demands.[24] As an accumulated assemblage of censorious accounts, they inform us of perhaps something lying at the foci of the institution itself. This is intimated by Hanna Holborn Gray's 2009 *Clark Kerr Lectures* who, quoting Laurence Veysey's superlative account of the rise of the American University in the late 19th century (*History of the American University*), stresses that as contemporary universities become "more intensely competitive ... they have become more standardized, less original, less fluid."[25] The rise of such intellectual critique of the university's intellectual space, whilst not historically uncommon,[26] is nonetheless significant in regard to its tenor and arguably points towards a

---

22 Consider the increasing and varied forms of critique levied at the institution which belies its normative values of intellectual freedom. Stefan Collini makes this clear in his estimation of working conditions of academics, "The experience of being a senior academic now ... may seem to more closely resemble that of being a middle-rank executive in a business organization than it does that of being an independent scholar or freelance teacher, while the conditions of work of junior and temporary staff in some unfavourable institutions may ... suggest comparisons with those of staff in a call centre." Stefan Collini, *What Are Universities For?* (New York: Penguin, 2012), 19.
23 Zygmunt Bauman, *Liquid Modernity*, (Cambridge: Polity, 2000), 5–9.
24 Such critique forms part of a "crisis literature" in educational studies which comments upon many of such developments. Bill Readings, *The University in Ruins* (Cambridge, Massachusetts: Harvard University Press, 1997); Julie A. Reuben, *The Making of the Modern University: Intellectual Transformation and the Marginalization of Morality* (London: Chicago University Press, 1996); Michael S. Roth, *Beyond the University: Why Liberal Education Matters* (New Haven: Yale University Press, 2015).
25 Hanna Holborn Gray, *Searching for Utopia: Universities and the Their Histories* (The Clark Kerr Lectures on the Role of Higher Education in Society) (London: University of California Press, 2012), 79.
26 Of particular interest here is the *Carmina Burana* dated to the 13th century, serves as a vital and vibrant account of early academic life during of the rise of the universities in the Latin West. Cf. Robert S. Rait, *Life in the Medieval University* (Cambridge: Cambridge University Press, 2012), 13–40.

superintendent castigation of the institution. This we may entitle as a "problem of the imagination" wherein, if taking these critiques cumulatively, they point towards misgivings of how and why we create knowledge belying the workings of academic imagination itself.[27] Peter Murphy, a prominent contemporary theorist of institutional imagination, takes the position further by contending that the university has failed to deliver on its promise of being imaginative and innovative in the modern "Knowledge Society." He summarises his position by arguing:

> The promise of post-industrialism was innovation. The primary cause of modern economic growth, the theory went, was innovation. Innovation is the social application of the power of creation. Modern societies that lack the capacity for creation struggle socially and flounder economically. The theory was not wrong. The extended economic stagnation in many OECD countries that follow 2008 was a symptom of depressed innovation. But this despondent state pointed to a deeper problem: namely that the post-industrial "knowledge society" ... *had stopped innovating on a large scale* – or rather it has never lived up to its self-image as an innovating epoch ... The university was the symbolic core of the post-modern age. It embodied its desires. It presented its aspirations. It was emblematic of the knowledge and infliction that, supposedly, elicited the technological and sociological innovations that energised economies and enlarged social prosperity ... *Yet in reality growth, prosperity and ideas proved to be much scarcer than in the industrial age.*[28]

The notion that imagination itself lies at the fulcrum of the construction of knowledge is not uncommon and is an idea more recently revived in the philosophy of mind.[29] However, its relationship to knowledge and the university remains relatively unexplored and partly at the detriment of that institution. In the present context, to infer that the university has an imagination problem refers not to the proliferation of information, access to knowledge or the production of academic work, nor the decline of 'good' ideas necessarily. The production of academic research and its dissemination are rather consequences of intellectual creativity, derived from the increasing competitiveness of modern scholarship, pressures of funding and academic review, the rise of audit cultures within universities etc. The problem of imagination refers rather to a situation in which the institution is growing globally, in myriad ways, and

---

27 Tom Nichols, *The Death of Expertise: The Campaign against Established Knowledge and Why it Matters* (Oxford: Oxford University Press, 2017), 70–104.
28 Peter Murphy, *Universities and Innovation Economies: The Creative Wasteland of Post-Industrial Society* (Abingdon: Routledge, 2015), 1, italics added.
29 Kind and Kung, *Knowledge Through Imagination*, 1–40.

becoming ever important to the intellectual, social and economic well-being of modern nations, and is equally coming under ever critique, from both those within and outside its walls. The "problem of imagination" is then an accumulative statement of these developments which find their consequences in, and not limited to, how academics think about and produce knowledge, questions over the purpose of education and the ultimate meaning of the actualized individual etc. If there is a problem of imagination, born out of the modern university, perhaps an unlikely philosophy of education we may call upon can be found in the work of Ashraf. A question then remains, is what then are the potential secular consequences of religious ideas?

Whereto Islamisation?

What the ruminations of an Islamic thinker such as Ashraf bequeath these critiques is not at first evident. To speak from what may seem an insular and redundant call towards a medievalism or limpid revivalism of Islamic epistemic ideas, in which the values and ideas of Islamic civilization are at once propitious for the circumstances of our world today, seems premature. In this sense it is a critique which marks itself off and away from more compatibilist trends found elsewhere in the discussion of religious offerings within a secular view of the world. The strength and legacy of the Islamisation thesis may lie then not only in its potential implementation but also as an aggregate of critiques housing a superordinate account of knowledge, learning and self-actualization within the parameters of modernity. To take this stance allows, firstly, for it to be considered as an initial and prominent offering of the role of Islamic education in a world where much of these ideas had been lost in the West (or rather were not considered). Secondly, its presence in a broader historical critique of modernity and finally, the unexpected parlance it has with the issues of the university—that match the criticisms of the academic world more generally. It is in this later incarnation of the thesis namely, the secular consequences of religious sentiments which may potentially, and unexpectedly, foment new uses of Ashraf's ideas.

Whilst the contemporary critique literature of education is diametrically distanced from a theocentric restoration of learning, there are certain concatenations between what is proposed by Ashraf and the critiques of the modern 21st century university. It is what George Steiner eloquently terms the "nostalgia for the Absolute"[30] in that it is the filling of the void left in the wake of grand narratives (such as religion, art, mythology etc.) whose retreat from social life does not elide their social yearning. In this sense, Islam, as a kind of counterbalance, offers an antipodal case, since as a world religion it does not seem to have succumbed, in the same manner, the same fate as other religions.

---

30 George Steiner, *Nostalgia for the Absolute (The CBC Massey Lectures)* (Scarborough: House of Anansi Press, 1997), 1–11.

In regard to the secular West and its global influence, problems which have emerged from the undergrowth and lay claim to Ashraf's desire to urge and make incandescent Islam's import to modern life.

> The problem for Muslims is therefore far more complex than the problem of substituting secularist concepts by Islamic concepts drawn from the *Qurʾān* and the *Sunnah*. Already large-scale modernization is going on in all Muslim countries. This modernization of environment is inevitably coupled with some form of mechanization and, where possible, with industrialization. Even countries ill-equipped to afford it are compelled to industrialize and welcome technology. Can education preserve and transmit orthodoxy through those Islamic concepts that we are expecting scholars to formulate, even when the environment, including its society, has been modernized and technology is creating a technological mentality?[31]

Where the means of "transmitting orthodoxy" are no longer guaranteed by the governance which legitimates their existence, there is a growing interest concerning the role of religion in education.[32] Much of the contemporary literature on the modern university, its purpose or "idea," bear upon stolid critiques of its inability to forge an identity outside the long gaze of the Knowledge Economy. The theologian Mike Higton for example, synthesises Christian values operating within a secular educational arena suggesting a typification of the latter, in which the necessary views of religious leanings are made necessary to speak to spiritual ideals of education and the semblance or balance it may provide.[33] Whether such attempts at rapport with the modern secularity of the university are tenable is not guaranteed however. Intimating a desire and acknowledging the challenge of such an endeavour, academic reflections on the university ingress their way to the elemental nodes of what education is. And in this regard, Ashraf's considerations are propitious, not least being shared in some insignificant degree by many such theorists. For Ashraf this specifically means that education serves to instil and promulgate "the sensibility of pupils in such a manner that in their attitude to life, their actions, decisions and approach to all kinds of knowledge, they are governed

---

31 Syed Ali Ashraf, *New Horizons in Muslim Education* (Kent, UK: Hodder and Stoughton, and Cambridge: The Islamic Academy, 1985), 12.
32 The role of religion in the university remains a consistently lively area of discussion specifically as it potentially commends interests in a broader vision for the scope of intellectual inquiry and the commensurability of the institution to host paradisciplinary meanings for education. See Jon H. Roberts, and James Turner, eds., *The Sacred and the Secular University* (Princeton: Princeton University Press, 2000); C. John Sommerville, *The Decline of the Secular University* (Oxford: Oxford University Press, 2006).
33 Mike Higton, *A Theology of Higher Education* (Oxford: Oxford University Press, 2012), 143–170.

by the spiritual and deeply felt ethical values of Islam."[34] Our present concern is considering three such elements wherein Ashraf's ideas are particularly indicative of contemporary discourse and serves fecund means of ameliorating those discourses. These being firstly, the ontology of humankind's existence, conceptualizing the essential pedagogic encounter between teacher and student and finally, the ends of education.

'Humankind' as the Presupposition of Education

All education presupposes, whether consciously articulated or otherwise, a conception of the human being and their place within being. Often manifest at an oblique angle through the curriculum or otherwise, it is the articulation of questions which pertain to the presuppositions of how, why and what education ought to be and render the innate capabilities of the individual in due accord with those ideas.[35] To the extent that without such conceptions, equally we may argue, it is impossible to educate, as education invariably presumes a knowledge of the self. Whether offered by religion, philosophy, culture etc., contemporary education, argues Ashraf, seeks to exploit the conception of man as a secularly rational, individually motivated and evolutionary superior being. As an existential marker, this conception of secular man helps to breathe life into a curriculum which is equally invested in its pursuits and diminutive notions of worldly success. In this regard, Ashraf will argue that:

> Believing as it does that the true aim of education is to produce men who have faith as well as knowledge, the one sustaining the other, Islam does not think that the pursuit of knowledge by itself without reference to the spiritual goal that man must try to attain, can do humanity much good. Knowledge divorced from faith is not only partial knowledge, it can even be described as a kind of new ignorance. The man who has lost his faith in God is not recognized by Islam as a man whose knowledge can be described as deep.[36]

In this sense, the merger of ethics and epistemology, between virtue and learning, whilst a natural alliance for conceptions of Islamic education, is almost entirely devoid of importance in today's education for Ashraf. His account alternatively mirrors the moral accrual of moral virtues through learn-

---

34 Husain and Ashraf, *Crisis in Muslim Education*, 1. Cf. R. S. Peters, *Education and the Education of Teachers* (London: Routledge, 2010), fn. 12.
35 In the conception of learning from the medieval Latin West, we find a useful example from the encyclopedic work *Hortus Decliarium* as an allegoric representation helping situate the learner within the spectrum of the knowledge. In particular, see picture 'The Seven Liberal Arts' (*Philosophia et septem Artes Lierales. Hortus Deliciarum: Seven Liberal Arts (folio 32r)* German Manuscript ca. 1170 CE Strasbourg (now destroyed), accessed March 8, 2021, https://www2.oberlin.edu/images/Art310/10624.JPG.
36 Husain and Ashraf, *Crisis in Muslim Education*, 37–38.

ing as is the case with a great number of pre-modern cultures.[37] However, judgements on the "depth" of knowledge which discords its union with faith does not necessarily have to mean religious faith (as is Ashraf's primary motivation here) but rather the extoling of faith in whose incandescence the venture of learning is illuminated. But modern (secular) learning is faced with a problem of harnessing faith in regard to the shifting certainties of modernity. In this sense, the edifice of the modern university is set upon the values of faith in reason, the individual spirit, certainty in the scientific method etc. Yet, questions remain however, as to how we may continue in laudation of such secular "articles of faith" when indeed their certainties are being ever challenged, and in unprecedented ways. If we may extend Ashraf's idea to give voice to contemporary discontents in the philosophy of science, it seems evident that certainty in the expectations of scientific knowledge is increasingly under threat.[38] The philosopher of science, Steve Fuller, echoing the problems of the modern ecological rift humanity faces and its relevance in modern academic life, conceives of a reversal of what he calls a "Karmic" vision of humanity towards an "Anthropic" conception of human life, marked by the legacy of the Abrahamic traditions. In the latter, he argues, there is a greater concordance with conceptions of human life and nature since

> The challenge comes not from science per se, but from an elective affinity between Neo-Darwinian science, biotechnology, and the three "karmic" religions, Hinduism, Buddhism, and Jainism. The basis of this affinity, which I call Karmic Darwinism, would reduce the difference between humans and other life forms, thereby minimizing the significance of humanity's place in nature.[39]

Fuller continues, arguing that:

Redressing the balance in favour of the anthropic perspective means breathing new life into the idea of human progress. But this will require taking the closeness of humans to God more seriously than many currently seem prepared to do. Monotheists have been protective of the sanctity of human life, and hence have traditionally opposed suicide, euthanasia, and abortion, while the secular descendants in bio-

---

[37] This is paralleled in ancient Judaic conception of wisdom as is evident here. The pedagogical tools were similarly given to embody the student as one who has gained understanding (lit. to know). This "knower of knowledge" is partly what is being mirrored in the Islamic conception of formal education. James L. Kugel, "Ancient Israelite Pedagogy and its Survival in Second Temple Interpretations of Scripture," in *Pedagogy in Ancient Judaism and Early Christianity*, eds. K. Martin Hogan, M. Goff, and E. Wasserman (SBL Press: Atlanta 2017), 16–18.

[38] Martin Rees, *Our Final Century* (New Hampshire: Arrow, 2003).

[39] Steve Fuller, "Karmic Darwinism: The Emerging Alliance Between Science and Religion," *Tijdschrift voor Filosofie* 64, no. 4 (2002): 697.

medicine have struggled to delay the moment of death as long as possible.[40]

Thinkers such as Fuller and their critique (and potential abjuration of orthodox ideas of humanity) are useful as an exploration of contemporary thinking in academia, and whilst they do not intend to redeem religious sensibilities or a theocentric vision of life, they call to unresolved questions which lie at the foundations of the modern university, articulating, at least in a broad sense, what it means to be human. Here again, we see the relevance of Ashraf as being part of a critique which sees the valuation of humanity, drawn from both physical and metaphysical plains, as necessary to the conception and inculcation of education. It seems, at least in the arena of social thought and the rise of AI theory, rising ecological threats, etc., that such questions are ever apropos.

Student and Teacher Relations

While Ashraf recognizes the pervasiveness of a secular *nomos* dominating the vista of modern social life its power, he ruminates, can however be limited by the Muslim imagination through the careful introspection of "simple" acts and ideas of education and learning.[41] That educational relations should be harnessed, which ennoble both the teacher and the student, anchor much of his ideas on pedagogy, and are key to segueing from secularity. In Ashraf's pronouncements on the matter, there ought to be an interpersonal relationship which harkens to a traditional premodern Islamic mien wherein the teacher acts as a moral persona; a maestro conducting the very elements of pedagogical exercise essential for the development of the student. He argues further for the idea of the teacher as a nurturer (*murabbi*) of human capabilities and potentials:

> For this reason in Islam the teacher was required not only to be a man of learning but also to be a person of virtue, a pious man whose conduct by itself could have an impact upon the minds of the young. It was not only what he taught that mattered; what he did, the way he conducted himself, his deportment in class and outside, were all expected to conform to an ideal which his pupils could unhesitatingly accept.[42]

Such an assessment of the teacher is one which nominates an entirely positive, as well as essential, repose to the teacher who can harness and nurture the innate capabilities of the student. The teacher, as the Prophet of Islam is considered in Islamic belief, is an indispensable guide to the self-realization

---

40 Fuller, "Karmic Darwinism," 697.
41 Ashraf, *New Horizons*, 82.
42 Husain and Ashraf, *Crisis in Muslim Education*, 104.

of the learner. Again, whilst Ashraf's assessment is not unique, it certainly remains a perceptible and continuing presence in the ideas and analysis of educational thought. For example, an earlier exploration of this idea in modern social theory is continued by Émile Durkheim who (re)introduces the importance of the moral quality of the teacher into his sociology of education.[43] More recently, the extensive influence of John Hattie's quantitative analysis of factors governing student performance claims that it is the teacher who stands demonstratively as key to the success of students. Such research has helped to give to rise to, amongst other things, the importance of teacher training and teaching excellence.[44]

In terms of teaching methodology, an important contribution from Ashraf is the manner by which the individual teacher is also an epistemic gateway towards an understanding of how a consilience of knowledge may exist, which remains otherwise unstated. The teacher, in other words, brings to life that which is dormant and nascent in the landscape of knowledge.[45] This important idea is iterated in other contemporary arguments such as in the work of the philosopher Alasdair MacIntyre who, speaking of the modern university, similarly stresses the importance of the teacher in this regard, a vehicle for expositing truths:

> To whom then in such a University falls the task of integrating the various disciplines, of considering the bearing of each on the others, and of asking how each contributes to the overall understanding of the nature and order of things? The answer is "No one," but even this answer is misleading. There is no sense in the contemporary American University that there is such a task, that something that matters is being left undone. And so the very notion of the nature and order of things, of a single universe, different aspects of which are objects of inquiry for the various disciplines, but in such a way that each aspect needs to be related to each other, this notion no longer informs the enterprise of the contemporary American University. It has become an irrelevant concept.[46]

---

43 Émile Durkheim, *The Evolution of Educational Thought: Lectures on the Formation and Development of Secondary Education in France*, trans. Peter Collins (New York: Routledge, 2009), xviii.

44 See John Hattie, *Teachers Make a Difference, What is the Research Evidence?* (Australian Council for Educational Research (ACER), Melbourne, Australia: October 2003).

45 Similar ideas are expressed in educational thought regarding the teacher, often as a counter to the normative view of the instructor as a fairly dormant instrument in the pedological moment. For a counter view see Daisy Christodoulou, *Seven Myths About Education* (London: Routledge, 2014), 27–46.

46 Alasdair MacIntyre, *God, Philosophy, Universities: A Selective History of the Catholic Philosophical Tradition* (London: Rowman & Littlefield Publishers, 2009), 16.

Specifically, the importance of the teacher as mediator in the process of imparting a religious consciousness, catches the relevance of Ashraf in contemporary discourses since the brilliance of the instructor manages such expectations. Compare the following passage as an example of the teacher who extols the importance of metaphysical presuppositions to knowledge within learning to utilize its potential:

> Teachers are nowadays accustomed to regard each subject as an independent unit to be taught from the point of view generated in the West. Each subject has its own discipline, no doubt, but when from the theoretical point of view its basic ideas are at variance with Islam, we have to question the validity and adequacy of that branch of knowledge. All branches of knowledge acquired by man with the help of his own intellectual endeavours or through his own emotional experiences cannot but be partial in comparison with God-given knowledge.[47]

This 'strong' version of the Islamisation thesis inspires the pedagogic moment to respond to the demands of a secular world, in so far as knowledge has been delimited, for Ashraf, by secular overtures. Whilst there is no doubt that secular ideas are themselves antipodal to sacred ones, they can be mediated since in Ashraf's epistemic account there is no *a priori* distinction apparent in his philosophy of knowledge, since all knowledge is of Divine benefaction. This leads to secular disciplines as bearing a natural "neutrality" and reconcilable to theocentric priorities. It is therefore possible to argue, in the tussle between these grand cultures of knowledge that

> Two [secular and religious] systems should merge into one system provided the basic philosophical foundations are what we have already discussed and at the same time most of the religious subjects should exist for specialization. Each student should acquire all the basic knowledge required for a Muslim and this knowledge should be organized on the principles of continuity, sequence and integration and taught up to graduate level. But from the secondary level onwards students should be allowed to specialize in different higher branches of perennial knowledge till he or she reaches the university stage.[48]

This theory of knowledge, whether successful in the final assessment as grounding schooling, premises an Islamic liberal education and seeks to show how knowledge can be pursued by modern Muslims. The question of integration, and succession of historical ideas of the sacred in knowledge continue to be propitious in Muslim thought. Ashraf's account stands, again, not as a unique or even a first enunciation of Islamic values and educational theory

---

47 Ashraf, *New Horizons*, 42.
48 Ashraf, 45.

though one which opens a contextual misalignment that may occur in the seeking of such ends. It is then arguably both refreshingly open ended as well as consciously aware of the limitations to be found within specific national contexts and social proclivities that might hinder such ideas.

The Ends of Education

The final idea in Ashraf's work to be discussed as part of his legacy offers the reader to entertain Islamic education as fulfilling human potential *in toto*. How and why this is done stands as clear in Ashraf's thought namely, the acquisition and embodiment of knowledge such that education is a sacrament anticipating Divine benefaction. Placed in conversation with philosophical discourses, as they have emerged in the 20th and early 21st centuries, this chimes with discerning how the ends of learning accentuate innate potentials of an individual. However, this is perhaps not merely, as mentioned by George Steiner, a "nostalgia for the Absolute." Taking Ashraf's prescience for contemporary educational discourse, there is less "nostalgia" and more anxiety for clarity and substance as it concerns the ends of learning. This arguable failure of modern education, and higher education in particular, may well lie in that which is less obvious and nascent to the endeavour of all learning namely, that of the imagination. In his account of the modern university and its attitude to educating the minds of the young, Ron Barnett concludes that

> The contemporary debate of higher education is, then, both narrow *and* is marked by an insecurity about how we might move forward. We require, therefore, in the first place, a *proliferation* of ideas of the university, if only to begin to demonstrate that things could be other than they are. The imagination can be a powerful agent for opening up thinking and for freeing the university from its self-imposed conceptual shackles. And we require the boldest of ideas; ideas that are not "cabined, cribbed, confined."[49]

For Ashraf, this imagination is given breath through recalibration of the given *moment* between thought and action, between knowing and doing (ʿilm and ʿamal). In the absence of such melding of epistemic and moral values, a kind of stale humanism emerges which while still presumes universal values has no means to harvest its fruits. For Ashraf it is an alienating and alienated principle from which we begin the educational journey. Alasdair MacIntyre,[50]

---

49 Ronald Barnett, *Imagining the University* (London: Routledge, 2012), 5, italics in the original.
50 The importance of the ends of learning are also not lost within modern secular education and the desire conceiving the ends in human flourishing as necessarily revalued in world of neoliberal political reframing of our educational systems, in particular in the West.

in this regard, reflects upon this dissension within the landscape of the university today arguing that

> For by either limiting mention of God from the curriculum altogether ... or by restricting reference to God to departments of theology, such universities render their secular curriculum Godless. And this Godlessness is ... not just a matter of the subtracting of God from the range of objects studied, but also and quite as much the absence of any integrated and overall view of things.[51]

Continuing in the themes of this inquiry, the importance of philosophy as acting between the fissure of theological, social and scientific worldviews is ever important.

> The fragmentation of enquiry and the fragmentation of understanding are taken for granted. So that, if philosophy is to put them in question, as any theistic philosophy must, it must not only engage in distinctively different types of enquiry but provide those enquiries so far as it can, with a different type of academic setting.[52]

Commenting on the ends of education, Ashraf similarly mentions that "The values of adaptability, experimentation, and tolerance (as opposed to dogma) must be embedded in the new system. This will, in all probability require the institution of *ijtihad* or interpretation of the Islamic law."[53] Here the importance of setting comparisons between scholars such as Ashraf and MacIntyre helps shape the manner of the inquiry and which may grant the possibility which would make such grand integrative and porous discourses possible. Ashraf's reclamation of an Islamic tradition in this sense sets a precedent by its desire for educational clarity, for both the beginnings and ends of learning within modern secular contexts. Again, whilst it may be less productive to infer those ideas as solutions to the panoply of educational problems faced by Muslims, they are nonetheless to be viewed as rendering theoretical possibilities. It is then evident that whilst the broader theoretical scheme of the Islamisation of knowledge has fared less well through historical practice, there is nonetheless evidence to suggest that the recommendations in certain elements of the theorization still hold ground. Seyyed Hossein Nasr, being an early protagonist of these ideas, alongside Ashraf, argues that the formulation of smaller concentrated and rigorous training institutes has proven its flourishment with the rise of Muslim liberal colleges in the western hemisphere as well as in the Muslim world:

---

51 MacIntyre, *God, Philosophy, Universities*, 17.
52 MacIntyre, 18.
53 Husain and Ashraf, *Crisis in Muslim Education*, 46.

There is the possibility to create from scratch small centers of learning, not of the size of a large *madrasa* with ten thousand students, but small units of Islamic education operating at an intellectually advanced level and incorporating some nontraditional subjects that could be integrated into an Islamic system through the so-called 'Islamization' of knowledge. The concept of Islamization of knowledge is something that many, including myself, have been speaking about for fifty years and has involved so far mostly rhetoric with little actually being done as far as creating integrated Islamic educational systems are concerned. However, there are now attempts to implement here and there such ideas including in the US and in Iran; for example, there is a major movement to Islamize the humanities taught in universities; yet even there one does not, as yet, see many concrete results on a large scale.[54]

This could be extended to argue, though unconnected to the Islamisation debate, that the importance of indigenous and authentic accounts of religious knowledge and education have a place in modern education, as is evidenced by the contemporary rise of centers of Islamic Theology across mainland Europe as based in universities.[55] The development of such specialist institutions in the West, in particular, gives credence to the growth of Islamic institutional expressions of knowledge and flourishment. The most evident and lasting contribution of theorists such as Ashraf and Nasr, in this sense, is being amongst the first to articulate what would be and becomes an evident question within the conception and practice of Islamic education over the following thirty years, since the publication of their initial works. In this sense, it should be lauded as an authentic and indigenous articulation drawn from the native soil of Islamic thought, belief and practice into the mainstream discourses (and discontents) pertaining to education in the West.

Conclusions and Reclamations

The place and global stature of modern educational systems in the world has perhaps surpassed even the expectations of Ashraf and the generation of his co-collaborators, with its social prestige and borderless reach. Perhaps they would be more surprised by the fact that their critiques of western soci-

---

54 Seyyed Hossein Nasr, "Philosophical Considerations of Islamic Education—Past and Future: Interview with Seyyed Hossein Nasr," in *Philosophies of Islamic Education: Historical Perspectives and Emerging Discourses*, eds. Mujadad Zaman, and Nadeem Memon (New York: Routledge, 2019), 21.
55 Bekim Agai, and Armina Omerika, "Islamic Theological Studies in Germany: A Discipline in the Making," in *The Piety of Learning: Islamic Studies in Honor of Stefan Reichmuth*, eds. Michael Kemper, and Ralf Elger (Brill: Leiden, 2017).

ety, and late modernity more generally, would run in comity with the broader social appraisals of the late 20th century. Perhaps further is the serendipitous expectation of Ashraf's argument for Islamic education as mirrored, in their own refracted and oblique manner, with contemporary discontents with educational philosophy in the 21st century. Yet despite such relevance to contemporary discourses, the work of Ashraf stands above claims of commensurability since he very much veers his work towards ontological shores, directed by Islamic foundations. To argue then, as he does, that "Man has not become better a man by going to the Moon"[56] is the acknowledgement of secular man who stands as alien to Islam's conception of humanity, as any extraterrestrial. He raises the challenge of Muslim thinkers to dare and think beyond their circumstances in order to draw upon the great heritage of Islam and redeem its legacies for today.

Knowledge without humanity is in some ways Ashraf's incitement to reclaim that heritage and in so doing, forge a new rapprochement with the world of learning. As Wadad Kadi has shown, that historical mention of educational practice animates important philosophical constellations for us even today since "the differences between the *studia humanitatis* and the disciplines developed in Islamic civilization become narrower and the similarities significant. Leaving aside the religious disciplines, ... and concentrating on the non-religious disciplines, we note that the *studia humanitatis* fields thrived enormously in Islamic civilization."[57] These connections to a higher form of knowing, is in Ashraf's account, a call to better know ourselves in the light of scriptural guidance and embodiment of the Prophetic nobility (*sunnah*). In so doing, the melding of the "word" and "spirit" of religious life meet in the heart of the individual, whether as a mature master or nervous neophyte—the honour of knowledge is best rendered through an enlightened soul.

Bibliography

Agai, Bekim, and Armina Omerika. "Islamic Theological Studies in Germany: A Discipline in the Making." In *The Piety of Learning: Islamic Studies in Honor of Stefan Reichmuth*, edited by Michael Kemper, and Ralf Elger, 330–357. Brill: Leiden, 2017.

Ashraf, Syed Ali. *New Horizons in Muslim Education*. Kent, UK: Hodder and Stoughton, and Cambridge: The Islamic Academy, 1985.

---

56 Husain and Ashraf, *Crisis in Muslim Education*, 81.
57 Wadad Kadi, "The Humanities through Islamic Eyes: The Beginnings," in *Knowledge and Education in Classical Islam: Religious Learning between Continuity and Change*, edited by Sebastian Günther, 43–58. Brill: Leiden, 2020), 50.

Al-Attas, Syed Muhammad Naquib. *Islam and Secularism*. Kuala Lumpur: ISTAC, 1993.
Barnett, Ronald. *Imagining the University*. London: Routledge, 2012.
Bauman, Zygmunt. *Intimations of Postmodernity*. New York: Routledge, 1992.
Bauman, Zygmunt. *Liquid Modernity*. Cambridge: Polity, 2000.
Christodoulou, Daisy. *Seven Myths About Education*. London: Routledge, 2014.
Collini, Stefan. *What Are Universities For?* New York: Penguin, 2012.
Durkheim, Émile. *The Evolution of Educational Thought: Lectures on the Formation and Development of Secondary Education in France*. Translated by Peter Collins. New York: Routledge, 2009.
Dzilo, Hasan. "The Concept of 'Islamization of Knowledge' and its Philosophical Implications." *Islam and Christian-Muslim Relations* 23, no. 3 (2012): 247–256.
Fuller, Steve. "Karmic Darwinism: The Emerging Alliance Between Science and Religion." *Tijdschrift voor Filosofie* 64, no. 4 (2002): 697–722.
Ganeri, Jonardon. *The Lost Age of Reason: Philosophy in Early Modern India 1450-1700*. Oxford: Oxford University Press, 2014.
Gray, Hanna Holborn. *Searching for Utopia: Universities and the Their Histories (The Clark Kerr Lectures on the Role of Higher Education in Society)*. London: University of California Press, 2012.
Halevi, Leor. *Modern Things on Trial: Islam's Global and Material Reformation in the Age of Rida, 1865-1935*. New York: Columbia University Press, 2021.
Hattie, John. *Teachers Make a Difference, What is the Research Evidence?* Australian Council for Educational Research (ACER), Melbourne, Australia: October 2003, 1–17.
Higton, Mike. *A Theology of Higher Education*. Oxford: Oxford University Press, 2012.
Hortus Deliciarum, German Manuscript (folio 32r) ca. 1170 CE, Strasbourg, https://www2.oberlin.edu/images/Art310/10624.JPG.
Husain, Syed Sajjad, and Syed Ali Ashraf. *Crisis in Muslim Education*. Kent, UK: Hodder and Stoughton, and Jeddah: King Abdulaziz University, 1979.
Kadi, Wadad. "The Humanities through Islamic Eyes: The Beginnings." In *Knowledge and Education in Classical Islam: Religious Learning between Continuity and Change*, edited by Sebastian Günther, 43–58. Brill: Leiden, 2020.
Kind, Amy, and Peter Kung, eds. *Knowledge Through Imagination*. Oxford: Oxford University Press, 2016.
Kugel, James L. "Ancient Israelite Pedagogy and its Survival in Second Temple Interpretations of Scripture." In *Pedagogy in Ancient Judaism and Early Christianity*, edited by K. Martin Hogan, M. Goff, and E. Wasserman, 15–58. SBL Press: Atlanta, 2017.
Mabud, Shaikh Abdul. "World Conferences on Muslim Education: Shaping the Agenda of Muslim Education in the Future." In *Philosophies of Islamic Education: Historical Perspectives and Emerging Discourses*, edited by Nadeem A. Memon and Mujadad Zaman, 129–43. New York: Routledge, 2016.
MacIntyre, Alasdair. *God, Philosophy, Universities: A Selective History of the Catholic Philosophical Tradition*. London: Rowman & Littlefield Publishers, 2009.
Milton, John. *Paradise Lost*. London: Penguin, 2014.

Murphy, Peter. *Universities and Innovation Economies: The Creative Wasteland of Post-Industrial Society.* Abingdon: Routledge, 2015.

Nasr, Seyyed Hossein. "Philosophical Considerations of Islamic Education—Past and Future: Interview with Seyyed Hossein Nasr." In *Philosophies of Islamic Education: Historical Perspectives and Emerging Discourses,* edited by Mujadad Zaman, and Nadeem Memon, 17–25. New York: Routledge, 2019.

Nasr, Seyyed Hossein. *Traditional Islam in the Modern World.* London: Kegan Paul International Ltd., 1987.

Nasr, Seyyed Hossein. *The Need for a Sacred Science.* New York: SUNY Press, 1993.

Nichols, Tom. *The Death of Expertise: The Campaign against Established Knowledge and Why it Matters.* Oxford: Oxford University Press, 2017.

Niyozov, Sarfaroz, and Nadeem Memon. "Islamic Education and Islamization: Evolution of Themes, Continuities and New Directions." *Journal of Muslim Minority Affairs* 31, no. 1 (2011): 5–30.

Parlett, David., *Selections from the 'Carmina Burana': A Verse Translation.* London: Penguin, 1996.

Peters, Richard Stanley. "Education and the Educated Man." *Journal of Philosophy of Education* 4, no. 1 (January 1970): 5–20. https://doi.org/10.1111/j.1467-9752.1970.tb00424.x.

Peters, Richard Stanley. *Education and the Education of Teachers.* London: Routledge, 1977.

Rait, Robert S. *Life in the Medieval University.* Cambridge: Cambridge University Press, 2012.

Readings, Bill. *The University in Ruins.* Cambridge, Massachusetts: Harvard University Press, 1997.

Rees, Martin. *Our Final Century.* New Hampshire: Arrow, 2003.

Reuben, Julie A. *The Making of the Modern University: Intellectual Transformation and the Marginalization of Morality.* London: Chicago University Press, 1996.

Roberts, Jon H., and James Turner, eds. *The Sacred and the Secular University.* New Haven: Princeton University Press, 2000.

Rosenthal, Franz. *Knowledge Triumphant: The Concept of Knowledge in Medieval Islam.* Leiden: Brill, 2007.

Roth, Michael S. *Beyond the University: Why Liberal Education Matters.* New Haven: Yale University Press, 2015.

Saeed, Abdullah. "Fazlur Rahman: A Framework for Interpreting the Ethico-legal Content of the Qurʾan." In *Modern Muslim Intellectuals and the Qurʾan,* edited by Suha Taji-Farouki, 37–66. Oxford: Oxford University Press, 2006.

Shabistarī, Maḥmūd. *Garden of Mystery: Gulshan-e Rāz of Mahmud Shabestari.* Translated by Robert Abdul Hayy Darr. Cambridge: Archetype, 2007.

Sommerville, C. John. *The Decline of the Secular University.* Oxford: Oxford University Press, 2006.

Stehr, Nico, and Bernd Weiler, eds. *Who Owns Knowledge? Knowledge and the Law.* New Brunswick: Transaction Publishers, 2008.

Steiner, George. *Nostalgia for the Absolute (The CBC Massey Lectures).* Scarborough: House of Anansi Press, 1997.

Chapter 18

Education of the Interior: Reflections on the Legacy of Syed Ali Ashraf[1]

Nadeem A. Memon

Introduction: Challenges to Islamic Education Renewal

This tribute to Syed Ali Ashraf begins with his deep concern over the loss of, what he called, "education of the interior." Ashraf's tireless contributions to the field of Islamic schooling were rooted in the need for moving beyond ritualistic religious studies, bifurcated curriculum, and an overemphasis of the mind over the spirit. Sadly, his concerns remain relevant today. This chapter offers a recounting of some of Ashraf's essential priorities for Islamic schools and then outlines three perspectives on Islamic schooling that extend his contributions.

Arguably the most common reference point for contemporary research on Islamic schooling is the First World Conference on Muslim Education held in Makkah, Saudi Arabia in 1977. This landmark conference and the notable series of conferences that followed have shaped the discourse on the aims of contemporary Islamic/Muslim education/schooling.[2] Whether referencing these conferences serves as an acknowledgement of an intellectual asset or as a point of departure, the fact remains that these conferences served as a catalyst in contemporary educational thought about teaching Islam, Islamization of higher education, and by virtue the aims and objectives of K-12 Islamic/Muslim schooling and education. Although the legacy of the late Syed Ali Ashraf extends beyond these conferences, they mark among the most no-

---

1 Sections of this paper have been published in Nadeem A Memon, "Islamic Pedagogy for Islamic Schools," in *Philosophy of Education*, ed. Kathy Hytten (New York: Oxford University Press, 2021).
2 Shaikh Abdul Mabud, "World Conferences on Muslim Education: Shaping the Agenda of Muslim Education in the Future," in *Philosophies of Islamic Education: Historical Perspectives and Emerging Discourses*, eds. Nadeem A. Memon and Mujadad Zaman (New York: Routledge, 2016), 129–43.

table contributions he left us. Ashraf played a significant role in convening the conferences but also in capturing the dialogue and recommendations forward through a series of publications that are so commonly referenced in contemporary research.[3]

Discussions in the world conferences largely emphasized Islamization of higher education but it was Ashraf's tireless efforts that transferred key ideas by the proponents of Islamization to make those ideas accessible and applicable at a primary and secondary school level. He also carried the heavy concern of Muslim students broadly acknowledging that no matter how much effort is put into Islamizing curriculum for K-12 Islamic schools the vast majority of Muslim students will continue attending public schools and hence attention must equally be focused there. For both systems—state and private—he emphasized the need for textbooks and syllabi to centre an Islamic worldview but equally acknowledged whole system concerns including a concern for teacher education, reconstructing curriculum, and assessment. Ashraf's contribution, albeit broad, left no leaf unturned.

Ashraf feared most the prevalence of a secular worldview, one where "education of the interior" is ignored and in the absence of any religious foundation. Ashraf, like Al-Attas and Nasr and other contemporaries of his age, emphasized the importance of an Islamic worldview—not merely appending Qurʾān and Ḥadīth to existing secular curricula. He defined Islamic education as "an education which trains the sensibility of pupils in such a manner that in their attitude to life, their actions, decisions and approach to all kinds of knowledge, they are governed by the spiritual and deeply felt ethical values of Islam."[4] In relation to Islamic education curriculum, Ashraf called for a new classification of knowledge, demarcated between (a) perennial knowledge derived from the canonical religious texts and (b) acquired knowledge that would include all other forms of knowledge yet presented in ways consistent with an Islamic worldview. He felt that such a curriculum had not been achieved to date because of the inability to reconcile such an approach with their adopted western liberal curriculum. These ideas reflected in many ways the essence of the Islamization of knowledge movement of his time in relation to school-based curriculum.

Ashraf also raised a scathing critique of the existing Islamic education curriculum of his time that remains by and large relevant today. He argued for instance that: (a) Islamic education leaves out the spirit and focuses far too heavily on ritual practice; (b) that "The present tendency to equalize all sub-

---

[3] Syed Sajjad Husain and Syed Ali Ashraf, *Crisis in Muslim Education* (1979); Syed Muhammad al-Naquib al-Attas, *Aims and Objectives of Islamic Education* (1979); Muhammad Hamid al-Afendi, and Nabi Ahmed Baloch, *Curriculum and Teacher Education* (1980). All these books were published by London: Hodder and Stoughton and Jeddah: King Abdulaziz University.

[4] Syed Sajjad Husain and Syed Ali Ashraf, introduction to *Crisis in Muslim Education*, 1–5.

jects in status and esteem" is problematic and that in a faith-centered school, the cultivation of faith must be the central preoccupation of the curriculum; (c) that there must be coherence across the curriculum, for example, teaching financial interest in Islamic Studies as being forbidden and then teaching that interest is essential to our global economy in economics classes gives students irreconcilable contradictory views; (d) "religious studies courses gradually become wider and wider in scope, range, and depth" but there is little attempt to organise courses, textbooks and teaching methods to enable students "to think for themselves about religion and build up within themselves powers of resistance to irreligious and disruptive forces" leading to the absence of clearly articulated outcomes; and (e) the need to consider the "mental development of children and the goal of education, in order to achieve continuity, sequence, and integration."[5] These five critiques remain important challenges to Islamic education curriculum and school renewal.

Teaching Islam: Current Challenges

Ashraf's call for curriculum renewal related to teaching Islam came from decades of commitment to British Islamic schools and collaborative efforts on supporting Muslim students in state schools. Granted much of his reflections and recommendations was based on professional experience and anecdotal evidence, his ideas reflected common sentiments among Western Muslim academics, educators, and parents concerned about the state of schooling for Muslim students. There is limited empirical research in the area of teaching Islam in schools but from what does exist, there remains striking consistencies with Ashraf's ideas. Recent studies about teaching Islamic Studies in Australian Islamic schools, for example, affirm the commonly presumed fear that students find the way Islam is taught disinteresting, irrelevant to their contexts, and dogmatic.[6] Studies of Muslim learners in state/public schools similarly found that Islam is being taught in ways that "does not represent their own experiences and interpretations of the faith."[7] Whether in private Islamic school settings or public schools where religion is discussed in humanities subjects, there exists a challenge of how Islam and Muslims are framed. One Australian Imam and current principal of one of the country's most established *madrasahs*, reflected on his own experience in an Islamic school and the current teaching of Islam in schools today:

---

[5] Syed Ali Ashraf, *New Horizons in Muslim Education* (London: Hodder and Stoughton and Cambridge: The Islamic Academy, 1985), 40–43.

[6] Mohamad Abdalla, "Islamic Studies in Islamic Schools: Evidence-Based Renewal," in *Islamic Schooling in the West: Pathways to Renewal*, eds. Mohamad Abdalla, Dylan Chown, and Muhammad Abdullah (Cham: Palgrave Macmillan, 2018), 257–284.

[7] Robert Jackson et al., *Materials Used to Teach about World Religions in Schools in England* (Research Report DCSF-RR197). UK: University of Warwick, 2010), 10.

Reflecting upon my personal experience as a child being educated in an Islamic school in Victoria, the Islamic discourse that we were exposed to as young Australian Muslims was, to a variable extent, disengaging, and unfortunately, little progress has been made in recent years. Religious instruction is mainly about the Islamic Studies period whereby narratives of the Prophet and his companions are put before the students as pure historical events. Basic jurisprudence is taught essentially as the dos and don'ts, without much insight into the rationale for these laws, which leads to the understanding that true faith should manifest itself in all walks of life, including our personal dealings, social lives, and all types of interactions. The subtle message that is conveyed through this approach is that the teachings of Islam are predominantly confined to the parameters of worship, whereby the manifestation of our religious identity only becomes evident by attending the daily prayers, by paying the annual *Zakaat*, by observing fasting during the month of Ramadan or perhaps when pilgrimage is performed.[8]

Elleissy aptly describes the general state of Islamic studies in Islamic schools globally—one where emphasis is placed on ritual practice in a manner disconnected from the broader schooling contexts in which learners are being educated. Winter in his own reflections of the educational dilemma argues that given the wide epistemological spectrum among Muslim communities, modern day madrasahs have become more consumed in a dialectical defence of theological positions over an inspirational curriculum.[9] Equally, he argues that state schools (speaking of the UK context) "have transmitted a vague but emotive sense of Muslim belonging, but have not easily inculcated compassion, aesthetics, or wisdom or the deep dialectical reasons for adherence."[10] Similarly, in his study of syllabi and textbooks that teach about religion in the United Kingdom, with a particular focus on Islam and Muslims, Thobani argues that what is most commonly used is the "five pillars approach." In this approach, the most commonly addressed topics include:

(1) doctrinal (Allah, the Qur'an, the *sunna*, *jihad*, divine judgement); (2) ritual (the five pillars, mosques, festivals, rites of passage); (3) ethical (*zakat*, helping the needy, caring for the environment); (4) mytho-

---

8   Abdullah Elleissy, "Attaining the 'Islamic' in Islamic Schools," in *Islamic Schooling in the West: Pathways to Renewal*, eds. Mohamad Abdalla, Dylan Chown, and Muhammad Abdullah (Cham: Palgrave Macmillan, 2018), 229.
9   Tim Winter, "Education as 'Drawing Out': The Forms of Islamic Reason," in *Philosophies of Islamic Education: Historical Perspectives and Emerging Discourses*, eds. Nadeem A. Memon, and Mujadad Zaman (New York: Routledge, 2016), 31.
10 Winter, "Education," 33.

logical (the founding story of Muhammad, the prophets, angels); (5) experiential (revelation, the night journey, suffering, evil and death); (6) social (family, marriage and divorce, the role of women, dress and food). In general, the contents make minimal reference to the major denominations and schools of interpretation in Islam, and the global diversity within Muslims. There is admittedly an inclusion of topics which fall outside these dimensions, such as citizenship education, global issues, religion and science, art and culture, and what it means to be a Muslim in Britain, but these appear marginally and infrequently.[11]

Putting aside public debates about the extent to which religious education (whether confessional or non-confessional) should be taught in State/public schools,[12] the fact is that the approach to teaching Islam in both contexts remains one-dimensional and unengaging from a learner's perspective. Some contemporary critiques also reflect, in some respects, Ashraf's insistence on prioritizing the spirit over ritual practice.

Extending Discourses on Islamic Education

In honour of Professor Ashraf's contributions to the field of Islamic Education, the following section outlines three broader current themes in the field that extend his foundational conceptualizations: (a) multi-perspectivity, (b) curriculum orientations and (c) education of the interior.

Multi-perspectivity

Among the extensions to Ashraf's contribution in the field is a move toward distinguishing exactly what is meant by religious education. Berglund offers an important typology that reflects the direction that most critical, constructivist educators are calling for and is now increasingly being reflected in religious education circles. She puts forth a typology of Islamic education programs that provide, what she labels as, education *into*, education *about*, or education *from* religion. Further, she defines each as:

> Education *into* religion introduces the pupil to a specific religious tradition, with the purpose of promoting personal, moral, and spiritual development as well as to build religious identity within a particular tradition. Many confessional approaches emphasize learning *into* re-

---

11 Shiraz Thobani, "The religious–Secular Interface and Representations of Islam in Phenomenological Religious Education," *Oxford Review of Education* 43, no. 5 (2017): 615.
12 In some contexts (e.g. Canada, United States, Australia) public or state schools refers to schools that are government funded and free i.e., no tuition for residents and citizens. In the United Kingdom public schools are fee paying private schools.

ligion, or learning how to live in accordance with specific religious tenets and practices. Education *about* religion utilizes a more or less academic examination of various religious traditions. This approach contextualizes religion within the comparative study of religions, history, and sociology. Education *from* religion takes the personal experience of the pupil as its principal point of departure. The idea is to enhance students' capacity to reflect upon important questions of life and provide an opportunity to develop personal responses to major moral and religious problems. In other words, students learn *from* different religious traditions and outlooks of life."[13]

The first two, education *into* and education *about* reflect the commonly held understanding about confessional and non-confessional teaching or education for faith formation versus education about comparative religion. However, the final conception she puts forward of "education *from* religion" proposes a trajectory that is growing widely in broader discourses of education that puts learners at the centre and shapes curricula around learner lifeworlds.[14] Research on "funds of knowledge" and "culturally responsive pedagogy" create space for the cultural, ethnic, racial, spiritual, and religious assets that a learner brings to classrooms in a way that privileges marginalized worldviews and learner experiences. In public school classrooms where inclusive and equitable education defines aspiration and good teaching, such an approach challenges inequitable treatment and misrepresentation of Muslim learners. However, these learner-centered educational discourses will raise (and are already raising) important questions about the implications for faith-formation or confessional religious studies where a particular, normative, or dominant view of a faith tradition is privileged.

Thobani raises similar concerns, that in both public (state) and private school settings, whether Islam is being taught for faith formation or from a non-confessional phenomological approach, teaching about Islam and Muslims largely overlooks the "denominational, ethnic, linguistic, and cultural diversity among Muslims . . . [and] historical and political considerations related

---

13 Berglund, Jenny. *Publicly Funded Islamic Education in Europe and the United States*. The Brookings Project on U.S. Relations with the Islamic World, Analysis Paper, no. 21. (US: Centre for Middle East Policy, 2015), 5, https://www.brookings.edu/wp-content/uploads/2016/06/Final-Web-PDF.pdf.

14 Lew Zipin, "Dark Funds of Knowledge, Deep Funds of Pedagogy: Exploring Boundaries between Lifeworlds and Schools," *Discourse: Studies in the Cultural Politics of Education* 30, no. 3 (2009); Susanne Gannon, Robert Hattam, and Wayne Sawyer, eds., *Resisting Educational Inequality—Reframing Policy and Practice in Schools Serving Vulnerable Communities* (Australia: Routledge, 2018); Django Paris, and H. Samy Alim, *Culturally Sustaining Pedagogies: Teaching and Learning for Justice in a Changing World* (New York: Teachers College Press, 2017).

to interpretations of Islam."¹⁵ The Toledo Guiding Principles for Teaching Religion call for an emphasis on "multi-perspectivity" that is also largely absent in the teaching of Islam. Thobani argues that:

> Emergent conceptions of education about religions, cultures, and beliefs, as reflected in the above reports, suggest the need for approaches to belief systems based on the principles of inclusivity, pluralism, and multi-perspectivism, as does the phenomenology of religion, but with much greater emphasis on connecting religion with other subject areas in the curriculum such as history, the social sciences and humanities, and the arts.¹⁶

He goes on to acknowledge that although a deep multi-perspective approach may not be realistic the need to move "beyond a simplistic rendering of Islam and Muslims" remains and that the use of dialogic pedagogy is one way of rethinking the way religion is taught.¹⁷

The need to make Islamic education relevant to our current contexts and in ways that centers the varied identities and perspectives held within Muslim communities has been raised by a number of contemporary scholars. Abd-Allah argues that the "Islamic legal tradition must not be seen as a program of detailed prohibitions and inhibitions but made relevant to the day-to-day imperatives of our lives with an eye to fostering positive identity and dynamic integration into American society."¹⁸ Sahin calls for a reflective Muslim paideia that facilitates the "indigenous Islamic expressions of being European and European articulations of Islam."¹⁹ And Kazmi insists that "One major distinction is that while the Islamic tradition is one, there are as many Muslim traditions as there are Muslim societies. It would be wrong, however, to view the Islamic tradition as a meta-narrative or meta conversation."²⁰ Each of these perspectives acknowledges the centrality of the Islamic tradition/legal tradition as an overarching and guiding construct but one that also provides great malleability in speaking to the diverse contexts and experiences in which Muslim communities reside.

---

15 Shiraz Thobani, "The religious-Secular Interface and Representations of Islam in Phenomenological Religious Education," *Oxford Review of Education* 43, no. 5 (2017): 615.
16 Thobani, 616.
17 Thobani, 617.
18 Umar Faruq Abd-Allah, "Islam and the Cultural Imperative," *Cross Currents* 56, no. 3 (Fall 2006), 370.
19 Abdullah Sahin, "Critical Issues in Islamic Education Studies: Rethinking Islamic and Western Liberal Secular Values of Education," *Religions* 9, no. 11 (2018): 20, https://doi.org/10.3390/rel9110335.
20 Yedullah Kazmi, "Islamic Education: Traditional Education or Education of Tradition?" *Islamic studies* 42 (2003): 283.

Curriculum Orientations

Levisohn raises a further critical consideration that complements multiperspectivity when teaching religion, what he refers to as curriculum orientations. Borrowing from studies of other subject areas such as English, he argues that any subject can be approached from "fundamentally distinct understandings of the subject."[21] Grossman, for example, suggests three orientations to the study of English[22] and Holtz outlines nine orientations for teaching Bible.[23] Levisohn defines a curriculum orientation as:

> An orientation is not a technique or method of teaching, and not merely an attitude held by the teacher, and not an approach to *studying* a subject. Instead, a teaching orientation is a conceptual model of teaching that subject. It is a teacher's fundamental stance toward a particular subject that encompasses a conception of purposes (of teaching that subject) and a set of paradigmatic practices. These purposes and practices hang together; an orientation has internal coherence. An orientation can be pursued well or it can be pursued poorly; an orientation is not, itself, good or bad. As part of our understanding of an orientation, we assume that any subject can have multiple orientations— but we do not assume that the multiple orientations are mutually exclusive (either in their purposes or their practices). Nor do we assume that orientations are fixed and eternal. On the contrary, the menu represents the range of stances that, we claim, are present at this moment in this place.[24]

Some of the salient points Levisohn raises are that (a) orientations are conceptual models of teaching a subject that (b) are not mutually exclusive or hierarchical.[25] Although a study of Islamic Studies curriculum orientations may not exist (to my knowledge), anecdotally, it is evident that multiple orientations exist and have historically existed. The oft-quoted exposition of Ibn Khaldun about madrasah curriculum in Spain and Morocco differing in their approaches alludes to orientations. A review of contemporary Islamic schools and Islamic Studies textbooks would point to emerging curriculum orientations also. Anecdotally, from my own work in and reflections on the field of Islamic schools, I suggest there are at least five emerging curriculum orientations in the field of Islamic schooling in the West.

---

21 Jon A. Levisohn, "A Menu of Orientations to the Teaching of Rabbinic Literature," *Journal of Jewish Education* 76, no. 1 (2010): 5.
22 Pamela L. Grossman, "What are we talking about anyway? Subject-matter knowledge of secondary English teachers," in *Advances in Research on Teaching*, vol. 2, *Subject Matter Knowledge*, ed. Jere E. Brophy (Greenwich, CT: JAI Press, 1991), 245-264.
23 Levisohn, "A Menu of Orientations."
24 Levisohn, "A Menu of Orientations," 13.
25 Levisohn, 11-13.

The first of these is the *Madrasah Approach* where religious studies is the focal point. The overall outcome is to produce learners who have memorized the Qurʾān, are well versed in Islamic beliefs and legal rulings through a deep study of classical texts, and are able to serve in Muslim communities as religious leaders and religious studies teachers. In this approach, there is not only most often a clear divide between religious and secular studies but the emphasis on the former far outweighs the amount of time and attention paid to the latter.

The second emerging curriculum orientation is one I refer to as the *Appended Approach*. This approach is largely a reaction to the *Madrasah Approach* for over-emphasizing religious studies and at the same time a reaction to secular public schooling for discarding confessional religious studies altogether. The *Appended Approach* seeks to balance an academically competitive secular education that meets (if not exceeds) all nationally mandated measures of educational success while providing a learning environment that is faith-centered. In this orientation, the Islamic studies emphasis is often less subject-oriented but rather embedded into the school culture through a faith-inspired code of conduct, communal prayer, and community-based service learning. Islamic Studies is formally taught but often with less allocated time and attention than what is given to core national curriculum subject areas. The emphasis of Islam is, therefore, seemingly "appended."

A third emerging approach is the *Integrated Approach* that is highly influenced by the Islamization Project of Al-Faruqi and also articulations of the world conferences. This approach seeks an "Islamic perspective in every subject."[26] The integrated orientation seeks to connect religious and secular studies so that learning is not divided, bifurcated, or viewed in the minds of learners as disconnected.[27] An integrated orientation has been achieved in multiple ways in Islamic schools thus far. Some educators draw on Islamic perspectives sporadically and when appropriate, others plan specific intersections in advance, some focus on cross-curricular themes and work collaboratively with colleagues to develop integrated learning maps, and yet others integrate through student-initiated project-based learning. The integrated curriculum orientation, as all orientations, have a range of varieties but this orientation in particular arguably has the largest spectrum and shades.

The fourth orientation is also rooted in the early conceptualizations of Islamization but emphasizes a nuance to integration. I label this orientation as the *Grounded Orientation* where the focal point begins from the Islamic world-

---

26 Freda Shamma, "Islamic Worldview and Curriculum Development," in *Islamic Schooling in the West: Pathways to Renewal,* eds., Mohamad Abdalla, Dylan Chown, and Muhammad Abdullah, 117–127 (Cham: Palgrave Macmillan, 2018), 122.

27 Shaikh Abdul Mabud, "The Emergence of Islamic Schools: A Contextual Background," in *Islamic Schooling in the West: Pathways to Renewal*, eds. Mohamad Abdalla, Dylan Chown, and Muhammad Abdullah, 11–34 (Cham: Palgrave Macmillan, 2018), 12.

view and then moves outward. This is also where it has been argued that Faruqi and Nasr parted in their conceptualizations of Islamization. The common ground between the two was a call for the reconstruction of knowledge that responds to "the increasing awareness of modernity as a worldview; a worldview that marginalizes religiously inspired ones by depriving knowledge of its teleological and sacred qualities."[28] But Nasr held the position that Muslims cannot simply adopt modern scientific knowledge into an Islamic worldview—in other words, integration cannot be one into the other. Nasr emphasized the importance of beginning with teaching Islamic philosophy in the early years of primary and secondary schools.[29] Following this, some aspects of logic, metaphysics, and ethics should be taught all prior to introducing western or oriental philosophies. And "the treatment of Western thought, although very elementary at this stage, should still be critical, and neither apologetic nor defensive."[30] The *Grounded Orientation* is evident in multiple contemporary curriculum initiatives such as the Ghazali Children's Project[31] and the Qurʾānic worldview curriculum framework of Elma Harder.[32]

The fifth approach is what I would call either the Identity or *Character Orientation*. Popularized in North American Islamic educational circles by the work of Dawud Tauhidi's Tarbiyah Project, this orientation emphasizes the "crisis in values and character development." Tauhidi eloquently articulated what is on the minds of most Islamic school educators which is that students lack a clear moral compass and are "disoriented spiritually."[33] He popularized an emphasis on *tarbiyah* (nurturing wholeness) through his writings, workshops, but most clearly through his leading one particular Islamic school toward implementation. He argued that Islam is not being taught as a way of life and that current Islamic Studies efforts are ineffective in inspiring Muslim children because teaching Islam is focused on "conveying information about Islam." He too drew inspiration from the Islamization archive in challenging the "pervasive influence of secular materialism." The Character Orientation draws from formal Islamic Studies but privileges values-based learning over practices. This orientation focuses on integrating Islamic values thematically throughout the curriculum and school ethos.

---

28 Ali Zaidi, "Muslim Reconstructions of Knowledge and the Re-enchantment of Modernity," *Theory, Culture & Society* 23, no. 5 (2006): 71.
29 Seyyed Hossein Nasr, "Islamic Pedagogy," *Islam & Science* 10, no. 1 (Summer 2012): 7–24.
30 Ashraf, *New Horizons*, 66.
31 Ghazali Children's Project, Fons Vitae, Louisville, Kentucky, accessed July 26, 2023, https://ghazalichildren.org/
32 Elma R. Harder, *Concentric Circles: Nurturing Awe and Wonder in Early Learning - A Foundational Approach* (Sherwood Park, Alberta: Al-Qalam Publishing, 2006).
33 Daud Tauhidi, *The Tarbiyah Project: A Renewed Vision of Islamic Education* (Canton, MI: Tarbiyah Institute, 2006), 8.

To reiterate Levisohn's perspectives, these orientations are not mutually exclusive or hierarchical in any way. Nor are they a trajectory of development. What these orientations, however, do achieve is broadening our understanding of the complexity of Islamic schooling and specifically complicate, in a positive sense, the task of curriculum renewal that Ashraf called for. Suffice it to say that more thorough empirical studies of the curriculum orientations of Islamic Studies in K-12 Islamic schools deserves attention and a mapping of these orientations as has been done in Jewish school curriculum[34] that provides clarity on the varied aims and aspirations.

Education of the Interior

It is a commonly held position that the purpose of education in the Islamic tradition is "nurturing and cultivating a virtuous form of life" and that the role of an educator is to "draw out" every learner's *fiṭrah* (natural inclination) toward goodness.[35] True learning is not the accumulation of tidbits of knowledge but the "deepening of our ontological consciousness."[36] The critique of contemporary Islamic school settings is that when it comes to religion, teaching remains "overwhelmingly dialectical, not inspirational," largely because religion is reduced to a subject of inquiry rather than an overriding philosophy of education.[37] The way forward for Islamic education settings is to reconnect with a form of learning that recognizes the innate knowledge within all human beings, our *fiṭrah* or natural inclination, which cannot be taught per se but rather must be drawn out. Cultivating *fiṭrah* requires pedagogies of recollection and reflection. A pedagogy of drawing out also requires a "heartfelt interaction between teachers and learners" for the spiritual aspirations to be achieved.[38] Sabani et al. draw on Nasr's conviction that knowledge of the secular and sacred are inseparable, that the ultimate purpose of learning is to know God, and that to know God requires spiritual consciousness, humility, and self-efficacy.[39] These parameters require the teacher committed to Islamic pedagogy to be an embodiment, aspirationally and wholeheartedly, similar to the aspired relationship between parent and child where knowledge of religion is lived. In this sense the essence of Islamic pedagogy is to form the human person, holistically—mind, body, and soul.[40]

---

34 Barry W. Holtz, *Textual knowledge: Teaching the Bible in Theory and Practice* (New York: JTS Press, 2003); Levisohn, "A Menu of Orientations."
35 Winter, "Education," 26.
36 Winter, 30.
37 Winter, 31.
38 Noraisikin Sabani, Glenn Hardaker, Aishah Sabki, and Sallimah Salleh, "Understandings of Islamic Pedagogy for Personalised Learning," *International Journal of Information and Learning Technology* 33 no. 2 (2016): 80.
39 Sabani et al., "Understandings of Islamic," 80.
40 Glenn Hardaker, and Aishah Ahmad Sabki, "Islamic Pedagogy and Embodiment: An Anthropological Study of a British Madrasah," *International Journal of Qualitative Studies in Education* 28, no. 8 (2015): 873, 876.

In response to the insistence that Islamic education is inherently holistic already premised with the end goal being to know God, and for learning to be focused on personal, spiritual growth, Ahmed and Sabir put forth a model of Islamic education entitled Shakhsiyyah Islamiyyah with British Muslim learners in mind. The principles of a *shakhsiyyah* education (personal character education) are designed to ensure that holistic education is seamless and that it "incorporates all types of knowledge and learning that is needed to live as a Muslim in the contemporary world."[41] Among the principles of *shakhsiyyah* education are the centrality of reconnecting with one's intention for learning, *qidwah* or leading by example, *ḥalaqah* or dialogic oral pedagogy, *minhaj al-dirāsī* referred to as an integrated thematic curriculum, and *taqdīr* to emphasize formative self-assessment as the overriding impetus of evaluation.[42] Shakhsiyyah requires a high level of personal relationship building between teacher and student, taking into consideration the learner's needs in order to support their self- and spiritual development.

For Islamic schools that may not have an appetite for a robust holistic model such as *shakhsiyyah* but that acknowledge the centrality of spiritual development to an Islamic pedagogy, a redefinition of an Islamic school ethos could also be considered. In describing what an Islamic school ethos should entail, Trevathan is critical of the Islamic schools that define their ethos by the obvious, outward rhythm of religious observance such as Islamically appropriate dress or uniforms for boys and girls. Schools need to shift from the emphasis on what he refers to as the "outward *sunnah* [religious way]" to an "inward *sunnah*" that fills the spirit. To challenge the overt culture of academic competition that defines global educational culture, including in Islamic schools, Trevathan suggests that fostering a school culture of humility is more aptly aligned to education in the Islamic tradition. Humility, he argues, is integral to Muslim "beingness" and "should be the heart of Muslim education."[43]

In an Islamic pedagogy that aspires to deepen ontological consciousness, it is evident that the role of the teacher and therefore the school ethos is critical. For *fiṭrah* to be drawn out, the school ethos, structure, curriculum, and educator consciousness must all align with the overarching educational aims of Islamic pedagogy.

The centrality of character development to Islamic education is known. Yet, the challenges in contemporary Islamic schools in fostering what

---

41 Farah Ahmed, and Tahreem Sabir, "Developing Shakhsiyah Islamiyah: Personalised Character Education for British Muslims," in *Rethinking Madrasah Education in a Globalised World*, ed. Mukhlis Abu Bakar (London: Routledge, 2018), 119.
42 Ahmed, and Sabir, "Developing Shakhsiyah Islamiyah," 119.
43 Abdullah Trevathan, "Muslim Ethos in Muslim Schools," in *Islamic Schooling in the West: Pathways to Renewal,* eds. Mohamad Abdalla, Dylan Chown, and Muhammad Abdullah (Cham: Palgrave Macmillan: 2018), 114.

Trevathan refers to as a disposition rooted in the Islamic concept of *akhlāq* remains a struggle for many, if not most Islamic schools.[44] In my own work related to teacher development and school renewal with Islamic schools from the United States to Australia and from Pakistan to the Maldives, an urgent priority expressed is the need for training teachers on "handling student misbehaviour." Part of the challenges are attributed to deficit sentiments held toward learners—common rationales given for misbehaviour being learner inability, unwillingness, lack of parental involvement, or assumed negative home cultures.[45] As Trevathan states: "Whatever the case may be, Muslim educators are clearly struggling."[46] As an emerging field of Islamic schooling, blame can be placed internally on parents and communities or externally on global youth cultures, but at some point, we must turn to ourselves as educators to question whether change may actually need to begin with ourselves.

A way forward for us as educators in addressing what feels like an epidemic of misbehaviour may not lie in "best practices" or innovative character education programs laced with rewards and restorations of justice—it may very well begin with reconnecting with our own sense of purpose. If, as Winter insists, the task of a Muslim educator is not simply to impart knowledge but to cultivate religious awareness—escaping "from the city of reason to the wilderness where God can be found"[47]—shouldn't we as educators be aspirants of this journey ourselves first? Arguably, an education of the interior cannot be imparted through curricular interventions or schoolwide policies alone. A schoolwide ethos reflected in a collective commitment by all educators to acknowledge our own "unfinishedness" combined with collective aspirations of travelling the path of seeking[48] may very well be the shift in thinking required for the future of Islamic school educators. The oft lamented fragmentation of learning in Islamic educational settings where the teaching of Islam is largely relegated to a subject of study has equally implicated the fragmentation of learning in the minds of educators. Fragmentation is not just curricular or structural in terms of subjects of study. But perceptions of educators have equally come to assume that the role of a science, mathematics and English teacher is to be a *muʿallim* (one who imparts knowledge) and the

---

44 Abdullah Trevathan, "Akhlaq (Character): Curriculum Realities and Ideals," in *Curriculum Renewal for Islamic Education: Critical Perspectives on Teaching Islam in Primary and Secondary Schools*, eds. Nadeem A. Memon, Mariam Alhashmi, and Mohamad Abdalla (New York: Routledge, 2021), 78–79.
45 Dylan Chown, and Omaira Alam, "Towards Authentic Behaviour Management Models for Islamic Schools—A Framework Synthesizing Research," *Islam and Civilisational Renewal* 7, no. 2 (2016): 188–202.
46 Trevathan, "Akhlaq (Character)," 77.
47 Winter, "Education," 30.
48 Ramzy Ajem, and Nadeem Memon, *Principles of Islamic Pedagogy: A Teacher's Manual*, Islamic Teacher Education Program (Canada: Razi Group, 2011), 27–32.

role of the *murabbī* (nurturer of souls) is left for those who teach religion formally. If the role of a Muslim educator is to be both *muʿallim* and *murabbī*, then two inevitable questions arise: (a) how are the science, math, and English educators in Islamic schools being prepared to be *murabbīs* and (b) are religious studies educators given the agency and autonomy to teach beyond the script and be responsive to learners as a *murabbī*?

An education of the interior must begin with educating ourselves as educators of our interior. The gap in character education programs is the assumption that educators do not require it themselves. To experience *dhawq* (tasting spiritual awareness) as Winter explains[49] requires an environment that embodies it, around fellow educators that are committed to it, and be given facilitated opportunities to engage with one's spirituality. Fostering a schoolwide ethos of this sort may not be possible through a prescriptive series of steps and guidelines. However, I would contend that there are rhythms of the school day and structural opportunities that must be made available for educators to reconnect spiritually if they are to embody an education of the interior. Such instances must begin with opportunities to learn about and engage with spiritual self-awareness in the Islamic tradition. Professional learning communities, facilitated reading groups, or educator dialogues can be opportunities to engage with Islamic conceptions of the soul, natural inclination, spiritual refinement, chivalry, controlling desires, and responsibilities of sister/brotherhood to name a few. There are no shortages of practical spiritual primers in both classical and contemporary Islamic educational thought and practice that can be drawn upon if an Islamic pedagogy is to transform our hearts. Engaging with treatises that enliven an education of the interior then ought to be coupled with the realities of educational practice in Islamic school settings. Perennial questions such as some of the following can inform educator dialogue: (a) what is our role as educators in Islamic schools, (b) what should we as educators hold ourselves accountable for, (c) can/should *akhlāq* (character) of students be measured, (d) does one's spiritual state oscillate and if so, how does that oscillation implicate our "akhlaqial" expectations of students?

An education of the interior must begin with ourselves as educators acknowledging that *tawḥīd* (God consciousness) cannot be imparted if one does not embody such consciousness themselves. The role of an educator in an Islamic school setting is not solely then to impart education but to partake in an educational journey themselves. Alkouatli explains that essential to education in the Vygotskian sense is for educators to embody "final forms" that then influence the learner.[50] She explains with an example related to

---

[49] Winter, "Education," 32.
[50] Claire Alkouatli, "Considering Human Development in Islamic Education," in *Curriculum*

language where an adult reflects a "final form" of being able to speak and influences a child who may only babble initially but will come to appreciate the "final form." From an Islamic conception of human development and particularly related to fostering an education of the interior, Vygotsky's "final form" requires nuance. One's own spiritual development, God-consciousness and sense of wholeness "is an ongoing process of self-, spiritual-, and social-transformation."[51] From this perspective, educators in Islamic schools must acknowledge we are forever unable to achieve a 'final form' yet must always continually be in a process of spiritual self-development. Therefore, as Islamic schools and education settings continue to blossom across the globe, a central consideration must shift from imparting *tarbiyah* to students to fostering an "education of the interior" within ourselves as educators.

Closing Thoughts

I would like to close by returning to the legacy that Syed Ali Ashraf has left us. There is no doubt that the discussions of the World Conferences on Muslim Education that he, among others, spearheaded have informed both research and practice of Islamic schooling today. A careful reading and constructive consideration, if not critique, of those initial ideas continue by many. And for others, those world conferences serve as a point of departure and distinction. In the 40 years since, the field of Islamic education/schooling and educational thought broadly has also evolved. The push toward rethinking the complex task of fostering faith-forming religious studies has been challenged and nuanced. And the complexities of what we know as Islamic schools have equally evolved into distinct orientations that often overlap. Where we are now, I think, is a space between what Nasr refers to as divergence and convergence. In a relatively recent interview with Nasr, he speaks to the interplay between divergent approaches of Islamic education and yet a tradition of teaching and learning that offers a unifying convergence. He explains,

> [T]here exists (by the principle of necessity and not accidentally) divergent ways through which one can understand Islamic education. This is manifest, for example, in the ways curricula, disciplines, and academic structures are apparently different from one another in Persia, Turkey, or Malaysia, etc. However, there are also, and often more importantly, convergent ways in which these ostensible differences become secondary to what may be thought of as a continuing theme or 'pattern' to Islamic education. This is essential to remember con-

---

Renewal for Islamic Education: Critical Perspectives on Teaching Islam in Primary and Secondary Schools, eds. Nadeem A. Memon, Mariam Alhashmi, and Mohamad Abdalla (New York: Routledge, 2021), 183.

51 Alkouatli, "Considering Human Development," 195.

sidering the manner in which the destructive influences of modern life have ruptured and often destroyed premodern Islamic ideas of knowledge, the sacred, identity, and life. That we can still speak of a functioning and vibrant idea of Islamic education in the 21st century is itself remarkable. Whatever may be said of the differences in the practice of Islamic education in various countries, there is a unifying inheritance, which remains consistently 'Islamic.'[52]

I feel we are at a point in our journey of Islamic schooling in the West where rearticulating this "unifying inheritance," and these universal Islamic principles of learning and teaching that define education in the Islamic tradition need to be reflected upon. Not, as Nasr points out, to create a uniform, monoculture of schools or curricular approach. Rather, we do so to achieve what Nasr so eloquently has said, "when we think about Islamic education, we must think of 'diversity within unity.'"[53]

Bibliography

Abdalla, Mohamad. "Islamic Studies in Islamic Schools: Evidence-Based Renewal." In *Islamic Schooling in the West: Pathways to Renewal*, edited by Mohamad Abdalla, Dylan Chown, and Muhammad Abdullah, 257-284. Cham: Palgrave Macmillan, 2018.

Abd-Allah, Umar Faruq. "Islam and the Cultural Imperative." *Cross Currents* 56, no. 3 (Fall 2006): 357-375.

Ahmed, Farah, and Tahreem Sabir. "Developing *Shakhsiyah Islamiyah*: Personalised Character Education for British Muslims." In *Rethinking Madrasah Education in a Globalised World*, edited by Mukhlis Abu Bakar, 118-34. London: Routledge, 2018.

Ajem, Ramzy, and Nadeem Memon. *Principles of Islamic Pedagogy: A Teacher's Manual.* Islamic Teacher Education Program. Canada: Razi Group, 2011.

Al-Afendi, Muhammad Hamid, and Nabi Ahmed Baloch, eds. *Curriculum and Teacher Education*. London: Hodder and Stoughton and Jeddah: King Abdulaziz University, 1980.

Alkouatli, Claire. "Considering Human Development in Islamic Education." In *Curriculum Renewal for Islamic Education: Critical Perspectives on Teaching Islam in Primary and Secondary Schools*, edited by Nadeem A. Memon, Mariam Alhashmi, and Mohamad Abdalla, 181-198. New York: Routledge, 2021.

Ashraf, Syed Ali. *New Horizons in Muslim Education*. London: Hodder & Stoughton, and Cambridge: The Islamic Academy, 1985.

Al-Attas, Syed Muhammad Naquib, ed. *Aims and Objectives of Islamic Education*. London: Hodder and Stoughton and Jeddah: King Abdulaziz University, 1979.

---

52 Nasr, 17.
53 Nasr, 18.

Berglund, Jenny. *Publicly Funded Islamic Education in Europe and the United States*. The Brookings Project on U.S. Relations with the Islamic World, Analysis Paper, no. 21. US: Centre for Middle East Policy, 2015. https://www.brookings.edu/wp-content/uploads/2016/06/Final-Web-PDF.pdf.

Chown, Dylan, and Omaira Alam. "Towards Authentic Behaviour Management Models for Islamic Schools—A Framework Synthesizing Research." *Islam and Civilisational Renewal* 7, no. 2 (2016): 188–202. https://doi.org/10.12816/0035196.

Elleissy, Abdullah. "Attaining the 'Islamic' in Islamic Schools." In *Islamic Schooling in the West: Pathways to Renewal*, edited by Mohamad Abdalla, Dylan Chown, and Muhammad Abdullah, 227-238. Singapore: Palgrave Macmillan, 2018.

Gannon, Susanne, Robert Hattam, and Wayne Sawyer, eds. *Resisting Educational Inequality—Reframing Policy and Practice in Schools Serving Vulnerable Communities*. Australia: Routledge, 2018.

Ghazali Children's Project. Fons Vitae, Louisville, Kentucky. Accessed July 26, 2023. https://ghazalichildren.org/.

Grossman, Pamela L. "What are we talking about anyway? Subject-matter knowledge of secondary English teachers." In *Advances in Research on Teaching*, vol. 2, *Subject Matter Knowledge*, edited by Jere E. Brophy, 245–264. Greenwich, CT: JAI Press, 1991.

Hardaker, Glenn, and Aishah Ahmad Sabki. "Islamic Pedagogy and Embodiment: An Anthropological Study of a British Madrasah." *International Journal of Qualitative Studies in Education* 28, no. 8 (2015), 873–886. https://doi.org/10.1080/09518398.2014.917738.

Hardaker, Glenn, and Aishah Ahmad Sabki. *Pedagogy in Islamic Education: The Madrasah Context*. Bingley: Emerald Publishing Limited, 2018.

Holtz, Barry W. *Textual knowledge: Teaching the Bible in Theory and Practice*. New York: JTS Press, 2003.

Husain, Syed Sajjad, and Syed Ali Ashraf. *Crisis in Muslim Education*. Jeddah: King Abdulaziz University, 1979.

Jackson, Robert, Julia Ipgrave, Mary Hayward, Paul Hopkins, Nigel P. Fancourt, Mandy Robbins, Leslie Francis, and Ursula McKenna. *Materials Used to Teach about World Religions in Schools in England*. Research Report DCSF-RR197. UK: University of Warwick, 2010.

Kazmi, Yedullah. "Islamic Education: Traditional Education or Education of Tradition?" *Islamic studies* 42 (2003): 259-288.

Levisohn, Jon A. "A Menu of Orientations to the Teaching of Rabbinic Literature." *Journal of Jewish Education* 76, no. 1 (2010): 4-51.

Mabud, Shaikh Abdul. "World Conferences on Muslim Education: Shaping the Agenda of Muslim Education in the Future." In *Philosophies of Islamic Education: Historical Perspectives and Emerging*, edited by Nadeem A. Memon and Mujadad Zaman, 29-43. New York: Routledge, 2016.

Mabud, Shaikh Abdul. "The Emergence of Islamic Schools: A Contextual Background." In *Islamic Schooling in the West: Pathways to Renewal*, edited by Mohamad Abdalla, Dylan Chown, and Muhammad Abdullah, 11-34. Singapore: Palgrave Macmillan, 2018.

Mohamad Abdalla, Dylan Chown, and Muhammad Abdullah, eds. *Islamic Schooling in the West: Pathways to Renewal*. Singapore: Palgrave Macmillan, 2018.

Nasr, Seyyed Hossein. "Islamic Pedagogy." *Islam & Science* 10, no. 1 (Summer 2012): 7-24.

Nasr, Seyyed Hossein. "Philosophical Considerations of Islamic Education—Past and Future: Interview with Professor Seyyed Hossein Nasr." In *Philosophies of Islamic Education: His-*

torical Perspectives and Emerging Discourses, edited by Nadeem A. Memon, and Mujadad Zaman, 17-25. New York: Routledge, 2016.

Paris, Django, and H. Samy Alim. *Culturally Sustaining Pedagogies: Teaching and Learning for Justice in a Changing World.* New York: Teachers College Press, 2017.

Sabani, Noraisikin, Glenn Hardaker, Aishah Sabki, and Sallimah Salleh. "Understandings of Islamic Pedagogy for Personalised Learning." *International Journal of Information and Learning Technology* 33 no. 2 (2016): 78-90.

Sahin, Abdullah. "Critical Issues in Islamic Education Studies: Rethinking Islamic and Western Liberal Secular Values of Education." *Religions* 9, no. 11 (2018). https://doi.org/10.3390/rel9110335.

Shamma, Freda. "Islamic Worldview and Curriculum Development." In *Islamic Schooling in the West: Pathways to Renewal,* edited by Mohamad Abdalla, Dylan Chown, and Muhammad Abdullah, 117-128. Singapore: Palgrave Macmillan, 2018.

Tauhidi, Daud. *The Tarbiyah Project: A Renewed Vision of Islamic Education.* Canton, MI: Tarbiyah Institute, 2006.

Thobani, Shiraz. "The religious–Secular Interface and Representations of Islam in Phenomenological Religious Education." *Oxford Review of Education* 43, no. 5 (2017): 612-625.

Trevathan, Abdullah. "Muslim Ethos in Muslim Schools." In *Islamic Schooling in the West: Pathways to Renewal,* edited by Mohamad Abdalla, Dylan Chown, and Muhammad Abdullah, 129-150. Cham: Palgrave Macmillan: 2018.

Trevathan, Abdullah. "Akhlaq (Character): Curriculum Realities and Ideals." In *Curriculum Renewal for Islamic Education: Critical Perspectives on Teaching Islam in Primary and Secondary Schools,* edited by Nadeem A. Memon, Mariam Alhashmi, and Mohamad Abdalla, 77-92. New York: Routledge, 2021.

Winter, Tim. "Education as 'Drawing Out': The Forms of Islamic Reason." In *Philosophies of Islamic Education: Historical Perspectives and Emerging Discourses,* edited by Nadeem A. Memon, and Mujadad Zaman, 26-42. New York: Routledge, 2016.

Zaidi, Ali. "Muslim Reconstructions of Knowledge and the Re-enchantment of Modernity." *Theory, Culture & Society* 23, no. 5 (2006): 69–91.

Zipin, Lew. "Dark Funds of Knowledge, Deep Funds of Pedagogy: Exploring Boundaries between Lifeworlds and Schools." *Discourse: Studies in the Cultural Politics of Education* 30, no. 3 (2009): 317-331.

Chapter 19

The Moral Theory of Five Cosmic Values: Islamic Moral Theory Based on Reason and Revelation

Mashhad Al-Allaf

Morality and Imaginative Insights

There are three hundred people in a boat sailing on the sea. They realize their safety is at risk, and they can only save the lives of the majority by throwing ten people overboard. Would it be morally right for them to kill ten people in order to save two hundred and ninety?[1]

In any moral dilemma, we not only need moral principles by which to justify the moral judgment, but also the rules by which to resolve the conflict between two distinct moral actions. This chapter presents my attempt to offer an Islamic moral theory based on the "five cosmic values" (Religion, Life, Intellect, Procreation, and Property) that guide to the right action in moral education. The theory also presents the absolute moral imperative, and rules for breaking the rules.

I should briefly mention here that the five values were presented in the eleventh century by the Shāfiʿī scholar Imām al-Ḥaramayn al-Juwaynī (1028–1085) as the objectives (*Maqāṣid*) of the Islamic law, then it was well developed and enhanced by his eminent student Imām Abū Ḥāmid al-Ghazālī (1058–1111). In the fourteenth century the theory of *Maqāṣid* was further elaborated and enhanced (based on al-Ghazālī's work) by the Mālikī jurist Imām Abū Isḥāq al-Shāṭibī from Granada (1320–1388) in his famous book *al Muwāfaqāt*. The theory was first established and developed in the area of the principles of Islamic jurisprudence (*ʿIlm Uṣūl al-Fiqh*), however my research here is to take

---

1 I took this case study from al-Ghazālī's book *Al-Mustaṣfā min ʿilm al-uṣūl* (Beirut, Lebanon: Muʾassasat al-Risālah, 1997), vol. 1, p. 421. The number of 300 people is my addition.

the basics of the theory and rebuild a contemporary theory in the area of ethics to be used as a theory for moral judgments in contemporary Islamic Moral Philosophy under the title: The Theory of The Five Cosmic Values.

Education in general assumes a scheme of moral values that operates as a point of reference; the theory of five cosmic values sets the theoretical and philosophical structure of such a scheme or framework and argues that both reason and revelation can be the very foundations of it. The theory also offers the philosophical justification of moral judgments.

The moral action is closely related to the meaning of life and how we ought to live; it is about how to construct and reconstruct the internal image that will constitute the trait of the personality. The term "ethics" (akhlāq) in the Arabic language is derived from the root kh-l-q (خ-ل-ق) and the word "creation" (khalq) is also derived from the same root. Thus, there is a linguistic connection between the two words, suggesting that "creation" is the work of God while moral action (khuluq) is how a person is morally constructing (and reconstructing) their life—it is the moral action that is the responsibility of each person in creating their own inner image. When a Muslim looks upon themselves in a mirror, they are directed to pray, according to a ḥadīth of the Prophet: "O Allah, just as You have made my external features beautiful, make my character beautiful as well."[2] This indicates there is an external image, and there is an internal image that human beings should work on and beautify by good actions. Islamic teachings often direct the imperative of cultivating the inner self more than the exterior aspects of the "I" which shape our identity. In Ṣaḥīḥ Muslim it is reported that the Prophet (pbuh) said, "Allah does not look at your outward appearance and your wealth, rather He looks at your hearts and deeds."[3] The heart is taken to be the focal point of ethical contemplation since it is considered the faculty of cognition.[4] The Qurʾān makes a clear difference between the sight that belongs to the eyes and the insight that belongs to the heart.[5]

By the "heart", Muslim scholars do not mean the biological heart that pumps blood to the body. They refer to the heart as a spiritual entity with the ability of knowledge, and it has a kind of connection to the biological heart, in a way that is unknown. However, this heart is essential to the health of the entire body. "There is a lump of flesh in the body; if it becomes good, the whole body becomes good, and if it is corrupted, the whole body becomes corrupted. And indeed, it is the heart."[6] This is important to education because the educated should be involved in this process of purifying the soul in order to achieve the goals of moral education. Moral action can be defined as the *autonomous action*

---

2 *Musnad Aḥmad*, 3823, 24392, 25221.
3 *Ṣaḥīḥ Muslim*, 1356.
4 Qurʾān 7:179.
5 Qurʾān 22:46.
6 *Ṣaḥīḥ al-Bukhārī*, 52.

of creating (or re-creating) oneself. This partly means that the educated are morally responsible for their actions because they freely choose to do so. There are well-known definitions for the term *akhlāq* in the Islamic literature, such as that given by Ibn Miskawayh (932–1030), and by Imām Abū Ḥāmid al-Ghazālī (1058–1111) and also by ʿAlī ibn Muḥammad al-Jurjānī (1339–1414) in his *Book of Definitions* (*Kitāb al-taʿrīfāt*). *Akhlāq* is defined as a well-established structure in the soul from which actions emanate without much thinking or reflection. For example, the truthful person will not spend too much time thinking about whether they should tell the truth or not, such an action of telling the truth should emanate rapidly and spontaneously.

The teacher should embody the manual and thus existentially reflect nobility they wish to see in the character of their student. Self-education is the best education because it gives the educated the ability to be by imagining himself or herself in certain ways, and then seriously engage in the process of crafting that image. This kind of moral imagination (as the tendency and inner thought to improve the traits of the personality and purify the soul) can be enhanced by curricula of the arts and sciences, especially literature, arts, philosophy, history, music, mathematics, and religion.

The Theory, Impartiality, Worldview and Education

Man is born with the inclination towards both immorality and righteousness[7] whilst education transforms a person into a moral being. Moral values are crucial elements in education, and as such, they require a theoretical framework for their foundation and the justification of moral judgments. Since an essential part of education is passing the values from one generation to another, an educational theory must present a general scheme which reflects the worldview of the culture itself and its scientific, philosophical, and religious principles. The worldview must offer a clear vision of the most essential issues and questions related to the meaning of life, the value of man, the purpose of existence, and death. The theory I am presenting here is based on an Islamic worldview which considers both reason and revelation as equally important sources in establishing the ultimate obligation of moral actions. The theory takes at its core the reality and dignity of human beings, considered autonomous, recognizing the necessity for social coherence. This theory aims to establish the supreme principle of morality as the main source of moral obligation. The theory starts by setting the moral rules as axioms that both reason and revelation agree upon, then advances the concepts necessary for the foundation of ethics. The theory sets general guidelines on how we ought to live and what constitutes the ultimate perfection of human beings. The the-

---

[7] "And the soul, and He who formed it. And inspired it to its immoralities and its righteousness. Successful is he who purifies it. And failing is he who corrupts it." (Qurʾān 91:7–10).

ory also overcomes some problems in the deontological ethics of Immanuel Kant (1724-1804) and other ethical theories by focusing on the idea that moral values must be absolute and not relative. If moral values are relative, then there is no sense in passing these values from one generation to another since the two generations will disagree on certain values and have moral conflict. If moral values are relative to cultures and different cultures have different moral codes, for example, in the cultural relativism of Melville J. Herskovits (1895-1963), then there will be a disagreement regarding the moral judgments themselves. We know that philosophers disagree on the sources of moral obligations and moral judgments; for example, an action might be considered morally wrong according to deontological ethics but may be justified as morally right according to utilitarianism (of J. S. Mill, 1806-1873). Reason itself gives preference to what we "ought" to do, and that is because "reason" and its rational judgments are presumed to be "impartial." However, one's reason can morally justify an action as right, and at the same time, another philosopher can justify the same action as morally wrong. This leads to relativism, which leads to a confused, if not chaotic, moral life.

I present a theory that shows that reason alone is insufficient for moral education (especially in theories such as those of deontological ethics, utilitarianism, and the like). At the same time, reference to revelation alone (such as that of the Divine Command Theory) deprives religion of the intellectual dimension embedded in its teachings. As a result, the theory intends to show that there is no contradiction between reason and revelation, and the values of both are essential in education. I believe *that which is divinely imperative is rationally imperative, but rationally imperative is not necessarily divinely imperative.* But what does constitute moral obligation? What is the standard for "ought" and "ought not"? Philosophically speaking, moral judgments can be based on reason alone, or religion alone, or on both reason and revelation such as that in Islam or can be based on customs and norms of a culture such as that of the theory of Cultural Relativism. I will present first the foundation of my theory:

The Foundations of the Theory of the Five Cosmic Values

The Human Dignity

Every person is a representative of the entire human race, and that which insults, or harms one person insults and harms the human race. The good deed for one is a good deed for all. Humans have been endowed with dignity, meaning dignity does not depart from them even after death because dignity is based on humanity and not on rationality or cognitive abilities. Even though humans are eligible for this dignity by reason, it is not permissible for any person to act against his or her own dignity because this dignity is not owned by the person, it is from God, first, and second, since humanity has a share in it, the individual has no right to nullify it.

Likewise, a person has no right to take away the dignity of any other person, even if that person has lost his rational abilities since this dignity is the legislation of God Almighty, as mentioned in the Qurʾān (17:70) and secondly, it pertains to all of humanity, and thirdly, if this person is absent of his mind and cognitive abilities, then the other person is fully in their mental and moral capacity, and they are responsible for this dignity. *Preserving human dignity is the first and unconditional moral responsibility.* Thus, we may first formulate the axiom of dignity: *Whether dead or alive, every human being enjoys a special honour that exceeds all recognized values known on earth. This sublime status and honour is called "human dignity," that every person merely deserves as such or as a human being.*

The respect for human dignity is unconditional, and its violation, under whatever circumstances, is unjustified. Unfortunately, human beings have squandered each other's dignity (due to seeking superiority or unduly exercising power), and in their best circumstances, human beings give "value" to each other. However, this "value" is insufficient to express the dignity that a human being deserves. God, may He be glorified and exalted, has endowed humans with a position that exceeds "value" and that is "dignity," in the Almighty's saying: "Indeed, We have dignified the children of Adam, carried them on land and sea, granted them good and lawful provisions, and privileged them far above many of Our creatures" (Qurʾān 17:70, trans. Abdullah Yusuf Ali).

Many things take their importance from their "value," but this is not true for humans because humans do not take their place from a system of human values, but from a supreme and transcendent source.

People are born crowned with dignity, but they are threatened everywhere and at all times by eliminating this dignity. Human legislative systems may legislate articles related to human rights but not to human dignity. Preserving rights is not necessarily preservation of dignity (a person may be granted a certain right with contempt, hatred, or humiliation of dignity), but preserving human dignity includes the preservation of right categorically.

I strongly believe that it is morally wrong to display photos, videos, and films (on TV or social media) of the killing of human beings, even if the killing is not real, as such movies and dramas conceptually destroys human dignity and provides a visual facility (on the level of perception) for the possibility of the actual happening of such actions later. Human actions occur first in the minds on the level of conception before they occur outside in reality. Thus, it is also morally unacceptable to depict and show a person being beaten in films and videos.

The Presumption of Innocence

It is important to discuss the original state of human beings in terms of duty and moral responsibility with regard to the rights of other people. In this theory, and according to the principles of jurisprudence (*uṣūl al-fiqh*) as explained by Muslim scholars, man is originally presumed innocent, i.e., man is not condemned and is not morally and legally accountable unless they infringe the rights of others or themselves. The formulation of this rule is *the original status of presumed innocence*. Originally, man is not condemned and is not bound by any right of others. His responsibility becomes bound by the fall of others' rights on him or by the occurrence of his moral action related to others' rights or the right of man to himself.

Morality: Will and Intention

A good intention alone is considered an absolute good, even if no moral action comes from it. Prophet Muhammad (pbuh) said: "The value of an action depends on the intention. A man will be rewarded only for what he intended."[8] Good intention is rewarded because it is good in itself, even if it is not yet actualized in moral action. The act of the "will" is good when it corresponds to the principles of the teaching of God. In other words, it is good when it is "willed" according to principles of reason, because *in the religion of Islam, true and valid rational reasoning harmonizes with the word of God*. In this sense submitting the will of man to the will of God becomes a rational act, and not an act of blind faith. God commands what is beneficial to humanity and what is reasonable, such as, being nice to your neighbours, and prohibition of theft and that of killing.

Good will does not necessitate a good action; thus, the good will be enhanced if it translates itself into action against all temptations and inclinations of the soul. This has been echoed by what Kant (1724–1804) wrote at the beginning of the first section of his book, *Groundwork for the Metaphysics of Moral*: "There is no possibility of thinking of anything at all in the world, or even out of it, which can be regarded as good without qualification, except a good will."[9]

Imām Abū Ḥāmid al-Ghazālī (1058–1111) had elaborated on this topic in his book on *Intention, Sincerity, and Truthfulness* of his encyclopedic work, *The Revival of the Religious Sciences*:

> Know that intention (*niyya*), will (*irāda*), and purpose (*qaṣd*), are synonymous of terms with a single connotation. Each state and attribute of the heart bound by two things: knowledge and action . . . for man

---

8   *Ṣaḥīḥ al-Bukhārī*, 1; this Ḥadīth is also agreed upon and is narrated by Muslim.
9   Immanuel Kant, *Grounding for the Metaphysics of Morals*, trans. James W. Ellington (Indianapolis/Cambridge: Hackett publishing company, Inc., 1981), 7.

has no desire for what he does not know. He must know. Nor can he act without willing. Therefore, there must be a will. Will signifies the rousing of the heart towards what it thinks accords with (its) goal, be it present or future.[10]

Despite the difficulty of defining these concepts, we can say that the intention itself is a description of an internal state of the emanation of the soul, which responds not by means of determination, but by way of orientation and inclination, and sometimes as a wish. The good intention remains important because it reflects the tendency towards the moral readiness that exists in the soul.

Then Imām al-Ghazālī introduces the concept of motivation and inclination into the definition of intention, saying that: "Intention, then, is an intermediary attribute. It consists of the will and the motivation of the self through the precept of the desire and the inclination for whatever agrees with the goal, be it present or future."[11] Kant says: "For the will stands, as it were, at a crossroads between its a priori principle, which is formal, and it is a posteriori incentive, which is material; and since it must be determined by something, it must be determined by the formal principle of volition, if the action is done from duty—and in that case every material principle is taken away from it."[12] It seems that what al-Ghazālī calls "intention," "will" and "purpose," Kant calls "will." Kant's ideas echo al-Ghazālī on the importance and the position of the will.

For its importance, the rule of intention can be presented in the following way:

Rule of Intention: Matters are measured by the intentions

Here, the word "matters" includes speech and actions. This rule in this linguistic formulation is known to Muslim scholars and is based on Prophet Muhammad's (pbuh) saying: "Actions are judged by intention."[13] It should be noted that if the act is based on goodwill and infringes upon other people's rights, then this good intention does not nullify others' rights. Every person is morally and legally bound by what they say and do. For Imām al-Ghazālī, an intention that is devoid of any attachments, interests, goals, consequences, etc. deserves to be called a pure intention, which is good in itself and serves as the main source and inspiration for moral action and a measure of it. This is similar to what Kant mentioned: "A good will is good not because of what it

---

10 Abū Ḥāmid al-Ghazālī, *Intention, Sincerity, and Truthfulness*, trans. Anthony F. Shaker (Cambridge: The Islamic Text Society, 2016), 11. This is Book 37, part 4 of Al-Ghazālī's *Iḥyā' 'ulūm al-dīn* (The Revival of the Religious Sciences).
11 Al-Ghazālī, *Intention, Sincerity, and Truthfulness*, 13.
12 Kant, *Grounding for the Metaphysics of Morals*, 13.
13 Ṣaḥīḥ al-Bukhārī, 1.

effects or accomplishes, nor because of its fitness to attain some proposed end; it is good only through its willing, i.e., it is good in itself."[14]

The Will and its Two Preconditions: Knowledge and Freedom

The "will" and the good intention to lead to the right actions presuppose two a priori conditions which are (1) that its absence (non-existence) leads to the absence of the moral action and (2) that its existence does not lead to the existence of the moral action. In other words, these two conditions are: first, to have true and correct knowledge about the course of moral action, and second, freedom to choose that specific moral action.

Precondition 1: The presumption of knowledge

Rational philosophers think that this presumption can be achieved through reason alone. Of course, reason is an important source of knowledge, but how do we know that rational knowledge in the field of ethics is correct? What is the standard of its truth? According to Kant, this act of reason can be achieved by universalization: "Since I have deprived the will of every impulse that might arise for it from obeying any particular law, there is nothing left to serve the will as principle except the universal conformity of its actions to the law as such, i.e., I should never act except in such a way that I can also will that my maxim should become a universal law."[15]

Nevertheless, how do we morally justify those who want to make their actions, such as committing adultery, as a "universal law" based on the personal freedom claimed as the right for all consenting rational, autonomous adults? The reason might formulate a universal law against itself and humanity because committing adultery threatens procreation (also, it is against human dignity because it uses the human body as means to satisfy the lust of the soul; it is also an act of dishonesty). It contradicts, as we will discuss, one of the five cosmic values. This reflects a weakness in ethics based on reason alone. Therefore, for the "will," there must be a correct knowledge on which the actions of people can be based, and this type of comprehensive and beneficial knowledge must be:

- From a sublime source, possessing cognitive abilities higher than those of human beings.
- It must be more objective than those subjective desires of people and should not serve the interests of certain political parties, business groups, ethnicities, social classes, and nationalities.
- It must go beyond the spatial and temporal limits.
- It does not contradict reason.

---

14 Kant, 7.
15 Kant, 14.

In short, it comes from revelation (being a sublime source, as stated above) and is completely consistent with reason in every place and time. The intention must have knowledge that guides it. This knowledge is derived from the rational ability to understand life and the meaning of existence. To understand the five cosmic values and the purpose of human existence, and then to act accordingly achieve justice to all. The absolute moral law embedded in the five cosmic values represents the absolute good for all. It addresses man as a rational being who has the freedom to act with an inclination towards either good or evil inherent in human nature. Thus these five values address him with reason and bind him by reason, so if a man chooses not to be in harmony with these five cosmic values (for example, causing harm to others), then he has abdicated his moral responsibility in front of the society, but if he did this harm in secret, or with a hidden intention, then this implies that he knows that his action is immoral for which he has concealed his action.

Precondition 2: The presumption of freedom

The "will" of doing any moral action presupposes the existence of "freedom" of the will to do so. This freedom is the causal condition of moral action. But the philosophical issue of "freedom of will" has been under the philosophers' examination for more than two thousand years without reaching any convincing or satisfactory answer. Among those philosophers, Immanuel Kant, discussed the issue in his book, *The Critique of the Pure Reason,* under one of his antinomies, and said that reason can offer an argument and a counter-argument to the "free will"; as a result, reason cannot take a side. The issues were moved outside the pure reason's epistemological boundaries to be taken as a necessary presumption for morality, as Kant discussed in his book, *The Critique of Practical Reason*. In his book *Groundwork of the Metaphysics of Morals,* Kant returns in the third section entitled, "The Transition from the Metaphysics of Morals to the Critique of Pure Practical Reason," pages 176–178, to the discussion of the issue with a sense of agnosticism:

> The subjective impossibility of explaining freedom of the will is the same as the impossibility of discovering and explaining an interest which man can take in moral laws. Nevertheless, he does indeed take such an interest, the basis of which in us is called moral feeling. Some people have falsely construed this feeling to be the standard of our moral judgment, whereas in contrast, it must rather be regarded as the subjective effect that the law exercises upon the will, while reason alone furnishes the objective grounds of such moral feeling.[16]

Kant raised the question about the very possibility of the moral imperative, but how is a categorical imperative possible? His answer was that it is

---

16 Kant, 59.

possible to presuppose that it is based on the idea of "free will." However, this answer left Kant in a weak position of begging the question because we can easily question him, how do we justify the assumption of "free will" itself? Kant's answer that there is no way for human reason to understand this presumption is apparent when he says:

> Thus, the question as to how a categorical imperative is possible can be answered to the extent that there can be supplied the sole presupposition under which such an imperative is alone possible—namely, the idea of freedom. The necessity of this presupposition is discernible, and this much is sufficient for the practical use of reason, i.e., for being convinced as to the validity of this imperative, and hence also of the moral law; but how this presupposition itself is possible can never be discerned by any human reason.[17]

With more clarification, Kant expresses the lack of any epistemological basis for "freedom" as a causality of the "will": "It is just the same as if I tried to find out how freedom itself is possible as the causality of a will. For I thereby leave the philosophical basis of explanation, and I have no other basis."[18]

Thus, Kant returns to give the practical reason what it is deprived of the pure reason. The justification for his thinking is based on the attempt to explain the possibility of the categorical imperative.

> But how pure reason can be practical by itself without other incentives taken from whatever source—i.e., how the mere principle of the universal validity of all reason's maxims as laws (which would certainly be the form of a pure practical reason) can by itself, without any matter (object) of the will in which some antecedent interest might be taken, furnish an incentive and produce an interest which could be called purely moral; or, in other words, how pure reason could be practical: to explain all this is quite beyond the power of human reason, and all the effort and work of seeking such an explanation is wasted.[19]

It seems that there is an epistemological impossibility, according to Kant, in explaining how the mere principle can by itself furnish an incentive and produce a purely moral interest; namely, this is beyond the ability of the human reasoning, as Kant said: "And so even though we do not indeed grasp the practical unconditioned necessity of the moral imperative, we do nevertheless grasp its inconceivability. This is all that can be fairly asked of a philosophy which strives in its principles to reach the very limit of human reason."[20]

---

17 Kant, 60.
18 Kant, 60.
19 Kant, 60.
20 Kant, 62.

For the above epistemological impossibility, Kant was forced to take the "freedom of the will" as a presupposition necessary for morality in his ethics: "Therefore if freedom of the will is presupposed, morality (together with its principle) follows by merely analyzing the concept of freedom."[21]

Kant's inconsistency on the question of a priori proof of freedom

Kant's moral philosophy is based on the idea of the categorical imperative. The categorical imperative is based on a prior assumption which is the idea of "freedom," which the "pure reason" had already excluded. Kant thinks that the idea of "freedom" is a presumed condition as a kind of causality of voluntary action belonging to living rational beings, Kant does not know how this happens, but he says:

> It is not enough to prove freedom from certain alleged experiences of human nature (such a proof is indeed absolutely impossible, and so freedom can be proved only a priori). Rather, one must show that freedom belongs universally to the activity of rational beings endowed with a will. Now I say that every being which cannot act in any way other than under the idea of freedom is for this very reason free from a practical point of view.[22]

The fact that "freedom" is generally related to the activity of a rational being does not necessarily require that it can be proven a priori since not everything rational is a priori. Likewise, it is impossible to provide theoretical proof for freedom, which is the second philosophical work that Kant did not accomplish. Therefore, Kant states (in the footnote of page 50) that to be freed from this burden of theoretical proof of human freedom, he accepts freedom only in the form of the presupposed idea upon which rational beings base their actions.

The only option left for Kant is to assume freedom and accept it as a postulate, as he says:

> We have finally traced the determinate concept of morality back to the idea of freedom, but we could not prove freedom to be something actual in ourselves and in human nature. We saw merely that we must presuppose it if we want to think of a being as rational and as endowed with consciousness of its causality as regards actions, i.e., as endowed with a will.[23]

Facing all these epistemological impossibilities in Kant's ethics and his agnostic position and being unable to provide any solutions to the issue of

---

21 Kant, 49.
22 Kant, 50.
23 Kant, 51.

morality and free will, the question may arise: how did Kant arrive at all these assumptions on which he built his moral system? If reason with its empirical knowledge was incapable of proving it, and logic with its inferential proofs could not prove it, then from where did Kant bring it? Did he bring it from religion?

It seems that Kant's justification for morality is pragmatic because he sees that in the kingdom of ends, we cannot be effective members in an ethical manner unless we are guided by the postulate of "freedom" and believe in it as if it were a "natural and undeniable law." It would have been better for Kant to say here as if it were a religious doctrine instead of saying it was a natural law. In this context, Kant uses words such as rational belief, as he says:

> Here then is the extreme limit of all moral inquiry . . . On the one hand, reason should not, to the detriment of morals, search around in the world of sense for the supreme motive and for some interest that is conceivable but is nonetheless empirical. On the other hand, reason should not flap its wings impotently, without leaving the spot, in a space that for it is empty, namely, the space of transcendent concepts that is called the intelligible world, and thereby lose itself among mere phantoms of the brain. Furthermore, the idea of a pure intelligible world regarded as a whole of all intelligences to which we ourselves belong as rational beings (even though we are from another standpoint also members of the world of sense) remains always a useful and permissible idea for the purpose of a rational belief, although all knowledge ends at its boundary. This idea produces in us a lively interest in the moral law by means of the splendid ideal of a universal kingdom of ends in themselves (rational beings), to which we can belong as members only if we carefully conduct ourselves according to maxims of freedom as if they were laws of nature.[24]

The Absolute Imperative in the Theory of the Five Cosmic Values

The defects in deontological ethics, i.e., the epistemological impossibility of proving the possibility of the categorical imperative, and the presupposing of the "freedom of the will" raise many questions about the very structure of a successful moral theory; I present here the theory of five cosmic values and its absolute moral imperative, which will overcome the difficulties in previous theories.

The absolute moral imperative in the theory of Five Cosmic Values

The absolute moral imperative in our theory of the five cosmic values can be formulated in the following way: *To act in such a way that preserves and exalts*

---

24 Kant, 61.

the five cosmic values; and to do so in a way that it does not violate or harm these five cosmic values. This absolute imperative indicates a categorical obligation that is not restricted to a specific culture, and it is non-utilitarian and non-circumstantial. That is, it is binding on all human beings without exception in every time and place and in perpetuity and continuity unless there is a case of necessity, as we will discuss later.

This absolute imperative includes two parts: the first is acting according to it, while the second part removes the harm. These five cosmic values in their hierarchy and their logical order in the Islamic tradition (for example in the writings of al-Juwaynī and al-Ghazālī) are:

- Religion
- Life
- Intellect
- Procreation
- Property

In short, an act is moral if it is consistent with, and not contradicting, the five cosmic values. That is, the action derives its moral (and even legal) legitimacy from its ability to preserve these five cosmic values and harmonize with them, and to protect them because the act, in this case, is beneficial to humanity as a whole. An act is considered immoral if it does not preserve and does not harmonize with these five cosmic values or threatens them because it is an act that is destructive to humanity as a whole. It is also a vice if the act does not reduce (as much as possible) anything threatening these cosmic values.

Everything that maintains and harmonizes with these five cosmic values is moral, and everything that contradicts and destroys them is an immoral act. Although these five cosmic values are derived from religion, the human intellect realizes their total value and legislates them for the welfare of humanity. For example, the third cosmic value (the intellect) is necessary for the existence of the human race. It is secured by lawful means of sustenance and protected against destruction by a set of rules and punishments. For example, anything that reduces the mind's ability to function properly, such as alcohol or any similar substance—whether drunk, eaten, smelled or injected—is prohibited. In the same way, to practise magic, palmistry, horoscope, and believing in superstitions are immoral acts. They block the intellect and deprive a person of rational thinking. Every person is supposed to think for himself or herself and plan their future, and no one is allowed to steal this ability from them or deviate them from it.

As for "property" (the fifth value) which is extremely useful and necessary for human life, Divine Law facilitates all lawful means for its acquisition. It is secured by defending the right of ownership and by penalizing theft. Theft is an immoral act because it threatens an important cosmic value, which is property. Ownership also extends to include intellectual property such as books, articles, computer programs, software, computer games, and the like.

"Life" is a major cosmic value and one of the highest priorities that should be preserved at all costs. It includes human and animal life and everything that has life. Life is secured by obtaining lawful means of sustenance such as food, marriage, medicine, shelter, etc. The way to protect it is through the enforcement of prescribed penalties provided by the Divine Law (*Sharīʿah*). For example, adultery, false accusation, killing, and suicide are prohibited. Therefore, whoever kills a soul, it is as if he killed all people or the entire human race. Every human being is a unique representative of humanity; if all perish except one person, this is the only person representing the human race among all other beings. Due to this importance of life, Islam considers it a top priority to be necessarily preserved and protected. And since human beings do not always abide by the rules and sometimes act against their own interests, Islam has enacted strict legislation to punish the act of murder. Likewise, the act of saving a soul is an ethical act urged by the teaching of Islam. The Qurʾān says:

> That is why We ordained for the Children of Israel that whoever takes a life—unless as a punishment for murder or mischief in the land—it will be as if they killed all of humanity; and whoever saves a life, it will be as if they saved all of humanity. Although Our messengers already came to them with clear proofs, many of them still transgressed afterward through the land (Qurʾān 5:32, trans. Abdullah Yusuf Ali).

What is worth noting here is the Qurʾānic word, the "soul" (*nafs*), instead of the word "person" because the word "soul" is inclusive of all ages and goes beyond any social, cognitive, or material class. As for the definition of "person," it is not easy to define it in philosophy, but every human being deserves dignity and respect. Human beings should be protected from harm even if they lack cognitive abilities for being very young or in a state of fainting, anesthesia, or amnesia, and comma, and for this reason, the word "soul" (*nafs*) is the most suitable term.

The source of moral judgments cannot be a human invention; otherwise, moral judgments become relative according to personal benefits or the benefits of groups of people, political parties, social classes, the computer elite, and corporations. This kind of obligation comes from God Almighty, addressed to all rational beings that are morally obligated due to their own human capacity.

The public interest (*maṣlaḥah*) or benefit of people is protected in the theory of the five cosmic values, through the Islamic law, in the following two ways: by offering or procuring benefits and by preserving or protecting them by setting rules and regulations including punishments for any act of violation.

Autonomy and the transcendental nature of the Absolute Moral Imperative

In this theory of the five cosmic values, there is an absolute moral imperative, by which I mean that which is valid for every human being regardless of colour, gender, race, religious belief, social level, economic status, and the like. It is not contingent upon a specific time or place, and in this sense it is absolute.

The absolute moral imperative is from religion, and it is itself the reason because human beings are rational beings and can interpret the meaning of moral obligation. Human beings are morally responsible because they act morally as autonomous beings according to rationality and free will. A person is an autonomous being because they do what is in the interest of human beings and human dignity; the person is free because they do what they deem to be rationally correct, even if it is against the desires of their soul, and thus their rational compliance with the law of the five cosmic values is in conformity with the religious command, because the moral imperative is true in itself (and not by any other consideration), is rational by all logical standards, and a legitimate right for everyone. Thus, man's servitude to God becomes an autonomous action and exercise of freedom.

Absolute moral law is transcendental because it transcends the limits and capacity of the human mind. It is from a transcendental source that transcends reason and experience, but it is open to reason and experience in understanding its universality and its necessity for human life. Revelation in this sense transcends reason. But can human reason legislate for itself that which satisfies its (reason's) notions and obtains the approval of people? The answer may be that the mind can do this, but in doing so if the mind itself is betrayed, harmed, or becomes treacherous to humanity, then it has committed an immoral act. An example is gambling. Both gambling and its legislation are morally wrong because gambling is destructive to the five cosmic values; it is based on greed and destroys the value of property by seeking quick profit with no effort of productive labour that is necessary for and contributive to the society. Gambling is also destructive to the second cosmic value (life) because gamblers end up with addiction, depression, offence, crimes, and suicide. The little benefit gained from gambling cannot outweigh the harm caused by it.

For a similar reason, usury is also immoral in the five cosmic values theory and prohibited by God's command because it destroys property and uses money as an end in itself or a commodity to be exchanged. Slavery, and discrimination based on colour (and other factors) are also immoral because they infringe the principle of human dignity.

The importance and the ranking of the Five Cosmic Values

The five cosmic values are necessary for human existence. Thus, every society should preserve and protect them; otherwise, human life would be harsh, brutal, poor, and miserable. These values have a practical hierarchy; the first of which is religion (spiritual value) and the last is property:

First, I would like to note that "freedom" cannot be considered as an independent cosmic value because "freedom" must the assumed as a cause of moral actions related to all five values above. The order of the five cosmic values, as stated earlier, is based on what is most essential for human society. Spirituality is the essence of a human being, and the power of belief is the strongest motivation in life, making religion occupy the first place in the hierarchy of values. Changing the priorities of the five cosmic values will lead to the creation of different societies, for example, placing property at the top of the hierarchy creates a material society, which lacks an understanding of the differentiation between means and ends, lacks spiritual values, is dominated by dishonest competition and cruelty in the process of seeking profits. It also leads to acts of pretending and pride in materialism. Changing the priorities of these necessities will lead to perplexity in moral life. The five cosmic values have global vitality, which reside in the fact that these values are necessary for every single culture regardless of whether it is Islamic or not. The failure to preserve them results in chaos for that culture, irrespective of its identity.

Is it possible that moral values based on religion be compatible with moral values derived from Pure Reason?

True knowledge from science and logic is supposed to harmonize with the truth of revelation. Let us take the example of the intellect:

According to revelation (*waḥy*), and the Islamic Divine Law (*Sharīʿah*), intellect is a necessity and must be preserved. Since alcohol nullifies intellectualization, alcohol and any other substance that can cause similar effects become prohibited. There might be some benefits in alcohol, as Qurʾān mentions; however, it also mentions that alcohol's harms overweigh its benefits, and thus it is prohibited.[25] A set of legislations must prevent its use because it inflicts harm on all society, family, and individuals (Fig. 1). Allah, in His absolute wisdom, legislates for human beings benefits that sometimes they cannot anticipate themselves.

Reason alone might prefer its own way of stating benefit and harm; however, the reason is limited to its methodology. The golden key to knowing benefit and harm is "experience," and the only road to it is "trial and error." Through experience, people discovered that alcohol caused harm and illness to individuals, young and old, and based on this, reason started to restrict the consumption of alcohol. With more experience, society realized that alcohol caused financial harm by affecting both the health and wealth of society; reason sought more alcohol regulation. Gaining more experience, reason realized that drinking and driving caused terrible damage to the life of people, prop-

---

25 Qurʾān 2:219.

erty, family, and society; thus, rational legislation went further in restricting the consumption of alcohol. With further experience because of advancement in science and medicine, the harm of alcohol started to manifest itself in other areas of life. Physicians realized that pregnant women who consume alcohol are destroying their fetuses physically and mentally. The harm inflicted on the fetus, the mother, the family, procreation, and society led to more restrictions on alcohol. However, although alcohol restriction is ongoing, it is not yet in the form of prohibition as in the Divine Law. After all, the route of reason in seeking more restrictions on consuming alcohol is continually confirming the beneficial aspect of the Divine Law legislation, showing no contradiction between reason and revelation in morality.

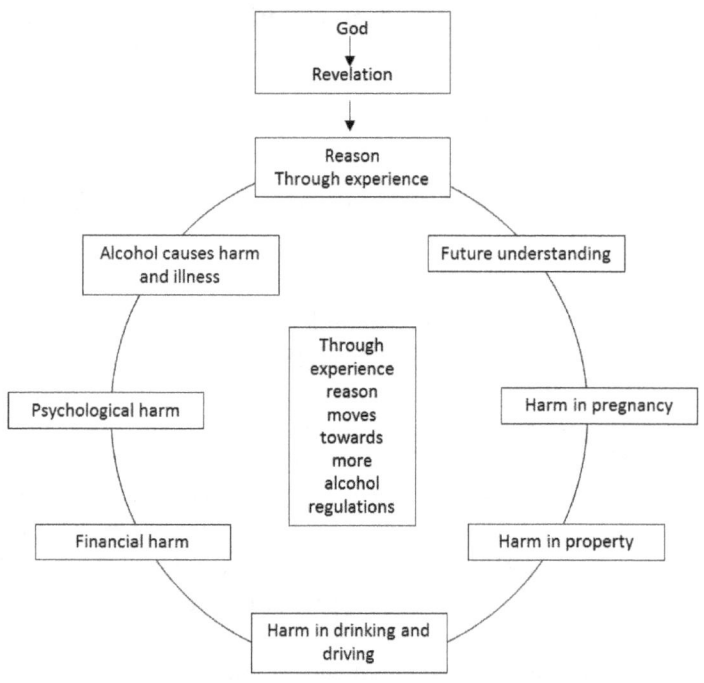

Fig. 1 Harmful effects of alcohol

In short, it seems that the mind revolves around its experience and converges on the judgment from the provisions of the *Sharīʿah*. Thus, the mind's path in searching for more restrictions on alcohol consumption constantly confirms the beneficial aspects of the Divine Law and the prohibition on the use of alcohol. Thus, it appears that there is neither contradiction nor disagreement between reason and revelation in this aspect. It follows therefore that the human intellect can legislate partial laws that are reasonable and binding. Still, it cannot legislate an absolute objective moral law that is binding on all human beings at all times.

Is it possible to break the absolute moral law by an action that will not be described as immoral?

I mentioned earlier that an action is morally right if it is consistent with preserving the five cosmic values and does not conflict with them or causes harm. But is it possible to break the absolute moral law by an action that will not be described as immoral? The answer, according to this theory, is "yes." A successful moral theory must also consider the human condition outside the area of free will, which we call the "necessities." Although the action is not in harmony with the theory, it is not considered an immoral act, either because of the absence of the freedom of the will or because of the necessity that prompted it. The rules for such actions are the following:

Rule 1: Cases of necessity make permissible what is normally forbidden or restricted

It is noted that the categorical imperative, according to Kant, has no exceptions. This weakness in deontological ethics was dealt with by W. D. Ross (1877–1971) in his book *The Right and the Good* where he discussed some general principles of what he called *"prima facie"* duty and its relation to the "actual or absolute duty".[26] In the theory of the five cosmic values, we can take into consideration the cases of "necessities" as it is possible, for example, to issue a verdict or legal opinion permitting abortion under the necessity of saving the mother's life, such as if her pregnancy is threatening her life. Despite a conflict with the cosmic value of procreation and that of life of the fetus, preserving the life of the pregnant mother is more important than preserving the life of the fetus because the mother is the source of it, and because we are more certain of her life. We are not sure of the life of the fetus who is alive in the mother's womb and does not possess an independent life. There are many details in the books of Islamic jurisprudence regarding the priorities and the importance of pregnant women. This chapter does not allow for such details. However, regarding the above rule, consideration should be given to the following:

First, that the exception of this act is contingent upon the state of extreme necessity only, as the permissibility of the act is restricted by the restriction that constituted it, this can be formulated as a sub-rule: *Necessity is determined by its particular circumstances.* The exception ceases immediately with the removal of this condition. Therefore, the sub-rule assumes another sub-rule that is formulated in this way: *What becomes permissible for a specific reason becomes impermissible when that reason ceases to exist.*

---

26 William David Ross, *The Right and the Good* (Oxford: Oxford University Press, 1930), 28.

Rule 2: Cases of necessities do not forfeit the rights of others

It should also be noted that one's necessity does not nullify the rights of others. In other words, it does not give a person the freedom to dispose of the rights of others. If he does, he is morally liable to make restitution or compensation to the victim. This is because compulsion is a compulsion for a person for that specific act, as it is against their will, but it is not permissible for the person to turn it into a voluntary act to harm others (or use others as a means to an end) which leads to the formulation of the following rule as a second rule: *Cases of necessities do not forfeit the rights of others*. And all the above is implicitly based on a general principle in the theory, which is: *Hardship secures lenience*. This is only related to hardship that is not associated with the devotional acts of worship because these acts are all within human beings' abilities, and God does not burden a soul beyond its ability.[27]

Deconstructing the Conflict between two moral actions: Priorities and Theory of Harm

An act might take place by way of compulsion without the freedom of the will that violates the absolute imperative in the preservation of the five cosmic values. However, it is not necessarily considered an immoral act, but the question is how to resolve the conflict between two contradictory moral actions?

Rules for removing harm

First, when two actions are in conflict, and one of them causes harm, then this rule must be followed: *harm must be removed*. The harm can be private or public. It is also permissible to prevent harm before it occurs as a preventive measure. Then the conflict can be removed according to this rule: *harm should be removed as much as possible (without causing damage)*. If the removal of the harm causes harm, then it defeats the purpose. The contradiction can be lifted by observing the above rule and the following sub-rule: *harm should not be removed by harm like it*. Accordingly, if there are two opposing harms, then this rule must be followed: *The greater of two harms is averted by assumption of the lesser, i.e., by choosing the lesser of the two harms*. But if private harm conflicts with public harm, then the resolution of the conflict is according to this rule: *Public harm or loss is averted by the private assumption of loss*. However, it is not permissible for any person to harm himself or herself according to this rule: *It is not permissible to do what will harm oneself*. According to the above rule, suicide, for example, is morally wrong and is prohibited; it is also morally wrong to injure oneself. But if a harm conflicts with interest, then the conflict can be resolved by following this rule: *Averting harm is to be preferred over procuring benefits*. In many cases the harm will be measured according to what it necessitates and case by case.

---

27 Qur'ān 2:186.

Case study: the abandoned ship. This case was mentioned at the beginning of this chapter. I should briefly say that in the case of the abandoned ship, al-Ghazālī thinks that the killing of the ten people cannot be morally justified by the principle of public interest or the safety of the majority because al-Ghazālī thinks that *maṣlaḥah* or public interest must meet three conditions: universality, necessity, and certainty. In the case of the abandoned ship none of them was met.

Case study: The School bus driver. A man suffers from epilepsy, and he is under treatment with a doctor, then he decided to apply for a job as a bus driver in a school to transport students from their homes to the school and back. The school administration decided to collect some information about his health condition after news reached it that he was being treated, but no one knew for what. Suppose the school administration asks his doctor for a medical report about his health condition and its history. Is it permissible for the doctor to reveal to them the type and history of the disease?

If the doctor did, he would violate the moral and legal obligation to preserve the privacy and confidentiality of patients' cases, and he would harm them. If he does not, he will harm many innocent students. So, what is the solution in such a situation? How is the conflict between these two actions resolved?

Rights: The consensus between two parties does not forfeit the rights of others

The personal agreement between two or more individuals does not invalidate the rights of others. Rights are principles and standards that are binding on everyone without exception, and laws protect them because they are an asset for the good of society, and it is not permissible to forfeit or waive them.

These rights are either the rights of God or the rights of people. It is not permissible for any person, regardless of their position, authority, or social status, to revoke these rights even if it was by mutual consent because they are not specific to him or her only, and they are related to human interests.

Example: Suppose that a married couple with children living an unstable marital life decide to separate on the understanding that the wife separates from the husband while abandoning her children. This mutual consent between the two parties does not nullify either spouse's right to see their children and spend time with them, nor the children's rights to be seen by their parents.

Example: A male and female a student at the university agreed to have sexual intercourse with mutual consent and without marriage or outside marriage. The mutual consent between them does not extinguish the right of punishment for adultery, because adultery spoils one of the five cosmic values that the absolute moral imperative intended to preserve, which is the cosmic value of procreation, and the punishment is a legitimate societal right to protect the public interests.

Is it possible for the action to be consistent in its outcome with the Five Cosmic Values but not be considered moral?

The five cosmic values theory urges the human soul to do all kinds of good in harmony with the five cosmic values. Still, the theory clearly distinguishes between the methodology of moral action and the teleology of this action. In other words, it distinguishes between the method of moral action and the goal of moral action. In this theory, the morally justified goals are those goals that human beings have reached with noble actions that do not violate any of the five cosmic values. Good intention does not change the moral status of a wrong or forbidden action.

Example: Feeding the needy and helping them is a noble moral act but feeding them with stolen money is an immoral act; rather, it deserves punishment as theft is prohibited. Also, feeding them to show off in front of people is an immoral act. Absolute moral law is concerned with the purity of intention, and the action that results from it is a noble ethical practice that refines the human soul.

Conclusion

The theory of five cosmic values presents to educators an Islamic moral theory that offers a rational criterion of solving moral problems in a way that is harmonious to Islamic teaching. The theory offers the absolute imperative for moral judgment that makes a clear demarcation between the right and the wrong action.

Bibliography

Al-Ghazālī, Abū Ḥāmid. *Al-Mustaṣfā min ʿilm al-uṣūl.* 2 vols. Beirut, Lebanon: Muʾassasat al-Risālah, 1997.

Al-Ghazālī, Abū Ḥāmid. *Intention, Sincerity, and Truthfulness.* Translated by Anthony F. Shaker. Cambridge: The Islamic Text Society, 2016.

Kant, Immanuel. *Grounding for the Metaphysics of Morals.* Translated by James W. Ellington. Indianapolis/Cambridge: Hackett publishing company, Inc., 1981

Ross, William David. *The Right and the Good.* Oxford: Oxford University Press, 1930.

Chapter 20

Spotlights on the Islamisation of Education from Syed Ali Ashraf's Perspective

Muḥammad Al-Sayyid Al-Sayyid Al-Ṣaftī

Islamisation of Education

Islamisation of education is an idea that has been extensively discussed following the First World Conference on Muslim Education held in Makkah in 1977. Professor Syed Ali Ashraf, to whom this work is dedicated, played the most dominant role in organising this and some other World Conferences that followed to discuss and sharpen philosophical arguments surrounding various aspects of Islamic education and its implementation in the modern world. Scholars who must be mentioned along with Syed Ali Ashraf for their remarkable contributions to the process Islamising education vis-à-vis the mainstream Western system of education include Syed Naquib al-Attas, Ismaʿil Raji al-Faruqi, and Seyyed Hossein Nasr who, like Syed Ashraf, had been working in the field of Muslim culture and tradition even before the organisation of the World Conferences. Muslim thinkers were deeply worried by the state of education in Muslim countries in the post-colonial period. After the formal independence of these countries many of them started to be ruled by governments that did not reflect the aspirations and wishes of the masses. Although these countries were formally independent, by and large they retained many of the colonial policies and especially the educational system remained as it was left by the imperialists. The nature of education that Muslims inherited from their colonial past has been vividly captured by Nakissa when he says:

> The empires promoted Western education for Muslims (especially elites), with the aim of exposing them to Western forms of knowledge and ideas about progress. It was expected that Muslims educated in this manner would gradually incorporate Western ideas about progress into their religious tradition, thereby fostering a reformed Islam.... It was also expected that Western education would weaken

Muslim religious belief, generating graduates less inclined towards fanaticism and *jihād* rebellion.[1]

The educational legacies that the Muslim countries inherited from their colonial rulers were marked by several important features. Firstly, the integrated holistic education system followed in Muslim lands was replaced by two streams of education—Western education that prepared students for worldly knowledge and madrasah system that imparted religious knowledge for producing the clergy. Ever since, the products of these two systems have been at loggerheads with each other over controlling the masses. Secondly, the main aim of education was to produce a class of people whose lifestyle and way of thinking would be in accordance with the wishes of the colonial masters and with little allegiance to the roots of their own faith. Finally, another feature was the government's neutrality on religious questions, which promoted secular education in the country while at the same time letting the madrasah education continue in an impoverished way. The dichotomy in these policies have been effectively maintained throughout the post-independent period with the secular education gaining ground. The education system they follow in Muslim countries is thus secular and Western—British or French. Consequently, in response to the growing influence of secularism and with the aim of preserving and revitalising Muslim culture and traditions across all aspects of life, diverse educational models promoting Islamisation have been put forth, both on local and global scales. These initiatives seek to instil Islamic values, morality, and spirituality, ultimately rekindling a sense of Ummatic consciousness.

Education in the Age of Imperialism

During colonial rule, the prevalent form of education in Muslim countries was Western secular education, imparted in schools and universities. This education provided students with rigorous training but often instilled doubts, leading some to embrace agnosticism or atheism. Thus, students shifted loyalty and respect from their country to the West. Our students rather looked at the colonisers of our countries as cultural emissaries and advocates of renaissance, who were essential for the development of our countries, and saw Islam as the cause of Muslim regression. Nowadays, our educated youths behave as if they do not belong to our homelands. In the past, young people were actively involved in resisting colonialists and imperialists, driving them out of their homelands. They viewed these foreign forces as invaders seeking to exploit their valuable resources and treasures. However, today, many youths perceive imperialists as agents of civilization and progress.

---

1 Aria Nakissa, "Liberalism's Distinctive Policy for Governing Muslim Populations: Human Rights, Religious Reform, and Counter-Terrorism from the Colonial Era Until the Present," *History Compass* 20, no. 9/e12748 (September 2022), https://doi.org/10.1111/hic3.12748.

So, education in the colonial era was distanced from religion. Since the English created English schools and universities, their education developed generations who did not maintain the national or religious spirit or thought about reforming their countries. One would not be astounded to read what Macaulay said: "We must at present do our best to form a class who may be interpreters between us and the millions whom we govern—a class of persons Indian in blood and colour, but English in tastes, in opinions, in morals and in intellect."[2] Zwemer, a prominent missionary leader, asserted that educational programs in Muslim countries prepared youths who did not know how to connect with God, leading them away from Islam. He argued that this was part of the colonialist agenda, aiming to create Muslims who were indifferent to their own well-being, their nation, and their religion, instead fostering a preference for comfort and laziness.[3]

Indeed, the education systems in Muslim countries have been estranged from Islamic principles since the onset of colonisation, and this disconnect persists even in the post-colonial era. Its objective was to lead Muslim youths toward agnosticism or atheism, isolating them from Islam's teachings. This initiative aimed to cultivate a generation of educated young individuals skilled in specific fields under the guidance of proficient instructors employing rigorous techniques. Unfortunately, this came at the cost of neglecting their own religious knowledge, leaving them with a skewed understanding of Islam and its core principles. Furthermore, it nurtured doubts within the hearts of these Muslim youths, making it challenging for them to embrace their faith and develop a deep love for their countries.

The colonial rulers introduced this educational system because they found it hard to evangelise Muslims and control their mind. Therefore, they decided to change the educational system. Zwemer says that as Muslims were avoiding Christian schools, it was necessary to create for them secular schools and make it easy for them to join such schools, for such schools would help eliminate the spirit of Islam in the students.[4]

---

2 Lord Macaulay published an official minute on the method of education in these countries on 2 February 1835 and was approved by William Bentinck on 7 March of the same year: "Minute by the Hon'ble T. B. Macaulay, dated the 2nd February 1835," Bureau of Education. Selections from Educational Records, Part I (1781–1839). Edited by H. Sharp. Calcutta: Superintendent, Government Printing, 1920. Reprint. Delhi: National Archives of India, 1965, 107-117.

3 Muḥammad Maḥmūd Ṣawwāf, *Al-Mukhaṭṭaṭāt al-Istiʿmāriyyah li-Mukāfaḥat al-Islām* (Dār al-Iʿtiṣām, 1963), 216-7.

4 *Al-Ghārah ʿalā al-ʿĀlam al-Islāmī*, 82 quoted in ʿAbd al-Raḥmān Ḥasan Ḥabannaka al-Maydānī, *Ghazw fīʾl-Ṣamīm: Dirāsah Wāʿiyah lil-Ghazw al-Fikrī* (Beirut, Damascus: Dār al-Qalam, 1982), 28.

Rise of Dichotomous Islamic Education and Muslim Response

The formal national and governmental education system in Muslim countries is only an extension of the Western system of education.⁵ The Western secular system of education affects all branches of knowledge. Especially, modern science is taught in such a way that impugns Islam and the Qurʾān, for this system was initially developed to promote the separation of religion and science and to spread the notion that science and religion are in conflict. As this dichotomy is against the principle of Islam, it was necessary that a pure Islamic education develops in response to this. It consists of the teaching of the Qurʾān and the Sunnah and rejecting every aspect of modern education that is contradictory to Islam.⁶ Syed Ali Ashraf stressed the need to develop a third form of education that combines modern education and religious one.⁷ Many scholars have been working on developing such a system.

Islamic education taught in the mainstream system of Muslim countries is inadequate and cannot resist the challenges that secularism poses to Islam. Religious education is a necessity for the survival of the religion, but the teaching of Islamic education is confined to mosques and seminaries, which have very important but recognisably limited roles. It is not appropriate to isolate religion from full participation in society. It is necessary to extend Islamic teachings to all levels of education, but a lack of sufficient knowledge of modern education, science and technology makes it difficult to achieve this in the modern world.

Professor Ashraf had a holistic approach to education. This holistic nature of education can be observed in a properly developed Islamic system of education that promotes spiritual, moral, intellectual, and physical development spanning the entire life.⁸ God the Almighty clarified in His noble Book that reflecting on God's creation and remembering God represents an act of worship: "Indeed, in the creation of the heavens and the earth and the alternation of the night and the day are signs for those of understanding. Who remember Allah while standing or sitting or [lying] on their sides and give thought to the creation of the heavens and the earth, [saying], 'Our Lord, You did not create this aimlessly; exalted are You [above such a thing]; then protect us from the

---

5   Hamid Hasan Bilgrami and Syed Ali Ashraf, *Mafhūm al-Jāmiʿah al-Islāmiyyah*, trans. ʿAbd al-Ḥāmid al-Khuraybī (Jeddah, KSA: Sharikat Maktabāt ʿUkāẓ lil-Nashr waʾl-Tawzīʿ, 1984), 33.
6   Bilgrami and Ashraf, *Mafhūm al-Jāmiʿah al-Islāmiyyah*, 33.
7   Syed Sajjad Husain, and Syed Ali Ashraf, *Azmat al-Taʿlīm al-Islāmī*, trans. Amīn Ḥusayn al-Ribāṭ (Jeddah, KSA: Sharikat Maktabāt ʿUkāẓ lil-Nashr waʾl-Tawzīʿ, 1983/1403), 35–36.
8   Muhammad Hamid Al-Afendi and Nabi Ahmed Baloch, *Al-Manhaj wa Iʿdād al-Muʿallim*, trans. ʿAbd al-Ḥāmid al-Khuraybī (Jeddah, KSA: Sharikat Maktabāt ʿUkāẓ lil-Nashr waʾl-Tawzīʿ, 1984), 149.

punishment of the Fire (Qurʾān 3:190-191).ʾ"[9] Similarly, thinking about God's creation to discover the scientific theories of the universe is an act of worshipping God the Almighty. We also read in God's Book about invitations to the human intellect to think and reflect: "Would you use intellect?"[10] "Would you think?"[11] "Would you see?"[12] "Would you remember?"[13]

Adam's Mission

Syed Ali Ashraf reminds us repeatedly that God, Mighty and Majestic, taught Adam all names:[14] "And He taught Adam the names—all of them (Qurʾān 2:31)." The children of Adam subsequently learned some of them through acquisition and trial. God's messengers came in succession to educate people. By virtue of knowledge, man has become the vicegerent of God on earth, and assumed the trust which the heavens, the earth, and mountains refused to do.[15] Thus, God gave His slave, Adam, may peace be upon him, capabilities to control the creatures and objects in the skies and on the earth. God the Almighty says: "It is Allah who subjected to you the sea so that ships may sail upon it by His command and that you may seek of His bounty; and perhaps you will be grateful. And He has subjected to you whatever is in the heavens and whatever is on the earth—all from Him. Indeed, in that are signs for a people who give thought (Qurʾān 45:12-13)."

As human beings are the knowers, the boundaries between the intellectual knowledge, the acquired knowledge, and Islamic religious knowledge tend to become blurred. The intellect discovers for man God's laws in the universe, i.e., the law of material objects or God's norm in the universe. As this law is discovered, knowledge is acquired so as to control matter. Man is not the maker or the creator of the law; he only discovers it. God the Almighty says: "It is not allowable for the sun to reach the moon, nor does the night overtake the day, but each, in an orbit, is swimming (Qurʾān 36:40)." This is God's cosmic law. So is God's legislation for man. Now, those who abide by God's law, are on the right track; and those who know God's law of material domain, they have more knowledge and have superior intellect. Knowledge that human beings acquire or create in the material domain is justified to the extent that it does not contradict their understanding of the revealed knowledge.

---

9   The translations of the Qurʾānic verses are taken from *Sahih International*.
10 Qurʾān 2:44, 76; 6:32; 7:169; 10:16; 11:51; 12:109; 21:10, 76; 23:80; 28:60; 37:138.
11 Qurʾān 7:179, 8:22, 45:5, 100-101.
12 Qurʾān 28:72; 43:51; 51:21.
13 Qurʾān 10:3; 11:24, 30. 16:17; 23:85; 37:155; 45:23.
14 Syed Ali Ashraf, *Āfāq Jadīdah fīʾl-Taʿlīm al-Islāmī*, Silsilat al-Taʿlīm al-Islāmī, trans. Amīn Ḥusayn al-Ribāṭ (Jeddah, KSA: Maktabat Dār al-Zamān lil-Nashr waʾl-Tawzīʿ, 1984), 11.
15 Qurʾān 33:72.

Therefore, Syed Ali Ashraf says that human beings are qualified to know about the universe endlessly.[16] God has subjected everything to human beings, but they have to know that they are created, are slaves of God, and that God sees them, wherever they are. God the Almighty says, "There is in no private conversation between three but that He is the fourth of them, nor are there five but that He is the sixth of them—and no less than that and no more except that He is with them [in knowledge] wherever they are (Qurʾān 58:7)." Also, God the Almighty says [in Luqman's words], "O my son, indeed if it [i.e., a wrong] should be the weight of a mustard seed and should be within a rock or [anywhere] in the heavens or in the earth, Allah will bring it forth (Qurʾān 31:16)." The Messenger, may God's peace be upon him, says, "If you cannot see Him, he is indeed seeing you."[17]

The cosmic laws are only from God's power and norm in the universe. Thus, searching for scientific truths—to know God's creation—becomes part of religion. Religion cannot be fully understood without the knowledge of some scientific truths. Intellect is necessary to understand the laws of religion, as it is necessary to know the scientific truths. Knowledge is required for reflection and worship. Religion or the laws of religion need an intellect that understands God's commands and prohibitions. As such, the scientific facts meet the religious facts. Scientific facts have been spoken of, referred to, or kept silent about by religion. No religious issue would ever conflict with a scientific issue, except when religion or science is misunderstood. Therefore, Syed Ali Ashraf, may God's mercy be upon him, says that education and teaching are inseparable in Islam. Also, a mere formal mixing between them is not an ideal education.[18]

Education can never be ideal except when scientific and religious methods fully integrate, so that there would be a comprehensive combination of religion, science, and ethics. Also, religion encompasses all life activities, along with belief in God, the Lord of the worlds. Each activity that one does is a religious activity for which one is rewarded by God the Almighty, as long as he does it sincerely for God alone. This is the meaning of the Qurʾānic verse, "And I did not create the jinn and mankind except to worship Me (Qurʾān 51:56)."

In his reflection and thinking, a Muslim worships God. Also, in his prostration and humility, a Muslim worships God. And in his work, a Muslim worships God. Likewise, providing youths with physical training is an act of worship, for the Prophet says: "A strong believer is better and more lovable to God than a weak believer."[19] Minds that are intelligent in understanding the religion and

---

16 Husain and Ashraf, *Azmat al-Taʿlīm*, 29.
17 Muḥammad ibn Ismāʿīl al-Bukhārī, *Ṣaḥīḥ al-Bukhārī, Kitāb al-Tafsīr, Bāb Inna Allāh ʿIndahu ʿIlm al-Sāʿah*, no. 4499, vol. 4 (Dar Ibn Kathir, Beirut, 1987), 1793.
18 Afendi and Baloch, *Al-Manhaj wa Iʿdād*, 149.
19 Abū al-Ḥusayn Muslim ibn al-Ḥajjāj, *Ṣaḥīḥ Muslim, Kitāb al-Qadar, Bāb fīʾl-Amr bil-Quwwah*

life are godly minds. Any moral act is an Islamic act that keeps people away from disobeying God. We read in the Qurʾān: "It is He who has sent among the unlettered a Messenger from themselves reciting to them His verses and purifying them and teaching them the Book and wisdom—although they were before in clear error (62:2)." So, God's words, "reciting to them His verses" indicate an auditory purification, "and purifying them" means a moral uplifting, "and teaching them the Book and wisdom" is a theoretical refinement and behavioral education that invoke the Prophet's example.[20]

The principles of this education exist in God's Sharīʿah. Therefore, God has preserved the source of this Sharīʿah: "Indeed, it is We who sent down the message [i.e., the Qurʾān], and indeed, We will be its guardian (Qurʾān 15:9)." God enjoined the Muslim community to apply this Sharīʿah: "And whoever does not judge by what Allah has revealed—then it is those who are the disbelievers (Qurʾān 5:44)," "And whoever does not judge by what Allah has revealed—then it is those who are wrongdoers (Qurʾān 5:45)," "And whoever does not judge by what Allah has revealed—then it is those who are the defiantly disobedient (Qurʾān 5:47)." So, those who intentionally do not judge by God's Sharīʿah are disbelievers, wrongdoers, and defiantly disobedient.

God has enjoined compliance with the Sharīʿah. Consequently, He enjoined that education must be inspired by it, for that which is ineluctable to fulfill an obligation is obligatory. Therefore, rejection of a Sharīʿah-inspired education is an act of disbelief, wrongdoing, and defiant disobedience of God, and thus disregarding the Sharīʿah is a total loss for education. The Muslim community loses when it leaves Islamic education. The cohesion of the Muslim community, which is maintained only through truth and patience, is likewise lost. God the Almighty says: "By the time! Lo! Man is in a state of loss; except for those who have believed and done righteous deeds and advised each other to truth and advised each other to patience (Qurʾān 103:1–3)."

Furthermore, Syed Ali Ashraf asserts Adam's mission as being a vicegerent of God on earth, entrusted with the responsibility of settling on the earth, worshipping God, and doing what pleases God. He says that Islamic education is "a trust that man bears until the Day of Resurrection."[21] He adds, "such an education was the mission of God's messengers, who were sealed by our Prophet Muhammad, may God's peace and blessings be upon him."[22] The comprehensive message of education continued from the Prophet's time, as God the Almighty says: "And do not forget your share of the world. And do good

---

wa-Tark al-ʿAjz, no. 2664, vol. 4 (Dar Ihya al-Turath al-Arabi, Beirut, 1972), 2052.
20 Maḥmūd ibn ʿAbdillāh al-Ālūsī, Rūḥ al-Maʿānī fī Tafsīr al-Qurʾān al-ʿAẓīm waʾl-Sabʿ al-Mathānī, vol. 10 (Beirut: Dār al-Fikr, 1978), 93.
21 Syed Ali Ashraf, Manuscript of Syed Ali Ashraf's Lectures, collected by Mahmud al-Hasan Yusuf (Dhaka: College of Religious Sciences, Dar al-Ihsan University), 17.
22 Bilgrami and Ashraf, Mafhūm al-Jāmiʿah, 38; Ashraf, Āfāq Jadīdah, 12.

as Allah has done good to you. And desire not corruption in the land. Indeed, Allah does not like corrupters (Qurʾān 28:77)."

Comprehensive Islamic Education Across Times

Comprehensive education also continued from the age of the Prophet through the rightly guided caliphs and the age of later caliphate. It continued until the Muslim states were occupied by European colonisers. The near total destruction of Islamic education in state schools, colleges and universities can be seen especially after the fall of the Ottoman caliphate in the First World War at the beginning of the twentieth century.[23] Under the comprehensive educational system, Muslim scholars would teach Islamic law, the Qurʾān, the Sunnah, medicine, and engineering which continued until the age that witnessed the beginning of modern sciences in Baghdad, Andalusia, and other Muslim countries. No double measures or partial treatment were involved as regards the teaching of such topics.[24] Muslims made remarkable contributions in various fields of knowledge when the European civilisation was in the Middle Ages. Some great Muslim minds are mentioned below.

Muslim Contributions to Science and Philosophy

Muslim scholars have significantly contributed to various fields throughout history. Below are some of the philosophers and scientists, along with the areas in which they made notable contributions:

1. Philosophy: al-Kindī (801–873), al-Fārābī (870–950), Ibn Sīnā (980–1037), al-Ghazālī (1058–1111), Ibn Rushd (1126–1198).
2. Mathematics: al-Khuwarizmī (c. 780–c. 850), Muḥammad ibn ʿĪsā Māhānī (c. 820–874), Abū-l Wafā al-Būzjānī (940–998), ʿUmar Khayyām (1048–1131), Naṣīr al-Dīn al-Ṭūsī (1201–1274).
3. Astronomy: al-Battānī (858–929), Ibn Yūnus (c. 950–1009), al-Zarqālī (1029–1100), Jābir ibn Aflaḥ (c. 1100–1150), Ibn Shāṭir (1305–1375).
4. Chemistry: ʿAlī, may God be pleased with him (600–661), Imām Jaʿfar al-Ṣādiq (699–765), Jābir b. al-Ḥayyān (760–815), Dhu-l-Nūn al-Miṣrī (c. 796–860), al-Jaldakī (c. 1308–c. 1350).
5. Physics: al-Fārābī (870–950), al-Bīrūnī (973–1048), Ibn al-Haytham (965–1040), al-Khāzin (c. 900–971), Quṭb al-Dīn al-Shīrāzī (1236–1311).
6. Medicine: al-Kindī (801–873), Abū Bakr al-Rāzī (c. 854–925), Ibn Sīnā (980–1037), ʿAlī b. ʿĪsā al-Kaḥḥāl (c. 940–1010), Ibn Zuhr (1094–1162).
7. Biology: ʿAlī al-Ṭabarī (810–861), al-Masʿūdī (912–957), Ibn Miskawayh (930–1030), Ibn al-Nafīs (c. 1208–1288), al-Ḍumayrī (1341–1405).

---

23 Bilgrami and Ashraf, *Mafhūm al-Jāmiʿah*, 45.
24 Husain and Ashraf, *Azmat al-Taʿlīm*, 67.

8. Botany and agriculture: al-Aṣmaʿī (739–831), al-Dīnawarī (815–895), Ibn al-Bayṭār (1197 1248), al-Ghāfiqī (?–c. 1165), Rashīd-ad-Dīn Ibn Sūrī (1177–1242).
9. Geography: Ibn Khurdādbih (820–912), al-Kindī (801–873), Muḥammad al-Idrīsī (1100–1165), Ibn Jubayr al-Andalusī (1145–1217), Ibn Baṭṭuṭa (1304–1368), Kâtip Çelebi or Ḥājjī Khalīfa (1609–1657).
10. Sociology: Ibn Khaldūn (1332–1406).

These scholars sowed the seeds of modern civilisation in Europe. When the Islamic forts collapsed in Europe, their research was transmitted to European institutions of learning at the beginning of the age of the Renaissance.

Dimensions of Secular Education in the Modern World

During the medieval era in Europe, which roughly spanned from the 5th to the 15th century, the church did hold significant influence over many aspects of life, including politics, culture, and education. While the church was indeed influential, Europe experienced a complex interplay of religious and secular powers during the medieval period. Martin Luther (1483–1546) ignited the struggle against the church, which was followed by the critiques of Descartes (1596–1650), Francis Bacon (1561–1626), Spinoza (1632–1677), John Locke (1632–1704), Jean-Jacques Rousseau (1712–1778), Voltaire (1694–1778), Nietzsche (1844–1900), Durkheim (1858–1917), and Karl Marx (1818–1883). Their dissent gave rise to atheist literature exploring themes such as the death of God, the Copernican revolution (1543), historical analysis of religious texts, the application of reason to revelation, the decline of religious influence, and its comparison to "opium of the masses." Mirabeau (1749–1791), a charismatic orator, spearheaded the revolution against the church, resulting in the weakening of its authority. In the aftermath, a consensus emerged to relegate religion to the realm of personal belief, advocating for a separation of church and state.

As a result of the ideas that led to the Renaissance, Christian religious dogma's domination of science began to decline. The Biblically-based scientific authority was increasingly challenged by the Renaissance and the Age of Enlightenment scientists and philosophers. Many of the scientific discoveries were against the theological understanding of the church and as a result, many scientists put their careers, and sometimes their lives, on the line in order to discover the truth.[25] The Enlightenment revolution demolished the church as well as anything supernatural.

---

25 Howard Kramer, "Seven Scientists Who Challenged the Church," *Complete Pilgrim* (January 1, 2019), https://thecompletepilgrim.com/seven-scientists-challenged-church/.

A scientific blow that was devastating to the church was Darwin's theory (1809-1772), which indicated that the diversity of life on earth came about through a process of procreation and gradual evolution. This theory is not accepted by Islam. There have been many secular criticisms of the Darwinian theory of evolution since it was published in 1859.[26] Over time, the Western world witnessed a secularisation of various academic disciplines. Freud (1856-1939) established his psychology on the principle that religion and morality do not exist. He introduced concepts like the Oedipus complex to address psychological issues, but such concepts were against religion and morals.[27] Emile Durkheim emphasised the idea of the collective mind or a collective consciousness that shapes the beliefs, values, norms, and moral boundaries of people.[28] Karl Marx, the father of communism, saw religion as the "opium of the people" used as a tool to control the masses.[29] Lastly, Jean-Paul Sartre (1909-1956) came up with his existentialism that emphasised individual freedom and human responsibility. He argued that people should liberate themselves from the constraints of religion because true human existence could only be validated through the exercise of individual freedom.[30] Thus, atheism spread in Europe, and religion was separated from science, politics, ethics, economics, legislation, literature and life. Scientific research did not accept religion to be part of it. The Western understanding was that science should be kept separate from religion.

Whatever the reasons, religion gradually lost its control on the education of people. Human rationality was given the highest authority to decide on the truth of any proposition, be it religious or otherwise. The promotion of doubt as a tool for scientific progress created fertile ground for the spread of agnosticism and atheism. If atheism was justified, given all the antecedent events, in Europe, there is absolutely nothing to justify it in Muslim countries. The call of Islam has been a call for knowledge and science since the advent of Islam. God the Almighty says: "Read in the name of your Lord, Who created (Qurʾān 96:1)." Also, Islam honours science and scientists, as God says: "Only those fear Allah, from among His servants, who have knowledge (Qurʾān 35:28)."

---

26 Michael Denton, *Evolution: A Theory in Crisis* (London: Adler & Adler, 1985); Michael Denton, *Evolution: Still a Theory in Crisis* (Seattle: Discovery Institute Press, 2016).
27 Oedipus Complex: each male baby has sexual feelings towards his mother, but finds his father a barrier between them, so he suppresses his sexual desire toward his mother, thus leading up to this complex. Electra Complex, proposed by Carl Jung: the female baby has sexual feelings toward her father, but finds her mother a barrier between them, so she suppresses her love of her father and hates her mother, thus leading up to this complex. See Muḥammad Quṭb, *Dirasāt fīʾl-Nafs al-Insāniyyah* (Beirut: Dār al-Shurūq, 1980), 247-49.
28 Muḥammad Quṭb, *Madhāhib Fikriyyah Muʿāsirah* (Beirut: Dār al-Shurūq, 1983), 115.
29 Quṭb, *Madhāhib Fikriyyah*, 101.
30 Quṭb, 516.

When science in Europe began to diverge from religion, European schools sought to separate the two as much as possible. This might be the reason why Professor Syed Ali Ashraf was upset with the secular system of education. He completed his study in England[31] and worked as a professor at British and American universities. He stayed in the United Kingdom for a long time and combated the secular educational system. He established the Islamic Academy in Cambridge in 1983 and Darul Ihsan University in Dhaka, Bangladesh in 1990 whose mission was to develop an Islamic system of education and combat secularism in education.

Professor Ashraf always asserted that science attests to belief in God the Almighty. The thing that saddened him most was the European thinkers' call to free science from religion. When he came back to the Islamic orient, he was even more sad to see the separation of religion and science in the Muslim countries. He did not like the separation in education between religious sciences and profane sciences, just as he did not see the superficial combination or mixing of both as an ideal education. He thought that ideal education is one that is based on a unified method of combining religious and profane sciences.[32] Separation of education and religion is to deprive Muslims of their spiritual power and lay them open to be exploited by others.

Along the same lines, Professor Ashraf believed that reason is God's light to man, on the basis of which man was entrusted with the responsibility of acting as God's vicegerent on earth. Adam, may peace be upon him, was a messenger whom God endowed with full knowledge of things: "And He taught Adam all the names (Qurʾān 2:31)." The children of Adam acquired knowledge through experiments. God subjected to them the earth and everything on it. The Qurʾān says that God created human beings on earth and subjected to them everything in the skies and on earth: "It is Allah who subjected to you the sea so that ships may sail upon it by His command and that you may seek of His bounty; and perhaps you will be grateful. And He has subjected to you whatever is in the heavens and whatever is on the earth—all from Him. Indeed, in that are signs for a people who give thought (Qurʾān 45:12–13)."

Objectives of Islamic Education from Syed Ali Ashraf's Perspective

Islamic education is meant to refine students' behaviour; it is not a means to gain knowledge only. Indeed, Islam seeks to bring up righteous people who

---

31 Muhammad Ahsanullah Mia, Muhammad Ismail Husain, Mahmudul Hasan Yusuf, Muhammad Shamsuddoha, and Shah Waliullah Farhad, eds., *Bôrenyo: Syed Ali Ashraf Smarok Grôntho* (Dhaka, Bangladesh: Faculty of Religious Education, Darul Ihsan University, 1999), 204.
32 Bilgrami and Ashraf, *Mafhūm al-Jāmiʿah*, 45–46.

endeavour to reform their families and communities as much as they can.[33] Man cannot dispense with the divine revelation if they want to be guided by the truth. It is only intelligent and willing minds that understand and follow God's commands and prohibitions.

Professor Ashraf wonders: Would democracy in education suffice in lieu of the divine revelation to educate and refine people?[34] We know to what extent disbelief, atheism, and permissiveness have entered democratic systems that are followed in most countries of the world today. He says that Western people, due to the secular education that is freed from religion, are trained to believe in rationality as the highest tool of human cognition. Using their rationality, some individuals or groups exhibit a desire for power and control over the world, often disregarding the potential risks to humanity as a whole. This ambition is reflected in the creation of deadly weapons and the exacerbation of irreversible climate change, environmental pollution and degradation.

History bears witness that the West has dominated the East, desacralised it, took away its resources, shed the blood of its people, violated their honour, and had no mercy on the children, women, and old people. It destroyed and eliminated people's cherished beliefs and traditions as much as it could, because of its secular education that has grown without religion and ethics. It has produced generations of professionals and youths who are good at their professions but have not succeeded in preventing a debauched lifestyle.[35]

To achieve an ideal educational system, the integration of Islamic sciences and modern sciences is paramount. This integration should extend beyond the mere content of curricula; it must permeate the entire Islamic environment encompassing homes, schools, society, media, and leadership. Such an immersive approach ensures that students witness the embodiment of Islamic virtues in practice. Without this holistic integration, there's a risk that students may fail to grasp the essence of virtue and consequently fail to detect moral shortcomings in society.

Education, if confined solely to the confines of mosques, often lacks real-world applicability. It is essential for education to extend its reach beyond religious institutions, as the broader societal context is where various transgressions and deviations often prevail. Therefore, education should not exist in isolation but should continually manifest itself in both individual and collective life within a nation.[36]

---

33 Husain and Ashraf, *Azmat al-Talʿīm*, 61.
34 Husain and Ashraf, 19.
35 Ashraf, *Manuscript*, 19.
36 Husain and Ashraf, *Azmat al-Taʿlīm*, 17; Bilgrami and Ashraf, *Mafhūm al-Jāmiʿah*, 56.

Principles of Curriculum Designing and Their Implementation

Through his writings Professor Ashraf maintains that Man-Nature-God relationship is a fundamental concept in developing an Islamic system of education, as human beings as God's creation have been placed on the earth where they have to interact with their surroundings in accordance with the commandments of God. This concept leads to the following three relationships:[37] (a) belief in and relationship with God, (b) relationship with people, and (c) relationship with nature. In this hierarchy of relationships human being's relationship with God the Almighty occupies the highest position.

Syed Ali Ashraf stresses the importance of establishing a college for religious sciences that should be responsible to ensure that the disciplines of humanities and sciences are developed and taught in accordance with the Sharīʿah. This college would thus supervise two colleges.[38] One college would be for the humanities, including languages and such subjects as psychology, sociology, politics, economics and other social sciences. Another college would be for sciences including medicine, engineering, natural sciences, etc. The supervision is intended to maintain an Islamic perspective in teaching humanities and physical and biological sciences. Some of the steps suggested by Syed Ali Ashraf to develop an Islamic education system are as follows:

1. The Islamic theory of education for every branch of knowledge must be developed and advocated by Muslim intellectuals who truly believe in it and would assiduously work to implement it.
2. Curricula must be prepared by scholars who can combine the Islamic Sharīʿah with authentic scientific knowledge so that Islamic knowledge and scientific theories are linked together profoundly, thus removing the dichotomy between the religious and profane sciences.[39]

---

37 Syed Ali Ashraf, *Nubdhah ʿan Ḥarakat al-Taʿlīm al-Islāmī: Taḥlīl Tārīkhī 1977-1999* (Cambridge: Islamic Academy, 1990), 27-8; also Husain and Ashraf, *Azmat al-Taʿlīm*, 84.
38 Ashraf, *Nubdhah ʿan Ḥarakat*, 27.
39 So long as natural sciences such as physics, chemistry, biology, etc. are concerned, it is easy to link their curricula with religion, for material sciences are consequences of God's power in man, animals, plants, mountains, skies, and the earth. "Then do they not look at the camels—how they are created? And at the sky—how it is raised? And at the mountains—how they are erected? And at the earth—how it is spread out?" (Qurʾān 88:17-20). The explanation of God's power in animals, the spheres, mountains and their minerals, the earth and its treasures, as well as man and his mind and thought—all of these are from God's signs: "In yourselves, would not you look?" (Qurʾān 51:21). But social sciences are difficult to Islamise. As for psychology, Freud's theory, for example, is detrimental to religion as it is based on the denial of religion and creation, the accusation of religion as being a sexual remnant of the Oedipus Complex and that creation is a sexual remnant of the Electra Complex, that man has no spirit that yearns for God and seeks His pleasure—all of which represents a theoretical construct that has nothing to do with science. It represents ignorance about the religious concept of

3. A generation of excellent and capable young teachers must be trained to deliver the Islamic education so developed.
4. These curricula need upright and determined students and teachers who should try their best to inculcate in them piety, quietness, manners, and motivation to receive such an ideal education.
5. For such a theory to be practised, the Muslim society must be prepared to apply the Sharīʿah, for the Sharīʿah demands education of the community and resistance to intellectual and behavioral deviations therein.

The success of such a system of education depends on the willingness of the community to observe the Sharīʿah, which is an obligation for the community. The worst type of wrongdoing is to legislate for oneself, while it is worthier to heed to God's law, for God's law in the universe is to be discovered and acted upon. It should not be disregarded in favour of modern theories. Also, God's legislative laws should not be replaced by man-made laws with the hope of attaining happiness and pleasure in this world. God knows His creatures best: "Does He who created not know, while He is the Subtle, the Acquainted (Qurʾān 67:14)?" This is to educate the community in the light of the Sharīʿah and to educate the students according to the Islamic theory of education. This way, education would be integrated theoretically at school and practically in society. The community would thus have a believing generation that is well versed in life affairs, fearing and watching God in secrecy and in public, as the Prophet says: "Perfection (iḥsān) is to worship God as if you see Him. If you do not see him, He is seeing you."[40]

Conclusion

We believe, Syed Ali Ashraf's Islamic educational movement constitutes a major Islamic revolution to change the Muslim community whose education has become corrupted, economics ruined, and generations instilled with doubt and incapacity by colonialism. His educational theory is a roadmap to rebuild Muslim institutions, develop Muslim youths, and restructure the Muslim society following God's Sharīʿah. It is a much-needed task and also a gift for the Ummah, as God says, "Indeed, Allah will not change the condition of a people until they change what is in themselves (Qurʾān 13:11)." It is only through the attainment of a proper system of education that Muslim community would attain enlightenment and fulfil God's purpose of creation of human beings. They wonder: when will this happen? Say: hopefully soon.

---

man and his mission. Therefore, psychology must be reformed before it is absorbed into educational curricula. Likewise, sociology and especially the perspective of Durkheim must be purified before they are combined with religious sciences.

40 Ṣaḥīḥ al-Bukhārī, Kitāb al-Tafsīr, Bāb Inna Allāh ʿIndahu ʿIlm al-Sāʿah, no. 4499.

Bibliography

Al-Afendi, Muhammad Hamid, and Nabi Ahmed Baloch. *Al-Manhaj wàl-iʿdād al-Muʿallim.* Translated by ʿAbd al-Ḥāmid al-Khuraybī. Jeddah, KSA: Sharikat Maktabāt ʿUkāẓ lil-Nashr wàl-Tawzīʿ, 1984.

Al-Ālūsī, Maḥmūd ibn ʿAbdillāh. *Rūḥ al-Maʿānī fī Tafsīr al-Qurʾān al-ʿAẓīm wàl-Sabʿ al-Mathānī.* Vol. 10. Beirut: Dār al-Fikr, 1978.

Ashraf, Syed Ali. *Āfāq Jadīdah fīʾl-Taʿlīm al-Islāmī.* Silsilat al-Taʿlīm al-Islāmī. Translated by Amīn Ḥusayn al-Ribāṭ. Jeddah, KSA: Maktabat Dār al-Zamān lil-Nashr wàl-Tawzīʿ, 1984.

Ashraf, Syed Ali. *Manuscript of Syed Ali Ashraf's Lectures.* Collected by Mahmud al-Hasan Yusuf. Dhaka: College of Religious Sciences, Dar al-Ihsan University

Ashraf, Syed Ali. *Nubdha ʿan Ḥarakat al-Taʿlīm al-Islāmī: Taḥlīl Tārīkhī 1977–1999.* Cambridge: Islamic Academy, 1990.

Bilgrami, Hamid Hasan, and Syed Ali Ashraf. *Mafhūm al-Jāmiʿah al-Islāmiyyah.* Translated by ʿAbd al-Ḥāmid al-Khuraybī. Jeddah, KSA: Sharikat Maktabāt ʿUkāẓ lil-Nashr wàl-Tawzīʿ, 1984

Denton, Michael. *Evolution: A Theory in Crisis.* London: Adler & Adler, 1985.

Denton, Michael. *Evolution: Still a Theory in Crisis.* Seattle: Discovery Institute Press, 2016.

Al-Ghārah ʿalā al-ʿĀlam al-Islāmī. Quoted in ʿAbd al-Raḥmān Ḥasan Ḥabannaka al-Maydānī. *Ghazw fīʾl-Ṣamīm: Dirāsah Wāʿiyah lil-Ghazw al-Fikrī.* Beirut, Damascus: Dār al-Qalam, 1982.

Husain, Syed Sajjad, and Syed Ali Ashraf. *Azmat al-Taʿlīm al-Islāmī.* Translated by Amīn Ḥusayn al-Ribāṭ. Jeddah, KSA: Sharikat Maktabāt ʿUkāẓ lil-Nashr wàl-Tawzīʿ, 1983/1403.

Ibrahimi, Iskandar Ali. *Al-Taʿlīm al-Islāmī fī Banglādesh Qadīman wa Ḥadīthan.*

Kramer, Howard. "Seven Scientists Who Challenged the Church." *Complete Pilgrim* (January 1, 2019). https://thecompletepilgrim.com/seven-scientists-challenged-church/.

Mia, Muhammad Ahsanullah, Muhammad Ismail Husain, Mahmudul Hasan Yusuf, Muhammad Shamsuddoha, and Shah Waliullah Farhad, eds. *Bôrenyo: Syed Ali Ashraf Smarok Grôntho.* Dhaka, Bangladesh: Faculty of Religious Education, Darul Ihsan University, 1999.

Nakissa, Aria. "Liberalism's Distinctive Policy for Governing Muslim Populations: Human Rights, Religious Reform, and Counter-Terrorism from the Colonial Era Until the Present." *History Compass* 20, no. 9/e12748 (September 2022). https://doi.org/10.1111/hic3.12748.

Quṭb, Muḥammad. *Dirasāt fīʾl-Nafs al-Insaniyyah.* Beirut: Dār al-Shurūq, 1980.

Quṭb, Muḥammad. *Madhāhib Fikriyyah Muʿāsirah.* Beirut: Dār al-Shurūq, 1983.

Ṣawwāf, Muḥammad Maḥmūd. *Al-Mukhaṭṭaṭāt al-Istiʿmāriyyah li-Mukāfaḥāt al-Islām.* Dār al-Iʿtiṣām, 1963.

Chapter 21

Literary Activities of Professor Syed Ali Ashraf

Mahmud Shah Qureshi

It is said that some people are born with a silver spoon in their month. Our experience of life tells us that some possess literature in their blood. Professor Syed Ali Ashraf is undoubtedly one of them. From the family annals it is discerned that the Syed family had connection with rich relatives, but our professor's father had rather led a modest life. He was an Inspector of Schools. With a master's degree in Arabic, he could do perhaps better. But he was not ambitious. His first and second sons were, on the contrary, highly ambitious but what the French would say, *en bon sens*, i.e., in good directions. Besides the high academic positions, the two sons—Syed Ali Ahsan and Syed Ali Ashraf—held, both were acclaimed nationally and internationally as the most eminent literary personalities of their country.

Syed Ali Ashraf had a very congenial formative phase. In school, college, and university or at home he breathed literary flavour. Moreover, during the 1940s, he found himself deeply involved in a movement, sometimes known as the *Renaissance Movement*. This was initiated at Calcutta by Bengali Muslim journalists, writers and educationists who thought it their duty to encourage the political leaders to provide guidelines to masses to achieve a homeland for the Muslims of British India. Within two years of the famous Lahore Resolution of the All-India Muslim League (1940), some young Bengali intellectuals of Dhaka University founded the *Purbo Pakistan Sahityo Sôngsôd* (East Pakistan Literary Society) in 1942[1] following their elders in Calcutta. The last group was successful in creating a deep awareness in the Bengali cultural arena. They had really brought a new spirit in the rather dull life of Dhaka. At least four annual conferences were held successively in 1942, 1943, 1944 and 1945 where local elites along with Hindu and Muslim literary figures participated.

---

1 *Banglapedia: National Encyclopedia of Bangladesh*, s.v. "Purba Pakistan Sahitya Sangsad," accessed April 17, 2024, https://en.banglapedia.org/index.php/Purba_Pakistan_Sahitya_Sangsad.

The Association was organized with Syed Sajjad Hussain (1920–1995) as President, Syed Ali Ahsan (1922–2002) as General Secretary and Syed Ali Ashraf as Joint Secretary. Although the last-named two brothers with their first cousin Syed Sajjad Husain (both from father's and mother's sides)[2] were holding the key positions in the organization, this was, however, not a family affair.[3] While young intellectuals like Sardar Fazlul Karim (1925–2014), Munier Chowdhury (1925–1971) and others cooperated with them whole heartedly, slightly older ones like Abdur Razzaq (c. 1914–1999) (later a sage, like university don) and Mazharul Huq[4] (later an eminent economist) also helped them in various ways. In order to propagate their ideas, the *Purbo Pakistan Sahityo Sôngsôd* published a newspaper, *Pakshik Pakistan* (Pakistan Fortnightly). One student leader, Nazir Ahmad (d. 1944), who was killed by his Hindu opponents, had earlier shouldered some of the burdens of the Association.

As Syed Sajjad Husain and Syed Ali Ahsan had to go out of Dhaka to join their destined jobs in the mid-1940s, so Ali Ashraf had, for a long time, to continue the arduous duties single-handedly. He was fortunate to have two young ladies for collaboration. They were his class friends or contemporaries—Asia (later, Mrs Syed Ali Ashraf) and Meher (later to become Mrs Kabir Chowdhury and a writer).[5] As it is well known, Syed Ali Ashraf was an extremely brilliant student of the University of Dhaka, and he received his bachelor's degree (with honours) and master's degrees in first classes. After the examinations were over, he was quickly appointed as a lecturer at the Department of English, University of Dhaka. He also got married with Asia who in the meanwhile also completed her master's in Arabic. This sophisticated lady was a distinguished artist, particularly noted for her watercolour paintings. It is well known in the close quarters that she remained a great source of inspiration all through our professor's life.

The legacy of the literary association may by summarized in the words of Professor Syed Ali Ashraf as to have "created such an enthusiasm by advocating that Muslim Bengali literature has a tradition of its own, that they have been ignored so far and that our writers should use the language really spoken and used by the Muslims, that a new trend in creative writing emerged."[6]

---

2   See Appendix 2 for Professor Ashraf's family tree showing his relationships with Syed Sajjad Husain and Syed Ali Ahsan.

3   For its impact, see M. S. Qureshi, *Culture and Development* (Dhaka: Dhaka National Book Center, 1982), 1–14.

4   For a discussion of the East Pakistan Literary Society and some of the people cited here, see Syed Sajjad Husain, *The Wastes of Time: Reflections on the Decline and Fall of East Pakistan* (Dhaka: Ashraf Husain on behalf Muslim Renaissance Movement and Nōtun Sofôr Prōkashōni, 1995), https://archive.org/details/WastesOfTime/page/n1/mode/2up.

5   *Wikipedia*, s.v. "Kabir Chowdhury," accessed April 17, 2024, https://en.wikipedia.org/wiki/Kabir_Chowdhury.

6   Syed Ali Ashraf, *Muslim Traditions in Bengali Literature*, 3rd ed. (Dhaka: Islamic Foundation, 1983), 95.

During the 1940s, Syed Ali Ashraf did not write many poems, he rather published several articles on language, literature and on current topics. However, he considered himself as a representative of pre-Pakistan poets who were exploring new Muslim consciousness. But his first collection of verses, *Choitro Jôkhon* published in 1958, seems to have presented much stylized form, inspired by English poets such as Robert Browning and others. He experimented with the forms of monologue[7] to express his romantic feeling without neglecting the realistic setting. He also demonstrated a remarkable ability to convey these emotions through highly condensed lines of poetry. Let us quote one example.

তাইতো তোমার প্রেম মনে প্রাণে কাঁপন জাগায়
ছন্দোময় তরঙ্গ উচ্ছ্বাস, হৃদয়ের তলদেশে
অলক্ষিতে গেঁথেছ শিকড়, তাই সে তারা শোভায়
ভাষায় ফুলেরা ফোটে প্রণয়ের স্বাপ্নিক আবেশে।
সংশয় রয়েছে তবু? তবে এই চুম্বন বিভায়
প্রেম সত্য দীপ্ত হোক দ্বিধ-অন্ধ রুদ্ধ চেতনায়।

[An approximate rendering in English: That is why your love stirs me in my mind and heart; there is a flow of rhymed waves, you have fixed your roots at the bottom of my heart. So the stars shine, flowers blossom with expressions of dreamy ambiance of love. Yet any doubt? Then let this feeling of kiss keep the subdued and hesitant existence of love true and enlightened.]

Besides nine sonnets and several other long and short poems, this book contains a rather long piece entitled 'Boni Adom' with six sections. This is a unique poem in Bengali as it reveals in modern idiom the Qurʾānic ideals of human beings, their qualities, and their defects.

In 1960, Professor Syed Ali Ashraf translated into Bengali *Love Poems*[8] of Claire Goll addressed to her husband Yvan Goll whose poems for his beloved wife were rendered into Bengali by Professor Syed Ali Ahsan. Twenty-two short poems of the renowned French romantic poet may find some resonance with the emotions previously conveyed in the translator's original poems of *Choitro Jôkhon*.[9]

---

7 Ashraf, *Muslim Traditions*, 5, 69.
8 "*Love poems* was published in a limited edition by their own Hemispheres press in 1947. It wasn't until after Yvan's death in 1950 that Claire gathered together the full collection of nearly sixty poems and published them first in French as *Dix Mille Aubes* and then in German as *Zehntausend Morgenröten*," 'Translators' Prefaces,' to *10,000 Dawns: Love Poems of Yvan and Claire Goll* with eight drawings by Marc Chagall, trans. Thomas Rain Crowe and Nan Watkins (Buffalo, NY: White Pine Press, 2004), 14–15.
9 Cf. Syed Ali Ahsan, "Syed Ali Ashrafer Kōbita," in *Syed Ali Ashrafer Kōbita* by Syed Ali Ashraf (Dhaka: Shilpōtōru Prōkashōni, 1991), 9–18.

Bisôngoti, published in 1974 is the second book of verses by Syed Ali Ashraf and this indicates a turning point in his poetic and spiritual career. The opening poems of the book eloquently capture the exquisite beauty of nature in Bangladesh. Some translations or adaptations of Ezra Pound and K. E. Cummins are also added.

The third book, *Hijrôt* (1984) truly reveals the spiritual realizations of our poet. We have here poems like "Asfala Saafeliin," "Labbaek," "Hajre Aswad," "Kaaba" and the like which take us deep into the feeling dear to the Muslims. The present writer fondly remembers the memories of his Ashraf Chacha[10] who, himself very ardently guided him to perform ʿUmrah during the last week of October 1977. By all means, these poems are like "emotion recollected in tranquillity" to borrow the words of Wordsworth.[11] Let us just read the first section of the poem "Tawaaf":

এখানে যে ঘূর্নন, এতো ঘূর্নন নয়, এ হচ্ছে সময়ের
সরল রেখাকে অতিক্রম করে চক্রবৃত্তের স্থির চাঞ্চল্যে
আত্মবিসর্জন। অতীত, বর্তমান ও ভবিষ্যতের
বন্ধন থেকে মুক্ত হয়ে, বায়তুল্লাহর স্থিরবিন্দুকে
অনাদি ও অনন্তের স্থির বিন্দু মেনে তারই
চতুর্দিকে বারম্বার নিজের সর্বস্বকে
নিয়োজিত করা।

[Literal translation of "Tawaaf": This *ronde* here is not a mere *ronde*; this is but self-sacrifice in fixed movements around the circle, by passing the straight line of time. Being free from the bondage of the past, present and future, considering the fixed point of *Baytullāh* (House of Allah) as the fixed point which has no beginning nor any end, let one engage his total self once and again around it.]

While *Hijrôt* was dedicated to the memory of Hazrat Baba Zaheen Shah Taji (*Raḥmatullāh ʿalayh*),[12] later Dr Ashraf published *Rubaiyat-e Zahini* (1991) from the inspiration of his Pir's (spiritual guide) teaching of Love. Some short poems in this book are eloquent expressions of a great spiritual leader in the tradition of old Persian masters.

Proshnottôr (1996) is his latest collection of poems. There are a few old and new verses dealing with the fundamental question of man's suffering due to his separation from the Ultimate Reality. But the poet also knows the answer.

---

10 Literally, "Uncle Ashraf" as the author is the son in law of Professor Ashraf's elder brother, Professor Syed Ali Ahsan.
11 William Wordsworth, "Preface to Lyrical Ballads" (1800).
12 See Chapter 34 of this book about Professor Ashraf's connection with this saint. *Raḥmatullāh ʿalayh* means "May the mercy of Allah be upon him." It is usual to write or utter this phrase after the names of saintly people.

Therefore, he invokes people to come near, in the concluding poem "Ore tora aay" (Oh, Ye come along), presented here with an approximate translation:

তিনি আর তুমি	He and you
এক বীজ ভূমি	Are the same field of seeds,
এক ফসলের ক্ষেত,	Same field of crop.
আমি সেই ক্ষেতে	In that field,
সারে জীবন্ত	With the manure's nourishment,
ফসল বোনার বেতা।	I am a cane for cultivating crops.
তাইতো আমাকে	So, I see myself
ফলন্ত দেখি	As fruit-bearing,
অবয়বহীন কায়া	A formless form.
তোমাকেই চেয়ে	Longing for you,
আমাকেই পাই	I discover myself.
এ কোন মধুর মায়া।	What a sweet experience!
এই মায়াতেই	This experience,
হৃদি মজ্জায়	Deep within my being,
প্রেমের উচ্চারণ,	Sparks the expression of love.
তোমারই ভিতরে	Within you
মহব্বতের	It blooms as the sea of affection.
সাগর উৎসারণা।	
সেই সাগরেই	Within that sea
ডুবিয়ে দিয়েছ	You've engulfed me,
বিলীন করেছ তুমি	You've dissolved me.
তিনি আর তুমি	He and you,
মিলিয়ে দিয়েছ	Together, have forged a singular realm
একক বিচর-ভূমি।	Of endless exploration.

Professor Ali Ashraf's poetical work is not too vast, but it is very profound and charged with spiritual overtone. His prose is rather expansive, encompassing both a remarkable quantity and exceptional quality. First of all, we should mention his *Kabyo Porichôy*, i.e., an introduction to the study of poetry, published in 1956, and this was his first book indeed. It is perhaps significant to mention here that the book was dedicated to his beloved wife, Asia.

In this book, he follows the principles of Matthew Arnold and tells us about the importance of criticism in society. The book is an excellent treatise for any student of literature, who would like to be informed about Western and Eastern methods. Concerning these matters, he published several other articles, in particular about stylistics. However, his doctoral dissertation at Cambridge, "Poetry and Its Audience in England from 1914 to 1945" has not yet been published either in English or in Bengali translation. This work was done with the contemporary theories of the sociology of literature, an unexplored field of research as yet.

Professor Ashraf made a singular contribution by collecting and compiling a book of letters of the great Bengali poet Kazi Nazrul Islam and their study in the early 1960s. A second edition was out in 1995. He also edited a *festschrift* on the poet entitled, *Homage to Nazrul Islam* (1972). Earlier, the Bangla Academy of Dhaka commissioned him to edit a collection of Golam Mostafa's verses. He provided a penetrating short study on this important Muslim poet of the twentieth century Bengal.

During the last days of his life Professor Syed Ali Ashraf was engaged in writing articles on many subjects. Only a few are published or publishable, for most of them are incomplete. However, his *Sôngsôd Juge*, an elaborate history of the literary society we discussed earlier and about the cultural scene of the 1940s in Dhaka, was probably never published. He has also written a book for children, *Chotoder Nobi Kahini,* published by the Islamic Foundation in 1985. This is about the prophets—from Prophet Ādam to Prophet ʿĪsā. It is as instructive as it is a pleasant reading for readers of all ages.

Professor Syed Ali Ashraf's two very important contributions to the historiography of Bengali literature is fortunately available in both Bengali and English. His *Muslim Traditions in Bengali Literature*[13] is a solid work on the Muslim position in Bengali society and culture. He earlier published one original paper on the subject in *Bangla Academy Potrika.* The second work is the translation of Dr Muhammad Enamul Huq's *Muslim Bangla Sahityo* published by Pakistan Publication, Karachi in 1962.

In addition to his numerous articles in English, which have been published in encyclopaedias and Western journals, as well as in his own publication, *Muslim Education Quarterly* (published by the Islamic Academy, Cambridge), this initial investigation into his aforementioned works suggests that he led a notably dynamic literary career, even delving into Bengali literature and associated topics. He used to hold occasional seminars under the auspices of the Islamic Academy of Darul Ihsan University. Many young and elderly poets and intellectuals participated in those with great enthusiasm.

To sum up this point, we can quote what Professor Abu Rushd, a writer of great repute had to say about his poetry:

বহু বছর ধরে দেশের বাইরে থাকলেও তিনি বাংলা কাব্যের ধারাবাহিকতা থেকে বিচ্ছিন্ন হয়েছেন একথা বলা যায় না। . . . ব্যক্তিগত প্রেম অতিক্রম করে তিনি স্বদেশ প্রেমে উদ্বুদ্ধ হয়েছেন, জীবনের হতাশা ও গ্লানি প্রবলভাবে মনের জোরের সঙ্গে অতিক্রম করে নিজের ধর্মের স্থায়ী আশ্রয় ও শীতল ছায়ায় এসে স্বস্তি পেয়েছেন।

---

13 Ashraf, *Muslim Traditions*.

কিন্তু যেটা কবি হিসেবে তার সবচেয়ে লক্ষ্যযোগ্য গুণ সেটা হলো তার নিজস্ব কণ্ঠছাপা . . . দেশজ প্রভাবের বাইরে কবি মাঝে মধ্যে আন্তর্জাতিকতাও অর্জন করেছেন।[14]

[Translation: Although living for a long time abroad, it cannot be alleged that he [Professor Ashraf] had been alienated from the traditions of Bengali poetry. . . . Transcending the sentiments of personal love, he is inspired with the love of his own country. By overcoming the despairs and disappointments of life with strong determination, he has found solace in the permanent shelter and cool shadow of his religion. But what is a most remarkable quality in him as a poet is his own poetic voice. . . . At times he even acquired international character notwithstanding the local influence.]

In conclusion, one might pose the question: educator, spiritual guide, or man of letters—which role best defines Syed Ali Ashraf? Perhaps all three facets intertwine seamlessly, for he was, fundamentally, a singular individual—a deeply humane and cultured one at that. However, his literary persona is intricately linked with both his individuality and his homeland. What is imperative now is to compile and meticulously edit his writings for a robust publication, ideally spanning one or two volumes. Undoubtedly, such an endeavour would significantly contribute to the enrichment of Bangladesh's cultural and intellectual history.

Bibliography

Ahsan, Syed Ali. "Syed Ali Ashrafer Kobita." In *Syed Ali Ashrafer Kobita* by Syed Ali Ashraf, 9–18. Dhaka: Shilpotoru Prokashoni, 1991.

Ashraf, Syed Ali. *Muslim Traditions in Bengali Literature*, 3rd ed. Dhaka: Islamic Foundation, 1983.

Banglapedia: National Encyclopedia of Bangladesh. s.v. "Purba Pakistan Sahitya Sangsad." Accessed April 17, 2024. https://en.banglapedia.org/index.php/Purba_Pakistan_Sahitya_Sangsad.

Husain, Syed Sajjad. *The Wastes of Time: Reflections on the Decline and Fall of East Pakistan*. Dhaka: Ashraf Husain on behalf Muslim Renaissance Movement and Notun Sôfor Prokashoni, 1995. https://archive.org/details/WastesOfTime.

Qureshi, Mahmud Shah. *Culture and Development*. Dhaka: Dhaka National Book Center, 1982.

---

14 Abu Rushd, "Having transcended personal love, he was inspired by a love for his motherland," in *Bôrenyo: Syed Ali Ashraf Smarok Grôntho*, eds. Muhammad Ahsanullah Mia, Muhammad Ismail Husain, Mahmudul Hasan Yusuf, Muhammad Shamsuddoha, and Shah Waliullah Farhad (Dhaka: Faculty of Religious Sciences, Darul Ihsan University, 19999), 154–55.

Rushd, Abu. In *Bôrenyo: Syed Ali Ashraf Smarok Grôntho*, edited by Muhammad Ahsanullah Mia, Muhammad Ismail Husain, Mahmudul Hasan Yusuf, Muhammad Shamsuddoha, and Shah Waliullah Farhad, 154–55. Dhaka: Faculty of Religious Sciences, Darul Ihsan University, 1999.

Wikipedia. s.v. "Kabir Chowdhury." Accessed April 17, 2024. https://en.wikipedia.org/wiki/Kabir_Chowdhury.

Wordsworth, William. "Preface to Lyrical Ballads" (1800).

Chapter 22

Between Utopia and Despair: The Impact of Environmental and Technological Millennialism on the Young

Magnus Bradshaw

Introduction

The work of Syed Ali Ashraf distinguishes the absolute and immutable values of Islam from the relative and fluid nature of secular values, and the implications of these as applied in the realm of education. Noting that they are based on radically different sets of principles, and that secular ideologies threaten the Islamic understanding of humanity, he argues that "It is impossible to compromise between Islam and secularism."[1] In the spirit of Ashraf, the present essay critically applies a theological perspective to the contemporary phenomena of environmental and technological millennialism, rooted in this fundamental distinction, whilst taking into consideration their impact on the young.

Ashraf was deeply concerned that the desire for power and control over nature has become a kind of madness. At the same time, he argued that technology is creating a dehumanizing "technological mentality," that societies are increasingly subordinate to its values and that technocracy ends up by creating a dangerous kind of hubris in humanity's self-image and in its relationship to God, as well as to the created world. He argued that humanity must regain control over technology, which can only be done by regaining the self-control that only faith and adherence to the disciplines of Islam can bring. Science and technology must not be rejected, but restrained and redirected so that they serve properly human and moral ends rather than contributing to the destruction of the environment and other harmful impacts.[2] At the same time,

---

1 Syed Ali Ashraf, *New Horizons in Muslim Education* (Cambridge: The Islamic Academy, 1985), 11.
2 Ashraf, *New Horizons*, 12, 13–14, 16–19, 86.

the origins and development of the topic under consideration here primarily relates to the modern West, and as such the religious context here is largely Christian. We should thus note here Ashraf's observation that "Islam asserts a long-standing universal tradition and reinforces the value scheme upheld by all world religions."[3] Underlying environmental and technological millennialism are a variety of secular ideologies and modes of thought which are often problematic from an Islamic perspective, if not completely incompatible with its beliefs and values. These include, but are not limited to, atheism, utopianism, progressivism, transhumanism, anarchism, Marxism and deep ecology. Given the impact of such belief systems on the young, whether direct or indirect, and taking into account Ashraf's concept of the Islamization of knowledge, it is important to discern appropriate Islamic approaches to these issues, whilst also considering ones that are inappropriate.

With its widespread fear of catastrophic destruction on multiple fronts—nuclear, ecological or technological threats—ours is indeed an "apocalyptic" time.[4] For Damian Thompson, we live in "an era of renewed dread," for there is a widespread perception of widespread social decay and a breakdown of order, of global anarchic tendencies.[5] The first detonation of an atomic bomb in 1945 was a pivotal event in the history of millennialism, particularly in regard to secular apocalypticism. It raised the possibility of an end to humanity similar to that depicted in Revelation and transformed the idea of an imminent end from the realm of personal belief and (to some) superstition, to an established fact, belief in which is entirely rational.[6] In the contemporary world there is a greater variety of apocalyptic belief than ever before, and these beliefs, whether ancient or modern, are more accessible than ever. As Philip Lamy notes, apocalypticism is manifest not only in religious and secular movements, but, in the "pop apocalypticism" that permeated American culture throughout the 1980s and into the 1990s.[7] This form of apocalypticism, one to which young people are increasingly exposed, is now part of the cultural mainstream in the West and beyond, and has become increasingly evident in the media of film, video games, fiction, the internet and conspiracy thinking, in which dystopian themes such as nuclear war, environmental disaster, moral decline, social collapse and the extinction of humanity are common.[8] According to Joanna Macy

---

3   Ashraf, 25.
4   Richard Bauckham, "Conclusion: Emerging Issues in Eschatology in the Twenty-First Century," in *The Oxford Handbook of Eschatology*, ed. Jerry L. Walls (Oxford: Oxford University Press, 2008), 684.
5   Damian Thompson, *The End of Time: Faith and Fear in the Shadow of the New Millennium* (London: Vintage, 1999), 356.
6   Daniel Wojcik, *The End of the World as We Know it: Faith, Fatalism, and Apocalypse in America* (New York: New York University Press, 1997), 97–118; Thompson, *The End of Time*, 13.
7   Philip Lamy, *Millennium Rage: Survivalists, White Supremacists, and the Doomsday Prophecy* (New York: Plenum Press 1996), v, vii.
8   Michael Barkun, *A Culture of Conspiracy* (Berkeley: University of California Press, 2013),

and Chris Johnstone a general state of anxiety and uncertainty regarding the state of the contemporary world and whether the world will be inhabitable in the future is "a pivotal psychological reality of our time."[9] Modern psychology now diagnoses "eco-anxiety," also referred to as "climate trauma" or "climate sorrow," with attendant emotions of fear, guilt, rage, and despair. This problem is now very widespread and is having a particularly worrying psychological impact on the young.[10]

The term "millennialism," whilst having a Christian origin, is now used in a scholarly context to refer to the belief that "in the imminent future there will be a transition—whether catastrophic or progressive—to a "collective salvation" . . . which will be accomplished by a divine or superhuman agent and/or humans working in accordance with a divine or superhuman plan."[11] Millennialism thus refers to a future "golden age" of indeterminate length referred to in many religions, and can also be applied to secular ideologies which believe in an impending new era of perfection.[12] "Millennialism" is closely associated with the related term "apocalypse" or "apocalypticism." Whilst the latter implies catastrophism and millennialism implies restoration, the two terms also include each other and are so closely related that they can be seen as interchangeable for the purposes of the present discussion.[13] In Islam, millennialism can be taken to mean both the events leading up to the end of the world, the moral and social chaos and inversion represented by Gog and Magog and the Antichrist, as well as the advent of the Mahdi and the return of Jesus, through whom order and justice are restored.[14]

The fact that thinking about the end of things is not just a religious concern but is also at work in a number of secular ideological contexts has recently become the focus of much academic interest. A number of scholars have argued that it was the Enlightenment that transformed and secularized millennialism in many ways.[15] In his seminal study, *The Pursuit of the Millennium*

10.
9   Joanna Macy and Chris Johnstone, *Active Hope* (Novato (CA): New World Library, 2012), 1.
10 Panu Pikhala, "Eco-Anxiety, Tragedy and Hope: Psychological and Spiritual Dimensions of Climate Change," *Zygon* vol. 53, no. 2. (2018): 545; David Wallace-Wells, *The Uninhabitable Earth* (London: Penguin, 2019), 136– 37.
11 Catherine Wessinger, "Millenialism in Cross-Cultural Perspective," in *The Oxford Handbook of Millennialism*, ed. Catherine Wessinger (Oxford: Oxford University Press, 2012), 3–24.
12 Catherine Wessinger, "Millennialism with and without the Mayhem," in *Millennium, Messiahs and Mayhem*, eds. Thomas Robbins and Susan J. Palmer (New York and London: Routledge, 1997), 47–59.
13 Eugen Weber, *Apocalypses: Prophecies, Cults and Millennial Beliefs Throughout the Ages* (London: Pimlico, 1999), 31.
14 David Cook, "Early Islamic and Classical Sunni and Shi'ite Apocalyptic Movements," in *The Oxford Handbook of Millennialism*, ed. Catherine Wessinger (Oxford: Oxford University Press, 2012), 267–83.
15 Nicholas Campion, *The Great Year: Astrology, Millenarianism and History in the Western*

(1957), Norman Cohn proposed that the religious millennial movements on which his study focused "bear a startling resemblance to the great totalitarian movements of our own day . . . the old symbols and the old slogans have indeed disappeared, to be replaced by new ones; but the structure of the basic phantasies seems to have changed scarcely at all."[16] The political millennialism associated with the French Revolution was later inherited by Karl Marx and others. It has been widely observed that Marxism and Nazism share structural similarities and key beliefs with religious millennialism—ideas of a final conflict between the forces of good and evil and the victory of chosen elite, whose sufferings are compensated for by a new life in a transformed world—and in general possess religious or pseudo-religious characteristics.[17]

Whilst religious millennialism always entails belief in an eternal salvation, however, this is not the case with secular movements, which are rooted in attempts at rational understanding with no connection to supernatural belief. Indeed, whilst religious millennialism entails the belief that a divine intervention will bring about the millennium, secular millennialism, being entirely this-worldly and historical, generally seeks to bring about the millennium through humanity's own efforts.[18] In this context, there is a close connection between the phenomena of secular millennialism, utopianism and the modern belief in progress.[19] Whilst secular millennialism is focused on "salvation" of a kind, and utopianism is more social and political in its emphasis,[20] the latter nonetheless also possesses many of the same quasi-religious features. The myth of progress is also closely related to utopianism and can indeed be defined as a form of utopianism or secular millennialism itself.[21] It should thus

---

Tradition (London: Penguin Arkana, 1994), 427; David Nash, "The Failed and Postponed Millennium: Secular Millennialism since the Enlightenment," *The Journal of Religious History*. 24, no. 1 (2000): 70–86; Richard Landes, *Heaven on Earth: The Varieties of the Millennial Experience* (Oxford: Oxford University Press 2011), 244.

16 Norman Cohn, *The Pursuit of the Millennium: Revolutionary Millenarians and Mystical Anarchists of the Middle Ages* (Oxford: Oxford University Press, 1970), xiv.

17 Cohn, *The Pursuit*, 307-8; Campion, *Great Year*, 427, 447; Frederick Baumgartner, *Longing for the End: A History of Millennialism in Western Civilization* (New York: St. Martin's Press, 1999), 210-212; Robert Ellwood, "Nazism as a Millennialist Movement," in *Millennialism, Persecution and Violence: Historical Cases*, ed. Catherine Wessinger (New York: Syracuse University Press, 2000), 241-60; John Gray, *Black Mass: Apocalyptic Religion and the Death of Utopia* (London: Allen Lane, 2007), 66– 69; Wessinger, "Cross-Cultural," 16; David Redles, "National Socialist Millennialism" in *The Oxford Handbook of Millennialism*, ed. Catherine Wessinger (Oxford: Oxford University Press, 2012), 529– 548.

18 Shklar, "Utopia," 110-111; Lamy, *Millennium Rage*, 95-96; Landes, *Heaven on Earth*, 21.

19 Damien Thompson, *Waiting for Antichrist: Charisma and Apocalypse in a Pentecostal Church* (Oxford: Oxford University Press, 2005), 174.

20 Sylvia Thrupp, "Millennial Dreams in Action: A Report on the Conference Discussion," in *Millennial Dreams in Action: Studies in Revolutionary Religious Movements*, ed. Sylvia L. Thrupp (New York: Schocken Books, 1970), 11– 27.

21 James Hughes, "Millennial Tendencies in Responses to Apocalyptic Threats," in *Global*

be noted that belief in progress and utopianism are closely related to the phenomena of environmental and technological millennialism, therefore we examine them in some detail here.

While we cannot provide here a detailed account of Islamic approaches to environmental or technological issues, some indications of these are necessary to provide context to our discussion. According to Seyyed Hossein Nasr, perhaps the most prominent commentator on environmental issues and the impact of technology in the Muslim world, since the nineteenth century much of the Muslim world has been trying to imitate Western ideologies, science and technology and forgetting its own heritage to the point that most Muslim intellectuals today effectively 'worship' science and technology. Such pseudo-religiosity entails the displacement of impulses and tendencies—which, according to Islam, were created to lead humanity back to God—into beliefs and activities incompatible with their legitimate functions. Unless humanity stays true to a spiritual understanding of itself, Nasr warns, technology and mechanization have the potential to dehumanize humanity, for "Rather than man deciding the value of science and technology, these creations of man have become the criteria of man's worth and value."[22] In regard to the environment, Nasr argues that the contemporary environmental movement lacks a sacred view of humanity and nature, and that our perspective on these must be re-sacralized and their spiritual significance understood.[23] For Nasr, the roots of the environmental crisis are spiritual and thus its solution can only be spiritual: "the ecological crisis is only an externalization of an inner malaise and cannot be solved without a spiritual rebirth of modern man."[24] Nasr's distinction between Pontifical Man and Promethean Man is particularly relevant here, for it helps to illustrate the difference between one perspective in which technology, for example, may usefully serve the legitimate needs of humanity, and another in which it has the potential to become a kind of idol. Pontifical Man is God's vicegerent, created in the "form of God," "bridge between Heaven and earth" and oriented towards the Eternal. Promethean Man, on the other hand, is "an earthly creature who has rebelled against Heaven and tried to misappropriate the role of the Divinity for himself." Promethean Man as a widespread phenomenon originated with the Renaissance in Europe; according to

---

Catastrophic Risks, eds. Nick Bostrom and Milan M. Cirkovic (Oxford: Oxford University Press, 2008), 73– 90; Michael Burdett, "The Religion of Technology: Transhumanism and the Myth of Progress," in *Religion and Transhumanism: The Unknown Future of Human Enhancement*, ed. Calvin Mercer and Tracey J. Trothen (Santa Barbara: Praeger, 2015), 131–48.

22 Seyyed Hossein Nasr, *Man and Nature* (London: Mandala, 1990), 19, see also 13.
23 Nasr, *Man and Nature*, 6, 14.
24 Nasr, 9.

Nasr, his innate nostalgia for the Eternal is misdirected in an endless variety of illegitimate ways, in the empty worship of a multitude of false absolutes.[25]

The Concept of Pseudo-religion

The concept of quasi-religious or pseudo-religious phenomena is thus a notion that can be identified in Islam. For Islam, human beings are innately religious in the sense that they possess a primordial nature (*fiṭrah*) which draws them to the divine. Before the creation, all human souls acknowledged the primordial covenant of the Day of Alast, on which they were asked: "Am I not your Lord?" (Qur'ān 7:172). Furthermore, they have been appointed as God's vicegerent (*khalīfatullāh*) on earth (Qur'ān 2:30). Given this innate thirst for the divine, everyone 'worships' in their own way and implicitly adheres to a metaphysical doctrine, whether this be valid or not. The unbeliever (*kāfir*) is etymologically one who "covers over" the truth within, and whose "religion" is therefore necessarily a false one, quite distinct from the *islām* (in the universal sense of monotheism and submission to the Divine Will) brought by all prophets. Amongst the phenomena that might be termed, to varying degrees, pseudo-religious from an Islamic perspective are the idolatry of pre-Islamic Mecca, the inverted religion inaugurated by the false Messiah or Antichrist (*al-Masīḥ al-Dajjāl*) of the end times, and indeed any form of *shirk*, the worship of anything other than God.

Historically, there have been attempts to create secular religions or to strip religion of its supernatural beliefs and turn it to purely socio-political ends. In the nineteenth century, French Positivists such as Auguste Comte tried to find a new religion, the Religion of Humanity, a form of technological millennialism in which humanity itself would be the object of worship. Ludwig Feuerbach and Karl Marx later taught that humanity should stop projecting its own qualities onto an imaginary God and instead become its own divinity.[26] These phenomena can in part be seen as precursors of the more widespread pseudo-religious movements associated with the twentieth century and the contemporary world. Matthias Behrens argues that religion necessarily has a metaphysical background and entails belief in and worship of a "transcendent divine" dimension, all of which "political religions" lack. Marxism and Nazism, for example, absolutize things that are relative and finite, never referring to the Ultimate Reality, but always to a finite one such as race and class, this being a feature of ideology rather than of religion. For Behrens, political

---

25 Seyyed Hossein Nasr, *Knowledge and the Sacred* (Albany: State University of New York Press, 1989), 160–62.
26 Thomas Molnar, *Utopia: The Perennial Heresy* (London: Tom Stacey, 1972), 68, 74, 84–85; David Noble, *The Religion of Technology* (London: Penguin, 1999), 83–84; Andrew Wernick, *Auguste Comte and the Religion of Humanity* (Cambridge: Cambridge University Press, 2001).

religions offer a form of purely historic "self-salvation" achieved through human action alone and with no need for divine grace. Whilst "pseudo-religions" can share certain features with genuine religions and attempt to fulfil those human needs that religion serves, they are unable to do this in the long term because they are inadequate substitutes and can in fact be seen as inherently anti-religious "non-religions."[27]

Employing an argument rooted in Sigmund Freud's model of repression, John Gray argues that the phenomenon of secular religions demonstrates that the religious impulse is as much innate to human nature as is sexuality and cannot therefore be eradicated. When the attempt is made to do so, it inevitably resurfaces in perverse and unhealthy forms, in this case a variety of quasi-religious secular cults which have developed in the void left by religion, and which are all the more extreme for the fact that the impulse underlying them had been repressed. According to Gray, we don't live in a truly secular age, for these forms of repressed religiosity play a central role in contemporary societies which, far from having left religion behind, have merely replaced it with a set of secular myths.[28] For example, the Jacobins, whilst rejecting religious belief, were in fact seeking a secular form of universal salvation, which, despite obvious differences, owed a considerable debt to Christianity. As Christianity declined, Gray argues, its eschatological teachings were repressed, only to return later in the form of revolutionary utopian movements promising that a purely this-worldly redemption was imminent.[29] Indeed, for Gray, the Enlightenment belief in a transforming revolution that will lead to a perfected society is itself drawn from Christianity, and "a continuation of religion by other means."[30] An important aspect of these quasi-religious phenomena is the fantasy of personal and millennial salvation which they present, whether these be political or scientific and technological.[31]

This phenomenon can also be observed in the relationship between progress, utopianism and life after death. According to Carl Becker, as faith in the existence of a paradise beyond death declined, belief in progress increased as a form of compensation for its loss.[32] Frank and Fritzie Manuel make the same argument in relation to utopianism, noting that "the unconscious material of the original myth was preserved."[33] The transhumanist philosopher Nick

---

27 Matthias Behrens, "Political Religion—a Religion?" in Hans Maier and Michael Schäfer, eds., *Totalitarianism and Political Religions*, vol. 2, *Concepts for the Comparison of Dictatorships* (Abingdon: Routledge, 2007), 225–32, 235–36, 237–38, note 2.
28 John Gray, *Black Mass*, 28, 42, 45–47.
29 Gray, 27–28.
30 Gray, 2.
31 John Gray, *Heresies* (London: Granta, 2004), 2, 41, 48.
32 Christopher Lasch, *The True and Only Heaven: Progress and its Critics* (New York: W. W. Norton & Company, 1991), 40.
33 Frank Manuel and Fritzie Manuel, *Utopian Thought in the Western World* (Oxford: Blackwell, 1979), 35.

Bostrom—transhumanism being the most recent manifestation of technological millennialism—provides an example of this phenomenon in his description of a blissful transhuman utopia which sounds very much like a secular paradise: "You could say that I am happy, that I feel good. You could say that I feel surpassing bliss. But these are words invented to describe human experience. What I feel is as far beyond human feelings as my thoughts are beyond human thought."[34] Thus, it seems that a desire for a personal immortality exists even amongst those whose beliefs are wholly secular and naturalistic, and that faith in progress has not been able to provide a satisfactory substitute.[35] As Michael Burdett observes, the "secularist faith" of transhumanism attempts to provide the hope that we can transcend our human limitations and overcome death, achieving salvation in a state of being akin to religious notions of glorification.

However, secular and religious understandings of immortality are profoundly different, for in contrast to religious doctrines of the afterlife, secular utopias such as transhumanism may envisage a form of salvation sometime in the future, but offer little for those who are living and dying now in a still very imperfect world.[36] Furthermore, while transhumanism envisages an indefinite extension in time, the religious view awaits a transfigured life that belongs to an eternity that transcends time altogether.[37] Thus transhumanism itself, with its supposedly rational quest for immortality through cryonics and other technological means—a hope which John Gray sees as more far-fetched than any of the faith-based tenets of religion[38]—can be seen as a pseudo-religious phenomenon, "an idolatrous religion proffering a counterfeit salvation."[39] In regard to utopianism in general, the Manuels observe that whereas paradise is created by God and the whole of creation is subject to His will, utopianism is a Promethean attempt to create a man-made paradise on earth in defiance of God's omnipotence and the created order.[40] For Krishan Kumar, this basic contradiction between the other-worldly emphasis of religion and the utopian concern with purely worldly matters, the City of Man rather than the City of God, is fundamental. Indeed, the utopian attempt to create a perfect society on earth can only be blasphemous from the religious perspective, for which salvation comes through enduring the trials of this imperfect world rather than

---

34 Michael Burdett, *Eschatology and the Technological Future* (Abingdon: Routledge, 2015), 97.
35 John Bozeman, "Technological Millenarianism in the United States," in *Millennium, Messiahs and Mayhem*, eds. Thomas Robbins and Susan J. Palmer (New York and London: Routledge, 1997), 139–58.
36 Burdett, *Eschatology*, 82, 100–102, 144.
37 Brent Waters, "Whose Salvation? Which Eschatology? Transhumanism and Christianity as Contending Salvific Religions," in *Transhumanism and Transcendence: Christian Hope in an Age of Technological Enhancement*, ed. Ronald Cole-Turner (Washington: Georgetown University Press, 2011), 24–36.
38 Gray, *Heresies*, 47, 50, 67.
39 Waters, "Whose Salvation?" 173.
40 Manuel and Manuel, *Utopian Thought*, 112.

arrogantly trying to usurp the divine omnipotence.[41] We now turn to examine some further themes of what might be considered "pseudo religion," focusing on the environment and technology, which, because neither is an appropriate object of worship, have the potential to take their place amongst "the myriad of pseudo-religions which abound in the West today."[42]

The Religion of Progress

Underlying technological millennialism in particular is perhaps the most pervasive form of secular millennialism today, the modern doctrine of progress, which originated as we currently know it with the Enlightenment philosophers of the late seventeenth and early eighteenth centuries.[43] It holds that it is a fundamental trend in history that things will get better in the future (meliorism) through the advancement of knowledge, science and technology. It may also entail belief in the moral improvement of humanity, and even the view that humanity will develop new and better physical, mental or spiritual capacities.[44] It has been widely argued that belief in progress functions as a secular substitute for the kinds of meaning traditionally provided by religion.[45] Christianity interprets history in a teleological way, with its focus on a meaningful future goal, and the modern doctrine of progress, despite its secular premises, is fundamentally indebted to this theological perspective. It has widely been seen as a secularized version of the Christian belief in Providence, for it envisages a kind of natural law whereby humanity ascends an inevitable spiral of development from age to age, with it now standing on the cusp of a utopian future.[46] Belief in progress can also take on the role of a theodicy, with the historical process being justified by its final result. However, in theological terms, this may risk becoming a form of collective self-deception, by allowing us to complacently turn a blind eye to the real evils and injustices which continue to thrive in a fundamentally imperfect world.[47] It is also a commonly held view amongst scholars that the doctrine of progress is a secularized version of religious millennialism.[48] The notion that God intervenes in history, as

---

41 Krishan Kumar, *Utopia and Anti-Utopia in Modern Times* (Oxford: Wiley-Blackwell, 1987), 10, 11, 22.
42 Mostafa al-Badawi, *Man and the Universe* (Amman: Wakeel, 2002), 91.
43 Sidney Pollard, *The Idea of Progress* (London: C.A. Watts & Company, 1968), 10; Campion, *Great Year*, 456.
44 Pollard, *Progress*, 9, 11, 12.
45 Pollard, 202–3; Gray, *Black Mass*, 2; Burdett, "Religion of Technology," 134.
46 Ernest Lee Tuveson, *Redeemer Nation: The Idea of America's Millennial Role* (Chicago and London: University of Chicago Press, 1968), ix–x; Karl Löwith, *Meaning in History: The Theological Implications of the Philosophy of History* (London and Toronto: University of Chicago Press, 1949), 60–61, 160; Lasch, *Heaven*, 40; Gray, *Heresies*, 2.
47 Bauckham, "Conclusion," 674, 677; Gray, *Heresies*, 5; Thompson, *End of Time*, 357.
48 Tuveson, *Redeemer*, ix–x; Robin Barnes, "Images of Hope and Despair: Western Apocalypticism: ca. 1500–1800," in Bernard McGinn, ed. *The Encyclopaedia of*

well as the millennial belief in a divinely ordained kingdom of justice to come, were transformed into the notion that humanity could save itself through its own efforts in the form of a gradual progress towards a utopian future.[49] Thus, for Karl Lowith, "The irreligion of progress is still a sort of religion, derived from the Christian faith in a future goal, through substituting an indefinite and imminent eschaton for a definite or transcendent one."[50]

Yet, in contrast to progressivism, religious millennialism has a very different understanding of human nature and the purpose of history. It teaches that a better world will come about through divine ordinance and grace rather than simply through human efforts at social reform. Its effects would include a deepening of piety and morality, not just a purely secular social harmony; it is God's Kingdom that will be established, not the kingdom of progressive humanity. In the new doctrine of progress, the Christian concepts of fall and redemption came to be applied collectively, with the historical process becoming the means whereby humanity might be "saved" through the advancement of knowledge and understanding.[51] For great Christian thinkers such as Augustine, on the other hand, "progress" could only be found in one's personal choice in the face of eternity of faith and piety over unbelief, in one's individual pilgrimage towards the celestial City: "The advance of men, for the great orthodox Christian thinkers, can only be spiritual if it is real and not delusive. Advances of a nonspiritual nature are but accidental accompaniments to the true progress."[52] This is all the more so because apocalyptic teachings concerning social and moral deviation in the end times clearly put a limit on any notion of an unambiguous progress in human affairs.[53] There is thus a fundamental distinction between the Christian faith in a transcendent salvation and the secular hope for worldly improvement.[54] As Jacques Ellul observes, "There is a great temptation today to confuse sociological evolution with spiritual progress. The Bible explicitly tells us that the history of mankind ends in God's judgment."[55] Karl Lowith likewise alludes to the dangers of "a mistaken Christianity that confounds the fundamental distinction between redemp-

---

    Apocalypticism, vol. 2, *Apocalypticism in Western History and Culture* (New York: Continuum, 1998), 143; Burdett, "Religion of Technology," 143.

49 Michael Barkun, *Disaster and the Millennium* (New Haven and London: Yale University Press, 1974), 184–85; Campion, *Great Year*, 500; Nicholas Campion, *The New Age in the Modern West: Counterculture, Utopia and Prophecy from the Late Eighteenth Century to the Present Day* (London: Bloomsbury, 2016), 24.
50 Löwith, *Meaning*, 114.
51 Tuveson, *Redeemer*, 7, 154–55.
52 Tuveson, 6–7; see also Löwith, *Meaning*, 84.
53 Tuveson, 7.
54 Tuveson, 53, 64–65; Bauckham, "Conclusion," 675.
55 Ted Peters, "Progress and Provolution: Will Transhumanism Leave Sin Behind?" in *Transhumanism and Transcendence: Christian Hope in an Age of Technological Enhancement*, ed. Ronald Cole-Turner (Washington: Georgetown University Press, 2011), 81.

tive events and profane happenings," the modern doctrine of progress being "Christian by derivation and anti-Christian by consequence."[56]

This said, the horrors of the World Wars, the ongoing threat of nuclear war, and the environmental crisis have meant that, for many, the Enlightenment belief in progress has been "irrevocably discredited by the traumatic experience of the twentieth century."[57] Indeed, in the contemporary world, it seems to have been partly replaced by a general feeling of anxiety about the future, a sense that we have reached an "end time," particularly in an ecological sense. In the contemporary world a progressive confidence in the future has also been replaced by a hedonistic focus on the present.[58] Indeed, apocalypticism may thrive today in part because it seems to be more in line with the troubled state of the contemporary world than an imminent consummation of optimistic secular notions of progress, whether Marxist, capitalist or liberal democratic.[59] Similarly, it has been argued that belief in progress stubbornly persists because the alternative is to fall into despair, such that faith in progress has become "the Prozac of the thinking classes."[60] Technological progress is very much included in this analysis, for it is evident that many of humanity's greatest problems—world war, nuclear weapons, environmental destruction—are intimately related to it. Indeed, The idea that science can create a better world, John Gray argues, is not supported by the evidence, but is rather an article of faith, as is the notion that the threats to humanity created by technological development can themselves be solved by further technological development.[61] The contemporary faith in technology does not take sufficient account of its negative unintended consequences and the human suffering, both physical and psychological that it causes,[62] nor the fact that it now represents a serious threat to the survival of humanity.[63] Thus, for Krishan Kumar, "It has been impossible to sustain for long the faith that the world is getting better and that, with the help of some more science and technology,

---

56 Löwith, *Meaning*, 202-3.
57 Joshua Searle, "The Future of Millennial Studies and the Hermeneutics of Hope: A Theological Reflection," in *Beyond the End: The Future of Millennial Studies*, ed. Joshua Searle and Kenneth G. C. Newport (Sheffield: Sheffield Phoenix Press, 2012),131; see also Campion, *Great Year*, 459-60; Bauckham, "Conclusion," 675; Michael Ashcraft, "Progressive Millennialism," in *The Oxford Handbook of Millennialism*, ed. Catherine Wessinger (Oxford: Oxford University Press, 2012), 55.
58 Bauckham, "Conclusion," 675.
59 Thompson, *End of Time*, 356; Gray, *Black Mass*, 186.
60 Gray, *Heresies*, 3; see also Pollard, *Progress*, 205.
61 Gray, *Heresies*, 4, 45.
62 Anthony O'Hear, *After Progress* (London: Bloomsbury, 1999), 105; Ashcraft, "Progressive Millennialism," 59-60.
63 Martin Rees, *Our Final Century* (London: Arrow Books, 2004); Richard Posner, *Catastrophe: Risk and Response* (New York: Oxford University Press, 2004); Nick Bostrom and Milan Ćirković, eds. *Global Catastrophic Risks* (Oxford: Oxford University Press, 2008).

it will get better still."⁶⁴ At the same time, from the point of view of religious faith, this loss of faith in progress can be seen as salutary, exposing the self-aggrandising nature of this belief and reminding us of the reality of human imperfection, as well as the primacy of the spiritual life.⁶⁵

Worshipping the Machine

Technological millennialism, which is deeply rooted in progressivism, can be defined as the belief that "technology will bring about a new golden age in the near future that will create a substantial, and permanent, fundamental improvement in the human condition."⁶⁶ Despite the secularizing impetus of technoscientific ideology, it has been argued that the current fascination with technology has its roots in religious impulses and continues to be driven by them.⁶⁷ According to David Noble, "The expectation of ultimate salvation through technology, whatever the immediate human and social costs, has become the unspoken orthodoxy, reinforced by a market-induced enthusiasm for novelty and sanctioned by a millenarian yearning for new beginnings."⁶⁸ The Industrial Revolution produced a quasi-religion of "machine worship,"⁶⁹ whilst more recently, the history of the United States in particular can be seen as a concerted attempt to create a sort of technological heaven on earth.⁷⁰ According to David Nye, technology is closely associated with the contemporary experience of the sublime, which is usually regarded as a religious emotion,⁷¹ whilst Robert W. Daly argues that people have a psychological tendency to attribute supernatural power to complex technological systems. Thus, as Burdett comments, "We experience the mystery of machines and the things that they can do in the same way that we experience the holy and religion."⁷²

In this regard, David Noble has described how the American space program was significantly motivated by and preoccupied with religious themes.⁷³ From its origins, spaceflight was always related to the notion of ascent to the heavens, and has also been seen as technological version of the Rapture, in which the saved ascend to Heaven.⁷⁴ Theologically, however, the space pro-

---

64 Kumar, "Apocalypse," 209–10.
65 Archbishop Rembert Weakland, "Hope in the Face of Crisis" in *Fearful Hope: Approaching the New Millennium*, ed. Christopher Kleinhenz, and Fanny J. LeMoine (Madison: University of Wisconsin Press, 1999), 187–188; O'Hear, *After Progress*, 94.
66 Bozeman, "Technological Millenarianism," 151.
67 Noble, *Religion of Technology*, 3; Burdett, *Eschatology*, 102.
68 Noble, *Religion of Technology*, 207.
69 Gregory Claeys, *Dystopia: A Natural History* (Oxford: Oxford University Press, 2018), 261.
70 Bozeman, "Technological Millenarianism,"155; Noble, *Religion of Technology*, 98–99; Burdett, *Eschatology*, 12.
71 David Nye, *American Technological Sublime* (Cambridge (MA): MIT Press, 1994), xiii.
72 Burdett, *Eschatology*, 54; see also Molnar, *Utopia*, 48.
73 Noble, *Religion of Technology*, 5.
74 Noble, 114–15.

gram can also be seen as manifesting a form of distorted transcendence, lacking in positive religious meanings, if not actually having a counter-religious significance. For Seyyed Hossein Nasr, the Space Program is an anti-spiritual exteriorization and materialization of the inner experience of spiritual ascent to the heavens, exemplified in Islam by the Night Journey (*miʿrāj*) of the Prophet.[75] What is more, the space program exemplified a culture more concerned with putting men on the moon than solving the world's problems, bent on escaping the present for the future, forgetting, as Lewis Mumford argues, that "As far as life values are concerned, one might trade all the planets of the solar system for a square mile of inhabited earth."[76] To justify space travel, Mumford contends, it is necessary to denigrate earthly life, whilst in reality the mysteries of life on earth still far outweigh those of the sterile, anti-human environments with which space travel concerns itself. Ultimately, he sees space exploration as a Faustian pact in which humanity is offered seemingly limitless power and control in return for submitting to its own anti-human creations.[77]

Even prior to the space program, Mumford was already convinced that the machine had come to displace both humanity and the natural world in its perceived significance. The mechanistic worldview of early modern science implied that there is no fundamental difference between machines and living organisms, and thus that the technocrats who invent and operate the machines, were akin to gods, 'creators' of life. The excessive domination of technology in our culture now dictated that humanity must willingly submit to the domination of machines and become more machine-like, or else become redundant. The machine itself ultimately came to be seen as superior to any other being, eventually becoming "the 'Supreme Power,' an object of religious adoration and worship."[78] Mumford's analysis appears to be borne out by Kevin Kelly's technophilic *What Technology Wants* (2010). Thus, for Kelly, technology is something akin to a substitute creation: "We can see more of God in a cell phone than in a tree frog";[79] it is implicitly divinized and presented as a legitimate object of worship: "The technium [Kelly's term for the entire technological system] is not God . . . But it contains more goodness than anything else we know"; for Kelly, technology is not only superior in intelligence to humanity, but effectively replaces humanity as *khalīfatullāh*, for it is "the way the universe has engineered its own self-awareness";[80] thus, humanity must learn to love technology, even to offer homage to it in quasi-religious acts of devotion: "In the future, we'll find it easier to love technology. Machines win our hearts

---

75 Nasr, *Man and Nature*, 19.
76 Lewis Mumford, *The Pentagon of Power* (New York: Harcourt, Brace and Javonovic, 1970), 49; see also Noble, *Religion of Technology*, 208 and Campion, *Great Year*, 2
77 Mumford, *Pentagon of Power*, 310–311, 313.
78 Mumford, *Pentagon of Power*, 24, 58, 72, 125, 283.
79 Kevin Kelly, *What Technology Wants* (London: Penguin Books, 2010), 358.
80 Kelly, *Technology*, 357–59.

with every step they take in evolution ... We will rhapsodize about this or that technology's charms and marvel at its subtlety. We will travel to it with children in tow to sit in silence beneath its towers."[81]

Humanity Divinized and Extinguished

According to Thomas Molnar, a distinctive feature of secular utopianism is that it cannot accept the imperfection of human nature or the fact that evil exists. It therefore seeks to alter and improve the very foundations of the human condition, which it believes to be malleable. Humanity's propensity to sin must be excised and its primordial innocence restored in the creation of a new, and ultimately divinized, human being. Because of its conservatism about the prospect of transforming human nature, religious belief is seen as a particular obstacle to realizing these hopes. As such, creation can only be mastered and remade if belief in God is replaced by faith in reason and science. Yet at the same time Molnar sees a kind of parody of the notion of a spiritual elect in utopians leaders who tend to see themselves as a purified vanguard, free of the limitations and standards that govern the masses, separating the blessed from the cursed and acting as if human perfection were already within reach. For Molnar, utopianism entails both the denial of God and the self-divinization of humanity. Whereas religions teach individual salvation through a God who transforms us, utopians seek a collective self-salvation for the whole of humanity, or a part of it, entirely through its own powers. The utopian temptation thus reiterates the original temptation of Eden and its later history reflects the story of the Tower of Babel, a Promethean humanity's attempt to reach the very heavens.[82]

These themes are implicit in the writings of Francis Bacon, the first thinker explicitly to link technoscience to progress and utopia. Bacon argued that the Fall could be reversed and the original Adamic state, with its accompanying power over nature, restored. He believed that the Millennium was imminent, and that technology had an important role to play in restoring human nature to its prelapsarian perfection. Later, Puritan Baconians took this a step further, hoping for more than a recovering of Adamic knowledge and the original purity of creation, aspiring instead to the divine knowledge itself and even to the making of a new creation, for it was believed that the original creation might be improved. In this way human beings were to go beyond the original endowment of Adam and effectively take on the role of gods, which Lewis Mumford refers to as "the undeclared ultimate goal" of modern science.[83] Indeed, in his utopian novel *New Atlantis* (1627), Bacon had already envisaged a time when

---

81 Kelly, 324–25.
82 Molnar, *Utopia*, 6, 9, 20, 44, 46, 57, 148–54, 159, 164–65, 193, 209, 237–40; see also Peters, "Progress," 71–73.
83 Noble, *Religion of Technology*, 50–53, 57, 66–67.

scientists would be able to create chimeras, which combined features of various species, and that this would be a sign of humanity's restored dominion over creation as a being with God-like powers.[84] David Noble sees more recent echoes of this program in the attitudes of both genetic engineers and the first atomic scientists and engineers. In awe of what they were unleashing and mesmerized by the power they were unleashing, the latter "viewed themselves, in almost a divine light, as the veritable saviors of mankind."[85] Such notions, albeit stripped of their religious associations, continue to thrive in the contemporary world. Thus, for the physicist Michio Kaku, humanity is on the verge of a transition from an Age of Discovery, in which humanity unlocked the secrets of nature, to an Age of Mastery, in which we will take control of nature and have god-like abilities.[86]

Transhumanism likewise echoes the common utopian belief that human nature, being subject to illness, ageing and death, is fundamentally unsatisfactory, and it seeks to transcend such limitations through technological enhancement, even to the point where human nature as we know it is left behind.[87] According to Ray Kurzweil, for example, the exponential growth of computing power since 1950 and the speed of technological change, particularly in the fields of robotics, genetics and nanotechnology, will increase to the point where human nature itself will be irreversibly transformed, an event which he calls the Singularity. Technology will ultimately allow humanity to transcend its own limitations by artificially transforming our bodies, greatly extending our lives, even 'uploading' our intelligence and entire personalities to computers and thus becoming immortal. In this 'transhuman' future of unimaginable splendor and perfection, humanity will eventually come to inhabit the entire universe.[88] However, this vision has been accused of illegitimately transgressing the boundary between religious and secular understandings of the future. Thus, Jürgen Moltmann and Ted Peters have made a theological distinction between two ways of seeing the future. The *futurum*, the perspective of futurologists, is a somewhat predictable development that results from present trends, whilst *adventus* is the dawning of a whole new reality, an eschatological future brought about by God's 'entry' into the temporal realm; it is only *adventus* (and God's grace), and not *futurum* that can transform human

---

84 Noble, 183.
85 Noble, 107.
86 Michu Kaku, *Visions: How Science will Revolutionize the Twenty-First Century* (Oxford: Oxford University Press, 1998), 9–10.
87 Ronald Cole-Turner, introduction to *Transhumanism and Transcendence: Christian Hope in an Age of Technological Enhancement*, by Ronald Cole-Turner, ed. (Washington: Georgetown University Press, 2011), 1–18.
88 Ray Kurzweil, *The Singularity is Near* (London: Duckworth, 2005); Peters, "Progress," 68–69; Ashcraft, "Progressive Millennialism," 59; Burdett, *Eschatology*, 90–91.

nature. For Peters, what transhumanists are really hoping for is *adventus*, but in reality, given their secular and materialistic premises, they can only legitimately expect *futurum*.[89]

Critics of transhumanism have also seen Kurzweil's Singularity as perhaps the ultimate example of technological dehumanization, for it seems to entail a significant loss of human identity and dignity, even in effect the end of humanity itself.[90] It thus seems to confirm the warnings of earlier critics of technological utopianism, who pointed to the possibility of just such an outcome.[91] Clearly transhumanism departs from a number of fundamental beliefs common to most of humanity: that conflict is an inevitable feature of human life, that worldly affairs can change for the worse as well as for the better, that the limitations of human nature exist for a reason and are unalterable.[92] Thus, for Ted Peters, transhumanists fail to take sufficient account of the role of moral evil in human affairs, that selfish human beings cannot easily be transformed into benevolent ones, that "No amount of increased intelligence will redeem us from what the theologians call *sin*."[93] It can seem that for secular utopians, the evil is always in others, never themselves; in their *hubris* they fail to perceive that "In the end, mastering the historical process would require human beings to master themselves, something they are very far from achieving."[94] Theologically, the varieties of technological millennialism continue to remind us that the human being can be 'divinized' in two superficially similar but incompatible ways that are in fact polar opposites. On the one hand the highest spiritual goal of Pontifical Man is to restore in himself the divine likeness, to live in the primordial state of the *fiṭrah*, whilst on the other, Promethean Man is a created being 'playing god' in an idolatrous and ultimately destructive way.

Environmental Millennialism

The view that humanity is having an effect on the environment that could ultimately have catastrophic consequences for civilization dates back to the mid-nineteenth century. It was shared by some Romantics, as well as authors such as Ralph Waldo Emerson and Henry David Thoreau. The modern environmental movement began with the publication of Rachel Carson's *Silent Spring*

---

89 Peters, "Progress," 74, 82; see also Burdett, *Eschatology*, 80.
90 Peters, "Progress," 76–78.
91 Jacques Ellul, *The Technological Society* (New York: Vintage, 1964); Nasr, *Man and Nature*, 13; Mumford, *Pentagon of Power*; Neil Postman, *Technopoly: The Surrender of Culture to Technology* (New York: Vintage, 1992), xii.
92 Molnar, *Utopia*, 229; Gray, *Black Mass*, 17; Burdett, *Eschatology*, 5.
93 Peters, "Progress," 80–82.
94 William Ophuls, *Immoderate Greatness: Why Civilizations Fail* (North Charleston: CreateSpace Independent Publishing, 2012), 1.

(1962), an apocalyptic presentation of the dangers of pesticides. Later works such as Paul Ehrlich's *The Population Bomb* (1968), and The Club of Rome's *Limits to Growth* (1972) presented human overpopulation and resource depletion as threats to the survival of humanity.[95] More recently, the apocalyptic potential of the "environmental crisis," particularly climate change, as a threat to the survival of humanity, or at least to civilization as we know it, is now widely understood.[96] Thus, as Globus and Taylor observe, "For the first time in history an apocalyptic fear, grounded in consensus science, had gained international visibility and legitimacy."[97]

Environmental millennialism has two distinct tendencies, albeit ones that can overlap or both be found within a given environmental group. The first, which can be termed the "humanistic," offers the hopeful prospect of small human communities living in harmony with a restored earth, and is anticipated in a way that is to some extent redemptive. This transformative and sometimes utopian perspective emphasises the importance of environmental activism and envisages the possibility of humanity successfully navigating the environmental crises of our time and establishing a more environmentally responsible civilization.[98] However, this more optimistic view now seems to be in retreat. In a recent study, Lisa Garfield argues that the environmental crisis is now widely seen as insoluble, and there are currently few detailed assessments of how a sustainable society could be brought about. Some environmentalists argue that nature is so damaged that it can no longer provide a basis for hopes about a better future. Thus, whilst environmental utopianism thrived in the 1970s and 1980s, in the contemporary world apocalyptic and dystopian assessments of our environmental predicament predominate.[99]

Given this increasing pessimism, a second tendency within environmental millennialism has begun to predominate. It tends to take a hostile view of civilization itself, particularly modern Western civilization, which it sees as inevitably heading for an apocalyptic ecological disaster and mass extinction of species. In some cases, it argues that the sooner that industrial civilization collapses, the better, as in this way more species and more wilderness

---

95 Frederick Buell, "A Short History of Environmental Apocalypse," in *Future Ethics: Climate Change and Apocalyptic Imagination*, ed. Stefan Skrimshire (London: Continuum, 2010), 14–15; Robin Globus and Bron Taylor, "Environmental Millennialism," in *The Oxford Handbook of Millennialism*, ed. Catherine Wessinger (Oxford: Oxford University Press, 2012), 629–31.
96 Globus and Taylor, "Environmental millennialism," 633–34; Wallace-Wells, *Uninhabitable Earth*.
97 Globus and Taylor, "Environmental millennialism," 634.
98 Martha Lee, "Environmental Apocalypse: The Millennial Ideology of 'Earth First!'" in *Millennium, Messiahs and Mayhem*, eds. Thomas Robbins and Susan J. Palmer (New York and London: Routledge, 1997), 120, 133.
99 Lisa Garforth, *Green Utopias* (Cambridge: Polity, 2018), 1, 19, 23, 155.

will be saved from destruction.[100] This more radical and misanthropic form of apocalypticism, which emerged notably within the Earth First! environmental movement, abandons all millennial hope and argues that humanity itself could not be reformed and might not survive these events, nor indeed does it deserve to.[101] Michael Shellenberger refers to the "anti-humanism" of this trend in "apocalyptic environmentalism," arguing that it is closely associated with a hatred of civilization and of humanity itself, as well as the view that the world would be better off without humanity, if it were governed by nature alone.[102] Thus, whilst humanistic environmentalists seek a transition to sustainability and fear the prospect of societal collapse, some apocalyptic environmentalists seek to actively bring this about. Probably the best known and most influential of them is Theodore Kaczynski, also known as the Unabomber. In his *Manifesto,* Kaczynski argues that the coming of civilization was a disastrous development, the Industrial Revolution even more so, and that it is thus necessary to revolt against modern civilization.[103] The recklessness and insanity of technological progress will inevitably result in disaster and the end of humanity, whether through environmental destruction or the loss of human dignity in a state of servitude to advanced technologies such as Artificial Intelligence or genetic engineering. Technological civilization must be brought to an end as rapidly as possible by means of a revolutionary movement so as to lessen the impact of this unavoidable catastrophe. Bringing down the techno-industrial system, with all the suffering that will cause, is morally justified to prevent these greater evils, for "only by accepting a massive disaster now can we avoid a far worse disaster later."[104]

This apocalyptic trend within radical environmentalism often includes a strongly misanthropic tendency. Thus, according to the Pentti Linkola, "Faith in humanity is the greatest of all follies," for "Man, no doubt, deserves even the most painful of labels: 'the cancer of the Earth,' a terrible mistake of evolution."[105] Linkola argues that in order to avoid the certain and imminent extinction of humanity, human population needs to be reduced to about 10% of what it is now.[106] To achieve this, there needs to be an enforced population reduction and deindustrialization of global society through a centralized authoritarian government of "a few wise individuals," whilst "Forms of boastful consumption must violently be crushed, the natality of the species violently

---

100 Lee, "Environmental Apocalypse," 124–25.
101 Lee, 128–33; see also Petti Linkola, *Can Life Prevail?* (London: Arktos Media, 2008).
102 Michael Shellenberger, *Apocalypse Never: Why Environmental Alarmism Hurts Us All* (New York: Harper, 2020), xiii, 270.
103 Theodore Kaczynski, *Technological Slavery: The Collected Writings of Theodore J. Kaczynski* (Port Townsend: Feral House, 2010), 171.
104 Kaczynski, *Technological Slavery,* 13–15, 124, 278.
105 Linkola, *Can Life Prevail?* 204, 161.
106 Linkola, 160–61.

controlled, and the number of those already born violently reduced—by any means necessary."[107] The prospect of the end of humanity, and its role in its own destruction, can thus encourage a misanthropic contempt for humanity, a growing view that there is something wrong with human nature itself, like a secular version of belief in original sin, though lacking the possibility of redemption associated with the religious view.[108] Thus, for Pascal Bruckner, we need to distinguish a form of environmentalism which is rational and democratic from another which is irrational and totalitarian. The latter suffers from the "infantile disease" of catastrophism, whilst presenting the human impact on the Earth as something akin to an original sin.[109]

The Religion of Nature

Manussos Marangudakis has argued that a variety of significant 20th century intellectuals looked to nature for the kind of personal and political guidance that had previously been provided by religion.[110] According to Michael Shellenberger, this attitude has become far more widespread in the contemporary world: "Environmentalism today is the dominant secular religion of the educated, upper-middle-class elite in most developed and many developing nations. It provides a new story about our collective and individual purpose. It designates good guys and bad guys, heroes and villains. And it does so in the language of science, which provides it with legitimacy."[111] Shellenberger argues that, whilst most environmentalists are secular in outlook, apocalyptic environmentalism has become a new religion in which nature acts as a substitute for God. In this new religion, environmentalists unconsciously adopt the Judeo-Christian morals and myths which remain so influential in Western culture, whilst scientists offer the moral guidance and interpretation of truth once provided by priests. While continuing to believe that they are driven by reason and science, in reality "secular people are attracted to apocalyptic environmentalism because it meets some of the same psychological and spiritual needs as Judeo-Christianity and other religions."[112] Thus, Kaczynski's *Manifesto* drew the attention of the anarcho-primitivist John Zerzan, who argues that nomadic hunter-gatherers lived in peaceful, egalitarian and sustainable communities which were healthier psychologically and physically than living under the alienated conditions of modern society. They thus provide evidence

---

107 Linkola, 205, 176.
108 James Schall, "Apocalypse as a Secular Enterprise," *Scottish Journal of Theology* 29 (1976), 361–62, 364–65; Daniel Wojcik, *The End of the World as We Know It* (New York: New York University Press, 1997), 146–47.
109 Pascal Bruckner, *The Fanaticism of the Apocalypse* (Cambridge: Polity Press, 2013), 2–3
110 Manussos Marangudakis, "Ecology as a Pseudo-Religion?" *Telos* no. 112 (1998), 119.
111 Shellenberger, *Apocalypse Never*, 263.
112 Shellenberger, 263–64.

that another way of life, a primordial state of being is possible, and we should seek to rediscover this.[113]

Whilst Kaczynski himself advocates not just reverence for but even worship of nature, so as to fill the spiritual emptiness of modern society, he also argues that anarcho-primitivists such as Zerzan romanticise hunter-gatherer societies rather than rationally and impartially studying them, selecting from the anthropological evidence to create a "mushy utopian myth . . . a kind of politically correct Garden of Eden."[114] He notes the quasi-religious features of the anarcho-primitivist myth, in which an original state of innocence gives way to a "fall" with the invention of agriculture and civilization in a way similar to the Christian myth of the Fall. The revolution and future utopia which the anarcho-primitivists hope for are akin to a Day of Judgment when Babylon falls, followed by the inauguration of the Kingdom of God when suffering comes to an end. In their willingness to struggle and even die for this earthly utopia, radical environmental activists are akin to the martyrs of early Christianity.[115]

Whilst environmental millennialism, whether it foresees catastrophe or utopia, may mimic faith, it does not seem to provide many of the benefits of religious belief. According to Shellenberger, whilst religious people benefit from an orienting set of ethical and spiritual principles which provide meaning and purpose to life and have been shown to be happier than their non-believing counterparts, these positive values are not found in apocalyptic environmentalism. Instead, it cultivates resentment, authoritarianism and unhappiness, all without meeting the spiritual needs of its adherents. In reality, it has its roots in an intellectual "culture of despair" that emerged after World War II, according to which reason and science reveal human life to be ultimately devoid of meaning and purpose.[116] Shellenberger argues that apocalyptic environmentalism has abandoned utopianism or rational hope for a vision of destruction, and it is now widely understood that this alarmism is contributing to the incidence of anxiety and depression, particularly among children. It was the prospect of environmental destruction that led to the young climate activist Greta Thunberg's depression. Such anxiety is understandable, given claims, such as that made by the British radical environmental movement Extinction Rebellion, that billions of people are going to die as a result of climate change. Roger Hallam, one of the founders of Extinction Rebellion, has stated that "Our children are going to die in the next ten to twenty years."[117] Whilst such statements are rejected by the majority of scientists, Extinction Rebellion—

---

113 John Zerzan, *Running on Emptiness: The Pathology of Civilization* (Port Townsend (WA): Feral House, 2002).
114 Kaczynski, *Technological Slavery*, 171, 157, 215.
115 Kaczynski, 169–71.
116 Shellenberger, *Apocalypse Never*, 264–66.
117 Shellenberger, ix, 22–23, 267, 273.

which Shellenberger argues has an obsession with death—has been invited into British schools to present their catastrophic vision to children.[118] Panu Pikhala likewise argues that this environmental apocalypticism, which over-emphasizes the disastrous aspects, is counter-productive because it is likely to increase eco-anxiety. The environmental message should instead be framed as "hope in the midst of tragedy," with religious belief playing an important role in providing meaning and hope in the face of widespread eco-anxiety.[119]

Conclusion: A Failed Millennium

We have argued here that the varieties of secular millennialism are pseudo-religious phenomena which, in addition to their inherently problematic characteristics, fail to fulfil the positive spiritual functions of traditional religious millennialism. These phenomena have a profound and increasing impact on the young, and the importance of addressing them in the context of Muslim education seems self-evident. As we have already suggested, an important dimension of religious millennialism is its ability to provide meaning by giving a cosmic significance to people's lives, explaining the purpose of human life and interpreting an underlying pattern behind global events. The chaotic nature of the present is no obstacle to faith, and indeed can be seen as a confirmation that "the time is nigh." From this perspective, the apocalypse is contained within a larger vision of order and harmony that offers the possibility of the transformation and redemption of the world. Despite the fear generated by anticipating the apocalyptic events, there is also hope, meaning and the prospect of personal salvation, as well as faith in God's just and benevolent providence.

On the other hand, from the empirical perspective of technological and environmental millennialism (as well as progressivism), according to which the Millennium must be brought about by human agency alone, it is a serious obstacle to faith and hope if humanity, rather than fulfilling its utopian potential, seems on the contrary to be creating a kind of dystopia. It is no surprise if there are tendencies to either escape into false hope and fantasies of salvation through technology, or retreat into misanthropy and despair at our seemingly insoluble environmental predicament. Being detached from any theological context, notably belief in an afterlife, contemporary secular apocalyptic visions lack the same ability to address the deeper meanings of human life and often represent an apocalypticism without hope.[120] Daniel Wojcik argues that

---

118 Shellenberger, 4, 22, 266.
119 Pikhala, "Eco-anxiety," 545.
120 Krishan Kumar, "Apocalypse, Millennium and Utopia Today," in *Apocalypse Theory and the Ends of the World*, ed. Malcolm Bull (Oxford: Blackwell, 1995), 200-244; Weakland, "Hope," 120–25; Lorenzo DiTommaso, "Apocalypticism and popular culture," in *The Oxford Handbook of Apocalyptic Literature*, ed. John J. Collins (Oxford: Oxford University Press 2014), 480–481.

secular apocalyptic beliefs lack the dimensions of morality and meaning given them by the religious, for in the absence of God or some other higher, ordering principle, history seems to lack ultimate purpose. The notion of a meaningless and unredemptive end to humanity is largely a phenomenon of the twentieth-century and is associated with a sense of resignation, despair and nihilism.[121] The prospect of the absurd and ultimately meaningless self-destruction of humanity through its own technological creations offers no possibility of a hopeful response, but rather, according to Robert Jay Lifton, only one of "psychic numbing," for "Within our present context . . . one perceives a threat of a literal, absolute end without benefit of a belief system that gives form, acceptance or solace to that idea."[122] For Robert Schall, the contemporary scientific apocalypticism lacks any sense of wonder or transcendence; in the present time of crisis we need to be reminded that the reality of the world is limited and that we are not merely earthly creatures. Only a religious perspective can preserve the traditional status of humanity and offer spiritual remedies to its predicament, whether these be forgiveness, self-sacrifice, gratitude or the practice of prayer.[123]

Bibliography

Ashcraft, Michael. "Progressive Millennialism." In *The Oxford Handbook of Millennialism*, edited by Catherine Wessinger, 44-65. Oxford: Oxford University Press, 2012.

Ashraf, Syed Ali. *New Horizons in Muslim Education*. Cambridge: The Islamic Academy, 1985.

Al-Badawi, Mostafa. *Man and the Universe*. Amman: Wakeel, 2002.

Barkun, Michael. *Disaster and the Millennium*. New Haven and London: Yale University Press, 1974.

Barkun, Michael. *A Culture of Conspiracy: Apocalyptic Visions in Contemporary America*. Berkeley: University of California Press, 2013.

Barnes, Robin. "Images of Hope and Despair: Western Apocalypticism: ca. 1500–1800." In Bernard McGinn, ed. *The Encyclopaedia of Apocalypticism*. Vol. 2, *Apocalypticism in Western History and Culture*. New York: Continuum, 1998.

Bauckham, Richard. "Conclusion: Emerging Issues in Eschatology in the Twenty-First Century." In *The Oxford Handbook of Eschatology*, edited by Jerry L. Walls, 671-90 Oxford: Oxford University Press. 2008.

---

121 Wojcik, *End of the World*, 1, 4, 10–11.
122 Robert Jay Lifton, "The Image of "the End of the World": a Psycho-Historical View," in *Visions of Apocalypse: End or Rebirth?*, eds. Saul Friedlander, Gerald Holton, Leo Marx and Eugene Skolnikoff (New York: Holmes and Meier, 1985), 163–64; Christopher Kleinhenz and Fanny LeMoine, "Introduction: Three Millennial Themes," in *Fearful Hope: Approaching the New Millennium*, eds. Christopher Kleinhenz and Fanny LeMoine (Madison: University of Wisconsin Press, 1999), 6.
123 Schall, "Apocalypse," 364–65, 369–70, 372.

Baumgartner, Frederick. *Longing for the End: A History of Millennialism in Western Civilization.* New York: St. Martin's Press, 1999.

Behrens, Matthias. "Political Religion—a Religion?" In *Totalitarianism and Political Religions.* Vol. 2, *Concepts for the Comparison of Dictatorships*, edited by Hans Maier and Michael Schäfer, 225–45. Abingdon: Routledge, 2007.

Bostrom, Nick, and Milan Ćirković, eds. *Global Catastrophic Risks.* Oxford: Oxford University Press, 2008.

Bozeman, John. "Technological Millenarianism in the United States." In *Millennium, Messiahs and Mayhem*, edited by Thomas Robbins and Susan J. Palmer, 139–58. New York and London: Routledge, 1997.

Bruckner, Pascal. *The Fanaticism of the Apocalypse.* Cambridge: Polity Press, 2013.

Buell, Frederick. "A Short History of Environmental Apocalypse." In *Future Ethics: Climate Change and Apocalyptic Imagination*, edited by Stefan Skrimshire, 13–36. London: Continuum, 2010.

Burdett, Michael. "The Religion of Technology: Transhumanism and the Myth of Progress." In *Religion and Transhumanism: The Unknown Future of Human Enhancement*, edited by Calvin Mercer and Tracey J. Trothen, 131–48. Santa Barbara: Praeger, 2015.

Burdett, Michael. *Eschatology and the Technological Future.* Abingdon: Routledge, 2015.

Campion, Nicholas. *The Great Year: Astrology, Millenarianism and History in the Western Tradition.* London: Penguin Arkana, 1994.

Campion, Nicholas. *The New Age in the Modern West: Counterculture, Utopia and Prophecy from the Late Eighteenth Century to the Present Day.* London: Bloomsbury, 2016.

Claeys, Gregory. *Dystopia: A Natural History.* Oxford: Oxford University Press, 2018.

Cohn, Norman, *The Pursuit of the Millennium: Revolutionary Millenarians and Mystical anarchists of the Middle Ages.* Oxford: Oxford University Press 1970.

Cole-Turner, Ronald. Introduction to *Transhumanism and Transcendence: Christian Hope in an Age of Technological Enhancement*, edited by Ronald Cole-Turner, 1–18. Washington: Georgetown University Press, 2011.

Cook, David. "Early Islamic and Classical Sunni and Shi'ite Apocalyptic Movements." In *The Oxford Handbook of Millennialism*, edited by Catherine Wessinger, 267–83. Oxford: Oxford University Press, 2012.

DiTommaso, Lorenzo, "Apocalypticism and Popular Culture." In *The Oxford Handbook of Apocalyptic Literature*, edited by John J. Collins, 473–10. Oxford: Oxford University Press 2014.

Ellul, Jacques. *The Technological Society.* New York: Vintage, 1964.

Ellwood, Robert. "Nazism as a Millennialist Movement." In *Millennialism, Persecution and Violence: Historical Cases,* edited by Catherine Wessinger, 241–60. New York: Syracuse University Press, 2000.

Garforth, Lisa. *Green Utopias.* Cambridge: Polity, 2018.

Globus, Robin, and Bron Taylor. "Environmental Millennialism." In *The Oxford Handbook of Millennialism*, edited by Catherine Wessinger, 628–46. Oxford: Oxford University Press, 2012.

Gray, John. *Heresies.* London: Granta, 2004.

Gray, John. *Black Mass: Apocalyptic Religion and the Death of Utopia.* London: Allen Lane, 2007.

Hughes, James. "Millennial Tendencies in Responses to Apocalyptic Threats." In *Global Catastrophic Risks*, edited by Nick Bostrom, and Milan M. Cirkovic, 73–90. Oxford: Oxford University Press, 2008.

Kaczynski, Theodore. *Technological Slavery: The Collected Writings of Theodore J. Kaczynski*. Port Townsend: Feral House, 2010.

Kaku, Michu. *Visions: How Science will Revolutionize the Twenty-First Century*. Oxford: Oxford University Press, 1998.

Kelly, Kevin. *What Technology Wants*. London: Penguin Books, 2010.

Kleinhenz, Christopher and Fanny LeMoine. "Introduction: Three Millennial Themes." In *Fearful Hope: Approaching the New Millennium*, edited by Christopher Kleinhenz, and Fanny LeMoine, 3–21. Madison: University of Wisconsin Press, 1999.

Kurzweil, Ray. *The Singularity is Near*. London: Duckworth, 2005.

Kumar, Krishan. *Utopia and Anti-Utopia in Modern Times*. Oxford: Wiley-Blackwell, 1987.

Kumar, Krishan. "Apocalypse, Millennium and Utopia Today." In *Apocalypse Theory and the Ends of the World*, edited by Malcolm Bull, 200–244. Oxford: Blackwell, 1995.

Lamy, Philip. *Millennium Rage: Survivalists, White Supremacists, and the Doomsday Prophecy*. New York and London: Plenum Press, 1996.

Landes, Richard. *Heaven on Earth: The Varieties of the Millennial Experience*. Oxford: Oxford University Press 2011.

Lasch, Christopher. *The True and Only Heaven: Progress and its Critics*. New York: W. W. Norton & Company, 1991.

Lee, Martha. "Environmental Apocalypse: The Millennial Ideology of 'Earth First!'" In *Millennium, Messiahs and Mayhem*, edited by Thomas Robbins, and Susan J. Palmer, 87–98. New York and London: Routledge, 1997.

Lifton, Robert. "The Image of 'the End of the World'": A Psycho-Historical View." In *Visions of Apocalypse: End or Rebirth?* edited by Saul Friedlander, Gerald Holton, Leo Marx and Eugene Skolnikoff, 151–70. New York: Holmes and Meier, 1985.

Linkola, Petti. *Can Life Prevail?* London: Arktos Media, 2008.

Löwith, Karl. *Meaning in History: The Theological Implications of the Philosophy of History*. London and Toronto: University of Chicago Press, 1949.

Macy, Joanna and Chris Johnstone. *Active Hope*. Novato (CA): New World Library, 2012.

Manuel, Frank, and Fritzie Manuel. *Utopian Thought in the Western World*. Oxford: Blackwell, 1979.

Marangudakis, Manussos. "Ecology as a Pseudo-Religion?" *Telos* no.112 (1998): 107–24.

Molnar, Thomas. *Utopia: The Perennial Heresy*. London: Tom Stacey, 1972.

Mumford, Lewis. *The Pentagon of Power*. New York: Harcourt, Brace and Javonovic, 1970.

Nash, David. "The Failed and Postponed Millennium: Secular Millennialism since the Enlightenment." *The Journal of Religious History* 24, no. 1 (2000): 70–86.

Nasr, Seyyed Hossein. *Knowledge and the Sacred*. Albany: State University of New York Press, 1989.

Nasr, Seyyed Hossein. *Man and Nature*. London: Mandala, 1990.

Noble, David. *The Religion of Technology*. London: Penguin, 1999.

Nye, David. *American Technological Sublime*. Cambridge (MA): MIT Press, 1994.

O'Hear, Anthony. *After Progress*, London: Bloomsbury, 1999.

Oliver, Kendrick. *To Touch the Face of God: The Sacred, the Profane, and the American Space Program, 1957–1975*. Baltimore: Johns Hopkins University Press, 2013.

Ophuls, William. *Immoderate Greatness: Why Civilizations Fail*. North Charleston: CreateSpace Independent Publishing, 2012.

Peters, Ted. "Progress and Provolution: will Transhumanism Leave Sin Behind?" In *Transhumanism and Transcendence: Christian Hope in an Age of Technological Enhancement*, edited by Ronald Cole-Turner, 63–86. Washington: Georgetown University Press, 2011.

Pikhala, Panu. "Eco-Anxiety, Tragedy and Hope: Psychological and Spiritual Dimensions of Climate Change." *Zygon* 53, no. 2 (2018): 545–69.

Pollard, Sidney. *The Idea of Progress*. London: C.A. Watts & Company, 1968.

Posner, Richard. *Catastrophe: Risk and Response*. New York: Oxford University Press, 2004.

Postman, Neil. *Technopoly: The Surrender of Culture to Technology*. New York: Vintage, 1992.

Redles, David "National socialist millennialism." In *The Oxford Handbook of Millennialism*, edited by Catherine Wessinger, 529–48. Oxford: Oxford University Press, 2012.

Rees, Martin. *Our Final Century*. London: Arrow Books, 2004.

Schall, James. "Apocalypse as a Secular Enterprise." *Scottish Journal of Theology* 29, (1976): 357–73.

Shellenberger, Michael. *Apocalypse Never: Why Environmental Alarmism Hurts Us All*. New York: Harper, 2020.

Searle, Joshua. "The Future of Millennial Studies and the Hermeneutics of Hope: A Theological Reflection." In *Beyond the End: The Future of Millennial Studies*, edited by Joshua Searle and Kenneth G. C. Newport, 131–47. Sheffield: Sheffield Phoenix Press, 2012.

Shklar, Judith. "The Political Theory of Utopia: from Melancholy to Nostalgia.' In *Utopias and Utopian Thought*, edited by Frank E. Manuel, 101–15. London: Souvenir Press, 1973.

Thompson, Damien. *The End of Time: Faith and Fear in the Shadow of the New Millennium*. London: Vintage, 1999.

Thompson, Damien. *Waiting for Antichrist: Charisma and Apocalypse in a Pentecostal Church*. Oxford: Oxford University Press, 2005.

Thrupp, Sylvia. "Millennial Dreams in Action: A Report on the Conference Discussion." In *Millennial Dreams in Action: Studies in Revolutionary Religious Movements*, edited by Sylvia L. Thrupp, 11–27. New York: Schocken Books, 1970.

Tuveson, Ernest Lee. *Redeemer Nation: The Idea of America's Millennial Role*. Chicago and London: University of Chicago Press, 1968.

Wallace-Wells, David. *The Uninhabitable Earth*. London: Penguin, 2019.

Waters, Brent. "Whose Salvation? Which Eschatology? Transhumanism and Christianity as Contending Salvific Religions." In *Transhumanism and Transcendence: Christian Hope in an Age of Technological Enhancement*, edited by Ronald Cole-Turner, 24–36. Washington: Georgetown University Press, 2011.

Weakland, Archbishop Rembert. "Hope in the Face of Crisis." In *Fearful Hope: Approaching the New Millennium*, edited by Christopher Kleinhenz, and Fanny J. LeMoine, 185–90. Madison: University of Wisconsin Press, 1999.

Weber, Eugen. *Apocalypses: Prophecies, Cults and Millennial Beliefs Throughout the Ages*. London: Pimlico, 1999.

Wernick, Andrew. *Auguste Comte and the Religion of Humanity*. Cambridge: Cambridge University Press, 2001.

Wessinger, Catherine. "Millennialism With and Without the Mayhem." In *Millennium, Messiahs and Mayhem*, edited by Thomas Robbins and Susan J. Palmer, 47–59. New York and London: Routledge, 1997.

Wessinger, Catherine. "Millenialism in Cross-Cultural Perspective." In *The Oxford Handbook of Millennialism,* edited by Catherine Wessinger, 3–24. Oxford: Oxford University Press, 2012.

Wojcik, Daniel. *The End of the World as We Know It.* New York: New York University Press, 1997.

Zerzan, John. *Running on Emptiness: The Pathology of Civilization.* Port Townsend (WA): Feral House, 2002.

Chapter 23

Natural Philosophy and Islamic Science: Is the Lack of Natural Philosophy the Reason for the Decline of Islamic Science?
Hazim Shah

Introduction

Islamic Science, or science in Islamic civilisation, flourished from the 9th to 14th century CE, and was more advanced than Western science. However, after the 14th century, science continued to develop in the West, mainly in the universities and culminating in the Scientific Revolution of the 17th century, while science in Islamic civilisation went through a period of decline. What were the reasons for this reversal of fortune? Several theories and explanations have been offered for the historical phenomena, one of which is the view that the lack of natural philosophy, which was a crucial element in the emergence of the new science, was negligible in Islamic Science mainly because of its rejection and censorship by the mainstream Ulama. In this article, I explore this question in some detail, and compare the role played by natural philosophy in the emergence of the new science in 17th century Europe. I argue that the "natural philosophy thesis" is problematic because the role played by natural philosophy in providing the theoretical or conceptual resources for the empirical development of science, and which shaped the character of modern-day science as found in physics and chemistry, occurred much later, i.e. in the 19th century, and was not yet a feature of the science of the 17th century.

The decline of Islamic Science, especially after the 14th century, has been attributed by several scholars such as Edward Grant, Floris Cohen, and Toby Huff to the decline of natural philosophy—especially Greek natural philosophy—in Islamic civilisation.[1] Al-Ghazālī's critique of Greek philosophy and

---

1 Edward Grant, *The Foundations of Modern Science in the Middle Ages* (Cambridge: Cambridge University Press, 1996); Edward Grant, *Science and Religion: 400 BC–AD 1550* (Baltimore: The Johns Hopkins University Press, 2004); Edward Grant, "The Fate of Ancient Greek

their Muslim followers such as Al-Kindī and Al-Fārābī, has often been cited as a major factor in the decline of natural philosophy in Islam. The decline of natural philosophy, in turn, has been adduced as a reason for the decline of Islamic Science in general, since natural philosophy was thought to be a necessary ingredient in the further advancement of science by providing the exact sciences the theoretical or conceptual resources for its further development. This argument is strengthened through a comparison with the development of science in the West, where it was claimed that the Scientific Revolution which occurred in Europe in the 17th century, was a product of the integration of natural philosophy, mathematics, and the experimental method.[2] It was the continued preservation of Greek natural philosophy and its further expansion in the medieval universities, which according to Edward Grant for example, was responsible for the emergence of modern science via the Scientific Revolution in the West and its non-emergence in Islam.[3]

In this article, I critically examine this thesis which I dubbed the "Natural Philosophy Thesis" (NPT) and argue that the thesis is problematic on several counts. In arguing against NPT, I will try to show that natural philosophy did not contribute directly to the Scientific Revolution of the 17th century. In fact, it was not until about the 19th century, with the development of the kinetic theory of gases, that natural philosophy in the guise of matter theory, i.e., kinetic corpuscularianism became effective as a conceptual tool or resource for empirical science. On the other hand, with respect to Islamic civilisation, some variant of natural philosophy did continue to exist, and in fact in the guise of Neoplatonism it was even considered acceptable by some Muslim thinkers, including the contemporary Muslim scholar, Seyyed Hossein Nasr. Thus, the precise role of natural philosophy in the development of modern science has to be carefully examined and a more nuanced treatment be given, before we can conclusively infer—if that is the case—that natural philosophy was the decisive factor in the rise of modern science in the West, and its decline in Islam.

The Natural Philosophy Thesis Stated and Explained

The thesis that natural philosophy—or rather its development—in Western civilization has been a major factor in the rise of modern science and the Scientific Revolution of the 17th century, has been advanced by several histo-

---

Natural Philosophy in the Middle Ages: Islam and Western Christianity," *The Review of Metaphysics* 61, no. 3 (2008): 503–526; Floris Cohen, *How Modern Science Came Into the World* (Amsterdam: Amsterdam University Press, 2010); and Toby E. Huff, *The Rise of Early Modern Science: Islam, China and the West* (Cambridge, Cambridge University Press, 1993), 68–69.

2 John Henry, *The Scientific Revolution and the Origins of Modern Science* (Basingstoke, Hampshire: Palgrave MacMillan, 2008); Grant, *Science and Religion*; Cohen, *How Modern Science Came into the World*.

3 Grant, *The Foundations of Modern Science*.

rians of science such as Edward Grant, Peter Dear, John Henry, and Floris Cohen.[4] Similarly, the lack or decline of natural philosophy in Islamic civilisation, especially after al-Ghazālī's critique of Greek natural philosophy, has been invoked as a reason for the decline of Islamic Science, and the reason why the Scientific Revolution did not take place in Islamic civilisation.[5] The reason as to why natural philosophy was crucial for the further development of science in the West, culminating in the Scientific Revolution, was offered by Edward Grant as follows:

> Before 1500, the exact sciences in Islam had reached lofty heights, greater than they achieved in medieval Western Europe, but they did so without a vibrant natural philosophy. In contrast, in Western Europe natural philosophy was highly developed, whereas the exact sciences were merely absorbed (from the body of Greco-Arabic scientific literature) and maintained at a modest level. After 1500, Islamic science effectively ceased to advance, but Western science entered upon a revolution that would culminate in the seventeenth century. What can we learn from this state of affairs?
>
> Let me propose the following: that the exact sciences are unlikely to flourish in isolation from a well-developed natural philosophy, whereas natural philosophy is apparently sustainable at a high level even in the absence of significant achievement in the exact sciences. One or more of the exact sciences, especially mathematics, was practiced in a number of societies that never had a fully developed, broadly disseminated natural philosophy. In none of these societies had scientists attained as high a level of competence and achievement as they had in Islam. Was then the subsequent decline of science in Islam perhaps connected with the relatively diminished role of natural philosophy in that society and to the fact that it was never institutionalized in higher education? This is a distinct possibility, if natural philosophy played as important a role as I attribute to it throughout this study. Thus in Islamic society, where religion was so fundamental, the absence of support for natural philosophy from theologians, and, more often, their open hostility toward the discipline, might have proved fatal to it and, eventually, to the exact sciences as well.[6]

---

4   Grant, *The Foundations of Modern Science*; Grant, *Science and Religion*; Grant, "The Fate of Ancient Greek Natural Philosophy"; Peter Dear, *The Intelligibility of Nature: How Science Makes Sense of the World* (Chicago: The University of Chicago Press, 2006); Henry, *The Scientific Revolution*; Cohen, *How Modern Science Came into the World*.
5   Edward Grant, *A History of Natural Philosophy* (Cambridge: Cambridge University Press, 2007).
6   Grant, *The Foundations of Modern Science*, 185–86.

Grant saw natural philosophy as providing the conceptual resources which was needed by the mathematical or exact sciences in order to transcend the limits of what Cohen referred to as "Alexandrian Science," that is science in the engineering tradition.[7] Most of the authors mentioned above, spoke of the integration or amalgamation of the three key areas or domains of knowledge, namely natural philosophy, mathematics, and the experimental method in the emergence of modern science. Floris Cohen, however, instead of emphasizing the "integration" aspect, spoke of the simultaneous "transformations" occurring in the three distinct domains—transformations which were necessary in order to bring about the eventual integration. As Cohen puts it:

> Thus the onset of the Scientific Revolution yielded three distinct modes of nature-knowledge ... If we wish to understand how modern science could arrive in the world, we must ask how, around 1600, these three almost simultaneous transformations could come about ... Three distinct driving forces propelled it forward. One was ... the 17th century practice of mathematization of nature experimentally sustained; another was ... the 17th century practice of fact-finding experimentation. And ... the unprecedented breaking down of barriers between the Galilean, the Cartesian, and the Baconian modes of nature-knowledge, leading in the 1660s to mid-1680s to three more revolutionary transformations marked by hugely productive mutual interaction.[8]

Cohen's qualification and refinement of the thesis notwithstanding, the main thrust of the thesis still lies in the claim that natural philosophy was crucial in the emergence of modern science in Europe in the 17th century. What the content of that natural philosophy was, the evolution and transformations it went through, and how it was "integrated" with mathematics and the experimental method—these are no doubt important details in understanding how modern science was historically forged, but at the end of it all what remains unchallenged is the significant role attributed to natural philosophy in the emergence of modern science.

The question which I wish to explore and challenge in this article, is precisely the role which has been attributed to natural philosophy in the rise of modern science in 17th century Europe, and the related claim that its lack or neglect in Islamic civilisation had been the cause of the decline of science in Islam. I will argue that natural philosophy in the form of matter theory, specifically kinetic corpuscularianism, did not directly contribute to the advancement of empirical science, until the discovery of the kinetic theory of gases in the 19th century. In the 17th century, as Cartesian mechanical philosophy, it

---

7   Cohen, *How Modern Science Came into the World*.
8   Cohen, xvi.

remained largely programmatic without empirical content, unlike Newtonian mechanics. It was theoretical or speculative, and not operational or capable of being empirically tested. In the form of "Mechanical Philosophy," it was more of an abstract worldview. In any case, Newton's and Descartes' natural philosophy were significantly different, which makes the "integration thesis" problematic, since on the one hand we have an operational Newtonian mechanics, and on the other hand we have a programmatic Cartesian natural philosophy, without the two being integrated. Similarly, it is questionable whether natural philosophy was really a major factor in the decline of Islamic Science, given that natural philosophy in some form continued to exist in Islam, and that as has been shown by Nasr for example, neo-Platonic natural philosophy could be harmonized with Islamic thought and Islamic science.

Criticisms of the Natural Philosophy Thesis

Although the NPT has been advanced in various forms by prominent historians of science as stated above, a closer scrutiny of the thesis reveals certain flaws, which makes the thesis rather problematic. In this section, I will put forward four main criticisms of the thesis.

The Scientific Revolution is a Rejection of Greek, Especially Aristotelian, Natural Philosophy

Although Greek natural philosophy, especially its Aristotelian variant, was sustained and developed in Europe during the Middle Ages, largely through being taught in the Faculty of Arts of the medieval universities, the Scientific Revolution was not the product of the extension of Greek natural philosophy, but rather, its rejection. As Edward Grant puts it:

> Why did Islamic education remain so static for seven centuries, while in the West, the analogous curriculum, based on medieval Aristotelian learning, was largely abandoned in the seventeenth century, after approximately four centuries, to be replaced by a new approach to science that is associated with the Scientific Revolution?[9]

Here, Grant clearly concurred with the views of earlier historians of the Scientific Revolution such as Herbert Butterfield[10] and Alfred Hall[11] who saw the Scientific Revolution as a turning point, a radical departure from Greek science and natural philosophy. In other words, Aristotelian science and natural philosophy could not have provided the much-touted natural philosophy-derived conceptual resource that led to the emergence of the New Science. The emergence of the New Science in the study of motion for instance, was not

---

9 Grant, "The Fate of Ancient Greek Natural Philosophy," 524.
10 Herbert Butterfield, *The Origins of Modern Science* (London: G. Bell & Sons, 1957).
11 Alfred R. Hall, *The Revolution in Science: 1500–1750* (London: Longman, 1983).

due to a further development of Aristotle's concept of motion, but by taking a different approach to the study of motion as was shown by Galileo. Unlike Aristotle, Galileo did not approach the subject in a philosophical or metaphysical manner, which Aristotle did by treating motion as a species of change considered as a metaphysical category. Motion was studied in a "piecemeal" manner by Galileo, epitomized by his study of free-fall motion, where the concepts can be operationalized, and measurements taken, as was done in his famous "inclined-plane experiment." There was no natural philosophy anywhere in sight. Yet apart from Copernican astronomy, it was Galilean, and later Newtonian, mechanics which gave substance to the Scientific Revolution. In neither astronomy nor mechanics did natural philosophy contribute to its revolutionary development.

Thus, Aristotelian natural philosophy was not incorporated into seventeenth century science, but rather abandoned. This leaves the "integrationist thesis" in abeyance. There are two points to be noted here; one is the time period, i.e., the 17th century, and the second the content of the natural philosophy that was supposedly integrated or amalgamated with mathematics and the experimental method. With regards to the 17th century, Aristotelian natural philosophy was no longer in fashion. It was replaced rather by "The Mechanical Philosophy" with its ontology of particles in motion across empty space and exemplified perhaps by Cartesian natural philosophy. Yet when talking about the content of the natural philosophy that was supposedly integrated with mathematics and the experimental method in the 17th century, we find that the Mechanical Philosophy was largely programmatic, and its concepts were not operational, just like Aristotle's concepts of nature. At best it was "preparatory," as perhaps suggested by Cohen's idea of the "transformation of natural philosophy" which later led to its integration with mathematics and experiment.

As Hugh Kearney argued in his book, *Science and Change: 1500–1700*, there were three traditions in science on the eve of the Scientific Revolution, namely the organic, the magical, and the mechanistic.[12] The organic tradition was based on Aristotelian science and natural philosophy, the magical tradition was associated with Renaissance science, and the mechanistic tradition related to the mechanical philosophy. The scientific revolution basically consisted in the replacement of the organic and magical tradition, by the mechanistic.

In comparison to science in Islamic civilization, what this implies is that, even if Greek philosophy was allowed to flourish in Islamic civilization, it would not have led to the scientific revolution since it was predicated on the rejection of Aristotelian natural philosophy. If anything, one could argue that al-Ghazālī's critique of Greek natural philosophy was not a disservice to the

---

12 Hugh Kearney, *Science and Change: 1500–1700* (New York: McGraw-Hill, 1971).

birth of modern science, because the Scientific Revolution itself was predicated upon the rejection of Greek science and natural philosophy.

The Integration between Matter Theory (Natural Philosophy) and Newtonian Mechanics Only Occurred in the 19th Century, and Not the 17th Century

The physics of the 17th century, which was based largely on Galilean and Newtonian mechanics, did not involve the incorporation of natural philosophy. In the 17th century, natural philosophy was in the form of matter theory. While Newtonian mechanics was "operational" and predictive, matter theory like the mechanical philosophy, was still programmatic and incapable of empirical predictions. Belief in it was rather a matter of faith, without any experimental support. And neither was matter theory, i.e., the natural philosophy of the day, integrated with Newtonian mechanics. As Stephen Gaukroger puts it, "matter theory was not yet integrated with Newtonian mechanics in the 17th century."[13] To quote Gaukroger:

> The issues here in large part hinged around the problem of how to integrate mechanics into matter theory. Mechanics deals with physical processes in terms of the motions undergone by bodies and the nature of the forces responsible for these motions. Matter theory deals with how the physical behavior of a body is determined by what it is made of, and in the seventeenth century it typically achieved this in a corpuscularian fashion, by investigating how the nature and arrangement of the constituent parts of a body determine its behavior. Mechanical and matter-theoretic approaches to physical theory are very different, they engage fundamentally different kinds of considerations, and on the face of it offer explanations of different phenomena.[14]

The key point to be observed here is that in the 17th century, natural philosophy in the form of matter theory, was not yet integrated with the mathematically-infused, experimentally-based Newtonian mechanics. In fact, that was to come much later, with the kinetic theory of gases in the 19th century. In other words, there was no integration yet between natural philosophy, mathematics, and the experimental method, as suggested by proponents of the NPT, in the 17th century.

Natural Philosophy Still Continued to Exist in Islamic Culture and Civilisation After Al-Ghazālī's Critique in the 11/12th Century

Despite Al-Ghazālī's famous attack on Greek philosophy through his major work, *Tahāfut al-Falāsifah* (The Incoherence of the Philosophers), natural phi-

---

13 Stephen Gaukroger, *The Emergence of a Scientific Culture* (Oxford: Oxford University Press, 2006).
14 Gaukroger, *The Emergence of a Scientific Culture*, 402.

losophy still continued to exist. The Spanish Muslim philosopher, Ibn Rushd (1126–1198 CE), a follower of Aristotle who came after Al-Ghazālī (1058–1111 CE), wrote his famous rebuttal *Tahāfut al-Tahāfut*, thus continuing the philosophical tradition in the Islamic world. Although many were aware of Ibn Rushd's reply to Al-Ghazālī, the fact that it came after the death of Al-Ghazālī and not during his lifetime, was not given sufficient emphasis. Had this fact been realized, then perhaps the impression that Al-Ghazālī had given Greek philosophy a death blow in the Islamic world, would not have remained.

Similarly, although the *Kalām* tradition in Islam is normally associated with Islamic theology and viewed as philosophy conducted in defence of the Islamic faith, yet it nevertheless uses philosophical methods of argumentation, which was sanctioned in Islam as *dalīl naqlī* or proof through reason. In fact, Ashʿarite atomism was a product of the *Kalām* school rather than *falāsifah*.[15] And it was indeed a form of natural philosophy, albeit connected with "Occasionalism" which makes horizontal causation problematic and hence not amenable to natural science.

In Safavid Iran in the 15th and 16th centuries, Greek natural philosophy continued to exist, but it did not bring about any scientific revolution in that part of the Islamic world despite the significant contributions made by Muslims of Persian origin in the Golden Age of Islamic science.

Thus, our brief survey of natural philosophy in the Islamic world after 1111 CE, i.e., the year of Al-Ghazālī's death, would indicate to us that natural philosophy, or more broadly, *falsafah*, was still alive in the Islamic world, even though it occupied a somewhat marginal status as compared to *Kalām* or traditional Islamic religious knowledge.

Natural Philosophy and Scientific Realism

Apart from the commonly cited argument concerning Al-Ghazālī's critique of Greek philosophy as the reason for the decline of philosophy in Islam, another important reason which has been advanced by Sabra, is the lack of a realist commitment to natural philosophy in Islam.[16] Sabra contrasted the religious approach of the theologians such as Al-Ghazālī, with that of the philosopher-scientist in the following manner. With regards to the religious view of secular knowledge, he wrote:

> There is only one principle that should be consulted whenever one has to decide whether or not a certain branch of learning is worthy of pursuit: it is the all-important consideration that "this world is a sowing

---

[15] Sabra, Abdelhamid I, "The Simple Ontology of Kalam Atomism: An Outline," *Early Science and Medicine* 14, no. 1–3 (2009): 68–78.

[16] Abdelhamid I. Sabra, "The Appropriation and Subsequent Naturalization of Greek Science in Medieval Islam: A Preliminary Statement," *History of Science* 25, no. 69 (1987): 223–243.

ground for the next"; and Ghazali quotes in this connection the Prophetic Tradition: "May God protect us from useless knowledge." The final result of all this is an instrumentalist and religiously oriented view of all secular and permitted knowledge. This is the view that accompanied the limited admission of logic and mathematics and medicine into the *madrasa* and the conditional admission of the astronomer into the mosque.[17]

In other words, the primacy of religious knowledge over secular learning holds in medieval Islamic culture. As for the "philosophical sciences" which is based on reason rather than revelation, Sabra has this to say:

> The philosophical sciences, *al-ulum al-hikmiyya*, had entered Islamic intellectual life under the banner of an articulated concept of *hikma* (or philosophical wisdom) which involved a doctrine of knowledge quite distinct from the view just outlined. According to this doctrine, the aim of theoretical investigation, whether mathematical, physical or metaphysical, was to ascertain the nature of all things as they are in themselves to the farthest extent possible, and the aim of the investigator was to gain knowledge of the truth for the sake of knowing the truth. The metaphysically inclined seeker after the truth, namely all the great philosophers of Islam . . . also believed that the ultimate value of all science was to perfect the human soul . . . But, for the philosopher and the philosophically committed scientist, this was not a state that transcended philosophical activity . . . Man's perfection thus lay in the perfection of his philosophical or scientific knowledge and the way to his salvation was none other than the way of science. By contrast, a logical consequence of Ghazali's view was . . . to put a curb on theoretical inquiry.[18]

Finally, Sabra put the "blame" on the "instrumentalist" approach of Muslim scientists as the reason for their inability to make further advances:

> Finally, with regard to instrumentalism, it should be noted that what we have to do with here is not a general utilitarian interpretation of science, but a special view which confines scientific research to very narrow, and essentially unprogressive areas. We may rightly admire the ingenuity, inventiveness and computational prowess in some of the works of the *muwaqqits* on timekeeping and the *qibla*; but we have to realize that breakthroughs . . . could only have occurred elsewhere—for example, in geometry and theoretical algebra, in observational

---

17 Sabra, "The Appropriation and Subsequent Naturalization of Greek Science," 239–40.
18 Sabra, 240.

and theoretical astronomy and in various branches of experimental science, all fields in which, it must always be remembered, the earlier *hakims* had made significant and rather promising advances.[19]

For Sabra, the reason why natural philosophy did not flourish or thrive in Islam is because of the lack or absence of a realist commitment in their theories of nature. This is because in Islam truth cannot be known purely through reason, and therefore philosophers whose only recourse to truth is through the use of reason, cannot possibly tell us the truth about nature. On reflection, the excellence of Islamic science is largely "Alexandrian" in nature—to use Cohen's phrase—where there is no question of realist ontological commitment to physical theories. To claim that truth about the natural world can be captured by philosophers through their theories of nature, raises the possibility of a clash with religious views of nature. This denial of philosophy's role to give us "truths of nature" through the natural philosopher's use of reason, it is claimed, provided a paralyzing disincentive for philosophizing in the Islamic world.

However, if we look at the history of Islamic astronomy, we find that Muslim astronomers and scientists, were not merely interested in a mathematical or instrumentalist model, but were also concerned with actual physical reality.[20] S. H. Nasr for example, has suggested that Muslim scientists such as Ibn Haytham adopted a realist approach towards science, which laid the basis for future European orientation towards science. To quote Nasr:

> But even more important in the long run for the philosophy of science, was Alhazen's insistence upon the crystalline nature of the spheres. In Greek science, while the Aristotelian insisted that the aim of science was to know the nature of things, the mathematicians and astronomers generally believed that their aim was to "save the phenomena." The Ptolemaic spheres were convenient mathematical inventions that aided calculation and had no physical reality. Perhaps the most important heritage that Islamic science bequeathed upon the West was to insist that the role of science, including mathematics, must be the search for knowledge of the reality and being of things. The emphasis upon the crystalline nature of the spheres by Alhazen was precisely a statement of this belief. Physics in Muslim eyes was inseparable from ontology.[21]

---

19 Sabra, 241–42.
20 David C. Lindberg, *The Beginnings of Western Science* (Chicago, The University of Chicago Press, 1992).
21 Seyyed Hossein Nasr, *Islamic Life and Thought* (Kuala Lumpur: Islamic Book Trust, 2010) 70–71.

Muslim astronomers were not satisfied with merely mathematical models, but instead were seeking for physical, causal explanations of astronomical phenomena. This clearly shows that they were not averse to realism with respect to scientific theory, given their attitude towards astronomical theory.

Seyyed Hossein Nasr on Natural Philosophy and Islamic Science

For Nasr, natural philosophy and Islamic Science are compatible, unlike the claim made by those who were critical of the view that natural philosophy was welcomed in Islam. However, the kind of natural philosophy which is compatible with Islamic Science is a neo-Platonic, religious or "perennial philosophy" that is more metaphysical in nature. Since Nasr considers himself a "Traditionalist" who defends Islamic metaphysics against the incursions of modern science with its mechanistic and reductionist worldview,[22] a closer look at his views on the relationship between natural philosophy and Islamic Science would also give us an insight into the thinking of medieval Muslim scientists who were engaged in a similar enterprise.[23] Basically, Nasr's objection to the inclusion of natural philosophy in Islamic Science, is more to do with the "type" of natural philosophy invoked, rather than an objection to natural philosophy *per se*. Nasr sees the "old science" as having a "cosmology" or "natural philosophy" which is compatible with a religious worldview. It was only with the rise of the "Mechanical Philosophy" in the 17th century that science adopted a worldview that is no longer in harmony with a religious view of the world. According to Nasr:

> The order of nature studied and explained by the traditional sciences not only corresponded to an aspect of reality, as seen concretely in the practical efficacy of certain forms of traditional medicine now avidly sought by many Westerners, but was also wed to the religious universe. . . .
>
> It was this common universe of discourse that was rent asunder by the rise of modern science as a result of which the religious view of the order of nature, which is always based on symbolism, was reduced either to irrelevance or to a matter of mere subjective concern, which made the cosmic teachings of religion to appear as unreal and irrelevant. Also, it was through the destruction of the unitary vision of the cosmos that the "laws of nature" became divorced from moral laws and the sciences of nature became divorced at their roots from the foundations of religious ethics. The consequence of this segmentation and separation was the alienation of man from an image of the Universe

---

22　See Seyyed Hossein Nasr, and Ramin Jahanbegloo, *In Search of the Sacred: A Conversation with Seyyed Hossein Nasr on his Life and Thought* (Santa Barbara, California: Praeger, 2010).
23　Grant, "The Fate of Ancient Greek Natural Philosophy."

created by himself but given a purely objective and nonanthropomorphic status and the surrender of nature as a mass without spiritual significance to be analyzed and dissected with impunity on the one hand and plundered and raped with uncontrolled avidity on the other. Thus, it is of the utmost importance to try to understand in depth how the modern scientific view of the order of nature was founded and how it has evolved during the past four centuries to the present day.[24]

Contrary to those who hailed the Scientific Revolution as a momentous episode in humanity's march towards progress,[25] Nasr saw the rise of modern science as a departure from the ideal state of "Islamic Science," which provides an enchanted view of the world thorough Islamic metaphysics and cosmology. According to Nasr:

> In fact it might be said that the main reason why modern science never arose in China or Islam is precisely because of the presence of metaphysical doctrine and a traditional religious structure which refused to make a profane thing of nature ... The most basic reason is that neither in Islam, nor India, nor the Far East was the substance and stuff of nature so depleted of a sacramental and spiritual character ... as to enable a purely secular science of nature and a secular philosophy to develop outside the matrix of the traditional intellectual orthodoxy. Islam, which resembles Christianity in so many ways, is a perfect example of this truth, and the fact that modern science did not develop in its bosom is not the sign of decadence as some have claimed but of the refusal of Islam to consider any form of knowledge as purely secular and divorced from what it considers as the ultimate goal of human existence.[26]

Thus, the presence of a metaphysical natural philosophy that is infused with religious symbolism, is in fact something which is welcomed in Nasr's view of Islamic Science. Looking at both al-Ghazālī and Nasr, I can therefore safely assume the following. What was rejected in medieval Islamic thought—following Ghazālī—was Greek natural philosophy, especially that attributed to Aristotle, the neo-Aristotelians, and the Atomists. As had been shown by Nasr, aspects of Greek philosophy such as Neoplatonism could be harmonized with an Islamic view of the universe. In other words, the rejection of Greek thought in Islamic Science was not a total rejection. Given that there are versions of Greek cosmology or natural philosophy which are compatible with Islamic

---

24 Seyyed Hossein Nasr, *Religion and the Order of Nature* (Oxford: Oxford University Press, 1996), 129.
25 Butterfield, *The Origins of Modern Science*, 190.
26 Seyyed Hossein Nasr, *Man and Nature: The Spiritual Crisis in Modern Man* (Chicago: ABC International Group, 1997), 97–98.

thought and Islamic science, our explanation for the incapability of Islamic Science to profit from the presence of (Neoplatonic) Greek philosophy has to be sought elsewhere, i.e., not in the contentious absence or neglect of natural philosophy in medieval Islam.

Nasr's idea of the "fusion" of natural philosophy into Islamic Science, however, is not similar to the manner in which natural philosophy is incorporated into Western science after the 17th century. In Western science, natural philosophy in the form of matter theory, is empirically testable and hence subjected to revision in the face of empirical evidence. There is no privileging of the metaphysical over the empirical. The sanctity of the metaphysical is not preserved in post-17th century Western science. This fundamental shift in the orientation of Western science is perhaps reflected in the attitude adopted by Kepler towards his study of astronomy. Initially, Kepler adopted a "metaphysical" approach by explaining the arrangement of the planets in the solar system in terms of the Platonic solids. However, he later abandoned this metaphysical view of the world when it could no longer accommodate the astronomical observations. In fact, later on he even abandoned the long-held "sacred" view of circular motion, adopting elliptical motion for the planets instead. Thus, despite his deep attachment to Plato's natural philosophy, fidelity to the facts of astronomy made him abandon the metaphysical in favour of the empirical. Even the once "sacred" circular motion of the ancients and medieval were abandoned in favour of "elliptical orbits."

The attitude taken by Nasr, and perhaps other like-minded Muslim thinkers in the past, would not have allowed such a transformation to occur in Islamic Science because it would result in an "impoverished" view of reality, despite the empirical success. This, according to my own conjecture, is also the reason why Muslim scholars in the past rejected Greek natural philosophy, and its concomitant amalgamation in Islamic Science. For had it been empirically confirmed, as was the case with Atomism in Western science, it would have to be accepted as part of the Islamic view of nature. On the other hand, cosy and enchanted theories of nature drawn from Islamic cosmology and metaphysics, would have to be abandoned if the empirical evidence dictates so. This contrasts with the approach taken by Kepler, who despite his earlier commitment to a Platonic metaphysics of the universe as shown in his model of the universe based on the five Platonic solids, abandoned it when it could no longer fit the astronomical facts. For Nasr, metaphysics is not revisable in the light of empirical data because metaphysical truth has a higher status. Kepler bit the bullet while Nasr and other like-minded Muslim scientists in the past, did not.

The Role of Natural Philosophy in Islamic and Western Science: Some Comparisons

While natural philosophy was eventually absorbed into Western science, leading to a synthesis of what Floris Cohen described as the "Athenian" and "Alexandrian" approaches to science,[27] where the former is in the philosophical tradition while the latter is in the instrumentalist or engineering mode, Islamic Science remained "Alexandrian" at best with achievements in mathematics, astronomy, optics, surgery, and the engineering feats of an al-Jazari. Although—as I have consistently argued—the thesis that natural philosophy is instrumental towards the emergence of modern science in the seventeenth century cannot be sustained, to deny the eventual amalgamation of natural philosophy in the form of matter theory, with mathematics and the experimental method to create the type of scientific theories found in the 19th and 20th centuries, is foolhardy.

Perhaps what can be said in favour of a modified natural philosophy thesis is that although it did not directly contribute towards the Scientific Revolution in the 17th century, whose defining moments were in the fields of astronomy and mechanics, it did eventually end up being integrated with mathematics and the experimental method to form the modern science that we know today. This is clearly seen in the case of the kinetic theory of gases in the 19th century, and the atomic theory in the 20th century. What distinguished the role of natural philosophy in Islamic and Western Science is that, in the West natural philosophy was allowed a "long waiting period" stretching back to the Middle Ages when it was taught at the medieval European universities in the Arts faculties.

On the other hand, natural philosophy, although not totally abandoned, was not cultivated to the same extent in Islamic civilisation. Historians of science such as Toby Huff and Edward Grant have cited al-Ghazālī and Ibn Khaldūn as two leading scholars in Islam, who rejected Greek natural philosophy as subjects which are not worth cultivating. However, to be fair to them, natural philosophy indeed did not provide any real contribution to the empirical sciences of that period. It was only as late as the 19th century that it became part of empirically testable theories. Even in the 17th century, the century of the Scientific Revolution, it remained largely programmatic in the form of the "Mechanical Philosophy," largely espoused by Descartes. What kept it going was a commitment to a certain view of nature, a nature that was "dis-enchanted"—to use Weber's phrase—without the empirical evidence or practice to sustain such a world picture. That world picture was largely drawn from Atomism, and the view that those basic particles or atoms move according to Newton's laws of mechanics. The long waiting period for natural phi-

---

27 Cohen, *How Modern Science Came into the World*.

losophy in the development of Western or modern science was not founded on reason or empirical evidence, but more on faith. Such faith only bore fruit as late as the 19th century, that is even after the First Industrial Revolution in Britain. But when it became coupled with empirical success and technological growth, the presence of "natural philosophy" in the form of abstract theories containing "theoretical entities" and descriptions of their behaviour, became the way to go in the leading science of the times, namely, physics.

The story in the Islamic world on the other hand, although it began in the realm of the cognitive, assumed a different status after the fall of the Abbasid Empire due to the Mongol invasion of 1258. External factors began to creep in, and became more influential in the development of science in the Islamic world.[28] Even if interest in natural philosophy had been sustained in the Islamic world, the lack of other factors such as continued institutional support in scientific endeavor and political patronage would have led to the decline of science in Islam in any case. This can be seen in the case of Iran, where unlike in the Sunni world, there was greater tolerance towards natural philosophy in Shīʿa Iran, with renowned philosophers such as Mullā Ṣadrā as late as the 17th century.

Conclusion

My critique of the Natural Philosophy Thesis (NPT) has come full circle. I started out by explaining what the thesis is and who its proponents are. I then argued that the thesis is problematic, and explained what the problems are. However, I did not totally abandon or reject the thesis, but qualified it by saying that such an integration of natural philosophy—in the form of matter theory—with mathematics and the experimental method, did occur but that its occurrence was much later, namely in the 19th rather than the 17th century. In the course of accepting this rather qualified or revised version of the thesis, I still maintain however, that the continued presence of natural philosophy in Islamic culture and civilization would not have given birth to modern science in Islamic civilisation, and neither was it a contributory factor to the rise of modern science in 17th century Europe.

In comparing the roles of natural philosophy in Western and Islamic science, I claim that it was the ability of natural philosophy to be put to the empirical test once it has become part of a scientific theory, which demarcated the way in which natural philosophy functioned in Western and Islamic science. In Islamic science and philosophy, natural philosophy occurred as cosmology and ontology, which cannot be subjected to experimental methodology. But although Islamic science did not take this last step which Western sci-

---

28 Ahmad Y. Al-Hassan, "Factors Behind the Decline of Islamic Science After the Sixteenth Century," in *Islam and the Challenge of Modernity*, ed. Sharifa Shifa Al-Attas (Kuala Lumpur: International Institute of Islamic Thought and Civilization, 1996).

ence did, it was however, spared a philosophico-cultural problem which later confronted Europe. This problem later appeared as "Eddington's problem of the two tables," i.e., the phenomenological table and the scientific table consisting of atoms in motion, and more recently as a topic in the philosophy of science known as the problem of scientific realism. The persistence of natural philosophy, construed as *epistêmê* rather than *technê*[29] in modern science, has confounded modern thinkers on the nature of physical reality and its relationship to our phenomenological world—the world of sense-experience, the world which we perceive in its experiential fullness. Islamic science, by refusing to subject metaphysics and ontology to experimental methodology, has preserved its worldview which gave it cultural stability and wholesomeness.

Western science on the other hand, has achieved its empirical success at a rather high price—that of cognitive instability with regard to its view of nature and physical reality. Its conception of the world now hangs on the coattails of scientists, especially physicists, and that conception can change depending on the experimental evidence and the paradigm accepted by the scientific community. But even that is problematic, since it assumes the acceptance of scientific realism, a position which is highly contested in the philosophy of science. The rejection of scientific realism does not confer much comfort either, especially for those who yearn for science to "tell us the truth about nature." What it means is that we do not have knowledge on the essential reality of the physical world, only "conjectures" (to use Popper's phrase) and conceptual models. At least by separating "cosmology"/natural philosophy from empirical science, the Islamic scientific tradition has managed to avoid this epistemologico-cultural calamity. Given the current state of flux in contemporary articulations of the nature of scientific theories, and the search for new models of science or even new ways of conceiving science, the practice found in Islamic science of the past could perhaps provide some guidance on how to produce a functioning science minus the cultural angst.

I met Professor Dr Syed Ali Ashraf personally when I was an undergraduate student at Manchester University in the mid-1970s, and attended a talk which he gave in London under the auspices of Federation of Student Islamic Societies (FOSIS). This article is therefore dedicated to his memory, and I have no doubt that he would have enthusiastically embraced scholarship exploring the intersection of Islam and science, particularly when viewed through a Muslim perspective.

---

29 Dear, *The Intelligibility of Nature*, 9.

Bibliography

Butterfield, Herbert. *The Origins of Modern Science*. London: G. Bell & Sons, 1957.

Cohen, Floris. *How Modern Science Came into the World*. Amsterdam: Amsterdam University Press, 2010.

Dear, Peter. *The Intelligibility of Nature: How Science Makes Sense of the World*. Chicago: The University of Chicago Press, 2006.

Gaukroger, Stephen. *The Emergence of a Scientific Culture*. Oxford: Oxford University Press, 2006.

Grant, Edward. *The Foundations of Modern Science in the Middle Ages*. Cambridge: Cambridge University Press, 1996.

Grant, Edward. *Science and Religion: 400 BC–AD 1550*. Baltimore: The Johns Hopkins University Press, 2004.

Grant, Edward. *A History of Natural Philosophy*. Cambridge: Cambridge University Press, 2007.

Grant, Edward. "The Fate of Ancient Greek Natural Philosophy in the Middle Ages: Islam and Western Christianity." *The Review of Metaphysics* 61, no. 3 (2008): 503–526.

Hall, Alfred R. *The Revolution in Science: 1500–1750*. London: Longman, 1983.

Al-Hassan, Ahmad Y. "Factors Behind the Decline of Islamic Science After the Sixteenth Century." In *Islam and the Challenge of Modernity*, edited by Sharifa Shifa Al-Attas. Kuala Lumpur: International Institute of Islamic Thought and Civilization, 1996.

Henry, John. *The Scientific Revolution and the Origins of Modern Science*. Basingstoke, Hampshire: Palgrave MacMillan, 2008.

Huff, Toby E. *The Rise of Early Modern Science: Islam, China and the West*. Cambridge, Cambridge University Press, 1993.

Kearney, Hugh. *Science and Change:1500-1700*. New York: McGraw-Hill, 1971.

Lindberg, David C. *The Beginnings of Western Science*. Chicago, The University of Chicago Press, 1992.

Nasr, Seyyed Hossein. *Religion and the Order of Nature*. Oxford: Oxford University Press, 1996.

Nasr, Seyyed Hossein. *Man and Nature: The Spiritual Crisis in Modern Man*. Chicago: ABC International Group, 1997 [1967].

Nasr, Seyyed Hossein. *Islamic Life and Thought*. Kuala Lumpur: Islamic Book Trust, 2010 [1981].

Nasr, Seyyed Hossein, and Ramin Jahanbegloo. *In Search of the Sacred: A Conversation with Seyyed Hossein Nasr on his Life and Thought*. Santa Barbara, California: Praeger, 2010.

Sabra, Abdelhamid I. "The Appropriation and Subsequent Naturalization of Greek Science in Medieval Islam: A Preliminary Statement." *History of Science* 25, no. 69 (1987): 223–243.

Sabra, Abdelhamid I. "Science and Philosophy in Medieval Islamic Theology." *Zeitschrift fur Geschichte der Arabisch-Islamischen Wissenschaften* 9 (1994): 1–42.

Sabra, Abdelhamid I. "The Simple Ontology of Kalam Atomism: An Outline." *Early Science and Medicine* 14, no. 1–3 (2009): 68–78.

Chapter 24

Syed Ali Ashraf:
The Spiritual-Intellectual Guide on Islam and English Literature
Nor Faridah Abdul Manaf

The Intellectual Guide

This chapter delves into Syed Ali Ashraf's perspectives on English Literature, emphasizing his profound appreciation for literary studies. It underscores his belief in the intrinsic value of literature, portraying it as a pivotal discipline that cultivates virtues and enhances cognitive abilities, thereby contributing to the development of strong character and critical thinking skills. However, he saw the need to approach it delicately in order to fully understand the vastness of Western civilisation which does not always run in conflict with Islamic thought. His literary analyses of Western texts consistently imbued them with an extra layer of depth, emphasizing the imperative of cross-cultural understanding and fostering peaceful and harmonious coexistence. The paper also demonstrates how Syed Ali Ashraf as a spiritual as well as an intellectual guide shares his thoughts on the concept of "tragic hero" in Shakespearean tragedies with a young postgraduate, desperately looking for a framework on reading Western texts with Islamic sensibility and wisdom.

Allah is All Merciful. My meeting with the late Syed Ali Ashraf was at the home of Abdur Rahman Doi. Professor Doi was then teaching at the International Islamic University Malaysia and was known for his great experience in researching and lecturing on Islamic Studies. Like Ali Ashraf, he worked hard in providing Muslim students with reliable information on and understanding of Islamic texts. Looking back, I was fortunate to meet both these scholars. I was a friend of Professor Doi's wife and was invited to a gathering at their place where Syed Ali Ashraf was a guest. As a young academic fresh from completing my studies in New Zealand and while pursuing my Diploma of Education at the International Islamic University Malaysia, I encountered Professor Ashraf's name and delved into his educational philosophy for the first time. Meeting him in person was a real blessing. The country was going through a crisis, and I spoke of a personality who we both knew. "He has changed," I said provocatively. "Well, the world has changed," he answered, calm on his face.

I knew then this was a real scholar who would not look at small things but would always look forward to a larger picture: how important it was for us to embrace change and live mindfully as Muslims—the Ummah was always at the heart of it all.

A few years afterwards, I was given the opportunity to continue my studies at the University of Liverpool in the United Kingdom and I chose to examine the cross-cultural and cross-philosophical thoughts between Islam and Christianity in Shakespearean tragedies, in line with my university's mission and vision on Islamisation of Knowledge as well as Integration of Knowledge which simply meant to look at the best both Islamic thought and Western thought could offer (as well as examine their differences).

I had always loved 16th Century British Literature. But in early 1990s, there were not much cross-cultural studies done as such as it is today. If Jerry Brotton's book, *The Sultan and the Queen: The Untold Story of Elizabeth and Islam* (2016) was published then, it would have made my academic life easier. I could have easily traced the influence Islam had on Elizabeth's Britain:

> England's fascination with the Islamic world went back even further than this first exchange of letters between the sultan and the queen. English merchants had begun doing business in Morocco and Syria as early as 1550s. Henry VIII often appeared at festivities "apparelled after Turkey fashion," dressed in silk and velvet and sporting a turban and scimitar.[1]

After spending a few months on the Master's taught program, it was time to fine-tune my thesis topic. I knew I needed to get some intellectual advice directly from the guru who was able to read Shakespeare with cross-cultural understanding. In those days, mobile phones and the Internet were not in existence, and I remember calling Syed Ali Ashraf from a phone box not far from my student hall. It must be destined. I got him on the first call. I told him I needed some advice on my thesis topic on Shakespeare. "Can I see you?" I asked. He said "yes" with not even a pause but mentioned that he was leaving a day after the following day. He asked if I had time to meet him at Cambridge the following day, because he had to fly back to Asia. I too said "yes" without thinking about how I would get to Cambridge. I had arrived in the United Kingdom just a couple of months ago and the thought of a woman in hijab,

---

1 Jerry Brotton, *The Sultan and The Queen: The Untold Story of Elizabeth and Islam* (New York: Viking Press, 2016), 4.

travelling alone at night on the train at a time when mobile phone did not exist didn't seem to be a problem when I said "OK" to Prof Ashraf. I must have caught on to his love and respect for knowledge and love for knowledge seeker. Either that or I was too desperate to get my thesis topic sorted out by a genius.

I met him as promised at 9 am the following day. He asked me when I arrived. When I told him when and where I stayed last night, he asked me why I didn't call him because he and his wife could have put me up at their place. Such was the humility of this great scholar. You must be reminded that when I met him in Kuala Lumpur, I was one of the many faces he met, and we spoke briefly. He would not have registered me. His generosity and kindness would be extended to any stranger in need. This testimonial is also given by others after his demise.

At the meeting in Cambridge, we spoke and discussed various possibilities before we agreed to a topic which was to examine the concept of "tragic hero" in Shakespearean tragedies from an Islamic perspective. The discussion continued till lunch hours when the good old Professor took me to Clare Hall, and we had lunch with other Cambridge University dons whom he happily introduced to me. I felt welcomed despite being a postgraduate sitting amidst great minds of Cambridge. I suspected that Professor Ashraf shared his Cambridge world with me to inspire me as a young researcher. He did not stop teaching even in those situations. From his conversations with me and with other professors, I gleaned insights into both everyday topics and more complex subject matters.

Then I was invited to his house where I met his wife, and we had time going for a walk along River Cam. It has been over 20 years, but their kindness and generosity still resonate in my memory.

Syed Ali Ashraf returned to Kuala Lumpur on numerous occasions I think, but I only saw him on one occasion. I had the opportunity to return his hospitality where my husband and I took him to dinner. I recall Syed Ali Ashraf's remark about Kuala Lumpur's streetlights: "Kuala Lumpur wants to be like New York. It wants to stay young and vibrant all the time." His comment elicited laughter, yet it also stirred deeper reflection within me. It seemed to highlight a reality we often ignored—the tendency to overlook underlying issues by focusing on superficial aspects. Despite the spontaneity of his remarks, every word he uttered carried significance, inviting further contemplation.

Ashraf on Islam and English Literary Studies

Syed Ali Ashraf emphasizes Islamic education rooted in a profound comprehension of the Qurʾān and the Sunnah. Central to his philosophy is the belief in humanity as Allah's vicegerent on earth, endowed with the capacity to govern the world wisely through the application of knowledge aligned with religious guidance. For Ashraf, there is no barrier to learning and it is this idea that he applies to the study of English Literature. For many, Islam and

English Literary Studies are strange bedfellows. However, as argued by Hafiz Masood, the discourse on Islam and English Literature is not something new. He has created an extensive bibliography on studies done on the discourse—from topics on the influence of Muslim literary traditions on the Europeans to works pertaining to the representations of Islam and Muslims in English Literature.[2] He also demonstrates how the interest on both Islam and English Literary Studies increased after September 11, 2001, citing various major conferences both in the United Kingdom and the United States. For example, the conferences held at Trinity College, Cambridge (2001) on "Between Empires: 'Orientalism' before 1600," Institute of English Studies, London (2002) on "Cultural Encounters between East and West," and Department of English, Reading (2004) on "Europe and the Islamic World: Cultural Transformations, 1453–1798." In recent years, the interest in Islam, English Literary Studies or discourse on Islam and Europe continues and courses as well as publications on the topic blossom. This includes works by Matthew Dimmock's *New Turkes: Dramatizing Islam and the Ottomans in Early Modern England* (2005) and Jerry Brotton's book, *The Sultan and the Queen: Untold Story of Elizabeth and Islam* (2016). This reflects the continued interest in the topic.

Syed Ali Ashraf who was trained in English Literature had long believed in the power of deep reflections but one which must, in the end, submit to the highest form of self-awareness which is the ability to read the Signs of God (āyātullāh). This awareness of Divine Unity (al-tawḥīd) cannot be achieved if man is not able to free himself/herself from the rigidity or constraints to think, reflect, read, and write creatively and imaginatively. However, Ashraf believes that this creativity will not be of any value if it is not able to comprehend the meaning of experience which the "spiritual self" reveals to it. For Ashraf, the imagination within oneself must establish ties between the Spirit and the self.[3] The writer must have faith in a Higher Reality to help him or her find a sense of purpose in life and in so doing, help others reflect on theirs.

This moral framework of values is necessary for Ashraf although he agrees that good literature can also be created by those not fully aware of the Divine Reality, but he asks how they would know what is good and what is evil if a certain moral framework is not in place. I wish to add, where does that knowledge of good and evil come from if not from religion? The old argument of doing art for art's sake or art for society continues to this day. In the past, George Sand (1804–1876) wrote that art for the sake of art was an empty phrase and she believed that the "artist's vocation is to send light into the hu-

---

2   Hafiz Abid Masood, "Islam in Medieval and Early Modern English Literature: A Select Bibliography," *Islamic Studies* 44, no. 4 (2005): 554, http://www.jstor.org/stable/20838992.
3   Syed Ali Ashraf, "Islamic Principles and Methods in the Teaching of Literature," in *Philosophy, Literature and Fine Arts*, ed. Seyyed Hossein Nasr (Kent, UK: Hodder and Stoughton, and Jeddah: King Abdulaziz University, 1982), 27.

man heart."[4] Sand's most celebrated novel *Consuelo* (1842) raises the questions on the role and responsibility of the artist and art. As documented by Linda Lewis (2003), Sand asks, in *Consuelo*, the following questions: "Who is the artist; what is the source of genius; what contribution should one make to the world by means of her art; are freedom and suffering necessary for the artist's development; and is the artist superior to the codes and rules of common, everyday humanity?"[5] In comparison to concerns raised by Syed Ali Ashraf, it seems that they share common grounds with regard to the function and role of literature. Friedrich Nietzsche also echoes the same thought when he says there is no art for art's sake. In his book, *Twilight of the Idols,* Nietzsche wrote,

> Once you exclude the purposes of sermonizing and improving people from art, it does not follow even remotely that art is totally purposeless, aimless, senseless, in short, *l'art pour l'art* [art for art's sake]—a worm swallowing its own tail. 'Better no purpose at all than a moral purpose!'—those are just words of passion. A psychologist, on the other hand, will ask: what does art do? Doesn't it praise? Doesn't it dignify? Doesn't it select? Doesn't it have preferences? All of this strengthens or weakens certain value judgments . . . Is this just incidental? accidental? completely unconnected to the artist's instinct? Or: isn't it the presupposition for an artist to be able to . . . ? Is the artist's most basic instinct bound up with art, or is it bound up much more intimately with life, which is the meaning of art? Isn't it bound up with the desirability of life? Art is the great stimulus to life: how could art be understood as purposeless, pointless, *l'art pour l'art?*[6]

Nietzsche refused to view art in such a narrow perspective as would other intellectuals across time and culture, such as *Léopold Sédar Senghor*, Chinua Achebe and Diego Rivera. Rivera for example thinks that the art for art's sake position would further divide the rich from the poor. He believes that such a position will only privilege the privileged and art if continued, will no longer convey the pulse of the people or society. Rivera believes that every artist is a propagandist, and this is alright be with. The association of propaganda with art became problematic because of "bourgeois prejudice." Rivera asserts that:

> Naturally enough the bourgeoisie does not want art employed for the sake of revolution. It does not want ideals in art because its own ideals

---

4   George Sand, "George Sand Quotes," BrainyQuote.com, accessed July 9, 2023, https://www.brainyquote.com/quotes/george_sand_119591.
5   Linda M. Lewis, *Germaine De Staël, George Sand, and the Victorian Woman Artist* (Columbia, Missouri: University of Missouri Press, 2003), 49.
6   Friedrich Nietzsche, *The Anti-Christ, Ecce Homo, Twilight of The Idols, And Other Writings*, trans. Judith Norman, eds. Aaron Ridley and Judith Norman (Cambridge: Cambridge University Press 2005), 204.

cannot any longer serve as artistic inspiration. It does not want feelings because its own feelings cannot any longer serve as artistic inspiration. Art and thought and feeling must be hostile to the bourgeoisie today. Every strong artist has a head and a heart. Every strong artist has been a propagandist.[7]

Rivera is brought into this discussion to demonstrate that despite differences of ideologies, certain aspects of his thought towards art overlap with those of Syed Ali Ashraf. Both (and others cited earlier) believe that art has a role. Art has some kind of responsibility. Syed Ali Ashraf is not alone in believing in the importance and role of creative works as a means for self-reflection and soul searching. In his article "The Aims of Education," Syed Ali Ashraf differentiates the meaning between education and instruction. For him, "Education helps in the complete growth of an individual's personality, whereas instruction merely trains an individual or a group in the efficient performance of some task."[8]

This idea is further extended to how he saw the importance of literature as a form of knowledge to guide and help shape the personality of a person. Literature is not neutral in character. As such, it is important to have a specific framework (Syed Ali Ashraf calls it "a scheme of literary criticism") to read literature along with the understanding of the concept of man provided by Islam.[9] He further reiterates that it is necessary for literary critics to have a concept of good and evil and for the Muslim writers and critics, that concept of good and evil must be that provided by the teachings of Islam, not just freely interpreted by individuals who may subscribe to all sorts of "isms." Alphonse Dougan in his article on "Good and Evil in Islam"[10] asserts that the Islamic definitions of good and evil are based on the purposes of creation and meaning of human life. The ultimate goal of life is to have a firm belief (*īmān*) in Allah, to know Allah (*maʿrifatullāh*) and to love Allah (*maḥabbatullāh*) and all these would not be convincing without the final submission (*islām*) to Allah—worshipping Him (*ʿibādah*). This means that whatever brings a person closer to Allah and will benefit him/her in the next world is good and whatever takes him/her away from Allah and incurs God's wrath is evil. Dougan gives an example of when good can be evil: abundant wealth and good health which make a person indulge in worldly desires and forget God. This act can be

---

7 Rivera, Diego, "The Revolutionary Spirit in Modern Art," *The Modern Quarterly* 6, no. 3 (1932): 57.
8 Syed Ali Ashraf, preface to *Aims and Objectives of Islamic Education*, ed. Syed Muhammad al-Naquib al-Attas (Kent, UK: Hodder and Stoughton and Jeddah: King Abdulaziz University, 1979), ix.
9 Ashraf, "Islamic Principles," 27.
10 Alphonse Dougan, "Good and Evil in Islam," *The Fountain Magazine* 50, (April-June 2005), https://fountainmagazine.com/2005/issue-50-april-june-2005/good-and-evil-in-islam.

self-destructive. Dougan cites the following verse of the Qurʾān which affirms that it is not wrong to be rich and wealthy but how one uses that wealth will determine whether the act is good or evil:

> Righteousness is not that you turn your faces toward the east or the west, but [true] righteousness is [in] one who believes in Allah , the Last Day, the angels, the Book, and the prophets and gives wealth, in spite of love for it, to relatives, orphans, the needy, the traveler, those who ask [for help], and for freeing slaves; [and who] establishes prayer and gives zakah; [those who] fulfill their promise when they promise; and [those who] are patient in poverty and hardship and during battle. Those are the ones who have been true, and it is those who are the righteous. (Qurʾān 2: 177, trans. *Saheeh International*).

In promoting teaching and reading English Literature using a moral framework, Syed Ali Ashraf expresses his concern over writers or critics who dogmatise.[11] He points out that any attempt to personalise any system of belief in a work of art would demand the readers to move away from the realm of pure literature into the realm of philosophical thought and Syed Ali Ashraf suggests that criticism should be kept "within the context of literature in so far as a picture of human life and events is concerned."[12] Literature today has become a transdisciplinary subject and justifiably so since literature reflects life and events surrounding it. In an article by Paul Sopčák, Massimo Salgaro and J. Berenike Herrmann entitled "Transdisciplinary approaches to literature and empathy," they argue that literary reading has "positive socio-cognitive effects and ethical import through its ability to promote perspective taking and moral reflection."[13] They also highlight that this can happen through a wide array of disciplines such as philosophy, psychology, sociology as well as legal and medical studies. I believe this is the stage where literature teaching and learning is now. While we try to keep true to literary elements and essence, we cannot help responding to local and global issues so that students could relate what is happening in their literary texts to what they see or go through themselves. It is through transdisciplinary approach that new forms of understanding could be achieved that would help students move away from Eurocentric interpretation of their literary texts.

Syed Ali Ashraf was instrumental in promoting faith-based education, and the aftermath of the Makkah conference in 1977[14] that he organised contin-

---

11 Ashraf, "Islamic Principles," 28.
12 Ashraf, "Islamic Principles," 28.
13 Paul Sopčák, Massimo Salgaro, and J. Berenike Herrmann, "Transdisciplinary approaches to literature and empathy: A special issue," *Scientific Study of Literature* 6, no. 1 (2016): 2, https://doi.org/10.1075/ssol.6.1.02sop.
14 This conference, called the "First World Conference on Muslim Education," was organized by Syed Ali Ashraf. See Shaikh Abdul Mabud, "World conferences on Muslim

ues to dominate the thinking of Muslim scholars and educationists around the world and the work on rebuilding what we have lost over time due to colonisation, poverty, and ignorance. While it might be easier to do this with some other disciplines—since the framework or terms of reference for those disciplines were already tested in the glorious past of Islamic civilisation, for example, Islamic economy through its system of *zakāh* and *waqf* among other things, medicine through the works laid out by Ibn Sīnā and other Muslim scientists—the question remains, how does one start to Islamise English literature? One must start with human experiences as captured by writers from different cultures. Language is after all only a tool. It may be Arabic, Malay, Urdu or any other language but its main function is to communicate and express. If we study a piece of literary work in any language including English, there should be no doubt that it could be studied from the perspective of Islam provided all the criteria recommended by Syed Ali Ashraf are met. The teacher must have a strong foundation of Islamic thought and must be a person who practises the religion. The teacher should also be well trained in the field so that in discussing moral values and virtues, he/she does not end up as a religious teacher instead of a teacher of literature. Such discussions provide opportunities for teachers with Islamic orientation to engage with often-confused Muslim youths in critical analysis of texts before coming to their own conclusion over what is proper/good and what is considered as improper.

This sense of propriety is very important in Islamic education. Syed Ali Ashraf wrote about the need of having our own Islamic literary criticism and hence, our own Islamic literary critics. This is still lacking, and we must make the most of what have been proposed by Muslim thinkers and philosophers like Syed Naquib Al-Attas, Syed Ali Ashraf, Seyyed Hossein Nasr, and Ismaʿil Raji al-Faruqi. Even then we do not have a textbook on their thoughts for easy reference which makes it difficult for a new teacher who may not have much exposure to Islam to be able to sustain the faith-based teaching approach as necessary. As highlighted by Syed Ali Ashraf, English literature could be seductive but the teacher as a critic must be able to navigate discussions on human limitations, evil temptations, and human's role as *khalīfatullāh* (vicegerent of Allah) so as to derive meanings from and contemplate on lessons from literary texts.[15] However, Syed Ali Ashraf also warns that literature should be treated as literature and not as a substitute for moral teaching. "Literature can never replace morality or religion," he says.[16] This does not mean that we are divorced from moral perception or moral contemplation. We read literary texts to explore all sorts of conditions some of which we can relate to and some we

---

education: Shaping the agenda of Muslim education in the future," in *Philosophies of Islamic Education: Historical Perspectives and Emerging Discourses*, eds. Nadeem A. Memon and Mujadad Zaman (New York & London: Routledge, 2016).
15   Ashraf, "Islamic Principles," 31.
16   Ashraf, "Islamic Principles," 36.

cannot. We read because we enjoy the language used and the beauty of language alone could transform an ordinary emotion into an aesthetic one and the power of emotion is that it could help us to contemplate and reflect deeply on a situation. Empathy is an end result of this deep reflection and contemplation.

In one of his articles, "Shariah and Tariqah,"[17] Syed Ali Ashraf points out that everything on earth is created for Man and Man is entrusted to fulfil obligations as outlined by the Qurʾān so that his/her status as the *khalīfatullāh* can be elevated. To do this, one needs Sharīʿah in which the outward form (external confession of belief (*īmān*) in the Oneness of God and observing other forms of ritual) must complement the inward virtue which "will lead one to the extinction (*fanāʾ*) of one's self into the Love of God and the Prophet."[18] Syed Ali Ashraf cites a few verses of the Qurʾān and sayings of the Prophet (pbuh) to reiterate his point on reaching this level of *fanāʾ*:

> When true Iman enters a man's soul he loves God and the Prophet more than himself, his family, clan, tribe or nation or entire humanity. That is what the Qurʾān tells us when it says: "Say! If your fathers and your sons and your brethren and your wives and your tribe and the wealth you have acquired and the merchandise for which you fear that there will be no sale and the dwellings you desire are dearer to you than Allah and His Messenger and striving in His Way, then wait till Allah bringeth His command to pass. Allah guideth not the wrongdoing folk." (9: 24)

The Prophet reinforces this statement by saying:

> "None of you can be a *muʾmin* until his love for me is more than his love for his parents, children and all the people of the world." It is only when this love enters the soul and real extinction takes place that a person worships God with all sincerity (*Ikhlāṣ*).

Man has been created to worship God as God states in the Qurʾān:

> "I have created Jinns and Man only to worship Me (or serve Me)." (51: 56)[19]

This understanding of why we are created by God is very important for us to understand the purpose of existence, and for Syed Ali Ashraf this is incorporated in his teaching philosophy. In the teaching of English, the role of language and literature is to heighten that understanding and feeling. Our in-

---

17 Syed Ali Ashraf, "Shariah and Tariqah," *Caribbean Muslims*, published March 8, 2013. https://www.caribbeanmuslims.com/?s=Syed+Ali+Ashraf.
18 Ashraf, "Shariah and Tariqah," para 5.
19 Ashraf, paras 5–7.

telligence comes through the spirit which Allah has blown into our soul and it is this which connects us to Him. The following of the Sharīʿah will lead us to the realisation of the Truth, Justice, Righteousness, Mercy, and Charity—the Attributes of God—within ourselves. He says,

> Through the Knowledge of these Attributes, he starts understanding the essence of Nature and his own true relationship with it. That is how man realizes that everything in existence is an *āyatullāh*, a sign or reflection of Reality. If we follow Sharīʿah properly then only we realize why Islam is called the natural religion (*Dīn al fiṭrah*).[20]

Syed Ali Ashraf was also much influenced by Imām Al-Ghazālī. Al-Ghazālī is known as a philosopher and theologian with Sufi inclination (follower of *ṭarīqah/taṣawwuf*). Al Ghazali's *Kīmyā-e Saʿādat* ("Alchemy of Eternal Bliss," originally written in Persian, outlines 40 steps on how to achieve gnosis and closeness to God and be in a state of eternal bliss). Equally impactful was his reading of Al Ghazali's *Iḥyāʾ ʿulūm al-dīn* (The Revival of Religious Sciences, written in Arabic of his personal religious experiences). *Iḥyāʾ ʿulūm al-dīn* came before *Kīmyā-e Saʿādat* and is a bigger work (40 volumes which deal with the principles and practices of Islam and demonstrate how these can be made the basis of a reflective religious life in one's attempt to attain the higher stages of Sufism). It is evident that Syed Ali Ashraf believed that life is a constant struggle between doing what is good and what is evil and these writings reflect the need to purify our *qalb* (heart). In *Iḥyāʾ*, Al-Ghazālī states that the heart or *qalb* has five obstacles to reaching Truth:

1. A natural defect of the heart as the heart of a child.
2. Impurities of sins owing to lusts (*shahawāt*).
3. When the heart is diverted to worldly matters, the brightness of Truth is not reflected in it owing to the object of enquiry not being directed towards it although it is pure and clean.
4. When the heart is veiled by its lusts so that it cannot gain the Truth.
5. When the heart is full of ignorance (*jahl*).[21]

Syed Ali Ashraf underscores the imperative of perpetual guidance for the purification of our innermost being, or *qalb*. He directs our attention to the era of the Prophet and the immediate post-Prophetic period, illustrating the profound interconnection between internal states and external behaviours evident in the teachings of the Caliphs. This alignment emphasises the authentic observance of Sharīʿah, where spiritual principles were intricately interwoven

---

20 Ashraf, para 9.
21 Che Zarrina Sa'ari, "Al-Ghazali's Views on the Heart, the Spirit and the Soul: A Comparison Between *Iḥyāʾ ʿUlūm al-Dīn* and *Al-Risālah al-Ladunniyyah*," *Jurnal Usuluddin* 7 (June 1998): 204, https://jice.um.edu.my/index.php/JUD/article/view/3301.

with practical conduct. The Prophet's companions, turned Caliphs after his death, did not merely rule the empire, but they also took care of their people's spiritual well-being and guided the new believers. Sharīʿah lost its grip when later rulers became more worldly than spiritual and failed to properly integrate both in their administration. As *qalb* is the source of knowledge, it is both the source and means of preservation and transmission of knowledge. To fully understand the internal meaning of Sharīʿah, a man's/woman's *qalb* must be purified.[22]

As an educator and spiritual guide, Syed Ali Ashraf was fully aware of why literature cannot replace religion to teach morality as this chapter has argued earlier. Nonetheless, he acknowledges that literature serves as a vital conduit for gaining deeper insights into human conditions and the essence of existence, if not for outright illumination, then at least to provoke contemplation on the meaning of existence.[23] It is also important to offer a variety of texts to the students so that they are aware that no writer has the absolute knowledge to Truth and that different writers have different ways of presenting views and have different interpretations of human conditions and characters.[24] He further emphasizes the significance of teaching literature, highlighting its role not only in cultivating students' artistic sensibility but also in nurturing their moral awareness. For Syed Ali Ashraf, in order to read with a sense of purpose, literary criticism is important; and for Muslims a moral framework is necessary to guide them to detect any moral deviation and the emergence of spiritual crises while also facilitating a deeper analysis of their underlying causes:

> The works of literature cannot by themselves provide a moral framework for exploration. Literature is not completely independent of life. ... In other words, there is always a referential framework and it becomes necessary that the writer, as a human being, who does not want to be influenced by all kinds of attitudes and who does not want to be moved in different directions by different writers, should evaluate the moral framework which he believes in and which provides complete guidance to the reader. ... The teacher and students can then objectively explore the moral frameworks of different writers and find how conflicting their judgments and realisations are. At the same time, this will be a highly instructive exploration for students if they are trying to find out how, in spite of the variety of realisations, these writers have been able to present truthful images about man in various situations.[25]

---

22 Ashraf, "Shariah and Tariqah".
23 Ashraf, "Islamic Principles," 23.
24 Ashraf, "Islamic Principles," 33.
25 Ashraf, "Islamic Principles," 34–5.

It is evident from the excerpt above that Syed Ali Ashraf is open to different literary ideals and thoughts as long as the teacher as a guide raises issues of cultural differences as well as different ways of seeing and thinking which exist among writers. There are many ways to arrive at the Truth. Some ways are shorter than others but for Syed Ali Ashraf, Sharīʿah coupled with ṭarīqah is a sure way to purify the *qalb* so that we are able to see things as they are.

Conclusion

In conclusion, the late Syed Ali Ashraf was not only a deeply committed Islamic intellectual, a literary critic, a poet but he was also a great spiritual guide. He passionately believed that literature cannot replace moral teaching or religion, but it can prompt thoughts which demand readers to think and reflect upon the purpose of life and where they are in the scheme of things as they read about various human conditions in their literary texts. My meeting with him was brief but the impact he had on me, as a person and as a student of Islam, is huge. May Allah place him among the righteous and in the highest form of Jannah (Paradise).

Bibliography

Ashraf, Syed Ali. Preface to *Aims and Objectives of Islamic Education*, edited by Syed Muhammad al-Naquib al-Attas, ix–xiv. Kent, UK: Hodder and Stoughton and Jeddah: King Abdulaziz University, 1979.

Ashraf, Syed Ali. "Islamic Principles and Methods in the Teaching of Literature." In *Philosophy, Literature and Fine Arts,* edited by Seyyed Hossein Nasr, 22–40. Kent, UK: Hodder and Stoughton, and Jeddah: King Abdulaziz University, 1982.

Ashraf, Syed Ali. "Education and Values: Islamic vis-à-vis the Secularist Approaches." *Muslim Education Quarterly* 4, no. 2 (1987): 4–16.

Ashraf, Syed Ali. "Shariah and Tariqah." *Caribbean Muslims*. Published March 8, 2013. https://www.caribbeanmuslims.com/Sharīʿah-and-tariqah.

Brotton, Jerry. *The Sultan and the Queen: The Untold Story of Elizabeth and Islam*. New York: Viking Press, 2016.

Dimmock, Matthew. *New Turkes: Dramatising Islam and the Ottomans in Early Modern England*. London: Routledge, 2005.

Dougan, Alphonse. "Good and Evil in Islam." *The Fountain Magazine* 50 (April-June 2005). https://fountainmagazine.com/2005/issue-50-april-june-2005/good-and-evil-in-islam.

Lewis, Linda M. *Germaine De Staël, George Sand, and the Victorian Woman Artist*. Columbia, Missouri: University of Missouri Press, 2003.

Mabud, Shaikh Abdul. "World conferences on Muslim education: Shaping the agenda of Muslim education in the future." In *Philosophies of Islamic Education: Historical Perspectives and Emerging Discourses,* edited by Nadeem A. Memon, and Mujadad Zaman, 129–143. New York and London: Routledge, 2016.

Masood, Hafiz Abid. "Islam in Medieval and Early Modern English Literature: A Select Bibliography." *Islamic Studies* 44, no. 4 (2005): 553–629. http://www.jstor.org/stable/20838992.

Nietzsche, Friedrich. *The Anti-Christ, Ecce Homo, Twilight of The Idols, And Other Writings*. Translated by Judith Norman. Edited by Aaron Ridley and Judith Norman. Cambridge: Cambridge University Press, 2005.

Rivera, Diego. The Revolutionary Spirit in Modern Art. *The Modern Quarterly* 6, no. 3 (1932): 51–7.

Sa'ari, Che Zarrina. Al-Ghazali's Views on the Heart, the Spirit and the Soul: A Comparison Between *Iḥyāʾ ʿUlūm al-Dīn* and *Al-Risālah al-Ladunniyyah*. *Jurnal Usuluddin* 7 (June 1998): 193–208. https://jice.um.edu.my/index.php/JUD/article/view/3301.

Sand, George. "George Sand Quotes." BrainyQuote.com. Accessed July 9, 2023. https://www.brainyquote.com/quotes/george_sand_119591.

Seyyed Hossein Nasr, ed. *Philosophy, Literature and Fine Arts*. Kent, UK: Hodder and Stoughton, and Jeddah: King Abdulaziz University, 1982.

Sopčák, Paul, Massimo Salgaro, and J. Berenike Herrmann. "Transdisciplinary approaches to literature and empathy: A special issue." *Scientific Study of Literature* 6, no. 1 (2016): 2–5. https://doi.org/10.1075/ssol.6.1.02sop.

Chapter 25

Islamic Scholarship: A Gateway to a Grand Destination[1]

Emajuddin Ahamed

It is my privilege to have been here this morning on this great occasion of Syed Ali Ashraf Memorial Lecture. This great occasion, having twin goals in view, is doubly blessed: This will help many a one to recollect with profound satisfaction Professor Syed Ali Ashraf's pioneering role in the field of Islamization of Knowledge, in the first place. Secondly, it may enthuse many others to carry forward what was begun by this great soul against heavy odds. Most importantly for us, he left us at a time when we needed him most. May Allah bestow His choicest blessings on him.

This international seminar is held at a time when some visible moves are afoot for bringing in a semblance of unity and solidarity among the Muslim states, and every one of us knows it, these states stand poles apart from one another both in political perception, economic viability, and intellectual development. You may remember that here at the Hotel Intercontinental, Dhaka, the second summit of D8 (Developing Eight), comprising Bangladesh, Egypt, Indonesia, Iran, Malaysia, Nigeria, Pakistan, and Turkey, was held on 1-2 March 1999. In that meeting, presided over by the Prime Minister of Bangladesh, heads of states, ministers, major dignitaries, and invited guests reiterated their faith in the Islamic way of life and their pride in the glorious Islamic heritage. They were concerned, at least apparently, with the increasingly growing economic misery of the *ummah*, getting worse every day.

In the Twenty-seventh Session of the Islamic Conference of Foreign Ministers (Session of Islam and Globalization) held in Kuala Lumpur from 27 to 30 June 2000, the politico-economic problems of the Muslim states were dis-

---

1 Presented at The Second Professor Syed Ali Ashraf Memorial Lecture held at Sundarban Hotel, Dhaka on 8 August 2000, sponsored jointly by the Islamic Academy, Cambridge and Darul Ihsan University, Dhaka, Bangladesh.

cussed in depth. They reaffirmed the need to take practical steps to reinforce economic cooperation among OIC Member States, particularly in the areas of trade, investment, and stock markets and technology, so as to achieve the ultimate objective of establishing a common Islamic market or any other form of economic complementarity.[2]

The political leaders and statesmen of these states have realized, at last, quite slowly though surely, that their positions are no better than merely marginal at the global level. None of these states has attained a world stature; none of these could be equated with any developed state of the West and what is worse, none of them is in a position to meet the challenges of this century. Consequently, in this new era of globalization and rapidly growing information technology closely associated with free and unfettered competition in all sectors of life, the only way they can survive as respectable social entities is through a creative multilateralism.

According to one estimate, the OIC member states account for only 10 percent of the total world trade though they constitute a little less than one-third of the United Nations in number. The Muslim leaders have also come to the painful realization that the Muslim states have remained underdeveloped despite possessing abundant resources, facing challenges in translating those resources into sustained development and prosperity—much like starved fish in a full and flowing river. Some such states as Indonesia, Saudi Arabia, Libya, Iraq and Kuwait are rich in natural resources, while others such as Bangladesh, Pakistan, Egypt and Turkey are quite rich in human resources, and these resources, natural and human, constitute the motive power of the modern civilization.

What are the reasons for this decadent state of the Muslim world today? Reasons are not far to seek. Instead of forging a common front on vital issues like engaging properly with the western powers, the leaders of some Muslim states are engaged in petty rivalries on trivial matters; sometimes they wage wasteful wars against one another; some of them remain satisfied with what they have and remain indifferent to others. Sometimes they prefer to depend, although unwittingly, on those who are not their real friends. As a result of animosity and indifference, the Muslim world remains divided among themselves and exposed to threat from the hostile powers. We should pay heed to the Islamic injunction to be united and not divided, and work whole heartedly, only then will we be able to attain success.[3] Malaysian Prime Minister Dr Mahathir Muhammed once remarked,

---

2   Organisation of Islamic Cooperation, "Final communique of the twenty-seventh session of the Islamic Conference of Foreign Ministers;" June 27-30, 2000, www.oic-oci.org/docdown/?docID=4291&refID=1205.
3   Qurʾān 3:103.

There are many things that we can do. There are many resources that we have at our disposal. What is needed is merely-the will to do it, As Muslims, we must be grateful for the guidance of our religion, we must do what needs to be done, willingly and with determination. Allah has not raised us, the leaders, above the others so we may enjoy power for ourselves only. The power we wield is for our people, for the ummah, for Islam. We must have the will to make use of this power judiciously, prudently, concertedly. Insyaallah we will triumph in the end.[4]

Time has therefore come for the OIC member states to take a bright vision of the future and expand its horizon of outlook so that it can strengthen itself and compete with other inter-state organizations from a position of strength. Time has come for the Muslim states to mobilize their resources so that they can emerge as a factor to be reckoned with in international politics, global economy, and world culture. Time has indeed come for the Muslim World to regain its historical role so that it can turn out to be a beacon, a lighthouse, a pole star, to the entire world.

This is possible through sustained efforts in perfecting life and living in the light of the holy Qur'ān. Islamic scholarship is the gateway to this grand destination. Everyone believes that it is not the Muslims that brought in glory to Islam; it is Islam that made the Muslims great, so let the light of Islam be the guiding spirit. At the beginning of this century, which appears to all intents and purposes to be the century of the Muslims, what is of prime significance is the resurgence of Islamic values and scholarship, and that is what can scrape off all the rust that has been accumulated over the engine of progress in these societies through centuries.

In such a stimulating company of the learned scholars from home and abroad may I think aloud that the intellectuals are the ones who have greater responsibility to lead others. Naturally, it behooves the Muslim intellectuals to play a creative role at this critical period of human history so that their wisdom, their new insights, and their new ideas can make the tasks of the political leaders and statesman a lot easier. The task of the intellectuals, however, should not be fabricated in the format of a jihad against the western scholarship; it should rather be in the form of revival of the spirit of Islam; it should take the form of liberating human energy by re-kindling the spiritual urge in the Muslim psyche, which made them search for truth in the days gone by and motivated them to strive for greater good for the humanity at large.

---

[4] Dr Mahathir bin Mohamad spoke at the opening of the tenth session of the Islamic Summit conference at Putrajaya Convention Centre on October 16, 2003, organized by the Organisation of Islamic Cooperation. Published in *The Sydney Morning Herald*, "Mahathir's full speech," October 22, 2003, para 58, https://www.oic-oci.org/confdetail/?cID=6&lan=en, and https://www.smh.com.au/world/mahathirs-full-speech-20031022-gdhmg3.html.

For the achievement of this lofty ideal, the Muslim World should concentrate mainly on an education or re-education process, because that is the essential tool for bringing about social changes. We must have not only the kind of instruction which is imparted these days—designed mainly for sharpening intellect in science and technology—but also have an amalgam of science and technology, on the one hand and religion and morality on the other, so that the material and spiritual aspects of life get lifted simultaneously and blended harmoniously. One would help humankind to establish their authority over the material world, while the other would develop their morality. This is the kind of instruction Islam has enjoined us, and this is what the Muslim world needs most and now. And this is what the Islamization of knowledge is all about. This kind of instruction is as important to the individual as to the collectivity of which they are a part. This is where a path-breaking momentous step has been undertaken by Professor Syed Ali Ashraf, and I believe, that has been a great leap forward for carving out a brave new world where Islam would regain its pristine glory, the Muslim *ummah*, their rightful place in the comity of nations, and Islamic civilization, its dignified role in shaping human conduct and activities in this century. We pray to Almighty Allah for enabling us to work on the instructions Syed Ali Ashraf has left behind both within and without Darul Ihsan University and redeem our debt to this immortal soul.

Chapter 26

Islamisation of Education: Contribution of Syed Ali Ashraf and a Global Muslim Perspective[1]

Ahmed Farid

This paper is in two parts. Part I attempts to recall the contribution of Syed Ali Ashraf towards Islamisation of education, his thoughts and writings and his role in organising the World Conferences on Muslim Education which have already started to impact the education of Muslims in different countries and hold promise for the future. Part II states the position of the *ummah*[2] in the contemporary world, the Muslim predicament and options, the inadequacy of their past response, a case for reorientation and the need for a more concerted effort to build on the work done so far.

I
Contribution of Syed Ali Ashraf

Here is a bird's eye view of the contributions of Syed Ali Ashraf in crystallising the ideas, concepts and methodology of the Islamisation of education. Undoubtedly, he was one of the foremost thinkers and an acknowledged authority in this area of critical importance for the *ummah*. He was a man of many talents—a scholar per excellence, a teacher, a thinker, an essayist, a poet, a literary critic, a visionary and a reformer. He was like a virtuoso, capable of playing diverse strands simultaneously and harmonising them into a symphony.

He assimilated the quintessence of thoughts of the greatest minds of Islamic scholarship and legacy and then recycled it in an elegant, modern diction. One finds in his writings an astounding combination of the knowledge

---

1 Presented at The Second Professor Syed Ali Ashraf Memorial Lecture held at Sundarban Hotel, Dhaka on 8 August 2000, sponsored jointly by the Islamic Academy, Cambridge and Darul Ihsan University, Dhaka, Bangladesh.
2 Global Muslim community.

of the lexicon of the Qurʾān, Ḥadīth, theology, jurisprudence, metaphysics, and mysticism. He readily appreciated art, literature, history, philosophy, and social thinking of the modern time. He possessed originality of thought and an erudite style of writing. He could easily grasp complex issues and express them with effortless grace and intellectual lucidity. Here are some excerpts of his writings:

> We needed a clear assessment of the shortcomings of the western concept of Man, of the sources and methods of acquiring knowledge in the West and of its specialised and hence partial worldview. We needed in short a new philosophical perspective with a new starting point derived from the Islamic alterative, an alternative that gives a comprehensive worldview and a methodology in which the material, the ethical and the spiritual approaches are integrated.[3]

> The problem of belief is created not by the discovery of new facts about life and nature, but by the hypotheses applied by researchers to interpret these facts. The only hypothesis that Islam demands is faith in God and the Prophet and the only process that it advises is action on the basis of the Absolute norm enshrined in the Attributes of God and exemplified through the character and conduct of the Prophet.[4]

> The Spirit (rūḥ) of Man therefore can control and guide the growth of Man only through tajdīd (renewal) and tazkiyah (purification). The renewal of Man's faith in God and the Prophet and hence in the Qurʾān and the Sunnah is achieved only when the mind is purified of false ideas, thoughts, desires, and devices. This renewal means the restoration of something of the primordial nature of Man and hence of the primordial vigour of Islam.[5]

Of his philosophy of education, here are some glimpses:

> Education must therefore provide the Muslims with the Knowledge of this worldview and the ways and means of getting it realised in life. This implies the prevalence of an education system which will guide the educated to create an ever-improving social order in the world so that the social, political, economic and cultural ethos allow faith (īmān) to be nurtured, knowledge (ʿilm: spiritual intellectual, moral and material) to be acquired freely according to the hierarchy of knowledge, doubts (shukūk) to be removed, justice (ʿadl) to prevail, wastage and

---

[3] Syed Ali Ashraf, "Editorial—The Islamic Frame of Reference: (B) The Intellectual Dimension," *Muslim Education Quarterly* 7, no. 1 (1989): 1–2.

[4] Syed Ali Ashraf, "Editorial—Recommendations of the Five World Conferences on Muslim Education: A Plan for Implementation," *Muslim Education Quarterly* 10, no. 1 (1992): 4.

[5] Syed Ali Ashraf, "Editorial—Recommendations of the Five World Conferences on Muslim Education: A Plan for Implementation," *Muslim Education Quarterly* 10, no. 1 (1992): 4.

misuse of energy (*isrāf*) to be restricted, greedy competitiveness (*ḥirṣ*) to be controlled, moderation (*iʿtidāl*) to prevail in society, contentment (*qanāʿah*) to be attained, transience of this life and the permanence of *ākhirah* (after-life) to be kept in view and fulfilment of God's Will through man's whole-hearted acceptance (*riḍāʾ*) of revelation to be achieved. *Ittibāʿ* (obedience) of the Prophet becomes then a pleasant thing to be sought for.[6]

He blazed a trail for the *ummah* in a less explored area of modern thought. He was an original thinker who had grappled with many intellectual problems of our time in an attempt to formulate a proactive, cohesive educational policy. He pointed out the inherent weakness of the "scientific worldview" and mentioned that some Western thinkers have also exposed the "serious flaws of empiricism and rationalism."[7] At times he differed with co-thinkers when he asserted: "Our problem is not that of Islamising existing branches of knowledge" and went on to stress that it is "that of learning how we can acquire knowledge in the real sense of Matter, Mind, Soul, Spirit, God and the whole creation, and their interrelationship. It is therefore a question of something other than 'reason' and 'logic' that we need. We shall have to explore the sources of knowledge established in Islam and the methodology followed in the past and in recent years by some eminent Muslim thinkers."[8]

He not only thought boldly but also acted bravely. He did not ponder and preach superciliously from an ivory tower on the intellectual sterility of some of his compatriots. Rather, he shared a concern with fellow intellectuals to identify the malaise of Muslim education in a bid to knead out a strategy and a plan of action. He walked the extra mile and beckoned to others to join in and redouble efforts to break out of a vicious circle. Seyyed Hossein Nasr speaks of Syed Ali Ashraf as one "who has been at the forefront in the recent endeavour to create an Islamic educational system . . . who has had much responsibility for the planning of the First World Conference on Muslim Education and those which followed."[9]

In the same vein Akbar Ahmed says, Ali Ashraf "belonged to that generation of South Asians who not only wrote in English but spoke the language with perfect diction—the Queen's English. . . . In the last decade of his life Ashraf made a significant contribution to education in Britain. Collaborating

---

6   Syed Ali Ashraf, "Editorial—Recommendations of the Five World Conferences on Muslim Education: A Plan for Implementation," *Muslim Education Quarterly* 10, no. 1 (1992): 5.
7   Syed Ali Ashraf, "Editorial—The Islamic Frame of Reference: (B) The Intellectual Dimension," *Muslim Education Quarterly*, 7, no. 1 (1989): 2.
8   Syed Ali Ashraf, "Editorial—The Islamic Frame of Reference: (B) The Intellectual Dimension," *Muslim Education Quarterly* 7, no. 1 (1989): 2.
9   Seyyed Hossein Nasr, foreword to *New Horizons in Muslim Education*, by Syed Ali Ashraf (Kent, England: Hodder and Stoughton and Cambridge: The Islamic Academy, 1985).

with Cambridge University, a series of seminars and books resulted. His approach... found an echo in British educationists."[10] Through this collaboration Ashraf hoped "to bring together all the important religions recognised in this country [UK] to maintain both unity and diversity."[11]

The very thought of organising the World Conferences on Muslim Education was an innovative idea. In order to persuade disparate groups to participate in them, it needed the imagination, courage, conviction, credibility, persuasive skills and organising abilities of an able catalyst. In each of the conferences held over a decade in different countries, Ali Ashraf had played a key role. Unfortunately, before further World Conferences could be held, he departed from this world. These conferences were landmark events in the intellectual history of the *ummah*. They caused a paradigm shift in thought on the whole question of education of Muslims. For Ashraf, it is not enough just to create an efficient man; the education system should also create a "good and righteous man." One major achievement was that the term "Islamic education" was redefined and there was a growing realisation of its comprehensive meaning beyond the teaching of the Qurʾān, Ḥadīth, Fiqh, science and technology. The term has been understood since to mean education in all branches of knowledge, taught from the Islamic perspective.

This concept was sanctified by the Makkah Declaration, signed by the heads of Muslim states or governments:

> We declare ourselves determined to cooperate in spreading education more widely and strengthening educational institutions until ignorance and illiteracy have been eradicated and to take measures aimed towards the strengthening of Islamic education curricula and to encourage research and *Ijtihad* among Muslim thinkers and *Ulema* while expanding the studies of modern sciences and technologies.[12]

An important point to note is that the heads of states being signatory to this great document, they have a historical responsibility to assist in its implementation. This is a responsibility not only of the governments, but also the entire community, wherever its members may be living.

The First World Conference on Muslim Education held in Makkah in 1977 noted that "Education should aim at the balanced growth of the total personality of Man through the training of Man's spirit, intellect, the rational self, feelings and bodily senses."[13] It classified knowledge into different categories

---

10　Akbar S. Ahmed, "Obituary: Professor Syed Ali Ashraf," *The Independent*, August 12, 1998, paragraphs 2 and 5.
11　Syed Ali Ashraf, preface to *Religion and Education: Islamic and Christian approaches*, eds. Syed Ali Ashraf and Paul H. Hirst (Cambridge: The Islamic Academy, 1994), xii.
12　Makkah Declaration by Heads of Muslim States at OIC, 1977.
13　*First World Conference on Muslim Education: Conference Book* (King Abdulaziz University, 1977), 78.

such as the "perennial knowledge" and "acquired knowledge" and identified the problems of different branches of knowledge including social, natural, and applied sciences. Its coverage included the dual system of education—secular and Islamic, women's education, and other related issues. One gap identified was the paucity of Islamic classics on education.[14] The responsibility then devolved on the Islamic Academy (Cambridge) to find suitable scholars to edit the classics and render them into English. Next, a need was felt to work on an "ideal-typical model" of Islamic education. The Second World Conference on Muslim Education (Islamabad, 1980) devoted its attention to the designing of the curriculum for the primary level and enunciating the broad principles for the secondary level. Once again, it was none but Syed Ali Ashraf who prepared the model curriculum for General Education.[15] In addition to this, he was the General Editor of a series of books published by King Abdulaziz University, Jeddah and Hodder and Stoughton, Kent (UK).[16] The Third World Conference on Muslim Education (Dhaka, 1981) focused on the preparation of textbooks. The Conference stated the "principles for ideal-typical courses and lesson-preparation." The major theme of the Fourth World Conference on Muslim Education (Jakarta, 1982) was the discussion of the teaching methodology and production of teacher education courses. The Fifth World Conference on Muslim Education (Cairo, 1987) reviewed the achievements and failures of the previous World Conferences and discussed the ways and means of implementing their recommendations. The sixth World Conference was in Cape Town (1996) and it was devoted to the preparation of model lessons and teaching guidelines based on the Islamic principles of education as developed at the First World Conference on Muslim Education.[17]

Ashraf adds that in line with the Islamic concept of Man and educational metaphysics, "education must be planned in such a way that it has a balanced interdisciplinary pattern."[18] Now many recommendations are available

---

14 *First World Conference on Muslim Education*, 78–87.
15 Syed Ali Ashraf, *New Horizons in Muslim Education* (Kent, England: Hodder and Stoughton and Cambridge: The Islamic Academy, 1985), 95–97.
16 The following six books in the Islamic Education Series were published by Hodder and Stoughton and King Abdulaziz University under the general editorship of Syed Ali Ashraf: (a) Syed Sajjad Husain and Syed Ali Ashraf, eds., *Crisis in Muslim Education* (1979); (b) Syed M. N. al-Attas, ed., *Aims and Objectives of Islamic Education* (1979); (c) Muhammad H Al-Afendi and Nabi A. Baloch, eds., *Curriculum and Teacher Education* (1980); (d) Isma'il R. Al-Faruqi and Abdullah O. Nasseef, eds., *Social and Natural Sciences: The Islamic Perspective* (1981).; (e) Mohammad W. Khan, ed., *Education and Society in the Muslim World* (1981), and (f) Seyyed Hossein Nasr, ed., *Philosophy, Literature and Fine Arts* (1982).
17 For a description of the World Conferences see: Shaikh Abdul Mabud, "World Conferences on Muslim Education: Shaping the Agenda of Muslim Education in the Future," in *Philosophies of Islamic Education, Historical Perspectives and Emerging Discourses*, eds. Nadeem A. Memon and Mujadad Zaman (New York and London: Routledge, 2016) 129–143.
18 Ashraf, *New Horizons in Muslim Education*, 5.

on conceptualisation, curriculum designing, textbook writing and teaching methodology. He suggested that some further steps were called for:

(i) The integration of the dual system at primary, secondary and university levels.
(ii) The restructuring of teacher education through the production of guidebooks for different subjects and revision of syllabi and courses on teacher education.

He reminds us that all aspects of human life are conditioned by his relationship with God. The development of our personality must be seen in the context of Man's relationships with God, Man and Nature. As far as education is concerned, the arrangement of subjects, development of the curriculum, and delivery of the subject matters should be planned with reference to Man as an individual, Man as a social being and Man as a being who has to live in harmony with Nature.

Syed Ali Ashraf did not confine himself to vague rhetoric or mere theorising but kept working on a clear, multi-dimensional plan of action for implementing the decisions and recommendations of the World Conferences. He worked in tandem with Shaikh Ahmad Salah Jamjoom and Abdullah Omar Nasseef to set up the Islamic Academy, Cambridge in 1983. In a parallel move, Isma'il Raji Al-Faruqi and Anwar Ibrahim co-founded the International Institute of Islamic Thought (IIIT) in 1981 with headquarters in Herndon, Virginia and launched the programme for the Islamisation of knowledge.[19] Ever since, these two institutions have poured out a golden cornucopia of ideas, books, and journals on Islamic thought for the modern world and have catalysed many seminars and conferences. Ali Ashraf suggested that what was needed was a basic plan so that theories about faith-based education could be nationally translated into practical realities. He kept writing thoughtful editorials in the *Muslim Education Quarterly*, highlighting the recommendations of the six World Conferences and identifying core issues such as the Islamic approach to education, the National Curriculum, moral development, the need for the Islamic frame of reference for Islamisation of education and its various dimensions. On the intellectual dimension, in his editorial comments he expressed his strong reservation about some views expressed by Abdul Hamid Abu Sulayman and Ziauddin Sardar on the "methodology" of implementing Islamic education. It would have been better to agree to disagree on such issues if unanimity of views was not forthcoming.

---

19 John L. Esposito, ed., "International Institute of Islamic Thought," in *The Oxford Dictionary of Islam* (Oxford: Oxford University Press, 2003), 139.

What Should Be Done Now?

Syed Ali Ashraf worked assiduously over three decades to conceptualise a novel and challenging idea and then launched a movement to put it into practice. His demise at a moment when his services were needed the most has inevitably created a vacuum, which will be difficult to fill. This is an irreparable loss. However, there is one consolation. He has left behind a legacy and indelible footprint for others to follow. Hence, any programme must consider the following: implementing the recommendations of the World Conferences on Muslim Education, supporting the publications of the Islamic Academy, and strengthening and helping the Darul Ihsan University, Dhaka.[20]

He produced many books and papers outlining the Islamic education movement and a roadmap for further action. Here are some highlights for further action based on his work.

(i) combine efforts of different institutions and organisations; they should work synergistically to Islamise education through cooperation and understanding.

(ii) find effective strategy and methodology to persuade the concerned governments, civil society, and foundations to consider the reports and recommendations of the six World Conferences on Muslim Education and initiate steps to implement them.

(iii) respond to the urgent need of producing basic theoretical works on the philosophy of education for every discipline, dealing with the concepts of *khilāfah* (vicegerency), *amānah* (trust) and *ʿilm* (knowledge); nature of humanity; the relationship between knowledge and values; and the relationship between education, the acquisition of knowledge and the total human personality.

(iv) plan education on an interdisciplinary pattern, establish interrelationships among three divisions of knowledge—religious sciences, human sciences, and natural sciences.

(v) classify knowledge and establish hierarchy of knowledge: religious, spiritual, moral intellectual, perennial, acquired, etc.

Ali Ashraf's book, *Islamic Education Movement: An Historical Analysis*, provides a wealth of information and a database that we can draw upon to capture his vision and master plan.[21] This invaluable document can serve as the basic building block for researchers, analysts, policy makers and activists to follow the trail blazed by him. They can add other components to enlarge it further to dovetail it into the emergent need of the Islamisation of education.

---

20 This chapter was written before the unfortunate closure of Darul Ihsan University in 2016.
21 Syed Ali Ashraf, *Islamic Education Movement: An historical Analysis* (Cambridge: The Islamic Academy, 1990).

Ali Ashraf sums up the impact of these conferences in the following words: "Thus the conferences have provided an ideal and suggested certain methods of achieving it. These recommendations and the papers presented at the conferences provide educationists and the authorities in Muslim countries with model and a plan of work. . . . a consciousness has already been generated and an Islamic Education Movement has been created. The seeds have already been scattered far and wide."[22] No better tribute could be paid to him than heightening this "consciousness" and nurturing these "seeds" already "scattered" so that they grow into lush green plants in the days to come.

II
A Global Muslim Perspective

Let us see the position of the *ummah* in the 15th century Hijri or 21st century of the new millennium. What is the global scene confronting the Muslim *ummah* today? The *ummah* is in a dilemma about whether to look forward or backward. Apparently, it is looking in the eye of a storm, which is violently pulling it out of its moral and cultural anchor and uprooting its spiritual habitat. Now the *ummah* is decadent and despondent. It is in decline. This decline has been in evidence for the past three centuries or so. Coincidentally, during this period Western societies have been in ascendance, certainly from the worldly point of view, which has not been a help to the former. Even in the postcolonial era, a cultural and intellectual assault on Islam goes on relentlessly. Edward Said observes, "Assiduous research has shown that there is hardly a prime-time television show without several episodes of patently racist and insulting caricatures of Muslims, all of whom tend to be represented in unqualified categorical and generic terms: one Muslim is therefore seen to be typical of all Muslims and of Islam in general."[23]

The Muslim response to this challenge has been reactive and inadequate. They were chagrined, shaken, and disoriented by the repeated reverses. In the field of education, the Muslim response generally has been to try to Westernise their societies by imitating the Western models. But some of them stuck to conservatism or carried on with an outmoded educational system, irrelevant to the need of the time. It is interesting that the prototype education system transplanted in Muslim lands did not create centres of excellence, comparable to their Western counterparts. There was "the inevitable failure of operating external forms without the inner loyalties of spirit."[24]

---

22 Ashraf, *New Horizons in Muslim Education*, 90-91.
23 Edward Said, *Covering Islam: How the Media and the Experts Determine How We See the Rest of the World* (New York: Pantheon Books, 1981), 69.
24 Wilfred Cantwell Smith, *Islam in Modern History* (London: Oxford University Press, 1957), 72.

The Muslim predicament is aptly described by Cantwell Smith, when he observes:

> Their recent history, it is not difficult for the return-to-Islam school to argue, has conspicuously demonstrated the ineptness of liberalism, its inability to lead the Muslims in practice to social justice or the good life. Few, whether Communist or Western, religious or secular, liberal or other, would disagree that something new is needed for that regeneration of which Islamic society, as the rest of us today, stands in need.[25]

And that, "In general it gradually became the conviction of even the Westernised Muslims that any reconstruction of their society to which they might aspire they must undertake themselves, without the help and even against the weight of Christendom."[26]

This was inevitable. After all, Western society and its institutions were built on a given vision. Similarly, the Islamic society, its conscience, its organisation, and institutions were also the product of a particular vision. As this vision became dim in the consciousness of the *ummah*, (on account of a variety of reasons), its society became weak and decadent. Gradually, Muslim intellectuals have come to conclude that the cause of its continued backwardness lies in its intellectual and methodological decline. Hence, a new approach, suitable for the present time, needs to be forged. This has been termed Islamisation. It is going to be a global phenomenon, involving the entire *ummah*. Of the general phenomenon of resurgence of Islam in the contemporary history, John Voll envisages that "with its unity and variety, its consensus and conflict, its continuity and change, Islam will continue in its fifteenth century to be a vital force in the world."[27]

It is indeed an ambitious undertaking to attempt to develop the *ummah* of Muslims and take them along the path of true advancement in future. Acquiring more knowledge and skill is a prerequisite for this. The Qur'ān begins its discourse with the word *Iqra'* (Read!) and the Holy Prophet (peace and blessings be upon him) constantly prayed for increase in knowledge. He said: "It is obligatory for each Muslim to seek knowledge."[28] He also said, "The superiority of the learned man over the devout is like that of the moon on the night when it is full, over the rest of the stars."[29] He told his followers that "Wisdom is the lost property of the believer, so wherever he finds it, then he is more worthy of it."[30] At this juncture, we must re-focus on this point and reinterpret these

---

25 Smith, 72.
26 Smith, 71.
27 John Obert Voll, *Islam: Continuity and Change in the Modern World* (Colorado: Westview Press, 1982), 357.
28 Kitāb al-Muqaddamah, *Sunan ibn Mājah*.
29 Kitāb al-ʿilm, *Sunan Abī Dāwūd*.
30 Kitāb al-ʿilm, *Jāmiʿ al-Tirmidhī*.

sayings of the Prophet to mean the desirability of going to the West or China or Japan or anywhere else for the acquisition of knowledge, scientific or of other types so long as such knowledge is not in conflict with the teachings of Islam. Basic science and its creation must become part of our civilisation.[31] Inspired by the spirit of Islam, our forebears assimilated all existing knowledge and achieved great advancement. There is no doubt that given determination, persistence, courage, perspective, careful planning, and an appropriate methodology, we can replicate this model today. In this respect, it will be relevant to refer to an observation of Edward Said:

> Cultures are not impermeable; just as Western science borrowed from Arabs, they had borrowed from India and Greece. Culture is never just a matter of ownership, of borrowing and lending with absolute debtors and creditors, but rather of appropriations, common experiences, and interdependencies of all kinds among different cultures. This is a universal norm.[32]

Nonetheless, the challenge is one of massive mobilisation of funds; creating human resources; physical, institutional and organisational infrastructure; making intellectual endeavour; research and development; cultural, artistic, scientific, and technological contributions as well as sustained effort at the grassroots level. Lobbying for support of the governments, UNESCO, the international community, and civil society should be sought as required.

One can take heart from the fact that, in line with the resolutions of the World Conferences on Muslim Education, International Institute of Islamic Thought has also chalked out an agenda. Some of its plans are:

(i) developing contemporary Islamic culture and methodology along with modern sciences and knowledge;
(ii) laying the foundation for the evolution of Islamic social sciences and humanities;
(iii) reviving the spirit of inquiry;
(iv) networking with the scholars, thinkers, leaders, and students through diverse organisations and the media;
(v) wide participation in various works and programmes of reformation, development, education, and publication.

Two major steps are: (i) classifying the legacy and (ii) achieving mastery of contemporary knowledge in the fields of social and human sciences.

No education system is value free. For this reason, a Western education engenders awe for the West in the mind of the pupil, and moreover, it often

---

31 Ahmed Farid, *An Encounter with Islam* (Dhaka: Islamic Foundation Bangladesh, 1995).
32 Edward W. Said, *Culture and Imperialism* (New York: Vintage Books, 1994), 217.

tends to make Muslim youth apologetic about their culture and history. To obliterate this inferiority complex from the Muslim's consciousness and instil a new orientation, the only option is Islamisation. One step towards Islamisation is a thorough grounding in Islamic spirit, legacy, and civilisation. To institutionalise it, the curriculum must have an Islamic value orientation as well as content. Knowledge of Arabic is essential. An additional need is the skill in or familiarity with one or more of the modern Western languages such as English, French, and German along with one's own mother tongue. Familiarity with Farsi will be an extra advantage.

There is an imperative need to arrive at a consensus on universal syllabi and curricula for the educational institutions of the *ummah* from school to university level. In this regard, the experiences of the successful Muslim schools in different parts of the world including America and Europe can serve as models. These schools offer a challenging academic course of study in which Arabic, national language, arts, mathematics, natural sciences, social sciences, and Islamic studies comprise the core subjects that are taught routinely. The curriculum is centred on Islamic principles and philosophy, while at the same time it incorporates the prescribed elements of different branches of knowledge in humanities, science, and technology. It is encouraging that students of these schools are experiencing success in the best universities anywhere.

Next is the question of higher education. Several Muslim universities have been established all over the world under either state patronage or sponsorship of private organisations and have achieved high standards. Some of them compare favourably with state universities, notwithstanding the vast resources diverted to the latter by the governments and donors. The International Islamic University Malaysia is an inspiring example among others. In addition, the Organisation of the Islamic Conference (OIC) has sponsored the Islamic Institute of Technology (IIT) at Gazipur, Dhaka in an attempt to bridge the technological gap.

Now let us examine the curriculum and syllabus to be administered at a standard Islamic university. It should aim at offering academically rigorous and professionally meaningful degree and postgraduate programmes to be taught by a qualified faculty. It must provide students with opportunities to increase their knowledge and understanding of the world and develop their individual skills and capabilities for learning, analysing, judging, creating, and communicating. A bachelor's degree, for example, will require about 124 credit hours of studies. Out of this, one requirement may be 36 credit hours of general education (GEd—university) comprising the following:

18 credit hours of Islamic studies including 9 credit hours of Arabic language;

6 credit hours of English/French /German language;

3 credit hours of computer literacy courses;

3 credit hours of fundamentals of mathematics;

6 credit hours of liberal arts course, say, in (a) the native language (e.g., Bengali for Bangladesh) and literature; and (b) their social, cultural, and economic history, as prescribed.

Then come the faculty/school/departmental requirements:

(i) core or compulsory courses;
(ii) elective courses (required for concentration or specialisation);
(iii) general education (GEd—departmental) courses required by the school/department;
(iv) free electives based on students' own choice.

These programs must endeavour to impart education in developing professional skills with an orientation of liberal arts and to sensitise students with higher values to make them successful in their career and to lead a full life.

The concept of Islamisation of knowledge and education emerged as a means of reaching a specific goal. The avowed aim of the Islamisation program is to remove from the education system the existing dichotomy between an "Islamic" approach and a "secular" approach. At the same time, it also aims at integrating the two systems into a vibrant unified system, suffused with the spirit of Islam. This is a very important chapter of the unfolding panorama of Islamic revivalism, which is in the words of Esposito, "producing a new class of modern-educated but Islamically oriented elites" and has become "a vibrant, multifaceted movement that will embody the major impact of Islamic revivalism for the foreseeable future."[33] It will be pertinent to state that many Muslim intellectuals are not yet aware of what is at stake. Either owing to acculturation or falling victim to an adverse media campaign, they are often found diffident or even averse to the very idea of asserting themselves. Muslims can be intellectually successful today, as they were yesterday, provided they adopt the right methodology and take recourse to "techniques, discourses, and weapons of scholarship and criticism once reserved exclusively for the European."[34]

If Islamisation of knowledge is a general idea, the Islamisation of education is a particular aspect of that idea. The latter is integrally connected with the former. To do away with any confusion, these terms should be defined and somewhat elaborated. Now, what is meant by "Islamisation"? Well, it upholds an ideal, an aspiration, a vision, and a program to present reality, truth, life,

---

[33] John L. Esposito, *The Islamic Threat: Myth or Reality* (Oxford: Oxford University Press, 1992), 23.
[34] Said, *Culture and Imperialism*, 243.

Man and knowledge to a contemporary audience in a language which a postmodern generation understands and appreciates. Esposito has called it the "Islamic reorientation."[35]

Islamisation is a process of cultural evolution—the culmination of an alternative cultural growth or flowering process—which will absorb all branches of knowledge, filter it and then disseminate it after establishing its concordance with the legacy and worldview of Islam. It might take a long time. But at its full efflorescence, this will rejuvenate the *ummah* and revive the full glory of Islam. This is a difficult but perfectly feasible goal. What is required is, interfacing all the efforts by different groups of people in their respective areas for their creative confluence in a vast arena. It is no more ambitious a project than an undertaking for replication of the achievements of the *ummah*'s forbears—who succeeded in assimilating diverse knowledge of ancient Greece, Iran, Mesopotamia, and India; and then, through a creative synthesis of their various elements with the revealed knowledge derived from the Qurʾān and Sunnah created the unique Islamic culture and civilisation. Its reference point is the Qurʾānic paradigm.

This is an enormous enterprise, involving globalised operations by a coalition of hundreds of people over time. The academia and the students must master the disciplines in social sciences, natural sciences, and technologies as well as in humanities—art, culture, and literature—and then integrate all this knowledge into the corpus of the Islamic legacy. This will inevitably call for selecting, eliminating, editing, amending, reinterpreting, and adapting, to make it compatible with the Islamic paradigm.[36]

The movement started in a trickle, gradually picked up a flow and kept meandering, often through a labyrinth of obstacles and dry sands. But its destiny is an ocean. It cannot stagnate. It must keep flowing, gather new momentum, and become an irresistible torrent, sweeping towards the ultimate flowering of a renewal of the ummah. It needs the involvement of every conscientious member of this huge community. This *ummah* consists of more than one billion people or one-fifth of humanity, living all over the world. The stakes are too high. Provided they remember that "Indeed, Allah will not change the condition of a people until they change what is in themselves" (Qurʾān, 13:11, trans. *Saheeh International*) and act on the teaching of this verse, they can unleash the power in them which will shape their destiny, *inshāʾ Allāh*.

---

35 John L. Esposito, *Islam: The Straight Path*, 3rd ed. (New York: Oxford University Press, 2005), 251.
36 (a) Ismāʿīl R. al-Fārūqī, *Islamization of Knowledge: General Principles and Workplan* (Herndon, Virginia: International Institute of Islamic Thought, 1982). (b) Abdul Hamid Abu Sulayman, "Editorial: From Islamization of Knowledge to Islamization of Education," *The American Journal of Islamic Social Sciences* 16, no. 2, (Summer 1999).

Bibliography

Abu Sulayman, Abdul Hamid. "Editorial: From Islamization of Knowledge to Islamization of Education." *The American Journal of Islamic Social Sciences* 16, no. 2 (Summer 1999).

Ahmed, Akbar S. "Obituary: Professor Syed Ali Ashraf." *The Independent*, August 12, 1998.

Ashraf, Syed Ali. *New Horizons in Muslim Education*. Kent, England: Hodder and Stoughton and Cambridge: The Islamic Academy, 1985.

Ashraf, Syed Ali. "Editorial—The Islamic Frame of Reference: (B) The Intellectual Dimension," *Muslim Education Quarterly* 7, no. 1 (1989): 1–9.

Ashraf, Syed Ali. *Islamic Education Movement: An historical Analysis*. Cambridge: The Islamic Academy, 1990.

Ashraf, Syed Ali. "Editorial—Recommendations of the Five World Conferences on Muslim Education: A Plan for Implementation." *Muslim Education Quarterly* 10, no. 1 (1992): 1–6.

Ashraf, Syed Ali. Preface to *Religion and Education: Islamic and Christian approaches*, edited by Syed Ali Ashraf and Paul H. Hirst, xi–xiv. Cambridge: The Islamic Academy, 1994.

Esposito, John L. ed. "International Institute of Islamic Thought." In *The Oxford Dictionary of Islam*. Oxford: Oxford University Press, 2003.

Esposito, John L. *The Islamic Threat: Myth or Reality*. Oxford: Oxford University Press, 1992.

Esposito, John L. *Islam: The Straight Path*, 3rd ed. New York: Oxford University Press, 2005.

Farid, Ahmed. *An Encounter with Islam*. Dhaka: Islamic Foundation Bangladesh, 1995.

al-Fārūqī, Ismāʿīl R. *Islamization of Knowledge: General Principles and Workplan*. Herndon, Virginia: International Institute of Islamic Thought, 1982.

King Abdulaziz University. *Conference Book: First World Conference on Muslim Education*. Jeddah and Mecca: King Abdulaziz University, 1977.

Mabud, Shaikh Abdul. "World Conferences on Muslim Education: Shaping the Agenda of Muslim Education in the Future." In *Philosophies of Islamic Education, Historical Perspectives and Emerging Discourses*, edited by Nadeem A. Memon and Mujadad Zaman, 129–143. New York and London: Routledge, 2016.

Nasr, Seyyed Hossein. Foreword to *New Horizons in Muslim Education*, by Syed Ali Ashraf. Kent, England: Hodder and Stoughton and Cambridge: The Islamic Academy, 1985.

Said, Edward W. *Culture and Imperialism*. New York: Vintage Books, 1994.

Said, Edward. *Covering Islam: How the Media and the Experts Determine How We See the Rest of the World*. New York: Pantheon Books, 1981.

Smith, Wilfred Cantwell. *Islam in Modern History*. London: Oxford University Press, 1957.

Voll, John Obert. *Islam: Continuity and Change in the Modern World*. Colorado: Westview Press, 1982.

Chapter 27

Syed Ali Ashraf's Contribution to Teacher Education in Bangladesh[1]

Mohammad Nurul Haq

Introduction

Islam emphasises right behaviour for good life in this world and happiness in life hereafter. The system of education supported by Islam encourages its followers, individually and collectively, to follow a complete code of life based on its moral and spiritual teachings. Hence an Islamic system of education does not admit of any dichotomy between the secular and the spiritual, whereas the Western system of education does not accept the spirituality that is associated with a religion or the supernatural realm as it does not recognise the absolutes of faith, revelation, and divine sovereignty. Consequently, teacher education in the Western system of education is based on concepts that deny or ignore revelation as the source of knowledge. The training of teachers is crucial, as they must *show the student the path to the future by means of proper guidance*. It is in this context that the production of the right kind of teacher—who occupies a central place in teaching and learning—is fundamental to the success of the movement for the Islamisation of Knowledge and Education. The contribution of Professor Syed Ali Ashraf to teacher education should be discussed from this angle.

Theoretical Framework

Professor Ashraf's views on the Islamic theory of education vis-à-vis the secularist view are as follows. All theories of education depend on the life-views: Islamic theory of education depends on the Islamic concepts of man, God and nature whereas secular education is guided by the secular concept of

---

[1] Presented at The Second Professor Syed Ali Ashraf Memorial Lecture held at Sundarban Hotel, Dhaka on 8 August 2000, sponsored jointly by the Islamic Academy, Cambridge and Darul Ihsan University, Dhaka, Bangladesh.

reality. The differences between the secularist and Islamic theories of education must be understood in accordance with the fundamental concepts enunciated below.

According to the secularist concept human beings are an evolved species who evolved from primitive to civilized existence, a conjecture based on the evolution of the instruments of civilization. The gradual evolution of human beings does away with the concept of the first man which is considered scientifically untenable. Values are regarded as social products which gives rise to beliefs in the evolution of values. It is accepted that social change will bring about change in the norm of values as there is nothing absolute. Hence the secularist does not believe in an intrinsic norm of values. Society determines the changing norm which therefore depends on publicly negotiable criteria. Hence the concepts of "good" and "evil" or "degeneration" and "reform" take on changeable meanings determined by society. Sceptical of a Creator, the next life, reward and punishment, the secularist trusts in human intelligence rather than in Divine Guidance.

Islam believes that human beings are created by God. They came into existence without evolution. Instruments of civilization have evolved but a human being is already endowed with the inner consciousness of Absolute values—such as Justice, Truth, Mercy, Love, etc.—values that are enshrined in the Names of God. Adam, the first man and first prophet possessed the norm of these intrinsic virtues ingrained in his soul. Hence the basic concepts of right and wrong, degeneration and reform become a necessity. Human beings as vicegerent (*Khalīfah*) of God is in constant need of Divine Guidance which has been conveyed to them by God's messengers.

Institutional Framework

In consonance with the fundamental concepts underlying the theory of Islamic education mentioned above, Professor Syed Ali Ashraf established the Institute of Teacher Education in 1994 as the first institute of Darul Ihsan University, Dhaka already founded by him in 1990. The institute started a BEd programme of 10-month duration for graduates in humanities, science and commerce, offering among others, such new courses as Our Islamic Heritage, Foundations of Islamic Education, History of Islamic Education, etc. to turn out right kind of teachers for our society. Besides, in the MEd programme initiated in 1995, the following new courses were introduced: Islamic Philosophy of Education, Re-designing our Curriculums and Syllabuses, Sociological and Psychological Foundations of our Education, Comparative Education in Islamic Countries, Planning and Financing our Education, Educational Research and Evaluation, and Guidance and Counseling for our Youth. He aimed at producing teacher educators, educational planners, administrators, and supervisors to assist in the growth and development of our new education system based on faith, knowledge and action.

Existing Secular System of Teacher Education in Bangladesh

The Teacher Training College, Dhaka was established in 1909 by the colonial government to train teachers for the secular secondary schools of the country. The curriculums and syllabuses prescribed were alien to our culture. To cite an instance, History of Education comprised education of ancient Athens and Sparta down to that of Great Britain. Students were thus deprived of the knowledge about their own history of education during the Muslim rule in Bengal, spreading over a long and glorious period of five centuries and a half. This omission was not accidental but deliberate.

Islamic education was formally introduced in Bengal in 1203 CE by the Muslim Commander Bakhtiyar Khilji and continued uninterrupted till the Battle of Plassey in 1757 when the country lost its independence through a conspiracy hatched by the imperialists in league with some native traitors. Following the loss of independence in 1757, the British adopted systematic steps to enslave the Muslims by abolishing the Islamic system of education. Some of those steps are mentioned below:

(i) Taking over the revenue administration of the country.
(ii) Replacement of Persian by English as the official language.
(iii) Introduction of the permanent settlement, depriving Muslims of their lands.
(iv) Abolition of the Muslim judicial system, and
(v) Misappropriation of Muslim educational endowments and foundations.

The above account explains the reason why the History of Education in Bengal was not included in the curriculums of the first Teacher Training College of the country and those of subsequently established ones. History bears out the fact that we are the descendants of the people who, during the Middle Ages, developed a viable education system that was free and universal, from primary to tertiary levels, while almost the whole of Europe was immersed in illiteracy. Furthermore, our forefathers created our mother tongue Bengali, expressed in both language and literature, of which we are rightly and justly proud.

Syed Ali Ashraf's Endeavours to Redesign the Existing BEd Curriculums

Professor Syed Ali Ashraf was fully aware of the limitations of the 10-month BEd programme. The duration was too short to be effective in turning out competent teachers with dedicated frame of mind. The contemporary situation worsened with the proliferation of so-called Teacher Training Colleges, established through private initiative with the sole purpose of making money. Before 1994, teacher education in Bangladesh, as in many countries worldwide, was under the complete control of the Ministry of Education. This is a common practice where governments regulate education to maintain standards. With the establishment of the so-called affiliating university, now named National University, the opportunists have managed to secure affiliations from this University for teacher training colleges, regardless of their educational standards. These colleges have sprouted up all across the country, posing a grave threat to the overall education system of Bangladesh, particularly in the realm of teacher education.

Sensing the above danger, Professor Syed Ali Ashraf decided, in consonance with the global practice, to offer a three-year BEd Honours programme which comprises such components as general education, subject specialization, professional preparation, professional laboratory experiences and student teaching. The Honours programme has been introduced posthumously since May 1999 in the Institute of Education, Darul Ihsan University. It may be mentioned that among the privately managed institutions of higher learning in this country, only Darul Ihsan University has ventured to embark upon the three-year BEd Honours programme following 12 years of schooling.

With the above end in view, he conducted several workshops, attended by the principals and the vice-principals of all the government Teachers Training Colleges all over Bangladesh from 1992 to 1994. He sent the redesigned curricula of the BEd programme to the vice-chancellor of the National University for implementation.

Simultaneously with the above efforts, he started redesigning the existing BEd curriculums in the light of Islamic theory of education. With this end in view, he used to hold workshops on different disciplines attended by senior faculty members of the departments of education. Unfortunately, he breathed his last before these curricular efforts, extending over a period from 1994 to 1998 were crowned with success.

Faith-Based Education

Besides his pioneering role in the movement for Islamization of education in the Muslim countries, he played an equally important role in launching another supplementary movement called, Faith-Based Education, in order to combat the worldwide evils of secular education by creating a common platform for the followers of all the major religions—Islam, Christianity, Judaism and Hinduism. Here too, he emphasized the need for properly educated teachers in the classroom.

Conclusion

The sudden demise of Professor Syed Ali Ashraf has left an irreplaceable void. He was a man of saintly character and was above all worldly temptations for power and position. He practised whatever he preached and was a towering personality among his contemporaries in intellectual and spiritual domains. The tale of his pioneering efforts in redesigning teacher education in the light of Islam as told above is not that of complete success due to the challenging circumstances in which he was working. Hence the question is: Where do we go from here? I think one effective way would be to march ahead by pooling together all the available resources in the Muslim countries in order to fulfil his dream of teacher education which was so dear to his heart as he sounded the warning, "without well-prepared educators, all attempts to Islamise knowledge and education will prove futile."

Chapter 28

Islamic Education in the Light of Professor Ashraf's Philosophy[1]

M. M. Roisuddin Ahammad

Introduction

Professor Syed Ali Ashraf eloquently expressed, "Education is the pathway to acquiring knowledge, a journey that leads to the holistic development of a human being."[2] He derives one of the most fundamental concepts of education from the verse of the Qurʾān where Allah says, "He taught Adam the names of all things" (Qurʾān 2:31).[3] The very first human, Adam, was a repository of knowledge. Allah blessed him with the wisdom of naming every element in the world, along with a profound understanding of their creation, growth, and eventual decay. Even if we cannot grasp an object merely by its name, we can discern its inherent characteristics. Through the act of naming, Allah bestowed upon Adam the knowledge of the existence of all things, and as each object is a manifestation of a unique divine quality, Adam gained the capacity to comprehend these qualities when Allah infused His divine attributes into his soul. This divine awareness is built in every soul as the Prophet (pbuh) asserted, "No child is born except on *al-fiṭrah* (innate nature) and then his parents make him Jewish, Christian or Magian."[4] Thus, the true essence of education lies in enabling individuals to perceive the authentic reality through knowledge and actions, fostering an awareness of their responsibilities towards the entire creation and the divine qualities of Allah.

---

1 This article is based on the author's PhD thesis entitled, *Syed Ali Ashraf: Jibon o kôrmo* (Syed Ali Ashraf: Life and Work). Translated by the Editor from the original Bengali version.
2 Syed Ali Ashraf, "Shikshar Uddeshsho," *Dainik Inqilab*, Dhaka, December 8, 1991, 6.
3 All Qurʾānic translations in this chapter are from Abdullah Yusuf Ali.
4 Ṣaḥīḥ al-Bukhārī, Book 65, Ḥadīth 297. See https://sunnah.com/bukhari:4775.

To cultivate virtuous individuals, we must first instigate transformative reforms within the realm of education. Such changes should strengthen faith and cleanse the minds of learners, purging them of hatred, malice, greed, deception, injustice, falsehood, and similar vices. Those undergoing such transformative experiences are more likely to embrace a life guided by divine principles. It is essential for them to gain insight into the practical implementation of religious systems across various aspects of life, such as in society, the state, economics, literature, and philosophy. Professor Ashraf holds that without such practical application, knowledge risks being confined to mere theoretical constructs on paper. He, therefore, put forward a roadmap for the development and application of Islamic education in the modern world through his lectures, seminars, and numerous writings. The following sections delve into different aspects of his educational philosophy and explore its real-world applications.

The Importance and Necessity of Education

The significance and indispensability of education in human life are immeasurable. Syed Ali Ashraf's theory of education is based on the Qurʾānic concepts of knowledge (ʿilm) and its acquisition, virtues (akhlāq) and purification (tazkiyah). The holy Qurʾān and Ḥadīth underscore the utmost importance of the pursuit of knowledge. The Qurʾān contains numerous verses emphasising the exploration of the depth of knowledge and its practical application to enhance human existence. This directive is echoed in various Ḥadīth as well. A retrospective analysis of history reveals that the cultivation of human qualities has been intrinsically linked to education. Every endeavour aimed at the welfare of humanity on earth has been propelled by the education of individuals.[5] In the very first verse that was revealed, the Almighty Allah enjoins humans to seek knowledge, declaring: "Read! in the name of thy Lord" (Qurʾān 96:1).

In Arabic, ʿilm translates to knowledge, representing a deep understanding gained through information. In the Holy Qurʾān and Ḥadīth, knowledge is not just about accumulating facts; it encompasses the wisdom that inspires belief in tawḥīd (Unitary Principle) and fosters awe of Allah. Obtaining knowledge is a religious obligation, and there are two types: farḍ ʿayn, compulsory knowledge that every Muslim must acquire, such as knowledge related to prayer, fasting, and faith, and farḍ kifāyah, a communal obligation where a select few can fulfil the requirement on behalf of the entire community, such as in-depth understanding of the Holy Qurʾān and Ḥadīth, or modern fields like medicine

---

5   Syed Ali Naqi, *Shikshar Islamikôron* (Dhaka: The Islamic Academy, Darul Ihsan University, 2002), 1.

and industry.⁶ However, Islam forbids knowledge that leads people away from the path of God or encourages sinful behaviour.⁷

The Prophet (pbuh) emphasised the importance of acquiring knowledge with the profound statement: "Facilitate things to people (concerning religious matters), and do not make it hard for them, and give them good tidings and do not make them run away (from Islam)."⁸ In this particular Ḥadīth, the directive is clear: to propagate Islam involves disseminating its true knowledge and information among the people. The instruction extends to ensuring that the policies and idealistic teachings of Islam reach everyone, emphasising the shared responsibilities of individuals. Moreover, there is a specific call to present Islamic education and knowledge in a manner that is both easy and lucid for students to comprehend.⁹ The Prophet (pbuh) further guides believers to seek a comprehensive understanding of the fundamental principles through ʿilm or knowledge. The holistic acquisition of knowledge concerning Islam is emphasised, highlighting the notion that without this essential knowledge, leading a proper life becomes an insurmountable challenge.

The significance of acquiring knowledge is stressed, suggesting that individuals who arm themselves with a thorough understanding of Islam are better equipped to make informed decisions in their lives. Conversely, a cautionary note is sounded against the potential pitfalls of ignorance. For instance, Islam warns against acquiring financial wealth through illegitimate means, cautioning that the pursuit of righteousness through subsequent charitable acts is a misguided notion; instead, it asserts that such actions result in sin. In contrast, the potential for earning virtue through small, legitimate donations is well documented in the Islamic literature. In essence, the Holy Qurʾān and Ḥadīth consistently emphasise the importance of knowledge, reminding us that it is not merely a personal quest but a fundamental obligation in the journey of life.¹⁰

This highlights the dual significance of acquiring and disseminating knowledge. It is incumbent upon us not only to acquire knowledge but also to share it with others, thereby illuminating society and the nation with the light of knowledge. Just as an uneducated society and nation cannot ensure the well-being of humanity, an individual's pursuit of knowledge alone cannot propel the progress of humanity. The welfare of humanity can only be achieved through collective efforts.¹¹ Each human being is considered the khalīfah or

---

6   Mawlana Nur Muhammad Azami, *Mishkat Sharif*, 2nd vol. (Dhaka: Imdadia Library, 1979), 3.
7   Azami, *Mishkat Sharif*, 4.
8   Ṣaḥīḥ al-Bukhārī, Vol. 1, Book 3, Number 69.
9   Muhammad Abdur Rahim, *Hadis Sharif*, 1st vol. (Dhaka: Islamic Foundation, 1984), 209.
10 Abdur Rahim, *Hadis Sharif*, 196–7.
11 Mawlana Mufti Muhammad Shafi, *Maʿārif al-Qurʾān*, vol. 8, trans. Muhiuddin Khan (Dhaka: Islamic Foundation, 1984), 959.

representative of the Almighty Allah, entrusted with many responsibilities. To fulfil these duties, knowledge is an absolute necessity. As the supreme creation, humans attain their eminence through acquiring talents, abilities, and above all, knowledge. Syed Ali Ashraf believed that the quest for knowledge is not just a personal endeavour but a universal imperative of paramount importance.[12]

Secular Education

Syed Ali Ashraf often speaks of the two prominent trends that can be discerned within prevailing educational methodologies. Firstly, there is an emphasis on practical knowledge and education, which equips individuals with the skills needed to lead a fulfilling life in this world. Secondly, religious education aims to foster a profound understanding of one's faith, facilitating the development of a genuinely virtuous human being.[13] However, it is worth noting that merely receiving a certificate upon completing one's education does not automatically transform a student into an ideal human being. Such individuals may still engage in immoral and inhumane activities. Rather than being considered truly educated, they should be regarded as proficient in a particular subject. This points to a deficiency in this education system's ability to produce ideal human beings.[14]

According to the perspectives of both secular and religious educational thinkers, the ultimate aim of education is to nurture exemplary human beings. To achieve this noble goal, we require teaching methods aligned with the philosophy of life. However, secular education often overlooks the significance of the human spirit, focusing on the acquisition of material wealth in worldly life. This system prioritises worldly knowledge and neglects divine revelations (*waḥy*) received by prophets regarding the elevation and degradation of the human spirit and character.[15] As such, it does not acknowledge faith or the pursuit of spiritual depths as educational objectives. This secular approach falls short in awakening the timeless intrinsic moral values inherent in human beings.

On the other hand, within the secular education system devised by colonialists, Muslim students often find themselves estranged from their religious beliefs rather than actively practising them. This educational paradigm fails to foster the development of ideal individuals, as it asserts that there is no divine creator; rather, it posits that individuals themselves are the architects

---

12 Naqi, *Shikshar Islamikôron*, 1.
13 Naqi, *Shikshar Islamikôron*, 1.
14 Syed Ali Ashraf, preface to *Aims and Objectives of Islamic Education*, ed. Syed Muhammad al-Naquib al-Attas (London: Hodder and Stoughton and Jeddah: King Abdulaziz University, 1979), ix–xiv.
15 Syed Ali Ashraf, "Shikshar Uddeshsho," *Dainik Inqilab*, Dhaka, October 31, 1991, 5.

of their world, devoid of any spiritual foundation. This approach marginalises the importance of emotions and lacks a commitment to eternal truths. The secular system, lacking a space for faith, inherently stymies any potential transformation of the human mind. Ethical values within this framework are considered mutable, subject to the fluctuations of societal norms.

This system operates on two foundational principles: first, the assertion of human independence, contending that an individual's education is solely contingent on their desires without external influence; and second, a pervasive scepticism, advocating acceptance only of what is proven through external methods of judgment and intellectual analysis, devoid of belief in anything unproven by scientific investigations. In the contemporary world, this approach has propagated widespread uncertainty. Syed Ashraf believed, to alleviate the uncertainties pervasive in modern civilisation, a transformative method is imperative—one that eradicates the aforementioned factors. This calls for an education system rooted in faith, an Islam-based approach, fostering an environment where students can evolve into ideal human beings.

In contrast, the godless and morally bankrupt secular education prevalent in some countries often fosters arrogance and intellectualism. Driven by a thirst for power and wealth seeking dominance even at the expense of humanity, they manipulate their leadership to exploit others, masquerading illegitimate actions as legitimate and engaging in wealth plunder, bloodshed, and the violation of purity. Their actions spare neither women, children, nor the elderly. Despite their professional advancements, they frequently fall short in the realm of ethics. In contrast, the true purpose of education is to mould individuals into carriers of ethical values who can help themselves and others.[16]

Islamic Perspective

Syed Ali Ashraf stressed that education rooted in religious ideals, particularly Islam, recognises the profound importance of faith and the cultivation of ethical values, striving to nurture individuals who are not only knowledgeable but also virtuous and spiritually connected. He argued that Western secular ideologies often lure individuals into a frenzy of self-interest, causing them to ignore ethical values and resulting ultimately in moral decay within society. To safeguard the younger generation from this degradation, he believed that education must instil in them the standards of humanity that religion has bestowed and that still persist within society. Religious ethical values should serve as the guiding principles for all forms of education, including economics, politics, literature, philosophy, and social sciences. According to him, the

---

16 Syed Sajjad Husain and Syed Ali Ashraf, eds., introduction to *Crisis in Muslim Education* (London: Hodder & Stoughton, and Jeddah: King Abdulaziz University, 1979), 1–5.

assimilation of modern knowledge can only be achieved when it is firmly rooted in the ethical values provided by religion.[17]

However, traditional religious education systems prevailing in our madrasahs, while focused on spiritual development, often lack efforts to enhance the welfare of life on earth and can struggle to convey the concept of an afterlife to the general populace. Nonetheless, during the golden age of Islam, the coordination of education for both worldly and spiritual domains was impeccable. Muslim scholars excelled in religious sciences while also mastering secular subjects. Their mission was to impart knowledge to the Muslim community with the goal of attaining success in this life and the hereafter. Notable figures from this era include Imām Ghazālī in philosophy, Al-Khwārizmī in mathematics, Al-Battānī in astronomy, Jābir ibn Ḥayyān in chemistry, Al-Bīrūnī in physics, Ibn Sīnā in medical science, Al-Masʿūdī in geography, Ibn Baṭṭuṭah in travelling, and Ibn Khaldūn in sociology.

Educational Dichotomy

In the early stages of the Islamic education system, there was no distinction between general knowledge and religious knowledge. However, during the colonial period, colonial powers strategically created a division between religion and science that weakened Islam and eroded the spiritual awareness of Islamic nations. This division ultimately led to the manipulation and subjugation of Muslims. Syed Ali Ashraf noted that during this period, some Muslim intellectuals in India foresaw the potential infiltration of various superstitions into Muslim society through English education. To counter this, they established two religious education institutions in Deoband and Saharanpur, aimed at safeguarding Muslims from the perceived detrimental effects of English culture. These efforts led to the emergence of a significant community of religious scholars deeply versed in religious education. However, these scholars struggled to reconcile the spiritual orientation of their religious education with the secular aspects of modern learning. Nevertheless, they did succeed in resisting the irreligious influences of British colonialism to a considerable extent.

Unfortunately, these intellectuals failed to recognise that English education could be a gateway to accessing the wealth of modern knowledge.[18] As a result, after the fall of imperialism and colonialism, the Islamic world, upon gaining independence, found itself disillusioned. Despite achieving political independence, the Muslim nations found themselves thwarted, unable to secure comprehensive autonomy in various domains. Consequently, the secu-

---

17 Isharaf Hossain, ed., "Syed Ali Ashrafer Gyan o Shikshar Islamikôron ebông Shiksha Dôrshon Bishôyôk Baithoki Alochôna," in *Intellectual Discourse* (Dhaka: Shikoṛayôn, 2002), 35.
18 Naqi, *Shikshar Islamikôron*, 5.

lar Western educational model, entrenched during the colonial era, persisted largely unchanged in the post-colonial period.[19] In contemporary educational practices, the Western secular system persists in sidelining Islam (or any religion for that matter) and, at times, launching attacks on the holy Qurʾān. This schism between scientific knowledge and religion emerged during a period when harmonising the two seemed insurmountable. The prevailing sentiment was one of opposition between religion and science, with the Western education system gaining prominence, causing a substantial decline in the significance of the Islamic education system.[20] Deliberate efforts were made to marginalise religious educators from active participation in the educational realm.

During this period, Islamic teachings, limited to the Qurʾān and Sunnah, faced neglect in the context of modern education. Even though there was a recognised need for religious education, the disjointed structure of modern education rendered lifestyles devoid of vitality and effectiveness. The fundamental efficacy of education was hampered within society. Through governmental initiatives, the prevalent education system, inclusive of Western education, underwent widespread expansion.[21]

As a result, Islamic education, though still nominally present, played a minimal role. Consequently, this education system struggled to counter the challenges posed by secularism to Islam. In many Islamic countries, educational institutions and universities primarily adopted Western secular education as the main system of education.[22] Even though students excelled in science-based lifestyles after obtaining higher degrees, seeds of doubt, disbelief, and atheism were planted in their minds. This led them to develop a fondness for Western cultures at the expense of their own heritage. The Western education system bred a generation distant from patriotic and religious sentiments, leading to a suppression of the need for reform in their homelands.

Holistic Integration

In this pivotal phase of our nation's transition, Syed Ali Ashraf committed himself to bridging the gap between modern education and Islamic education. Just as the practice of science simplifies and empowers practical aspects of human life, religious practice is essential for maintaining control over our inner inclinations. Science and technology equip us with abilities and efficiencies, while religion and ethics instil honesty and sanctity in us. One propels

---

19 Muḥammad Al-Sayyid Al-Sayyid Al-Ṣaftī, *Syed Ali Ashrafer Drishtite Shikshar Islamikôron: Ekti Pôrjalochôna*, trans. Mahmudul Hasan Yusuf from Arabic into Bengali (Dhaka: Darul Ihsan University, 2003), 7.
20 Al-Ṣaftī, 7.
21 Hamid Hasan Bilgrami and Syed Ali Ashraf, *The Concept of an Islamic University* (London: Hodder and Stoughton; Cambridge: The Islamic Academy,), 33.
22 Muhammad Abdurrabb, *Islami Shiksha Byabostha* (Dhaka: Education Society, 1999), 54.

us forward in life, while the other bestows inner peace. Science bolsters our self-confidence, while religion offers profound solace through submission to the Almighty Allah. Both are indispensable for a well-organised and enhanced life.[23] The coordination of these two realms is undeniably crucial. Without this synergy, personal lives remain unfulfilled, and social harmony deteriorates, potentially leading to global turmoil, conflict, and insecurity.[24]

Allah's Sharīʿah represents the divine policies concerning human beings. Those who adhere to the Divine Law find their actions in harmony with Allah's will. On the other hand, individuals who gain knowledge about the rules and disciplines governing material aspects of the universe experience enhanced cognitive development. Syed Ali Ashraf emphasises that humans are inherently prepared to acquire boundless knowledge about the universe, and while they have dominion over the material world, they should never forget their status as Allah's creations and servants.[25] Allah's presence is constant, as evident when He declares, "There are not three in a private conversation but that He is the fourth of them, nor are there five but that He is the sixth of them - and no less than that and no more except that He is with them [in knowledge] wherever they are." (Qurʾān 58:7). This reinforces the notion that even the smallest entity, whether within a stone, in the sky, or buried within the earth, is under His jurisdiction. This insight underscores that religion and science share common ground, as the universal rules, regulations, and paths discovered by science are, in themselves, manifestations of Allah's miracles. Understanding Sharīʿah requires intellectual acumen, and knowledge encompasses thoughts, research, and religious practices. To comprehend Allah's directives and prohibitions, intelligence is a necessary faculty. Thus, the realms of science and Sharīʿah are inherently interconnected, with no conflict between religious and scientific concerns.[26]

In Islam, human beings are seen as integral, and life and surrounding conditions are designed to harmonise with every aspect of life. The religious consciousness and worldly activities of individuals are never kept separate in Islam; coordination is encouraged in every aspect, linking family members, national citizens, and universal humanity. To enrich life, both the body and mind must be nourished. Just as science and technology enrich the body, ethics enrich the mind. This integration of religion and ethics with science and technology is a hallmark of Islam, setting it apart from other belief systems.

---

23 Emajuddin Ahamed, in "Syed Ali Ashrafer Gyan o Shikshar Islamikôron ebong Shiksha Dôrshon Bishôyôk Baithoki Alochôna," in *Intellectual Discourse* (Dhaka: Shikoṛayôn, 2002), 15.
24 Emajuddin Ahamed, "Syed Ali Ashrafer Gyan," 16.
25 Muhammad Hamid Al-Afendi and Nabi Ahmed Baloch, eds., *Curriculum and Teacher Education* (London: Hodder and Stoughton and Jeddah: King Abdulaziz University, 1980), 149.
26 Al-Afendi and Baloch, *Curriculum*, 149.

The pursuit of knowledge is deeply ingrained in Islam, and Syed Ali Ashraf aimed to Islamise education to foster this spirit.[27] He delineated the philosophy of Islamising education by replacing the modern secular approach to knowledge with a religious approach. His vision was that any reader who studies any subject could become a true human by acquiring both religious and modern knowledge if the underlying philosophy of the discipline studied is God-centred.[28] He committed himself to championing and safeguarding the Islamic education system worldwide, with the ultimate goal of nurturing genuine humanity. While he acknowledged that modern knowledge could produce top-level professionals in various fields, including medicine, law, aviation, and science, he contended that it alone could not shape true human beings. Therefore, he immersed himself in the educational movement to formulate a policy conducive to the development of genuine humanity. Through extensive research and logical reasoning, he demonstrated that fundamental aspects of Islamic education could indeed cultivate true humanity and tirelessly strived to free humanity from the clutches of corrosive moral degradation.

Syed Ali Ashraf recognised that only through the Islamisation of education could a fully developed educational system be realised. Consequently, he exerted considerable effort to implement a coordinated education system. His educational philosophy was rooted in spiritual principles, leading him to oversee the creation of textbooks and the training of teachers. Through this approach, he aimed to provide students with a well-rounded, fully developed education that was both grounded in Islamic values and spiritually enriching.[29] In the educational context, it is imperative to ensure that students are not exposed to contradictory values. The acquisition of knowledge about virtuous activities should not be marred by the observation of non-virtuous and reprehensible behaviour in society. A true Islamic education extends beyond the confines of the mosque, emphasising values of honesty and righteousness both inside and outside its walls. Islamic education should be seamlessly integrated into daily life and complemented by a comprehensive curriculum.

The foundational ethical values and awareness inherent in humanity are a divine endowment to every soul prior to birth. The principles of spiritual purity and the purification of sensual desires, including lust, are profoundly similar across various religions. When an individual places their faith in Allah, their soul experiences a significant transformation, leading them to seek truthfulness, relinquish lies, overcome pride, and conquer vices like lust, anger, greed, and gluttony. Any knowledge devoid of Islamic principles not only remains immature but also obstructs the progress of humanity, fostering a self-centred perspective. In Professor Ashraf's view, intellectualism-driven

---

27 Emajuddin Ahamed, "Syed Ali Ashrafer Gyan," 7.
28 Husain and Ashraf, introduction to *Crisis*, 2.
29 Naqi, *Shikshar Islamikôron*, 3.

scientific development and technological progress alone cannot offer solace to human civilisation and human life.[30] He advocated for education policies grounded in religion, which would give rise to a comprehensive understanding of human nature. Divine knowledge, he asserted, does not conflict with fundamental beliefs, nor does it impede the advancement of any field of knowledge. These educational methods are designed to integrate religious perspectives and concepts, exemplifying the concept of Islamisation of education.

Based on the aforementioned philosophy, Syed Ali Ashraf aspired to foster the true development of humanity through the acquisition and application of education. In the present day, global controversies and conflicts have permeated every aspect of our lives, from the personal to the societal, from the local to the international. Consequently, humanity worldwide finds itself in a state of disarray. Individuals' personalities are not maturing as they should, with some fixated on the pursuit of science and technology to meet material needs, while others focus exclusively on religious practices. This lack of balance has thwarted the realisation of our true potential. To fulfil our aspirations, it is imperative that we reconcile these two facets of life through profound modifications in the educational system, achieving a harmonious blend of science, technology, religion, and ethics. Islam, Syed Ali Ashraf argued, offers a model for achieving this harmonisation, and incorporating these principles into the educational system would result in a more complete education.[31] In this context, the genuine pursuit of knowledge becomes feasible, which Syed Ali Ashraf referred to as the "Islamisation of knowledge," the "Islamisation of education" and sometimes, "education of the interior."

His efforts to reorient the education system towards religious values extended beyond Bangladesh to the global arena. His rationale was that only religion has the power to instil a sense of justice and injustice in the human psyche. Those who embrace religion also consider moral and ethical principles. Therefore, Syed Ali Ashraf advocated for an education system founded on Islam, governed by divine principles, as a means of producing responsible citizens. He contended that without a well-structured education system, we cannot cultivate proper citizens. He emphasised that many young individuals, despite having religious awareness, often emerge from major educational institutions with a diminished sense of faith. Therefore, he advocated for changes in the education system through the Islamisation of education, always maintaining his unwavering faith in Allah, despite his modern philosophical outlook.[32]

---

30 Isharaf Hossain, ed., "Syed Ali Ashrafer Gyan," 35.
31 Emajuddin Ahamed, "Syed Ali Ashrafer Gyan," 16.
32 Muhammad Iqbal Hossain, "Smritite Ômlan Ômôr Tumi," in *Bôrenyo: Syed Ali Ashraf Smarok Grôntho*, eds. Muhammad Ahsanullah Mia, Muhammad Ismail Husain, Mahmudul Hasan Yusuf, Muhammad Shamsuddoha, and Shah Waliullah Farhad (Dhaka: Faculty of

Syed Ali Ashraf aspired to establish a foundation for the pursuit and application of knowledge illuminated by the principles of Islam. This vision stemmed from the inherent universality present in Islam, where all individuals are regarded as equals. Even in its instructions and the Medina Charter, which addresses followers of diverse religions, Islam advocates a profound sense of equality for the entire human race. The holy Qurʾān reinforces this concept, proclaiming, "O mankind! We created you from a single (pair) of a male and a female, and made you into nations and tribes, that ye may know each other" (Qurʾān 49:13). Allah intended for humanity to flourish universally, with a well-developed life accessible to all. In this verse, the Holy Qurʾān reminds humanity of its common origin from a pair of man and woman. It further articulates the purpose behind diversifying people into nations and tribes: to facilitate mutual understanding and connection. Allah's divine intention is for the global human race to flourish in a well-developed and meaningful life.

Central to this vision is the imperative role of an effective education system, as the comprehensive development of individuals hinges upon the acquisition of proper knowledge. Syed Ali Ashraf sought to foster an environment where the pursuit of knowledge, grounded in the fundamental teachings of Islam, becomes the cornerstone for the advancement and prosperity of the entire human race.[33]

Establishment of Educational Institutions

Syed Ali Ashraf's educational philosophy is intricately woven with the ideals of social reform. Recognising the transformative power of a profound understanding and embrace of Islamic principles, he envisioned a path towards an enlightened society, emancipated from baseless beliefs and superstitions. A crucial aspect of his vision was instilling Islamic values in the upbringing of young boys and girls, aiming to eradicate unfairness, injustice, and immorality from the fabric of society. To actualise this vision, Syed Ali Ashraf took proactive measures by promoting early education in maktabs and madrasahs. Understanding the importance of grounding children in Islamic teachings from a tender age, he initiated the establishment of educational institutions in various regions. One such notable endeavour was the creation of Shah Hafiz Furqaniah Madrasah in Alokdia village, Magura district, Bangladesh—his paternal settlement. This institution, named after his forefather Shah Hafiz, currently accommodates approximately one hundred students, both boys and girls. The madrasah operates with the support of funding from the Ashraf Charitable Trust and a team of dedicated teachers.

Religious Sciences, Darul Ihsan University), 74.
33 Emajuddin Ahamed, "Syed Ali Ashrafer Gyan," 15.

Throughout his career, Syed Ali Ashraf continued his commitment to education by founding institutions wherever he resided. While a comprehensive discussion of all these establishments is beyond the scope of this chapter, two prominent institutions will be briefly outlined below, shedding light on their respective aims and objectives.

The Islamic Academy

In June 1983, Syed Ali Ashraf established an educational charity known as the Islamic Academy in Cambridge, UK with the noble aim of promoting the integration of Islamic values into education. He was its founding director general. This organisation was involved in various activities including organising seminars, holding dialogues and publishing books while remaining associated with the Cambridge University Faculty of Education. The functional responsibilities of this organisation were handed over to a Board of Trustees with Ahmad Salah Jamjoom as its chairman.

Syed Ali Ashraf said that the purpose of the Cambridge Islamic Academy was to make education faith based in character. In other words, education, in all its forms, should be structured upon the principles rooted in religious beliefs about human nature and the Islamic ideals that guide the development of human character, with the goal of enabling individuals to become representatives of Allah (*khalīfatullāh*) on earth. This includes both theoretical education aimed at instilling moral values and the establishment of ethical standards for human-to-human and human-to-nature relationships. To achieve this overarching goal, he suggested several essential steps. First and foremost, it is imperative to incorporate the teachings and principles of humanity imparted by our religious beliefs into educational policies. Currently, various secular philosophies have distorted these fundamental concepts, leading to the erosion of our moral values. Consequently, we find ourselves entangled in various conflicts over the very essence of education. The Islamic Academy's core mission is to shield individuals from these conflicts and institute education policies grounded in faith. Secondly, the Islamic Academy aims to formulate curriculums and textbooks that align with these faith-based educational policies. Thirdly, it aims to revamp the current teaching methods to ensure the effective transmission of these values and principles. For this, the Academy was engaged in various activities such as conducting research, writing textbooks, holding interfaith dialogues and organising conferences and seminars.[34]

According to the Board's decision, liaison officers were appointed in several countries of the world, whose function was to carry on with the Islamic education movement in their own countries on behalf of the Islamic Academy, Cambridge. In Bangladesh, Professor Syed Ali Naqi was appointed as the liaison officer. He established a research-oriented organisation in Dhaka known

---

34 Isharaf Hossain, "Ekanto Sakshatkare Dr Syed Ali Ashraf," in *Bôrenyo*, 198.

as the Islamic Academy in 1983. The Bangladesh Islamic Academy regularly arranged a monthly seminar with the objective of Islamisation of education. Through this Academy, a book of poems dedicated to Prophet Muhammad (pbuh) was published. The first part of the history of Bengali literature written by Professor Syed Ali Ahsan was also published from here.[35]

Darul Ihsan University

In 1986 the Darul Ihsan Trust was set up through the initiatives of Ashraf Charitable Trust and Jamaʿat-e Madina Trust. In March 1988, an international curriculum committee was formed at the initiative of Bangladesh Islamic Academy and the cooperation of the Muslim World League (Rābiṭat al-ʿAlam Al-Islāmī) based in Makkah, Saudi Arabia. Syed Ali Ashraf was the chairman of this committee and Syed Ali Naqi was its member secretary. The other members of this committee were National Professor Syed Ali Ahsan, Dr Ayub Ali, Dr Mustafizur Rahman, Dr Hashim Mahdi, Shaikh Badruddin and Syed Abul Hasan Ali Nadwi. This committee convened a continuous series of meetings for fifteen consecutive days at the Darul Ihsan Trust's office in Dhaka. As a result of these meetings, a comprehensive curriculum was developed, grounded in an Islamic perspective and spanning from primary to tertiary education. To bring this curriculum to life, the Institute of Higher Islamic Studies was established, which started operating in October 1989. The inaugural meeting of the organisation's first governing body took place on December 27 and 28, 1989. At that time, Hussain Muhammad Ershad, the then President of Bangladesh, ceremonially inaugurated the campus of what was going to be Darul Ihsan University at Savar, Dhaka.[36] Later, when Professor Ashraf appealed to President Hussain Muhammad Ershad for the formal permission to establish Darul Ihsan University, the President issued a notification. In the absence of private universities in Bangladesh, Professor Syed Ali Naqi, in consultation with his brother Syed Ali Ashraf, brought curricula from various American private universities. The curriculum of Darul Ihsan University was created, based on the curriculum of Princeton University located in the New Jersey State of America, and in the month of July 1990 it was established as the first private university in Bangladesh,[37] and in 1993 this university got the formal government approval.

Regarding Darul Ihsan University's objectives, purpose, and programmes, Syed Ali Ashraf said in October 1994:

> Darul Ihsan University is a government approved private organisation. . . . I have donated to this organisation thirty-nine bighas of land. My Saudi friend, Shaykh Adil Batterjee, helped me purchase another four acres of land, and I am grateful to him.

---

35 Naqi, *Shikshar Islamikôron*, 13-14.
36 Naqi, *Shikshar Islamikôron*, 15.
37 Naqi, *Shikshar Islamikôron*, 16.

The primary objective behind the establishment of Darul Ihsan University is the practical realisation of my seventeen years of work for the establishment of fundamental educational principles, which encompass curriculum development, textbook production, and the formulation of pedagogical approaches rooted in ethical values derived from religion. In 1977, I organised the First World Conference on Muslim Education in Makkah on behalf of King Abdulaziz University. Subsequently, I organised other World Conferences on Muslim Education, addressing aspects like syllabus composition in Islamabad (1980), textbook development in Dhaka (1981), teacher training in Jakarta (1982), and helped with the conference on evaluation of the achievements of the previous conferences in Cairo (1987). Despite these international gatherings and their noble intentions of Islamising education, none of the proposed reforms were fully executed in any Muslim-majority country. Exceptions were found in Malaysia, where Dr Anwar Ibrahim made attempts, and in Brunei, where the education minister expressed an intention to do the same in their education policy. Given my advancing years, I aspire to demonstrate in my homeland that by implementing this educational approach, the acquisition and dissemination of a wide spectrum of contemporary knowledge can be profoundly enriched when anchored in ethical values bestowed by religion. The fundamental purpose of Darul Ihsan University is to actualise these innovative teaching methods....

We aim to demonstrate that the ethical values bestowed by religion underpin moral standards across all knowledge domains. We seek to awaken the students to the perspective that humans are not mere subjects of change; they possess the capacity to resist societal transformations, assess societal development . . . and chart new directions. In essence, they will be ready to engage in the pursuit of truth consistently.

Darul Ihsan University is committed to nurturing such students. To achieve this goal, the university has organised research efforts, revamped curricula, and authored new educational materials.[38]

According to Syed Ali Ashraf, knowledge can be divided into three parts. Following this classification, three faculties were opened at Darul Ihsan University and various subjects were included under them, as stated below.

1. Faculty of Religious Sciences: This faculty imparts the knowledge that is based on the relationships between Allah and human beings. The departments operating under this faculty are as follows: (a) Islamic Studies and

---

38 Syed Ali Ashraf, "Darul Ihsan Bishwobiddalôy: Laksho, Uddeshsho o Karjokrôm," in *Bôrenyo*, 178–180.

Daʿwah Department: It operates a BA (Hons.) course and an MA course. A diploma course was also run under this department. (b) Arabic Language and Literature Department: This department was opened in 2002. Here an MA course was operated along with a BA (Hons.) course.
2. Faculty of Humanities: The departments under this faculty are as follows: (a) English Department: In this department an MA course is run along with a BA (Hons.) course. (b) Business Administration Department. (c) Library and Information Science Department.
3. Faculty of Natural Sciences: The departments under this faculty are: (a) Computer Science and Engineering Department. (b) Information Technology Department.
   The Computer Science and Engineering Department was functional from the beginning. Later, the subject of Information Technology was included in this department.
4. BEd and MEd Courses. These courses are equivalent to those of Dhaka University, and the curricula closely mirror each other, with a distinctive approach where educational policies are explored by evaluating various theories from an Islamic perspective and subsequently elaborating on Islamic theories.[39]

Regarding the BEd and MEd courses, Syed Ali Ashraf said,

> While many training colleges in Bangladesh focus primarily on the history of education in India down to the present time, we take a broader view. Our goal is to expand our students' perspectives by providing an overview of global educational transformation. We commence by elucidating the historical foundations of education and how it was imparted in ancient civilisations. We then proceed to discuss the educational systems during the rise and fall of Egyptian, Chinese, Greek, and Hindu civilisations. Subsequently, we introduce students to the evolution of education with the emergence of Islamic civilisation and the changes in education influenced by modern Western civilisation. Our instruction concludes with the history of education in India, and especially the education trends of Bangladesh encompassing the Hindu period up to the present day. In pursuit of this goal, we are acquiring revised and updated textbooks that delve into the intricate history of education. Moreover, we teach our students the relationships between moral values and teaching methods, supported by a selection of carefully compiled books. These resources are intended for use not only within our institution but also across all teachers' training colleges in Bangladesh and the Institute of Education and Research (IER) at Dhaka

---

39 Information gathered and recorded through a personal meeting with Prof. Syed Ali Naqi on 1 July 2006.

University. To promote these innovative changes in teacher training, I conducted workshops for principals and vice principals of training colleges every Thursday during November and December of 1992....

Our vision is for Darul Ihsan University to be recognised as exceptional, setting a precedent among universities all over Bangladesh. We want to demonstrate through this university that through religion-based education it is possible to disseminate cutting-edge knowledge, and through this we can cultivate individuals who embody the ideals of humanity. Our ultimate aspiration is to guide future generations away from atheistic secularism, and instead, build a society founded on enduring ethical values.[40]

Syed Ali Ashraf established a model school called Darul Ihsan Model School in Dhanmondi, Dhaka. In order to align with contemporary educational trends, Professor Ashraf appointed a committee to develop English textbooks and design a comprehensive social studies curriculum catering to students aged five to twelve. He personally engaged with the children by employing innovative methods such as storytelling and visual aids, fostering a deep understanding and appreciation of Islam, our Prophet's (pbuh) life, our society, and our cultural heritage in a practical manner.[41]

Additionally, under the supervision of Darul Ihsan University, he established a residential madrasah, called Tahfizul Quranil Karim Fazil Madrasah, aimed firstly at boys aged seven to twelve. This madrasah emphasises Qurʾān memorization (ḥifẓ), alongside instruction in Arabic, Bengali, Mathematics, and English. For students aged twelve to nineteen, who have successfully memorised the Qurʾān, i.e., become ḥāfiẓ, the curriculum offers a comprehensive madrasah education program up to the ʿĀlim level. It is worth noting that the curriculum and textbooks of this madrasah are aligned with those of Al-Azhar University, a renowned institution that has officially recognised the syllabus of this madrasah. Upon completing the ʿĀlim examination, students can gain direct admission into Al-Azhar University.[42]

Conclusion

Syed Ali Ashraf was at the helm of the Islamic educational movement during his time. His educational policy was a remarkable coordination of the fragmented education system, unparalleled in modern times. He dedicated his entire life's talents, thoughts, awareness, hard work, and resources to acquiring and disseminating knowledge, becoming an extensive repository of wis-

---

[40] Syed Ali Ashraf, "Darul Ihsan Bishwobiddalôy: Laksho, Uddeshsho o Karjokrôm," in *Bôrenyo*, 180.
[41] Syed Ali Ashraf, "Darul Ihsan Bishwobiddalôy," 180–1.
[42] Syed Ali Ashraf, "Darul Ihsan Bishwobiddalôy," 181.

dom and insight.⁴³ He excelled in all facets of intellectual pursuits, but his lifelong dedication was to develop an ideal educational policy that harmonised the divided realms of education. Whenever discussions turned to educational systems, he probed into what enhancements could be made. He continuously explored educational methodologies that promoted physical, practical, and intellectual growth. His educational policy aimed to teach Islamic ethics while coordinating natural and human sciences. Ethics served as a guide to a healthy, attractive, and harmonious life. In his view, just as mastery of science and technology was necessary to control nature, combat diseases, and alleviate poverty, religious teachings were vital for reining in human vices such as greed and anger. He understood that without the harmony of modernity and religion, a nation's educational landscape could be overrun by undesirable influences, yielding no golden crops.⁴⁴

His international recognition far surpassed his fame in his homeland, where many failed to appreciate the brilliance of the lamp of his knowledge, despite its illumination. Throughout his life, he served humanity and disseminated valuable knowledge, with his greatest efforts directed towards the Islamisation of education, a contribution that remains unmatched.⁴⁵ He stood at the forefront of the movement to Islamise global higher education and was a leading advocate for the formulation of an ideal educational policy. Syed Ali Ashraf was a prominent figure among Muslim intellectuals who tirelessly strived to harmonise Islamic education with the modern thought patterns of the contemporary world.⁴⁶ He passionately believed that divine knowledge stands as the foundational pillar in the quest to cultivate ideal individuals, making the dissemination of this knowledge and the development of the requisite mental framework central to the main purpose of education. Without faith or belief, such mental preparedness remains elusive. The purpose of education is to awaken the faith (*īmān*) that lies dormant within the heart of every child.⁴⁷ Thus, education not only seeks to build faith but also endeavours to externalise, safeguard, and foster the means to delve deeper into the realms of faith.

Through his extensive experience, he came to a profound realisation that the Muslim world, even after gaining political independence from the Western powers, would remain bereft of true significance unless its educational system underwent a transformation. His lifelong dedication to researching

---

43 President Abdur Rahman Biswas, "Tar Moto Emon Manush ar Dekhina," in *Bôrenyo*, 24. *Abdur Rahman Biswas* (1 September 1926–3 November 2017) was a *Bangladeshi* politician. He was the *President* of *Bangladesh* from 1991 to 1996.
44 Emajuddin Ahamed, "Chôrom Muhurtei Take Hariyechi," in *Bôrenyo*, 24–25.
45 Shamsher Ali, "Islamic Shiksha Bistare Tar Ôbodan Ôtuloniyo," in *Bôrenyo*, 26.
46 Mawlana Obaidul Haque, "Islami Shiksha Andolon Chilo Tar Jiboner Sar Nirjas," *Bôrenyo*, 26.
47 Syed Ali Ashraf, "Shikshar Uddeshsho," *Dainik Inqilab*, December 14, 1991, 6.

educational reforms led him to engage in profound dialogues with prominent intellectuals across the Muslim world at international education seminars and conferences. He was also in constant dialogue with educationalists from other faiths while he was residing in the UK. Eventually, he harnessed these invaluable experiences to establish the Islamic Academy in Cambridge and Darul Ihsan University in Dhaka. Drawing from his extensive research and travels within his native and foreign lands, he firmly understood that achieving educational and cultural independence was the pivotal precursor to giving political independence its true meaning.[48]

Professor Syed Ali Ashraf emphasised that becoming an ideal person transcends the mere acquisition of information and knowledge; it necessitates the possession of refined behaviour. The goal of education is to shape the character and conduct of students. This is rooted in the broader objective of Islam, which aspires to produce ideal humans capable of effecting positive change within their families and, if possible, throughout humanity. Accepting the commandments and instructions of Allah becomes paramount for safeguarding against intellectual blunders, as intelligence is essential for comprehending the Sharīʿah.

Bibliography

Abdurrabb, Muhammad. *Islami Shiksha Byabostha*. Dhaka: Education Society, 1999.

Al-Afendi, Muhammad Hamid, and Nabi Ahmed Baloch, eds. *Curriculum and Teacher Education*. London: Hodder and Stoughton and Jeddah: King Abdulaziz University, 1980.

Ahamed, Emajuddin. "Chôrom Muhurtei Take Hariyechi. In *Bôrenyo: Syed Ali Ashraf Smarok Grôntho*, edited by Muhammad Ahsanullah Mia, Muhammad Ismail Husain, Mahmudul Hasan Yusuf, Muhammad Shamsuddoha, and Shah Waliullah Farhad, 24–25. Dhaka: Darul Ihsan University, 1999.

Ahamed, Emajuddin. In "Syed Ali Ashrafer Gyan o Shikshar Islamikôron ebông Shiksha Dôrshon Bishôyôk Baithoki Alochôna," in *Intellectual Discourse*. Dhaka: Shikoṛayôn, 2002.

Ali, Shamsher. "Islamic Shiksha Bistare Tar Ôbodan Ôtuloniyo." In *Bôrenyo: Syed Ali Ashraf Smarok Grôntho*, edited by Muhammad Ahsanullah Mia, Muhammad Ismail Husain, Mahmudul Hasan Yusuf, Muhammad Shamsuddoha, and Shah Waliullah Farhad, 26. Dhaka: Darul Ihsan University, 1999.

Ashraf, Syed Ali. Preface to *Aims and Objectives of Islamic Education*, edited by Syed Muhammad al-Naquib al-Attas, ix–xiv. London: Hodder and Stoughton and Jeddah: King Abdulaziz University, 1979.

Ashraf, Syed Ali. "Shikshar Uddeshsho," *Dainik Inqilab*, Dhaka, December 8, 1991.

Ashraf, Syed Ali. "Shikshar Uddeshsho." *Dainik Inqilab*, Dhaka, December 14, 1991.

Ashraf, Syed Ali. "Shikshar Uddeshsho." *Dainik Inqilab*, Dhaka, October 31, 1991.

---

48 Abdul Ghafur, "Ôsamanno Medhabi o Daksho Songôthok Syed Ali Ashraf," in *Bôrenyo*, 43.

Ashraf, Syed Ali. "Darul Ihsan Bishwobiddalôy: Laksho, Uddeshsho o Karjokrôm." In *Bôrenyo: Syed Ali Ashraf Smarok Grôntho*, edited by Muhammad Ahsanullah Mia, Muhammad Ismail Husain, Mahmudul Hasan Yusuf, Muhammad Shamsuddoha, and Shah Waliullah Farhad, 178–181. Dhaka: Darul Ihsan University, 1999.

Azami, Mawlana Nur Muhammad. *Mishkat Sharif*, 2nd vol. Dhaka: Imdadia Library, 1979.

Bilgrami, Hamed Hasan, and Syed Ali Ashraf. *The Concept of an Islamic University*. London: Hodder and Stoughton; Cambridge: The Islamic Academy.

Biswas, President Abdur Rahman. "Tar Moto Emon Manush ar Dekhina." In *Bôrenyo: Syed Ali Ashraf Smarok Grôntho*, edited by Muhammad Ahsanullah Mia, Muhammad Ismail Husain, Mahmudul Hasan Yusuf, Muhammad Shamsuddoha, and Shah Waliullah Farhad, 24. Dhaka: Darul Ihsan University, 1999.

Ghafur, Abdul. "Ôsamanno Medhabi o Daksho Sôngôthok Syed Ali Ashraf." In *Bôrenyo: Syed Ali Ashraf Smarok Grôntho*, edited by Muhammad Ahsanullah Mia, Muhammad Ismail Husain, Mahmudul Hasan Yusuf, Muhammad Shamsuddoha, and Shah Waliullah Farhad, 42–44. Dhaka: Darul Ihsan University, 1999.

Haque, Mawlana Obaidul. "Islami Shiksha Andolôn Chilo Tar Jiboner Sar Nirjas." In *Bôrenyo: Syed Ali Ashraf Smarok Grôntho*, edited by Muhammad Ahsanullah Mia, Muhammad Ismail Husain, Mahmudul Hasan Yusuf, Muhammad Shamsuddoha, and Shah Waliullah Farhad, 26. Dhaka: Darul Ihsan University, 1999.

Hossain, Isharaf. "Ekanto Sakshatkare Dr Syed Ali Ashraf." In *Bôrenyo: Syed Ali Ashraf Smarok Grôntho*, edited by Muhammad Ahsanullah Mia, Muhammad Ismail Husain, Mahmudul Hasan Yusuf, Muhammad Shamsuddoha, and Shah Waliullah Farhad, 196–99. Dhaka: Darul Ihsan University, 1999.

Husain, Syed Sajjad, and Syed Ali Ashraf, eds. Introduction to *Crisis in Muslim Education*, 1–5. London: Hodder & Stoughton, and Jeddah: King Abdulaziz University, 1979.

Hossain, Muhammad Iqbal. "Smritite Ômlan Ômôr Tumi." In *Bôrenyo: Syed Ali Ashraf Smarok Grôntho*, edited by Muhammad Ahsanullah Mia, Muhammad Ismail Husain, Mahmudul Hasan Yusuf, Muhammad Shamsuddoha, and Shah Waliullah Farhad, 73–74. Dhaka: Darul Ihsan University, 1999.

Naqi, Syed Ali. *Shikshar Islamikôron*. Dhaka: The Islamic Academy, Darul Ihsan University, 2002.

Rahim, Muhammad Abdur. *Hadis Sharif*, 1st vol. Dhaka: Islamic Foundation, 1984.

Shafi, Mawlana Mufti Muhammad. *Maʿārif al-Qurʾān*, vol. 8. Translated by Muhiuddin Khan. Dhaka: Islamic Foundation, 1984.

Al-Ṣaftī, Muḥammad Al-Sayyid Al-Sayyid. *Syed Ali Ashrafer Drishṭite Shikshar Islamikôron: Ekti Pôrjalochôna*. Translated by Mahmudul Hasan Yusuf from Arabic into Bengali. Dhaka: Darul Ihsan University, 2003.

Part II
Reminiscences

Chapter 29

Professor Syed Ali Ashraf: An Appreciation
Peter Mitchell

I first meet Professor Syed Ali Ashraf in 1974 at the University of Cambridge and worked closely with him on a number of his chosen projects. By any measure he was an outstanding person, showing clearly by his life and actions a combination of outstanding scholarship with deep personal piety. He appeared to be indefatigable, continually moving from one challenging enterprise to another. He seemed never to be defeated. When one avenue proved to be impassable, he immediately sought to find another. He was certainly fearless, being prepared to state his case clearly and courteously no matter how important or significant the figure he was approaching may be, whether it was a college president, the head of a Cambridge faculty, an archbishop or a leading politician.

My memories of him as a skilled negotiator are many. He was able to persuade a not very enthusiastic national awarding body to support very generously a project investigating the place and experiences of Muslim pupils in British schools. He was eager to win the cooperation of the various religious bodies of this country to formulate joint policies on educational matters that affected all. The result was a series of seminars on educational topics of mutual interest and even more significantly to encourage the participants to agree both on joint statements and recommended courses of actions that were published and widely circulated. He had the wisdom to see that in the British situation a united front of those who shared a religious perspective was possible without in any way compromising the beliefs and convictions of those who had participated. He held strongly that together they represented a body of opinion that could not easily be ignored and often represented a majority that because of its unnecessary silence was too often underestimated.

He had a particular gift of getting very diverse people to work together on common projects. So even where in a modern Western University Faculty of Education there were those who did not share his Islamic faith, he was able to win their respect and cooperation because they saw he was as dedicated to the cause of education as they were. For this reason, he and the Islamic Academy were able to become full partners with the Cambridge Faculty of Education on a series of projects that led to joint reports and publications, an outstanding achievement by any standard.

Near to Professor Ashraf's heart was the belief that religion had a central part to play in education, not only as a subject that itself deserved study at the highest level, but also as education's only reliable foundation. Belief in God and in the transcendent nature of reality, he thought, ought to inform the whole of education and provide a framework in which a more adequate education of the young could be fashioned. His many books and articles show how he worked out in detail how these insights could transform our whole approach to the curriculum, teaching methods, forms of assessment, our educational aims and objectives and the total ethos of educational institutions built on these principles. Without compromising in any way his own deeply held Islamic faith, he sought to cooperate with all those of good will who could help further this cause. For this reason, he actively pursued the formation of a faith-based education that could operate at all levels. I was able to see this in operation when he invited me to visit the University[1] he had helped to found and lead in Bangladesh. The students were lively and appreciative, and far from being the fanatics of popular myth, were open and responsive to the challenges of contemporary life. They were true followers of the Professor, who remaining firmly Muslim was prepared to learn what was valuable from others.

He had a ready pen and a fluent style. His teachers' manual on Islam[2] had a wide circulation in British schools and was appreciated for its clarity and insights. It undoubtedly helped teachers to give a truer picture of Islam to numerous pupils in the secondary schools of British society. Too often, he believed, a distorted view of Islam was presented to non-Muslim pupils, often unwittingly by hardworking but poorly informed teachers, who, if they taught Islam at all, stressed the outward form of Islamic and Muslim customs at the expense of its deeper religious truths. He was also convinced that the voice of Islam should be heard in the educational debates of our times in an articulate and intelligible manner. The *Muslim Education Quarterly* that he founded enabled Muslim scholars to articulate to an English-speaking audience their considered opinions on educational issues of all kinds and he was not afraid to give space to other people of goodwill in ways of mutual cooperation unusual if not unique amongst such journals. His own incisive editorials were always worth reading.

---

1   This is Darul Ihsan University, Savar, Dhaka, Bangladesh that Professor Syed Ali Ashraf founded it in 1990. The government of Bangladesh accredited it as a private university in 1993.
2   Syed Ali Ashraf, *Islam: Teachers' Manual,* The Westhill Project R.E. 5-16 (Cheltenham: Nelson Thornes Ltd, 1989).

As well as being committed to the cause of education, he was above all a man of deep personal faith. It was obvious that he took his religion very seriously. It shaped the way he lived. It was not just outward show but was a matter of the heart. He lived what he taught. God was to him a living reality. But he also saw what remained to be done. It helps to explain his great energy and the fact he did not spare himself. He was in the midst of all this effort, essentially a man of peace seeking the co-operation of all those of good will who would help achieve those goals he held most dear. He leaves us an example it would be difficult to emulate. Behind everything which he did and to which he was prepared to devote his energy and possessions was his conviction that religion and in particular Islam properly understood could help transform society for the better, but only if its principles were translated into every aspect of life. It was his deepest regret that even Muslim societies were slow to realise this truth and were too influenced by what he saw as the secular inroads of a totally materialistic view of life.

Professor Ashraf, therefore, both by his writings and life represented a living example of an expression of Islam too often ignored and overlooked in these turbulent times. A man essentially of peace he believed that by argument, scholarship, and example the truth of his religious and Islamic convictions could win the day. He showed that it was possible for Muslims to work cooperatively with all those of goodwill to build a better and more just society. This did not mean remaining silent over perceived wrongs and injustices. Protest, vigorous and articulate, was often needed however unpopular this might be. But this had to be accompanied by positive, constructive activity that demonstrated the possibility of a better way forward. He always advocated creative ways of acting and thinking that did not despise either the wisdom of the past or new knowledge and skills but sought instead to incorporate them into productive and fruitful ways of living. For this reason he was deeply committed to a university education that would encourage talented young Muslims to integrate their Islamic faith with the new insights of modern knowledge. He opposed an unthinking traditionalism that failed to respond to new teaching methods and the enlarged curriculum urgently needed if the new generation of Muslims was to adequately respond to the fresh challenges of the present. He therefore taught young Muslims, both men and women, to be faithful to their religious convictions but also to be unafraid of new knowledge and to seek to develop their God-given gifts to their maximum potential for the benefit of humanity and in the service of God. He also taught them to see other human beings not as potential enemies but as possible co-operators in working for the good of all.

This therefore was a creative way of peace, not submissive to the way things are, but seeking energetically to build a better, more just and more cooperative society and respecting and welcoming those who did share his, Professor Ashraf's, profound Islamic convictions. This was especially true of the sensitive way he approached those of other faiths. He had made a deep study of English literature. He appreciated the insights into the vagaries of human nature this provided. His was never a superficial approach to human life and the created world. He understood something of its complexities, its glories and darknesses, its beauties and perplexities, all seen as part of the mystery of the Divine creation, an expression of the Divine love. At heart he was a poet, exemplified by his many books of poetry, unfortunately not yet translated into English. It is one of the major tragedies of our times, that the picture of Islam that he conveyed, peaceable, creative, just, and cooperative, witnessing through its culture and achievements to a deeply religious, productive, and progressive way of life, should be lost in a storm of violence and recriminations. It is all too easy to point multiple fingers of blame and hostility. It is much harder to recreate this vision that Professor Ashraf and his like have bequeathed to us. But unless we can do so, our world will become an increasingly dangerous place for us all to live in. We owe it to Professor Ashraf and the example he has left us to ensure that this fate does not overtake us and that the way of peace with justice triumphs.

Chapter 30

A Few Memories of Syed Ali Ashraf at Cambridge: 1950–1952

Norman J. L. Howlings

The late Professor Ashraf's lasting legacy is the momentum generated by his tireless zeal in promoting serious thought—not only in the Muslim world, but among people of other religious faiths—about the desperate need in an increasingly secular and materialistic world to restore a spiritual dimension to education. To this end he bent all his energies, relentlessly travelling, lecturing, writing, and I have no doubt that he burned himself out in the process. During one of our last conversations, in May 1997, a chance remark of his led me to think that something was seriously amiss with his health, and I suggested that perhaps the time had come when he should begin to spare himself a little. His only answer was a smile.

I feel privileged to have been asked by the Islamic Academy to contribute to this commemorative volume; other contributors—indeed many readers—will have been more closely associated in recent years with Professor Ashraf and his work. What I have to offer is in no way a scholarly addition to any of the topics which were his special concern, but merely a few personal reminiscences of a valued friendship that continued for the best part of half a century, reminders of interests and facets of his personality that latterly may not always have been apparent.

It was at Cambridge in the Michaelmas term of 1950 that the Senior Tutor of Fitzwilliam House (now College), the late R. N. Walters, told me that he would like me to meet an interesting young scholar from Dhaka University who had come to read for the English Tripos. At the time I was in my third year at Fitzwilliam, one of the many older students who had come late to the University after war-time service in the Forces—referred to by W. S. Thatcher, the redoubtable Censor of Fitzwilliam, as his "returning warriors." I had graduated that summer and was now working for Part II of the English Tripos. The meeting duly took place in Norman Walter's room and although, sadly, I cannot now recall details of what we talked about, I retain a distinct impression of a neat, bearded, slightly-built young man, quietly spoken and self-contained, of serious demeanour though with a glint of humour in the eyes, and I was immediately aware of a questioning, scholarly mind. Scant entries in my diaries of the time remind me that we subsequently met regularly, often in the refectory of the University Library and that during the Spring and Summer of 1951 over frugal lunches of bread, cheese and a glass of water, our discussions ranged—among other matters—through 18th century aesthetic criticism, theories of the Imagination, and the work of Wordsworth and Coleridge. I see, too, that in January 1951, Ali (the name by which he was known by the small circle of his fellow-students) spent some days in Addenbrooke's hospital with bout of malaria and that during my visits to the hospital we read French, including the poetry of Baudelaire. I was puzzled by this at first: Baudelaire seems such an unlikely poet for Ali to have been reading. Jottings at the back of the diary, however, throw some light: students reading English had to take a paper in another language; besides, Ali wrote poetry himself and was interested in the way the French poet used strange images and an interplay of sense-impressions to evoke states of feeling not susceptible of more direct expression. Not long after, (22 February 1951) we attended a lecture by T. R. Henn on "The supernatural in Yeats" which led to further discussion of poetry as a vehicle of the numinous. I mention these instances to suggest that the direction of thought, the cast of his mind, is already so recognisable. (And a thought occurs to me: has anyone ever made a study of his Bengali poems?)

It was a valuable feature of the English Tripos in our time that its full designation was "Literature, Life and Thought" (whether it still is I do not know), and this encouraged breadth in one's reading, making it possible to relate the study of literature to the currents of thought and feeling of any given period. This suited Ali particularly well since for him the reading of literature was never an end in itself but made sense only when leading to a clearer perception of the human condition and a deeper understanding of our place in the total scheme of things. It was our great good fortune, therefore, that in the early 1950's a remarkable series of public lectures was being given by the Slade Professor of Fine Art, Nikolaus Pevsner, on Medieval and Renaissance Art. Ali and I attended the lectures regularly and they provided a stimulating context of thought in which to set the work of Chaucer, say, or of Shakespeare and his contemporaries. It was no doubt the Pevsner lectures that lay behind another diary entry for 1951. In May we went by train to London and visited the National Gallery and I recorded that I took him to see my favourite painting, the "Annunciation" by Crivelli, in which a group of merchants are talking—discussing business matters, no doubt—and only a small child sees the holy event which is taking place at the same time. Other paintings we looked at included the van Eyck "Portrait of Jan Arnolfini" and works by Bosch and Brueghel.

Although I did not record it, Ali must have returned to East Pakistan during the long vacation of 1951, but he was back in Cambridge for the Michaelmas term having brought his wife, Asia, with him. All who knew her will remember a gracious lady with a quiet sense of humour, sensitive, perceptive, highly intelligent and gifted: she painted delicate water colours, and as I write this, a blue stone pot of traditional Bengali design which she made for us stands in my hearth, and I am saddened at the thought of the prolonged illness that clouded her last years. But in 1951 the sun was still shining. I had married some years before and our second child was expected that Autumn. Diary notes that Asia and Ali came to tea with us on 15th October, and a treasured photograph from early 1952 shows us with the new baby. It was a sorrow to Ali and Asia that she was unable to have children, but during their later stay in England, when Ali came to work for his Ph.D., she found expression for her love for children in teaching.

I single out two further memories from the first phase of Ali's time in Cambridge. After taking Part II of the English Tripos, I had abandoned an intention to stay on for research and was now following the one-year post-graduate course to qualify as a schoolmaster. One of the lecturers on the course was Dr R. H. Thouless and I have a brief note of a lecture he gave on "perception" which again became the topic for discussion in the University Library. Thouless was opposed to mechanistic theories of mind and held perception to be an active process, the mind actively co-ordinating data received by the senses, bestowing a unity on them. This, we agreed, was pure Wordsworth and we reread the famous conclusion to chapter xiii of Coleridge's *Biographia Literaria* and Book II of Wordsworth's *Prelude*. The other memory is of a lecture by a Dr Bake on Indian music. This was familiar ground to Ali, but to me then it was a new experience. Dr Bake showed that fundamentally there was a marked similarity between the ragas of Indian music and the Western modes, which he illustrated with European folk melodies and Christian plainchant. If up to then Indian ragas had been unknown to me, plainchant was equally unfamiliar to Ali, and I was able to play him records (old 78's of course) of the monks of Solesmes abbey singing Gregorian chant.

These few memories—like snapshots in an old photograph album—provide, I hope, glimpses of Ali in those early years in Cambridge, reading widely, intellectually alert, eager to pursue a wide range of interests. We inevitably talked of religion, and I recall he once said that there were many ways of knowing God, and that he would like to experience the Christian way. I suggested we should both go to a service at Little St Mary's church one Sunday, but this never happened. I wish I could convey something of the flavour of his conversation. That he had firm ideas and belief goes without saying, but his manner was not dogmatic, and he was a good listener, with the habit of relating topics of discussion, whatever the subject, to a wise saying of some holy man or to parallel instances in folklore or ancient Sanskrit literature. Thus, on one occasion, on my objecting to the part played by coincidence in the plot of Thomas Hardy's novels, he questioned whether chance or coincidence ever occurred in life. Well yes, of course. And so to the poor fisherman arrested for being in possession of the king's ring. Yes Ali?—tell me more. The fisherman discovered the ring in the belly of a fish he had caught, the very ring lost by Sakuntala while bathing, the restoration of which to the king brought about their reunion and the recognition of Bharata as the heir. And then followed his hearty laugh, so characteristic of him throughout his life, a genial, human dimension of his profoundly serious nature. It was this good humour, friendly and comfortable, that endeared him to us—that small Fitzwilliam group (I think here particularly of Dick Wilkinson and Jim Harvey.)—and who ever since have remained touched by his spirit.

Chapter 31

Professor Syed Abu Nasr Ali Ashraf: A Friend I Miss Forever[1]

A. M. M. Azhar Hussain

It was the month of August 1940; I went to the then Government Dacca Intermediate College for admission into the I.A. class. Dr Momtazuddin Ahmed (later on, Vice Chancellor, Rajshahi University)[2] was the Principal of the College. In those days the present High Court Building used to house the Dacca Intermediate College. It is a magnificent building and was built to be the residence of the Governor of undivided Bengal Presidency. I cannot exactly remember, but there were three or four boys of my age in the office. A short-statured boy with sharp eyes and thick-glassed spectacles was next to me. I came to know that he was Syed Ali Ashraf, a brilliant student of Armanitola Government High School[3] and who did very well in the Matriculation examination. After a brief interview with the Principal, we were admitted to Section Four with Geography, History, and Economics and had to take two papers on English literature. We became friends soon and the bond which started in 1940 continued lifelong.

Ashraf was very studious with a wide range of general knowledge. He could argue with clear and precise logic on any subject for a long time. If I remember aright, he recited a self-composed poem at the condolence meet-

---

1 Presented at The Second Professor Syed Ali Ashraf Memorial Lecture held at Sundarban Hotel, Dhaka on 8 August 2000, sponsored jointly by the Islamic Academy, Cambridge and Darul Ihsan University, Dhaka, Bangladesh.
2 Momtazuddin Ahmed (1903–1971), born on 24 December 1903, was a philosopher and educationist. He obtained his BA (Honours) and MA in Philosophy in 1926 and 1927 respectively from the University of Dacca, and PhD from the University of London in 1937. He was the Principal of Dhaka College (now in Bangladesh) from 1939 to 1945 and the Vice Chancellor of Rajshahi University from 1957 to 1965.
3 Located at Armanitola in Old Dhaka, this school was established in 1904 by the British government as an experimental school of the only teacher training college of East Bengal at that time.

ing on Rabindranath Tagore in 1941 in the college. The meeting was presided over by Dr Momtazuddin Ahmed, the Principal and the chief guest was Dr R. C. Majumdar,[4] the then Vice Chancellor of Dacca University.

Over the years we came nearer, and I came to know him very closely. After his M.A., he became a lecturer at the University of Dacca and after a few years, joined the Department of English at Rajshahi University, but he did not stay there long and left for West Pakistan, to join the University of Karachi.

He studied at the University of Cambridge and had his B.A., M.A., and Ph.D. from there, and later on he was appointed a fellow of Claire Hall, Cambridge University. In between these years, I met him several times at Karachi. He was the Head of the Department of English at Karachi University for a long time. Then he moved to Saudi Arabia. While in Saudi Arabia, he was a Professor of English and later on the Head of the Department in Ummul Qura University in Makkah and he was there for quite a long time.

He was deeply concerned with the problem of Islamisation of education and with this idea in view he travelled widely popularising his new approach through giving lectures, writing books and articles, and attending conferences. I always admired his intellectual sincerity and his deep insight into spiritual matters. I used to think that perhaps those were his theoretical beliefs but by his death he has proved that he used to live on a higher plane which was beyond my reach by common logic. In many matters he was very near, but in some matters, he was moving on a different platform and perhaps very lonely there.

Indeed, he has popularised the Islamic concept of higher education, shedding new light on it to channel European education through a different route. He has proved that Western education can only be beneficial to us if we are deeply anchored in our own culture and religion. With this idea in view, he established a centre at Cambridge—the Islamic Academy—which regularly publishes a journal on education and Islamic culture, titled *Muslim Education Quarterly*, to which many well-known scholars have contributed.

Long before Darul Ihsan University became a reality, Ashraf and I used to talk about the shape of it at his Karachi residence and also at Dacca. Sometimes when I could not make a point clear and he was also in doubt, he would keep mum and then suddenly exclaim, "Azhar, there will be obstacles, but we will have to surmount those."

His dream is a reality now in the shape of Darul Ihsan University. However, we must be very cautious because we are surrounded by Godless education. I feel we will still have to walk miles and miles. I am confident that the sapling

---

4 Ramesh Chandra Majumdar (known as R. C. Majumdar, 1884–1980), born in Faridpur, Bengal Presidency, was a historian and professor of Indian history. He was the Vice Chancellor of Dacca University from 1937 to 1942.

he has nurtured will grow into a mighty tree, providing us shelter from the myriad distractions that pass for education in our society today. I consider Ashraf's greatest achievement is Darul Ihsan University where he put into practice his ideas which were burning in his mind for all these years.

His mind was very much alive. On the one hand he was a critic and on the other hand his mind was filled with poetic fervour. He has written many articles on Muslim education, and I consider *New Horizons in Muslim Education*[5] and *Crisis in Muslim Education*[6] as his most well-known books where he has pointed out the present ills of orthodox thinking and dangers of modern theories and advised all to come with an open mind. He has emphasised that we should not abandon Western education and isolate ourselves from the world, but rather integrate our culture and religion with it to achieve a balanced and optimal approach. It is only then that the object of our education will be achieved.

In the field of Bengali poetry, he is a new force. On the one hand the lilting of love is musically heard through the length and breadth of his poems, on the other a deep spiritual longing is expressed. His poems, such as "Asfala Saafeliin," "Hajre Aswad," "Kaʿba Sharif," "Hera," "Arafat," and "On the Road to Madina Munawwara," reveal the heart of a devotee who has completely surrendered to the will of Allah. Like T. S. Eliot, Ashraf has combined deep critical understanding and high poetic fervour in his prose and poems. His *Kabyo Porichôy* deals with the fundamental concepts of aesthetics in a very clear and lucid way.

I can summarise Ashraf's view on life from what I have seen in him and from his books that he was a person of very strong conviction and always believed that we may commit mistakes but if we are sincere in asking for the help of Allah, it will surely come.

Before concluding this short chapter, I would like to mention an incident which is quite interesting. It happened in 1964 or 1965 in Karachi. Ashraf was driving his Morris Minor car, and I was with him. It was evening and we were far away from the university campus. The car suddenly stopped and refused to move. Trying for half an hour I became worried and a bit afraid as it was getting dark, and night was creeping in. Ashraf was sure that some help would come. I felt hopeless and was almost at the breaking point. Then all of a sudden, the engine started—I don't know why nor could I explain how. We reached our destination late but safely. Ashraf told me later that he was praying all the time while I was toying with different gadgets of the car. His belief in prayer was serious and sincere.

---

5   Syed Ali Ashraf, *New Horizons in Muslim Education* (Kent, England: Hodder and Stoughton and Cambridge: The Islamic Academy, 1985).
6   Syed Sajjad Husain and Syed Ali Ashraf, eds., *Crisis in Muslim Education* (Kent, England: Hodder and Stoughton, and Jeddah: King Abdulaziz University, 1979).

Now he is no more, but I don't think he is far away from us. His educational philosophy that he tried to implement at Darul Ihsan and other institutions in the Muslim world is a significant symbol of his being and I am confident it will continue to serve the Ummah for time to come.

Bibliography

Syed Ali Ashraf. *New Horizons in Muslim Education.* Kent, England: Hodder and Stoughton and Cambridge: The Islamic Academy, 1985.

Syed Sajjad Husain and Syed Ali Ashraf, eds. *Crisis in Muslim Education.* Kent, England: Hodder and Stoughton and Jeddah: King Abdulaziz University, 1979.

Chapter 32

Reflections on the Life of Syed Ali Ashraf: Based on an Interview with His Sister-in-Law, Mrs Selina Ali

Muhammad Abdul Jabbar Beg

Accompanied by a Muslim teacher of Cambridge, F. M. Aziz, I had the opportunity to go to the house of Mrs Selina Ali, sister-in-law of the late Professor Syed Ali Ashraf on 29 December 2005 to interview her about the life and work of Syed Ali Ashraf. I interviewed her in the presence of her husband, Mushtaque Ali, their son, Fuad Ali and daughter, Nadia Ali. She narrated the life of Professor Syed Ali Ashraf, commenting on photographs from an album and newspaper cuttings that illustrated her brother-in-law's days in Karachi University and Cambridge. Professor Ashraf, I was informed, owned an expensive camera. He was a keen amateur photographer, and the album was made by himself. The following is a summary of her narrative.

Selina Ali told me that she was very cautious about communicating with anyone about her brother-in-law's life because she did not want any misinformation about Professor Ali Ashraf to be published.

She was fond of her elder sister, Asia Ashraf (wife of Syed Ali Ashraf) from an early age. The older sibling took her under her wing, and she became a member of Professor Ashraf's family. Ali Ashraf had no children of his own; Selina became a substitute daughter, and she regarded him as a father figure. She travelled with her sister and Ali Ashraf on their journeys from Dhaka to Karachi and to Cambridge and back. She fondly remembers the travels with her *Bubu* (elder sister in Bengali) and *Dula-Bhai* (brother-in-law in Bengali) by boat in a river in Comilla district in Bangladesh following their marriage. Professor Ashraf always loved travelling by rivercraft or boat and by ship. For instance, Ali Ashraf travelled from Bombay to England by ship. Ali Ashraf used this method of travelling when he came to the city of Cambridge as an undergraduate in the 1950s and later also as a postgraduate in English literature in the 1960s. It was then that he would take his family punting on the River Cam.

She talked about frequent picnics and the meetings with the academics who visited Ali Ashraf in Cambridge. Among them were Norman Howlings and his wife. While in Cambridge, Asia Ashraf completed her postgraduate certificate in education at Homerton College in 1952. As a hobby, Mrs Ashraf and Selina Ali attended an embroidery class in Cambridge, while Ali Ashraf enjoyed attending a book-binding class. When Ali Ashraf completed his PhD thesis[1] at Cambridge University his tutor bound it.

She remembers that her elder sister, Mrs Asia Ashraf set up a Nursery School on the roof of her house in Rajshahi, Bangladesh during Ali Ashraf's employment at the English Department at Rajshahi University. While Ali Ashraf was a Professor of English at Karachi University, he set up a modern language laboratory with 16 booths for teaching English at the University. Her brother-in-law was an affectionate man who raised some children of his relatives while at Karachi University. Syed Ali Ashraf, according to Selina Ali, was a very kind and methodical person (*ekjon gochalo manush* in Bengali). Unlike many religious people who looked untidy and disorderly, he was smart and well-dressed.

While he was a professor at Karachi University, he used to wear the attractive dress of Sherwani and Chost-Payjama (tight-fitting trousers) and always looked handsome and dignified. He trimmed his beard every week. Knowing the value of keeping personal records, Professor Ashraf compiled an album and kept diaries to remember memorable occasions.

Professor Ashraf easily befriended strangers whether they were writers or of other professions. For instance, once he met a motorcyclist, Abdus Salam who was travelling around the world on a private motorcycle. He became so fond of the Professor that he regularly sent him picture postcards from different countries he visited. Another person, Suraj Miah of Dhaka was a guitarist, whose musical talent was appreciated by Professor Ashraf so much that he was always welcome in Professor Ashraf's house. While a Visiting Professor in America he met the famous English writer, Aldous Huxley. They became good friends.

Another foreigner, Mr Amir Ali who spoke Swahili as his mother tongue, came from Tanzania. When Amir Ali travelled to India from Karachi University, Dr Ashraf gave him money to buy some English books on poetry and fiction written by eminent Indian writers. While studying at Karachi University Amir Ali asked Professor Ashraf to write books on English literature to be used by Swahili-speaking students and others. Professor Ali Ashraf was a family friend of many scholars of foreign nationalities including Professor Maita of Hawaii University. It is remarkable that Maita's family members were fond of music,

---

[1] The thesis entitled, "Poetry and its Audience in England from 1914 to 1945" by Syed Abu Nasr Ali Ashraf is available at Cambridge University Library and University of Cambridge Faculty of English. It was submitted at Cambridge University in 1964.

and they shared a common interest with the Ashrafs. It is therefore not surprising that during his teaching career at Karachi University Syed Ali Ashraf became a member of the prestigious Writers' Association called PEN (Poets, Essayists and Novelists) whose members included some French, Russian and Indian writers as well as the celebrated Urdu poet Faiz Ahmad Faiz. Professor Ashraf was a distinguished Professor of English, who was naturally well-informed about English literary works published in Pakistan. He used to write articles on the state of the art of English literature which existed in Pakistan.[2]

From Karachi University Ali Ashraf used to publish a quarterly journal called *Venture*, which attracted readers, contributors, and subscribers from different parts of the world. While a professor at Karachi University, he used to deliver lectures on summer courses organised by American Universities.

According to Selina Ali, Professor Ashraf came to Karachi in 1956. While at Karachi University Professor Ashraf promoted collaboration between academics of East and West Pakistan. This took the form of extending invitation to scholars from East Pakistan to Karachi University to moderate university examination papers and to attend national conferences in the federal capital of Pakistan. Such scholars included Syed Sajjad Husain[3]—a cousin of Ashraf and an authority on the English poet Rudyard Kipling—who was professor and head of the Department of English at Dhaka University; and Azizur Rahman Mallick, professor and head of the Department of History at Rajshahi University.

When Professor Ashraf moved to Karachi, he and his family used live in Nazimabad and later moved to a house on the campus of Karachi University. Professor Ashraf was a broadminded person who admired scholars of diverse cultural backgrounds which included some Western and certain Hindu scholars such as the poet Browning and Rabindra Nath Tagore. His wife, Asia Ashraf was very fond of Tagore's songs (widely known in Bengali as *Robindro Songiit*). Among his classmates at school and college were Hindus who, despite their migration to India, remained friends for life with Syed Ashraf. One such friend was Amlan Datta, who was born in Comilla, now in Bangladesh, in 1924 and later migrated to India, and died in Calcutta in 2010. Amlan Datta was a noted economist and held many academic and administrative posts in India including vice chancellor of Visva-Bharati University, Santiniketan in Birbhum district in West Bengal, India. Syed Ashraf maintained his connection with him till his last day. This was due to his liberal and tolerant outlook and love for

---

2   For example, see his compilations titled, "Pakistan," in *The Journal of Commonwealth Literature* in the following three successive years.

   1968: Volume 3, Issue 2, https://doi.org/10.1177/00219894693.2006.

   1969: Volume 4, Issue 2, https://doi.org/10.1177/00219894694.200812.

   1970: Volume 5, Issue 2, https://doi.org/10.1177/00219894705.201012.

3   See Appendix 2 for Professor Ashraf's relation with Syed Sajjad Husain.

men of diverse faiths. He maintained this outlook till the twilight years of his life. Whether this was due to his strength of character or poetic temperament, it is difficult to say.

Syed Ashraf went to Cambridge for his PhD in 1960 and was later joined by his wife, followed by Selina Ali. Mrs Asia Ashraf who was a teacher, taught at schools in Cambridge in early 1960's and later between 1974-1990. Ashraf had many friends among English professors during his life in Cambridge, when he used to attend annual conferences on Shakespeare at Stratford-upon-Avon. Ali Ashraf was not only a writer on English literature but also a poet in his mother tongue of Bengali. He produced a textbook on poetry called *Kabyo Porichôy* (lit. Introduction to the study of poetry) in Bengali. His fascination for poetry was perhaps the reason why he decided to do his PhD on "Poetry and its Audience in England from 1914 to 1945" at Cambridge University.

Professor Ashraf was not only a man of poetic and philosophic temperament but also a person who was very kind to people as well as animals. In his house at Karachi, he had a pet cat, which was named Diana. When this cat became sick he became distraught. He would nurse the animal feeding it regularly with fish, which he skinned and boned. He fed the cat in this way for weeks until it regained its health. This was an unusual story in Professor Ashraf's life. By narrating this and other stories in the life of Ashraf, Selina Ali was reminding us that he was an extraordinary person and there was something mysterious and philosophical in his life and personality. Among other things, Professor Ashraf was fond of his family. He was so kind to his sister-in-law (whom he affectionately called Shelly) that he arranged her marriage with Mushtaque Ali. The two families became so close that they went on pilgrimage (Ḥajj) to Makkah together.

Ali Ashraf performed his first pilgrimage most probably as early as 1958. He probably repeated his Ḥajj with his spiritual mentor, the late Pir Baba Zaheen Shah Taji.[4] It was either then or later that he took the photograph of *Al-Ḥajar al-Aswad* (the Black Stone) at the Kaʿbah. This photograph exists in his album.

It is often said that a picture is worth a thousand words. Mrs Selina Ali showed me the family album and recounted her memories of her brother-in-law. She also showed me some of his books (including a Persian book on Talisman which was bound by Professor Ashraf with his own hands). Among the exhibits were his PhD thesis and some other books. She also brought out some journals and articles of Professor Ashraf, including a memorial book in a special issue of a Bengali journal, *Sôkal* (or morning), which appeared in 1997 in Dhaka, Bangladesh. This journal included an introductory chapter on the highlights of Syed Ali Ashraf's life and work.

---

4   See Chapter 34 of this book regarding Baba Zaheen Shah Taji.

Mrs Selina Ali was proud to mention that Professor Muhammad Mahmood Ahmad[5] of Karachi University was the person who introduced Professor Ashraf to a Sufi, named Zaheen Shah Taji. This Sufi's own mentor was named Baba Yusuf Shah Taji who was a disciple of Baba Tajuddin Nagpuri. Baba Zaheen Shah Taji conducted the marriage (ʿaqd nikāḥ) ceremony of Miss Selina and Mushtaque Ali. With the passage of time Baba Zaheen Shah Taji became Ali Ashraf's spiritual teacher and Pir (spiritual master; lit. old man). The depth of Ali Ashraf's attachment to him was so great that Ali Ashraf dedicated a book of poems to him, entitled *Rubaiyat-i Zahini* (lit. Quatrains of Zaheen Shah Taji), a reminder of the celebrated *Rubaiyat* of ʿUmar Khayyām. Although not as famous as the latter, Ali Ashraf's Quatrains or *Rubaiyat-i Zahini* was nevertheless quite unique in Bengali literature.

I had the opportunity to see some photographs of Professor Ashraf's Sufi master, who helped him to enter the fold of Sufism in Pakistan. Among these photographs in the Ali Ashraf Album there is a photograph of Ali Ashraf on the day he was elevated from a novice (*murīd*) to the rank of a trained Sufi (*khalīfah*), when he gained his Turban from his Sufi mentor. It will be relevant and befitting to publish the Ashraf Album as a supplement to this memorial volume which will be published in the near future. Ali Ashraf's deep interest in Sufism explains why some Muslims in Cambridge and the Caribbean islands regard him as a Sufi Master of Cambridge and a preacher of Islam tinged with the theosophical teachings of Sufism. I gather that he was fond of some of the mystical teachings of Imām Abū Ḥāmid al-Ghazālī.

Professor Ali Ashraf regularly held *Dhikr* (lit. remembrance of Allah) sessions on Thursday evenings. He was an essayist and a poet whose books include an anthology of poems called *Ali Ashrafer Kobita* ("Poems of Ali Ashraf") and other books, such as *Proshnottôr* ("Questions and Answers"); *Bisôngoti*, as well as *Muslim Traditions in Bengali Literature*[6] and its Bengali version, *Bangla Sahitye Muslim Oitijhyo*. Ali Ashraf taught English literature at various universities, including the Universities of Rajshahi, Dhaka and Karachi in Pakistan and King Abdulaziz University in the Kingdom of Saudi Arabia. He was, like Sir Sayyid Ahmad Khan, the founder of a Muslim private university, called Darul Ihsan University in Dhaka, Bangladesh and became its founding vice-chancellor in 1990 when this university was established as the first private university in Bangladesh.[7] He taught Islamic philosophy of education at this university. This was the highest achievement and the crowning glory of his educational career. Besides, he was a Fellow of two Cambridge colleges (Clare Hall and Wolfson College). Apart from this, he was a member of the Faculty of

---

5 See Chapter 34 of this book for information on Professor Muhammad Mahmood Ahmad.
6 Syed Ali Ashraf, *Muslim Traditions in Bengali Literature* (Karachi University: Bengali Literary Society, 1960).
7 See Syed Ali Naqi, "Syed Ali Ashraf: Exploring Education through a Spiritual Lens," Chapter 14 of this book for the genesis of Darul Ihsan University.

Education at Cambridge University. In Cambridge Professor Ali Ashraf will be remembered as the founder of the Islamic Academy and the founding editor of the quarterly journal, *Muslim Education Quarterly* from 1983 until his death in 1998. Ali Ashraf was one of the most illustrious Asian students at the University of Cambridge. His life and literary work will immortalise his name.

Chapter 33

Dignity Wrapped up in Humility: A Tribute to Professor Syed Ali Ashraf

M. Harunur Rashid

Professor Syed Ali Ashraf was one of the most outstanding personalities of the twentieth century; a rare individual who was not only a scholar of English literature but also a Muslim philosopher of great distinction. He was a spiritual mentor, a Sufi saint who had a considerable following all over the world. As an educationist, he had a worldview which provided for a change in attitude in the backdrop of a materialistic world full of greed, chaos and confusion and showed the way which could train the total personality of man and bring about a transformation of the body and the spirit. He was a poet whose poems, like those of T. S. Eliot, resonate with his profound faith in Allah and His Prophet (pbuh) and his spiritual ecstasy.

He graduated from Fitzwilliam College, Cambridge and did his PhD from there. The field he chose for his dissertation was modern English poetry, an area deemed daunting even for a native scholar of English literature in the early nineteen sixties. He was an outstanding poet and authored a book in his native language on critical analysis of poetry. He started teaching at Dhaka University, and later moved to Karachi, where he spent most of his professional life at Karachi University. As a teacher of English literature, he was superb as borne out by some of my contemporaries at Fitzwilliam College who came from Karachi University in the mid-sixties.

Professor Syed Ali Ashraf was a multi-dimensional personality. He proved his worth as an educational administrator. While in Saudi Arabia working as a Professor of English and head of the department at King Abdulaziz University, Jeddah, he was successful in bringing together Muslim scholars from all over the world as one of the two organizing secretaries of the First World Conference on Muslim Education held in Makkah in 1977.[1] There were eight follow-

---

1   King Abdulaziz University, *Conference Book: First World Conference on Muslim Education:* (Mecca and Jeddah: King Abdulaziz University, 1977).

up World Conferences of Muslim Education in different capitals of the Muslim world. Professor Ashraf was the organizing secretary of the second, third and fourth of these conferences and an advisor to the fifth and the sixth conferences.[2] In 1980 he was appointed the first Director General of the World Centre for Islamic Education, set up by the Organization of the Islamic Conference in Mecca. By then he became a familiar name in the academia of the Muslim world.

I first saw him at a seminar organized by the Department of English, Dhaka University, in 1959. I met him first face to face in 1967 at the University of Chittagong where he went as a member of the selection board responsible for choosing successful candidates for English teacher appointments. I was an applicant for the post of Assistant Professor. When my turn came, I entered the room of the Vice-Chancellor, Dr A. R. Mallick and I was asked to take my seat. I saw Dr Ashraf seated across the table with his usual dignity and calm and plain clothes. Meanwhile, the telephone rang, and Dr Mallick picked up the phone and had a brief talk with someone. Dr Mallick turned to me and said, "Mr Rashid, I am sorry we can't interview you as I had a call from the Director of Public Instruction, Ferdous Khan, and he has asked me specifically not to interview you as you have a bond with the government for the scholarship on which you had gone for higher education." I could see a feeling of despair written large on the face of Dr Ashraf who turned to Dr Mallick and requested him to at least interview me. Dr Mallick was a strong personality known for his courage. He replied and said, "Dr Ashraf, if I had not received this personal call from the Director of Public Instruction, I would have interviewed him and perhaps even given him a tentative selection, subject to his obtaining release from the government." Dr Ashraf was terribly disappointed as I walked out of the room.

I met him nearly 20 years later in Casablanca, at the World Conference on the theme of "Unity in Diversity" sponsored by the Council of World Religions. This is what I wrote in an obituary in the *Dhaka Courier* published on 14 August 1998:

> In November 1987 I went to Casablanca to attend an Islamic conference on Sufism. The venue was Hyatt Regency hotel, and all the stalwarts of Islamic thought came from all over the world. I was not surprised to see Professor Syed Ali Ashraf along with his accomplished wife. He was by then a key figure in the Islamic world of letters.[3]

---

2 Shaikh Abdul Mabud, "World Conferences on Muslim Education: Shaping the Agenda of Muslim Education in the Future," in *Philosophies of Islamic Education: Historical Perspectives and Emerging Discourses*, eds. Nadeem A. Memon and Mujadad Zaman (New York: Routledge, 2016), 129–43.
3 Harunur Rashid, *Dhaka Courier*, 14 August 1998.

On the sidelines of the plenary, I had time to talk to him and get to know him better. He was a Sufi and had a great command over the inner and outer aspects of Islam. He spoke softly and explained the intricacies of ʿilm-e taṣawwuf (spiritual knowledge). He had a large following as a mentor (murshid) in Europe, America and Bangladesh. One day during a coffee break at this conference he sat opposite me at a separate table and gently proposed if I would become one of his disciples. He had listened to my paper which I delivered the day before and perhaps found something in the paper which dwelt on the concept of unity in diversity. I could not or rather did not give him a clear answer to his proposal. Noticing my indecision, he said that a real murshid could lead his disciple up to Sidrat al-Muntahā[4] in a spiritual journey. He understood my indecision and talked about other things. The real cause of my indecision was that I had before that met my murshid, Syed Rashid Ahmed Jaunpuri (R.A.),[5] though I was still waiting to be initiated as one of his murīds (disciples).

The next time I met him was at Clare College, Cambridge where he was a Fellow and he had invited me to lunch at the senior cafeteria. He gave me a delicious meal and talked about my academic programmes at home. The fourth time I met him and his wife was at their Cambridge home. It was a dinner, and both hosts worked tirelessly to ensure we (me and Maqsud, an undergraduate, who accompanied me) felt completely at home and comfortable. After dinner we had a relaxing tea. This was in July 1991 when I visited Cambridge to attend a seminar on Contemporary English Literature sponsored by the British Council at Christ's College during summer break of the University. This seminar gave me an opportunity to interact with some of the heavy weights of the twentieth century English literature including William Golding who autographed his book *Lord of the Flies* for me.

Dr Ashraf with his profound scholarship and acumen could have become one of the leading experts of research on English literature. Instead, he turned to Islamic thoughts, philosophy, and exoteric and esoteric aspects of Islam. He was drawn to Sufism even before he travelled to England for higher studies as is borne out by his early poems based on religious thoughts. I had read his *Kabyo Porichôy*[6] while I was an undergraduate at Dhaka University. That was one of the best books available on the art of criticism and understanding of poetry.

---

4   Sidrah in Arabic means the lote-tree and muntahā means the extreme edge or limit. Thus, literally, Sidrat al-Muntahā means "the Lote-Tree that is situated on the extreme edge or limit." ʿAllāmah Ālūsī al-Baghdādī in his Rūḥ al-Maʿānī has explained it thus. "At this the knowledge of every learned man comes to an end; whatever is beyond it is known to none but Allah." Syed Abul Aʿla Maududi, *Tafhīm al-Qurʾān* (Lahore: Idara Tarjuman ul Qur'an, 1946–1972), verse 53:14, http:www.englishtafsir.com/Quran/53/index.html.
5   R.A. stands for Raḥmatullāh ʿalaih, meaning "may Allah's mercy be upon him."
6   Syed Ali Ashraf, *Kabyo Porichôy* (Introduction to Poetry) (Dhaka: Mokarram Publishers, 1956).

He and his wife are buried just outside the mosque of the permanent campus of Darul Ihsan University in Ganakbari, Savar, Dhaka. I visited his *maẓār* (grave) once and offered *Fātiḥah*[7] on him. I could feel the peace and serenity that surrounds the place. He did his best to restore the lost glory of faith and knowledge of Islam, but Allah willed it otherwise and the Sufi saint's dream was shattered to pieces within eighteen years of his passing away when Darul Ihsan University was closed due to controversies surrounding its activities.

I am indebted to him in many ways. R. N. Walters was both his and my supervisor, though I did not continue to do my PhD under him. Mr Walters spoke highly of him. He once told me that Syed Ali Ashraf received star marks in his essay paper in his English Tripos. I could clearly see that he had put in a word for me to Mr Walters for my placement at Fitzwilliam as an undergraduate. Till then he had not seen me or known me personally. But he somehow developed love for me in such a way that while I was teaching later at Jahangirnagar University, Bangladesh he made me an honorary Professor of English of his Darul Ihsan University. This was an honour done to me and I was not required to deliver any lectures. Today when I look back at him, I can still see him with his profound looks and lovely face lit up with a heavenly smile.

In sum, I see him with profound respect as a rare individual. Allah had given him some extraordinary qualities which put him in the ranks of the great lovers of humanity. His belief in Islam was profound, but he looked on other religions with respect which his co-religionists failed to appreciate. He earned a lot of money but was free from the greed of earthly possessions. He gave away all his wealth for the good of his fellow beings irrespective of creed.

He was a poet with a difference. No one including Kazi Nazrul Islam and Farrukh Ahmad wrote the kind of religious poetry he wrote. His poems did not attempt to blend Hindu and Muslim myths, as Nazrul's did, nor did he, like Farrukh Ahmad, nostalgically revisit the glorious Muslim past. His poems were spontaneous expressions of spirituality, sometimes overflowing with ecstatic emotion of the Sufi kind. As a literary critic he tried to introduce readers to the essential components of poetry—sounds, rhythm, words, themes, and creation of an illusion endowed with sublimity freely quoting excerpts and ideas from I. A. Richards, Wordsworth, Coleridge, T. S. Eliot, A. E. Houseman, and the Chicago school of New Criticism. He was obviously influenced by I. A. Richards' Practical Criticism as can be seen from his approach to the appreciation of poetry. The last chapter of his *Kabyo Porichôy* is a readers' guide to the understanding of poetry, which he had a mind to develop into a separate book. That would have been an excellent guide to reading poetry if he could materialize his dream.

---

7 This practice involves reading *Sūrah al-Fātiḥah*, the first chapter of the Qurʾān, and asking Allah to send its reward to the spirits of the deceased.

As a Sufi saint he did not believe in making noises about his ascension into the higher realms of esoteric attainment, but I see him as a great Sufi saint of the first order of his time, perhaps of the last five hundred years. But Allah knows best.

Bibliography

Ashraf, Syed Ali. *Kabyo Porichôy* (Introduction to Poetry). Dhaka: Mokarram Publishers, 1956.

King Abdulaziz University. *Conference Book: First World Conference on Muslim Education.* Mecca, and Jeddah: King Abdulaziz University, 1977.

Mabud, Shaikh Abdul. "World Conferences on Muslim Education: Shaping the Agenda of Muslim Education in the Future." In *Philosophies of Islamic Education: Historical Perspectives and Emerging Discourses*, edited by Nadeem A. Memon and Mujadad Zaman, 129–43. New York: Routledge, 2016.

Rashid, Harunur. *Dhaka Courier*, 14 August 1998.

Chapter 34

In Memory of Syed Ali Ashraf: Reminiscences and Reflections

Muhammad Ahsan

Education is the mainstay for the sustained development of every country, and this is particularly true for the underdeveloped Muslim world. Unfortunately, in modern Islamic history, the Muslim world did not produce enough scholars and scientists who could develop and strengthen its educational system. The sad outcome of this situation needs no explanation. Professor Syed Ali Ashraf (1924–98) was an eminent Muslim intellectual who served in three countries, Pakistan, Saudi Arabia and the UK. In his view, Islamic education is not limited to teaching the Holy Qurʾān and Ḥadīth, rather it encircles the teaching of all disciplines in accordance with Islamic principles. The present article is an attempt to explore various aspects of the life of Professor Ashraf. It is mainly based on the author's visit to Karachi, Pakistan, where he met and interviewed several of his former students and colleagues, including Professor Masood Amjad Ali, Professor Zubair Bin Umar Siddiqui, Professor Manzoor Ahmad, Syed Hasan Mutahar, Professor Rafat Karim, and Professor Sharif al Mujahid as well as the present *Gaddī Nashīn* of *Tājī Khānqāh*.[1] All these people provided very useful information for this article which was not available from any other source.

In 1992, I was in Japan on a study programme and one day during my usual research work, I came across a monograph entitled, *New Horizons in Muslim Education* by Syed Ali Ashraf.[2] On its back cover, it was written that, "This monograph incorporates keynote papers which the author prepared for the three World Conferences on Muslim Education held in 1980, 1981 and 1982. These conferences originated from the First World Conference on Muslim Educa-

---

1 The prevailing spiritual head of a *Khānqāh* is called *Gaddī Nashīn*. In Urdu literature, *Gaddī* means a seat and the person who sits on that is called *Nashīn*. However, this term is specifically used for the current spiritual leader of a *Khānqāh* or tomb.
2 Syed Ali Ashraf, *New Horizons in Muslim Education* (Cambridge: The Islamic Academy, 1985).

tion held in Makkah in 1977. The theme of the monograph is the ideal-typical model for Islamic education, and it deals with the practical problems which a modern Islamic society will face in trying to implement this ideal. It provides an invaluable contribution to discussion on this vital subject." It was because of my great interest in this area that I went through this monograph and was much impressed by the scholarly approach adopted by the author as well as his efforts to bring about a silent educational revolution in the Muslim World.

It was the quality of this document which convinced me to purchase it soon after I completed reading it. This was my introduction in absentia with Professor Ali Ashraf as well as my imagination about his intellectual excellence. However, what I did not imagine at that time was that one day I would again refer to this book for the present memorial volume. The quality of this document can be judged in the words of Seyyed Hossein Nasr, an eminent Muslim thinker who wrote a foreword for this book. He says: "The monograph of Dr Syed Ali Ashraf, who has already done so much to further the cause of Islamic education, draws the attention of the intelligentsia of the Islamic world and especially those in a position of responsibility from an educational and also political point of view to the real issues involved and the questions which must be solved."[3]

I have always had a desire to meet Professor Ashraf but unfortunately, prior to the commencement of my association with the Islamic Academy Cambridge, he had passed away. Professor Ashraf spent around 17 years of his professional career (1956–73) as the Head of the English Department at the University of Karachi. For the past few years, I have had the desire to meet various people in Karachi who have had an academic or social relationship with Professor Ashraf. I wished to ask these people to recall their memories and share their views with me so that I could put this oral history on record. I am grateful to the Islamic Academy that assisted me in fulfilling my desire to visit these people in Pakistan and conduct interviews with them. During early 2008, I stayed in Karachi for a week and met various relevant intellectuals.[4]

Before I present the outcome of these meetings, it would be appropriate to write a few lines on the city of Karachi and the University. Although the modern history of Pakistan begins with its independence in 1947, various archives and scientific research indicate that this area has been inhabited for thousands of years. At the end of British rule, the country became an independent Muslim state with its two wings, namely East Pakistan and West Pakistan. Within its short history, the country passed through several crises. In 1971, its East wing became an independent country named Bangladesh. The history of Karachi is as old as the history of the South Asian region. It was a small fish-

---

3   Seyyed Hossein Nasr, foreword to *New Horizons in Muslim Education*, by Syed Ali Ashraf (Cambridge: The Islamic Academy, 1985), i–ii.
4   We are grateful to Professor Ashraf's former colleagues for their cooperation and help.

ing village at the time when Alexander camped there after a series of tough and bloody wars in the Indus valley. In 712, Mohamed bin Qasim, a young Arab general conquered it and establish Muslim rule.[5]

When Pakistan emerged as an independent country, Karachi with its classical and European styled buildings had become a metropolitan city due to which it was declared its first capital.[6] For this reason, it attracted and accommodated a huge influx of migrants and refugees which changed its demographic and cultural landscape. Although there were a number of benefits, this situation also created several problems such as maintenance of law and order in the city. Keeping aside these problems, this was the most suitable city to establish a new university for this newly born country. The University of Karachi started functioning in 1950[7] and it was housed in a few small buildings in the city's congested areas. In 1960, it was moved to its present premises and now it is the biggest university of the country.

The Department of English was established in 1955 and Professor Muhammad Ahsan Farooqui was its first head. The department was located in Shivjee Murarji building in Nanakwara, but in January 1960 when the university moved to its present campus, the department was housed on the first floor of the arts faculty building. As mentioned above, Professor Ashraf joined this department as its head in 1956 and remained here until 1973.[8] For this reason, during my tour to Karachi, my first stop was the English Department. Here, I met Professor Kaleem Raza Khan who was the Chairman of the department at that time. Professor Khan gave me a warm welcome and offered his full cooperation for this memorial volume. He gave me four issues of *Venture*, a scholarly journal edited by Professor Ashraf. I was pleased to see these issues published in 1961, 1969, 1970 and 1971. In these issues, there were articles written by him as well as Professor Masood Amjad Ali who, later, was my first interviewee for this project.[9] I must mention here that my tour to Karachi was an emotional and exiting experience. It provided me with an opportunity to hear various senior scholars who had been close to Professor Ashraf. The outcome of these meetings is presented in the following pages.

Professor Masood Amjad Ali

Professor Masood Amjad Ali joined the University of Karachi as a B.A. Honours student in 1957. There he studied a three-year Honours course and a one-

---

5 At that time, Karachi was called Daibal.
6 In 1958, the capital of Pakistan was shifted from Karachi to Rawalpindi and then to Islamabad in 1960.
7 Established in June 1951 by an act of Parliament.
8 Professor Ashraf joined the University of Karachi in 1956. At that time Professor Ahsan Farooqui was the chairman of the English Department. Later, Professor Ashraf took charge of the chairmanship from Professor Farooqui.
9 The photographs of various interviewees are also given within the respective texts.

year M.A. programme. After completing his M.A. programme in 1961, he was appointed Assistant Lecturer in the same department where he started to teach poetry and modern fiction. In 1964, he went to England on a Commonwealth scholarship. It was a one-year postgraduate course which he completed with a thesis. On his return, he continued teaching until 1999, when he retired from the university. After his retirement, he was re-employed by the university and continued to teach poetry and modern fiction.

"Professor Ali Ashraf had a different method of teaching," said Professor Amjad Ali. "He never delivered a long and heavy lecture on the subject; rather, used to ask questions of the students and encouraged them to explore the answers." He used to say to his students: "My job is not to solve your problems; rather, to create problems for you so that you can resolve them by yourself." This was a very interesting and unique method as in this way every student was given a chance to speak on various issues. Of course, some issues were debatable and on which some people used to agree while others did not. Professor Amjad Ali revealed that he still remembered that once Professor Ashraf was shocked when he told him that in his opinion *Lady Chatterley's Lover* was a religious book.[10] He asked him: "How do you say that it is a religious book?" Professor Amjad Ali replied: "It is because Lawrence believed in the holiness of the human body, soul and intellect. That's why, in certain ways it was not a pornographic writing because the book was not aimed at creating such feelings."

Masood Amjad Ali

In the same perspective, in 1960, there was also a heated debate in Cambridge University. This debate was led by Professor F. R. Leavis[11] who was also Professor Ali Ashraf's teacher when he was studying there. In these discus-

---

10 David Herbert Lawrence, *Lady Chatterley's Lover* (Florence: Privately Printed by the Tipografia Giuntina, 1928). Since its publication in 1928, Lawrence's novel *Lady Chatterley's Lover* had been banned in Britain. Even its publishing was not allowed in this country because of its sexual explicitness. For this reason, it was printed in Italy. However, with the passage of time and the gradual opening up of sexuality in British culture, the novel was allowed in the country in 1960. The story of this novel revolves around the relationship between an upper-class young married woman and the working-class gamekeeper who works for the estate owned by her husband. In fact, at that time, such relationship was considered a challenge to the prevailing social fabric of society. The defenders of this novel argue that the theme of *Lady Chatterley's Lover* is not the sexual passages that were the subject of such debate, but the search for integrity and wholeness.

11 F. R. Leavis, in full Frank Raymond Leavis, born July 14, 1895, Cambridge, Cambridgeshire, England, died April 14, 1978, Cambridge, English literary critic who championed seriousness and moral depth in literature and criticized what he considered the amateur belletrism of his time. See Adam Augustyn, "F. R. Leavis," in *Encyclopaedia Britannica*, last updated April 10, 2023, https://www.britannica.com/biography/F-R-Leavis.

sions, a variety of arguments were presented, both for and against this novel. Professor Leavis was a very strong defender of Lawrence. To put forward his arguments, Leavis wrote two books, one called *The Great Tradition*, while the other with the title *D. H. Lawrence: Novelist* was completely devoted to the study of this author. Interestingly, in the 1960s, in parallel to Cambridge University, similar discussions were also going on in Professor Ashraf's class in Karachi University. No doubt, such open discussions in a relaxed environment made his class very lively and informative. Although he did not agree with everything his students said, this was a very useful and practical teaching and learning environment which everyone enjoyed. "He was an affectionate and caring person," said Professor Ali, "He was a man of few words as he did not talk much, although it is generally said that teachers are professional talkers."

Professor Ashraf was a religious devotee and a practising mystic. He was a prominent *murīd*[12] of Baba Zaheen Shah Taji (1902–1978). There were some other leading intellectuals of Karachi including Professor M. M. Ahmad[13] who also belonged to the same religious circle. On several occasions, Professor Amjad Ali also visited Baba Zaheen Shah. He said that those religio-spiritual gatherings used to take place on Tuesday evenings followed by *maḥfil-e samā*[14] to be continued until late into the night. In spite of late-night sittings, on Wednesday morning, Professor Ashraf was always fresh to take up his class. In fact, he maintained a good balance between both sides of his life, i.e., an academic as well as a mystic. Keeping this balance was helped by the fact that he belonged to a religio-academic family due to which such characteristics were in his blood.

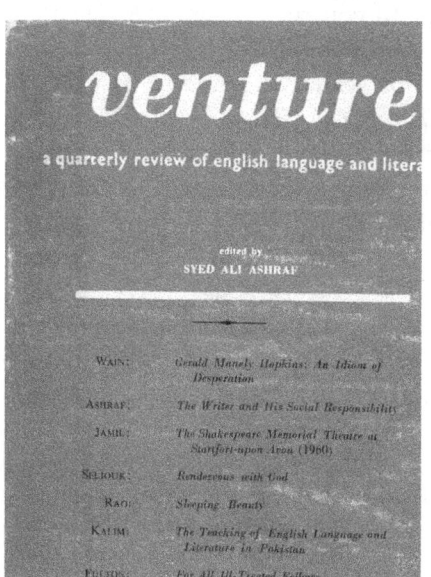

During his stay at Karachi University, Professor Ashraf also used to publish a journal called *Harvest*. This was mainly a student magazine as most of the contributions to this journal were from them. Unfortunately, after his departure from Karachi University, the magazine did not continue. As mentioned earlier, in addition to *Harvest*, he also used to publish a highly reputed literary journal named *Venture*. The quality of this journal can be judged from the fact that

---

12 *Murīd* is a specific term used in Islamic religious context which means a follower or disciple.
13 Professor M. M. Ahmad was Head of the Philosophy Department and was senior to Professor Ashraf.
14 Specific gatherings in which religious songs are sung to music and/or drums.

distinguished British and American intellectuals also used to contribute to it. These academic, literary and religious activities always kept Professor Ashraf extremely busy, and he had to manage a variety of activities simultaneously. His hard work combined with his academic excellence made him popular in intellectual circles in and outside of Pakistan. "This was the reason," said Professor Amjad Ali, "that once Stephen Spender,[15] a famous English poet, novelist and essayist who wrote mainly on themes of social injustice and the class struggle, came to visit Professor Ashraf in Karachi." In fact, it was his fantastic personality and professional expertise which created an exciting literary atmosphere in the Department of English. These were the qualities due to which he was highly respected among his colleagues.

Professor Zubair Bin Umar Siddiqui

Professor Zubair Siddiqui completed his M.A. in English in 1962 from the University of Sind. He started his professional life by joining Government College Sukkur as a Lecturer in English. With its very strong English Department, it was a well-established institution. He taught in this college for six years and then moved to England where he stayed for a period of two years. Later, he went to Saudi Arabia in 1969 and joined the Ministry of Education as an Inspector of Schools. After working elsewhere in the country, he then transferred to Makkah where he started teaching English.

Zubair Siddiqui

Professor Siddiqui revealed that his relationship with Professor Ali Ashraf started in Makkah as a neighbour. This was the time when, after leaving Pakistan, Professor Ashraf joined Umm al-Qura University.[16] Afterward, his cousin Syed Sajjad Husain[17] also joined him in Makkah. They all lived in different apartments of the same building and used to go to the same mosque. Interestingly, it can be considered a coincidence that during the early 1970s, two other prominent Pakistani intellectuals, i.e., Professor Jalil ud-Din Khan[18] and Professor Ghulam Ali Chaudhary,[19] both friends of Professor Ashraf, also joined him in

---

15 Stephen Spender had a strong interest in politics and declared himself a socialist and pacifist. In 1937, along with the International Brigades, he joined the Spanish Civil War. Harry Pollitt, the then Secretary General of the Communist Party of Great Britain, said to Spender: "Go and get killed; we need a Byron in the movement." Spender wrote of his experience of the war in his poems. In 1970, he joined University College London as a Professor of English and remained there for seven years.
16 At that time, this university was at an early stage of its formation.
17 Professor of English and former Vice Chancellor of Rajshahi and Dhaka universities in Bangladesh. See Appendix 2 of this book for his relationship with Professor Ashraf.
18 The then Head of the Department of English, University of Sind.
19 The then Head of the Department of English, University of Punjab.

Makkah. Obviously, such a gathering turned into a circle of friends. Professor Siddiqui, being the youngest in the group, always took pleasure in helping and serving his colleagues.

One thing which he particularly appreciates about Professor Ashraf is that despite his exceptional skill in the English language, high level of academic professionalism and expertise in Islamic studies, he was an extremely simple as well as a soft-spoken and kind-hearted man. He was a straightforward person and always preferred to wear traditional dress, eat with his hands, rather than using a knife and fork, and sit on the floor wherever it was possible. However, his humbleness, simplicity and softness never created any hurdle in his professionalism and expression. This can be judged from the situation that whenever he was talking in a professional or academic context, it seemed that he was a different person. Professor Ashraf had an open personality and in the case of religion, he never hid his close association with a specific line of *Taṣawwuf*.[20] Unfortunately, his religious line was not compatible with the Saudi Arabian government's official religious policy which is mainly based on the Salafī school of thought. Therefore, this difference created some problems for him during his stay in that country.

"As a neighbour, a close friend and a five-times-daily prayer fellow," said Professor Siddiqui, "I found him an outstanding person." Interestingly, in addition to a strong element of Islamic culture in his life, some reflections of Bengali traditions could also be traced in his personality. He continuously maintained these things throughout his life. Professor Siddiqui continued: "I was much junior to Professor Ashraf and due to his personal and professional qualities, I always had a great respect for him in my mind. I would also like to highlight the point that he worked so hard in his profession that his English lectures and writings were as good as a native scholar of this language."

Professor Manzoor Ahmad

Manzoor Ahmad

Professor Manzoor Ahmad's specialisation is Philosophy, and he has been teaching in Karachi for a number of years. Presently he holds two titles, i.e., Chairman, Executive Board, Usman Institute of Technology (Hamdard University, Karachi) and Rector, International Islamic University, Islamabad. He said as a joke: "Now if someone asks me what I do, my usual reply is that I am an engineer—engineer of education." In collaboration with Hakim Mohammed Said,[21] Professor

---

20 Spiritual and philosophical path of saints—a source of spiritual purification.
21 Hakim Mohammed Said (1920–1998) was a renowned scholar and physician of herbal indigenous medicines in Pakistan. He was the Governor of Sind province and established Hamdard Foundation in 1948. Hakim Said wrote numerous books and papers and

Ahmad was intensively involved in establishing some reputed educational institutions in Pakistan, such as Hamdard University of which he was the Founding Vice Chancellor. In addition, he also played an invaluable role in establishing Baqai Medical University, Karachi as well as the Usman Institute of Technology which is an engineering college with its focus on micro-engineering.[22]

Professor Ahmad was a close friend of Hakim Mohammed Said and Professor Ali Ashraf for a long time. He revealed that Hakim Said and Professor Ashraf knew each other from the late1960s. Professor Ahmad and Hakim Said were in Makkah and one day after morning prayer, Hakeem Said said that they should establish a university in Karachi. Professor Ahmad offered his full cooperation in this proposed project. Later on, they discussed this idea with several other intellectuals including Professor Ali Ashraf who was also very interested in this project. Professor Ahmad said that he knew Professor Ashraf very well although he was not his student; rather, he was a student of Professor M. M. Ahmad who was the professor of Philosophy and a close friend of Professor Ashraf at the University of Karachi. He passed his M.A. in Philosophy in 1955 and since 1956, when Professor Ashraf joined Karachi University, he had been meeting him mostly along with Professor M. M. Ahmad. In addition to his academic excellence and professional activities, Professor M. M. Ahmad was deeply interested in mysticism and was the disciple of Baba Yusuf Shah Taji.

Khānqāh Tājīyah

After the demise of Baba Yusuf Shah Taji, he continued his attachment with Baba Zaheen Shah Taji. Baba Zaheen Shah Taji was the successor of Baba Yusuf Shah Taji and was a very learned man.[23] With the passage of time, Professor M. M. Ahmad developed his mystic capabilities and influenced prominent people around him such as Professor Ashraf. Professor Ashraf was deeply involved in mysticism due to which he later became a *Khalīfah*[24] of Baba Zaheen Shah Taji. Baba Zaheen Shah Taji started a monthly magazine called *Tāj* published by *Khānqāh Tājīyah*.[25] The magazine had two sections, Urdu and English. Professor Ashraf used to be the editor of the Eng-

---

established Hamdard University in 1991.
22 Usman Institute of Technology (UIT) became a university—UIT University—in 2017.
23 Baba Zaheen Shah Taji was the *Khalīfah* of Baba Yusuf Shah Taji. After the death of Baba Yusuf Shah Taji, Baba Zaheen Shah Taji took over the position.
24 In mystic circles, the *Khalīfah* of a saint is considered a special representative of the saint.
25 Taji mystic institution based at the Taji *Khānqāh* is primarily a building for the gathering of a spiritual brotherhood for spiritual and educational training.

lish section. The magazine is still published today. *Khānqāh Tājīyah* also published several other books on religion.

Professor Manzoor Ahmad particularly highlighted the point that Professor Ashraf was a sweet and soft-spoken person and never raised his voice, nor did he ever enter into a warring argument with anybody. He always expressed himself in the shortest possible sentences. Professor Ahmad further said that: "I have very pleasant memories of Professor Ashraf. Once I also met him in Cambridge when he had settled there. He was a special man—a man of culture and human moral values—who impressed me." He further states that he never saw Professor Ashraf wearing a three-piece suit; rather, he was always seen in a Sherwānī[26] with a cap on his head. Professor Ahmad also narrates that after completing his M.A. in Philosophy, he started to teach in the same department. Coincidently, the Department of Philosophy and the Department of English were in close proximity due to which he used to see Professor Ashraf quite often. In addition, there was also a close circle of friends in Karachi University of which Professor M. M. Ahmad and Professor Ashraf were important members.

Syed Hasan Mutahar

Syed Hasan Mutahar graduated from Aligarh Muslim University, India and has worked in various institutions in Pakistan and Saudi Arabia. Presently, he is retired but still holds two prominent titles, i.e., an Advisor to the Muslim World League and Vice President of The Muslim World Almanac Research and Documentation Society in Makkah. He had known Professor Ali Ashraf since 1960, formally as well as informally. In 1960, Syed Mutahar went to London where he started to publish a newspaper titled, *Muslim News International*. He revealed that Naseem Ahmad, who later became the Secretary of Information, Government of Pakistan, was an advisor to this journal. However, because Ahmad did not have a strong ideological approach with regard to this journal, Syed Mutahar invited Professor Ashraf to participate in publishing this paper. At that time, Professor Ashraf was doing his Ph.D. at Cambridge University.

Syed Hasan Mutahar

In 1973, Syed Mutahar settled in Makkah where he worked as an editor for two newspapers published by the Muslim World League. He revealed that when Professor Ashraf came to Saudi Arabia, he stayed with him before get-

---

26 A long traditional coat which has been commonly used by South Asian Muslim men. Nowadays, due to the sweeping waves of globalisation which have significantly eroded several local cultures and norms, the tradition of wearing Sherwānī has more or less disappeared.

ting his own apartment. Later, he remained his neighbour throughout his stay in Makkah. In Syed Mutahar's view, Professor Ashraf was a reputed and respected person, both in the perspective of his professionalism and because of his Islamic thought. He had a strong religious belief, led a simple pious life and was very regular in offering his daily prayers. He had short beard and used to wear an Islamic cap. Many people in Karachi viewed him as the future Dean and Vice Chancellor of the University. He closely observed the events which led to the breakaway of East Pakistan from its West wing. He felt that there was a considerable socio-economic difference between the two parts of the country and that the East wing was not given its due share in administering the country. He used to feel uncomfortable about this situation.

In Syed Mutahar's view, Professor Ashraf possessed a polite and compassionate personality. He was a very hard-working person. In his conversation, he always used a minimum but adequate number of words. No doubt this was his art of speaking. He also said that, in 1977, Professor Ashraf's role in conducting the First World Conference on Muslim Education in Makkah was highly appreciated throughout the Islamic World. Due to such a noble work, he was also respected in the royal family of Saudi Arabia. Later on, at the time of his departure from Saudi Arabia, it was his reputation which enabled him to attract funds for establishing the Islamic Academy in Cambridge.

Syed Mutahar mentioned sadly that during Professor Ashraf's stay in Saudi Arabia, there were some people who complained about him to the Saudi authorities that he was a Sufi and was against the philosophy of Muhammad ibn Abd al-Wahhab.[1] It was the feeling of Professor Ashraf that some of the sympathisers of Jamaat-e-Islami[2] in Makkah were also involved in running a campaign against him. It was a hard time for him, and his employment contract was also not renewed by the concerned authorities. In this disappointing situation, Professor Ashraf wrote a letter of complaint to Sayyid Abul Ala Maududi[3] back in Pakistan in which he mentioned that a few people of his (Sayyid Maududi's) school of thought gave statements against him. Sayyid Abul Ala Maududi felt very uncomfortable by this situation and wrote two letters, one to Professor Ashraf in which he expressed his concern and sadness to him and another letter to the Saudi authorities clarifying that Professor Ashraf was an important Muslim scholar and a devoted educationist. It was due to the second letter that Professor Ashraf was reinstated in his position and remained there for a further few years.

---

1 Sheikh Muhammad ibn Abd al-Wahhab (1703–1792) was a prominent Arab theologian and scholar. The official religious policy of Saudi Arabian government is based mainly on his philosophy.
2 A religio-political party in Pakistan.
3 The author of numerous books and a famous politico-Islamic figure, Sayyid Abul Ala Maududi (1903–79) was a famous thinker. He was the founding chairman of Jamaat-e-Islami (an Islamic political party).

Syed Mutahar also happily shared that he had strong family ties with Professor Ashraf and also visited him in Cambridge. He regarded Professor Ashraf as a very pious man. Not only was he very regular in his five daily prayers, but he also used to offer *Tahajjud*[4] prayers on a regular basis. He was a great researcher and completed his various books during his stay in Saudi Arabia. Most of his books were on education with their main focus on the regeneration of the education system in the Muslim World. Luckily, he was not alone in this struggle; rather, he enjoyed the full support and cooperation of his cousin Professor Syed Sajjad Husain who was also teaching English in the same university in Makkah.

Professor Rafat Karim

Rafat Karim

Professor Rafat Karim is a former Chairman of the Department of English, University of Karachi. He has been associated with this university for 33 years. Currently he is the Registrar and Dean of the Faculty of Arts and Social Sciences, Greenwich University, Karachi. He is also the founding President of the Shakespeare Association of Pakistan established in 1997.[5] The society is a registered non-profit making organisation and is a corporate member of the International Shakespeare Association which is based at Stratford-upon-Avon. Professor Karim stated that he joined the University's English Department in November 1972 and at that time Professor Ali Ashraf was the Chairman of the Department of English. He had known Professor Ashraf since 1963 when he was a B.A. Honours student. At that time Professor Ashraf was on study leave, working towards his Ph.D. at Cambridge University.

"Professor Ali Ashraf was a much-respected scholar not only within Karachi University but also in Karachi city," said Professor Karim. He was a short-statured person, who always wore Pakistani traditional dress, having a short beard along with the usual cap on his head. With these characteristics, his appearance and physique were purely Asian and Muslim. It was amazing to see that such a simple man was so perfect in speaking English. After his return to Karachi from Cambridge, he introduced a new M.A. programme in English Linguistics, and it happened to be the first time in the academic history of Pakistan that such an M.A. was available in the country. He was the first academic who introduced the concept of functional English in Pakistan. Professor

---

4   An optional/supererogatory prayer performed during the night. The best time for performing *Tahajjud* prayer is the last part of the night.
5   The achievements of the Association can be judged from the fact that within one year of its inception, it organised a very successful four-day international conference on Shakespeare.

Ashraf enjoyed a very good relationship with the British Council and with the assistance of the Council, he established a separate section for English Linguistics in the Department. In addition, he also established the first well-equipped laboratory of English teaching with its focus on phonetics and pronunciation. This programme has continued to date. Professor Ashraf also taught English literature, linguistics, poetry and Shakespeare.

Professor Karim said that group conflict is a feature common to all institutions; unfortunately, the Department of English at Karachi University was no exception in this regard. In this type of situation, the loyalties of junior staff also became divided.[6] It meant that either you were with Professor Ashraf or with the other camp. Professor Karim always tried to maintain a neutrality and to promote professional values due to which he earned enormous respect and appreciation in the mind of Professor Ashraf. This can be judged from the fact that when Professor Ashraf left Pakistan, he gave his classes to Professor Karim who was the most junior members of staff at the time. Professor Karim was proud of this appreciation and considered it a great honour.

Professor Karim regarded Professor Ali Ashraf as an extremely dignified and composed person. He knew the art of showing respect to others and earning respect from them. Many people liked to be in his company. Junior members of staff and students always felt comfortable and relaxed in his meetings. Professor Karim also said that in a short period of time, he and Professor Ashraf developed a cordial family relationship. He recalled that during 1973, when Professor Ashraf's sister-in-law Selina[7] got married, he (Professor Ashraf) requested him to spare his car for a few days. This was a brand-new Vauxhall Victor car recently bought by Professor Karim's father. Professor Karim was pleased to offer his car as well as the services of his driver for the marriage ceremony. By the same token, he recalled that in 1993, when he went to Cambridge University for a seminar on Shakespeare, Professor Ashraf warmly received him, and he was humbled by his hospitality.

Professor Sharif al Mujahid

Professor Sharif al Mujahid's specialisation is journalism and mass communication. In 1955, he joined Karachi University as Assistant Professor and taught there until 1976. He is named as a "Distinguished National Professor" by the Higher Education Commission of Pakistan and is also the Honorary Director of the Archives of Freedom Movement, University of Karachi. He established the Department of Journalism at the International Islamic University, Malaysia; Department of Journalism at Karachi University and Quaid-i-Azam Academy, an autonomous institution at Karachi which conducts research on

---

6 Professor Karim said that this division was purely based on personal and professional rivalry, and it had nothing to do with ethno-linguistic backgrounds.
7 Selina used to live with Professor Ashraf and his wife, Asia.

Mohammad Ali Jinnah, the founder of Pakistan. He is the author of many books, monographs, reports, research papers and articles for various encyclopaedias. Due to his exceptional academic contributions over five decades, he has been awarded the Aizaz-i-Kamal/Fazilat in 2001, and Sitara-i-Imtiaz in 2006 by the Government of Pakistan.[8]

Professor Mujahid informed me that he knew Professor Ali Ashraf when he arrived at Karachi University in 1956. His greatest assets were his English accent as well as his doctorate from Cambridge. In his view, he was a more religious person as compared to his elder brother, Professor Syed Ali Ahsan, although both had a short beard.[9] However, in contrast, Syed Ali Ahsan—who was head of the department of Bengali of University of Karachi—was more social and cultural in his personality. Professor Mujahid also disclosed that professionally and socially he was very close to Professor Ashraf and Professor Ahsan. Both brothers lived side by side in Nazimabad No. 2. At that time, there was an organisation named "Congress for Cultural Freedom" founded by Stephen Spender. Professor Ashraf and Syed Ahsan[10] were its active members and they established its office in the same building. The Congress regularly published a monthly journal called *Encounter*. It is worth mentioning that most of the present buildings and blocks of Karachi University were constructed during the 1960s. Prior to that, various departments of social sciences were in congested commercial areas of the city. As the Department of Journalism and the Department of English were quite close to each other, he had many chances to meet Professor Ashraf most evenings.

Sharif al Mujahid

Professor Mujahid particularly highlighted the point that due to his extraordinarily compassionate personality Professor Ashraf made a lot of friends all over the world. In his view, during his early life, Professor Ashraf was a modern progressive person and used to wear a three-piece suit. However, with the passage of time, he changed a great deal. This can be judged from the fact that afterwards, he always wore traditional dress along with a cap on his head. In 1985, Professor Mujahid went to Cambridge for a research project and stayed in Professor Ashraf's house for a day. The last time Professor Mujahid met him was in 1992 in Kuala Lumpur where he came for a viva at the University of Malaya. At that time, he wore an Arab dress. When Professor Mujahid

---

8 https://archives.sindhculture.gov.pk/shariful_mujahid/
9 As mentioned above, Syed Ali Ahsan was the head of Bengali Department at Karachi University and retained this position until 1960. Afterwards, he went to Dhaka where he was appointed the Director of Bangla Academy.
10 With its main office in Paris, the Congress was an international non-profit making organisation. Syed Ali Ahsan was very active in this Congress and was made its Secretary General.

asked him about this change in his dress, he replied with his usual smile: "It's easy and comfortable."

A Short Visit to the Mystic World

As I have mentioned earlier, it was a great pleasure for me to meet former colleagues and friends of Professor Ashraf who, in fact, are also the most senior intellectuals of Pakistan. However, despite these exciting meetings, my satisfaction was incomplete until I explored some aspects of his mystic life. For this reason, I wanted to visit the *Khānqāh* of the late Baba Zaheen Shah Taji and meet the present *Gaddī Nashīn*. The *Khānqāh* is situated in Mewashah[11] graveyard which is close to the Lyari River. This is the biggest and the oldest graveyard of the city and has immense historical significance. Interestingly, in this graveyard, different faith communities[12] have reserved their specific sections for burials. Therefore, Mewashah can be considered a composition of several small graveyards.

Baba Zaheen Shah Taji

Historically, the area in which this graveyard is situated had been considered a relatively up-market locality in the city. However, unfortunately at present, due to its high level of deprivation and crime, this is one of the most neglected and underprivileged areas of Karachi. During my stay in Karachi, I asked a few taxi drivers to take me there, but none of them was willing to do so because of security concerns. I thought about how the time had changed. It had not been risky to go there during Professor Ashraf's time. Anyway, after continued efforts, I was able to find transport to go there. It was a Thursday morning and only a few people were there. The *Khānqāh* is situated at the edge of the graveyard and the amazing thing was that it was very well maintained. The present *Gaddī Nashīn*, Hazrat

Baba Atif Shah Taji

---

11 With regard to its name 'Mewashah,' it is said that during the colonial period, a saint called Syed Abdul Kabir (1715-1865) took up residence in Karachi. Since he used to distribute, among his devotees, all the fruit (*Mewah*) he received from his admirers, he came to be known as Mewashah.

12 These major communities are Bohris, Khoja Sunnat Jamaat, Junagarh Memon Jamaat, Saudagaran-e Delhi, Malabar Muslims, Ismailis and Okhai Memon Jamaat. It is noteworthy that in addition to the ordinary deceased, a large number of dignitaries and non-Muslims are also buried here, for instance, various Sufis and saints, Arabs, members of the royal family of Afghanistan, Christians and Jews.

Baba Atif Shah Taji sits there on each Tuesday morning. However, on my request, he honoured me and came especially to the *Khānqāh* to see me. Baba Atif is a young man and he had not met Professor Ashraf, although he knew of him well.

The Taji mystic chain is a branch of the Sunni School of thought and Syed Muhammad Tajuddin (1861-1925) was its founder. He was also commonly known as Tajuddin Baba, and was a descendent of Hazrat Ali, fourth of the "rightly guided" (*rāshidūn*) caliphs. He was born in Nagpur, India in 1861. At the age of 15, he completed his study of Arabic, Urdu, Persian, and English. He was a kind-hearted man and led an extremely simple life. At the time when Professor Ashraf was in Karachi, Baba Zaheen Shah Taji was the *Gaddī Nashīn*. Baba Zaheen Shah was a very learned man and extensively wrote on various issues. His most famous book entitled, *Tājul-Awliyāʾ* is on the life history and mystic philosophy of Tajuddin Baba. He also translated two important works of Ibn ʿArabī, *Fuṣūṣ-ul-Ḥikam* and *Al-Futūḥāt al-Makkiyyah* and Manṣūr al-Ḥallāj's *Kitāb-ut-Ṭawāsīn* in Urdu.

As mentioned earlier, Professor M. M. Ahmad, a close friend of Professor Ashraf was the head of the Department of Philosophy, University of Karachi.[13]

---

13 A brief overview of the life history and spiritual journey of Professor M. M. Ahmad can best be described in the words of Professor A. B. A. Haleem who was his uncle and had been Vice Chancellor of the University of Karachi and the University of Sind, and the Pro-Vice Chancellor of Aligarh Muslim University. He writes: "Muhammad Mahmood Ahmad was born in Bihar on 15th January 1906. In 1923, that is, at the age of 17, he passed his Matriculation Examination of the Patna University. His success at the Matriculation Examination was followed by two important events of his life. The first was a visit to Nagpur for the purpose of paying homage to Hazrat Baba Tajuddin (1861-1925). He remained at Nagpur for several days and obtained the blessings and benediction of the saint. There is a family tradition to the effect that Hazrat Baba Tajuddin entrusted Mahmood's spiritual training to another Pir who was none other than Hazrat Baba Yusuf Shah Taji. The Second event of note was his admission to the Aligarh Muslim University. He remained at Aligarh as a student from 1923 to 1930 and passed his I.A., B.A., M.A., and LL.B. examinations. During this period he came under the influence of Maulana Sulaiman Ashraf—a man of great learning and piety. Mahmood attended regularly the lectures which the Maulana used to deliver on *Tafsīr* and often visited him at his house and benefited from his conversation. . . . In 1944, he was appointed a civilian member of the 57 Service Selection Board and rendered valuable service in the selection of personnel for commission in the armed forces. When the board was wound up, he was appointed in 1946 as a Staff Officer (Major) in the Directorate of Education at GHQ India. In 1947, after the creation of Pakistan, he was transferred from GHQ to the post of Director of Education at Military Academy, Kakul, and was given the rank of Lt-Colonel. In 1952, he was appointed Reader in Philosophy at the University of Karachi and in 1955 was made a professor. As a Reader as well as Professor, he was the Chairman of the Department of Philosophy and had to build it up from scratch. He worked as Dean of the Faculty of Arts for four years and acted as Vice Chancellor of the university between 1961 to 1965 for various periods. Before finishing his career as a teacher, he held the Agha Khan Chair of Islamic Studies at the American University of Beirut for two years (1965-67)." See: Abu Bakr Ahmad Haleem, "Muhammad Mahmood Ahmad—A

Due to his mystic belief, he was already associated with Baba Zaheen Shah Taji. With respect to age and professional career, Professor M. M. Ahmad was senior to Professor Ashraf. In fact, it was he who introduced Professor Ashraf to Baba Zaheen Shah Taji. In 1957, after performing his *Umrah*,[14] Professor M. M. Ahmad died in Jeddah and was buried in Makkah. In 1969, Baba Zaheen Shah published his memorial volume, both in Urdu and English. During my visit to Karachi, I was given its copies. The English volume was edited by Professor Ashraf while the Urdu version was edited by Baba Zaheen Shah Taji.[15] In the English volume, Professor Ashraf says:

> We [Professor Ashraf and Professor M. M. Ahmad] met again in 1956[16] when I joined Karachi University as a Head of the Department of English. When he became the Dean of the Faculty of Arts, our meetings became more frequent and I came to know him better. But our intimacy became deeper and my respect and love for him increased when he started taking a keen interest in my spiritual wellbeing. My spiritual guide had died in June 1957 when I was in America. It had so upset me that I had practically given up reading and writing and was spending most of my time in the mosque.... It was he who took me to Baba Zaheen Shah Taji Saheb and it was his considerate and loving company that helped me a great deal in regaining my balance and composure.[17]

Professor Ashraf further narrates: "He [Professor M. M. Ahmad] had devoted his whole life and energy towards the acquisition of Knowledge of God through his intellectual and his spiritual endeavours, and towards the use of his knowledge for the benefit of his fellow-beings. Thus he combined within himself both Marifat[18] and Shariat,[19] internal knowledge and external behaviour. This was possible because from the very beginning of his life, God had not only endowed him with the necessary ability but also given him adequate opportunity to transform himself into a real mystic."[20] In the view of Baba Za-

---

Memento," in *In Memory of Dr. M. M. Ahmad: Reminiscences and Reflections*, ed. Syed Ali Ashraf (Karachi: Taj Publications, 1969), 17–20.

14 Lesser pilgrimage to Makkah.
15 I am thankful to Professor Manzoor Ahmad and the *Khānqāh* for providing me English and Urdu volumes of this publication, respectively.
16 It was in 1953 that Professor Ashraf met Professor M. M. Ahmad for the first time in a conference held in Dhaka.
17 Syed Ali Ashraf, ed., *In Memory of Dr. M. M. Ahmad: Reminiscences and Reflections* (Karachi: Taj Publications, 1969), 85–92. Baba Zaheen Shah Taji was the chief editor of this memorial volume. It can be safely said that as the editor of this publication, Professor Ashraf also chose its title. In this perspective, I personally liked the same wordings for the title of this chapter.
18 *Ma'rifah*, the mystical intuitive knowledge of spiritual truth.
19 *Sharī'ah*, the Islamic law governing all aspects of life.
20 Ashraf, *In Memory of Dr. M. M. Ahmad*, 3–4. Professor Ashraf further states that: "At

heen Shah Taji, "Dr had truly submitted his being, his intellectual and emotional self to the will of Allah. His whole being had thus became Islamic and all discrepancy between his thought and action had disappeared.... While joining the University of Karachi, he had laid down a condition, which was accepted by the Syndicate that if he ever took a loan from the university, he would not pay any interest on it, nor would he take any interest on the provident fund that he would get after his retirement."[21]

Muhammad Mahmood Ahmad

Similar views are also expressed by Seyyed Hossein Nasr, who says: "Dr. M. M. Ahmad lived a life of inner purity and died as a *Mu'min*.[22] Although, his loss is very great both for Pakistan and the world of Islam, his life was successful in that he lived according to principles and thus inspired all those who came to know him as a teacher or friend. And finally, in the 'House of the Beloved,' he found Beloved whom he sought all of his life."[23] Professor Manzoor Ahmad revealed that, "One of the subjects which Dr. M. M. Ahmad taught with great interest was Philosophy of Religion to his final year students of M.A. He himself was deeply involved in this subject... Though he very strongly believed in what he taught, he was not authoritative in his approach. He always invited his students and listeners to think for themselves."[24] These views highlight that the religio-mystic factor was dominant in Professor M. M. Ahmad's personality,[25] and that this was the spiritual base due to which Professor

---

Aligarh, he [Professor Ahmad] came in contact with two eminent scholars devoted to Islam: Maulana Sulaiman Ashraf and Professor Zafar Hasan. At an early age, he had gone to get the blessings of Baba Tajuddin. It was not surprising that his spiritual training would ultimately be in the hands of Baba Tajuddin's most beloved disciple, Baba Yusuf Shah Taji and then his disciple, Baba Zaheen Shah Taji."

21 Baba Zaheen Shah Taji, "Dr. Ahmad—A Saint," in *In Memory of Dr. M. M. Ahmad*, 5–15. This article was originally written in Urdu and then translated into English by Kazi A. Kadir.
22 *Mu'min* is an Arabic term means a "believer" in Islam.
23 Ashraf, *In Memory of Dr. M. M. Ahmad*, 25–27.
24 Ashraf, 93–102.
25 Ashraf, 32–34. Another important and interesting point about Professor M. M. Ahmad is revealed by Syed Amiruddin Qidvai. He narrates: "True, the name of Pakistan was coined by Chowdhry Rehmat Ali and is associated with him. But few know that Mahmood Bhai [Professor M. M. Ahmad] and Dr. Mohammad Afzal Hussain Qadri, Dean, Faculty of Sciences, Karachi University, were intimately associated with Chowdhry Rehmat Ali's

Ashraf, Professor M. M. Ahmad and Baba Zaheen Shah Taji were very close to each other.

Intellectual Excellence of Professor Ashraf

The above discussion presents various reflections on Professor Ashraf's life. It highlights a number of dimensions of his personality, particularly his high level of human and moral values, academic eminence, expertise in research, reforming the educational system of Muslim countries and, his spiritual thoughts and practices. No doubt, on the whole, all these factors also reflect his intellectual excellence. Here, at the conclusion of this chapter, I would like to re-visit his monograph referred to earlier in which he says: "The aim of education, according to the *ummah* in general, is to produce a good Muslim who is both cultured and expert—cultured in the sense that he knows how to use knowledge for his spiritual, intellectual and material progress, and expert in the sense that he is a useful member of the community."[26] An important question which arises here is: how can such objectives be achieved? In his view: "a hierarchy of knowledge has to be established. All branches of knowledge are not of equal status. Spiritual knowledge has the highest priority. As morality is based on that knowledge, as it governs Man's individual and collective behaviour, and as material progress depends on basic universal values, knowledge of moral values is next in importance. Then comes intellectual knowledge, or knowledge that leads to the discipline of intellect. Knowledge that controls and disciplines human imagination, and knowledge that helps Man to gain control over bodily senses, follow."[27]

While emphasising the importance of this issue, he says:

> Education is a purposeful activity directed to the full development of individuals. A norm of values is therefore essential in all educational planning, be that norm secularist or humanist or Marxist or religious. Islam provides an objective norm for all educationists. 'Is-

---

work. The three of them were instrumental in getting inserted a note on Pakistan into the *Encyclopaedia Britannica*. Chowdhry Rehmat Ali was in constant correspondence with Mahmood Bhai and often sought his advice on matters of mutual interest. My first meeting with Chowdhry Rehmat Ali took place when he was staying at Mahmood Bhai's house in Aligarh . . . . I would be failing in my duty if I do not relate, for the purpose of keeping the records straight, that it was Mahmood Bhai (Afzal Bhai and I were also with him) who had explained the Pakistan plan to Quaid-i-Azam Mohammad Ali Jinnah at Meerut in March in 1939. Later we were called to Bombay by Quaid-i-Azam to present the plan in all its details at the meeting of the Muslim League. The Quaid-i-Azam liked it and having weighed all the pros and cons of the matter, he allowed the Pakistan Resolution to be moved at the Lahore session of the All-India Muslim League. Seven years later Pakistan was born."

26 Ashraf, *New Horizons in Muslim Education*, 39.
27 Ashraf, 51.

lamic education,' I said in my introduction to *Crisis in Muslim Education*, 'is an education which trains the sensibility of pupils in such a manner that in their attitude to life, their actions and decisions and approach to all kinds of knowledge, they are governed by the deeply felt ethical values of Islam.'[28]

He further argued that, "If Muslim society can tackle these problems, the secularised West will definitely revise their conclusions about 'secularism' and think again and thus find a new, more fruitful, dimension in their intellectual, emotional and social process in order to save their society from total disintegration."[29] This argument clearly indicates that the term 'Islamic Education' does not just mean the teaching of the Qurʾān, Ḥadīth and Fiqh;[30] rather, it encompasses the teaching of all disciplines in line with Islamic principles. This was the vision of Professor Ashraf which he attempted to propagate throughout the Muslim World.

Bibliography

Ashraf, Syed Ali, ed. *In Memory of Dr. M. M. Ahmad: Reminiscences and Reflections*. Karachi: Taj Publications, 1969.

Ashraf, Syed Ali. *New Horizons in Muslim Education*. Cambridge: The Islamic Academy, 1985.

Augustyn, Adam. "F. R. Leavis." In *Encyclopaedia Britannica*. Last updated April 10, 2023. https://www.britannica.com/biography/F-R-Leavis.

Baba Zaheen Shah Taji. "Dr. Ahmad—A Saint." In *In Memory of Dr. M. M. Ahmad: Reminiscences and Reflections*. Karachi: Taj Publications, 1969.

Haleem, Abu Bakr Ahmad. "Muhammad Mahmood Ahmad—A Memento." In *In Memory of Dr. M. M. Ahmad: Reminiscences and Reflections*. Karachi: Taj Publications, 1969.

Lawrence, David Herbert. *Lady Chatterley's Lover* (Florence: Privately Printed by the Tipografia Giuntina, 1928).

Nasr, Seyyed Hossein. Foreword to *New Horizons in Muslim Education*, by Syed Ali Ashraf. Cambridge: The Islamic Academy, 1985.

---

28 Ashraf, 24.
29 Ashraf, 1.
30 Islamic jurisprudence, an elaboration of Islamic law which is based on the Qurʾān and Ḥadīth.

Chapter 35

Professor Syed Ali Ashraf: A True Believer

Rhoda Jal Vania

"Why do you always wear cotton saris?"
"Why, what's wrong with wearing cotton saris? I would have thought that as a Bengali, you would approve."
"Oh yes, I do! In your application you said you were a Zoroastrian by faith, and I am told that young women from your community, as from the Christian community, mostly wear dresses."

"The reason," I said, "is my living in East Pakistan for a few years when my father was posted there some years ago. I found these cottons beautiful, cheap and very comfortable for our climate. So I have continued wearing them after returning to Karachi."

"Ah! That's good," he said. "You wear them like a Bengali girl. I will call you my Bengali student in the department."

With this conversation, a few days after I joined the Department of English at the University of Karachi in 1956 to do my Masters, started a long friendly association with Mr Ashraf as we called him then. He had arrived in Karachi a few weeks earlier from East Pakistan to head the English Department at this new Federal University.[1] Soon he invited me to meet his wife and young school-going sister-in-law.[2] The childless couple had brought her to live with them in Karachi and though they never adopted her officially, Selina was to prove to be more than a real daughter to them until the end of their lives. "They do not know Karachi or many people here and would welcome your friendship, advice and help," he told me. My parents were also glad to meet them and add them to our list of Bengali friends in Karachi. By the time I left

---

1 University of Karachi was established through the parliament as a Federal University in 1951.
2 Her name is Selina. See Muhammad Abdul Jabbar Beg, "Reflections on the Life of Syed Ali Ashraf: Based on an Interview with His Sister-in-Law, Mrs Selina Ali," Chapter 32 of this book on her memories of Professor Ashraf.

the University two years later, a close friendship had been forged between the two families, as we found we had many interests in common.

I also found that some friends in East Pakistan, who had later become his students, spoke glowingly of him as a teacher of literature. I was to discover this myself also. Sensitive to literature, he not only taught literature but also enjoyed literature and wanted his students to enjoy it also. He was always ready to 'talk' literature even outside classes. He read literature well and like me enjoyed reading his favourite poems and passages from drama and prose aloud. These sessions remain a happy memory from that period. I often wished later that he had continued to concentrate on teaching literature, perhaps a selfish wish, because it was my prime interest. But by the time I began to teach in the department a few years later, Mr Ashraf's energies were shared by other interests.

The two new contending interests were education and Islam, and the two were closely connected. They were the result of Professor Ashraf's attempt to address the problems around him. He had taken over a small, new department which had been functioning in a makeshift manner in makeshift premises for about two years before he arrived. The conditions were very different from what he had known in East Pakistan. The students who varied in age and background were different too. Most of them had lost precious years during the upheavals at the time of the Partition of India and came from families who had been battered in one way or another. As a result, many like me, were working part-time to meet educational expenses. Professor Ashraf also discovered that very few were there for the pure love of literature. In those days a certain prestige was attached to a Master of Arts in English and students who intended to enter the civil or foreign services, join multinationals, or even go into professions such as law very often completed this degree for the purposes of a basic liberal education. This was a legacy of the British period.

However, the world had changed radically since the Partition of India and so had our educational needs. Most teachers in the English Departments had studied literature before the Partition under British professors. Bewildered by this new crop of students and falling standards they generally felt that before long the English Departments would become departments where foreign literature would be taught in translation or be closed down. The government and popular uninformed opinion wanted to replace the colonial language with Urdu in all sectors. The staff therefore tried to maintain standards and roll along as well as they could.

Professor Ashraf was not a person who would just roll along. Like some others he believed that neither could English be abandoned completely nor was it desirable to do so. Urdu was not the mother tongue of the majority and not all Pakistanis could use it comprehensibly. As a responsible academic and Head of the English Department of Pakistan's only Federal University he thought it was his duty to tackle this important and complex problem in the best interest of education in the country. He made no hasty or egocentric decisions. He started by visiting educational institutions at all levels. He studied the syllabi, talked to English teachers and even observed classes. The falling standards, the very large classes and the government's disinterested ignorance had resulted in a feeling of helplessness and frustration amongst the teachers of English in schools and colleges and they were anxious that their problems be addressed. They therefore welcomed Professor Ashraf's suggestion that as a first step an English Teachers Association be formed immediately. His Bengali background made him more aware of the need to retain the English language and he wanted to make sure that it was taught and learnt properly. Many Bengalis spoke a little Urdu but hardly any West Pakistani spoke or understood Bengali. The only means of communication between the two wings of Pakistan both at the official and individual levels was very often English. The disastrous emotional decision to declare Urdu as the only national language had resulted in violent rioting[3] which Professor Ashraf had observed at close quarters in East Pakistan. The language problem thus touched every facet of national life and if it was not handled carefully and correctly it would destroy the educational fabric we had inherited at the time of the Partition and make it impossible to formulate a proper educational policy for the future.

Professor Ashraf was not an influential man, nor did he have any financial backing. In fact, to some extent, he was an outsider. It was through sheer hard work and sound honest thinking that he achieved what he did. In West Pakistan, his department started a language programme and established the first language laboratory with modern equipment with the help of the British Council. Teachers were sent to language training centres abroad for training and the English syllabus was revised. The language problems were not solved before he left Pakistan. Because of the incorrect policies of the government, they remain unsolved even thirty years after Professor Ashraf's departure from Pakistan.[4] It goes to Professor Ashraf's credit that in the fifties he moved in the right direction and created an awareness of the magnitude of the problem. He also, in a way, sacrificed his own career in literature for what he thought was the greater good.

It is at this point that he also turned to a more formal study of his religion because the educational issues that filled his mind were those of Muslim education. He noticed a growing decline in character and morality and in order to check this through education he wanted to make sure that he drew the correct conclusions and so made the correct decisions. Always a good Muslim, Professor Ashraf had never been a conservative or radical Islamist and disapproved of fanatics. I remember his once asking me complainingly why people thought he was a *Mawlānā*.[5] I had said jokingly that it might be because he kept a beard at

---

3   The Language Movement of East Bengal/East Pakistan.
4   This chapter was written in 2001.
5   Lit. "our master." Especially in Bangladesh, India and Pakistan the word *Mawlānā* is used

a young age when not many people grew beards. He laughed and confided that he had not grown it for religious reasons. Continuing honestly, he explained that he had a very boyish face and was afraid his students would not take him seriously when he started teaching university students. He found that a beard made him look older, so he had kept one from then on. Professor Ashraf was not a religious ascetic either. He appreciated the beautiful and good things in life and believed in Keats maxim: "Beauty is Truth, Truth Beauty."[6] He said he had studied English Literature because of its excellence and because he had found its concerns universally moral. He believed this study had improved his moral judgment and saw morality as the end of all religious and literary study. That is why when he turned to a more profound study of Islam, he chose the Sufi tradition and as his mentor a religious scholar who was also a good poet and one of the most intelligent men I have met.[7]

Professor Ashraf never did anything by halves. Once he had chosen the work on which to expend his future energies and found a person who could guide him in this work, he became immersed in this work. These new interests formed a powerful convergence of divine and pragmatic values that were to remain a diving force for the rest of his life. His faith in God and his mentor who was to pilot the way to the sacred goals he had chosen became unshakable. I remember an incident in late 1964 which illustrates this faith in a frightening manner. One morning he got up for *Fajr* prayers,[8] slipped and had a bad fall. When I reached the University to teach an 8 a.m. class I was told what had happened and that Mrs Ashraf wanted me to go to their house on the campus immediately. I found him in a semi-conscious state. The University doctor had visited and said the head injury had caused a cerebral haemorrhage and asked Mrs Ashraf to take him to a specialist in a Karachi hospital immediately. She was in tears as hours had passed and he was still at the campus, which was more than twelve miles away from the hospital. She did not drive, and no public transport was available. When I asked the reason why he was still not taken to hospital, she said that he had directed her to inform his religious brotherhood and do what his mentor advised. They had come immediately and pronounced that it was not a haemorrhage. They decided to start special prayers at their *mazār*[9] immediately and return soon. I ran back to the department for the help of colleagues who had by then arrived for classes. After much

---

    as an honorific title for a learned Muslim scholar educated in madrasah.
6 John Keats, "Ode on a Grecian Urn," *Annals of the Fine Arts*, vol. 4 (London: Sherwood, Neely & Jones, 1820), 639.
7 This was Baba Zaheen Shah Taji. See Muhammad Ahsan, "In Memory of Syed Ali Ashraf: Reminiscences and Reflections," Chapter 34 of this book on this mentor of Professor Ashraf.
8 This is the first of the five mandatory Islamic prayers, to be performed anytime between the moment of dawn and the beginning of sunrise.
9 A *mazār* is a mausoleum or shrine, typically that of a saint or notable religious leader.

argumentation he was taken to the hospital after noon. The delay could have caused complications or worse.

Though a visionary, Professor Ashraf was also a very practical man, one could even say a worldly man with a natural human ambition of wanting to better his life and the lives of his family members and associates. To many, this seemed to run counter to his religiosity. But his absolute faith in God and the prophets and saints had led him into understanding that God prevents any conflict between the spiritual and the pragmatic in life. In time, his vision of a better life was increasingly founded on the moral beliefs of Islam. He did not create or want to create any utopias of his own. With complete faith he planned his work and every action in the light of Islamic teachings. If there was the slightest doubt regarding the legitimacy of any thought or desire it was squashed immediately. No attempt was made to justify it. No conflict was engendered. This total surrender of individual personality—and he had possessed a strong definable personality—became a self-willed process of annihilation as the years passed until many aspects of the nature of my old teacher of literature became unrecognisable.

In the late sixties I resigned from the University and a short time later went to the States for my doctorate. Soon afterwards the political upheaval in the country created a situation that made Professor Ashraf leave the department, first on long leave and then permanently when he saw there was not going to be any early end to the turmoil. He resigned for personal reasons and moved to England, a country he had come to love. Since his student days he had enjoyed the beauty of its countryside, its rich traditions of intellectual liberalism; the magnificent architecture of its old universities, aristocratic houses, churches, and cathedrals; its well-stocked libraries and bookstores. He was particularly fond of Cambridge where the Ashrafs eventually settled. He made me share his fondness for that peaceful and beautiful University town by giving me several guided tours of the place when I spent some days with them there. He used to say what many Muslims were to repeat, that he found it easier to be a good Muslim in England than in Pakistan. Mrs Ashraf had also trained there and after leaving Pakistan taught in a school in Cambridge until she retired. They had many friends there who helped him rescue a great many senior Bengali academicians trapped and nearly killed during the Bangladesh war of independence.

Though both the Ashrafs continued to write to me whenever they could, we met just a couple of times after the seventies and did not meet at all in the last ten years of his life. For this reason, I have dwelt only on those early years when I worked closely with them and came to know them well in Karachi. At that time, he was already a senior faculty member and seemed to have reached the top of the ladder by this appointment to the Federal University of Pakistan and being recognised countrywide as a good teacher, writer and administrator. But from this point in time nearly fifty years later it seems a transitional period in which he was preparing himself for what he was to achieve after he left Pakistan. The making of the man, the figure he became, should interest those who knew him only after this period as I would like to read of his later work about which I know very little. This account should show that what he achieved was predictable and not unexpected. He was set in that direction since the sixties.

There are two other reasons I have thought it fit to describe how and why there was such a change and shift in his life and professional interests. On the whole, we live in a very negative world and anybody as positive as Professor Ashraf with his indefatigable energy and drive would quite expectedly alienate some if not many. Our Professor had his share of detractors. Two observations, heard repeatedly since he left Karachi from a great many people, have bothered me for a long time because they are incorrect and unfair. Here, I would like to clarify these slurs in memory of my old teacher, colleague and friend to complete this account of those transitional years in his life. People have charged him of deserting his country and his profession for a better life and that he got involved with Saudi Arabia in order to exploit their newfound prosperity for his own self-interests. Anybody who really knew Professor Ashraf should know this is false and unjust. People had the right to disagree with his beliefs and work and even disassociate themselves from these. They had the right to disapprove of his enthusiasm and magnificent obsessions. But nobody had the right to accuse a man who was working towards positive goals of the insincerity and dishonesty implied in such observations. I would like to expand on what I have already been saying in order to remove these misconceptions.

Professor Ashraf did not desert his profession or Pakistan for gain and greener pastures. He did his utmost to stay and continue his work but conditions that he did not create were beyond his control. The break-up of the country and the sealing of the borders between Pakistan and the new Bangladesh where most of his family lived had made communication with the family, friends and old colleagues nearly impossible. They needed his help, as conditions there were really bad. He left to help others and not himself and did succeed in arranging for and extending considerable help to families in dire straits who might not have pulled through without this help. He did not leave for greener pastures either. He had no job in Cambridge and had to look after a house full of dependants. It was fortunate that Mrs Ashraf had a full-time teaching job. They all lived a Spartan life and Mrs Ashraf rationed the food to balance the budget. Though based in America, I was working on a part of my doctoral research at the British Museum during this period and was often in London. I could not help or even visit them often as I myself was trying to stay afloat doing odd jobs but was aware of what was going on. This was not only the time of the painful birth of Bangladesh but also of the Vietnam war and even affluent America was in a bind. Because of circumstances Professor Ashraf, like others had stepped out into a war-torn world full of hardships.

I also know that no large aid was promised by Saudi Arabia when he left Karachi and the security of a permanent job. Trying to build a new educational infrastructure in their country, the Saudis could offer temporary work to the academic refugees from Bengal. They really did not have suitable positions for these highly qualified people. I remember one of this group telling me that when they first went they had to share rooms and just had a bed, a table, a stool pretending to be a chair and a typewriter each. Most of what they earned was sent to their families. As there were no women in the household and their food budget was limited, they all had health problems. As soon as conditions improved, they returned to Bangladesh.

Professor Ashraf's association with Saudi Arabia continued because of his interest and experience of adapting and evolving a modern educational system in keeping with the religious and cultural values of an Islamic society. The Saudi Arabian government approved of his approach and ideas, more so than Pakistan ever had and employed him on contract to guide them whenever help was needed. There was therefore no change in the work he had been trying to do in Karachi, beyond the requirements of a different locale. In course of time this proved to be fortunate for Professor Ashraf because Saudi Arabia seemed to be more receptive to his ideas and appreciative of what he did for them. They supported him increasingly, yet he never settled there. If he made some money, he worked hard intelligently and deserved what he earned. He also ploughed back most of it in projects trying to improve the lives of Muslims worldwide through the correct kind of education in keeping with modern Islamic ideals.

It is sad that he had passed away suddenly before the affairs of the Islamic university[10] he founded in his native Bengal, the culmination of his life's work, were settled to his satisfaction. It was an enormous undertaking, which took his life, and one can only hope that the younger individuals he has trained succeed in accomplishing his mission, so that his efforts do not go to waste. It was his personal contribution to Muslim Education, which will always be remembered. May he now rest in eternal peace, the peace and rest he never allowed himself in this life. He will be missed by many Muslims and non-Muslims who valued the light of Knowledge, which in religious terms is eternal truth, as he did. All the prophets, philosophers and thinkers of the world have recognised this light of Knowledge as revealing and defining the essential nature of God.

---

10 This is Darul Ihsan University, Savar, Dhaka.

Chapter 36

Dr Syed Ali Ashraf: Memoirs of a Student

Farogh Naweed

I came to know Dr Syed Ali Ashraf when I spent two years to do my M.A. in English from the University of Karachi during the years 1956 to 1958. Dr Ashraf was the Head of the English Department, which in those earlier formative years of Pakistan, was housed in a derelict building in Nanak Wara area of Karachi near Khori Garden. All the four Departments of languages, including English, were housed in that building near the city courts. The other departments were that of Urdu, Arabic and Persian.

My first encounter with Dr Ashraf took place in a rather bizarre manner. I had done my graduation from Multan, my hometown in Pakistan, after migration from India in 1947 and having secured first class marks in English, the natural and obvious choice would have been to seek admission to M.A. classes in Punjab University at Lahore. However, my late father had some other designs and plans for his eldest son. He wanted me to do law for which I had no fascination. As a compromise it was decided that I should join regular M.A. classes in the English Department and do law in evening classes. This arrangement at that time in 1956 was possible in Karachi alone and that is how I landed in that city. I joined evening classes of LL.B. at S. M. College without any difficulty. I was confident that with first class marks in English in B.A. from Punjab University, I would be able to get admission into M.A. English classes without much fuss. I duly applied for admission but was surprised that my name was not there on the list of successful candidates put on the notice board of the Department. So, one fine day I mustered courage and decided to see the Head of the English Department to find out the reasons for denial of admission to me. Since I had never met the Head of the English Department, as a raw young man who was barely eighteen years old at that time and was feeling a bit timid in a city comparatively cosmopolitan and bustling with activity, I had visualized the Head of the Department to be a smart, Europeanized, modern, clean shaved and fashionably attired person. With this mental picture I ventured into the precincts of the English Department on that fateful day and came across a person who was just the opposite of the picture I had conjured in my mind. The gentleman I came across was wearing a Sherwani, sporting a thick black beard, had a squint in his eyes and wore conspicuous thick glasses. I ventured and accosted the gentleman to guide me to the Head of the Department. Prompt came the reply in a voice and pronunciation that was immaculate and perfect, "I am the Head of the Department!" For a few moments I felt frozen in my shoes. But then I must have uttered something to explain the predicament of my name being dropped from the list of successful candidates despite having a good academic record. Dr Ashraf took me to his office there and then, and everything was resolved satisfactorily. I could discern a faint smile on his swarthy lips because what had actually transpired was that due to some clerical mistake (which is quite common in Pakistan), my name was included in the list of successful girls! Throughout my two years in the English Department, I was to see time and again Dr Ashraf's passionate concern for the welfare of the students who were under his custody.

The second distinctive trait that was conspicuous in his behaviour was his concern for the moral upbringing of students. Boys and girls sat separately in the classroom and despite hidden resentment, the segregation of sexes was enforced strictly. One could discern natural liking and appreciation for those girls who wore burqa or hijab.

One particular incident in this regard is etched in my memory. During the two years stay in the Department of English, we had two Fulbright Professors of English through the courtesy of Ford Foundation. In 1957 it was Dr Andrey Chew,[1] a great authority on medieval poetry, who relished teaching us Chaucer. In 1958 it was the turn of Dr Celesta Wine,[2] a professor in her late forties with a twinkle in her eyes who introduced us to Robert Frost. The Department was to go to Hawkesbay beach for its annual outing. Everyone was to assemble in the Department from where a chartered bus was to take us to our destination. Dr Wine came clad in an outrageous bikini at that time with a loose fitted gown thrown over. Dr Ashraf was simply aghast, took her to a corner and whispered something the students could not hear in her ears. But everyone heard

---

1   Professional Activities Division, International Educational Exchange Service, *Department of State International Educational Exchange Program: American Lecturers and Research Scholars Receiving United States Government Awards Under the Fulbright Act 1956-57 Academic Year* (Department of State, USA, September 14, 1956), 27, https://libraries.uark.edu/specialcollections/fulbrightdirectories/1956%20-%201957.pdf.

2   Professional Activities Division International Educational Exchange Service, *Department of State International Educational Exchange Program: American Lecturers and Research Scholars Receiving United States Government Awards Under the Fulbright Act 1957-58 Academic Year* (Department of State, USA, August 23, 1957), 26, https://libraries.uark.edu/specialcollections/fulbrightdirectories/1957%20-%201958.pdf. See also: Ron Chepesiuk, "The Winthrop College Archives and Special Collections: Selected Resources for the Study of Women's History," *The South Carolina Historical Magazine* 82, no. 2 (Apr. 1981): 163.

loud and clear what Dr Wine said to Dr Ashraf, "In the States I don't even wear this one." Everyone went for the annual picnic, but Dr Ashraf simply refused to go as his sense of morality was hurt deeply. The basic Islamic tenets and teachings were so deeply ingrained in him that despite having lived in Western society and culture, there could be no compromise on Islamic moral values.

After I left the University there was minimal contact. The events, which unfolded in our national history, were rather painful. With the dismemberment of Pakistan and resultant loss of East Pakistan, it must have been extremely painful for a sensitive East Pakistani to continue to live in Karachi though Dr Ashraf was too emancipated and enlightened a person to be bothered by prejudices. Just at that time when final examinations were over, an event took place which tested the strength of Dr Ashraf's character as a teacher and Head of the English Department. Somehow, the students came to know that Dr Wine was examining our Essay paper. Four or five students including me decided to approach her with this news and try to solicit some information about our marks. Dr Wine was staying in Hotel Metropole, the only hotel where the foreigners preferred to stay at that time. So, while the rest of the boys went to wait at Café Grand just opposite Hotel Metropole (I think this café is still functioning), three of us knocked at Dr Wine's room. She was quite pleased to see us and shared her experiences of recent travel to Srinagar in occupied Kashmir. When we came to the crunch question, she was bold enough to admit that she had recently graded thirty-one essay papers of the Final M.A. Class. She was kind enough to tell me that she recognized my handwriting and I had stood first in the paper by securing sixty-three marks out of hundred. When Kaleem (later Dr Kaleemur Rehman and Head of the English Department) wanted to know about marks obtained by him one could see Dr Wine at her mischievous best. She said she could not recollect exactly but he had obtained either sixty-two or thirty-eight marks! That was her way of settling score with Kaleem who was pulling the leg of his professor in the class.

There was still time for our results to be announced officially and I was under pressure from my father to return to my hometown Multan. So, one day I approached Dr Wine at Hotel Metropole and requested her to issue me a testimonial, as I would be soon leaving for Multan. I thought she would be reluctant because officially the results were yet to be declared. But to my surprise she agreed willingly and typed out a testimonial there and then. I made the mistake of bragging about my securing first position in the Essay paper and showed the testimonial to a couple of close friends including Kaleem who beseeched me to let him have the testimonial for a day which I foolishly did. It never came back to me. But what happened I was to learn later. Kaleem presented this testimonial to Dr Ashraf. It could have triggered a catastrophe. Dr Ashraf spoke to Dr Wine who stuck to her ground. In her opinion there was nothing wrong in her issuing the testimonial before the result was officially declared. Meanwhile, oblivious of all this, I went to Dr Wine and pretended that the testimonial she had given me had been inadvertently lost. She was gracious enough to type and issue me another one, which I cherish and is still with me.

Dr Ashraf never spoke to me about this incident, but as a good administrator he did not allow things to go out of hands. I am sure he must have put this incident out of his mind because when the final results were out, he was kind enough to offer me the post of a lecturer in the English Department purely on the basis of merit. Kaleem had overall stood first, I was second and Rhoda Vania was third. Dr Ashraf offered lectureship to the first three position holders. By the time the results were announced I was back to Multan and had joined Emerson College and later I was to sit for competitive examination and join first State Bank of Pakistan and later Civil Service of Pakistan.

I remember having met Dr Ashraf in the airport lounge either in Karachi or Islamabad on a couple of occasions. But this time, I was posted as Deputy Secretary (Banking) in the Ministry of Finance, and I remember having told Dr Ashraf that under a Presidential Directive we had undertaken Islamization of banking. By that time Dr Ashraf was working on Muslim education or something of the sort and he shared some papers in this regard with me. No wonder he was later appointed as the first Director General of the World Center for Islamic Education established under OIC. The last time I came into telephonic contact with him was in 1993. I had some problems with my eyes, and somebody recommended Dr Scott in Cambridge. I had an appointment with him, and he eventually operated upon my eyes for which I had to stay at Lea Hospital in Cambridge for two to three days. When I regained consciousness after the operation in the hospital, I could see a bouquet of flowers in the corner of the room and when the nurse read out the name of the sender, I found it was Dr Ali Ashraf!

When I look back, Dr Syed Ali Ashraf emerges as a person who had rare qualities of head and heart. He was basically a simple person with grooming in modern education. He was deeply religious but never narrow-minded. He was deeply religious who was enamoured with the metaphysical world, but progressive and modernistic ideas in other cultures were always welcome. Islamic teachings were a beacon of guiding light for him and with acquisition and awakening of new vistas of knowledge, there were endeavours to interpret the teachings of Islam to meet the challenges of present times. No wonder a major part of his life was dedicated to the evolution of an Islamic Education System that could be a motivating force for the Muslim countries and Ummah. I recollect how emotionally involved he seemed while teaching Mathew Arnold's *Culture and Anarchy*. Arnold says that culture is "a pursuit of our total perfection by means of getting to know . . . the best which has been thought and said in the world."[3] If anyone came nearer to this definition of a cultured person, it was Dr Syed Ali Ashraf. May his soul rest in peace.

---

3   Matthew Arnold, preface to *Culture and Anarchy: An Essay in Political and Social Criticism*

Bibliography

Arnold, Matthew. Preface to *Culture and Anarchy: An Essay in Political and Social Criticism*, iii-lx. London: Smith, Elder and Co., 1869.

Chepesiuk, Ron. "The Winthrop College Archives and Special Collections: Selected Resources for the Study of Women's History." *The South Carolina Historical Magazine* 82, no. 2 (Apr. 1981): 143-172.

Professional Activities Division, International Educational Exchange Service. *Department of State International Educational Exchange Program: American Lecturers and Research Scholars Receiving United States Government Awards Under the Fulbright Act 1956-57 Academic Year.* Department of State, USA, September 14, 1956. https://libraries.uark.edu/specialcollections/fulbrightdirectories/1956%20-%201957.pdf.

Professional Activities Division International Educational Exchange Service. *Department of State International Educational Exchange Program: American Lecturers and Research Scholars Receiving United States Government Awards Under the Fulbright Act 1957-58 Academic Year.* Department of State, USA, August 23, 1957. https://libraries.uark.edu/specialcollections/fulbrightdirectories/1957%20-%201958.pdf.

(London: Smith, Elder and Co. 1869), viii.

Chapter 37

Remembering Syed Ali Ashraf

Muhammad Abdul Jabbar Beg

Let me begin with a disclaimer. I do not know Professor Ali Ashraf's life and work sufficiently to be able to write about him with some degree of certainty; nevertheless, I met him many times in the United Kingdom and during 1993-1994 attended some seminars at Homerton College and Fitzwilliam College, Cambridge, on "faith-based education" sponsored jointly by the Islamic Academy in Cambridge and the University of Cambridge Department of Education. I also interviewed him several times in January and April 1996. Ali Ashraf was the Founding Director of the Islamic Academy in Cambridge, which publish a quarterly Journal, *Muslim Education Quarterly*. He also founded Darul Ihsan University in Dhaka, Bangladesh—a private institution of which he was the Vice Chancellor for a few years before his death.

Historical Background

Ali Ashraf was born to Syed Ali Hamid, an Inspector of Schools, and his wife Qamrunnigar Khatun.[1] About his parents, he confessed: "As far as my mother is concerned, she was not a scholar. The only thing I can say is that she never beat her children. We (i.e., Ali Ashraf and his siblings) always had tremendous reverence for her. As regards my father, he was very reserved, and we were very afraid of him. He was a very straightforward, honest and a highly confident person". Ali Ashraf said that his great grandfather studied Islamic subjects at Al-Azhar University in Cairo. He also said, "Our forefather, Shah Ali

---

[1] There is some confusion concerning Professor Ali Ashraf's birth date. According to an essay in a book dedicated to his memory entitled, *Bôrenyo: Syed Ali Ashraf Smarok Grôntho* (p. 202), Ali Ashraf was born in the house of his maternal grandfather in Dhaka on 30th January 1924. However, Ali Ashraf personally told me that he was born on 31 December 1924 (at 3 A.M.). According to an obituary by Dr S. A. Mabud published in *Muslim Education Quarterly*, no. 3, vol. 15, 1998 and Akbar S. Ahmed in the London newspaper, *The Independent* dated 13 August 1998 (online version 13 August), Ali Ashraf was born on 1 January 1925.

Baghdadi, who came to India, and who is now buried in Dhaka, belonged to the Sufi line [i.e., order]." Following his claim of a genealogical link with Shah Ali Baghdadi, I discovered the following in *A History of Sufism in Bengal* by Muhammad Enamul Haq:

> In the village of Mirpur in Dacca lies the tomb of this saint (i.e. Shah Ali Baghdadi, who died before 1480 A.D.). His title indicates that he was an inhabitant of Baghdad, but otherwise nothing definite is known about him. According to Mr. B. C. Allen, this saint died in 1577; but in the absence of reliable historical evidence, we are unable to accept the accuracy of this date. Adjoining the present shrine of the saint there is an old mosque, which according to an inscription in it, dates its foundation to the year 885 A.H./1480 A.D., which was during the reign of Yusuf Shah (1478–82 A.D.). It is a well-known fact that almost all mosques adjoining *dargāhs* (i.e. tombs of Sufis) in Bengal were built after the death of the saints or during their lifetime. So, it can be fairly presumed that the saint Shah Ali Baghdadi, died before the year 1480 A.D."[2]

It is with a heavy heart and tender feelings that I write this biographical sketch of Professor Ashraf. Though I am not a hagiographer, I must admit that he stood out among the Bengali-speaking Muslims who lived in Cambridge during the twentieth century. Ali Ashraf was bilingual and expressed his ideas as effectively in Bengali as in English. He did not belong to the class of *ʿulamāʾ*, that is, Islamic theologians. He had no professional qualifications in Qurʾānic Studies (*ʿulūm al-Qurʾān*), Ḥadīth literature (*ʿulūm al-ḥadīth*), Islamic Jurisprudence (*fiqh*) or Islamic history (*tārīkh*). Yet he had a deep knowledge of Islam which he gained informally. He was sympathetic towards the Islamic heritage of Bengali Literature as is demonstrated in his Bengali book, *Muslim Traditions in Bengali Literature*.[3]

His poetic talent was recognized in Bangladesh.[4] Moreover, he belonged to the mainstream Muslim poets of Bengal, such as Kazi Nazrul Islam, Farrukh Ahmad, Ghulam Mustafa and Al-Mahmud. As a descendant of Shah Ali Baghdadi, he acquired spiritual knowledge of Islam from his family at an early age, and later came in contact with some great spiritual masters who guided him along the path to spiritual fulfilment. These spiritual masters authorized him as their *khalīfah* (successor) to initiate others into the Sufi path (*ṭarīqah*). Ali Ashraf taught his disciples modes of supplication and contemplation (*dhikr*) of God so as to generate love for Him and attain His nearness. He was a strict

---

2 M. Enamul Haq, *A History of Sufism in Bengal* (Asiatic Society of Bangladesh, 1975), 233.
3 Syed Ali Ashraf, *Muslim Traditions in Bengali Literature* (Karachi University: Bengali Literary Society, 1960).
4 See, Syed Ali Ashraf, *Syed Ali Ashrafer Kobita* (Dhaka: Shilpotoru Prokashôni, 1991).

follower of Sharīʿah, that is, the revealed law of Islam. Bengal is littered with graves of saints that attract worshippers. These include the tombs of Shah Jalal in Sylhet, Karamat Ali in Rangpur, Shah Makhdum in Rajshahi, Chehel Ghazi (40 warriors) in Dinajpur, and the alleged tomb of Bayazid Bustami in Chittagong. The mystic cult of Bengal concentrates its attention on graves or tombs of past Sufis or even alleged mystics who never existed to the extent that their devotees start to worship their graves. Ali Ashraf was totally opposed to such anti-Islamic practices. The Prophet said, "Verily, when a righteous man among them would die, they would build a place of worship over his grave and carve these images within it. They will be the worst to Allah on the Day of Resurrection."[5] Imām Mālik reported in Al-Muwaṭṭaʾ that Allah's Messenger said: "O Allah! Do not make my grave into an idol that is worshipped. Allah's anger is severe upon a people who turned the graves of their Prophets into places of worship (mosques)."[6] However, the visiting of graves has been instructed by the Prophet (peace be upon him). Ibn Masʿūd reported: "The Messenger of Allah (peace and blessings be upon him) said, 'I had prohibited you from visiting graves, but you may visit them now. Verily, they will weaken your attachment to the world and remind you of the Hereafter.'"[7] Ali Ashraf used to visit the tomb of his ancestral saint, Shah Ali Baghdadi from time to time. Having said all that, I must admit that my primary purpose in writing this short biography is to evaluate his intellectual legacy.

In the course of my interviews with him in 1996, I reminded him that my former Cambridge professor, Robert B. Serjeant, had written a book on the Sayyids of Hadramaut.[8] I asked him whether he would like to write a book on the Sayyids of Bangladesh. He showed an interest in the subject but confessed that although he did not have the time to write such a work himself, he would like some of his colleagues at the Darul Ihsan University to supervise either an M.Phil. or a Ph.D. thesis on the history of the Sayyids of Bangladesh. When I asked him again, he told me that the subject was being seriously considered by scholars. I sensed that he was not particularly enthusiastic about the project (probably for personal reasons). I also suggested to him that the Muslims of Bengal would be grateful to Ali Ashraf if he would consider penning an autobiography. I reminded him of Carlyle's dictum that "The History of the world is but the Biography of great men."[9] I argued that a scholar of his standing would know more than anyone else about his life. Hence an autobiography would be his important legacy. He told me with humility that as nobody would be inter-

---

5 Ṣaḥīḥ al-Bukhārī, Kitāb al-ṣalāt, no. 343.
6 Imām Mālik, Al-Muwaṭṭaʾ, Kitāb qaṣar al-ṣalāt fī al-safar, no. 85.
7 Sunan Ibn Mājah, Kitāb al-Janāʾiz, Bāb mā jāʾa fī ziyārat al-qubūr, no. 1571.
8 Robert Bertram Serjeant, Saiyids of Ḥaḍramawt (London: School of Oriental and African Studies, 1957).
9 Thomas Carlyle, "The Hero as Divinity," in On Heroes, Hero-worship, & the Heroic in History (London: James Fraser, 1841), 47.

ested in his life, it would be a waste of time to write it. I am sad that because he did not take up my suggestion, we shall never know the full story of his life. I then proposed that it would be one of his major contributions to Qurʾān Studies if he would translate the whole Qurʾān into simple English, something that no person from East Bengal had ever achieved. After some persuasion, he agreed to translate the Qurʾān into English provided at least two competent Islamic scholars (ʿulamāʾ) would work with him. I was heartened to hear his response. At the end of the interview, I asked him again about what his ultimate legacy would be: a history of the Sayyids, an autobiography or a new translation of the Qurʾān. He told me that he intended to do the latter project. Unfortunately, Ali Ashraf died within two years of my interviews. His wife, Asiah Khatun, who became disabled, also passed away within a few years. Alas, he could neither write an autobiography, nor a history of the Sayyids, nor could he translate the Qurʾān. When he died leaving behind neither children nor an autobiography, I was broken hearted. I kept quiet for a while before writing this biographical essay.

In the early 1990s I met Professor Ashraf informally at Friday (Jumuʿah) prayers in Corpus Christi College, Cambridge. Occasionally, he used to lead the Jumuʿah prayers. Massoud Shadjareh, an Iranian political activist, who had lived in Cambridge for many years and worked at the Cambridge Community Centre, used to attend these Friday prayers and serve Shish Kebabs to the attendees. I enjoyed some of these social and spiritual gatherings that followed the prayer service. It is probably appropriate to add that I also attended some sermons (khuṭbah) delivered by Ali Ashraf (as Imām of the Friday prayers) at the 205 Gilbert Road Mosque in Cambridge. In one of these sermons, he discussed the spiritual significance of eating ḥalāl (lit. lawful) food. It was here that he would conduct some religious activities and evening dhikr sessions in which tamarind seeds (as rosary beads) were used by the participants to keep count of how many times dhikr (lit. remembrance of God) utterances were made. I witnessed the recital of sacred formulas of Astaghfirullāh (7 times), Bismillāh al-Raḥmān al-Raḥīm (19 times), Sūrah al-Fātiḥah (3 times), Sūrah al-Ikhlāṣ (10 times), Āyat al-Kursī (once), Subḥān Allāh (33 times), Al-ḥamdu lillāh (33 times), Allāhu Akbar (34 times), Allāhumma ajirnī min al-nār (7 times), and ṣalāt on the Prophet (11 times) followed by a supplication.[10]

Personally, I was not much interested in such activities, but occasionally attended these dhikr sessions in a private room or house. Many adolescents and some adults attended these activities. It was at 8 p.m. (Bangladesh time)

---

10 Astaghfirullāh—I seek forgiveness from Allah. Bismillāh al-Raḥmān al-Raḥīm—In the name of God, the Most Gracious, the Most Merciful. Sūrah al-Fātiḥah—1st chapter of the Qurʾān. Sūrah Ikhlāṣ—112th chapter of the Qurʾān. Āyat al-Kursī—Chapter 2, verse 255 of the Qurʾān. Subḥān Allāh—Glory be to Allah. Al-ḥamdu lillāh—Praise be to Allah. Allāhu Akbar—Allah is the Greatest. Allāhumma ajirnī min al-nār—O Allah, protect me from the hellfire. Ṣalāt—blessings on the Prophet.

on 15 August 1995 that my father Al-Hajj Dr Mirza Maqbool Hossain Beg passed away in Dinajpur, Bangladesh, and I requested Professor Ali Ashraf to arrange a prayer session for his departed soul. I provided delicious food for those who attended the session. I was grateful to Professor Ali Ashraf for his role in presiding over the *fātiḥah* and *duʿāʾ* (lit. supplications). After the death of my father, I suffered from depression and sought his advice to overcome my sorrow. He told me to recite a short supplication: (*Rabbi*) *annī massanī al-ḍurru wa-Anta arḥam al-rāḥimīn* (Qurʾān 21:83) (O Lord, distress has seized me, and You are the Most Merciful of those who show mercy).

Professor Ali Ashraf believed in spiritual healing. On one occasion when I visited his house in Cambridge, I saw him practising his healing craft. When a man arrived complaining of a severe headache, he silently recited something and blew on the top of his head. A few minutes later the headache disappeared. This surprised me.

I discovered that Professor Ali Ashraf was a scholar with a profound religious outlook who prayed five times a day. In this respect there was something special in his character and personality. It is known from eyewitnesses that he never missed his daily prayer. One day I was with him on a double-decker bus when he performed his late afternoon prayer (*ʿaṣr*). I was stunned by this. He maintained his ablution (*wuḍūʾ*). It was due to his upbringing, and later his discipleship of some spiritual masters that made him a true follower of Sharīʿah (the revealed law of Islam) and *ṭarīqah* (spiritual path), and he did not see any contradiction between them.

One of my friends told me that on one occasion they were descending in a lift from a multistorey car park in Cambridge, when it got stuck. It was then early evening prayer time (*maghrib*) and Ali Ashraf performed his ritual *maghrib* prayer inside the confined space of the lift. It would be no exaggeration to say that Ali Ashraf always performed his prayers on time, whether he was on a bus, train, boat, or aeroplane. This shows his great sincerity and unshakable conviction in the faith and practice of Islam. He was not ostentatious in his dress and was an amiable person. He was an ascetic person who lived a life in moderation.

Towards the end of his life, I felt that he would not be with us much longer. Out of curiosity I asked him through my friend, F. M. Aziz to let me interview him about his life and work. He reluctantly agreed and over lunch at his home I asked him about his life and creative work. I was primarily interested in his career as a professor in Pakistan, Saudi Arabia, and Cambridge. This interview lasted more than one afternoon. With his permission, I recorded the interviews. As a historian, I am interested to know the truth about people. What astonished me most was that at the end of one session Professor Ashraf asked me whether I would like to hear him recite his own poems. I said I would, after which he recited many of his poems in Bengali that had been published in the anthology *Syed Ali Ashrafer Kobita* mentioned earlier. I recorded his recitation and have listened to it again and again—and feel that I have lost a friend whom I will never meet again. May God bless his soul and grant him Paradise in the hereafter (ākhirah). I have prayed for him despite my personal differences with him in religious matters.

Professor Ali Ashraf has been one of my mentors (in a limited sense of the term). He published half a dozen of my articles on the Companions of the Prophet (Ṣaḥābah), aspects of architecture, Islamic science, and on King Abd al-Aziz Ibn Saʿud, a dozen reviews of books on Islam, history, minorities, and education, four obituaries of Muhammad Hamidullah, Majid Khadduri, Muhammad Mohar Ali and Kazi Din Muhammad. I liked him as a scholar, writer and poet. He was a follower of Ḥanafī madhhab (School of Law). I was far from it. He was also a follower of Sufi Shaykhs. As a simple Muslim, I disapprove of pseudo-Islamic Mysticism (or Sufism). I believe Sufism is not Islam in its pristine form. It is a corrupt form of religious practice which has its origin in un-Islamic sources, such as Neoplatonism, Gnosticism, Monasticism and even Buddhism. I believe in the simple version of Islam as found in the Holy Qurʾān and the Sunnah (practice) of the Prophet Muhammad (peace be upon him). I belong to a group known as Ahl-e Ḥadīth or Ḥanbalī, which is also known as Salafī or Muwaḥḥidī. Despite my difference of opinions with him on religious matters, I have profound respect for him for the sincerity of his faith, simplicity of his life, profundity of his thought, his spiritual insight, and his gentle manners.

Ali Ashraf was a keen photographer and left an album which is now being looked after by his sister-in-law, Selina Ali and her husband Mushtaque Ali, who live in London. In 1996 I was photographed with Professor Ali Ashraf in his Cambridge home by a relative, F. M. Aziz mentioned earlier.

Ali Ashraf was a prolific writer and the founding editor of a journal entitled *Muslim Education Quarterly*, which was published in Cambridge starting from 1983. He also edited an anthology of poems by Ghulam Mostafa (1897–1964), a well-known poet of Bengal, who was born at Manoharpur in the district of Jessore and was a schoolteacher by profession. A graduate of Ripon College in 1918, Ghulam Mostafa began teaching at Barakpur Government High School in 1920. He received his Bachelor of Teacher's Training from David Hare Training College in 1922 and after a long career, retired as Headmaster of Faridpur Zila School in 1949. Ghulam Mostafa was a prolific writer and poet and Ali Ashraf, as an admirer of his distinctive literary works, paid the following tribute to his genius:

> Though Ghulam Mostafa had started writing just before Nazrul Islam came into the field, he continued to produce poetry after independence. Five of his poetry books were published before 1947: *Raktarag* (1924), *Khoshroj* (1929), *Kavya-Kahini* (1932), *Sahara* (1936) and *Hasnahena* (1938). After 1947 his translation of *Mosaddas-e-Hali* (1949), *Shikwa, Jawab-e-*

Shikwa (1960), *Kalam-e-Iqbal* (i.e., the poems of Muhammad Iqbal) and al-Quran (in parts) (1957) kept the tradition of translations of Urdu, Arabic and Persian literature alive. These were successful translations. In 1958 his philosophical poem Bani Adam was published. His Tarana-e-Pakistan (anthem of Pakistan) came out in 1948. He also brought out an anthology of his poetry selected by him called *Bulbulistan*. A selection of his best poems edited with a critical introduction by Syed Ali Ashraf was published by Bengali Academy in 1967. Three different facets of human sensibility had a great impact on his poetic consciousness: the Muslim mind as it was evolving during his life-time, love and the vivacity of youth. The impact of the first type of sensibility led to the production of two types of poems—the occasional poems which reflected the ephemeral and transitory socio-political events of the Muslim world and their impact on the Muslim mind of the Sub-continent and those good poems which presented the universal themes, ideals and myths affecting Muslim life, and also permanently influencing all human beings. In the first category fall such poems as 'Shadhin Mishar' (Independent Egypt), 'Hindu-Muslim', 'Vijoy-Ullash' (the joy of victory), and 'League-Vijoy' (the victory of [the Muslim] League). These had occasional value and appeal to the Muslim community only.

To the second category belongs such poems as 'Eid-Utsab', 'Manush' (Man) and 'Bani Adam' (the sons of Adam). Some of the narrative poems in the *Kavya-Kahini* written on Muslim themes in imitation of Tagore's *Katha-o-Kahini*, in which incidents and situations drawn from Hindu myths and history are depicted, can also be placed in this category because in spite of their typical Muslim perspective they deal with eternal human problems. Ghulam Mostafa succeeded in universalising the situations and themes in the other poems such as 'Eid-Utsab' by presenting it as a symbol of purity, love and joy. Similarly, in 'Manush' (Man) he depicts the Quranic concept of Man's creation, his choice between good and evil and his fall. Thus, the story deals with the universal problem of Man caught in the eternal conflict between the forces of Good and Evil. *Bani Adam* is a long poem in blank verse that deals with this problem. But what is precise and concise in 'Manush' (Man) becomes rather diffuse in this poem. In spite of this limitation this is a bold attempt. He succeeds better as a love-poet. His love-poems depict the sorrows of separation, the joy of the consummation of reciprocal love and the peace and happiness of domestic life. 'Pasher Barir Meye' (lit. the girl in my neighbour's house), 'Bhushan', 'Kurano Manik', 'Premer Joy', and poems in *Sahara* and *Hasnahena* deal with these aspects of love. In another type of love-poem the poet explores the source of love and finds human love only as a reflection of Man's love for Beauty. Sometimes the poet finds this love for Beauty in conflict with his love for a specific individual. This theme was explored by Tagore and Nazrul Islam before him and he seems to be imitating them. The third type of poems written by Ghulam Mostafa deals with youth and its glory. The total performance places him in the category of good poets. His acute observation, accurate and adequate presentation and command over rhythm prove his craftsmanship. But he did not seem to respond to the cultural conflict through which East Bengali educated community was passing since 1947."[11]

Professor Ashraf's critical evaluation of Ghulam Mustafa's poems evolved from his own commitment to poetry in general and Bengali poetry in particular. Besides his anthology, *Syed Ali Ashrafer Kobita*, he also published *Rubaiyat-i Zahini*, (Srijan Prokashoni Ltd., Dacca, December 1991), which was dedicated to his spiritual mentor Zaheen Shah Taji; another anthology of Bengali poems was *Proshnottôr* (lit. question and answer) (Bud Publications, Dhaka, 1996); Ashraf also published *Kabyo Porichôy* (Introduction to poetry) (Dacca, 1956). Among Ali Ashraf's other books, mention should be made of the Bengali *Bangla Sahitye Muslim Oitijhyo* (Dacca, 1962) and its English version *Muslim Traditions in Bengali Literature*. Besides these, he has written two books on Kazi Nazrul Islam: *Homage to Nazrul Islam* (English) (Bengali Department, Karachi University, 1972), and *Nazrul Jibone Premer Ek Notun Ôddhay* (lit. A new chapter in the love-life of Nazrul Islam) (second edition, Karachi and Dacca, 1995). Over and above these publications, we owe to Professor Ali Ashraf two notable articles, including "Bengali Poetry Since Independence," in *Pakistan Quarterly*, vol. XV, parts 1 and 2, 1967, and an essay, "Bengali Drama" in *The Reader's Encyclopaedia of World Drama*, edited by John Gassner and Edward Quinn (New York: Thomas Y. Crowell, 1969).

It was while Professor Ali Ashraf was employed as Head of the Department of English at King Abdulaziz University at Makkah (1974–77) that he proposed to King Faisal ibn Abd al-Aziz the idea of holding a World Conference on Muslim Education. This project was approved by the Saudi Government and as a result the First World Conference on Muslim Education was held in Makkah in 1977. Over three hundred scholars attended the conference and Ali Ashraf was appointed Secretary of the Follow-up Committee.[12] It was then decided that he be appointed chief editor of a proposed six-volume edition of the papers presented at this conference. These six books in the "Islamic Education Series" were published by Hodder and Stoughton and King Abdulaziz University under the general editorship of Syed Ali Ashraf. It has been claimed that

---

11 Syed Ali Ashraf, *Literature, Society and Culture in East Pakistan 1947 to 1971* (Karachi: Karachi University, 1973).
12 Shaikh Abdul Mabud, "World Conferences on Muslim Education: Shaping the Agenda of Muslim Education in the Future," in *Philosophies of Islamic Education, Historical Perspectives and Emerging Discourses*, eds. Nadeem A. Memon and M. Zaman (New York: Routledge, 2016), 129–43.

the importance of this first series "lies in the exposition of basic educational problems in the Muslim world, in the formulation of the methodology for the solution of these problems and in making the readers of the East and the West appreciate that modern Muslim mind which is also devoutly religious."[13] The Makkah Conference on Muslim Education was a turning point in the new collective rethinking on the education system in the Muslim world. Professor Ali Ashraf played an important part in awakening the reform of the Muslim educational order the world over.

There were three other books in "Islamic Monograph Series." They are, *New Horizons in Muslim Education* by S. A. Ashraf (1985), *The Concept of an Islamic University*, which was jointly written by H. H. Bilgrami and S. A. Ashraf (1985), and *Islamic Sociology: An Introduction* by Ilyas Ba-Yunus and Farid Ahmad (1985). Ashraf also contributed an erudite article entitled, "Universities" to *The Oxford Encyclopaedia of the Modern Islamic World* (edited by John Esposito, New York: Oxford University Press, 1995). This article, which was probably the most important ever written by him, was largely based on the monograph, *The Concept of an Islamic University*. Ashraf's only book for children, and by far his most popular book, was entitled *The Prophets* (London: Ta-Ha Publishers, 1980). It draws our attention to the Messengers of God from Adam to Jesus. Another lesser-known work was a booklet entitled, *The Qur'ānic Concept of History*, which was published by the Islamic Foundation in Leicester in 1980. Let me quote a few sentences from this book to conclude this essay:

> Adam is a completely new creation endowed with spiritual knowledge and blessed with the duty of a Prophet for his children. We do not get any details about his life. We are informed of his two sons, Abel and Cain. The next picture is of human corruption and the destruction of all unbelievers by a great flood at the time of another Prophet, Noah.
>
> From the Qur'ān it appears that there was a time when all people were of the same colour. But Allah divided them into different groups having different colours because he wanted that they should know each other and through that knowledge understand the purpose of creation and the glory of Allah.
>
> From Noah till the last Prophet there is a continuous line of Prophethood and human history, with the rise and fall of nations integrally related to faith and Man's behaviour, his acceptance or denial of the Message that Allah has sent through His Prophets. Political authority is shown to have been linked up with the moral and spiritual conduct of Man. The life of the last Prophet, peace be upon him, proves beyond all doubt that all authority ultimately belongs to Allah. He chooses those who obey Him and fight for His cause. When a nation disobeys Allah

---

13 Appears on the back dust cover of each of the six books in the series.

and upsets the code of life granted by Him then Allah sends warnings to that nation in the form of natural calamities. But if the nation does not repent and becomes more hard-hearted then He sends human beings to destroy those people. He also sows the seeds of discord among those nations which give up His code and proudly and arrogantly pose to be self-sufficient.

There is thus a Divine plan in history. Increase in wealth or a higher standard of living does not mean real happiness. Real happiness consists in pure living, in humility, in resignation to the Will of Allah, and in fighting in His path in order to establish His kingdom on the earth. Any nation that becomes morally degenerated is bound to fall and lose its greatness."[14]

God knows everything.

Bibliography

Ashraf, Syed Ali. *Literature, Society and Culture in East Pakistan 1947 to 1971*. Karachi: Karachi University, 1973.

Ashraf, Syed Ali. *The Qurʾānic Concept of History*. Leicester: The Islamic Foundation, 1980.

Carlyle, Thomas. "The Hero as Divinity." In *On Heroes, Hero-worship, & the Heroic in History*. London: James Fraser, 1841.

Haq, M. Enamul. *A History of Sufism in Bengal*. Asiatic Society of Bangladesh, 1975.

Mabud, Shaikh Abdul. "World conferences on Muslim education: Shaping the agenda of Muslim education in the future." In *Philosophies of Islamic Education, Historical Perspectives and Emerging Discourses*, edited by Nadeem A. Memon and M. Zaman, 129–43. New York: Routledge, 2016.

Mabud, Shaikh Abdul. "Obituary: Professor Syed Ali Ashraf." *Muslim Education Quarterly* 15, no. 3 (1998): v-vi.

Mia, Muhammad Ahsanullah, Muhammad Ismail Husain, Mahmudul Hasan Yusuf, Muhammad Shamsuddoha, and Shah Waliullah Farhad, eds. *Bôrenyo: Syed Ali Ashraf Smarok Grôntho*. Dhaka, Bangladesh: Faculty of Religious Education, Darul Ihsan University, 1999.

Serjeant, Robert Bertram. *The Saiyids of Ḥaḍramawt*. London: School of Oriental and African Studies, 1957.

---

14   Syed Ali Ashraf, *The Qurʾānic Concept of History* (Leicester: The Islamic Foundation, 1980), 8–9.

Chapter 38

My Memories of Professor Dr Syed Ali Ashraf
Imran N. Hosein

Professor Dr Syed Ali Ashraf, the eastern-trained Sufi Shaikh who was also a Western-trained scholar of English language and literature, has a remarkable record as an energetic and much-travelled spiritual master and guide, who touched the hearts and changed the lives of thousands, even in my native Caribbean Island of Trinidad which he visited, perhaps, a dozen times. The fragrance of his wise and gentle words and the light of his loving spiritual touch, still linger on in many hearts in the island so many years after his death. I saw him literally raise dead hearts back to life, again and again, as he poured raindrops into those parched hearts with whom he made spiritual contact. Large numbers of Muslims became his spiritual disciples as they flocked to him from far and wide. Some even caused him some distress as they brought their worrisome baggage with them, yet I never heard him raise his voice in a display of anger, nor ever lose his cool in trying moments. The most that he did was to refuse to shake hands and embrace someone whose errant ways needed to be firmly corrected.

Most of the Islamic organizations in Trinidad also sought his assistance and accepted his guidance in their conduct of the affairs of the Muslim community—even in their relations with the Government of Trinidad and Tobago. He was particularly helpful in his efforts to assist those who had the responsibility for teaching in Islamic schools and colleges, while conducting several seminars devoted to Muslim education, and assisting in the preparation of a syllabus for such studies.

What is it that explains that Sufi magnetism which is so conspicuously absent in the rival *Salafi* version of Islam, and which functioned in such a wondrous way in Syed Ali Ashraf in spontaneously attracting a multitude of hearts that were parched and longing for raindrops from above? The answer is located not only in Sufism's insistent spiritual interpretation of the universe, but even more so in the constant interaction which it ignites with the *Samāwāt*, or worlds of space and time which lie beyond our material universe. Several verses of the Qur'ān both indicate the possibility of such interaction, as well as invite the believers to embark on such a spiritual quest. Here are two such verses:

$$\text{يَا مَعْشَرَ الْجِنِّ وَالْإِنسِ إِنِ اسْتَطَعْتُمْ أَن تَنفُذُوا مِنْ أَقْطَارِ السَّمَاوَاتِ وَالْأَرْضِ فَانفُذُوا لَا تَنفُذُونَ إِلَّا بِسُلْطَانٍ}$$

(Qur'ān 55:33)

The Qur'ān addresses the assemblies of Jinn and human beings as follows:

> If you believe that you are capable of traversing the different regions of the *Samāwāt* and the earth, proceed with the effort; however, you will not be able to do so unless you receive authority from Allah Most High.

(This is an explanation, rather than a translation, of the above verse—since the miraculous Arabic text of the Qur'ān cannot be translated to any other language.)

$$\text{الَّذِي خَلَقَ سَبْعَ سَمَاوَاتٍ طِبَاقًا مَّا تَرَى فِي خَلْقِ الرَّحْمَنِ مِن تَفَاوُتٍ فَارْجِعِ الْبَصَرَ هَلْ تَرَى مِن فُطُورٍ ثُمَّ ارْجِعِ الْبَصَرَ كَرَّتَيْنِ يَنقَلِبْ إِلَيْكَ الْبَصَرُ خَاسِئاً وَهُوَ حَسِيرٌ}$$

(Qur'ān 67:3–4)

> Hallowed be He Who has created seven *Samāwāt* in full harmony with one another: You cannot find any defect in the creation of Allah Most Gracious. Return with your *baṣar* (i.e., internal sight), in search of defects—do you see any defect? You may return again and again with your *baṣar* in your search for defects in Allah's creation, but be warned that your *baṣar* will return to you, again and again, and yet again, dazzled and truly defeated.

Dr Ali Ashraf's continuous travels in the world of spiritual *reality* which lies beyond the material *form* of things in this universe may have commenced in attachment to the rivers, the rain, the flowers, and the serenity of his native Bengal. His internalization of that external beauty and serenity may also have contributed to the development of his remarkably humble, serene and magnetic personality. We once went for an early morning walk with him in the enchantingly beautiful Trinidadian valley of Santa Cruz, after the *Ṣalāt al-Fajr* (the morning prayer), and we found him pausing time and again as we walked, to admire and to comment on flowers along the way. "This one," he said, "is called *Rani ki Taria*" (the Queen's crown). In fact, when we walked with Dr Ali

Ashraf that morning, I suspect that we also walked with the flowers and rivers, and all the tumultuous beauty which Allah gave to Bengal, and which seemed to constantly flow from his heart and mind.

I once travelled with him on spiritual errand to Khairpur, a city in Sindh in Pakistan, which was remarkable for its resemblance to *Yathrib,* also known as *Madīnat al-Nabī*.[1] We slept side by side on mattresses laid on the floor, and I was blessed to observe from very close, the unadorned *natural* simplicity in the way of life of a true Sufi who was in no way discomforted in having to share private space. He had told us that he woke from sleep every morning at 3, and when I saw him rise from his mattress in the early morning, and I checked the time, it was indeed 3. He even spent a few days with me and my family in our apartment in Karachi, prior to our travel to Khairpur, and we witnessed the parallel to the Sunnah of sweeping the floor oneself, when he insisted on going into the bathroom himself, and washing his own inner clothing.

I saw in my learned teacher, the Sufi Shaikh, Maulana Dr Muhammad Fazlur Rahman Ansari (1914–1974), the same harmonious embrace of all that was enchantingly beautiful in nature, and consequent harmonious integration of all dimensions of his personality. This erudite Sufi Shaikh himself personally chose all the trees that were planted on the compound of the Islamic Center in Karachi where the Aleemiyah Institute of Islamic Studies was established, and the trees all had different colours and different shapes of leaves. This wondrous diversity of colours and shapes not only integrated harmoniously with each other to bring rest and comfort to our eyes and souls, but it also mirrored his methodology for study of the Qurʾān.

The Sufi Shaikh could, perhaps, confide in us that trees, flowers, rivers, clouds, and stars can speak, and they can say to us that *when we learn to read and understand the pages of the book of nature, it will help us to read and penetrate the pages of the Book of Allah!* Nature speaks to us, and we must learn to listen if we are to ever touch parched hearts and pour raindrops into them!

I want to tax the gentle reader's patience to narrate an incident concerning a colleague of Dr Ali Ashraf, who was also a colleague of Dr Ansari. He straddled, like they both did, the two worlds of Western and Islamic scholarship, with a spiritual embrace, and he struggled to respond to the challenges posed by the West to the world of Islam. I narrate the event *only* because it offers dramatic evidence of the importance of interaction with spiritual *reality* which is located just beyond the material *form* of things in nature, and which I found located in the very core of Dr Ali Ashraf's spiritual personality.

I narrate an event which occurred in the life of the eminent Pakistani philosopher-jurist, Mr A. K. Brohi, who also articulated the spiritual quest in Islam with unmatched eloquence. He once asked me to take him to the cemetery because he wanted to visit the grave of a colleague of his, Mr Kamal Faruqi,

---

1   This is the city of Madinah in Saudi Arabia.

who died while he, Mr Brohi, was away from Karachi. I took him there one morning, and when we reached Kamal Faruqi's grave, Mr Brohi behaved very strangely for a long time while I stood silently by, observing him. He kept on sniffing at the air, as if in search of something. Nature was speaking to him, and it seemed as though he was struggling with the message that was being sent to him. That strange and mysterious conversation between Mr Brohi and nature continued for more than half an hour until he abruptly said to me: "Let us leave now." He never spoke a word as I drove him to his home.

I finally discovered what the conversation was all about when Mr Brohi died a short time later, and when I attended his funeral, I watched in utter amazement as he was buried on the very spot on which he had stood for so long that day, as if transfixed, in mysterious farewell conversation with nature.

Dr Ali Ashraf, the Sufi Shaikh, like other spiritual luminaries through the ages, had eyes with which to see what others could not see, ears to hear when others could not hear, and spoke with words which could be transported beyond the stars. He once gave me an exceptional explanation of the verse of the Qurʾān in which Allah Most High responded to the plea of Nabī Ibrāhīm (A.S.) for an explanation of how He (Most High) gave life to the dead.

"If we can train a bird to answer to our call," said Dr Ali Ashraf, "so too can Allah Most High programme every cell of our body to answer to His call; and when, on resurrection day, He calls us all back to life, every cell will all answer to His call." Here is the verse of the Qurʾān:

وَإِذْ قَالَ إِبْرَاهِيمُ رَبِّ أَرِنِي كَيْفَ تُحْيِي الْمَوْتَى قَالَ أَوَلَمْ تُؤْمِن قَالَ بَلَى وَلَكِن لِّيَطْمَئِنَّ قَلْبِي قَالَ فَخُذْ أَرْبَعَةً مِّنَ الطَّيْرِ فَصُرْهُنَّ إِلَيْكَ ثُمَّ اجْعَلْ عَلَى كُلِّ جَبَلٍ مِّنْهُنَّ جُزْءًا ثُمَّ ادْعُهُنَّ يَأْتِينَكَ سَعْيًا وَاعْلَمْ أَنَّ اللَّهَ عَزِيزٌ حَكِيمٌ ۝

(Qurʾān, 2:260)

And, lo, Abraham said: "O my Sustainer! Show me how Thou givest life unto the dead!" Said He: "Hast thou, then, no faith?" (Abraham) answered: "Yea, but [let me see it] so that my heart may be set fully at rest." Said He: "Take, then, four birds and teach them to obey thee; then place them separately on every hill [around thee]; then summon them: they will come flying to thee. And know that God is almighty, wise."

The Islamic scholar, Muhammad Asad, has given the same explanation of the above verse:

My rendering of the above parable is based on the primary meaning of the imperative ṣurhunna ilayka ("make them incline towards thee" i.e., "teach them to obey thee"). The moral of this story has been pointed out convincingly by the famous commentator Abū Muslim (as quoted by Rāzī): "If man is able—as he undoubtedly is—to train birds in such a way as to make them obey his call, then it is obvious that God, Whose will all things obey, can call life into being by simply decreeing, 'Be!'"[2]

It would take the likes of a Sufi Shaikh of the spiritual elevation and intellectual caliber of Shaikh Shahidullah Faridi or Maulana Muhammad Abdul Aleem Siddiqui to comment further on Dr Ashraf's spiritual status and achievements, and hence I do not qualify to offer further comment on this subject.

Nor do I have competence to comment on Dr Ali Ashraf's academic career as a Professor of English Literature and Chairman of the Department of English at the University of Karachi, where I first came to know him. I was a young student in 1965 reading for a BA Honours degree in Philosophy in the adjoining Department of Philosophy, and I often caught glimpses of him as we shared the same floor of the building. I was even blessed, on rare occasions, to sit in his classroom as he taught us the remarkable language and literature which surely played a role in making Britain great.

But he was a friend and colleague of my teacher and Shaikh of blessed memory, Maulana Ansari, and it was because of that connection with Islamic scholarship and the Islamic spiritual quest, rather than through English language and literature, that he took a special interest in me, and we eventually drew closer. We would meet on those rare occasions during the period 1965–1971 when he would visit the Aleemiyah Institute of Islamic Studies to meet with Dr Ansari, and also to share some time with us, students, who had come to study Islam from many different parts of the world. Indeed, the most brilliant student of all, Muhammad Alamgir, was a Bengali Muslim like himself.

I met him again in 1977 when I travelled from Geneva to visit Makkah for ʿUmrah, as well as to conduct research for my PhD thesis on the OIC (Organization of the Islamic Conference, now renamed Organization of Islamic Cooperation), and I spotted him while I was at the Kaʿbah. We had not met since I departed Pakistan in 1971, and I was unaware that he had moved from Karachi to take up the position of Professor and Chairman of the Department of English at King Abdulaziz University in Makkah. He took me by the arm and gently guided me, the way a shepherd guides a solitary sheep, to his residence, which turned out to be a simple sparsely furnished apartment close to the Kaʿbah which he shared with the Vice Chancellor of a university in Bangladesh. He insisted that I share a meal with him. These two distinguished scholars, one of whom was a Sufi Shaikh, then proceeded to leave me speechless in amazement as I watched them get to work to prepare a simple meal which I would eventually share with them.

---

2 Muhamamad Asad, *The Message of the Qurʾān* (Gibraltar: Dar al-Andalus Limited, 1980).

Dr Ali Ashraf showed some interest in my research work pertaining to a critical evaluation of the political organization of the Muslim world in post-Caliphate Islam but did not express his own views on the subject. He may, perhaps, have felt that I was yet too green to digest the spiritual *reality* which explained the contemporary political disarray in the world of Islam.

Years later I got an unforgettable taste of that spiritual *reality* when he took me with him on a visit to the grave of the erudite Sufi Shaikh, Baba Zaheen Shah Taji, located at some distance outside of the city of Karachi. After we had offered our *Duʿāʾ*[3] at the grave of the Shaikh, I was again reduced to speechless amazement while I sat, as quiet as a mouse, in the corner of a room in an adjoining building, and he engaged in a profound and hours-long exchange of views with Baba Taji's successor (whose name I do not recall). They must have traversed several parallel universes that memorable night as they conversed with each other in chaste Urdu; but because of difficulties of language, I could savour only part of the intellectual and spiritual feast that was laid before me. They talked for so long that I may even have fallen asleep while they were talking and may even have done some travelling myself while sleeping; but I do remember that he shared with me the news, sometime later, that he had a personal experience of the *Rafraf khuḍr* mentioned in *Sūrah al-Raḥmān* (Qurʾān 55:76). He did not disclose to me whether they were "green cushions," or "carpets" or even "meadows," as some commentators have opined, or even something else.

I am conscious of the fact that he pursued his doctoral studies in English Literature at Cambridge University in the UK, and that he may even have taught at that University. I also know that he maintained a close attachment with Britain, and with Cambridge, all through his life. He even established "The Islamic Academy" in Cambridge, which played an important role in organizing international conferences on Islamic Education. He once took me with him to Cambridge, where I visited the Academy, and met with his educated and articulate wife. In fact it was soon after I met him in Makkah that he also became Director-General of World Centre for Islamic Education in Jeddah, Saudi Arabia in 1980, and as a consequence he was now able to direct greater effort in organizing world conferences on Islamic Education. He had already organized the First World Conference on Muslim Education in 1977, and now the Second, Third and Fourth World Conferences were organized in 1980, 1981 and 1982 respectively.[4]

---

3   Prayer, supplication, invocation of God.
4   Mabud, Shaikh Abdul, "World Conferences on Muslim Education: Shaping the Agenda of Muslim Education in the Future," in Nadeem A. Memon and Mujadad Zaman, eds., *Philosophies of Islamic Education, Historical Perspectives and Emerging Discourses* (Routledge, 2016), 129–143.

My Memories of the Cairo (Fifth) World Conference on Muslim Education, 1987

I attended the Fifth World Conference on Muslim Education which Dr Ali Ashraf helped to organize in Cairo, Egypt, in 1987, and relived nostalgic memories of the year that I had lived as a student in that city twenty-three years earlier. Memories floated down the river as I took morning walks alongside the Nile. I also used aroma as my guide as I searched the streets of Cairo to eventually find a shop selling ground Yemeni coffee (*Bun Yamanī*).

Maulana Dr Waffie Muhammad of Trinidad, who was a student of Maulana Ansari, also attended that conference. I remember presenting a paper at the conference on the subject of "Theocentricity and Islamic Education" and then having to defend, unsuccessfully so, my use of the word "God," for "Allah."

I met in the conference such distinguished scholars as Professor Seyyed Hossein Nasr, Martin Lings and Dr Malik Badri, all of them for the first time. I even took some time off from the conference to visit the famous blind Egyptian Islamic scholar, Shaikh Abdul Hameed Kishk. It is an indication of the stature that Dr Ali Ashraf occupied in the world of Islamic scholarship that he could succeed in attracting a veritable galaxy of illustrious scholars of Islam to attend that memorable conference in which I could meet with Dr Malik Badri, the supreme expert in the world in the field of Islamic psychology. I never got a chance to have a personal meeting with Professor Hossein Nasr, although I participated in some casual group discussions with him, but I was lucky to strike gold with Martin Lings.

I was troubled by the views expressed by René Guénon and the group of "perennial" Sufi scholars who were inspired by him, i.e., Guénon. They included such names as Frithjof Schuon, Titus Burckhardt, Le Guy Eaton, Hossein Nasr and Martin Lings. Schuon was, perhaps, the foremost disciple of Guénon, and he had written his *magnum opus* entitled *The Transcendent Unity of Religions*. Even while we all recognized the transcendent unity of Truth, I had significant difficulties with the view that *one universal community of faith, united by perennial truth, would emerge at the end of history*. Martin Lings was, perhaps, the foremost disciple of Schuon, and I felt that I should not lose the opportunity to have an exchange of views with him which might ease my troubled mind. I therefore chose to knock on his door in our hotel one morning just after *Ṣalāt al-Fajr*, only to be greeted by a clearly upset Martin Lings. He had spent most of the night awake in *Dhikr* and was now trying to get some sleep. He was clearly irritated by the disturbance caused to his sleep. I hurried in embarrassment to escape, only to be surprised at breakfast later that morning when he searched for me, and having found me, joined me for breakfast with profound apologies for his earlier display of irritation. We spent an hour or more in unhurried discussion on what must be considered to have been a very tough subject for a young novice like me. Most of the time we spent together that morning was devoted to the following verse of the Qurʾān for which I sought from him an explanation compatible with the views of the Sufi school to which he belonged:

$$\text{وَأَنزَلْنَا إِلَيْكَ الْكِتَابَ بِالْحَقِّ مُصَدِّقًا لِّمَا بَيْنَ يَدَيْهِ مِنَ الْكِتَابِ وَمُهَيْمِنًا عَلَيْهِ فَاحْكُم بَيْنَهُم بِمَا أَنزَلَ اللَّهُ وَلَا تَتَّبِعْ أَهْوَاءَهُمْ عَمَّا جَاءَكَ مِنَ الْحَقِّ لِكُلٍّ جَعَلْنَا مِنكُمْ شِرْعَةً وَمِنْهَاجًا وَلَوْ شَاءَ اللَّهُ لَجَعَلَكُمْ أُمَّةً وَاحِدَةً وَلَٰكِن لِّيَبْلُوَكُمْ فِي مَا آتَاكُمْ فَاسْتَبِقُوا الْخَيْرَاتِ إِلَى اللَّهِ مَرْجِعُكُمْ جَمِيعًا فَيُنَبِّئُكُم بِمَا كُنتُمْ فِيهِ تَخْتَلِفُونَ}$$

(Qurʾān 5:48)

And unto thee have We revealed the Scripture with the truth, confirming whatever Scripture was before it, and a watcher over it. So judge between them by that which Allah hath revealed, and follow not their desires away from the truth which hath come unto thee. For each We have appointed a divine law and a traced-out way. Had Allah willed He could have made you one community. But that He may try you by that which He hath given you (He hath made you as ye are). So vie one with another in good works. Unto Allah ye will all return, and He will then inform you of that wherein ye differ. (Trans., Pickthall)

Thirty-five years have passed since we sat together that morning for a lengthy exchange of views, and I am relieved that I was correct in being troubled by views which, I have now come to recognize, are in conflict with the Qurʾān—but this will have to be explained *Inshāʾ Allāh*, in another essay.

English Literature

There is much in English literature which, when viewed from the perspective of Islam, is both valid, and valuable, and it would be foolish of anyone to embark on a wholesale condemnation of that literature. I was myself inspired by Longfellow's "A Psalm of Life" which I memorized as a schoolboy. His words still ring in my ears:

Tell me not, in mournful numbers,
Life is but an empty dream!
For the soul is dead that slumbers,
And things are not what they seem.
Life is real! Life is earnest!
And the grave is not its goal;
Dust thou art, to dust returnest,
Was not spoken of the soul.

Despite the above, it would nevertheless be a matter of great importance for us if this outstanding Sufi Shaikh, who was also a scholar of English Literature, had located in English literature any evidence which confirmed Britain to be the island of *Tamīm al-Dārī* (see my book, *Jerusalem in the Qur'ān*). After all, the essence of Sufism, or *Taṣawwuf*, is located in internal intuitive spiritual insight *(al-Baṣīrah),* and it was this capacity to penetrate beyond *external appearance* to reach the *internal reality* of things which characterized the spiritual luminaries of mankind all through the ages. I would not be surprised if it transpires that Dr Ali Ashraf did discover some evidence in English Literature of a satanic epistemological agenda being pursued for the eventual secularization of knowledge, and of the process of modern education. Such evidence would, of course, have great eschatological value, even though it would not detract from the importance of learning the English language.

A Vision

A committee appointed in early 1984 to prepare a program of events through which we could commemorate Dr Ansari's death on the tenth anniversary of his departure from the world, met in Karachi in early 1984 and decided to invite Dr Ali Ashraf to travel from UK to Pakistan to address the most important commemorative event which was held at Karachi's Intercontinental Hotel. I will forever regret not having a recording of that important address in which he recognized the importance of Maulana Ansari's unique Islamic scholarship, and its abiding legacy. And it was while he was delivering his address before a large and distinguished audience on that occasion that I had a vision of Dr Ansari (repeated 4 times before Dr Ali Ashraf concluded his address) which confirmed to me that the two men were engaged in the identical struggle of responding appropriately—both intellectually and spiritually—to the ominous challenges to Islamic civilization which had come from modern godless Western civilization. Allah Most High intervened during that address of Dr Ali Ashraf to convey that message to me through a vision.

I remember inviting Dr Ali Ashraf, a few months later, to make his first ever visit to my native island of Trinidad in order to address the 1st ASJA Islamic Seminar on the topic of "Islam and Western Civilization." (ASJA is an acronym for Anjuman Sunnatul Jamaat Association, i.e., *Sunnah wal Jamā'ah*.) The seminar was held in September 1984 at the ASJA Girls College in San Fernando. Dr Ali Ashraf left no stone unturned in his address as he warned of the great dangers posed by the godless epistemological foundations of modern Western civilization. His address mirrored the glorious intellectual contributions of Dr Kalim Siddiqui and Dr Malik Badri who fearlessly blazed the same trail in exposing the psychological, political and economic *Kufr* of Western civilization.

It was certainly in pursuit of a comprehensive response to the enormously dangerous challenges posed to the process of education in Islam that Dr Ali Ashraf organized those important international conferences and seminars on the subject of Muslim Education; but he also went on to establish the *Muslim Education Quarterly* which he published from Cambridge. His dream may have been for that Quarterly journal to become the cornerstone on which succeeding generations of Islamic scholars would continue indefinitely to construct a new house for Muslim education. Such a new house would offer adequate protection from the relentless and monstrously destructive attacks launched by the modern West, and by the legions of secularized Muslim scholars who were educated and trained to function as their Trojan horses in the world of Islam.

The Fast Lane

Nature moves slowly, and the human heart, mind and memory are calibrated to move in harmony with nature. It is only when we learn to 'think,' that we can become thinkers capable of understanding and penetrating the knowledge bestowed on us in the Qurʾān. *Dajjāl* is using television, the "smart phone" and many other brilliant inventions, to cause our children in particular, as well as most of the rest of us, to become addicted to living in the *fast lane* of life that he has created and is thus destroying our capacity to 'think.' How so?

The blessed Prophet (pbuh) had warned us of that *fast lane* in which a whole year passes as if it were just a month, and a whole month as if it were just a week, and a whole week as if it were just a day, etc. (*Musnad Aḥmad*). The result is that our present generation of so-addicted children live their lives imprisoned in the "here" and "now"—aimlessly drifting in whichever direction the *fast wind* blows—and incapable in later life of either reading history, or in anticipating what lies ahead. They would adamantly refuse to spend even a single day in a Muslim Village located in the *slow-moving* remote countryside. Indeed they would protest that they will die if they had to live in such a place! We can therefore expect a world tomorrow in which less and less people would be capable of 'thinking'—and hence it will be a world with less and less thinkers!

I must confess that I already find careless *laissez-faire* indifference in some who had listened so attentively to Dr Ali Ashraf, and had felt his loving spiritual touch, and I have fear of what we can expect from the generations which will come, in the face of ever-increasing danger to faith which has constantly been emerging from the modern West.

Limits of Contemporary Sufism?

Why is it that the Sufi magnetism which changed lives so spontaneously and dramatically, could not build and sustain over time a community of believers who would *establish* the *Dīn* (religion), even in micro-communities, and thus remain faithful to Allah Most High despite the tests and trials of the modern age? Why is it that men like Maulana Abul Aʿla Maududi and Dr Israr

Ahmed could successfully build exemplary model communities in the *Jamaat-e-Islami* and *Tanzeem-e-Islami* which still struggle with commendable integrity and discipline to establish the *Dīn*, while Sufi gatherings display a lamentable elasticity with no appetite for resisting *Dajjāl*, even when he brings forth the last people who would follow him, i.e., the modern feminist revolution? What is it that explains the limits of contemporary Sufism in responding to the challenges of the modern age?

My response, offered as gently as possible, is that while contemporary Sufism can awaken dead hearts by touching the emotional cords located in the emotional being, and can ignite a spiritual journey which can transport us (with *Baṣīrah*, i.e., internal sight) to worlds beyond the material universe, it seems to lack the eschatological explanation from the blessed Qurʾān of contemporary reality. Such an explanation would have opened the eyes of the Sufis to the enormously dangerous changes taking place, for example, in the world of money. There are, of course, other dangerous changes taking place, besides the monetary, in the new financial world of banks for example, and in the post-Caliphate system of political organization, with which the West has imprisoned the rest of the world. The sad reality is that neither Sufi nor *Salafī* were able to even recognize, these last one hundred years, that the monetary system of paper-money which came to the world of Islam from *Dajjāl's*[5] mysterious Judeo-Christian Zionist alliance, was bogus, exploitative and *Ḥarām*. Neither Sufi nor *Salafī* offered any valid response to that monetary system which eventually reduced Bangladesh, as well as most of the rest of the non-European (i.e., Western European) world, to wretched miserable poverty. Cryptocurrencies and Bitcoin, (I choose to describe them as *casino money*), are now poised to replace today's bogus, fraudulent, and utterly *Ḥarām* paper-money. When they do so, most of mankind will eventually be imprisoned in a monetary Guantanamo from which very few can escape—regardless of whether they are Sufi or *Salafī*.

The inescapable implication is that Muslims have continuously betrayed the blessed Qurʾān these last one hundred years and must now hasten to direct primary attention to the Qurʾān in an earnest effort to penetrate and understand the *reality* of mysterious events which have been continuously unfolding in what must be recognized to be the last count-down in *Ākhir al-Zamān*—the End of Time. All that now remains to occur before *Dajjāl* appears in person and Jesus returns to kill him, are the *Malḥamah* or Great War,[6] and the conquest of Constantinople.

---

5   The *Dajjāl* (*al-Masīḥ al-Dajjāl*) is the liar who leads people astray, the messiah of misguidance who will tempt people by means of the signs that he is given. He will appear towards the End of Time.

6   *Al-Malḥamah al-Kubrā* is an apocalyptic great battle to occur in the end times according to Islamic eschatology.

Did the blessed Prophet (pbuh) not declare that "the best of you are those who (devote their lives) to study the Qurʾān and (then) to teach it?" Did he not complain to Allah with these sorrowful words?

$$\text{وَقَالَ الرَّسُولُ يَا رَبِّ إِنَّ قَوْمِي اتَّخَذُوا هَذَا الْقُرْآنَ مَهْجُورًا}$$

(Qurʾān, 25:30)

And on that Day the Messenger of Allah will complain: O my Lord-God! My people have surely deserted this Qurʾān and have hence treated it as a thing that is discarded!

If we are to preserve and build on the glorious legacy left by this outstanding Sufi Shaikh, I suggest that an effort be made to build such small communities in the countryside (rather than towns or cities) which would take complete control of the education of children in order to ensure that education is built on the foundations of the blessed Qurʾān. When those who live in such villages, bond with each other in a loving fraternity of believers, such a community might succeed in preserving that which was lovingly bestowed upon them by spiritual luminaries of the likes of Dr Syed Ali Ashraf.

If we are to bring forth from our Muslim communities, those who would walk in the spiritual trail blazed by Dr Ali Ashraf, we may well have to commence that spiritual journey by learning how to talk to trees, and how to listen when they talk to us. After all, we must not forget that Allah Most High, declared in the Qurʾān (71:17) that *He brought us forth from the earth as (or in the likeness of) trees and plants,* and every farmer knows the importance of protecting his nursery plants. Did Prophet Muhammad (pbuh) not inform us that Allah never sent a Prophet who was not (at some time or the other) a shepherd (*Ṣaḥīḥ Bukhārī*)? Is it not through interaction with plants and animals, as well as in taking proper care of our children, that we inculcate the humility that is indispensable for touching the hearts of mankind?

Dr Ali Ashraf Was Disturbed by My Developing Thought

It is clear that in his last years Dr Ali Ashraf was disturbed by the direction in which my Islamic scholarship was developing. He was disturbed that I was treading intellectual terrain and reaching conclusions which departed from the Islamic scholarship which had preceded me. The outstanding Islamic scholar, Dr Israr Ahmed, who was his contemporary, also felt the same way about my developing thought; and even today, more than twenty-five years later, most scholars of Islam either reject my views on Islamic eschatology or refrain from any positive comment. In fact, at that time—more than twenty-five years ago—I was just beyond the formative stage of developing my eschatological scholarship on *Dajjāl*, the false Messiah, and on Gog and Magog, and I was slowly constructing, brick by brick, my house of Islamic eschatology. Neither was I aware at that time of my destination, nor was he—hence, perhaps, his discomfort. I persisted in my effort, despite his discomfort, to understand the *reality* of the historical process in *Ākhir al-Zamān*, until I was eventually rewarded, by Allah's Kindness and Grace, to understand several verses of the Qur'ān which delivered the very foundation of Islamic eschatology. Only then was I able to interpret, for example, the *shadow* mentioned in the Qur'ān (77:30) which had three parts, as *Dajjāl's* master-plan to eventually *rule* the world, stage-by-stage, through a movement from a *Pax Britannica* and *Pax Americana* to a *Pax Judaica*, and to publish, within just a few years of Dr Ashraf's death, my first book in Islamic eschatology entitled *Jerusalem in the Qur'ān*.

I am sustained in my eschatological scholarship by the abiding conviction that whatever is truth will survive and will abide, even if a lonely scholar has to tread troubled waters, and whatever is false and misguided will eventually be exposed and rejected.

Sunset

There are many, I believe, who felt the way I felt, that Dr Ali Ashraf brought both dazzling sunshine and heavenly raindrops with him wherever he went, and that he brought to our lives an unforgettable moment in time—when it appeared as though time itself had stopped still—so we could savour *endless time*. And so when he died in the UK, and the news reached me in New York, it was as though the sun had set and darkness had fallen upon the earth. But twenty-five years after his death, it remains clear that timeless *Nūr* (Light) which comes from Allah will continue to linger on in the world long after the stars have gone to sleep.

I visited his grave in Bangladesh where he now rests next to his dear wife, and prayed for them both, and I pray that at least some of those who read this essay may also, one day, be able to visit him where he now rests, and also pray for them both—husband and wife. *Āmīn!* May Allah Most Kind have Mercy on his soul and forgive him his sins. *Āmīn!* And may Allah also accept his pioneering work for extricating Muslim education from the secular abyss into which it is still being led by modern godless Western civilization, and his noble work for restoring its spiritual foundations that are located in the blessed Qur'ān. May Allah Most High grant that his work might continue to blossom in the loving hands of the scholars who have succeeded him. *Āmīn!*

There are, of course, immense obstacles to be overcome if Dr Ali Ashraf's work in Muslim education is to further blossom, even in my native Caribbean Island of Trinidad where those who have the knowledge and competence to guide the process of Muslim education in our Muslim schools and colleges are banned by *Dajjāl's* schoolboy leaders from doing so. But we must have patience, and must persevere, despite all obstacles, since the alternative to perseverance would be the possible loss of coming generations of Muslims.

Chapter 39

Professor Syed Ali Ashraf: Visits to Trinidad

Waffie Mohammed

Professor Syed Ali Ashraf visited Trinidad for the first time in 1984. He was invited by the Anjuman Sunnatul Jamaat Association (ASJA) to deliver the keynote address on the topic, "Islam and Western Civilization" at a one-day seminar held at the ASJA Girls' College in San Fernando, Trinidad. Before his coming to Trinidad, he was known by both Maulanas Imran Nazar Hosein and Siddiq A. Nasir. They had both met him at the University of Karachi in Pakistan and at the World Center for Islamic Education in Jeddah, Saudi Arabia. It was Maulana Imran Nazar Hosein who suggested to ASJA that the Professor was the most competent person to deliver the feature address at the proposed seminar.

Professor Ashraf was very impressed with the work that Muslims were doing in Trinidad and continued to visit this country many times afterwards. He came to these shores on at least eight occasions, viz. in 1984, 1985, 1986, 1988, 1989, 1993, 1997 and 1998. During his second visit, he began reactivating the spiritual dimension of those who had given their allegiances (*bay'ah*[1]) to the spiritual teachers who had visited Trinidad before—Shaykhs like Maulana Abdul Aleem Siddiqi[2] and Maulana Dr Fazlur Rahman Ansari.[3] He found that many of the *murīds*[4] had the *dhikr*[5] in their *qalb*.[6] He also began giving *dhikr* to others who were interested.

---

1 *Bay'ah* is oath of allegiance to a particular Sufi Shaykh, which marks the initiation into the Sufi order.
2 Muhammad Abdul Aleem Siddiqi, born on 22 August 1954 in Meerut, India and died on 3 April 1892 in Madina.
3 Muhammad Fazlur Rahman Ansari, born in Saharanpur, India, on 14 August 1914 and died in Karachi on 3 June 1974.
4 A *murīd* (lit. committed one) is a novice of a Sufi order; disciple.
5 The practice of *dhikr* focuses on remembering Allah in one's heart.
6 The spiritual heart.

It became necessary to entrust someone with the charge of conducting the *dhikr* sessions during his absence, and Maulana Dr Waffie Mohammed was so designated. Later on, upon his fourth visit in 1988, he appointed Hajji Kamaluddin Ghanny and Haji Aleem Mohammed to assist Dr Waffie. Professor Ashraf realized that in the beautiful island of the Republic of Trinidad a lot of major Islamic activities were possible and as a result, he tried to improve the condition of the Muslims both theologically and spiritually.

His efforts in Trinidad were centered on three main areas of activities. These were:

- To bring together the spiritual groups and to assist them in reaching their goal, that is, to attain *maʿrifah*,[7] and to initiate others in the spiritual path.
- To assist the Muslims in establishing a well-coordinated theological programme by developing a theological institution with a strong external links.
- To develop a syllabus and accompanying materials for faith and value-based education, both in the denominational primary and secondary schools, as well as in the government primary and secondary schools.

During each of his visits, he worked energetically in pursuing these programmes with the hope of having some tangible results in the shortest space of time. The results of his efforts can be summarized as follows:

Spiritual Supervision

Upon his visit in 1984, the Professor Ashraf found that Muslims were attached to numerous spiritual orders. The largest group was from the Qādiriyyah Order with the *murīds* having as their Shaykh either Maulana Abdul Aleem Siddiqui or Maulana Dr Fazlur Rahman Ansari. Maulana Dr Waffie Mohammed, who was a *murīd* of Maulana Dr Fazlur Rahman Ansari, was given *ijāzah*[8] by his Shaykh to accept *murīds* in the Qādiriyyah Order. The other group with a significant number of followers was the Naqshbandī Order, with Haji Muhammad Yusuf Francis[9] being their Shaykh. Haji Francis was alive at the time of Professor Ashraf's visits. There were a small number of followers of the Tijānī Order and a few more *murīds* with *mashāikhs*[10] from India and Pakistan. Professor Ashraf used to visit Haji Francis every time he came to Trinidad,

---

7   Gnosis; spiritual realization, experience.
8   Permission and authorization to initiate others into the Sufi path.
9   Born on 28 August 1903, in St. James, Trinidad and died on 17 April 1993. He hailed from a devout Roman Catholic family and accepted Islam in 1925. He lies buried in St. James cemetery, Trinidad.
10 Master of a spiritual order. Also used for religious scholars.

and they both had a very cordial relation, as they were both *murīds* of the late Shaykh Manzoor Hussain[11] who resided in the holy city of Madinah.

In 1985 Maulana Dr Waffie Mohammed gave his allegiance (*bayʿah*) to Professor Ashraf and entrusted all his *murīds* to his care. Some made remarkable spiritual progress and one of Dr Waffie's students, Hajji Kamaluddin Ghanny, was given permission to conduct *dhikr* sessions. Professor Ashraf, who was a Shaykh of the Naqshbandī order, accommodated the *murīds* from all the spiritual orders in his *dhikr* and meditation sessions, as he informed the people that he had a spiritual request from Maulana Dr Fazlur Rahman Ansari to assist his *murīds* as well. His famous instruction to all those who sat with him was, "concentrate on your *qalb*," that is, your spiritual heart.

Professor Ashraf authorized those who were given the permission to conduct the *dhikr* sessions to accept new *murīds*' oaths of allegiance (*bayʿah*) on his behalf. As time went by, he found that one of the brothers, that is, Hajji Kamaluddin Ghanny was beginning to exceed the expectations required of a *murīd*, so he withdrew the *ijāzah* that was given to him, leaving only two brothers to sit in front of the groups at the time of meditation.

The Professor used to conduct the *dhikr* sessions in three main centers in Trinidad. In the north it was in a mosque with a beautiful scenic location called Santa Cruz. It was located in a valley between the mountains of the northern range. Every morning, brothers and sisters from all over the country used to journey to that mosque to attend the *Fajr*[12] prayer in *jamāʿah*[13] with him and then to sit in *murāqabah*[14] with him until sunrise. His daily schedule was to pray *tahajjud*[15] and *Fajr*, sit in *murāqabah*, take breakfast, take a little rest, and then meet *murīds* or go on visits. After lunch and *Ẓuhr ṣalāt*, he would take some rest and then offer the *ʿAsr* prayer, then he met *murīds*, and might journey to other places to give talks. He used to conduct *murāqabah*[16] after *Maghrib* prayer and then he would return to retire for the night.

In the central part of the country, the gatherings used to be in one of the many mosques. These included San Juan, Curepe, Tacarigua, Warrenville, Marabella, Princes Town, Macoon Street, San Fernando, and La Romaine. In the South it was nearly all the time at the Avocat Masjid. Besides these centers, the Professor visited many *jamāʿahs* (religious gatherings) and some of the

---

11 Born on 31 December 1899 in Khairpur, India and died on 15 April 1988 in Karachi, Pakistan. He was buried in Madinah.
12 Five mandatory prayers in Islam are: *Fajr* (dawn payer), *Ẓuhr* (midday payer), *ʿAsr* (afternoon payer), *Maghrib* (sunset payer) and *ʿIshāʾ* (night payer).
13 Congregation.
14 *Murāqabah* is a spiritual method of 'observing' and 'watching' in a state of stillness whereby the aspirant concentrates on their heart to gain insight into their relationship with their Creator.
15 Supererogatory (*nafl*) prayers offered normally after midnight.
16 It is a spiritual exercise of meditation whereby the aspirant (*murīd*) strives to empty the heart of all thoughts and concentrates on the Name of Allah.

primary and secondary schools in the afternoon. Wherever he used to pray, he used to carry on the *dhikr* sessions and delivered inspiring speeches to the congregations.

In order to help the newcomers understand about *dhikr* and *murāqabah*, the Professor, along with one of his *murīds*, Dr Waffie Mohammed, prepared a booklet entitled *Meditation*. This booklet was printed on behalf of Jamaat-e Madina which was founded by Shaykh Dr Badiuzzaman of Chowmuhani, Noakhali, Bangladesh. The Professor himself was the Amīr of this Jamaat here in Trinidad. This book contains six important chapters and other information necessary for the initiated to understand all about meditation, *hadiyyah*,[17] *dhikr* and *murāqabah*. This booklet was and continues to be distributed to all *murīds*. It was later revised and reprinted in Bangladesh. It is being reprinted here in Trinidad whenever necessary and is always available to new *murīds*. It is a very helpful book for anyone wishing to understand what *bayʿah* is and how to carry on the spiritual exercises.

Professor Ashraf made meditation and *murāqabah* meaningful to the spiritual seekers (aspirant, *murīd*) or travellers (*sālik*) who seek to progress from the realm of seeking into the realm of perception and finding, that is, those who were desirous of attaining nearness to Allah through *dhikr*. He made them understand that in order to progress spiritually one must satisfy certain conditions. These are outlined in the booklet as follows:

- The seeker on the spiritual path should follow the Sharīʿah.
- The seeker must have sincerity and purity of intention and realize that good fortune depends on His (Allah's) pleasure and bad luck is caused by His displeasure.
- The meditator must have complete concentration while meditating.
- The meditator should keep their attention on the source of grace (*faiḍ*) and the region where it arrives.
- The meditator needs to be aware of the stages they are crossing in *murāqabah*.

Many of his *murīds* were able to activate the five spiritual points (*laṭāʾif*, sing. *laṭīfah*). Some were given the five different lights (*nūr*),[18] and some had the good fortune of ascending.[19]

---

17 Lit. offerings; asking Allah to send the rewards of a virtuous act—such as the recitation of some blessed words, *sūrahs* or formulas from the Qurʾān or Ḥadīth—upon the soul of the spiritual masters and other Muslims.
18 Each of the five *laṭāʾif* is associated with a particular colour of light (*nūr*).
19 Known as *ʿurūj* in Sufi terminology, when the aspirant traverses different spiritual realms.

Theological Education

Professor Ashraf was very happy to find full-time and part-time theological institutions in this country. He visited the Darul Uloom which is a full-time theological institution managed by the Tabligh Jamaat. This institution is located in the central part of Trinidad and caters for young boys and girls housed in separate buildings. This institution caters for young students who are desirous of doing academic as well as theological education. It is registered with the Ministry of Education as a denominational school.

The other theological institution that Professor Ashraf visited was the Haji Ruknuddeen Institute of Islamic Studies (HRIIS). This was a part-time theological seminary and was run by the Anjuman Sunnatul Jamaat Association. Maulana Dr Waffie Mohammed, who was at the time the Director of the Regional Office of the Muslim World League, was the principal.

Professor Ashraf had liked this institution very much and on two occasions delivered the keynote address at the graduation ceremonies to the students who had successfully completed the two-year diploma course. On the second occasion the theme of his lecture was "Education and Values: Islamic vis-à-vis the Secularist Approaches."[20] It was a very enlightening speech, and in it he outlined many important areas worth considering if the education system is to help improve the lives of these students by making them better adults in the morrow. He concluded his presentation with the following message:

> Islam thus provides basic universal foundations of the norm, helps parents and teachers to be conscious of the 'intrinsic' worth and character of human nature, and make children conscious of it gradually through the cultivation and strengthening of faith through a process of the learning, experiencing and broadening of different spheres of Knowledge and through increasing awareness of the intimate relationship between God, Man and Nature and the gradual unfolding of its manifestation to children through graded courses at individual, societal, worldly and universal levels of existence.[21]

As the Professor was always the guest of the Anjuman Sunnatul Jamaat Association (ASJA) of Trinidad and Tobago, he attempted to connect the ASJA's theological institute, that is, the Haji Ruknuddeen Institute of Islamic Studies (HRIIS) to Al-Azhar in Cairo and Nadwatul Ulama in India, in whatever way it was possible and also to find a suitable principal from one of these institutions for HRIIS. He was hoping that if a suitable full-time principal was appointed, HRIIS could become a full-time theological institution, which could have met

---

20 Syed Ali Ashraf, "Education and Values: Islamic vis-à-vis the Secularist Approaches," *Muslim Education Quarterly* 4, no. 2 (1987): 4.
21 Syed Ali Ashraf, "Education and Values," 13.

the requirements of enrolling students from the other Caribbean islands as well.

In his search for a principal, he took along with him Hajji Zainol A. Khan, who was the first vice-president of ASJA for most of the Professor's visits in Trinidad, to Egypt, Makkah, Madina and India.[22] He also appointed Dr Aleem Mohammed of Trinidad as a member of the Board of Trustees of the Islamic Academy in Cambridge and of the Darul Ihsan University in Dhaka, Bangladesh. By so doing he was developing a direct connection between the theological institutions in Trinidad and his own theological institution, Darul Ihsan in Bangladesh as Dr Aleem Mohamed was then one of the important members of the ASJA's Executive Committee and a member of the Board of HRIIS.

Professor Ashraf was also contemplating having a memorandum of agreement between HRIIS and Darul Ihsan University whereby the HRIIS students could study the degree courses of Darul Ihsan University and sit their exams as external students. However, that programme was in the initial stage and the details had to be worked out. Unfortunately, the programme did not materialize, as the change of administration in ASJA prevented further pursuit of what was initially decided, and the Professor passed away before having further discussions on the subject with the new Executive Committee of ASJA.

Faith and Value-Based Education

Professor Ashraf was very interested in developing syllabuses for the country's primary and secondary schools. He wanted to have "an integrated system of education so that the future generations may be made fully conscious of the essential norm of humanity and may get the benefits of the cultivation of faith in God." He openly preached that education should be faith based. For example, in his presentation at the second graduation ceremony of the HRIIS, he began his address with the following remarks:

> The aims and functions of education are integrally related to the concept of man, the purpose of human existence, and the goal and destiny of mankind. The Islamic and the secularist approaches are fundamentally different in these spheres. They seem to meet and coalesce occasionally in external peripheries, but their roots are different and antagonistic. Islam is rooted in faith in God, the Prophet and in the Hereafter. Secularism is rooted in a tentative faith in the evolution of a conscious, willing, rational man and other living creatures and the rest of the universe, out of a Godless, causeless, completely non-rational, inert matter.[23]

---

22 See Chapter 39 for Prof Ashraf's visit to Cairo, Jeddah, Makkah and Delhi with Zainol Khan for this purpose.
23 Syed Ali Ashraf, "Education and Values," 4.

Through ASJA he was able to convince the government of Trinidad and Tobago that education is a twofold process—one is "acquiring external knowledge breeding extrinsic faith and the other, through internal realization of the intrinsic meaning and worth of that knowledge in training man to play his individual, societal, cultural and civilizational role in a world perspective."[24]

He was able to impress upon the government that such a programme was designed to assist the future generation to be more mindful of their rights and responsibilities as members of society. As a result, a three-day seminar was planned. This seminar was coordinated by the Inter-Religious Organization and the Ministry of Education of Trinidad and Tobago. The Honorable Prime Minister of Trinidad and Tobago opened the first day's proceedings and the Minister of Education stayed during the entire proceedings of the first day.

The aims and objectives and the philosophical principles of education that Professor Ashraf developed for discussion at the conference were as follows:

1. Education should aim at the balanced development of the total personality of individuals through the integrated flowering of the spiritual, moral, ethical, intellectual, emotional, imaginative, and physical selves.
2. In order to achieve this aim, the educational policymakers should derive from religion the essential norm of humanity, the purpose of human existence, and the final goal of human achievement as a whole-hearted servant of God ready to serve God through their selfless service to humanity and their benevolent control over external nature.
3. This goal can be achieved through common commitment to an agreed form of pluralism and the explicit recognition by all groups of the four common beliefs as follows:
4. Belief in the transcendental essence of a Deity, (b) belief in the existence of the spiritual dimension in each human being, (c) belief in the eternal and fundamental values such as Truth, Justice, Righteousness, Mercy, Love, Compassion, and care for all creation which are to be found reflected and developed in the human self and the need for them to be encouraged, nurtured, refined, and developed, and (d) belief in the need for Divine (or transcendental) guidance.
5. As faith in God strengthens a person's wholehearted commitment to such values, it is the duty of educational policymakers to make explicit provisions for the nurturing of faith in God through the teaching of the essence of religions (Religious Education) to all students and also through the provision of religious instruction in distinctive faiths to pupils belonging to different faiths.
6. The common core of values should also include respect for the cultural and religious beliefs and practices of different groups, the pursuit of coop-

---

24 Syed Ali Ashraf, "Education and Values," 9.

eration, the peaceful resolution of personal and social disagreements and respect for the natural environment and natural resources.
7. It should also include the proper use of standard English as a common language and provide equal opportunity for all pupils to attain mastery of this language, as a means of clear communication for organized, rational thoughts and emotive expressions, and the reinforcement of aesthetic and religious sensibilities.
8. For the progressive development of the society in terms of its shared values, the common core should also include a system of revisable practices and democratic political procedures, provided the basic norm of values and their realization in practice as commonly accepted and preached by religions are upheld through education.
9. Education should promote the search for truth and the form of inquiry and justification appropriate to different kinds of knowledge and experience. The prime end in all areas is not the development of doubt or skepticism but the achievement of commitment and assent, freely given an appropriate ground. Education is not and cannot in practice be understood as concerned with each child individually constructing a body of beliefs, for all of which they have personal justification. It is concerned with each pupil coming to understand the need for his beliefs to be appropriately grounded.
10. Because of their complex interrelations, education must necessarily be concerned with the progressive development of pupils' spiritual, moral, intellectual, imaginative, social, emotional, and physical capacities or their cognitive, affective, and conative aspects. It should attend responsibly to all their dimensions and their interrelations.
11. The acquisition of knowledge is the means of achieving the above aims. The whole gamut of human knowledge should therefore be divided into three categories on the basis of a human being's relationship with God, with other human beings and with external nature including natural beings.
12. For these three branches, basic concepts in all branches of human sciences and natural sciences should be derived from the principles given in religious sciences. At present secularist concepts completely ignore the concepts given in religious sciences, which are mainly derived from God-given knowledge.
13. Knowledge of these concepts can be found in the work already done by Hindu, Christian, Bahá'í and Muslim educationalists and thinkers in the last thirty years. For further conceptual work the government is hereby advised to fund research to formulate such concepts.
14. As the secularist concepts, on the basis of which humanities, social sciences and natural sciences are often taught, completely ignore the religious concepts and propagate openly anti-religious concepts, it has become nec-

essary to formulate concepts from the knowledge that religion gives about human nature, about the eternal values and the consciousness which is ingrained into them and about how faith in God and love of God strengthen a human being's love for those values.

Thus, the scientific concept of history ignores the moral law that pervades the historical panorama, the law that makes us conscious of God's quality of justice operative in the universe and teaches nations and races to be good. Similarly, the secularist concept of democracy, which makes people the sovereign, lacks the ultimate universal and eternal norm of innate values that religion teaches by asserting the sovereignty of God.

The government is therefore urged to get the conceptual research done so that proper textbooks could be prepared on the basis of concepts that the religious concept of human nature helps us to formulate.

15. Science education needs to be based on the concept that freedom to do all research is limited by the overarching concept of God-given natural laws for the universe which should not be violated as this would lead to unimaginable disasters. The present concept of a large number of modern scientists that nature is not created by God but is an evolved imperfect phenomenon which human beings can try to make perfect should be replaced by the concept of creation and God-given laws which scientists should discover and teach and use for their research.

16. Young people in our society are already exposed to the bewildering variety of attitudes and assumptions presented by the mass media. There should be education in media values with reference to the essence of values taught by all religions so that this may help them become critically aware of these influences on their lives, to discover how appropriate the potentiality is for good which also resides in the mass media and to reject their more destructive and harmful offerings. In this matter, close cooperation should be arranged between the teachers and the parents. At the same time, the government should establish a set of publicly agreed values and standards in which religions should cooperate. This ought to be encapsulated in regulatory structures against which the productions of the media should be judged and to which it should be held accountable. In order to achieve this end, cooperation of the media be given the force of law.

The conference made recommendations and a committee was appointed by the government to pursue the aims and objectives of education as enunciated above. A new syllabus was developed, and the appropriate materials to be used as teaching aids are currently being assembled.

The conference made recommendations under the following heads:

- Suggested common value framework for the curriculum:
- Beliefs and values: Intellectual, emotional, and social.

- Suggested guidelines for implementing the curriculum objectives.
- The content of value-based curriculum.
- Textbook revision.
- Recommendation for teacher education.

Professor Ashraf was very concerned about the continuation of his mission in this part of the world, and he urged Dr Waffie Mohammed to make sure that the *murīds* continue to receive attention. He then departed from these shores on his way home but was taken by Allah while he was in that country. May Allah bless his soul.

Chapter 40

Reminiscing on Professor Syed Ali Ashraf
Zainol A. Khan

In February 2013 Professor Shaikh Abdul Mabud, Director General of the Islamic Academy of Cambridge, wrote to me advising that the Academy was planning to publish a Commemorative Volume in cherished memory of his predecessor, the late Professor Syed Ali Ashraf (may Allah be pleased with him). He invited me to submit an article to be included in the publication, and suggested I chose from a number of themes, one of which was "Personal Memories of Professor Ashraf." I accepted the invitation and subsequently submitted the following essay.

How I Became Acquainted with the Name

I first became acquainted with the name Syed Ali Ashraf when I saw a short article entitled "Iman and Islam" written by a person carrying that name in a publication some forty or more years ago. What struck me were the words "M.A. Cantab" appearing in brackets after the name. Having been born in a country which had been part of the British Empire and followed the British political and educational systems, I said to myself: "This article has to be good because the author is a graduate of one of the most prestigious universities in the world." So, I decided to read the article and was not disappointed, either with the contents (from which I learnt a great deal) or with the succinct way in which it was written as, indeed, one would expect from a graduate of Cambridge University.

The contents of the article made an indelible impression on me so much so that I reproduced it subsequently in one of the issues of the "Trinidad and Tobago Eid-ul-Fitr Annual" which I edited for many years. In addition, I would paraphrase its contents when I was sometimes called upon to address the audience at small Islamic functions. When some decades later I did have the privilege of meeting the author of the article (who was then a professor at the University of Cambridge) and having him as my house guest on many occasions I once reminded him of the article, but he could not recall it.

My First Encounter with the Professor

In late 1984 I visited Australia and New Zealand and while on my return journey I spent a week in Karachi as a guest of the World Federation of Islamic Missions and its affiliate, the Aleemiyah Institute of Islamic Studies, which was founded by the late Dr Fazlur Rahman Ansari in honour of the late Maulana Abdul Aleem Siddiqui[1] (May Allah be pleased with them both). At the time I held the position of the first Vice President of the Anjuman Sunnat-ul-Jamaat Association (ASJA) and Chairman of its Propagation Committee.

During my visit to Karachi, I held discussions with Shaikh Imran Nazar Hosein (a Trinidadian who was among the first group of graduates of the Aleemiyah Institute and was at the time a Lecturer there) with a view to his returning home for a few weeks for the purpose of conducting a series of lectures and seminars. Shaikh Hosein was amenable to the suggestion and a few weeks later he arrived in Trinidad to conduct the programmes.

While finalising his programme, the Shaikh informed me of the capabilities of one Professor Syed Ali Ashraf of Cambridge University and suggested that the professor should be invited to conduct a seminar in Trinidad and Tobago. I thought the idea was a very good one. The Shaikh advised that he could contact the professor by phone. I obtained the approval of the President of the Association immediately after which the Shaikh rang the professor from my home. After speaking to the professor for a few minutes the Shaikh introduced me to him over the phone, then passed the phone to me so I could formally invite him to visit the country for a week as a guest of the Association in order to conduct the seminar. I did so, and we agreed on the dates of his arrival, the seminar and his departure. He further told me that he would like to conduct some *murāqabah* (meditation) sessions while he was in Trinidad and requested that they be arranged.

I must confess that when speaking on the phone with the professor I was immediately impressed as his voice and manner of speaking conveyed the impression to me that, besides being knowledgeable in the academic and Islamic areas, he had an amiable disposition and would be easy to get along with.

The Professor's First Visit to Trinidad

On the professor's arrival in the country the President of ASJA and I awaited him in the restricted Customs area and recognised him immediately as he

---

1   Maulana Siddiqui paid a six-month visit to Trinidad in 1950 as part of one of his world tours. He was accompanied by his son-in-law, Dr Fazlur Rahman Ansari, who carried out the duties of Private Secretary. Maulana Siddiqui passed away in 1954 in Madinah at the age of 63 after performing the Hajj. Dr Ansari paid three further visits to Trinidad and was elected Sheikh-ul-Islam in 1974 following the demise of Haji Ruknuddeen. As he was resident in Karachi, a local Muslim Advisory Council was established and worked under his directions. He died in Karachi in 1974.

stood in the Immigration line waiting to be attended to. It was easy to identify him as he wore a sherwani and a Jinnah cap. He saw the President and me, both of whom wore *kurtas* and *topees*, smiled and waved to us.

We met the professor after he passed through Immigration and welcomed him to our country. I cleared him through Customs (where I had worked during my first ten years in the Public Service and still had some contacts) and we escorted him to the public area where a number of people were waiting to welcome him. I then drove him to my home where he was my guest during his week's visit. Joining us at dinner that night were a few people including the President of ASJA and Shaikh Hosein.

The seminar was scheduled for the following Sunday. During the week the professor visited some of the ASJA's Primary schools, addressed a meeting of schoolteachers and met members of the ASJA Executive Committee. Traditionally, lectures to the Muslim community related to Islamic topics. As the seminar to be conducted by the professor was on a non-traditional subject, it was thought it might attract only a very small audience. However, a nearly full hall of participants assembled (about 175 people of different backgrounds and ages) on that Sunday morning to hear the professor deliver his lecture, which was followed by numerous questions and lively discussions.

Visits to Haji Muhammad Yusuf Francis[2]

As I mentioned previously, during my first telephone conversation with the professor he had indicated that he would like to conduct some *murāqabah* sessions while in Trinidad. I deduced from that request that he was a Shaikh of a Sufi order. I subsequently found out that he belonged to the Naqshbandi Order. Very early during his first visit to the country he told me that he must pay a visit to Haji Francis, a revert to Islam. We did so and the professor made it his duty to pay his respects to Haji Francis during all his subsequent visits to the country.

---

2 I first made acquaintance with Haji Francis (1903–1993) in the mid-forties when I became involved in Islamic activities. Haji Francis became a revert to Islam in 1925. Subsequent to his reversion, his siblings also reverted to Islam. He started a group involving Muslim youths called "The Muhaidhudeen Young Men's League" in the capital city which was very active in projecting Islam. He became involved in one of the Sufi Orders (Naqshbandi) and was able to attract a group of people who met once a week for *murāqabah* sessions. In the early sixties he visited Madinah where he spent about two years with his Shaikh. I would meet him at various functions and briefly before the Jumʿah *ṣalāt* at the Jama Masjid, Port of Spain while I was working. In addition, I would consult him for guidance on what course of action I should take on a number of occasions. I do not know how the professor became aware of the activities of Haji Francis and can only surmise it was through his international connections.

Courtesy Call on the President of the Republic of Trinidad and Tobago

Justice Noor Mohammed Hassanali, a retired Appeal Court Judge, was elected to the position of President of the country on March 19th, 1987. During his visit later that year the professor told me that he would like to make a courtesy call on the President, who was a Muslim. I made the necessary arrangement with the President, with whom I had been acquainted for a number of years and accompanied the professor on the visit.

After the usual courtesies were exchanged the professor advised the President of his involvement in the effort to further faith-based education in the United Kingdom and other countries and of the seminar he was due to conduct in this connection at the Hilton Hotel. The President, who had a keen interest in education and had in fact been a teacher at a Secondary School for a few years before leaving the country to study law, wished the professor success in his efforts.

Dinner and Tea with His Compatriots

My wife had been actively involved on a voluntary basis in a number Islamic activities for most of her adult life. One such area was imparting Islamic religious instructions at the University Private School, a task which she thoroughly enjoyed and performed for twenty-eight years. The school catered primarily for the children of the academic and lay staff of the St. Augustine Campus of the University of the West Indies. The academic staff was drawn from various parts of the world.

During one of the professor's earlier visits my wife told him that there was a Bangladeshi lecturer attached to the University, a Dr Aberdeen, whose child attended her Islamic class. The professor expressed interest in meeting the family, so my wife contacted the child's mother whom she had met on a few occasions at the school and invited the family to have dinner with us. They accepted our invitation and the professor happily conversed with them and relished the Bangladeshi-style fruit dessert Mrs Aberdeen brought. During the dinner Dr Aberdeen told the professor that there were about three or four other Bangladeshis lecturing at the University besides himself. The professor informed Dr Aberdeen that he would like to meet with them also. As a result, we had them all over for tea one afternoon. As I recall they brought some Bangladeshi delicacies with them which the professor thoroughly enjoyed. The professor was very happy in the company of his compatriots and was all smiles on those two occasions.

Mrs Ashraf Accompanies the Professor on a Few of His Visits

Mrs Ashraf accompanied the professor on at least two of his visits to Trinidad. On the first occasion both were our guests for the period of their visit.

My wife, who was at the time President of the ASJA Ladies Section, invited the members of the Executive Committee to have tea at our home in order to meet Mrs Ashraf. Besides the social aspect of the visit, this gave Mrs Ashraf an insight into the activities of the group.

Murāqabah Sessions

At the beginning of this article I mentioned that when I extended an invitation to the professor over the phone to visit the country for the purpose of conducting a seminar, he indicated to me that he would like to organise some *murāqabah* sessions during his visit. As mentioned also, during his first visit he made it his duty to pay his respects to Haji Francis who had conducted such activities for many years but was now failing in health.

The professor was able to attract a fairly large group of people to join in this exercise, perhaps about a hundred or so, as evidenced by the number of people who would be at the airport to meet him on the occasions of his arrivals and departures. These sessions were conducted mostly coinciding with the *Fajr ṣalāt* (morning prayer) at two different venues, one of which was far from my home. This necessitated his staying at one of his *murīds* (disciples) in the area. As a result, after a few years, when visiting the country he would come to my home directly from the airport, have dinner with a few guests and leave about eleven next morning for the home of one of his *murīds*, returning to my home about eleven on the morning of his departure, have lunch with some guests, after which I would take him to the airport to catch his flight back home.

The Professor Attends Rabita (Muslim World League) Conference

The professor arrived for his annual visit to Trinidad in 1989 a few days before a two-day Rabita Conference for the Caribbean and South America was due to be held. He was my house guest at that time, and I advised him of the Conference and that I would be attending it as a delegate of my Association. When he learned that Dr Abdullah Omar Nasseef, Secretary General of Rabita (Rābiṭat al-ʿālam ail-islāmī), was due to attend he became very excited. He told me that Dr Nasseef and he had taught at the same University in Saudi Arabia for a number of years and a close relationship existed between them. He expressed the desire to attend the Conference and I told him that he should contact the local Director of Rabita, whom he knew very well, in order to obtain an invitation so he could attend. The Director advised him that the issuing of invitations was under the purview of the Secretary General and that the professor's request would be put to him when he arrived, which was the evening before the Conference was due to start. Very late on that evening the local

Director rang the professor and informed him that Dr Nasseef had approved his request.

Accordingly, the professor attended the two-day Conference and sat at the table with the delegates of ASJA. When the delegates broke for *Ẓuhr ṣalāt* (midday prayer) and lunch on the first day I was separated from the professor while proceeding to the prayer hall. After the *ṣalāt* was completed, I could not see the professor because of the large number of delegates and accordingly proceeded to the dining hall with the expectation of finding him there. After looking around for a while I saw the professor and Dr Nasseef sitting at a table having lunch. The professor saw me and motioned for me to join them, which I did. We were later joined by two officials of Rabita. The professor and Dr Nasseef carried on a light conversation during lunch, mostly about old times together. However, from their conversation and reactions to each other I came to the conclusion that they were very close friends. Dr Nasseef invited the professor to visit with him in his suite after dinner that night as we left the table to return to the Conference Hall.

After dinner the professor asked me to accompany him to Dr Nasseef's room. I agreed as the professor was my house guest and was travelling to and from the Conference with me. Again, both of them were smiling and laughing while they spoke, obviously reminiscing about some events in the past. After about an hour we took leave of Dr Nasseef, with the professor and Dr Nasseef embracing tightly in the Islamic fashion for a long time, both obviously with the thought "When will we meet again?"

The Professor at the Dining Table

Prior to the professor's arrival in the country my wife sought advice from Shaikh Hosein on the professor's preferences for meals. She was told, among other things, that he liked stewed fish with "kitcherie" (rice cooked together with split mung bean or lentil) and a vegetable known locally as "lowkie" (marrow or bottle gourd in some countries). My wife was familiar with it as her mother used to cook it. After we were married my mother-in-law would sometimes send some cooked "lowkie" for us but, not being a lover of vegetables or one to venture into eating food to which I was not accustomed, I never partook of it. My wife loved it, however. At that time, I used to go to the market on weekends to purchase fresh vegetables and similar produce (my wife, of course, making a list of her needs). "Lowkie" was not easily available as it was used mainly by older people of East Indian descent. I was eventually able to locate one or two vendors who stocked the item when it was available and obtained it whenever the professor was our guest.

As regards his daily routine, the professor occupied the bedroom next to the one my wife and I occupied. The bedroom was also adjacent to the prayer room cum library. I would often hear some movements in his room in the early hours of the morning, which indicated that he was awake. When I went to the prayer room for the *Fajr ṣalāt* I would on most occasions find him already there waiting for me. We would converse until the *Fajr ṣalāt* was performed, after which he would return to his room. He would normally come out of his room after having a shower about half an hour after sunrise, have a cup of coffee and some crackers, then return to his room for a while. He would come out about an hour and a half later to have breakfast, which consisted mainly of a soft-boiled egg and toast. I was never a lover of soft-boiled eggs but had to have one to keep the professor's company while he was having his. Since that time whenever my wife gives me a soft-boiled egg at breakfast I think of the professor. We never had guests for breakfast and quite often the professor would call my wife by her first name, telling her to come and join us at the table. Initially she would decline but eventually the professor became like one of the family and eventually she would have no hesitation in joining us at the table.

We would normally have guests for lunch. Over the years they included the Presidents of the three Muslim organisations, a former senior member of the Cabinet of the country, a Pakistani national who had been taught by the professor at Karachi University and was the local Manager of a foreign bank, a number of Imams and field workers in the cause of Islam. My wife would consult the professor on the menu for the day and he would tell her to prepare a simple meal. My wife, however, would prepare a variety of dishes and when we sat at the table she would come and explain what was contained in the various dishes. The professor would shake his head and tell her she should not have taken so much trouble. Then I, with a serious look on my face, would quip: "Professor, you know it's only when you are here that I get good food to eat." At this, the professor would laugh heartily, shake his head sideways in disagreement, and respond: "No. No."

During one of the professor's visits we had as our luncheon guests four of the first graduates of the Aleemiyah Institute of Islamic Studies, Karachi, Pakistan. They were, Shaikh Ali Mustafa, a Surinamese revert of African descent who had served as a missionary in a number of countries and was on a short lecture tour of Trinidad; Maulana Siddique Ahmad Nasir of neighbouring Guyana, who was in Trinidad to conduct a series of lectures; Maulana Dr Waffie Mohammed, a Trinidadian, who was the local Director of Rabita; and Shaikh Imran Nazar Hosein, also of Trinidad.

I believe it was the first time these scholars were all meeting together since their graduation many years before. The guests arrived shortly before noon, and we sat on the porch and engaged in light conversation until it was time to offer the *Ẓuhr ṣalāt*. We used my living room for this purpose as it would have been somewhat crowded to perform the prayer in my prayer room cum library. We then had lunch after which we sat on the prayer mats in the living room (which had not yet been removed) to have coffee and dessert. The whole atmosphere was one of informality, especially with the former classmates sometimes reminiscing about their experiences while studying together. Everyone was in a happy spirit, talking about a variety of subjects, laughing, and having snacks. I saw the professor in a different light then, not as the staid University lecturer or Shaikh or religious leader, but as an ordinary human being who could relate comfortably with those around him. This atmosphere prevailed for a few hours until the guests had tea and left shortly after four.

The Professor and the New Bedsheet

All wives like to keep a neat house and to pamper their guests, notwithstanding their financial limitations. My wife is no exception. We were preparing for the imminent arrival of the professor on the occasion of his annual visit and my wife decided that she wanted a new bed sheet and pillowcases to match the colour of the recently re-painted bedroom walls. After my usual objections as to why a new sheet was necessary (which, as expected, were overruled) we went to the nearby department store where she purchased a set she found suitable. The items were duly washed, pressed, and fitted on the bed on the afternoon of the professor's expected arrival.

The professor arrived on time, performed the required ṣalāt, dined, then retired to his room early to recuperate after the long (nine hours) journey by air. When the professor came by the kitchen door the next morning to let us know he was up and to have his usual cup of coffee and crackers, both my wife and I enquired if he had had a good night's rest. To our surprise he stated that he could not sleep during the night as there was the image of a butterfly on the sheet. Now, both my wife and I are aware of the restrictions of Islam in this respect, and we endeavour to follow them. We told the professor we were not aware of this and went to his room with him to examine the sheet. At first we could not discover the image but on close examination we realised that what we considered to be a simple pattern was in fact very faint images of a butterfly. So my wife bought a new set of sheets, had them washed and ironed, and replaced the set which was on the professor's bed.

Mission to Egypt, Saudi Arabia and India

(a) *Background to visits*

The ASJA had been sending students to study at great expense at the Aleemiyah Institute of Islamic Studies in Karachi, Pakistan, since its establishment by the late Dr Fazlur Rahman Ansari (R.A.)[3] in 1964. This fell eventually under the purview of the writer in his capacity as Chairman of the ASJA's Propagation Committee. The necessity for the establishment of an Institute for Islamic Studies locally therefore arose from the late 1970's but did not materialise for some years. However, in the mid-eighties the writer was able to get the

---

3   R.A. stands for *Raḥmatullāh ʿalaih*, which means "Allah's mercy be upon him."

Association to agree to the establishment of such an institution, to be named after the late Haji Ruknuddeen, former Qadi and Sheikh-ul-Islam. A Board of Directors was established for this purpose, with the writer as Chairman. The Board commenced organising part-time residential courses in 1986 and when the professor became aware of its existence, he suggested later it should have a link with the Darul Ihsan University which he was at the time in the process of establishing. The professor then proposed that the Institute should operate on a full-time basis and liaise with Maulana Abul Hasan Ali Nadwi,[4] a world-renowned Islamic scholar and writer, in this respect. This was agreed to as a result of which the Maulana recommended Dr Majid Ali Khan[5] of Jamia Millia Islamia for the position of Principal of the Institute.

During the professor's visit to Trinidad in 1990 the ASJA agreed that he and I should travel to a number of countries and meet certain officials, as indicated below, for the purpose of having the Haji Ruknuddeen Institute of Islamic Studies (HRIIS) functioning on a full-time basis. The professor arranged the travel schedule and the appointments for the middle of November. I met him in London and we visited the Saudi Embassy for him to renew his visa and for me to obtain one. We visited the Egyptian Embassy later for the same reason. (I had obtained my Indian visa in Trinidad).

(b) *Cairo, Egypt*

The arrangements for our stay in Cairo and for a meeting with the Minister for the Affairs of Al-Azhar University were made by a friend of the professor who was himself a retired professor at the University and was then operating a bookstore specialising in Islamic books for university students. All I can recall of his name is that it began with the letter "B," hence I will refer to him as Professor B. He booked us in the Al-Hussein Hotel, which is very near to the Al-Hussein Masjid, in which there is a shrine containing the head of Imam Hussein (R.A.). The professor and I were forced to share a large room with two single beds and toilet facilities as the celebration of the martyrdom of Imam Huseiin (R.A.) was due to take place in a few days. As a matter of fact, our booking was accepted on the condition that we leave by a certain time.

We visited Professor B at his bookshop at around 11.00 the morning after our arrival, as he had invited us to have lunch with him. When the two professors met, I got the distinct impression from the way they greeted each other

---

4 Maulana Abul Hasan Ali was a distinguished scholar who was internationally recognised for his work in the field of Islam. He received many honours from different parts of the world, including being given the key to the Kaʿbah in order to enter it whenever he wanted.

5 Dr Khan had taught for nearly five years at the ASJA Boy's College, San Fernando, Trinidad and was subsequently awarded the Second Prize in a world competition initiated by Rabita for his submission on the life of the Prophet Muhammad (pbuh).

and conversed that they had not only known each other for a considerable length of time but were also close friends. Shortly after our arrival at the bookstore we were joined by two sisters-in-faith who had travelled from Alexandria by train that morning specially to meet the professor. From the way that the professor and the sisters exchanged greetings and conversed during their stay with us I concluded that they were *murīds* of his and may have attended *murāqabah* sessions and/or seminars conducted by him. The sisters appeared to have a high degree of respect and admiration for the professor. The sisters spent about three hours with us before leaving to catch a train to return to Alexandria.

The following day the professor and I met with the Minister, and we made separate requests, through an interpreter, for teachers from Al-Azhar University for the Darul Ihsan University in Bangladesh and the Haji Ruknuddeen Institute of Islamic Studies in Trinidad, respectively. The Minister was very sympathetic to our requests, explaining that there were over five thousand graduates of Al-Azhar who were assigned to various organisations in different parts of the world for the purpose of performing *daʿwah* and whose salaries were paid by the government. He went on to explain the conditions under which missionaries were assigned to overseas bodies. The meeting ended with the Minister promising to give careful consideration to the two requests.

We visited the Al-Hussein Masjid to perform our *ṣalāt* as often as possible. After the *ṣalāt* on one occasion the professor and I visited the shrine where the Imam's head is buried in order to offer *duʿāʾ* (supplication). The professor offered the *duʿāʾ*, which lasted for about ten minutes, in a very low voice. I glimpsed at him occasionally and noticed that he was very emotional, his face taking on different expressions during the course of his supplication. I was reminded somewhat of the supplications offered by Haji Francis at religious functions in Trinidad. This could perhaps be explained by the fact that they were both Shaikhs of the Naqshbandi Order.

After spending three days and nights in Cairo, we donned our *Iḥrāms* and boarded a plane for Jeddah to continue our mission.

(c) *Saudi Arabia*

We were met on our arrival at Jeddah Airport by one of the *murīds* of the professor, a Bangladeshi, who had taken a few days leave from his job in order to transport us during our visit. We had dinner at his home, after which he drove us to Makkah Sharīf, where we stayed in an apartment[6] rented by the

---

6 The professor told me that he had rented the apartment, which was very near the Ḥaram Sharīf, while lecturing in at a University in Makkah and on moving from the country he had kept the tenancy because of his frequent visits to Makkah. He further said that the owner of the building had given all the tenants in the building notice to vacate it so

professor. On arrival in Makkah we both of course performed 'Umrah, though at different times. The following day we travelled to Jeddah where we first met the Chairman of the Islamic Academy with whom the professor had an appointment to discuss progress being made in connection with efforts to raise funds for acquisition of the property adjoining the Academy's headquarters in Cambridge. The chairman informed the professor that he had written to a number of people soliciting a specific amount by way of donation from each for the project and that if half of them responded favourably sufficient funds would be received to purchase the proposed building. The chairman expressed confidence that their objective would be achieved.

We then visited the Islamic Development Bank (IDB) where I had an appointment with a Drs. Mohammed to discuss the delay in dealing with the release of funds already approved for the construction, furnishing and equipping of an extension to the HRIIS. Drs. Mohammed advised that this matter was not within his portfolio and took us to the head of the relevant section. It turned out that no action had been taken on the matter but the head of the section, after perusing the file, told us that all the requirements had been met for the release of the funds and promised to expedite the matter. We returned to Makkah after having a late lunch at the home of a Trinidadian brother who worked at the IDB.

I do not believe that either the professor or I would have been happy if we had reached Jeddah, performed the 'Umrah and did not read *ṣalāt* in Masjid al-Nabawī and also visit the tomb of the Noble Prophet (pbuh). This we did the following day. We were driven to Jeddah Airport from where we flew to Madinah Sharīf. We took a taxi to a hotel very close to the Masjid to book a room for a few hours so that we could freshen-up. The face of the front desk clerk at the hotel broke into a huge smile on seeing the professor, and he let out a loud "Welcome Professooor! Assalāmu 'Alaikum." The professor's face broke out into an equally big smile and he replied to the greeting, following which they heartily shook hands. (I concluded from the way they greeted each other that the professor was a regular guest at the hotel). After the professor signed the Register we went to our room, made fresh ablutions, and then walked the short distance to the Masjid. We waited in the Masjid making *dhikr* (remembrance of Allah) until it was time for the *Ẓuhr ṣalāt*. After performing the *ṣalāt* in *jamā'ah* we went to the shrine of the Noble Prophet (pbuh) in order to make *du'ā'* and send salutations to him. We continued by performing the same rites before the graves of Haẓrat Abū Bakr As-Ṣiddīq (R.A.) and Haẓrat 'Umar Al-Fārūq (R.A.). After offering two *raka'āt ṣalāt* in Riyāḍ ul-Jannah we performed

---

that a modern multi-storey structure could be erected. The professor however wanted to retain the tenancy because of its convenience and attempted to have the rent paid regularly. The owner however refused to accept it.

dhikr for a while again before we returned to the hotel, checked out, took a taxi to the airport and boarded our flight to Jeddah.

Having completed our objectives in Jeddah, we then flew to New Delhi the next day in order to continue our mission.

(d) *Delhi*

In Delhi we stayed at the Hyatt Regency Hotel where we were able to obtain separate rooms. Shortly after we checked in at the hotel the professor contacted Dr Majid Ali Khan, who had been recommended by Maulana Abul Hasan Ali Nadwi to fill the position of Principal of the HRIIS. The following day we met with Dr Khan at the office of the Managing Director of Kutub Khana Azizia, booksellers and publishers, and started discussions with him. We broke for *Ẓuhr ṣalāt*, which was read in the Jama Masjid opposite us and returned to the office for lunch. We then hired a taxi which, under Dr Khan's directions, took us on a brief tour of the Parliament Buildings, President House and a few other places of interest before returning to our hotel late in the afternoon.

While en route to Delhi the professor had told me that it would be a pity if we reached India and did not visit the shrine of Kwaja Moinuddin Chishti in Ajmir and also the Taj Mahal in Agra. I agreed with him entirely. On arriving at our hotel, the professor went to a travel agency office in the lobby and enquired about a tour to Ajmir. We were informed that it would take a full day and involved taking a taxi to the railway station at six in the morning, catching a train at a particular time for the long journey to Ajmir and after visiting the shrine, returning to Delhi during the night. The professor made the necessary bookings for us to go but on checking with the travel agency for the tickets for our train journey the next morning we were told that there was a problem with the train schedule that day and our proposed tour would have to be cancelled. We were naturally disappointed, especially as another arrangement could not be made due to our limited stay in Delhi.

However, we were able to visit the Taj Mahal in Agra. Dr Khan made arrangements with the owner of a taxi to drive us there and accompanied us on the visit. We left the hotel about seven in the morning, arriving at the monument some four and a half hours later. While touring the monument we went to the basement (now closed to the public) where the bodies of the Emperor Shah Jahan and his wife, Mumtaz Mahal, are preserved. While standing before the remains of the couple the professor commented that millions visited the tomb every year and wondered whether any offered *duʿāʾ* for them. He said that we should, then raised his hands and offered an appropriate supplication. I raised my hands and joined him in it.

After our tour of the building, we proceeded to the adjoining masjid where we offered our *Ẓuhr ṣalāt*. We then had lunch at a nearby restaurant and started on our return journey around four o'clock. However, after about three hours the car started developing mechanical problems while we were on a highway. Fortunately, the driver was able to coax the vehicle along until we reached a village and located a mechanic who was able to complete repairs after working on the vehicle for about three hours. We then continued our return trip to Delhi, arriving at our hotel around one in the morning.

The following afternoon we went to Dr Khan's home to have tea with about ten to twelve of the senior academics at the Jamia Millia Islamia, where Dr Khan lectured. The professor gave a brief presentation on the advantages of faith-based education and entertained questions from them. The discussions had to be curtailed however when it was time to perform the Maghrib ṣalāt. The professor and I had previously been invited to stay on for dinner, which we did. After dinner we continued our previous discussion on the offer to Dr Khan to accept the position of Principal of the HRIIS, with Dr Khan requesting time to consult his family before arriving at a decision. We then performed the ʿIshāʾ ṣalāt after which we returned to our hotel.

(e) *Lucknow*

We flew to Lucknow the next morning to meet with Maulana Abul Hassan Ali Nadwi, former Rector of the Nadwatul Ulema, who had recommended Dr Khan for the position of Principal of the HRIIS. We arrived in Lucknow at about eleven in the morning and were met at the airport by an official of the institution. We were driven to the institution and escorted to separate rooms. The professor was ushered to his room first. The door was wide open, and I naturally looked in. It was a very large room with an unusually large bed, which was covered with a beautiful bright-coloured bedspread. It was obvious that the institution thought very highly of the professor and had spread the "red carpet" for him. I smiled, looked at the professor and said: "Professor! You are being given royal treatment today." The professor smiled back weakly at me (I believe he might have been embarrassed at the arrangements) and I left and was escorted to my room. We refreshed ourselves and when we heard the adhān (call to prayer) for the Ẓuhr ṣalāt we came out of our respective rooms, where we met an official in the corridor who escorted us to the masjid on the compound. After the ṣalāt, the official led us to a large room in a building where a number of people, including the Maulana, were gathered. The professor and the Maulana heartily embraced each other and had a brief conversation before we were introduced to the others in the room, who were senior members of the academic staff.

We then sat, in Islamic tradition, on the carpeted floor to have lunch. There were a large number of small containers, each with a different item of prepared food, spread on the floor. This was the pattern for lunch and dinner during the three nights and four days we stayed at the institution. It appears to me, in retrospect, that whenever the Maulana visited the institution, he would have his meals with senior members of the academic staff, with each one bringing a small quantity of whatever had been prepared in his home and sharing it with the others.

At Nadwatul Ulema the professor met an old friend and colleague, Dr Abdullah Abbas Nadwi (then retired), who was a distinguished scholar and writer. The professor spent two mornings with him compiling a syllabus for the HRIIS. I sat in at the meetings but could not make much contribution as this area was outside my scope.

Both the professor and I wanted to do some shopping, he for his wife and niece and I for my wife. We were taken to the stores one afternoon by an official of the institution for this purpose (see next section).

The Maulana invited the professor to visit his home in Bareilly (some thirty or forty miles away) to spend a day with him. The professor asked me to accompany him on the visit the next day but I declined, feeling they would want to have some time together to reminisce. The professor was away for most of the day. The next morning, having concluded our business at Nadwatul Ulema, we returned to Delhi.

(f) *We part company*

With our visit to Lucknow, our mission was then completed.

The following day we left for different destinations: I, early in the morning for London and, after a few days, back to Trinidad and, later in the day, the professor to Bangladesh in connection with matters relating to Darul Ihsan University. The professor came down to the front desk of the hotel with me to see me checked out after which I expected he would have gone up to his room. He did not but walked down the steps of the hotel with me to my waiting taxi. We embraced each other for a while before I entered the taxi. It was a sad parting as a close bond had grown between us during his visits to Trinidad and strengthened during the two weeks or so we had spent together. I looked back through the glass of the car as the driver moved off and saw the professor waving for some time before turning and starting to mount the steps to enter the hotel.

The Expert in Ladies Wear

I must confess that I am not familiar with the preferences of the opposite sex. Shortly after I was married some fifty-nine years ago it was my wife's (Laila's) birthday, so I went to the cosmetic counter of a reputable local store, purchased (on my limited salary as a public servant) a well-known international brand of perfume which was highly advertised, had it gift-wrapped and then presented it to my wife lovingly. She unwrapped the gift, opened the perfume, then told me that she did not like the scent. Well, from that time I left the gift selection for her initially to one of her sisters (most of whom lived nearby) and then, when our children grew up, one of our two daughters. When both girls were married and lived abroad, my eldest son took over this highly skilled art and still does the needful whenever the occasion arises.

My wife wears Islamic garments based mainly on the Pakistan-Indian shalwar-kameez fashion so when the occasion arose for the professor and me to go to a number of countries, including India, she naturally wanted me to purchase some outfits for her. Not being accustomed to purchasing garments for her I accordingly took along one of her outfits which fitted her well and also made copious notes about the colours, styles etc. she would like. While on our mission to the various countries I told the professor that if the occasion arose, I would like to do some shopping for my wife and he replied that he would also like to do some for his wife and niece.

During our three day stay at Nadwatul Ulema in Lucknow arrangements were made for a member of the staff to take us to the shopping district. As we visited various stores the professor would choose suitable items for his wife and niece (at which he seemed to be accustomed). When we visited the stores which stocked an assortment of shalwar and kameez he would look carefully at the items as the attendant held them up for us to obtain a proper view, and would make comments such as "Laila will not like this" or "This will not suit Laila" in which case the garment would be rejected. When he felt a garment was suitable for my wife he would comment "This will fit Laila" or "Laila will love this" and put it aside to be paid for. I thanked the professor for undertaking a task which I would have failed at and, indeed, my wife was enthused when she saw the professor's selection.

The Power of *Du'ā'*

While travelling with the professor in 1990 I had a personal experience with his prowess in the spiritual field when we landed at Jeddah Airport. The invasion of Iraq by the Western countries was then imminent and there was very strict security at the airport. There were long lines of passengers waiting to be cleared by Customs Officers with most passengers' baggage being thoroughly examined. I was in front of the professor in the line when he tugged at my *Iḥrām* and told me to stand behind him. I did as he wished, after which he pulled our suitcases together. I could then hear him whispering some words softly. I looked at his face and saw his eyes closed and his lips moving. He was obviously offering an appropriate *du'ā'* for us to be cleared by Customs without any difficulty. He finished the *du'ā'* by leaning slightly over the suitcases and blowing over them. When he reached the Customs Officer, the officer spoke briefly with the professor and then cleared us without inspecting our suitcases.

I will mention here the experience a prominent local businessman related some years ago at a small function he held at his residence to mark Eid ul-Fitr and the award to him of an honorary LLD degree by the University of the West

Indies. In his welcome address to the guests the host alluded to a recent fire in his local plant, saying that he was out of the country when his wife telephoned him and informed him of the fire which was then spreading rapidly. Continuing, he said he immediately telephoned Professor Ashraf, who advised him to offer a particular *du'ā'*, which he immediately did. He kept in continuous contact with his wife on the phone so that he could be apprised of developments at the factory and very soon afterwards she informed him that the direction of the heavy breeze, which was spreading the fire rapidly through the factory, suddenly changed to the opposite direction, resulting in the fire no longer being a threat to the whole premises and the damage being contained.

I was aware that the businessman had a very close personal relationship with the professor and had no doubt about what he related, especially having regard to my own experience at Jeddah Airport.

The Two Seminars on Faith-Based Education

The professor conducted two seminars on faith-based education in Trinidad.

The first seminar: The first was towards the end of 1987, shortly after a new party had been elected to power. It was a Thursday morning with the professor who was due to leave the country the following Monday. At breakfast the professor told me that he would like me to arrange a meeting with the new Minister of Education, a former Principal of a well-recognised government-assisted Boys Secondary School, with the view of having faith-based education introduced in the education system in the country. I informed the professor that it would be difficult to make an appointment with the Minister before his departure at such short notice, but he insisted that I at least try. I did and was able to reach the Minister, with whom I had a very good rapport as we had served together on the Executive Committee of the Anti-Apartheid Organisation of Trinidad and Tobago. I explained my reason for calling to the Minister who advised that he had a very busy schedule as he was due to leave the country the next afternoon on government business. He, however, agreed to meet us at 8 a.m. for half an hour the next morning.

The professor and I went to the Minister's office at the appointed time and the professor briefly explained the concept and importance of faith-based education. We raised the question of the Minister's attending a seminar on the subject to be sponsored by the ASJA and he promised to give the opening address. Two days were fixed in consultation with him, and the professor accordingly returned to the country to conduct the seminar. I made appropriate arrangements, liaising with the heads of religious organisations, who I knew through my involvement in the Inter Religious Organisation of Trinidad and Tobago. The leaders of about fifteen bodies and two other representatives from each organisation were invited to the two-day seminar which was held at the Hilton Hotel and Conference Centre. I chaired the various sessions of the seminar which was very well attended. The Minister delivered the feature address and was so interested in the subject that he remained the entire morning, only having to leave to attend the regular weekly sitting of the House of Representatives after lunch. Discussion was at a high level, and I was especially surprised at the quality of the presentations and suggestions made by all participants, especially representatives of the smaller bodies.

The second seminar: The second seminar was held under the auspices of the Inter Religious Organisation at the Royal Plaza Hotel in August 1993 during the professor's annual visit to the country. I was First Vice President of the IRO at that time and when I became aware of the dates of the professor's visit to the country, I suggested to them that they should sponsor a seminar along the lines of the one held previously by the ASJA. They readily agreed. I presided over the opening session of the two-day seminar which was formally opened by the Prime Minister of Trinidad and Tobago, the Hon. Basdeo Panday. Like the first seminar, all discussions were of a high standard.

Recommendations were made to the government after both the seminars but in spite of promises made no positive action was taken as neither of the parties in power at the time was re-elected after their term of office expired.

Lingering Memories

I knew the professor from 1984 until his sudden demise in 1998. I consider it not only a privilege but also a blessing from *Allāh Ta'ālā* to have known him, to have had him as my house guest every year during that period, and to have spent over two weeks travelling with him. My wife and I still have vivid memories of him, a few of which have been recorded above. I pray that *Allāh Subḥānahu wa Ta'ālā*, in His Infinite Grace and Mercy, will make his grave spacious for him and grant him a place among His honoured ones in the afterlife.

Chapter 41

Visionary Legacy: The Life and Dreams of Professor Ashraf

A. K. M. Mohiuddin

Professor Syed Ali Ashraf was a singular figure in Bangladesh, whose sudden departure during his slumber at the Cambridge Islamic Academy on 7 August 1998 left a void difficult to fill. His passing marked a loss not only for his homeland but for the global Muslim community, as his multifaceted contributions spanned academia, literature, Islamic scholarship, and education. Professor Ashraf embodied a rare amalgamation of virtues. He excelled as a student, distinguished himself as a revered educator, showcased his literary prowess as a poet and critic, gained international acclaim as an Islamic scholar, and undertook the noble task of founding educational institutions, thereby leaving an indelible mark as a spiritual luminary.

However, his paramount ambition lay in his visionary dream: to conceptualise and implement an educational paradigm tailored to the needs of the world's Muslim populace. Over the course of twenty-two relentless years, he dedicated himself fervently to realising this vision. His dream, too profound for mere words to encapsulate, centred on addressing what he identified as the core predicament plaguing the Muslim ummah: education. Professor Ashraf astutely recognised that the prevailing educational landscape was antithetical to nurturing Muslim identity and societal cohesion. He discerned the urgent need for a reformed educational framework that not only shielded against cultural erosion but also poised Muslims to thrive in the contemporary and future global milieu.

His analysis revealed a historical chasm in Islamic educational evolution, wherein traditional madrasah pedagogy and blindly adopted Western models fell short of meeting the exigencies of Muslim life. In essence, Professor Ashraf's legacy beckons the Muslim world to bridge this schism, to forge an educational trajectory rooted in Islamic heritage yet adaptive to contemporary realities. His life's work epitomises a clarion call for educational renewal—a call that resonates not only within the corridors of academia but also within the hearts of millions striving for a revival of Muslim thought and identity. He recognised the imperative of revitalising Muslim education to align it with contemporary global standards. Yet, the enormity of this task, matched only by its weighty responsibility, did not deter him; rather, he embraced it with full cognisance of its magnitude. Professor Ashraf's insights transcended mere whims; they were grounded in logic and rationality, setting him apart from his contemporaries.

While many espoused their own educational methodologies for Muslims, few could articulate the rationale behind their approaches or elucidate their practicality. In stark contrast, Professor Ashraf meticulously elucidated the reasoning behind his educational philosophies through his writings in the Cambridge Islamic Academy's *Muslim Education Quarterly* and other platforms. His intellectual prowess and clarity of vision positioned him as an unparalleled authority on Muslim education, not just within Bangladesh but also on the global stage.

Aware of the shortcomings of both Western education and traditional madrasah pedagogy, Professor Ashraf initiated a groundbreaking endeavour in Savar's Bolibhodro (in Dhaka) to establish an alternative primary and secondary education system. This ambitious undertaking, although underappreciated by many, held profound significance in addressing the deficiencies of existing educational paradigms. Despite his myriad commitments, he recognised the paramount importance of this venture, albeit constrained by the demands of his other endeavours. In retrospect, the establishment of the organisation in Savar for young boys represented a pinnacle of Professor Ashraf's educational vision, eclipsing, I think, even the founding of a university in its transformative potential.

The most disheartening aspect of the life of this altruistic individual, wholly dedicated to the long-term betterment of Muslims worldwide, was the lack of support and cooperation he received from segments of society, particularly those who purportedly championed Islam. Regrettably, even among our esteemed ulema, there was a failure to grasp the significance and value of his endeavours. In matters of education, they lacked the breadth of knowledge, depth of experience, and emotional acuity necessary to comprehend Professor Ashraf's vision, plans, and considerations. Thus, those expected to understand him most profoundly understood him the least. He was a saintly figure, revered by his devotees, yet often misunderstood.

Having collaborated with him for one year and eight months, I witnessed firsthand his solitary journey in pursuing the noblest aspirations of his heart and the formidable challenges of their realisation. He departed from this world burdened by this profound sorrow, but the magnitude of the loss incurred by Muslims worldwide due to our failure to comprehend and support him cannot be adequately expressed. Individuals of his calibre are rare, and only Allah knows when such a luminary will grace us again. May Allah grant him a place of honour and blessing. Ameen.

Chapter 42

In Remembrance of Syed Ali Ashraf

Tosun Bayrak

In 1978, we went to Hajj with my family. During the circumambulation of the Kaʿbah, we were practically knocked down by a group of brothers, who were rushing towards the black stone as if chasing an elephant with their spears in their hands. May Allah forgive me, I was quite annoyed. My wife, an American woman who had become a Muslim two years before, told me later that day that I should have forgiven their behaviour, because they did not know what they were doing, as they unfortunately were uneducated. "After all," she said, "they were not rushing to a Macy's sale or to a bank. They were doing what they were doing for Allah's sake." Indeed, she was right. Most of the things we do which are detrimental to ourselves as Muslims are due to the lack of education in the Islamic world today, where hundreds of millions of people remain illiterate.

Professor Syed Ali Ashraf was the most sincere, best willed and selfless warrior in the battle of this injustice to ourselves, members of a religion to whom the first word of Allah Most High was the order: "Read."[1] To this day, I do not know how he chose us to attend a conference at Durham University, I believe in 1980, where he received us most graciously with a gentle, sincere smile which beautified his face. I later discovered he remained this way even in the most unpleasant conditions. Brothers of many paths attended that conference: Sunnīs, Shīʿīs, and Aḥmadīs from many corners of the world. He treated them with equal warmth and understanding, but alas, many did not return the same feeling. Much of the conference consisted of disagreement, mostly based not on real issues, but on the manifestation of our egos.

At dinner time, a period of social interaction, people gather around tables, each group upholding their own convictions while opposing those of others. Syed Ali Ashraf's table was the exception: we talked about and hoped for unity in Islam. We were honoured to be invited, and occasionally people who were

---

[1] Qurʾān 96:1.

tired of bickering escaped and found refuge with us. The conference ended with agreement to disagree, in spite of his indefatigable effort to foster unity. It was on that occasion that he kindly offered us membership on the Editorial Advisory Board of the *Muslim Education Quarterly*, of the recently established Academy in Cambridge. This organization, its activities and publications, and its encouragement to Islamic educators and scholars under his tutelage, has served considerably to cure the lack of education in the Muslim world.

At that time, Syed Ali Ashraf had the idea of rewriting textbooks in all subjects for Muslim schools from an Islamic point of view. He proposed to us to write a book on the history of World Art in Islamic terms, which unfortunately we have not yet been able to do. During those few days in Durham our respect for his sincerity, our appreciation for his knowledge and goodwill, and our love for his kindness, character and friendship were already established. On his request, we wrote a piece on Islamic calligraphy, which was published in the *Muslim Education Quarterly*.[2]

We did not have the pleasure of seeing him again until the spring of 1987, when he invited us and two scholars of our choice to another conference in Cairo.[3] We proposed our friends Dr Ragip Frager,[4] a renowned psychologist, the head of the Institute of Transpersonal Psychology in California, and Shems Friedlander,[5] a writer who had written books on Mawlānā Jalāluddīn Rūmī and Mawlawiyyah.[6] We were received at the airport by Syed Ali Ashraf and brought to a wonderful hotel. Here we found numerous scholars from all over the world, including Seyyed Hossein Nasr, and Martin Lings, who impressed me with an Arabic costume as well as his wonderfully sensitive and scholarly book on our Prophet (peace and blessings be upon him).[7]

Syed Ali Ashraf served everybody not only as an organizer and a guide, but also almost as a servant and a waiter during our communal breakfasts. We remember him bringing food to our tables with a smile and a good word.

The atmosphere was again dominated by our egos, although we heard many scholars giving very impressive talks about their particular subjects.

---

2   Tosun Bayrak, "Art: The Islamic Approach," *Muslim Education Quarterly* 1, no. 4 (1984): 30-43.
3   This was the Fifth World Conference on Muslim Education held in Cairo, Egypt in March 1987.
4   Ragip Frager al-Jerrahi al-Halveti holds a PhD in Psychology from Harvard University, and is the Founder and President Emeritus of Sofia University (formerly known as the Institute of Transpersonal Psychology) in Palo Alto, CA.
5   Shems Friedlander was an American Islamic scholar, Sufi master, visual artist, filmmaker, author, and an emeritus professor of practice at the American University in Cairo.
6   Mawlawiyyah is the Turkish Mevlevi Order of Sufis founded in Konya by Mawlānā Jalāluddīn Rūmī.
7   Martin Lings, *Muhammad: His Life Based on the Earliest Sources* (Cambridge: Islamic Texts Society, 1983).

One of those was Dr Ragip Frager's talk on Sufi principles in Freudian psychology, which was very well received.

Our talk was on the deficiency of our secular public education systems, which were still under the influence of the English and the French colonial school systems in occupied Muslim countries, which aimed to prepare students for being government clerks, but not for any higher positions in the future. We had witnessed this in Morocco when independence was finally obtained, and there was subsequently a great deal of difficulty in finding educated people even to fill ministerial and high administrative posts. In more Westernized countries like Turkey, secular public schools totally ignored religious education, which left young people without an identity. Obviously, our talk was not well received by many except for Syed Ali Ashraf.

During this conference we remember that we were asked to support him in a meeting with the Saudis to raise money. We arrived on time and waited for hours to be received by our Saudi hosts. But when we were accepted into their quarters, we were chastised for being late. Yet, Syed Ali Ashraf with his sweet smile smoothed the situation very quickly. And later he explained that they were right: although we were announced when we came on time, and they agreed to see us a few hours later, the meeting started late because of us. That was he: conciliatory, humble, intelligent, and selfless.

After that we exchanged a few letters, but we did not see him again. We read his articles and his books, and we believe he has done good work in the service of God Most High. May Allah reward him, have mercy on his soul and accept him in His paradise. Āmīn.

Conclusion
Shaikh Abdul Mabud

This book features essays contributed by Professor Ashraf's friends, colleagues, relatives, disciples, and other scholars, many of whom had personal interactions with him in various roles. Many contributors to this book have shared incidents involving their personal interactions with Professor Ashraf. In these encounters, they were struck by the depth of sincerity, sense of urgency, genuine compassion, and empathy he displayed. They have noted that he was equally at ease in his interactions with dignitaries, scholars, friends, families, and strangers. His simplicity and magnanimity attracted everyone. He firmly believed that an educator should possess not only profound intellectual capabilities but also uphold good moral principles. In his view, morality is inseparable from education; it is an essential component of its very definition.

Some contributors have explored Professor Ashraf's spiritual practices and demonstrated how they were integral to his daily life. He never isolated spirituality from theology; instead, he integrated Sharīʿah and Ṭarīqah both in his educational pursuits and in his own religious practices. He argued that without this integration, Muslim cultural and civilisational advancement would be hindered. While emulating Professor Ashraf's religious practices may be challenging, educational activities should, at the very least, align with both the theological and spiritual dimensions of Islam. Education should not overlook or deny what lies beyond the visible world. The unseen world, which can only be realised with spiritual insight, is an integral part of reality that God manifests as His signs both in external nature and within the inner recesses of human beings, and education should incorporate at least some aspects of it. He firmly believed the idea that education, lacking spirituality and centred solely on worldly gains and excessive control over nature, fails to satisfy human inner needs and is detrimental to human development.

Through these essays, Syed Ali Ashraf emerges as an able teacher, a wise mentor, a spiritual guide, an efficient organiser, a skilled negotiator, and most importantly, as a person full of compassion and concern for others. The contributors have described him as an educationalist, as a poet and as a spiritual guide. As a visionary and an educationalist, he laid the foundation of the worldwide movement in Muslim education through the organisation of the World Conferences on Muslim Education and through his subsequent writings and lectures. As observed by more than one contributor, he forged a new path in Bengali poetry, offering a wholly innovative direction to explore. As a spiritual guide he touched the lives of many in different countries of the world. Professor Ashraf possessed a multi-dimensional personality, making genuine contributions in the fields of literature, education, and Islamic culture. He transcended the boundaries of Bengali or English literature, delving into diverse traditions and cultures. His vision embraced a universal truth underlying all traditions. Faith was his ultimate stronghold, providing him with immense strength and unwavering conviction. In line with his ancestors, he delved deeply into the inner aspects of Islam, transcending sectarian boundaries to embrace all that is true and beautiful. For him, modern education was not a hindrance but a tool to rediscover the essence of faith, nourished by love for God and the Prophet. He traversed the globe with the message of Islam and Islamic education, advocating for an education that fosters balanced growth in both material and spiritual realms.

As the essays in this book show, instead of being confined to narrow thinking, Professor Ashraf remained open and responsive to the challenges of contemporary life. He asserted that the aim of education is twofold: to acquire external knowledge that fosters extrinsic faith, and to achieve internal realisation of the intrinsic meaning and worth of that knowledge. This dual purpose is crucial in training individuals to fulfil their roles within society, culture, and civilisation, both from individual and a global perspectives. True education is goal-oriented and centred on God, the Transcendent Reality. It involves a holistic approach where humans engage their rational and spiritual faculties to comprehend this reality. Such education guides individuals toward a moral and spiritual life, grounded in Divine guidance, with a keen awareness of accountability on the Day of Judgement. As noted by some contributors, Professor Ashraf embodied moral uprightness living by a code of ethics rooted in principles and integrity. He believed that values are not only essential for personal growth but also crucial for shaping the future generation.

Professor Ashraf's religious approach to education places acquired knowledge, whether in the social sciences, the humanities, or the natural sciences, within a broader and deeper perspective that goes beyond the human constructs of the social and material worlds. It acknowledges the moral and spiritual dimensions of human personality, utilising a cognitive tool that transcends mere reason and resides within the innermost part of the human being. He thought that the true human peculiarity and individuation does not lie in the biology but in something embedded deep within the recess of the human soul. This personal core lies hidden within us and gradually blossoms into our physical and sentient life. He truly believed that "Teaching the whole person," a commonly heard rhetoric, remains unattainable unless due attention is given to the interior of the human being. He showed that secular philosophy of education has failed to address the existential, moral, and spiritual aspects of human life that is so sacred. Its negation of Divinity, reductionist views, prioritising rationality at the expense of spirituality, promotion of consumerism, neglect of inner wellbeing, and contribution to environmental degradation and social inequality are destructive of humanity. Throughout his life, he advocated for a holistic approach that integrates material concerns with spiritual, ethical, and social dimensions of human existence and can save human beings from the dangers they face in the modern world.

What becomes clear from the essays in this book is that Professor Ashraf tirelessly worked to dispel myths about Islam being fanatical, retrograde, and rigid, aiming to win people over with his firm conviction and powerful writing. He consistently promoted creative ways of acting and thinking, valuing both the wisdom of the past and new knowledge and skills, seeking to incorporate them into productive and fruitful living. Equally critical of the misrepresentation of Islam on the one hand and unbridled secularism on the other, he endeavoured to integrate Islamic faith with modern insights. Most of his educational endeavours focused on effectively addressing the fresh challenges of the present moment. Professor Ashraf believed that by focusing on shared goals such as societal justice and environmental stewardship, education can promote harmonious living and peaceful coexistence. His approach to embracing cultural and faith diversity emphasises both unity and diversity. Religions can maintain their uniqueness while coming together to address societal challenges. By presenting a unified front, they underscore the importance of spirituality and faith-based perspectives in tackling contemporary issues. This approach serves as a response to secularism, highlighting the relevance and impact of religious beliefs and practices in modern life.

Having been associated with him for twenty-four years, I had the opportunity to observe him closely. I found him to be a person full of warmth and kindness. He fulfilled his commitments and obligations with utmost care and was ready to help and support all those in need. I found that despite his astounding accomplishments, he was easily accessible to people of all sectors of society, sharing his wisdom with whoever he came into contact with. Professor Ashraf's piety is evident in every aspect of his life: I have prayed with him in the train and on the station platform, joined him in long prayers in Masjid al-Ḥaram, or seen him muttering prayers or concentrating in silent devotion when in difficulty, or healing people. I have found his devotion unwavering, guiding his every action, whether personal, social, or academic, even if it entailed personal loss. It did not take me long to find him as someone so close to my heart that I could trust him and confide in him and could look up to him for any help or guidance in personal matters. I have noticed how he held his own spiritual masters in highest esteem which I believe was a source of strength for him. His simplicity, combined with his religiosity, was truly magnetic. He inspired those around him towards a better life and a more compassionate world. His knowledge was vast and diverse that he acquired with his dedicated study, rich experience, and spiritual devotion. I hope that this book will help preserve the valuable legacy left by Professor Ashraf by documenting his ideas, contributions, and relentless struggle to establish an enlightened form of education. This education aims to help Muslims fulfil their purpose of existence, which is none other than the worship of God, the Lord of the worlds. Hopefully, future generations will ponder over his legacy and utilise it in meaningful ways. This may involve reinterpreting Professor Ashraf's ideas or finding new ways to apply his principles to contemporary issues.

Afterword
Anwar Ibrahim
Prime Minister of Malaysia

The late Professor Syed Ali Ashraf was a paragon of erudition, grace and wisdom. His life whispers the tales of a weighty but utterly fulfilling journey from the vibrant streets of Dhaka to the hallowed halls of global scholarship.

More than mere literary critic and poet, as some might be tempted to pigeon-hole him into, Syed Ali whirled with words and wisdom, shaping the minds and spirits of those who wandered in the garden of knowledge. Beneath the vast canopy of his thoughts, we gain passage to spiritual understanding and worldly insight. Like stars in the intellectual firmament, his works continue to guide us, illuminating the path to a more enlightened future.

In today's rapidly evolving world, marked by the relentless advance of artificial intelligence, Syed Ali's vision for an education steeped in values and spirituality has become increasingly pertinent. As AI technologies grow more sophisticated, taking over mechanical, mathematical, and even some creative aspects of knowledge, the essence of what makes us human—our values, ethics, and spiritual understandings—must be cultivated more diligently than ever within educational paradigms.

Syed Ali's advocacy for an Islamisation of education, emphasising a balanced integration of faith and worldly knowledge, provides a critical framework for contemporary education systems worldwide. This is essential in an era where AI's capabilities can potentially diminish the human role in various fields, making it imperative that education not only imparts cognitive skills but also nurtures ethical, moral, and spiritual dimensions of human life. This is no technophobic outburst but an earnest caveat: Such an education can equip individuals to use AI responsibly and ethically, ensuring that technology serves humanity positively and does not erode ethical boundaries or the value of human intuition and emotion.

Understanding different religious and ethical frameworks is crucial for global cooperation, peace, and harmony. In this regard, Syed Ali's interfaith pathway to education—recognising and respecting the values across different religions—fits in snugly towards advancing a more inclusive, empathetic, and culturally aware society. This approach has become particularly significant amid the reckless deployment of identity politics by the forces of obscurantism and voices of rack and ruin not only in the West and the Muslim world, but also across the globe at large.

Education of the Interior: Essays in Honour of Professor Syed Ali Ashraf is a comprehensive compilation of analyses and tributes dedicated to the life, work, and legacy of Syed Ali. Kudos to the eminent contributors for ensuring that this festschrift reflects the pervasive influence and enduring impact of Syed Ali's work not only on themselves but also on individuals, communities, and institutions far and near. Beyond the shadow of a doubt, it is a fitting testament to his legacy as a scholar, educator, and spiritual guide. Let us remember him not just in words, but in the rhythm of our daily lives and the courage of our convictions.

Appendix 1:
Syed Ali Ashraf: Chronology of Events

1924	30 January. Syed Ali Ashraf was born in Agla Purbo Para, Nawabganj, Dacca, British India.[1]
1931	He Moved to Dacca city from Agla with his family.[2]
1932	He was admitted to Armanitola Government High School, Dacca.
1940	He passed the Matriculation Examination from Armanitola Government High School, Dacca.
1940	He was admitted to Government Dacca Intermediate College, Dacca.
1942	He passed the IA examination from Government Dacca Intermediate College, Dacca.
1942	He was admitted to the Department of English, Dacca University for a BA (Hons) in English.
1943–1944	Joint Secretary of Purbo Pakistan Sahitya Sangsad (East Pakistan Literary Society).
1944–1945	Secretary of Purbo Pakistan Sahitya Sangsad.
1945–1947	Vice-president of Purbo Pakistan Sahitya Sangsad.
1945	He passed BA (Hons) in English from Dacca University, Dacca.
1946	He passed MA in English from Dacca University, Dacca.
1946	15 November. He was formally initiated into Sufi path (Naqshbandiyyah ṭarīqah) by taking oath of allegiance (bayʿah) to Hazrat Haji Ghulam Muqtadir (RA) of Khulna.
1947–1953	Lecturer in English, Dacca University, Dacca.
1948	He married Asia Khatun, daughter of Mohor Ali of Chandpur.
1949	1 October. He left Dacca for the UK for higher education.
1950–1952	He was admitted to Fitzwilliam College, University of Cambridge, as an Affiliated Student, where he pursued English Tripos and earned a BA degree.
1953–1954	Reader in English, Dacca University, Dacca.
1955	Cambridge University MA was conferred on him.
1955–1956	Reader and Head, English Department, Rajshahi University.

---

1 His full name was "Syed Abu Nasr Ali Ashraf." See "Introduction," note 6. Also, Chapter 37: Muhammad Abdul Jabbar Beg, "Remembering Syed Ali Ashraf," note 1.
2 In 1982, the English spelling of the city was officially changed from Dacca to Dhaka.

1956–1965	Reader and Head, English Department, Karachi University.
1957	He met Hazrat Baba Zaheen Shah Taji (RA) in Karachi and became his disciple.
1960–1964	He pursued his PhD at the University of Cambridge and successfully obtained it in 1964.
1965–1973	Professor and Head, Department of English, University of Karachi.
1971	Visiting Professor of English, Harvard University, Cambridge, Mass., U.S.A., Summer School.
1973–1974	Fellow, Clare Hall and Supervisor of English, University of Cambridge.
1974	Visiting Professor of English, New Brunswick University, Fredericton, Canada.
1974–1977	Professor and Head, English Department, King Abdulaziz University, Makkah Branch.
1975	He moved with his family to his own house at 23 Metcalfe Road, Cambridge.
1977	He was appointed an Organising Secretary of the First World Conference on Muslim Education held in Saudi Arabia.
1977–1982	Professor of English, King Abdulaziz University, Jeddah.
1978	1 June. Hazrat Dr Badiuzzaman of Mirwarishpur, Noakhali, Bangladesh offered him the *Khilāfah* from himself.
1980	He was appointed the Organising Secretary of the Second World Conference on Muslim Education held in Islamabad, Pakistan.
1980	4 December. Hazrat Dr Badiuzzaman offered Syed Ali Ashraf the *Khilāfah* in Qādiriyyah, Chishtiyyah, Naqshbandiyyah and Mujaddidiyyah *ṭarīqahs* on behalf of Jamāʿat-e Madīnah. Dr Badiuzzaman also appointed him as the president of Jamāʿat-e Madīnah in his absence.
1980–1982	He was appointed Director General, World Centre for Islamic Education set up by OIC (Organisation of Islamic Conference), Makkah, Saudi Arabia.
1981	He was appointed the Organising Secretary of the Third World Conference on Muslim Education held in Dhaka, Bangladesh.
1982	He was appointed the Organising Secretary of the Fourth World Conference on Muslim Education held in Jakarta, Indonesia.
1982–1984	Fellow of Wolfson College, Cambridge University.
1982–1992	Visiting Professor, Department of Education, University of Cambridge, Cambridge, U.K.
1983–1998	He founded the Islamic Academy in Cambridge in 1983 and served as its Director General until his passing.

1989	He established the Institute of Higher Islamic Studies in Dhaka, which was later renamed as the Institute of Higher Islamic Learning.
1990–1998	He founded Darul Ihsan University in Dhaka, Bangladesh in 1990 and served as its Vice-Chancellor until his passing.
1992	He founded Tahfizul Quranil Karim Fazil Madrasah at Bolibhadro, Savar, Dhaka, Bangladesh.
1997	He sold his house at 23 Metcalfe Road and moved to 205 Gilbert Road, Cambridge, which served as the headquarters of the Islamic Academy. He resided here for a few months before passing away.
1998	7 August. He passed away at 205 Gilbert Road, Cambridge.
1998	10 August. Syed Ali Ashraf was laid to rest on the campus of Darul Ihsan University at Bolibhadro, Savar, Dhaka, Bangladesh.

Appendix 2
Family Tree of Syed Ali Ashraf

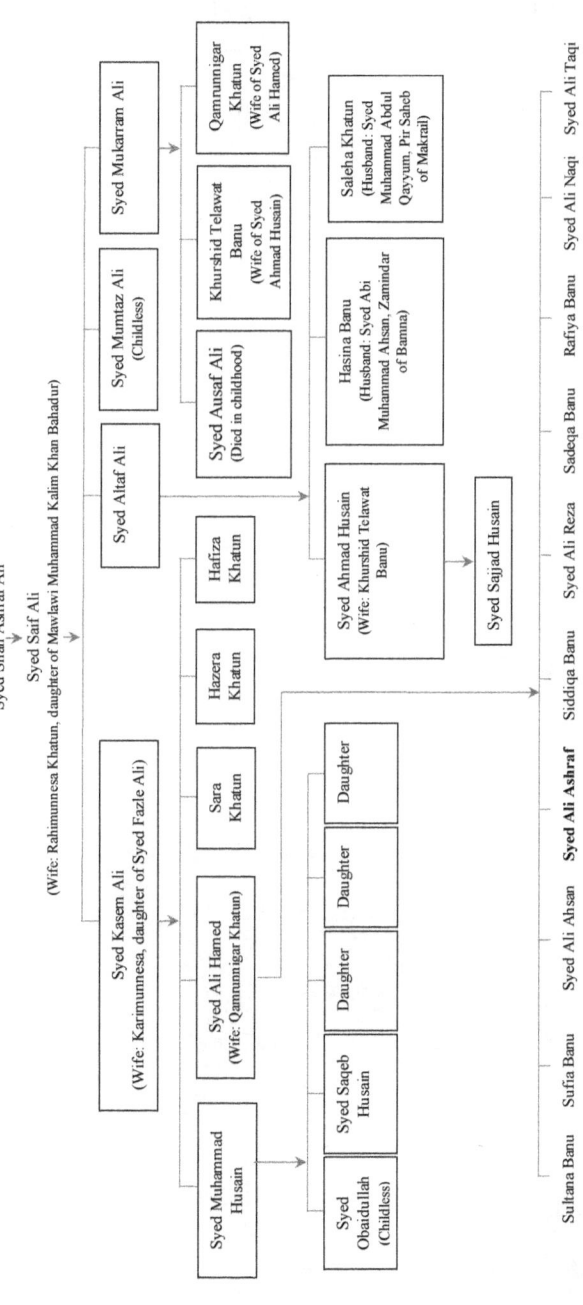

Note: Shah Ali Baghdadi, a 19th level descendant of the fourth caliph of Islam, Ali ibn Abi Talib, came to Delhi with some disciples in 813/14 AH (1412 CE) at the age of twenty. He left Delhi and travelled to the village of Kasba Girdah in Fatehabad Pargana (Faridpur district) which was conquered by the Muslims during the reign of Jalaluddin Muhammad Shah (1415–1433). (*Banglapedia*, s.v. "Shah Ali Baghdadi (R)"). Shah Ali Baghdadi died in c. 1480 and was buried in Mirpur, Dhaka. This family tree is taken from: Syed Ali Ahsan, *Hôzrot Shah Ali Boghdadi* (Dhaka: Syed Ali Naqi, 1996), 16–21.

Contributors

Roisuddin Ahammad

Dr Roisuddin Ahammad obtained his PhD from Rajshahi University in 2007. The topic of his doctoral research was "Syed Ali Ashraf: Life and Work." He received his Dākhil Certificate in 1984 and ʿĀlim Certificate in 1986. In 1988 he obtained his Fāḍil degree from Choigharia Senior Madrasah, Magura in Bangladesh. He received his BA (Honours) and MA in Islamic Studies from Rajshahi University in 1992 and 1993 respectively. Currently, he is serving as Assistant Professor at Kazi Salima Haque Women's College in Mohammadpur, Magura.

Emajuddin Ahamed

Professor Emajuddin Ahamed earned his PhD degree in political science from Queen's University, Ontario, Canada. He taught political science at the University of Dhaka, first as a senior lecturer and then as a professor. He served as the vice chancellor of Dhaka University from 1992 to 1996. He became the vice-chancellor of the University of Development Alternative in 2002. Ahamed received several academic awards including Ekushey Padak, Jatiya Shahitya Sangshad Gold Medal, Zia Sangskritik Gold Medal, and Michael Madhushudan Datta Gold Medal.

Akbar S. Ahmed

Professor Akbar Ahmed is the Ibn Khaldun Chair of Islamic Studies at American University in Washington, D.C. and the former Pakistani High Commissioner to the UK and Ireland. He served as the First Distinguished Chair of Middle East and Islamic Studies at the U.S. Naval Academy in Annapolis, MD. He has taught at Cambridge, Harvard and Princeton Universities. He is the author of over a dozen award-winning books including a quartet of studies published by Brookings Press examining relations between the West and the World of Islam after 9/11: *Journey into Islam: The Crisis of Globalization* (2007), *Journey into America: The Challenge of Islam* (2010), *The Thistle and the Drone: How America's War on Terror Became a Global War on Tribal Islam* (2013), and *Journey into Europe: Islam, Immigration, and Identity* (2018).

Muhammad Ahsan

Professor Dr Muhammad Ahsan is Deputy Vice-Chancellor (Academic) of International Open University, The Gambia. Having graduated from four countries (Pakistan, Japan, Holland and UK) Dr Ahsan has worked in two continents (Asia and Europe) and has over thirty years of experience of research and teaching in various capacities. He has made notable contribution in the fields of international relations, globalisation, political economy, development studies and education. In addition to authoring several books, Dr Ahsan has produced many reports and research papers published in various refereed international journals. His publications include *Sexuality Education from an Islamic Perspective* (co-author, 2020), *Writing Thesis and Academic Articles: A Practical Handbook for Researchers* (2017) and *The Ummah and Global Challenges: Re-organising the OIC* (2006).

Syed Ali Ahsan

Syed Ali Ahsan, the eldest brother of Professor Syed Ali Ashraf, was a Bangladeshi poet, writer and academic. He was the Director General of Bangla Academy from 1960–66. In 1966, he was invited to become adviser to the Secretariat of UNESCO. He was the Vice-Chancellor of Jahangirnagar University (1972), Rajshahi University (1975) and Darul Ihsan University (1998). Syed Ali Ahsan was Minister of Education, Culture, Sports and Religion in the cabinet of President Ziaur Rahman in 1977. He was awarded Ekushey Padak (1982) and Independence Day Award (1987) by the Government of Bangladesh and was selected as the National Professor of Bangladesh (1987). He was an adviser to the Nobel prize committee for literature from 1976 to 1982.

Syed Farid Alatas

Dr Farid Alatas is Professor in the Department of Sociology at the National University of Singapore. His recent publications include *Applying Ibn Khaldun: The Recovery of a Lost Tradition in Sociology* (Routledge Advances in Sociology), 2014 and *Ibn Khaldun* (Makers of Islamic Civilization), Oxford University Press, 2013. He has also contributed to scholarly journals and essay collections, several articles on Ibn Khaldun, with particular emphasis on the application of his concepts and methodology in contemporary issues in the social sciences, educational philosophy, and culture.

Mashhad Al-Allaf

Dr Mashhad Al-Allaf is Associate Professor of Ethics, Logic, Philosophy of Science, and Islamic Studies at American University of Ras Al Khaimah, UAE. He holds a doctoral degree from the USA in Modern Philosophy: Science and Metaphysics (1995). He has taught at Washington University, and St. Louis University. He is the author of several works, including *The World and My Philosophy*, (2020, Arabic); "Logic and Theism" chapter in *Theism and Atheism: Opposing Arguments in Philosophy,* eds. Joseph Koterski, S.J. and Graham Oppy (2019); and *Locke's Philosophy of Science and Metaphysics* (2007). He taught different courses in the USA for about 20 years on Logic, Islamic Philosophy, Modern Philosophy, and Philosophy of Science and Technology. Specifically, he has taught at Washington University, and St. Louis University.

Osman Bakar

Osman Bakar is currently Distinguished Professor and Al-Ghazali Chair of Islamic Thought at the International Institute of Islamic Thought and Civilization (ISTAC), International Islamic University Malaysia. He is author and editor of 38 books and numerous articles on various aspects of Islamic civilization, comparative religion, and interreligious dialogues. He is listed in the past one decade as one of the 500 Most Influential Muslims in the world.

Tosun Bayrak

Sheikh Tosun Bayrak al-Jerrahi al-Halveti was an author, translator, and Sufi. He served as a government official in Ankara, Honorary Consul of Turkey in Morocco and was the Sheikh of the Jerrahi-Halveti Order in America. He studied Biological Sciences at Robert College, Istanbul; Art, Architecture, and Art History in the Studios of Bernard Leger and *André Lhote* in Paris; Architecture at the University of California, Berkeley; and History of Art at the Courtauld Institute of Art, London. He received a Master's in Fine Arts from Rutgers University. He was Professor of Art and Art History at Fairleigh Dickinson University, New Jersey.

Muhammad Abdul Jabbar Beg

Dr Muhammad Abdul Jabbar Beg earned a PhD degree in the Middle Eastern Studies from the University of Cambridge. He was a lecturer (1974) and an Associate Professor (1979) of Islamic History at the Universiti Kebangsaan Malaysia (UKM); and an Associate Professor (1986–1990) in the Department of History at the Universiti Brunei Darussalam. He was a visiting scholar at the University of Cambridge; lectured on Middle Eastern History at the University of the Third Age in Cambridge (1999–2004) and taught at the Markfield Institute of Higher Education, Leicestershire as an Associate Professor (2001). He contributed many entries to *The Encyclopaedia of Islam* (new edition) and published several books on Islamic civilization.

Magnus Bradshaw

Magnus Bradshaw has a PhD from the University of Birmingham on apocalypticism in Western Sufism which he is currently preparing for publication. His previous publications include "From Humanism to Nihilism: The Eclipse of Secular Ethics" (*Muslim Education Quarterly*, Vol. 24, No. 1 and 2, 2011) and "Conforming to the Real: Frithjof Schuon on Morality" (*Sacred Web*, 30 and 31, 2012–2013).

Ahmed Farid

Ahmed Farid was a member of the civil service of Pakistan and Bangladesh. In his career, he took up many different roles in the government and participated in many high-level multilateral negotiations, seminars and conferences representing Bangladesh. He was seconded to the United Nations Economic and Social Commission for Asia and the Pacific (ESCAP) from 1975–83. He served as the Permanent Secretary at the Ministries of Jute, Planning, and Science and Technology between 1985 and 1989. He was the Bangladesh Ambassador to UAE in 1989-93. He was also a vice chancellor of the University of Science and Technology, Chittagong. He contributed several articles on Islam and the Muslim Ummah.

J. Mark Halstead

J. Mark Halstead is Emeritus Professor of Education at the University of Huddersfield and a Senior Associate Member of the Oxford Centre for Islamic Studies. He was educated at Oxford University, where he read English and then Oriental Studies, and at Cambridge University, where his PhD thesis was on "The Education of Muslim Children in the UK." He was Professor of Moral Education and Associate Dean for Research and Innovation at the University of Plymouth until 2006, and then Research Professor and Head of Department at the University of Huddersfield's School of Education. He has supervised more than 20 doctorates and has written on a wide variety of topics including Islamic education, Muslims in Britain, faith schooling, moral, spiritual and multicultural education, philosophy of education, culture and values in education, the hidden curriculum, and the language of spirituality.

Mohammad Nurul Haq

He served as Treasurer of Darul Ihsan University and was also the Director of its Institute of Teacher Education. Additionally, he acted as Pro Vice Chancellor for a period.

Imran N. Hosein

Imran N. Hosein was born in Trinidad in 1942. He studied Islam briefly at *Al-Azhar* University, Cairo, before becoming the student of Maulana Dr Muhammad Fazlur Rahman Ansari at the Aleemiyah Institute of Islamic Studies in Karachi, in 1964. He studied Philosophy at the University of Karachi, and International Relations at the Institute of International Relations of the University of the West Indies, and the Graduate Institute of International Studies, Geneva. He has become a prolific writer with two dozen books already published—many of them devoted to Islamic Eschatology. His publications include *Dajjāl, the Qurʾān and Awwal al-Zamān* and *Methodology for the Study of the Qurʾān*. He is now writing his second book on *Dajjāl* entitled, *From Jesus the True Messiah to Dajjāl the False Messiah—a Journey in Islamic Eschatology*. His books can be viewed at his website: www.imranhosein.org and ordered from his bookstore: www.imranhosein.com. He can be reached at inhosein@hotmail.com.

Norman J. L. Howlings

Norman Howlings was head of the English Studies department at Huddersfield Polytechnic (now University) at the time of his retirement in 1981 and was a tutor with the University of the Third Age (U3A) since it started in Huddersfield in 1984. He was recognized as "a tutor who has given his time freely for decades to help others." When he reached the age of 90, he was presented with a copy of the *Times* newspaper from the day he was born by Huddersfield U3A president Mrs Margaret Fearnley at their AGM held at St Patrick's Catholic Centre, Trinity Street.

A. M. M. Azhar Hussain

Professor A. M. M. Azhar Hussain was professor of economics at Rajshahi University, Bangladesh. He taught at Darul Ihsan University, Dhaka, Bangladesh for a few years and later became its vice chancellor. He was a lifelong friend of Professor Syed Ali Ashraf.

Anwar Ibrahim

The Most Honorable Dato' Seri Anwar Ibrahim is the 10th prime minister (2022-) of Malaysia. He held many government posts in the late 20th century. In 1971 he founded the Muslim Youth Movement of Malaysia, serving as its president until 1982. He served as minister of culture, youth, and sports (1983), agriculture (1984), and education (1986–91) before being appointed minister of finance (1991–98) and deputy prime minister (1993–98). He held lecturing positions at the University of Oxford; Johns Hopkins University, in Baltimore, Maryland; and Georgetown University, in Washington, D.C. He was conferred the degree of Doctor of Laws, honoris causa by the University of the Philippines. He authored several books, including *The Asian Renaissance* (1996).

Iftekhar Iqbal

Iftekhar Iqbal (PhD, Cambridge) is Associate Professor of History at the Universiti Brunei Darussalam and works in environmental and intellectual history. Prior to joining UBD, Iqbal held teaching or research appointments at the University of Dhaka, King's College London and Humboldt University Berlin. He is recipient of several fellowships including the British Academy Visiting Fellowship and Georg Forster Fellowship from Humboldt Stiftung. Iqbal's publications include *The Bengal Delta. Ecology, State and Social Change 1840–1945*

(Palgrave Macmillan, 2010) and articles published in journals such as *Journal of Asian Studies, Modern Asian Studies*, and *Environment and History*.

Ahmad Salah Jamjoom

Shaikh Ahmad Salah Jamjoom was an Islamic thinker, notable economic expert, a successful businessman and a generous philanthropist, who made great contributions in three specific fields: Islamic education, Islamic finance and banking, and memorization of the Qurʾān. He was Finance Minister in the Cabinet of King Saud bin Abdulaziz of Saudi Arabia in early Sixties; and later, Minister of Commerce in the Cabinet of King Faisal bin Abdulaziz. Shaikh Ahmad was a key figure in organizing the Word Conferences on Muslim Education, the setting up of the World Centre for Islamic Education, the foundation of the Islamic Academy, Cambridge and in the establishment of Darul Ihsan University in Dhaka, Bangladesh.

Zainol A. Khan

Zainol A. Khan was born in San Fernando, Trinidad in 1929 and was a Public Servant. He wrote five books on various aspects of Islam and published extensively on Islam in the local press. He was involved in multi-faith activities for over three decades and served in various positions in the Inter Religious Organisation (IRO) of Trinidad and Tobago. He was listed in *Who's Who-Trinidad and Tobago 1991* and was awarded a "Certificate of Merit for Distinguished Services to Religion and Public Service" by the International Biographical Centre, Cambridge, England in 1991.

Asiyah Kumpoh

Asiyah Kumpoh is an Assistant Professor at the Faculty of Arts and Social Sciences, Universiti Brunei Darussalam. Her current research and publications focus on Brunei history, conversion narratives, the Brunei Dusuns and diasporas in Brunei. Among her latest publications are The Bruneian Concept of Nationhood in the 19th and 20th Centuries: Expression of State Sovereignty and National Identity (with Nani Suryani Abu Bakar, *Brunei Museum Journal* 2021, 79–84) and Globalisation, Education and Reform in Brunei Darussalam (co-edited with L.H. Phan, R. Jawawi, K. Wood and H. Said, Palgrave Macmillan, 2021).

Shaikh Abdul Mabud

Professor Shaikh Abdul Mabud has been based at Sultan Omar 'Ali Saifuddien Centre for Islamic Studies, Universiti Brunei Darussalam (UBD) since 2015. Concurrently, he is Director General of the Islamic Academy, Cambridge, UK, a post he holds since 1999. Prior to joining UBD, he was Professor of Islamic Studies at The Muslim College, London, UK (2015) and Professor of Islamic

Philosophy at Islamic College for Advanced Studies, London (2005–2007) and Research Instructor at University of Utah, Salt Lake City, USA (1981–1983). He was the editor of Cambridge-based educational journal, *Muslim Education Quarterly*, and has published numerous articles on Islamic education, science, and religion. He holds a PhD in Physics and a Postgraduate Certificate in Education, both from the University of Cambridge.

Nor Faridah Abdul Manaf

Professor Nor Faridah Abdul Manaf, formerly Professor of English at English Language and Literature Department, Kulliyyah of Islamic Revealed Knowledge and Human Sciences, and Deputy Rector for Internationalization and Global Network at International Islamic University Malaysia, has over 33 years of teaching experience. Some of her books include *Imagined communities revisited: critical essays on Asia-Pacific literature and cultures* (co-edited, 2009), and *Travel Poetry* (2019). Prof Faridah won Gold award for leadership given by Kulliyyah of Islamic Revealed Knowledge and Human Sciences in 2020.

Nadeem Memon

Dr. Nadeem Memon is an Associate Professor at the Centre for Islamic Thought and Education (CITE) at the University of South Australia (UniSA). At CITE/UniSA, Nadeem serves as a Course Coordinator for the Graduate Certificate in Education (Islamic Education), the first online graduate education program for educators in Islamic schools globally. His research focuses on teacher education with particular emphasis on Islamic Pedagogy, comparative faith-based schooling, philosophy of religious education, and culturally responsive pedagogy. In his research program, Nadeem is a Chief Investigator on an Australian Research Council (ARC) Discovery Grant (2022-2025) on Culturally Responsive Schooling. Nadeem holds a PhD in Theory and Policy Studies in Education from the Ontario Institute for Studies in Education (OISE) at the University of Toronto, Canada. He currently lives in Adelaide, Australia with his wife and son.

Peter Mitchell

Peter James Mitchell was a University Lecture in Education at the University of Cambridge and Life Fellow, Hughes Hall at the same university. He was responsible for the PGCE students specialising in the teaching of Religious Studies in secondary schools. He contributed to a range of courses for undergraduates in religious studies, the philosophy of education, the philosophy of religion, world religions and research methods concerned with investigations into the upbringing of children in faith communities as well as philosophy of education courses concerned with values in education and the relationship between religion and education.

Waffie Mohammed

Dr Waffie Mohammed is the Principal of Markaz al Ihsaan Institute of Islamic Theology, Trinidad. He obtained his M.A. in Islamic Studies and PhD in Comparative Religion from Karachi University. He also holds a *Darajah Al-Kāmil* in Islamic Studies from Aleemiyah Institute of Islamic Studies, Karachi. He served as the Director of the Muslim World League Regional Office for the Caribbean and Central America. For a few years he was the Principal and Advisor to the Board of Haji Ruknuddeen Institute, Trinidad and Tobago. During the 1980's he was a Senator in the Parliament of Trinidad and Tobago.

A. K. M. Mohiuddin

Former Professor of Rajshahi University English Department. He was also Professor of English Language and Literature at Darul Ihsan University, Dhaka.

Safti Muhammad

Dean, Faculty of Religious Studies, Darul Ihsan University, Dhaka, Bangladesh. He was from Egypt and educated at Al-Azhar.

Syed Ali Naqi

Syed Ali Naqi, a brother of Prof Syed Ali Ashraf, earned a B.A. (Honours) and an M.A. in History from Dhaka University. He taught at Jagannath College and Dhaka College in Dhaka. In 1995, he was appointed Pro-Vice-Chancellor of Darul Ihsan University, and in 2005, he became its Vice-Chancellor. He played a major role in establishing Darul Ihsan University and was one of the founding members of Darul Ihsan Trust.

Seyyed Hossein Nasr

Professor Seyyed Hossein Nasr is a world-renowned scholar on Islam and is currently a University Professor at the George Washington University. He has published over fifty books and hundreds of articles in numerous languages and translations. He graduated from Massachusetts Institute of Technology with an undergraduate degree in Physics and Mathematics. Nasr is the only Muslim to be included in the Library of Living Philosophers. His academic work extends from classical Islamic philosophy, Islamic science, Sufism, and critique of modernity to interfaith relations, Islam-West relations, and the environmental crisis. He was the first Muslim scholar ever to be invited to give the prestigious Gifford Lectures, which were later published as *Knowledge and the Sacred* (1981).

Abdullah Omar Nasseef

Abdullah Omar Nasseef has held many important positions in Saudi Arabia including serving as Vice-President of the Kingdom's Shura Council, President of King Abdulaziz University, and Secretary-General of the Muslim World League (1983-1993). He was the Secretary-General of the International Islamic Council for Dawa and Relief, (IICDR) which is composed of more than one hundred Islamic organizations from all around the world and headquartered in Cairo, Egypt. He was the President of the Muslim World Congress and chairman of the Oxford Centre for Islamic Studies. He was the Vice-Rector of King Abdulaziz University when the First World Conference on Muslim Education was organised by this university. Along with Professor Syed Ali Ashraf and Shaikh Ahmad Salah Jamjoom, he played a key role in organising the first four World Conferences on Muslim Education.

Farogh Naweed

Farogh Naweed obtained his Bachelor's degree from Emerson College, Multan (1953-56) and M.A. in English from Karachi University (1956-58). He was Additional Secretary, Prime Minister's Secretariat, Islamabad, Government of Pakistan for ten years.

Mahmud Shah Qureshi

Mahmud Shah Qureshi is an essayist, translator, and scholar. He has published over 40 books, the first one being *Chinnamul* (1958). He held many positions during his long academic career. He obtained his doctorate degree from the Sorbonne University with distinction (1965). His French work, "Etude sur l'evoulution intellectuelle chez les Musulmans du Bengale" was published in 1971 and an English version in 2016 entitled, "The Crescent and the Lotus: A Study on the Intellectual History of the Muslims of Bengal (Upto 1947)". A contributor to French and Bengali encyclopaedias, he specialises on writers particularly Syed Ali Ahsan, Syed Waliullah, Andre Malraux and others. He received numerous honours and awards from the French Government.

M. Harunur Rashid

Born in 1939, Mohammad Harunur Rashid was educated at the universities of Dhaka, Bangladesh and Cambridge, UK. He has taught English literature and language at government colleges, Chittagong University, Jahangirnagar University and North South University. He was appointed Director General of Bangla Academy in 1991 and President of the same Academy in 2007. He was elected President of World University International, Geneva in 1984. He was also elected President of the Asiatic Society of Bangladesh in 1998. He contributed to the national newsweekly, *Dhaka Courier* for twenty-five years and was its chief editor during 1999. A translator of repute, he has translated some classics from English, French and Malay into Bengali. He has also translated some modern Bangladesh poetry into English. He was drawn to Sufism in the late eighties and has written extensively on his mentor's views on and philosophy of Islam.

Ghulam Nabi Saqeb

Professor Ghulam Nabi Saqeb served as an Assistant Professor at King Abdulaziz University, Saudi Arabia, as Professor at the International Islamic University Malaysia and Head of the Department of Education at the National University of Modern Languages, Pakistan. He joined the Muslim World League (Rābitat al-ʿĀlam al-Islāmī) in 1984 and was seconded to the University of London Institute of Education, where he established a unit on Islamic Education for the promotion of higher degree research on this subject. He published a few books, including *Modernization of Muslim Education in Egypt, Pakistan and Turkey*, and over two dozen articles in learned journals. He was the Assistant Organising Secretary of the First World Conference on Muslim Education which was held in Makkah in 1977.

Mohammad Hazim Shah

Prof Mohd Hazim Shah holds a Bachelor's degree from the University of Manchester, a Master's degree in Philosophy from the London School of Economics, and a PhD in the History and Philosophy of Science from the University of Pittsburgh, USA. He is currently serving as a Professor in the School of Languages, Civilisation, and Philosophy, College of Arts and Sciences, at the Universiti Utara Malaysia. Prior to this, he was a Professor of the History and Philosophy of Science at the Department of Science and Technology Studies, University of Malaya, Kuala Lumpur. He was appointed as a member of the "Science and Islam Task Force," headed by the former secretary-general of the Organisation of Islamic Cooperation (OIC), Professor Dr Ekmeleddin Ihsanoglu (2015/2016). He was a Visiting Research Fellow at the University of Melbourne, Australia (1993), and at the University of Cambridge (2008).

Sarah Smalley

Dr Sarah Smalley taught for 14 years in two Cambridgeshire secondary schools. From 1990 she worked for Cambridgeshire County Council first as Advisory Teacher, then as Adviser for Religious Education, supporting policy development and providing in-service training for teachers across the age range. She obtained an M.A. in Area Studies (Middle East) at the School of Oriental and African Studies of London University in 1990. Between 2004 and 2006 she served as Chair of the Association of Religious Education Inspectors, Advisers and Consultants. From 2007 to 2015 she led the work of the RE Council of England

and Wales, working with members of faith and belief communities across England and Wales, members of parliament, academics, and teachers to promote the understanding and improvement of RE in schools and colleges. She is now retired but continues an active involvement in education as a school governor.

Brenda Watson

Brenda Watson is a retired educational consultant who currently writes on a wide variety of topics concerned with values and beliefs, philosophy and religion. A former lecturer at Didsbury College of Education, she became Director of the Farmington Institute in Oxford for several years before doing consultancy work. She has written a number of books including *Education and Belief* (1987), *Priorities in Religious Education* (ed. 1992), *Truth and Scripture* (2004) and, with Penny Thompson, *The Effective Teaching of Religious Education* (second edition 2006). Her recent articles include, in the philosophy journal *Think*, "Belief and Evidence, and How It May Aid Reflection concerning Charlie Hebdo" (Spring 2016).

James Kinnier Wilson

James Kinnier Wilson (b. 27 November 1921, d. 22 December 2022) was a British Assyriologist. He was Eric Yarrow Lecturer in Assyriology, from 1955 until 1989, and Emeritus Fellow, Wolfson College, University of Cambridge. He was appointed Lecturer in Assyriology, Durham University (1950), researcher at The Oriental Institute, University of Chicago (1951-52), Lecturer and then Assistant Professor, University College, Toronto (1953-55) and Chairman, Faculty of Oriental Studies, Cambridge (1965–67). His publications include *The Wisdom and the Beauty: A Selection of Short Passages from the Qur'an.* (Shepheard-Walwyn, 2007) and *Towards Novaluation: God's Work and Ours at the End of the Age* (Janus Publishing Company, 2010). He used to live in Cambridge.

Rhoda Jal Vania

Rhoda Jal Vania was a student of Professor Syed Ali Ashraf at Karachi University. She spent her childhood in Lahore and her formative years in Chittagong before she moved with her parents to Karachi. Rhoda Vania did her PhD in Literature from the University of Minnesota and returned to Pakistan to teach at Karachi University. She became a professor at the English Department of Karachi University, and later also worked at the Indus Valley School of Art and Architecture and The Lyceum, Karachi. After retirement she was Principal of Beaconhouse School System for a while, taught A level Literature at St Michael's for a term and then worked for the University Grants Commission in Islamabad. She was associated with the Lyceum School since its inception and served as its Board member, and as Principal when needed.

Mujadad Zaman

Dr Mujadad Zaman is Assistant Professor of Education at Boğaziçi University (Türkiye). He researches the philosophy of education with a broad focus on questions of how and why we learn across cultures. Specifically, he works on the history of pedagogy, classical Islamic learning, aesthetics, and craft education as well as the role and purpose of the modern 21st century university.

Index

A

Abraham, Prophet 152, 158, 182, 183, 184, 514
Abrahamic faiths 61, 276
afterlife 7, 16, 139, 145, 158, 162, 164, 188, 199, 268, 354, 355, 368, 432, 514, 550
Al-Ghazali 22, 23, 90, 93, 95, 96, 100, 101, 142, 145, 149, 304, 306, 309, 310, 316, 323, 332, 374, 376, 379, 380, 381, 385, 387, 400, 463
Aquinas, Thomas 23, 139
Aristotle 81, 118, 124, 238, 239, 379, 381, 385
artificial intelligence 365, 560
astronomy 195, 203, 221, 379, 383, 386, 387, 432
atheism 119, 222, 326, 327, 333, 334, 336, 349, 433, 442, 568
Al-Attas, Naquib xvii, 13, 19, 20, 25, 26, 43, 44, 45, 46, 47, 48, 52, 53, 54, 56, 87, 91, 94, 96, 97, 99, 100, 102, 103, 107, 109, 139, 140, 166, 198, 203, 235, 269, 284, 287, 301, 325, 388, 390, 396, 398, 402, 412, 430, 444

B

Bacon, Francis 81, 108, 333, 361, 377
Bible 182, 185, 190, 191, 203, 240, 243, 247, 258, 260, 262, 263, 293, 296, 302, 357
British education system 8, 15, 137, 155, 156, 159, 164
British Islamic schools 288, 297
Buddhism 15, 24, 32, 36, 118, 158, 189, 204, 206, 232, 236, 237, 254, 255, 276, 506

C

Catholic 85, 91, 160, 168, 190, 191, 257, 278, 284, 525, 571
Christianity 14, 24, 33, 47, 66, 87, 136, 155, 156, 158, 187, 190, 191, 192, 193, 194, 195, 196, 197, 198, 202, 203, 206, 209, 232, 236, 247, 257, 258, 259, 260, 261, 276, 284, 354, 355, 356, 357, 366, 367, 372, 375, 385, 390, 392, 425
civilization, Western 29, 31, 32, 33, 36, 47, 129, 142, 364, 375, 519, 523
civilizational dialogue 29, 32, 33, 34, 37
colonialism xiii, 41, 70, 228, 269, 326, 327, 338, 432
communism 59, 64, 67, 230, 334, 349, 351, 353
Confucianism 32, 33, 63, 68, 198
consumerism 8, 29, 68, 75, 81, 82, 119, 135, 212, 231, 236, 295, 319, 558
cosmology 51, 384, 385, 386, 388, 389
critical thinking 21, 137, 140, 391

D

Darwin, Charles 238, 240, 334
democracy 8, 9, 60, 61, 68, 70, 81, 157, 336, 532
Divine Names 50, 55
Divine Unity 51, 52, 55, 394
Durkheim, Emile 278, 284, 333, 334, 338

E

educational philosophy 16, 21, 29, 79, 137, 144, 159, 221, 235, 238, 283, 392, 428, 435, 437, 458, 568
educational reform 39, 148, 165, 269
empiricism 82, 83, 105, 106, 111, 140, 240, 410
English Literature 22, 121, 391, 393, 394, 397, 398, 403, 450, 455, 459, 460, 461, 462, 463, 465, 467, 481, 492, 515, 516, 518, 519, 557, 575
Enlightenment 6, 81, 143, 190, 229, 231, 333, 350, 351, 354, 356, 358, 371
environmental crisis 37, 75, 228, 229, 231, 233, 236, 237, 238, 276, 277, 336, 349, 352, 358, 364, 365, 366, 367, 558, 574
Eurocentrism 187, 190
evolution 142, 144
extremism 36, 41, 68, 72, 74, 245, 249, 250

F

faith-based education xvi, 14, 155, 159, 169, 170, 171, 172, 173, 174, 175, 176, 177, 178, 179, 180, 212, 225, 241, 397, 413, 448, 501, 537, 546, 549
First World War 119, 332
fitrah 353, 363
free will 312, 313, 315, 318, 321
Freud, Sigmund 81, 231, 334, 337, 354, 555

G

Gaddafi, Muammar 62, 74
globalization 59, 64, 68, 126, 129, 405
Greek philosophy 101, 374, 379, 380, 381, 385, 386
Gulf War 63, 65

H

Hajj xvi, 123, 505, 553
Hinduism 15, 24, 63, 66, 158, 195, 196, 197, 203, 205, 206, 232, 236, 276, 425
human consciousness 40, 50
humanism 31, 81, 101, 139, 140, 142, 151, 156, 157, 160, 188, 280, 364, 365, 487
humanities 231, 282, 288, 292, 337, 417, 418, 420, 423, 531, 557
human rights 87, 130, 133, 139, 308
Hussein, Saddam 59, 62, 63, 64, 74

I

Ibn al-ʿArabī 50, 51, 56
Ibn Khaldun 34, 38, 45, 93, 100, 142, 149, 198, 201, 203, 204, 293, 333, 387, 432, 567, 568
ijtihād 18, 19, 60
Indonesia 58, 59, 60, 64, 67, 69, 225, 404, 405, 563
Industrial Revolution 359, 365, 388
inner spirit 82
Institute of Islamic Thought 53, 90, 94, 96, 102, 112, 186, 203, 388, 390, 413, 417, 420, 421, 569
interfaith xvi, 14, 235, 237, 438, 560, 574
Islamic civilization 33, 34, 35, 36, 37, 42, 43, 49, 60, 73, 129, 273, 283, 379, 407, 519, 569
Islamic eschatology 350, 353, 520, 521, 522, 523
Islamic law 4, 5, 6, 19, 21, 35, 51, 60, 82, 88, 93, 98, 99, 100, 135, 145, 146, 215, 216, 221, 222, 281, 304, 309, 317, 319, 320, 331, 332, 337, 338, 399, 400, 401, 402, 434, 444, 485, 488, 502, 503, 505, 527, 556
Islamic philosophy 51, 52, 120, 295
Islamic Revival 40, 41, 42, 44, 45, 46, 48, 69
Islamic Revolution 53, 69, 338
Islamization of knowledge 52, 53, 54, 55, 94, 95, 102, 103, 235, 269, 282, 284, 287, 349, 404, 407, 420, 421

J

Judaism 14, 24, 32, 36, 66, 87, 139, 158, 191, 206, 236, 237, 258, 259, 260, 276, 284, 425

K

Kant, Immanuel 81, 82, 250, 263, 307, 309, 310, 311, 312, 313, 314, 315, 321, 324
Khomeini, Ayatollah 59, 69, 74
King Faisal 11, 41, 222, 508, 572

L

liberalism 81, 108, 137, 229, 416, 493
literary criticism 4, 396, 398, 401

M

madrasah 6, 45, 148, 288, 289, 293, 326, 432, 437, 442, 492, 551, 552
Makkah Conference 12, 27, 40, 41, 43, 44, 45, 46, 47, 48, 49, 51, 52, 53, 54, 55, 397, 509
Malaysia xvi, 9, 10, 19, 26, 41, 44, 45, 53, 56, 67, 69, 96, 198, 203, 225, 300, 391, 392, 404, 418, 440, 481, 560, 569, 571, 573, 576
Marx, Karl 69, 195, 333, 334, 351, 353
Maududi, Abul Ala 467, 479, 520

mechanical philosophy 377, 378, 379, 380, 384, 387
metaphysics 30, 142, 232, 240, 295, 384, 385, 386, 389, 409, 412
Middle Ages 29, 59, 118, 133, 193, 204, 250, 332, 351, 370, 374, 375, 378, 387, 390, 424
Middle East 59, 74, 96, 210, 291, 302, 567, 576
millennialism 348, 349, 350, 351, 352, 353, 355, 356, 357, 359, 363, 364, 367, 368, 372
morality 8, 17, 23, 87, 100, 101, 104, 105, 126, 128, 138, 139, 145, 149, 150, 151, 152, 153, 162, 164, 166, 173, 229, 233, 234, 280, 305, 306, 307, 312, 314, 315, 319, 320, 326, 334, 357, 369, 398, 401, 407, 430, 438, 441, 478, 487, 491, 492, 498, 556
Muslim world xiii, 5, 6, 7, 11, 13, 35, 36, 39, 41, 42, 43, 46, 52, 53, 55, 59, 60, 62, 65, 67, 70, 71, 72, 82, 90, 97, 110, 130, 136, 137, 195, 204, 228, 267, 281, 352, 381, 383, 388, 392, 405, 406, 407, 412, 432, 439, 443, 444, 451, 458, 466, 470, 471, 478, 479, 480, 488, 507, 509, 516, 528, 538, 551, 553, 554, 561, 574, 575, 576

N

nationalism 32, 36, 196, 236
natural philosophy 374, 375, 376, 377, 378, 379, 380, 381, 383, 384, 385, 386, 387, 388, 389
natural sciences 50, 53, 102, 221, 231, 238, 337, 414, 418, 420, 531, 557
neoplatonism 375, 378, 384, 385, 506
Newton, Isaac 378, 379, 380, 387

O

Orientalism 66, 193, 194, 195, 196, 202, 203, 204, 394
Ottoman 35, 60, 61, 332, 394

P

Palestine 36, 74, 213
perennial philosophy 33, 384, 517
Plato 81, 175, 386
pluralism 83, 89, 138, 155, 156, 157, 159, 163, 188, 207, 213, 249, 262, 292, 530
poetry 9, 16, 69, 74, 116, 118, 119, 120, 121, 122, 123, 124, 175, 193, 342, 344, 345, 346, 450, 452, 457, 460, 462, 465, 467, 468, 473, 481, 497, 506, 507, 508, 557, 576
Popper, Karl 106, 389
positivism 95, 101, 105, 109, 111, 231, 254, 353
post-colonial 39, 40, 41, 45, 52, 54, 69, 228, 325, 327, 433
post-modern 65, 73, 82, 242, 254, 272, 420
progressivism 81, 349, 357, 359, 368
Prophet Muhammad 16, 20, 35, 69, 83, 86, 92, 97, 123, 125, 130, 146, 150, 152, 215, 219, 277, 309, 310, 331, 439, 506, 522, 542

Q

Qur'ān xvii, 1, 4, 7, 8, 13, 16, 17, 18, 19, 20, 21, 22, 24, 35, 37, 40, 49, 50, 51, 60, 61,

INDEX

69, 70, 71, 74, 79, 82, 85, 86, 88, 92, 98, 104, 111, 117, 121, 125, 128, 130, 131, 132, 133, 134, 135, 136, 137, 142, 144, 145, 147, 148, 149, 150, 152, 158, 163, 184, 185, 220, 221, 222, 224, 232, 233, 239, 240, 241, 243, 246, 265, 266, 268, 274, 287, 289, 294, 305, 306, 308, 317, 319, 322, 328, 329, 330, 331, 332, 334, 335, 337, 338, 339, 353, 393, 397, 399, 405, 406, 409, 411, 416, 420, 427, 428, 429, 433, 434, 437, 442, 445, 467, 468, 470, 488, 502, 504, 505, 506, 509, 512, 513, 514, 515, 516, 518, 519, 520, 521, 522, 523, 527, 553, 570, 571, 572

R

rationality 6, 18, 84, 89, 109, 138, 140, 142, 143, 145, 159, 164, 165, 307, 318, 334, 336, 552, 558
Reformation 60, 190, 191, 242
Renaissance 31, 81, 190, 333, 352, 379, 452
Resurrection 331, 503

S

Saladin 63, 64
Salafi 476, 506, 511, 521
Saudi Arabia xiii, xv, xvi, 9, 10, 11, 41, 63, 67, 79, 136, 219, 222, 286, 405, 439, 456, 463, 465, 470, 475, 478, 479, 480, 494, 495, 505, 513, 516, 524, 538, 541, 543, 563, 572, 575, 576
Schuon, Frithjof 23, 31, 32, 33, 38, 230, 239, 243, 517, 569
science and technology 21, 42, 54, 133, 141, 238, 328, 352, 356, 358, 407, 411, 434, 436, 443
Science, Western 383, 387, 390
Scientific Revolution 374, 375, 376, 377, 378, 379, 380, 385, 387, 390
Second World War xiii, 59, 119, 228, 367
secular philosophy 87, 138, 157, 165, 385, 558
Sharīʿah 4, 5, 6, 19, 21, 35, 60, 88, 98, 99, 100, 135, 145, 146, 215, 317, 319, 320, 331, 337, 338, 399, 400, 401, 402, 434, 444, 485, 503, 505, 527, 556
Shia 66, 199, 388, 553
socialism 186, 242
social sciences 51, 64, 187, 191, 221, 231, 238, 292, 337, 417, 418, 420, 431, 482, 531, 557, 568
spirituality 9, 18, 24, 73, 78, 87, 88, 89, 126, 139, 142, 147, 162, 171, 221, 226, 237, 299, 300, 326, 422, 468, 556, 558, 560, 570
state schools 159, 161, 288, 289, 290, 332
Sufism 2, 3, 4, 5, 22, 50, 51, 56, 79, 80, 97, 118, 119, 121, 124, 148, 217, 218, 219, 220, 222, 400, 463, 465, 466, 467, 468, 469, 479, 492, 502, 506, 510, 511, 513, 514, 515, 516, 517, 518, 519, 520, 521, 522, 524, 525, 527, 536, 554, 555, 562, 569, 574, 576
Sunnah 4, 7, 8, 13, 16, 17, 20, 21, 22, 24, 60, 86, 98, 104, 109, 135, 136, 142, 148, 150, 163, 268, 274, 283, 297, 328, 332, 393, 409, 420, 427, 433, 506, 513, 519
Sunni 66, 199, 350, 370, 388, 484, 553
supernatural 188, 189, 199, 200, 202, 241, 333, 351, 353, 359, 422, 452

T

terrorism 58, 61, 74, 128, 129, 130, 207, 213, 246, 247, 249, 251
theology 19, 49, 50, 51, 55, 100, 162, 236, 281, 381, 409, 556
theory of evolution 6, 139, 238, 239, 240, 276, 334, 423
traditional civilization 30, 31, 32, 33, 37
traditionalism 22, 53, 449
transhumanism 349, 354, 355, 363

U

ummah 39, 41, 45, 46, 47, 131, 404, 406, 407, 408, 410, 411, 415, 416, 418, 420, 487, 551
United Nations 41, 61, 130, 405, 417, 570
utilitarianism 139, 231, 232, 307
utopianism 349, 351, 352, 354, 355, 361, 363, 364, 367

www.ingramcontent.com/pod-product-compliance
Lightning Source LLC
Chambersburg PA
CBHW031304150426
43191CB00005B/70